W9-DCV-907

THEORIES OF HUMAN COMMUNI-CATION

SECOND EDITION

THEORIES OF HUMAN COMMUNICATION

SECOND EDITION

Stephen W. Littlejohn
Humboldt State University

Wadsworth Publishing Company
Belmont, California
A Division of Wadsworth, Inc.

Communications Editor: Kristine Clerkin

Production: Del Mar Associates

Designer: John Odam

Copy Editor: Jerilyn Emori

Technical Illustrator: Stephen Harrison

Printed in the United States of America

1 2 3 4 5 6 7 8 9 10—87 86 85 84 83

ISBN 0-534-01280-9

Library of Congress Cataloging in Publication Data

Littlejohn, Stephen W.
Theories of human communication.

Bibliography: p.
Includes index.
1. Communication I. Title. P90.L48
001.5 82-21938 ISBN 0-543-01280-9

Acknowledgments
13, 15–16: From *The Conduct of Inquiry* by Abraham Kaplan. Copyright © 1964. Reprinted by permission of Harper & Row Publishers. **41–42, 71:** From *Communication Quarterly,* "Alternative Perspectives for the Study of Human Communication: Critique and Response," by Jesse Delia. Copyright © 1977. Reprinted by permission of *Communication Quarterly.* **30–32:** From *The Ghost in the Machine* by Arthur Koestler. Copyright © 1968 by Arthur Koestler. Reprinted by permission of Macmillan Publishing Co. and A. D. Peters and Co. Ltd. **50–52:** From *Symbolic Interactionism: Perspective and Method* by Herbert Blumer. Copyright © 1969. Reprinted by permission of Prentice-Hall, Inc. **60–65, 71:** From *Communication Rules: Theory and Research* by Susan B. Shimanoff. Copyright © 1980 by Sage Publications. Reprinted by permission of Sage Publications. **66–67, 69–70, 72:** From *Communication Action and Meaning* by W. Barnett Pearce and Vernon Cronen. Copyright © 1980 by Praeger Publishers. Reprinted by permission of Praeger Publishers. **69:** From *Genetic Psychology Monographs,* "The Development of Listener Adapted Communication in Grade-School Children from Different Social-Class Backgrounds," by Kerby T. Alvy. Copyright ©1973. Reprinted by permission of The Journal Press. **78, 84:** From *The Psychology of Language* by J. A. Fodor, et al. Copyright © 1974 by McGraw-Hill, Inc. Used with permission of McGraw-Hill Book Company. **87–88:** From *Kinesics and Context* by Ray Birdwhistell. Copyright © 1970 by the University of Pennsylvania Press. Reprinted by permission of the University of Pennsylvania Press. **96–97:** From *Philosophy in a New Key* by Susanne Langer. Copyright © 1942 by Harvard University Press. Reprinted by permission of Harvard University Press. **99:** From *American Psychologist,* "On Understanding and Creating Sentences," by Charles Osgood. Copyright © 1963. Reprinted by permission of The American Psychological Association and the author. **101:** From *The Measurement of Meaning* by C. Osgood, G. Suci, and P. Tannenbaum. Copyright © 1957 by the Board of Trustees of the University of Illinois. Reprinted by permission of the University of Illinois Press. **116, 118:** From *The Mathematical Theory of Communication* by Claude Shannon and Warren Weaver. Copyright © 1949 by the Board of Trustees of the University of Illinois. Reprinted by permission of the University of Illinois Press. **123–124:** From *Communication: The Study of Human Interaction,* "Human Information Processing," by C. David Mortensen. Copyright © 1972 by McGraw-Hill. Reprinted by permission of McGraw-Hill Book Company. **135:** From *Studies of Rhetoric and Public Speaking in Honor of James Albert Winans,* "The Literary Criticism of Oratory", by Herbert Wichelns. Copyright © 1925 by Appleton-Century-Crofts. Reprinted by permission of Prentice-Hall, Inc. **168, 170, 172:** From *Explorations in Interpersonal Communication,* "A Relational Approach to Interpersonal Communication," by Frank E. Millar and L. Edna Rogers. Copyright ©1976. Reprinted by permission of Sage Publications **171:** From *Human Communication Research*, by Malcolm Parks. Copyright © 1977. Reprinted by permission of International Communication Association and the author. **174:** From *Leaders of Schools: FIRO Theory Applied to Administrators* by Will Schutz. Copyright © 1977. Reprinted by permission of University Associates. **174, 175, 177:** From Firo: *A Three-Dimensional Theory of Interpersonal Behavior* by William Schutz. Holt, Rinehart and Winston, 1958. Reprinted as *The Interpersonal Underworld.* Copyright © 1966, Science and Behavior Books. Reprinted by permission of Science and Behavior Books. **178–179:** From *Frame Analysis: An Essay on the Organization of Experience* by Erving Goffman. Copyright © 1959 by Erving Goffman. Reprinted by permission of Doubleday and Company. **179–180:** From *The Presentation of Self in Everyday Life* by Erving Goffman. Copyright © 1959 by Erving Goffman. Reprinted by permission of Doubleday and Company. **182–184:** From *Self and Others* by R. D. Laing. Copyright © 1969. Reprinted by permission of Tavistock Publications. **185–187:** From *The Psychology of Interpersonal Relations* by Fritz Heider. Copyright © 1958. Reprinted by permission of the author. **187–190:** From *American Psychologist,* "The Process of Causal Attribution," by Harold Kelley.Copyright ©1973. Reprinted by permission of The American Psychological Association and the author. **193–195:** From *Of Human Interaction* by Joseph Luft. Copyright © 1969 by the National Press. Reprinted by permission of Mayfield Publishing Company (formerly National Press Books). **202–203:** From *The Acquaintance Process* by Theodore M. Newcomb. Copyright © 1961. Reprinted by permission of Holt, Rinehart and Winston, CBS College Publishing. **211–213:** From *Perspectives on Communication in Conflict,* "A Transactional Paradigm of Verbalized Social Conflict", by C. David Mortensen. Copyright © 1974. Reprinted by permission of Prentice-Hall, Inc. **217–218, 222–227:** From *Group Dynamics: The Psychology of Small Group Behavior* by Marvin E. Shaw. Copyright © 1981. Reprinted by permission of McGraw-Hill Book Company. **232–235:** From *Small Group Decision Making* by B. Aubrey Fisher. Copyright © 1980. Reprinted by permission of McGraw-Hill Book Company,. **237–239:** From *Victims of Groupthink* by Irving L. Janis. Copyright © 1972. Reprinted by permission of Houghlin Mifflin Company. **255–256, 258:** From *Communicating and Organizing* by Farace, Monge, and Russell. Copyright © 1977. Reprinted by permission of Addison-Wesley. **266–268:** From *The Medium is the Massage* by Marshall McLuhan and Quentin Fiore, produced by Jerome Agel. Copyright © 1967. Reprinted by permission of Bantam Books. **266–269:** From *Understanding Media* by Marshall McLuhan. Copyright © 1964. Reprinted by permission of McGraw-Hill Book Company. **291–293:** From Communication Research, "A Dependency Model of Mass Media Effects", by S. J. Ball-Rokeach and M. L. De Fleur. Copyright © 1976. Reprinted by permission of Sage Publications.

Contents

Preface

The study of human communication involves copious and diverse scholarship. This is both a blessing and a curse. It is a blessing because it has provided a rich source of ideas and insights into an elusive theme of human life. It is a curse because it has led to disarray and confusion about what is known. The field of communication badly needs integration. This book is the result of a project begun about ten years ago to bring together in a single volume many of the major theories of communication from various fields. The aim of the project is to make the insights of these theories more accessible to the student of communication and to provide a framework in which theoretical contributions can be compared, evaluated, and integrated.

The first edition of *Theories of Human Communication* was an initial step in this direction. The first edition summarized and organized many theories related to various themes of communication. Two major weaknesses were apparent in that edition. First, although theories were organized according to topic, little integration resulted. Second, theories were summarized, but no evaluation was presented. This edition seeks to overcome these difficulties.

This second edition retains the essential features of the first. It summarizes a large number of theories from several disciplines. Each theory is treated separately, so that the student can clearly see the focus and contribution of each. Extensive footnotes and references provide tools for further exploration of the theories and topics included.

Several new features have been added to the text to enhance its usefulness. After looking through the present edition, you will not doubt that it constitutes a major reworking of the original. The discussion of theory in the first two chapters has been expanded and updated; an important addition is the discussion of philosophical issues, which sets the stage for analysis of theories.

Perhaps the most important addition is the evaluation of the theories. Evaluative criteria are developed in Chapter 2, and these are applied directly or indirectly to the theories in each chapter. For the most part I attempted to capture the spirit of published criticism, but in cases where such criticism was not readily available, I took the role of critic to develop original evaluation.

At the end of each chapter is a new section summarizing what we know about the chapter's theme. These sections are not intended as point-by-point summaries. Nor are they detailed lists of facts or suppositions about aspects of communication. Rather, these brief sections are intended to present in general form the consensus of most knowledgeable scholars about the theme of the chapter. In other words these sections present points of general agreement or abstractions supported by the majority of theories in an area.

In addition, the capstone chapter has been completely revised. Its new aim is to present an assesssment of the status of communication theory at this time. It is a very personal statement with which others may or may not agree. Here I present my analysis of the field of communication, the status of communication theory at this time including its strengths and weaknesses, and a projection for the future of communication theory.

You will notice in this edition that most of the topics of the earlier version remain intact, presented in roughly the same order. However, there is considerable shift in emphasis from one theme to another. For example, theories of interpersonal communication, relevant to dyadic interaction, have been expanded into two chapters to reflect the relative increase in the amount of theory building in that area. In fact the conceptualization of communication contexts has been reworked slightly, as reflected in chapter titles, because of what I believe are changing perspectives in the field.

Theories of Human Communication is a highly selective effort. I wish to present enough material to depict the breadth of the field and to allow the student to see similarities and differences among theories, but to include all major theories related to communication would have been impossible. The need to remain current required that several new theories be added. The addition of this new material along with analysis and evaluation required that other theories be dropped for space reasons. I felt that certain old theories should be retained, because they were either highly influential or foundational. Even though such theories are no longer in vogue, they provide a sense of tradition and theory development. In the main, however, I have kept the book as up to date as possible. I made heavy use of anthologies, surveys of literature, and other secondary treatments to guide my selections and summaries, deferring as much as possible to experts in each area.

In summary, I see the second edition as a logical and necessary step in the development of a long-term project on the integration of human communication theory.

I would like to express my appreciation to the people who helped create this book: to Kevin Howat for his faith in the value of the project; to Sandra Craig and Nancy Sjoberg for their book sense and managerial skills; to Jerilyn Emori for her tireless editorial eagle eye; to John Odam and Steve Harrison for their design and artistic talents; to Karen Massetti-Miller and Sammy Reist for their keen attention to documentary detail; and to Charlotte Brown for a beautiful manuscript.

I am especially indebted to Richard N. Armstrong, State University of New York, Brockport; Fred L. Casmir, Pepperdine University; Kenneth N. Cissna, University of South Florida, Tampa; Forrest Conklin, University of Northern Iowa; John E. Crawford, Arizona State University, Tempe; Frank Dance, University of Denver; Loren Dickinson, Walla Walla College; Robert Emmery, California State University, Fullerton; Lawrence Frey, Wayne State University; Blaine Goss, University of Oklahoma; Mark Hickson, Mississippi State University; Stephen King, San Diego State University; Rebecca Rubin, Cleveland State University; R. C. Ruechelle, California State College, Stanislaus; Roger Smitter, Albion College; John Sutterhoff, California State University, Chico; and Gordon Whiting, Brigham Young University.

Mostly, I would like to thank my best friend, colleague, and wife Karen Foss for her encouragement and concern, urging and respite, criticism and confidence.

PART

I

INTRODUCTION

CHAPTER

1 The Nature of Communication Theory

As long as people have wondered about the world, they have been intrigued by the mysteries of their own nature. The most commonplace activities of our lives—those realms of human nature we take for granted—become puzzles of the largest magnitude when we try to conceptualize them. The study of how people relate to one another has occupied a major portion of the world's mental energy.

Communication is intertwined with all of human life. Any study of human activity must touch on communication processes in one form or another. Some scholars treat communication as central, while others take communication for granted without making it the focus of their study. In this book we are concerned with the idea of communication as central to human life. Our guiding question is how scholars in a wide variety of traditions have conceptualized, described, and explained human communication.

In a sense this book describes a part of our quest to understand ourselves. Specifically, it is a synthesis of many contemporary theories of communication. The book does not provide *the* answer to questions we ask about communication, but it does present several answers that have been proposed. In other words this book does not complete the puzzle of communication but illustrates how some of the pieces have been shaped and joined.

What Is Communication Theory?

In one sense any attempt to explain or represent a phenomenon is a theory. As discussed in the next chapter, a theory is someone's conceptualization of an observed set of events. Communication professors often ask their students to devise explanations of certain aspects of communication. This task is a theory-building exercise because it involves stating clearly what is believed to be happening in communication. Indeed, everybody operates by theory much of the time. Our theories consist of ideas that guide us in making decisions and taking actions. Sometimes we are wrong; our theories are flawed. At these times we may modify what we think the world is like.

Although the word *theory* can be used to describe the educated guesswork of laypersons, academics use the word somewhat differently. Scholars make it their work to study a particular kind of experience with a keen eye. A theory is the scholar's construction of what an experience is like, based on systematic observation. Theory in this sense is the scholar's best representation of the state of affairs at any given time. As you will see in the next chapter, theory building is not an easy task. A great deal of focused observing, hypothesizing, and revising is required.

The term *communication theory* usually refers to the body of theories that makes up our understanding of the communication process. Much disagreement exists about what constitutes an adequate theory of communication. In this book you will read about a wide variety of theories. These theories are discussed in terms of their philosophical assumptions, their claims about what communication involves, and their strengths and weaknesses. You will find a basis for making your own decisions about which theories should and should not be included in our body of knowledge about communication.

Why Study Communication Theory?

Besides fulfilling the student's curiosity about communication—meeting the need to know—the study of communication theory is valuable on other grounds. Communication is one of our most pervasive, important, and complex clusters of behavior. The ability to communicate on a higher level separates human beings from other animals. Our daily lives are strongly affected by our own communication with others as well as by messages from distant and unknown persons. If there is a need to know about our world, that need extends to all aspects of human behavior, especially communication.

Specifically, an understanding of systematic theories of communication is an important step toward becoming a more competent, adaptive individual. Often when the student asks how to become a better communicator, the teacher provides a list of recipes. This approach is a beginning, but the communication process is too complex to be approached entirely on the level of simplistic guidelines. Although recipes may help, what the student needs to learn about sending and receiving messages and relating to others is an understanding of what happens during communication and an ability to adapt to circumstances. The study of communication theory is a way to obtain this understanding.

A colleague of mine used to say that the study of communication theory will cause the student to see things never seen before. N. R. Hanson writes: "The paradigm observer is not the man who sees and reports what all normal observers see and report, but the man who sees in familiar objects what no one else has seen before."[1] This widening of perception, the unhitching of blinders, helps one transcend habits and become increasingly adaptable and flexible. To borrow some analogies from Kuhn: "Looking at a contour map, the student sees lines on paper, the cartographer a picture of a terrain. Looking at a bubble-chamber photograph, the student sees confused and broken lines, the physicist a record of familiar subnuclear events."[2] The basic justification for studying theories of communication is that they provide a set of useful conceptual tools.

The Academic Study of Communication

Communication theory is diverse because communication itself is always present and complex. Looking for the best theory of communication is not particularly useful inasmuch as communication is not a single, unified act but a process consisting of numerous clusters of behavior. Each theory looks at the process from a different angle, and each theory provides insights of its own. Of course, all theories are not equally valid or useful, and any particular investigator may find a specific theory or theories more useful for the work to be undertaken. We should welcome rather than avoid a multitheoretical approach to the complex process of communication.[3]

An obstacle to a multitheoretical approach is the tendency to view communication from the narrow confines of specific academic disciplines. Because disciplines are somewhat arbitrary, disciplinary divisions do not necessarily provide the best method of packaging knowledge. This statement is not meant to suggest that one should avoid identification with a traditional discipline but only that interdisciplinary cooperation is essential. University courses related to communication are found in many departments, just as the theories described in this book represent a wide array of

1. N. R. Hanson, *Patterns of Discovery* (Cambridge: At the University Press, 1961), p. 30.

2. Thomas S. Kuhn, *The Structure of Scientific Revolutions* (Chicago: University of Chicago Press, 1970), p. 111.

3. For an excellent case in favor of multiple approaches to communication, see John Waite Bowers and James J. Bradac, "Issues in Communication Theory: A Metatheoretical Analysis," in *Communication Yearbook 5*, ed. Michael Burgoon (New Brunswick, N.J.: Transaction Books, 1982), pp. 1–28.

disciplines. As Dean Barnlund indicates: "While many disciplines have undoubtedly benefited from adopting a communication model, it is equally true that they, in turn, have added greatly to our understanding of human interaction."[4] Remember that when people tell you they are communication experts, they are saying little. Their primary interests may be in the sciences or the arts, mathematics or literature, biology or politics.[5]

Although scholars from a number of disciplines share an interest in communication, the scholar's first loyalty is usually to the general concepts of the discipline itself. Communication is generally considered subordinate. For example, psychologists study individual behavior and view communication as a particular kind of behavior. Sociologists focus on society and social process, seeing communication as one of several social factors. Anthropologists are interested primarily in culture, and if they investigate communication they treat it as an aspect of a broader theme. Do we conclude from this that communication is less significant as an academic study than behavior, society, and culture? Of course we do not.

In recent years scholars have recognized the centrality of communication and have emphasized it in their research and theory. Some of these scholars were trained in traditional disciplines. Others learned in academic departments called communication or speech communication. Regardless of their original academic homes, these scholars have come together in the new field of communication. They have flipped the scholarly coin to make traditional themes support rather than dominate the study of communication. The field of communication is characterized not only by its focus on communication per se but also by its interest in the entire breadth of communication concerns. The work of the International Communication Association and the Speech Communication Association typifies what is happening in this field.

Although many theories relate to aspects of communication, only a few deal with communication itself. Most of our understanding of communication arises from theories produced in the traditional disciplines. This book includes theories that relate directly to communication as a process and those that contribute to our understanding of communication less directly. The field of communication is so young that it has not produced much theory, so our knowledge of communication still relies primarily on an eclectic approach. This situation is changing, however, and in a few years we will see more direct theorizing about communication. In discussions of theories in this book, the relevance of each theory to the broader study of human communication is explained.

Defining Communication

Because of its complex, multidisciplinary nature, communication is difficult to define. The word *communication* is abstract and, like all words, possesses multiple meanings.[6] Scholars have made many attempts to define communication, but seeking a single working definition may not be as fruitful as probing the various concepts behind the term. The term *communica-*

4. Dean Barnlund, *Interpersonal Communication: Survey and Studies* (New York: Houghton Mifflin, 1968), p. v.

5. The multidisciplinary nature of the study of communication is emphasized in numerous sources, including George Gordon, *The Languages of Communication* (New York: Hastings House, 1969), p. ix; Franklin Knower, "The Development of a Sound Communicology" (unpublished manuscript); C. David Mortensen, *Communication: The Study of Human Interaction* (New York: McGraw-Hill, 1972), p. 22; Kenneth Sereno and C. David Mortensen, "A Framework for Communication Theory," in *Foundations of Communication Theory* (New York: Harper & Row, 1970).

6. For discussions of the multiple meanings of the term *communication*, see as example Gordon, *Languages*; Mortensen, *Human Interaction*; Thomas R. Nilsen, "On Defining Communication," *Speech Teacher* 6 (1957): 10–17. One hundred twenty-six different definitions of communication can be found in Frank E. X. Dance and Carl E. Larson, *The Functions of Human Communication* (New York: Holt, Rinehart & Winston, 1976), Appendix A.

tion can be used legitimately in a number of ways. Frank Dance takes a major step toward clarifying this muddy concept.[7] He discovered fifteen distinct conceptual components in the various definitions. Table 1.1 summarizes the components and provides an example for each. In addition Dance found three points of "critical conceptual differentiation," which form the basic dimensions along which the various definitions differ. The first is *level of observation*. Definitions vary in level of abstractness. Some definitions are broad and inclusive; others are restrictive. The second dimension is the inclusion or exclusion of *intentionality*. Some definitions include only intentional message sending and receiving; others preclude intention. Third is the factor of normative *judgment*. Some definitions include a statement of evaluation; other definitions do not contain such implicit judgments of quality.

Dance's conclusion is important: "We are trying to make the concept of 'communication' do too much work for us."[8] He calls for a *family of concepts*. The theories included in the following chapters, seen collectively, represent a step in the direction of specifying the members of this family of concepts.

An Organizing Framework

Communication theories can be classified in a number of ways. We could, for example, divide theories according to the disciplines in which they were developed. However, such an organizing pattern would probably not be beneficial, as discussed earlier. Instead, in this book theories are organized according to domain. A theory's domain is its topic or subject, or the aspect of communication covered by the theory. This method of organizing theories is advantageous because it allows us to employ elements of communication as guides for using the different theories, moving systematically from one aspect of communication to another. After all, the goal of this book is not merely to summarize a number of theories but to build an understanding of communication in the process.

The theories in this book are divided into three types of domains. The first type includes *general theories* of communication, theories designed to capture the general nature or essence of communication. The second type includes *thematic theories*, those that deal with certain pervasive themes present in most communication events regardless of the setting. The third type consists of *context theories*, theories that apply specifically to a particular setting of communication.

General theories appear in Part II of this book. Three classes of general theories are covered: system theory, symbolic interactionism, and rules theory. System theory captures the holistic, relational nature of the communication process, emphasizing ways in which elements interrelate to establish an indivisible whole. Symbolic interactionism stresses the ways in which humans define themselves, others, and situations by exchanging messages. Rules theory deals with socially derived guidelines for communication behavior.

Part III presents four broad themes of communication that apply to all contexts: language, meaning, information, and persuasion. Language includes verbal and nonverbal signs. Meaning involves the human response to symbols. Information consists of how messages are

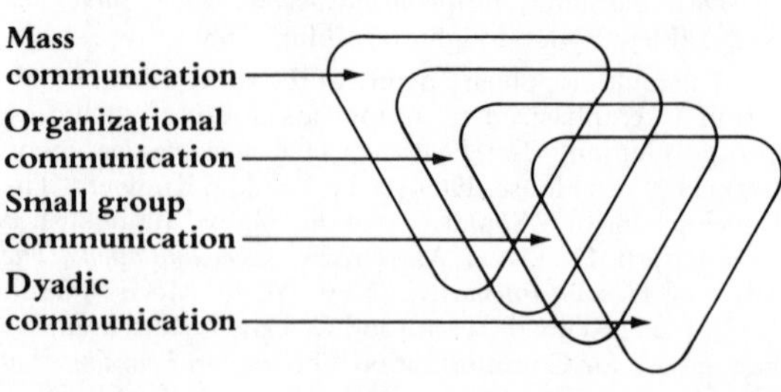

Figure 1.1. Hierarchy of contexts.

7. Frank E. X. Dance, "The 'Concept' of Communication," *Journal of Communication* 20 (1970): 201–10; also Dance and Larson, *Functions*.

8. Dance, "Concept," p. 210.

TABLE 1.1
Conceptual components in communication

1. Symbols/Verbal/Speech	"Communication is the verbal interchange of thought or idea" (Hoben, 1954).
2. Understanding	"Communication is the process by which we understand others and in turn endeavor to be understood by them. It is dynamic, constantly changing and shifting in response to the total situation" (Anderson, 1959).
3. Interaction/Relationship/Social Process	"Interaction, even on the biological level, is a kind of communication; otherwise common acts could not occur" (Mead, reprinted 1963).
4. Reduction of Uncertainty	"Communication arises out of the need to reduce uncertainty, to act effectively, to defend or strengthen the ego" (Barnlund, 1964).
5. Process	"Communication: the transmission of information, idea, emotion, skills, etc., by the use of symbols—words, pictures, figures, graphs, etc. It is the act or process of transmission that is usually called communication" (Berelson and Steiner, 1964).
6. Transfer/Transmission/Interchange	"The connecting thread appears to be the idea of something's being transferred from one thing, or person, to another. We use the word 'communication' sometimes to refer to what is so transferred, sometimes to the means by which it is transferred, sometimes to the whole process. In many cases, what is transferred in this way continues to be shared; if I convey information to another person, it does not leave my own possession through coming into his. Accordingly, the word 'communication' acquires also the sense of participation. It is in this sense, for example, that religious worshipers are said to communicate" (Ayer, 1955).
7. Linking/Binding	"Communication is the process that links discontinuous parts of the living world to one another" (Ruesch, 1957).
8. Commonality	"It (communication) is a process that makes common to two or several what was the monopoly of one or some" (Gode, 1959).
9. Channel/Carrier/Means/Route	"The means of sending military messages, orders, etc., as by telephone, telegraph, radio, couriers" (*American College Dictionary*).
10. Replicating Memories	"Communication is the process of conducting the attention of another person for the purpose of replicating memories" (Cartier and Harwood, 1953).
11. Discriminative Response/Behavior Modifying Response	"Communication is the discriminatory response of an organism to a stimulus" (Stevens, 1950).
12. Stimuli	"Every communication act is viewed as a transmission of information, consisting of a discriminative stimuli, from a source to a recipient" (Newcomb, reprinted 1966).
13. Intentional	"In the main, communication has as its central interest those behavioral situations in which a source transmits a message to a receiver(s) *with conscious intent to affect the latter's behaviors*" (Miller, 1966).
14. Time/Situation	"The communication process is one of transition from one structured situation-as-a-whole to another, in preferred design" (Sondel, 1956).
15. Power	"Communication is the mechanism by which power is exerted" (Schacter, 1951).

used to reduce uncertainty and to make predictions and decisions. Persuasion encompasses the ways in which individuals change in transactions with others.

Part IV deals with contextual theories, theories that aim to explain aspects of communication appearing in particular settings. Four contextual domains are included: dyadic, group, organizational, and mass communication. Dyadic, group, and organizational contexts are basically interpersonal, while the mass context is mediated; that is, conducted through an intervening channel. Communication contexts are conceived of as a hierarchy. Each higher level includes important aspects of lower levels within it. Mass communication, for example, necessarily involves organizational communication, group communication, and dyadic communication. Figure 1.1 illustrates the hierarchy of contexts.

Many communication scholars would add a fifth context to this analysis: *intrapersonal,* or communication within the self. Certainly, this addition is valid, but it is not included here for two reasons. First, few theories address this level directly. Second, intrapersonal communication is so pervasive that it cuts across all other contexts, making it a universal theme. Communication theories most relevant to intrapersonal communication deal with language, meaning, information, and persuasion. Part III of the book itself might be considered a summary of intrapersonal communication theories.

To further visualize the contextual model of domain, consider the two dimensions of domain illustrated in Figure 1.2. The vertical dimension consists of themes that cut across contexts, and the horizontal dimension includes contexts in which all the themes operate. Thematic theories cover topics relevant to the rows, and context theories cover topics relevant to the columns. General theories attempt to capture the general nature of the process, cutting across both columns and rows.

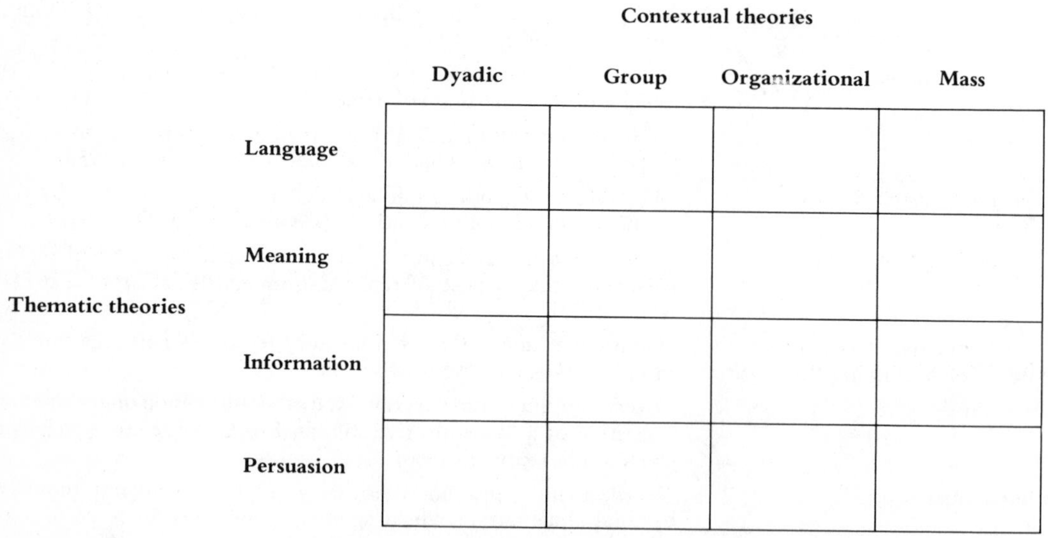

Contextual theories

Thematic theories		**Dyadic**	**Group**	**Organizational**	**Mass**
	Language				
	Meaning				
	Information				
	Persuasion				

Figure 1.2. Theoretical domains.

CHAPTER

2 Theory in the Process of Inquiry

In the study of human communication, as in all branches of knowledge, it is appropriate, even compelling, to ask ourselves: How did we come to profess what we know or think we know? The questions of truth, discovery, and inquiry is a particularly important place to begin this book because each of the chapters presents a kind of truth. Every theorist represented here has taken a stab at truth.

This chapter discusses the process of developing knowledge. Knowledge does not just spring into being. Rather, it is the product of hard work, with scholarship taking a central role in its generation. First we will discuss inquiry as a general process, including the nature of scholarship. Then we will take a closer look at theory as a part of inquiry. Later we will examine central philosophical issues related to communication theory, concluding with a discussion of the criteria for evaluating theories.

The Process of Inquiry in Communication

A Basic Model of Inquiry

Inquiry involves processes of systematic, disciplined ordering of experience that lead to the development of understanding and knowledge. Inquiry is what scholars do to "find out." Inquiry is not just one process, of course. Many modes are used, but all are distinguished from mundane or common experience. Inquiry is focused; it involves a planned means or method and it has an expected outcome. The investigator is never sure of the exact outcome of inquiry and can anticipate only the general form or nature of the results.

These scholars also share a general approach to inquiry that involves three stages.[1] The first and guiding stage of all inquiry is *asking questions*. Gerald Miller and Henry Nicholson, in fact, believe that inquiry is "nothing more . . . than the process of asking interesting, significant questions . . . and providing disciplined, systematic answers to them."[2] These authors outline common types of questions asked by the scholar. Questions of *definition* call for concepts as answers, seeking to identify what is observed or inferred (What is it? What shall we call it?). Questions of *fact* ask about properties and relations in what is observed (What does it consist of? How does it relate to other phenomena?). Questions of *value* probe aesthetic, pragmatic, and ethical qualities of the observed. Such questions result in value judgments about phenomena (Is it beautiful? Is it effective? Is it proper?).

The second stage of inquiry is *observation*. Here the scholar experiences the object of inquiry. Methods of observation vary significantly from one tradition to another. Some scholars observe by examining records and artifacts, others by personal involvement, others by using instruments and controlled experiment, others by taking testimony. Whatever form is used, the investigator employs some planned method for answering the questions.

The third stage of inquiry is *constructing answers*. Here the scholar attempts to define, to describe and explain, to make judgments. This stage, which is the focus of this book, is usually referred to as *theory*.

1. The process of inquiry is described in Gerald E. Miller and Henry Nicholson, *Communication Inquiry* (Reading, Mass.: Addison-Wesley, 1976).

2. Ibid, p. ix.

Students naturally tend to think of the stages of inquiry as linear, occurring one step at a time, but inquiry does not proceed in this fashion. Each stage affects and is affected by the others. Observations often stimulate new questions, and theories are challenged both by observations and questions. Theories lead to new questions, and observations are structured in part by existing theories. Figure 2.1 illustrates the interaction among the stages of inquiry.

Types of Scholarship

The preceding section discusses inquiry in general terms, ignoring the distinctions between the many types of inquiry. These types stem from different methods of observation and lead to different forms of theory. Methods of inquiry often are grouped into three broad forms of scholarship: scientific, humanistic, and social scientific.[3] Although all of these forms of scholarship share the common elements discussed in the previous section, they also have major differences.

Scientific Scholarship. Science often is associated with objectivity. This association is valid or not, depending on how you view objectivity. If by objectivity you mean suspension of values, then science definitely is not objective. However, if by objectivity you mean standardization, then science is indeed objective; or, more accurately, it aims to be objective. The scientist attempts to look at the world in such a way that all other observers, using the same methods, will see the same thing in a given observation. Replications of a study will yield identical results. Remember that such objectivity is the goal-ideal of science but that it is not always achieved.

Science is consistent with the philosophical position that the world has form and structure apart from differences between individual observers. The world sits in wait of discovery. Where the scholar has reason to believe that a phenomenon exists in the world, the goal is to observe that phenomenon as accurately as possible. Since no divinely revealed way exists for knowing how accurate one's observations are, the scientist must rely on agreement among observers. This reliance is why objectivity or replicability is so important in science. If all trained observers report the same results, we can be assured that the phenomenon has been accurately observed. Because of the emphasis on discovering a knowable world, scientific methods are especially well suited to problems of nature.

Humanistic Scholarship. While science is associated with objectivity, the humanities are associated with subjectivity. Science aims to standardize observation; the humanities seek creative individuality. If the aim of science is to reduce human differences in what is observed, the aim of the humanities is to understand individual subjective response.

While science is an "out there" activity, humanities stress the "in here." Science focuses on the discovered world; humanities focus on

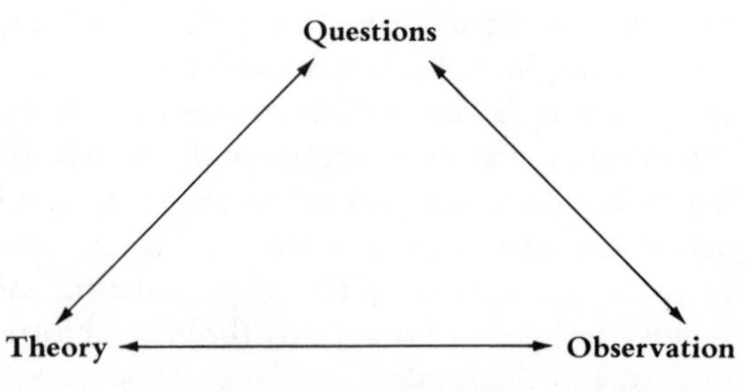

Figure 2.1. The stages of inquiry.

3. An excellent, though somewhat different, discussion of scholarship can be found in Ernest G. Bormann, *Theory and Research in the Communicative Arts* (New York: Holt, Rinehart & Winston, 1965). For more detailed discussions of the forms of scholarship presented in Bormann, see Nathan Glazer, "The Social Sciences in Liberal Education," in *The Philosophy of the Curriculum*, ed. Sidney Hook (Buffalo: Prometheus Books, 1975), pp. 145–58; James L. Jarrett, *The Humanities and Humanistic Education* (Reading, Mass.: Addison-Wesley, 1973); Gerald Holton, "Science, Science Teaching, and Rationality," in *The Philosophy of the Curriculum*, ed. Sidney Hook (Buffalo: Prometheus Books, 1975), pp. 101–18.

the discovering person. Science seeks consensus; humanities seek alternative interpretations. Humanists often are suspicious of the claim that there is an immutable world to be discovered. The humanities scholar tends not to separate the knower from the known. The classical humanistic position is that who one is determines what one sees. Because of its emphasis on the subjective response, humanistic scholarship is especially well suited to problems of art, personal experience, and values.

This discussion is not intended to lead you to believe that science and humanities are so far apart that they never come together. Almost any program of research and theory building includes some aspects of both scientific and humanistic scholarship. The differences mentioned relate to the primary thrust of the two groups of scholarship; points of cross-over also exist between them. At times the scientist is a humanist, using intuition, creativity, interpretation, and insight. Ironically, the scientist must be subjective in creating the mechanisms that will eventually lead to objective observation. Research design is a creative process. At times the humanist, in turn, must be scientific, seeking facts that enable scholars to understand the experiences to which ultimately they will respond subjectively. As we shall see in the next section, where science leaves off and humanities begin is not always clear.

The Special Case of the Social Sciences. A third form of scholarship is social science. Many social scientists would not separate this type of scholarship from science, seeing it instead as an extension of natural science. In fact, numerous methods used by social scientists are borrowed from physics. Social science, however, is a world apart. Paradoxically, it includes elements of both science and humanities, but it is different from both.

Social scholars attempt to understand human beings as objects of study. They seek to observe and interpret patterns of human behavior. In practice scholars distinguish between behavioral science and social science, the former referring to individual behavior and the latter to human interaction. For our purposes these two branches are combined.

In order to understand human behavior, the scholar must observe it. If behavioral patterns do in fact exist, then observation must be as objective as possible. In other words, the behavioral scientist, like the natural scientist, must establish consensus on what is observed. Once the behavioral phenomena are accurately observed, they must be explained or interpreted. Interpreting may be confounded by the fact that the object of observation, the human subject, is itself an active, knowing being. Unlike objects in the natural world, the human subject is capable of having knowledge, of possessing values and making interpretations. Can "scientific" explanation of human behavior take place without consideration of the "humanistic" knowledge of the observed person? This question is the central philosophical issue of social science.

Controversy about the nature of inquiry into human life is common in social science. In previous years the majority of social scientists believed that scientific methods alone would suffice to uncover the mysteries of human experience. Today most social scientists realize that while scientific methods are an important aspect of their scholarship, a strong humanistic element is present as well. Specifically, the individual subjective response must be considered in understanding how people think and evaluate.

The study of communication is a social science. It involves understanding how people behave in creating, exchanging, and interpreting messages. Consequently, communication inquiry combines both scientific and humanistic methods. The theories covered in this book, as examples of social science, vary significantly in their use of the languages of science and humanities. Traditionally in the field of speech communication, humanistic theories of communication have been referred to as *rhetorical theory* and scientific theories as *communication theory*. This distinction is not particularly useful. All of the theories we will discuss deal with human communication; both humanistic and scientific theories are worthy of inclusion in our body of knowledge about human communication.

In the field of communication there is no universal agreement on the limits of science and humanities. We are far from consensus on the questions that can and should be approached scientifically and those that should be the focus of humanistic methods. In the final analysis scholars defend the traditions in which they are trained and which they enjoy the most. These issues of scholarship are taken up in more detail later in the chapter under the heading of philosophical issues.

The Nature of Theory

What is theory? Uses of the term range from farmer Jones's theory about when his pullets will start laying eggs to Einstein's theory of relativity. People sometimes use the term *theory* to mean any unsubstantiated guess about something. Too, theory often is contrasted with fact. Even among scientists, writers, and philosophers the term is used differently.

Theory is often distinguished from *model*. In a broad sense the term *model* can apply to any symbolic representation of a thing, process, or idea. We thus encounter models of the human figure, trains, and planes. On the conceptual level are models that represent ideas and processes. Such models may be graphic, verbal, or mathematical. In any case a model is usually viewed as an analogy to some real-world phenomenon. Thus models are interpreted metaphorically so that the model builder attempts to draw symbolic parallels between structures and relationships in the model and those in the modeled event or process.[4]

Leonard Hawes reviews several common distinctions between the concepts of *model* and *theory*.[5] Most distinctions actually are misconceptions, he believes. He defines a theory as an *explanation* and a model as a *representation*. For him, models merely represent aspects of the phenomenon without explaining the interrelationships among the parts of the modeled process.

In this book we will not pursue the distinctions between theories and models of communication.[6] The purpose of the book is to represent a wide range of thought about the communication process. Therefore the term *theory* is used in its broadest sense as *any conceptual representation or explanation of the communication process.* The intent is not to distinguish between those representations called models and those called theories, though technical differences may exist.

As you will see in the following pages, many conceptual representations are available. In their most general form, however, all are attempts of various scholars to represent what is conceived as important in the process of communication. Two generalizations can be made about theories.

First, all theories are abstractions. Theories of communication are not themselves the process being conceptualized. As a result every theory is partial; every theory leaves something out. Theories focus on certain aspects of the process at the expense of other aspects. This truism about theory is important because it re-

4. Max Black, *Models and Metaphors* (Ithaca: Cornell University Press, 1962), chap. 13.

5. Leonard Hawes, *Pragmatics of Analoguing: Theory and Model Construction in Communication* (Reading, Mass.: Addison-Wesley, 1975), pp. 122–23.

6. For definitions of the terms *theory* and *model*, see Dean C. Barnlund, *Interpersonal Communication: Survey and Studies* (New York: Houghton Mifflin, 1968), p. 18; Bormann, *Communicative Arts*, p. 96; Karl W. Deutsch, "On Communication Models in the Social Sciences," *Public Opinion Quarterly* 16 (1952): 357; Calvin S. Hall and Gardner Lindzey, *Theories of Personality* (New York: Wiley, 1970), pp. 9–10; Gerald R. Miller, *Speech Communication: A Behavioral Approach* (New York: Bobbs-Merrill, 1966), pp. 52–53; C. David Mortensen, *Communication: The Study of Human Interaction* (New York: McGraw-Hill, 1972), p. 29; Frank E. X. Dance and Carl E. Larson, *The Functions of Human Communication* (New York: Holt, Rinehart & Winston, 1976), p. 3; Hawes, *Pragmatics*, pp. 28–29.

veals the basic inadequacy of theory. No single theory will ever reveal Truth. The creator of a theory attempts to point out and explain what is believed to be important, nothing more.[7]

Second, all theories must be viewed as constructions. Theories are created by people, not ordained by God. Theories represent various ways in which observers see their environments, but theories themselves are not reality. Many readers and theorists forget this principle, and students often are trapped by the conception that reality can be seen in this or that theory. Abraham Kaplan writes: "The formation of a theory is not just the discovery of a hidden fact; the theory is a way of looking at the facts, of organizing and representing them. . . . A theory must somehow fit God's world, but in an important sense it creates a world of its own."[8]

Let us take an analogy from biology. Two observers using microscopes may see different things in an amoeba, depending on their theoretical points of view. One observer sees a one-celled animal; the other sees an organism without cells. The first viewer stresses the properties of an amoeba that resemble properties of all other cells—the wall, the nucleus, the cytoplasm. The second observer concentrates on the analogy between the amoeba and other whole animals. This observer sees ingestion of food, excretion, reproduction, mobility. Neither observer is wrong. Their theoretical frameworks simply stress different aspects of the observed object.[9] Because of the fact that theories and models are constructions, questioning a theory's *usefulness* is wiser than questioning its *truthfulness*.[10] This statement is not intended to imply that theories do not represent reality, but that any given "truth" can be represented in a variety of ways, depending on the theorist's orientation.

The Functions of Theory

Eight important and overlapping functions of theory can be identified: (1) the organizing and summarizing function, (2) the focus function, (3) the clarifying function, (4) the observational function, (5) the predictive function, (6) the heuristic function, (7) the communicative function, and (8) the control function.[11]

The first function of theory is to organize and summarize knowledge. We do not see the world in bits of data. Humans need to organize and synthesize the world. Patterns must be sought and connections discovered. Theories and models are one way of accomplishing this organization of knowledge. An added benefit of this function is theory's contribution to cumulation in knowledge. The student, practitioner, or scientist does not have to start anew with each investigation. Knowledge is organized into a body of theories, and the investigator begins a study with the organized knowledge of generations of previous scholars.

The second function is that of focusing. Theories, in addition to organizing data, focus attention on important variables and relationships, as a map depicts terrain. From the overall surface a map points out recreation spots, communities, picnic grounds, and shopping centers. To the persistent question of "What will I look at?" the theory points out areas for investigation.

Third, theories provide the advantage of clarifying what is observed. The clarification not only helps the observer to understand relationships in communication but to interpret specific events. Theories provide guideposts for interpreting, explaining, and understanding the complexity of human relations.

Fourth, theories offer an observational aid.

7. For discussions of the partial nature of theories, see Miller, *Speech*, p. 52; Lee Thayer, "On Theory-Building in Communication: Some Conceptual Problems," *Journal of Communication* 13 (1963): 217–35.

8. Abraham Kaplan, *The Conduct of Inquiry* (San Francisco: Chandler, 1964), p. 309.

9. Examples from N. R. Hanson, *Patterns of Discovery* (Cambridge: At the University Press, 1961), pp. 4–5.

10. See Hall and Lindzey, *Theories*, pp. 10–11.

11. This listing is a synthesis of functions gathered from a variety of sources. See Barnlund, *Interpersonal Communication*, p. 18; Irwin B. J. Bross, *Design for Decision* (New York: Macmillan, 1953).

Closely related to the focus function, the observational function points out not only what to observe but how to observe. Especially for those theories that provide operational definitions, the theorist gives the most precise indication possible about what is meant by a particular concept. Thus by following directions the reader is led to observe details elaborated by the theory.

The fifth function of theories, to predict, is one of the most widely discussed areas of scientific inquiry. Many theories allow the inquirer to make predictions about outcomes and effects in the data. This ability to predict is important in the applied communication areas such as persuasion and attitude change, psychotherapy, small group dynamics, and organizational communication. Teachers work toward developing skills and abilities to improve communication competence. Various communication theories aid this process by enabling the student to substitute well-founded predictions for good guesses.

The sixth theoretical function, the heuristic function, is also frequently discussed. A familiar axiom is that a good theory generates research. The speculation forwarded in theories of communication often provides a guide as to the direction the research will take and thus aids in furthering the investigation. This heuristic function of aiding discovery is vital to the growth of knowledge and is in a sense an outgrowth of each of the other functions of theory.

Seventh, theories serve an indispensable communicative function. Most investigators want and need to publish their observations and speculations for other interested persons. Theory provides a framework for this communication and provides an open forum for discussion, debate, and criticism. Through the communication of numerous explanations of the phenomena we study, comparison and theory improvement become possible.

The eighth function of theories is control. This function grows out of value questions, in which the theorist seeks to judge the effectiveness and propriety of certain behavior. Such theory is often referred to as *normative*, in that it seeks to establish norms of performance. Much theory, of course, does not seek to fulfill this function at all, remaining on the *descriptive* level.

Theory Development and Change

Although it is important to understand that the theory is an abstraction from reality, realizing the functional relationship between the two is also necessary. Theory is not a purely abstract entity with little relationship to actual experience. In fact, theory and experience interact continually for the ultimate improvement of both. Irwin Bross's excellent model of this theory-experience relationship is shown in Figure 2.2.[12]

From original experiences (including research), we formulate our symbolic models. We

12. Bross, *Design*, pp. 161–77.

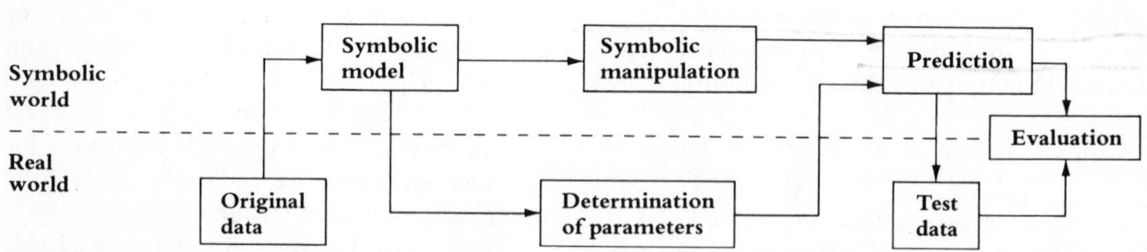

From *Design for Decision* by Irwin Bross. Copyright © 1953 by the Free Press, a corporation. Reprinted with permission of the publisher.

Figure 2.2.

are able to think through and manipulate variables in our heads, while at the same time focusing on specified parameters in the real world. From the interaction of these two, predictions are made, tested, and verified. Over time the models change, grow, and improve, as illustrated in Bross's more extended diagram shown in Figure 2.3. Thus good theory development is a constant process of testing, formulating, and retesting.

This testing-retesting process stresses the need for research, which is vital to theory development in three interconnected ways. Research allows for (1) specific investigating of facts that are singled out as important, (2) testing the theory's predictive usefulness on real events, and (3) further developing and articulating the theory.[13]

Theories may change in three important ways. The first is *growth by extension*. Here knowledge is expanded piece by piece, moving from an understanding of one bit of reality to an adjoining bit. This is the process of adding new concepts to the old. On the other hand, the second way, *growth by intension*, is the process of developing an increasingly precise understanding of concepts or single bits of knowledge.[14] Kuhn, in a monograph on scientific revolutions, describes the third process of change, *revolution*.[15] Over time researchers in an area of study increase their knowledge through extension and intension. At some point an extraordinary case is discovered that runs counter to prevailing assumptions of the theory in use. At this point a crisis develops, leading to the development of a new theoretical approach. The new theory represents a different way of looking at the world, a way that competes with the original theory. Gradually, the revolutionary theory is accepted by more and more members of the field until it becomes the primary theoretical approach. Often during the years when a new theoretical approach is being formulated, theorists who support the old approach become defensive, protecting their many years or entire lifetimes of work that may be at stake.

The scientific revolution described by Kuhn often requires redefinition of an entire field of knowledge. Previous areas of study may die; others may be born; new weddings may occur. "What were ducks in the scientist's world before the revolution are rabbits afterwards. The man who saw the exterior of the box from above later sees its interior from below."[16] Theory in any field, including communication, is crucial for the formal investigation of phenomena. Kaplan states this idea: "What is

13. Thomas S. Kuhn, *The Structure of Scientific Revolution* (Chicago: University of Chicago Press, 1970), pp. 25–27.

14. Kaplan, *Conduct*, p. 305.

15. Kuhn, *Structure*.

16. Ibid., p. 111.

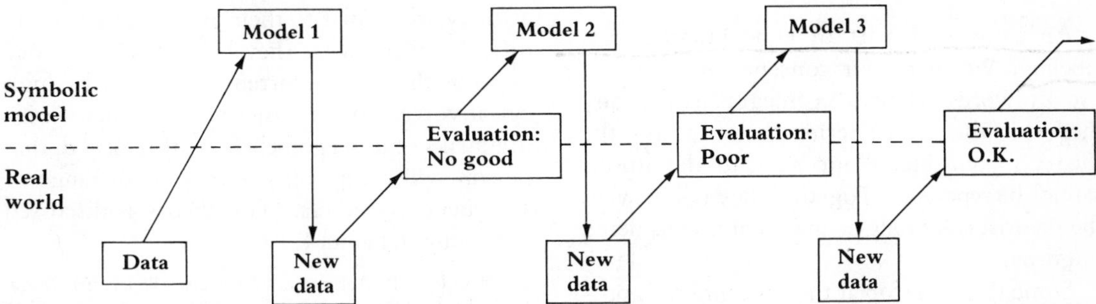

From *Design for Decision* by Irwin Bross. Copyright © 1953 by the Free Press, a corporation. Reprinted with permission of the publisher.

Figure 2.3.

rooted in the particularity of fact comes to flower in the generalization of theory—or else it fails to seed."[17]

Concepts in Theories

The first and most basic aspect of a theory is its set of *concepts*. We as persons are by nature concept-processing beings. Our entire symbolic world—everything known—stems from concept formation. Kuhn writes: "Neither scientists nor laymen learn to see the world piecemeal or item by item; . . . both scientists and laymen sort out whole areas together from the flux of experience."[18] Although the process of conceptualizing is complex, basically it consists of grouping things and events into categories according to observed commonalities. The communication theorist observes many variables in communication and classifies and labels them according to perceived patterns. The goal of theory is to increase the usefulness of its concepts. Kaplan describes the process:

> As knowledge of a particular subject-matter grows, our conception of that subject-matter changes; as our concepts become more fitting, we can learn more and more. Like all existential dilemmas in science, of which this is an instance, the paradox is resolved by a process of approximation: the better our concepts, the better the theory we can formulate with them, and in turn, the better the concepts for the next improved theory. . . . It is only through such successions that the scientist can hope ultimately to achieve success.[19]

An important part of conceptualizing is labeling. We mark our concepts by symbols, usually words. Hence, an integral part of any theory is the set of terms that captures the theory's concepts. Concepts and definitions cannot be separated. Together they tell us what the theorist is looking at and what is considered important.

Some theories stop at the concept level, providing only a list of concepts and definitions without explaining how the concepts interrelate or affect one another. Such theories are known as *taxonomies.* (Note that many scholars believe that taxonomies are not theories.) Introductory communication texts often include basic models that list the "parts" of the communication process, including such concepts as source, message, receiver, feedback, and so forth. The best theories, however, go beyond concepts to provide explanations, statements about how concepts interrelate. These explanations tell us why variables are connected. Theories that stop at the concept level are primitive at best, since the goal of theory building is to provide an understanding of how a phenomenon operates.

Explanation in Theories

The Principle of Necessity. A phenomenon is explained to the extent that regularities in the relationships among concepts are identified. An explanation designates some force among variables that makes particular outcomes *necessary*. Explanations vary according to the type of necessity believed to exist. There are three types.[20]

Causal necessity occurs in a causal relationship. Here the theory states that an antecedent event determines the behavior of a subsequent event: A is believed to cause B. This kind of explanation involves if-then reasoning. Suppose, for example, that you wished to explain why people sometimes perceive statements that actually are similar to their own beliefs as quite different from what they believe. One theory explains that this occurrence is caused by high ego involvement. In other words, when an individual's central ego beliefs are threatened, that person will accept only a very small range of statements by others. (This theory is discussed in detail in Chapter 8.)

17. Kaplan, *Conduct*, p. 119.
18. Kuhn, *Structure*, p. 28.
19. Kaplan, *Conduct*, p. 53.
20. Based on P. Achinstein, *Laws and Explanation* (New York: Oxford University Press, 1971); see also Donald P. Cushman and W. Barnett Pearce, "Generality and Necessity in Three Types of Theory about Human Communication, with Special Attention to Rules Theory," *Human Communication Research* 3 (1977): 344–53.

The second type of explanation employs *practical necessity*. Because this form of explanation applies primarily to human social interaction, it is often used in communication theories. It suggests that a person may choose to behave in a particular way to meet goals. One's choice is affected by a variety of pressures from self, others, and situation. In causal necessity behavior is determined by previous conditions, with the person responding *passively*. In practical necessity the person *actively* selects courses of action to achieve some future state. In causal explanation the subsequent event is explained by the antecedent event. In practical explanation the antecedent event is explained by the subsequent event. For example, you would be using practical necessity if you explained that people construct messages in particular ways because they wish to achieve identification with an audience. (This theory is discussed in Chapter 4.)

The third form of explanation relies on *logical necessity*. This form of explanation is more difficult to understand. A theory using logical necessity as a basis for explanation consists of a series of interlocked statements about a phenomenon. One state of affairs is seen as a logical consequence of the acceptance of other statements. In the other two forms of explanation, a linear link in time is assumed: A causes B, or A leads to B. In logical necessity such is not the case. Logical necessity relies on a series of internally consistent definitions and a set of correlations or correspondences among events. As an example consider the following series of theoretical statements:

1. A complementary relationship exists when the behavior of one person follows naturally from the behavior of another.

2. This condition exists when the relational rules are both understood and accepted by the partners.

3. Power is the ability to control relational rules.

4. One-up behavior asserts control over the relational rules.

5. One-down behavior accepts control by the other in a relationship.

6. In a complementary relationship the person who consistently behaves in a one-up fashion has the power.

In the above example each statement is necessary if you believe the other statements in the series; a logical, necessary relationship exists among statements. Further, this series of statements leads us to accept a positive correlation between power, one-up behavior, and control. This correlation is made to seem necessary not because of an established consistent link between one event and another in time but because of the logic of the whole system of definitions. (This theory is presented in more detail in Chapter 9.)

Laws, Rules, and Systems. Traditionally in the field of communication, theories have been separated into three types, depending on their primary method of explanation. Although such a typology is neat, it has been criticized in recent years for presenting a false picture of theoretical differences.[21] Because the laws-rules-system trichotomy is prevalent in the literature, we will discuss it briefly. However, the next section, on theory typology, covers a system that is superior for analyzing theory based on modes of explanation.

Law theories are believed to rely primarily on causal necessity, embodying the spirit of science. They make use of covering laws that specify universal causal relations among variables.[22] *Rules theories*, which rely on practical necessity, are believed to be more humanistic, claiming

21. This controversy is well summarized in Ernest Bormann, *Communication Theory* (New York: Holt, Rinehart & Winston, 1980), chap. 7.

22. For discussion of this approach, see Charles R. Berger, "The Covering Law Perspective as a Theoretical Basis for the Study of Human Communication," *Communication Quarterly* 25 (1977): 7–18.

that people actively choose and change rules. Rules theorists are seen as doubting the viability of covering laws in communication.[23] In between lies the *systems approach*, which purportedly relies on logical necessity. This type of theory is believed to center on the logical relations among elements of a holistic system. Such theories stress the intercorrelation among events.[24]

A Theory Typology. Doubt has been cast on the utility of this laws-rules-systems trichotomy. Differences may not be as clear as suggested by its advocates. Although the covering law approach clearly embodies a scientific epistemology, the difference between systems and rules appears to be more a matter of generality or abstractness than method of explanation. Besides, there are important differences in explanation even among theories that are classed as systems or those classed as rules. For example, rules theorists disagree among themselves as to how much power rules exert over people's actions, and system theorists equivocate about whether systems relations are causal, correlational, or both. Keep in mind that we are not discarding the terms *laws, rules*, and *systems*. (In fact, this book has chapters on both rules and systems.) The problem lies in using these labels together as a trichotomy to designate particular forms of explanation.

Therefore, this book does not discuss theoretical differences in terms of laws, rules, and systems. Rather, two dimensions are used: differences in method of explanation and differences in generality. On the generality dimension, two types of theory are presented. *Analytic* theories assume that any phenomenon is best understood as a composite of finely screened elements. The aim of such theory is to reduce the whole down to its knowable parts. *Synthetic* theories are more abstract, focusing on general patterns and interrelationships.[25] Analytic and synthetic theories can be further divided into different types, depending on the method of explanation used. Although analytic theories tend to be causal and synthetic theories tend to be practical, crossovers often occur, as we shall see momentarily. Figure 2.4 outlines eight resulting types of theory, including two types that are nonexplanatory.

Philosophical Issues in the Study of Communication

Communication Metatheory

Metatheory, as the prefix *meta-* suggests, is a body of speculation on the nature of inquiry that goes beyond the specific content of given theories. It addresses such questions as what should be observed, how observation should take place, and what form theory should take. Metatheoretical debates are a natural consequence of uncertainty over the status of knowledge in a field. In the last decade or so, metatheory has dominated the communication field. Communication scholars have come to question the adequacy of their methods, precisely because of the problems of social science summarized earlier in this chapter.[26]

Philosophy as a discipline deals with problems of knowledge and reality. Philosophy questions the basic assumptions and methods of proof used in generating knowledge in all walks

23. For a discussion of this approach, see Donald P. Cushman, "The Rules Perspective as a Theoretical Basis for the Study of Human Communication," *Communication Quarterly* 25 (1977): 30–45.

24. For a discussion of this approach, see Peter R. Monge, "The Systems Perspective as a Theoretical Basis for the Study of Human Communication," *Communication Quarterly* 25 (1977): 19–29.

25. This analysis adapted from Vernon E. Cronen and Leslie K. Davis, "Alternative Approaches for the Communication Theorist: Problems in the Laws-Rules-Systems Trichotomy," *Human Communication Research* 4 (1978): 120–28.

26. For another discussion of metatheory, see John Waite Bowers and James J. Bradac, "Issues in Communication Theory: A Metatheoretical Analysis," in *Communication Yearbook 5*, ed. Michael Burgoon (New Brunswick, N.J.: Transaction Books, 1982), pp. 1–28.

of life. Thus the kind of metatheoretical discussion that has occurred in communication in recent years constitutes an important philosophical analysis of communication research and theory. This philosophical examination is somewhat complex, yet it can be grouped into three major themes: epistemology, ontology, and perspective. These areas are discussed below.

Issues of Epistemology

Epistemology is the branch of philosophy that studies knowledge. Epistemologists ask how humans know what they claim to know. Epistemologists question observations and claims as a way of understanding the nature of knowledge and the processes by which it is gained. Any good discussion of inquiry and theory will inevitably come back to epistemological issues.

Because of the diversity of disciplines involved in the study of communication and the resultant divergence of thought about research and theory, epistemological issues are important in this field. Some of the most basic of these issues can be expressed as questions.[27]

To what extent can knowledge exist before experience? Many theorists believe that all knowledge arises from experience. We observe the world and thereby come to know about it. Yet

27. This analysis from Stephen W. Littlejohn, "Epistemology and the Study of Human Communication" (Paper delivered at the Speech Communication Association, New York City, November 1980). See also Littlejohn, "An Overview of Contributions to Human Communication Theory from Other Disciplines," in *Human Communication Theory: Comparative Essays*, ed. Frank E. X. Dance (New York: Harper & Row, 1982), 247–49. For a somewhat different approach, see W. Bennett Pearce, "Metatheoretical Concerns in Communication," *Communication Quarterly* 25 (1977): 3–6.

Explanation dimension	Generality dimension →	Analytic theories	Synthetic theories
	Causal explanation	Type 1 Theories low in level of abstraction using causal explanation	Type 2 Theories high in level of abstraction using causal explanation
	Logical explanation	Type 3 Theories low in level of abstraction using logical explanation	Type 4 Theories high in level of abstraction using logical explanation
	Practical explanation	Type 5 Theories low in level of abstraction using practical explanation	Type 6 Theories high in level of abstraction using practical explanation
	Nonexplanatory	Type 7 Taxonomies low in level of abstraction	Type 8 Taxonomies high in level of abstraction

Figure 2.4. Types of theory.

is there something in our basic nature that provides a kind of knowledge even before we experience the world? Many philosophers believe so. This kind of "knowledge" would consist of inherent mechanisms of thinking and perceiving. For example, strong evidence exists that children do not learn language entirely from hearing it spoken. Rather, they may acquire language by using innate models to test what they hear. (We will discuss this idea more in Chapter 5.)

To what extent is knowledge universal? Is knowledge certain, there for the taking by whoever is able to ascertain it? Or is knowledge relative and changing? The debate over this issue has persisted for hundreds of years. Communication theorists vary in terms of assumptions about the certainty of truth. Those who take a universal stance will admit to errors in their theories, but they believe that these errors are merely a result of not yet having discovered the complete truth. Relativists would have us believe that knowledge will never be certain because there is no universal reality that can be comprehended.

By what process does knowledge arise? This question is extremely complex, and the debate on the issue lies at the heart of epistemology. There are at least three positions on the issue. Mentalism or *rationalism* suggests that knowledge arises out of the sheer power of the human mind. This position places ultimate faith in human reasoning. *Empiricism* states that knowledge arises in perception. We experience the world and literally "see" what is going on. *Constructivism* believes that people create knowledge in order to function pragmatically in life. People project themselves into what they experience. Constructivists believe that phenomena in the world can be fruitfully conceptualized many different ways, knowledge being what the person has made of the world.

Is knowledge best conceived in parts or wholes? Gestaltists teach that true knowledge consists of general, indivisible understandings. They believe that phenomena are highly interrelated and operate as a system. Analysts, on the other hand, believe that knowledge consists of understanding how parts operate separately.

To what extent is knowledge explicit? Many philosophers and scholars believe that you cannot know something unless you can state it. Knowledge is thus seen as explicit. Others claim that much of knowledge is hidden, that people operate on the basis of sensibilities that are not conscious and that they may not even be able to express. Such knowledge is said to be tacit.[28]

The way in which scholars conduct inquiry and construct theories depends largely on their epistemological assumptions. Many basic positions arise from the issues just described. These positions can be called *world views*. Numerous fine distinctions can be made among these positions, but our discussion groups them into two broad opposing world views that affect thinking about communication.[29]

World View I. This tradition is based on empiricist and rationalist ideas. It treats reality as distinct from the human being, something that people discover outside themselves. It assumes a physical, knowable reality that is self-evident to the trained observer.

Discovery is important in this position; the world is waiting for the scientist to find it. Since

28. See Michael Polanyi, *Personal Knowledge* (London: Routledge and Kegan Paul, 1958).

29. This particular two-fold analysis is supported in part by Georg H. von Wright, *Explanation and Understanding* (Ithaca: Cornell University Press, 1971) and Joseph Houna, "Two Ideals of Scientific Theorizing," in *Communication Yearbook 5*, ed. Michael Burgoon (New Brunswick, N.J.: Transaction Books, 1982), pp. 29–48. Many other schemes have been devised to classify epistemological approaches. See for example Stephen Pepper, *World Hypotheses* (Berkeley: University of California Press, 1942); B. Aubrey Fisher, *Perspectives on Human Communication* (New York: Macmillan, 1978); Kenneth Williams, "Reflections on a Human Science of Communication," *Journal of Communication* 23 (1973): 239–50; Barry Brummett, "Some Implications of 'Process' or 'Intersubjectivity': Postmodern Rhetoric," *Philosophy and Rhetoric* 9 (1976): 21–51; Gerald Miller, The Current Status of Theory and Research in Interpersonal Communication," *Human Communication Research* 4 (1978): 175.

knowledge is viewed as something acquired from outside oneself, World View I is often called the *received view*. Objectivity is all important, with investigators being required to define the exact operations to be used in observing events. Most mainstream physical science is World View I, and much behavioral and social science follow suit. The method used involves hypothesizing a state of affairs and carefully testing the hypothesis through observation. Further hypotheses are then deduced. Bit by bit theory is developed and knowledge grows.

World View I aims to make lawful statements about phenomena, developing generalizations that hold true across situations and over time. Scholars in this tradition try to reveal how phenomena appear and how they work. In so doing the scholar is highly analytical, attempting to define each part and subpart of the object of interest.

What, then, characterizes communication theory and research in World View I? First, such research tends to use behavioristic methods cultured in psychology. Researchers follow strict operations so that actual behavior can be observed. Second, World View I communication theory seeks covering laws. It attempts to come up with universal statements about communication. Third, communication research and theory in this tradition tend to be analytic, breaking down the process into small pieces. Fourth, this kind of theory and research seek causal, mechanistic explanations of communication events. Fifth, this research and theory images the human being as a reactive object.

World View II. This tradition takes a different turn by relying heavily on constructivism, viewing the world in process. In this view people take an active role in creating knowledge. A world of things exists outside the person, but the individual can conceptualize these things in a variety of useful ways. Knowledge therefore arises not out of discovery but from interaction between knower and known. For this reason perceptual and interpretive processes of the individuals are important objects for study.

World View II attempts not to uncover universal laws but to describe the rich context in which individuals operate. It is humanistic in that it stresses the individual subjective response. Knowing is interpreting, an activity everybody is believed to engage in. Many theories of communication take a World View II stance, being based on the assumption that communication itself is a vital vehicle in the social construction of reality.[30]

In sum, the following qualities characterize the communication theory and research of World View II. First, interpretation is stressed, rather than objective observation. Second, tacit processes as well as overt behavior are uncovered. Third, research and theory in this tradition emphasize social knowledge via symbolic interaction. In other words, knowledge is seen as arising from the use of symbols in communication with other people. Further, this research and theory tends to be humanistic, stressing individual differences. Finally, this view attempts to capture communication as process.

Issues of Ontology

While epistemology is the study of knowledge, ontology is the branch of philosophy that deals with the nature of being, or more narrowly, the nature of the phenomena we seek to know.[31] Actually, epistemology and ontology go hand in hand, since our conception of knowledge depends in part on our notions about the nature of the knowable. In the social sciences ontology deals largely with the nature of human existence. Thus ontological issues in the study of

30. See for example Peter Berger and Thomas Luckmann, *The Social Construction of Reality* (Garden City, N.Y.: Doubleday, 1966); Alfred Schutz, *The Phenomenology of the Social World*, trans. George Walsh and Frederick Lehnert (Evanston, Ill.: Northwestern University Press, 1967).

31. For a discussion of ontology, see Alasdair MacIntyre, "Ontology," in *The Encyclopedia of Philosophy*, ed. Paul Edwards (New York: Macmillan, 1967), vol. 5, pp. 542–43.

communication deal with the nature of human social interaction.

Ontological issues are important because the way a theorist conceptualizes communication depends in large measure on how the communicator is viewed. All communication theories begin with assumptions about being. Issues in this area reflect disagreements about the nature of human experience. Three issues are important.[32]

To what extent do humans make real choices? Although all investigators probably would agree that people perceive choice, there is a long-standing philosophical debate on whether real choice is possible. On one side of the issue are the determinists, who state that people's behavior is caused by a multitude of prior conditions and that humans are basically reactive and passive. On the other side of the debate are the teleologists, who claim that people plan their behavior to meet future goals. This school sees people as decision-making, active beings who affect their own destinies. Middle positions also exist, suggesting either that people make choices within a restricted range or that some behavior is determined while other behavior is a matter of free will.

To what extent is communication contextualized? The question is whether behavior is governed by universal principles or whether it depends on situational factors. Some philosophers believe that human life and action are best understood by looking at universal factors; others believe that behavior is richly contextual and cannot be generalized beyond the immediate situation. The middle ground on this issue is that behavior is affected by both general and situational factors.

To what extent are humans interpreting beings? This issue relates to problems of meaning. Some theorists believe that humans behave in accordance with stimulus-response principles, strictly reacting to pressures from the environment. Others believe that people are thinking interpreters. According to the second view, people create meanings and use these meanings to interpret and understand situations in which they find themselves.

Although numerous ontological positions can be seen in communication theory, this book groups them into two basic opposing positions: actional and nonactional. *Actional theory* assumes that individuals create meanings, they have intentions, they make real choices. The actional view rests on a teleological base, which says that people make decisions that are designed to achieve goals. Theorists of the actional tradition are reluctant to seek covering laws because they assume that individual behavior is not governed by universal prior events. Instead, they assume that people behave differently in different situations because rules change from one situation to another.

Nonactional theory assumes that behavior basically is determined by and responsive to past pressures. Covering laws are usually viewed as appropriate in this tradition; active interpretation by the individual is downplayed.

Issues of Perspective

Perspective involves the proper substantive coverage of theories of communication. In other words, the perspective of a theory is its angle or focus. Perspectives to a large extent are correlated with epistemology and ontology because how the theorist views knowledge and being affects the perspective of the theory. Any theory of communication provides a particular perspective from which the process can be viewed. A perspective is a point of view, a way of conceptualizing an area of study.[33] Earlier in this chapter you learned that all theories are abstractions and constructions. The configuration of a theory depends on the perspective of the theorist. This perspective guides the theorist in choosing what to focus on and what to leave out, how to explain the process, and how to conceptualize what is observed. Aubrey Fisher states the idea: "Clearly, a concept that is trivial or irrelevant or even ignored in one perspective

32. For an ontological discussion of communication theory, see Bowers and Bradac, "Issues."

33. For a discussion of perspective, see Fisher, *Perspectives*, pp. 57–85.

may suddenly leap into importance when one applies an alternative perspective."[34] In fact, a fuller, more complete picture of the process can be obtained by switching perspectives, which is certainly one of the methods of this book. Although theoretical perspectives can be conceptualized in a number of ways, the following four labels best describe the major divisions of the field.[35]

Behavioristic Perspective. This perspective, which comes from the behavioral school of psychology, stresses stimulus and response. Communication theories that use this perspective tend to emphasize the ways that individuals are affected by messages. Such theories tend to conform to World View I assumptions, and they are usually nonactional.

Transmissional Perspective. Transmissional theories view communication as the transfer of information from source to receiver. They use a linear model of movement from one location to another. This perspective stresses communication media, time, and sequential elements. Generally it is based on World View I and nonactional assumptions.

Interactional Perspective. This perspective recognizes that communicators respond reciprocally to one another. While the metaphor of the transmissional perspective is the line, the circle captures the interactional approach. Feedback and mutual effects are key concepts. Such theories typically are World View II; they may be actional or nonactional, depending on the degree to which communicators are thought to be active choice makers.

Transactional Perspective. This perspective stresses sharing. It sees communication as something in which all participants actively engage. Theories of the transactional perspective stress context, process, and function. In other words communication is viewed as highly situational and as a dynamic process that fulfills individual and social functions. This perspective emphasizes holism, imagining communication to be a process of sharing meaning. Transactional theories tend to espouse World View II assumptions, and they use actional explanations.[36]

How to Evaluate a Communication Theory

As you encounter theories of communication, you will need a basis for judging one against another. Here is a list of some criteria that can be applied to the evaluation of any theory.[37] Remember that no theory is perfect; all can be faulted. Therefore the following criteria are goal-ideals.

Theoretical Scope

A theory's scope is its comprehensiveness or inclusiveness. Theoretical scope relies on the principle of generality.[38] This principle states that a theory's explanation must be sufficiently general to cover a range of events beyond a single observation. People continually provide explanations for events, but their explanations are not always theoretical. When an explanation is a mere speculation about a single event, it is not a theoretical explanation. However, when an explanation goes beyond a single instance to cover a range of events, it is theoretical. Normally, the more general a theory, the better it is.

Two types of generality exist. The first is the coverage of a broad domain. Theories that meet the test of generality in this way deal with many phenomena. A communication theory that meets this test would explain a variety of communication-related behaviors. A theory

34. Ibid., 61.

35. Adapted from David M. Jabusch and Stephen Littlejohn, *Elements of Speech Communication* (Boston: Houghton Mifflin, 1981), pp. 12–24. Fisher's (*Perspectives*) model is somewhat different.

36. Perhaps the most thorough discussion of this perspective can be found in Mortensen, *Communication*.

37. Evaluation is discussed in greater depth in Bross, *Design* pp. 161–77; Deutsch, "On Communication Models," 362–63; Hall and Lindzey, *Theories*, chap. 1; Kaplan, *Conduct*, pp. 312–22; Kuhn, *Structure*, pp. 100–101, 152–56; Mortensen, pp. 30–34.

38. Achinstein, *Laws*; Cushman and Pearce, "Generality."

need not cover a large number of phenomena to be judged as good, however. Indeed, many fine theories are narrow in coverage. Such theories possess the second type of generality. Although they deal with a narrow range of events, their explanations of these events apply to a large number of situations. Such theories are said to be powerful.

Consider two contrasting examples. The theory of Kenneth Burke, (discussed in Chapter 4) as a theory that covers a broad range of phenomena, is a good example of the first type of generality. Many aspects of communication can be explained by the categories of Burke's theory. His categories, however, rely on understanding specific aspects of particular situations. Although this theory follows the principle of generality in terms of breadth of coverage, it does little to explain specific behavior across situations. In contrast, information theory, as explained in Chapter 7, covers very few communication-related themes, but its propositions for measuring the capacities of communication channels and the requirements of messages apply in a large number of transmission situations. As such, it is a good example of the second kind of generality.

Appropriateness

Is the theory's perspective appropriate for the theoretical questions the theory addresses? For example, the behavioristic perspective is not appropriate for questions related to meaning. Some theories of meaning, which are indeed behavioristic (see Chapter 6), can be faulted for lack of appropriateness. Their epistemological assumptions are inadequate for the domain they purport to cover.

Heuristic Value

Does the theory have potential for generating research and additional theory? One of the primary functions of theory is to help investigators decide what to observe and how to observe it. For example, a major contribution of Bales's interaction process theory (Chapter 11) is that it has spawned much research and further theorizing about group communication. Even Bales's critics find his ideas useful as springboards to develop new concepts.

Validity

Validity often implies truthfulness. In evaluating theories, however, validity is better conceived of as consistency, since the truthfulness of a theory may never be known. Two forms of consistency can be evaluated in a theory. *Internal consistency* is the degree to which the tenets of a theory are consistent with the researcher's observations. *External consistency* is the degree to which the theory's claims are supported by other theories in the same domain. External consistency also may be called concurrent or consensual validity. Milton Rokeach's theory of attitudes, beliefs, and values is strong in both internal and external validity (see Chapter 8). An intricate theory, it has many propositions, forming a highly consistent web of claims. At the same time the theory receives much support from other theories of cognition, attraction, self-concept, and attitude.

Parsimony

The test of parsimony may be called logical simplicity. If two theories are equally valid, the theory with the simplest logical explanation is said to be the best. For example, although classical information theory can be faulted on other grounds, it is highly parsimonious. A few core assumptions and premises lead logically to a variety of claims about channels, signals, messages, and transmission.

What Do We Know about Communication Theory?

In summary, what can we say about communication theory? Theory is an integral part of the process of inquiry, which also includes asking questions and making observations. These three elements are strongly interconnected. Inquiry and theory vary depending on the type of scholarship with which they are associated. Scientific scholarship stresses objectivity. Humanistic scholarship stresses subjectivity. Social science attempts to understand the human being as an object of study; it includes elements of both science and humanities. The chief problem of social science inquiry is the degree to which scientific methods are appropriate for revealing human behavior.

What is a theory? We know that a theory is constructed by a human observer. A theory is always abstract and always leaves something out of its observations. Theories function to organize and summarize knowledge, to focus observation, to clarify what is seen, and to provide methods for observation. They also help to predict, to generate research, to communicate ideas, and to control. Theories are not immutable: Because of research, theories change and grow by intension, extension, and revolution.

Theories are based on concepts and explanations. Concepts are groups of observations sharing common elements and a common name. Explanations point out the relationships among concepts, relying on causal, practical, or logical necessity. Theories can be compared according to their levels of generality and methods of explanation.

Philosophical issues in the study of communication are reflected in metatheory. Metatheory deals with issues of epistemology, ontology, and perspective. Two general epistemological positions are apparent in communication literature. World View I is basically scientific in orientation, stressing the ways in which knowledge about communication can be "received." World View II is basically humanistic, emphasizing the ways in which individuals create knowledge for personal and social use. The two basic ontological positions in communication are the actional and nonactional. Actional theories stress humans as choice-making beings; nonactional theories present people as passive and reactive. Four perspectives are apparent in communication theory: (1) the behavioristic perspective, which focuses on stimulus and response; (2) the transmissional perspective, which stresses linear sending and receiving of messages; (3) the interactional perspective, which includes feedback and mutual effect as central concepts; and (4) the transactional perspective, which centers on shared meaning.

As you proceed through this book, keep in mind the basic criteria for judging theories: scope or generality, appropriateness or suitability, heuristic value or research-generating ability, validity or consistency, and parsimony or logical simplicity. In the next chapter, we begin our survey of theories by examining system theory and cybernetics.

PART

GENERAL THEORIES

CHAPTER

3 General System Theory and Cybernetics

This book is organized around three broad domains of communication theory: general theories, thematic theories, and contextual theories. Part II covers three general theoretical approaches that attempt to capture the communication process as a whole. This chapter deals with system theory and the next chapter discusses symbolic interactionism and rules theory.

System "theory" is more a perspective or general approach than a theory per se. It provides a way of looking at the world that can help us better understand communication.[1] The system approach is discussed in the domain of general theory because it is especially useful in capturing the general nature of the communication process. It is useful in narrower domains as well, such as information theory, which is discussed as a theme of its own in Chapter 7. Nearly every chapter that follows includes theories that use system concepts. Interpersonal, group, and organizational settings are especially well served by system theory.

In this chapter we will take a brief look at the system concept, with particular focus on general system theory and cybernetics. The latter portion of the chapter outlines some system qualities of communication. Other system-oriented theories are presented in upcoming chapters.

Fundamental System Concepts

What Is a System?

A system is a set of objects or entities that interrelate with one another to form a whole. One of the most common distinctions is between closed and open systems.[2] A *closed system* is one that has no interchange with its environment. It moves toward progressive internal chaos (entropy), disintegration, and death. The closed-system model most often applies to physical systems, which do not have life-sustaining qualities. An *open system* is one that receives matter and energy from its environment and passes matter and energy to its environment. The open system is oriented toward life and growth. Biological, psychological, and social systems follow an open model. General system theory deals with systems primarily from this open perspective. When we speak of systems in this chapter, we are concerned only with the open model.

From the simplest perspective a system can be said to consist of four things.[3] The first is *objects*. The objects are the parts, elements, or members of the set. These objects may be physical or abstract or both, depending on the nature of the system. Second, a system consists of *attributes*, or the qualities or properties of the system and its objects. Third, a system must possess internal *relationships* among its objects. This characteristic is a crucial defining quality

1. For excellent discussions of general system theory (GST) and other systems approaches, see Peter Monge, "The Systems Perspective as a Theoretical Basis for the Study of Human Communication," *Communication Quarterly* 25 (1977): 19–29.

2. A. D. Hall and R. E. Fagen, "Definition of System," in *Modern Systems Research for the Behavioral Scientist*, ed. Walter Buckley (Chicago: Aldine, 1968), pp. 81–92; Anatol Rapoport, "Foreword," in Hall and Fagen, "Definition," pp. xiii–xxv. For an excellent short description of open versus closed systems, see Ludwig von Bertalanffy, *General System Theory: Foundations, Development, Applications* (New York: Braziller, 1968).

3. Hall and Fagen, "Definition."

of systems and a primary theme in this chapter. A relationship between objects implies a mutual effect (interdependence) and constraint.[4] This idea will be elaborated later. Fourth, systems also possess an *environment*. They do not exist in a vacuum but are affected by their surroundings.

The advocates of general system theory maintain that biological, psychological, and social systems possess certain common qualities. In fundamental ways these signposts define the system concept. These qualities are not mutually exclusive; they obviously overlap and to a large degree help to define one another.

Wholeness. A system by definition constitutes a unique whole.[5] Part and parcel of the system concept is the attitude of holistic thinking. In order to understand this idea, examine for a moment the opposite view—physical summativity. In the summative model the whole is merely a collection with no unique qualities of its own, like a box of stones. But in a system the whole is an integration of parts.

Interdependence. The reason we must view a system as a whole is that its parts interrelate and affect one another. Elements A and B may be separate when viewed apart from the system, but in combination a mutual interaction is present between them, the result of which is different from each element individually. The parts of a system are correlated, and the correlation can be thought of as a *constraint*. An object, person, concept, or other part of a system is always constrained by its interdependence with other parts. In a summative model this interdependent relationship does not exist. Instead, parts are conceived of as *in*dependent elements. (Dependence-independence actually should be thought of as a continuum, with various parts in the system having differing *degrees of freedom*.) As a result of interdependence, a change in one part of the system will produce changes throughout the system.

The idea of interdependence is easily illustrated in a family situation. If a family is a system of interacting individuals, each member is constrained by the actions of the other members. While each person has freedom, the members are also more or less dependent on one another. The behaviors in a family are not independent, free, or random, they are patterned and structured. What one family member does or says follows from or leads to an action of another.

Hierarchy. One of the most important qualities of a system is hierarchy.[6] This principle is the theme of Arthur Koestler's *The Ghost in the Machine*, as reflected in the following excerpt:

> There were once two Swiss watchmakers named Bios and Mekhos, who made very fine and expensive watches. Their names may sound a little strange, but their fathers had a smattering of Greek and were fond of riddles. Although their watches were in equal demand, Bios prospered, while Mekhos just struggled along; in the end he had to close his shop and take a job as a mechanic with Bios. The people in the town argued for a long time over the reasons for this development and each had a different theory to offer, until the true explanation leaked out and proved to be both simple and surprising.
>
> The watches they made consisted of about one thousand parts each, but the two rivals had used different methods to put them together. Mekhos had assembled his watches bit by bit—rather like making a mosaic floor out of small coloured stones. Thus each time when he was disturbed in his work and had to put down a partly assembled watch, it fell to pieces and he had to start again from scratch.
>
> Bios, on the other hand, had designed a method of making watches by constructing, for a start, sub-assemblies of about ten components, each of which held together as an independent unit. Ten of these sub-assemblies could then be fitted together into a

4. Walter Buckley, "Society as a Complex Adaptive System," in Buckley, *Modern Systems Research*, pp. 490–513.

5. Rapoport, "Foreword"; Hall and Fagen, "Definition."

6. For excellent discussions of hierarchy, see Donna Wilson, "Forms of Hierarchy: A Selected Bibliography," *General Systems* 14 (1969): 3–15; Arthur Koestler, *The Ghost in the Machine* (New York: Macmillan, 1967); W. Ross Ashby, "Principles of the Self-Organizing System," in *Principles of Self-Organization*, ed. Heinz von Foerster and George Zopf (New York: Pergamon Press, 1962), pp. 255–78.

sub-system of a higher order; and ten of these sub-systems constituted the whole watch. . . .

Now it is easy to show mathematically that if a watch consists of a thousand bits, and if some disturbance occurs at an average of once in every hundred assembling operations—then Mekhos will take four thousand times longer to assemble a watch than Bios. Instead of a single day, it will take him eleven years. And if for mechanical bits, we substitute amino acids, protein molecules, organelles, and so on, the ratio between time-scales becomes astronomical; some calculations indicate that the whole life-time of the earth would be insufficient for producing even an amoeba—unless he [Mekhos] becomes converted to Bios' method and proceeds hierarchically, from simple sub-assemblies to more complex ones.[7]

Every complex system consists of a number of subsystems. The system therefore is a series of levels of increasing complexity. The idea of system hierarchy can be illustrated by the "tree" model in Figure 3.1.

Koestler describes system hierarchy as the *Janus effect*: "The members of a hierarchy, like the Roman god Janus, all have two faces looking in opposite directions: the face turned toward the subordinate levels is that of a self-contained whole; the face turned upward toward the apex, that of a dependent part. One is the face of the master, the other the face of the servant."[8]

Koester's coined term for a system (hierarchy) is *holon*. The individual in society is a social holon, consisting hierarchically of cells, organs, organ systems, and body and is part of the larger group, culture, and society.

Self-regulation and Control. System theory provides a teleological perspective. Teleology, as described in Chapter 2, is the philosophy that attributes happenings to future goals or purposes. Systems are most often viewed as goal-oriented organisms. They are governed by their purposes. What happens in a system is controlled by its aims, and the system regulates its behavior to achieve the aims. The parts of a system must behave in accordance with its rules or canons and must adapt to the environment on the basis of feedback. This aspect of system functioning, known as *cybernetics*, will be taken up in detail in the next section.

7. Koestler, *Ghost*, 45–47.

8. Ibid., p. 48.

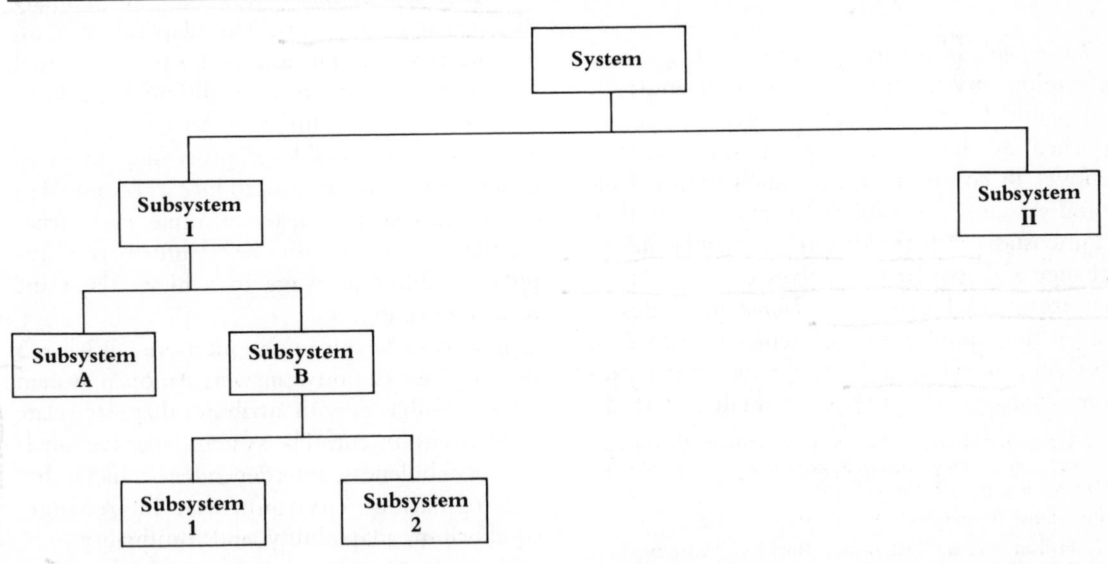

Figure 3.1. System hierarchy.

Interchange with the Environment. An open system by definition interacts with its environment. It takes in and lets out matter and energy. Thus systems are said to have *inputs* and *outputs*. This concept follows logically from the ideas of hierarchy and cybernetics. A particular element can be included in the system or the environment depending on the focus of the observer. An element in the environment will affect the elements of the system in the same way that a suprasystem would affect its subsystems and vice versa. The system affects the environment; the environment affects the system.[9]

Balance. Another quality of systems is balance or homeostasis.[10] This quality is related to self-regulation and system organization. In order to avoid the fate of a closed system—increasing entropy—the open system must maintain itself, stay in balance, hold its own. It must work to do this. One of the primary tasks of many interacting subsystems is that of maintaining balance in the system. The system must be capable of sensing deviations from the "assigned" norm and of correcting these tendencies. The section on cybernetics covers this aspect of systems in detail.

Change and Adaptability. Because it exists in a changing environment, the system must be adaptable.[11] This adaptability often is accomplished by the homeostatic quality described above. In complex systems such as sociocultural systems, adaptability involves more than homeostasis. Advanced systems must be able to change and reorder themselves on the basis of environmental pressures. *Homeostasis* designates the equilibrium maintenance feature of systems; *morphogenesis* designates the structure-changing aspect.[12] A. D. Hall and R. E. Fagen describe three kinds of structured change that might occur over time in the process of morphogenesis.[13] The first is *progressive segregation*, a process of movement from wholeness toward summativity, movement along the continuum of dependence-independence toward division among subsystems. This kind of change may lead to greater differentiation of subsystem function. *Progressive systemization* is the opposite—movement toward interdependence among parts. Both kinds of changes can occur in the same system simultaneously or sequentially. *Progressive centralization* (or *decentralization*) may also occur in systems and may take place simultaneously with segregation or systemization. In progressive centralization a particular subsystem tends to become more and more important in guiding the system; with other subsystems thus becoming more dependent on this *leading part*. This quality of adaptability and change points up the dynamic nature of the complex, open system.

Equifinality. Finality is the goal achievement or task accomplishment of a system. Equifinality means that a particular final state may be accomplished in many ways and from many different starting points. The adaptable system, which has a final state as a goal, can achieve that final state in a variety of different environmental conditions. Inputs never equal outputs. The system is capable of processing inputted data in different ways to produce its output.[14] In classroom instruction, for example, an instructor may relate the same basic information (inputs) in different ways to achieve the same results (outputs).

In answer to our initial question, "What is a system?" we can now answer: An open system is a set of objects with attributes that interrelate in an environment. The system possesses qualities of wholeness, interdependence, hierarchy, self-regulation, environmental interchange, equilibrium, adaptability, and equifinality.

9. Gordon Allport, "The Open System in Personality Theory," in Buckley, *Modern Systems Research*, pp. 343–50; Hall and Fagen, "Definition."

10. Ashby, "Principles."

11. Hall and Fagen, "Definition," Buckley, "Adaptive System"; Koestler, *Ghost*.

12. Buckley, "Adaptive System," p. 493.

13. Hall and Fagen, "Definition," pp. 85–86.

14. Bertalanffy, *General System Theory*, chap. 3.

What Is Cybernetics?

Cybernetics is the study of regulation and control in systems, with emphasis on the nature of feedback.[15] An important feature of open systems, as we have just seen, is that they are regulated, that they seek goals, and that they therefore are purposeful. This special area of system functioning is claimed as the territory of cybernetics.

Cybernetics deals with the ways systems (along with their subsystems) use their own output to gauge effect and make necessary adjustments. The simplest cybernetic device consists of a sensor, a comparator, and an activator. The sensor provides feedback to the comparator, which in turn provides guidance to the activator. The activator in turn produces an output that affects the environment in some way. This fundamental process of output-feedback-adjustment is the central theme of cybernetics.

The field of cybernetics was developed by Norbert Wiener and his associates.[16] Wiener's primary discipline was mathematics, but he considers cybernetics to be an interdisciplinary area: "The most fruitful areas for the growth of the sciences were those which had been neglected as a no-man's land between the various established fields."[17] Wiener's early work on computers and neurology led him to see patterns of control behavior, which he believes to be significant. Wiener discusses the beginnings of cybernetics in the early 1940s:

> [We] had already become aware of the essential unity of the set of problems centering about communication, control, and statistical mechanics, whether in the machine or in living tissue. On the other hand we were seriously hampered by the lack of unity of the literature concerning these problems, and by the absence of any common terminology, or even a single name for the field. . . . We have decided to call the entire field of control and communication theory, whether in the machine or in the animal, by the name of *Cybernetics*.[18]

Obviously, feedback mechanisms specifically and behavior in general vary in their degree of control complexity. In an early article Rosenbleuth, Wiener, and Bigelow provide a model of this increasing complexity.[19] In the model (Figure 3.2) the most basic distinction is between *active* and *passive* behavior. An organism displaying active behavior is the primary source of the energy involved in the behavior. The active organism itself provides the stimulus. In passive behavior the organism receives inputs or stimuli. Passive behavior is primarily a response to outside energy. Within the category of active behavior, a further division can be made between *purposeless*, or random, and *purposeful* behavior. Purposeful behavior is directed toward an objective or aim; random behavior is not. As we have indicated, cybernetics is interested in purposeful levels of behavior in systems. All purposeful behavior requires feedback; the nature of the feedback may be more or less complex, as indicated in the model.

Purposeful behavior may be further subdivided into *complex* and *simple* feedback mechanisms.[20] In the simple condition the organism uses feedback in a restricted sense but does not modify or adjust behavior in the course of acting. Complex systems, however, use positive and negative feedbacks to adjust and adapt during the action itself. This dynamic level will be explained in more detail in the discussion of feedback loops and networks. Further, complex systems may be *predictive* or *nonpredictive*. Predictive behavior is based on anticipated position

15. Rollo Handy and Paul Kurtz, "A Current Appraisal of the Behavioral Sciences: Communication Theory," *American Behavioral Scientist* 7, no. 6 (1964). Supplementary information is found in Gordon Pask, *An Approach to Cybernetics* (New York: Harper & Row, 1961); G. T. Guilbaud, *What Is Cybernetics?* (New York: Grove Press, 1959).

16. For a historical review see Norbert Wiener, *Cybernetics or Control and Communication in the Animal and the Machine* (New York: MIT Press, 1961), pp. 1–29.

17. Ibid., p. 2.

18. Ibid., p. 11.

19. Arturo Rosenbleuth, Norbert Wiener, and Julian Bigelow, "Behavior, Purpose, and Teleology," *Philosophy of Science* 10 (1943): 18–24 (reprinted in Buckley, *Modern Systems Research*, pp. 221–25).

20. I have changed the original nomenclature here to avoid confusion and inconsistency with previous word usage in this chapter. The authors' intent is unchanged.

or response rather than actual position or response. As a good hunter knows, you do not aim at the running animal; rather, you anticipate where it will be when the bullet reaches it. Finally, prediction itself is more or less accurate, as indicated by the final distinction in the model, *orders of prediction*.

A simple model of feedback is represented in Figure 3.3. As previously indicated a part of the output from the system is returned as feedback, and certain internal controls or adjustments take place. In Figure 3.3, B is an energy source directing outputs to C. A is the control mechanism responding to feedback from C. Depending on the complexity of the system and the nature of the directedness of output, the control mechanism itself is restricted in the kind of control it can exert. Figure 3.4 illustrates some possibilities.[21]

The first model in Figure 3.4 illustrates a situation where the signal itself is modified (for example, amplified) by A. The high-pitched squeal in a loudspeaker system is an example. The next model illustrates a simple switch such as a thermostat or circuit breaker. The third model illustrates selection control in which A chooses a channel or position on the basis of criteria. In a guided missile, for example, the guidance system may specify turning in one direction or another, based on feedback from the target.

The process of system regulation through feedback involves several facets. The regulated system must possess certain control guidelines. The control center must "know" what environmental conditions to respond to and how. It must possess a sensitivity to aspects of the environment that are critical to its goalseeking.[22]

Feedback basically may be classified as positive or negative, depending on the way the system responds to it. Negative feedback is an error message indicating deviation; the system adjusts by reducing or counteracting the deviation. Negative feedback is the most important type of feedback in homeostasis, for the princi-

21. Adapted from Guilbaud, *Cybernetics.*

22. Walter Buckley, *Sociology and Modern Systems Theory* (Englewood Cliffs, N.J.: Prentice-Hall, 1967), pp. 52–53.

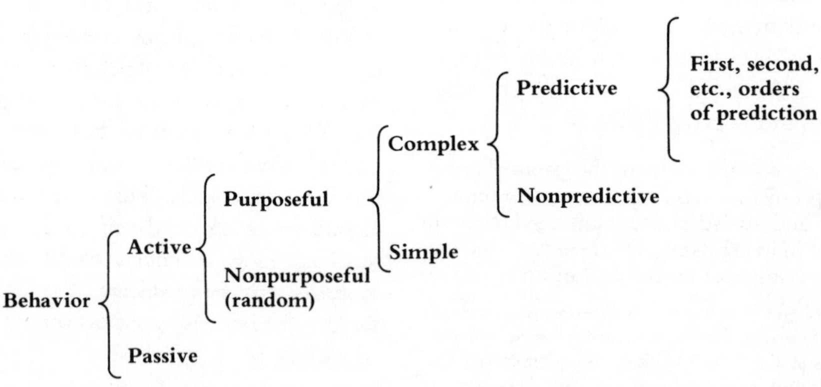

Figure 3.2. Model of cybernetic complexity.

ple of deviation-counteracting is the focus of traditional cybernetics. A system can also respond by amplifying or maintaining deviation. When this happens, the feedback is said to be positive. This kind of interaction is important in morphogenesis, or system growth (for example, learning). The inflationary cycle in economics is an example of positive feedback effects. The growth of a city is another. In communication when a speaker receives negative feedback from a listener, the speaker knows he or she is missing the aim. Negative feedback from a fellow communicator usually calls for a shift in strategy to close the gap between how the speaker wants the listener to respond and the actual response. Whether in mechanical or human systems, the response to negative feedback is "Cut back, slow down, discontinue." Response to positive feedback is "Increase, maintain, keep going."

Our discussion of feedback thus far has given the impression that a system responds as a unit to feedback from the outside. This impression is realistic only for the simplest systems such as a heater-thermostat arrangement. As a series of hierarchically ordered subsystems, advanced systems are more complex. A subsystem at any moment may be part of the larger system or part of the environment.[23] Further, we know that subsystems respond to one another in mutual interdependence. As a result the concept of feedback is expanded for complex systems. In a complex system a series of feedback loops exist within and among subsystems, forming networks. At some points the feedback loops are positive, at other points negative. But always, consistent with the basic feedback principle, system output returns as feedback input. No matter how complicated the network, one always comes back to the beginning.

23. Magoroh Maruyama, "The Second Cybernetics: Deviation-Amplifying Mutual Causal Processes," *American Scientist* 51 (1963): 164–79 (reprinted in Buckley, *Modern Systems Research*, pp. 304–138.

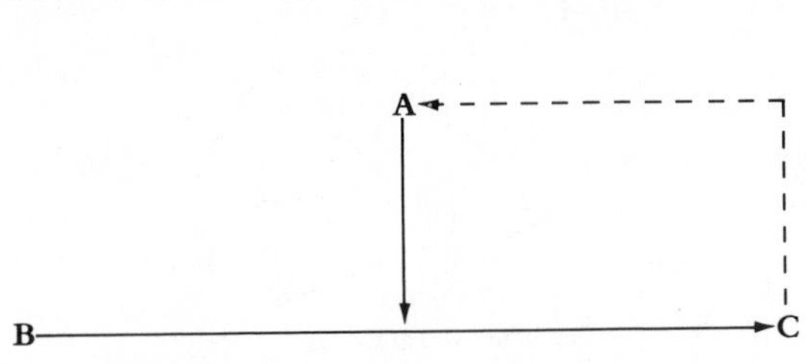

Figure 3.3. A simple feedback model.

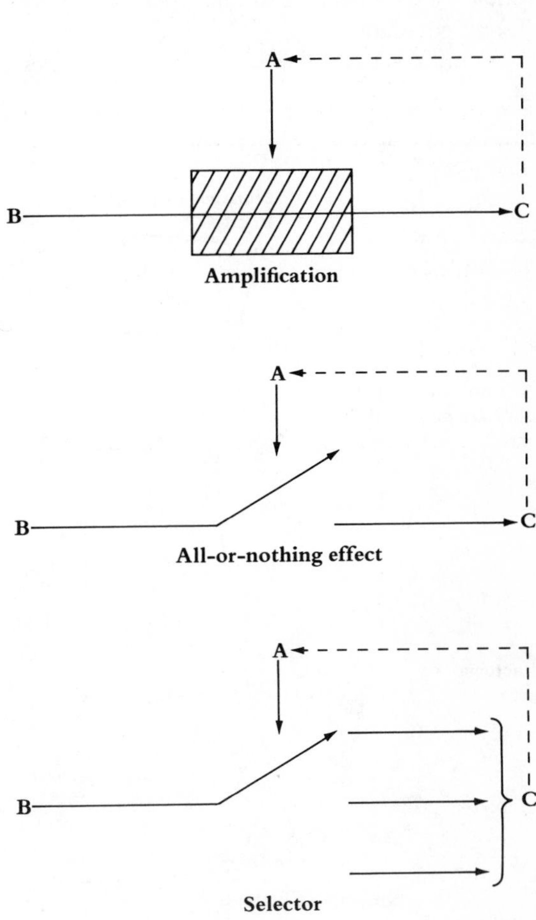

Figure 3.4. Illustrative control models.

A simple illustration of a system network is the example of urbanization in Figure 3.5.[24] In this figure the pluses represent positive relationships, the minuses negative relationships. In a positive relationship the variables increase or decrease together. In a negative relationship as one increases, the other decreases. For example, as the number of people in the city (P) increases, modernization also increases. With increased modernization comes increased migration, which in turn further increases the population. This relationship is an example of a positive feedback loop. A negative relationship is illustrated by the effect of the number of diseases (D) on population (P).

As our discussion up to this point indicates, cybernetics is a central concept in system theory. Feedback and control relate inextricably to the essence of open-system theory. The cybernetic elements of control, regulation, and feedback provide a concrete explanation of such system qualities as *wholeness* (a portion of the system cannot be understood apart from its loops between subsystems); *interdependence* (subsystems are constrained by mutual feedbacks); *self-regulation* (a system maintains balance and changes by responding appropriately to positive and negative feedbacks); *interchange with the environment* (inputs and outputs can be largely explained in terms of feedback loops).

Although these cybernetic concepts originated in the fields of physiology, engineering, and mathematics, they have tremendous impli-

24. Ibid.

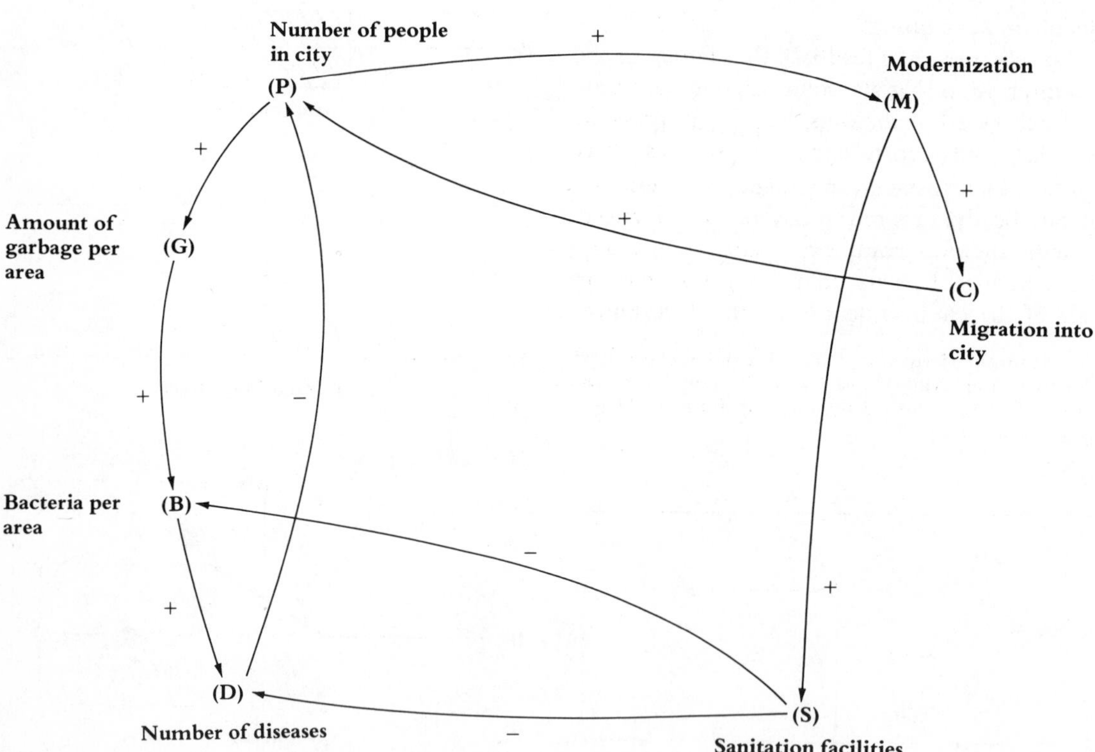

From *American Scientist*, "The Second Cybernetics," by Magorah Maruyama. Copyright © 1963. Reprinted by permission of the publisher.

Figure 3.5. A simplified feedback network.

cations in the behavioral and social sciences as well.[25] As Wiener states, "This principle [feedback] in control applies not merely to the Panama locks, but to states, armies, and individual human beings. . . . This matter of social feedback is of very great sociological and anthropological interest."[26]

Principles of cybernetics lead to one of the purported advantages of system theory; namely, that it is broad enough to allow various alternative explanatory logics.[27] As Peter Monge puts it, "Systems theory provides an explanatory framework that is capable of incorporating both behavioral and action positions.[28] He believes this incorporation is so because the basic teleology of systems, made possible by their cybernetic functions, may be of two types.

First, the system may achieve an end or goal by responding automatically to negative feedback, much as a heater responds to a thermostat. This off-on behavior displays causal necessity and follows nonactional ontology. Second, some systems or subsystems may behave with intention, actively choosing one of many possible courses of action to arrive at an end state. Human social systems, in contrast to physical systems such as the thermostat or guided missile, are viewed as purposeful in this way. This kind of explanation employs practical necessity and is highly actional in ontology. Hence, purpose may be explained by two alternative logics, and system theory is believed to accommodate either of these.

Therefore what distinguishes system theory from other approaches is its high level of generality and emphasis on interrelationships among elements, not on the type of necessity employed. This idea is controversial, as we shall see in the criticism section of this chapter.

General Systems Theory as an Approach to Knowledge

General system theory (GST) is a broad, multidisciplinary approach to knowledge based on the system concept. GST was developed primarily by Ludwig von Bertalanffy, a well-known biologist.[29] Basically, GST postulates concepts governing systems in general and applies these generaliations to numerous phenomena.[30] Here is how Bertalanffy describes GST:

> It seems legitimate to ask for a theory, not of systems of a more or less special kind, but of universal principles applying to systems in general.
>
> In this way we postulate a new discipline called *General System Theory*. . . .
>
> General System Theory, therefore, is a general science of "wholeness" which up till now was considered a vague, hazy, and semi-metaphysical concept. In elaborate form it would be a logico-mathematical discipline, in itself purely formal but applicable to the various empirical sciences.[31]

Bertalanffy first conceived of GST in the early 1920s.[32] At that time he began to think about biology in organismic terms, but this proved an unpopular approach. Not until after World War II did he feel comfortable about publicizing his system ideas. After the war he promoted his view primarily through lectures and symposia. Bertalanffy describes the criticism he faced:

> The proposal of system theory was received incredulously as fantastic or presumptuous. Either—it

25. See Karl Deutsch, "Toward a Cybernetic Model of Man and Society," in Buckley, *Modern Systems Research*, pp. 387–400.

26. Norbert Wiener, *The Human Use of Human Beings: Cybernetics and Society* (Boston: Houghton Mifflin, 1954), pp. 49–50.

27. For a listing of these logics, see Peter Monge, "The Systems Perspective as a Theoretical Basis for the Study of Human Communication," *Communication Quarterly* 25 (1977): 19–29.

28. Ibid., p. 28.

29. For a biographical and bibliographical sketch of Bertalanffy, see "Ludwig von Bertalanffy," *General Systems* 17 (1972): 219–28.

30. For an example of formalized GST, see Masanao Toda and Emir H. Shuford, "Logic of Systems: Introduction to a Formal Theory of Structure," *General Systems* 10 (1965): 3–27.

31. Bertalanffy, *General System Theory*, pp. 32–37.

32. For a brief survey of the history of GST, see Bertalanffy, *General System Theory*, chap. 1.

was argued—it was trivial because the so-called isomorphisms were merely examples of the truism that mathematics can be applied to all sorts of things . . . or it was *false* and *misleading* because superficial analogies . . . camouflage actual difference. . . . Or, again, it was philosophically and methodologically *unsound* because the alleged 'irreducibility' of higher levels to lower ones tended to impede analytical research.[33]

Bertalanffy persisted, however, and in 1954 the Society for General Systems Research was born.[34] Like most other movements, GST is not a singular theory developed by one person. While GST itself was promoted by Bertalanffy, others were doing similar work in other fields. The two most important cognate areas, which were developed almost simultaneously with Bertalanffy's work, were Norbert Wiener's cybernetics and Shannon and Weaver's information theory. In fact, these three approaches so completely support one another that they are like tributaries of the same river. Since information theory is a narrower approach, we will consider it separately in Part III. Keep in mind, though, that it is part of the broader GST perspective. Cybernetics, on the other hand, is clearly a macro approach and is so closely tied to system theory that we must consider it in this chapter.

Another closely allied area is systems science. The systems sciences are applied technological fields, including systems engineering (development of people-machine systems), operations research (control of personnel, machines, materials, and money), and human engineering (work-efficiency development). Bertalanffy took these fields to be evidence for the viability of his more general perspective: "Concepts like wholeness, organization, teleology, and directiveness appeared in mechanistic science to be unscientific or metaphysical. Today they are taken seriously and as amenable to scientific analysis."[35]

A primary aim of GST is to integrate accumulated knowledge into a clear and realistic framework. General system theorists attempt to do this through the principle of *isomorphism*. An isomorphism is a structural similarity between two models or between an abstract model and an observed phenomenon. Two systems that are widely different are said to be isomorphic if their behaviors are governed by the same principles. A generalized model such as GST attempts to elucidate these principles. Following is an example:

An exponential law of growth applies to certain cells, to populations of bacteria, of animals or humans, and to progress of scientific research measured by the number of publications in genetics or science in general. The entities in question . . . are completely different. . . . Nevertheless, the mathematical law is the same.[36]

The need for greater integration of knowledge in many areas such as communication is critical. Kenneth Boulding provides a compelling argument for the use of GST as an integrator of knowledge:

The need for general systems theory is accentuated by the present sociological situation in science. . . . The crisis of science today arises because of the increasing difficulty of such profitable talk among scientists as a whole. Specialization has outrun Trade. Communication between the disciplines becomes increasingly difficult, and the Republic of Learning is breaking up into isolated subcultures with only tenuous lines of communication between them. . . . One wonders sometimes if science will grind to a stop in an assemblage of walled-in hermits, each mumbling to himself words in a private language that only he can understand. . . . The spread of specialized deafness means that someone who ought to know something that someone else knows isn't able to find it out for lack of generalized ears.

It is one of the main objectives of General System Theory to develop these generalized ears.[37]

33. Ibid., p. 14. For a thorough review of GST criticism and rebuttal, see Ludwig Bertalanffy, "General System Theory—A Critical Review," *General Systems* 12 (1962): 1–20 (reprinted in Buckley, *Modern Systems Research*, pp. 11–30).

34. The Society's yearbook, *General Systems*, has been published annually since 1956. It is an excellent compilation of theoretical and applied work in GST.

35. Bertalanffy, "A Critical Review," p. 14.

36. Bertalanffy, *General System Theory*, p. 33.

37. Kenneth Boulding, "General Systems Theory—The Skeleton of Science," in Buckley, *Modern Systems Research*, p. 4.

Communication as a System

System theory and cybernetics are abstract theories. In other words, they provide a set of logics about things in general without specifying what those things are. They do not become communication theories until someone applies them to human interaction per se. Many theorists have done precisely that. In this book several system theories of communication are presented. Most of these, however, deal with particular communication settings. For example, in Chapter 9 on interpersonal communication, the work of the Palo Alto group is discussed. Their theory, based on system principles, lays the groundwork for much of our thinking on communication in relationships. In Chapter 11 on group and organizational communication, two important system approaches are discussed. Fisher's ideas on group communication deal with the ways that interaction in groups follows system patterns and phases. The approach of Farace, Monge, and Russell deals with organizations as systems of communication networks. Clearly, system theory has had a major impact on the field of communication.

One of the strongest advocates for the system approach to communication is B. Aubrey Fisher. In his book *Perspectives on Human Communication* he applies system concepts to communication in what he calls the pragmatic perspective.[38] His work, summarized in this section, constitutes a general system view of communication. From his pragmatic perspective Fisher emphasizes four aspects of communication: individual behavior, sequential interaction patterns, content and relationship dimensions, and the social system.

Behavior is important as the smallest unit of analysis in the communication system. Individuals communicate by behaving in ways that have potential for eliciting meanings in others. Since communicators have no direct access to the thoughts, feelings, and meanings of other people, these variables, which are internal in the individual, are not considered to be basic in person-to-person contact. Rather, external acts are the sole vehicles for linking individuals in the communication system. Fisher refers to this principle as externalization. He does not mean to imply that internal variables such as attitudes, values, and emotions are not important. In large measure they shape how an individual behaves. From a system point of view, however, the behavior itself is what counts. Consider for example, an assembly line worker in a factory. This worker has many feelings, thoughts, emotions, attitudes, and values that are important in determining her behavior. Coworkers and superiors, however, have no way to know what is happening inside this person except by observing her actual behaviors. Through observation other workers will assign meaning to some of what she does and says.

The second focus of the pragmatic perspective, according to Fisher, is *sequential interaction patterns*. Although individual behavior is the most basic unit of analysis, observing individual behavior is not sufficient for understanding the communication system. Instead, one must consider sets of acts that are linked to one another in the stream of interaction. Two methods of analyzing behavior in communication situations have been employed.[39] The first is the human system model. Here one observes individual behaviors in an attempt to reveal an understanding of the person as a subsystem of communication. Fisher prefers the second method, the interact system model, which takes as the basic unit of analysis the *interact*, a set of linked acts. Analysis of this kind is necessary for understanding actual communication. The interact, or set of acts, is one person's behavior followed by the behavior of another. Such behavior usually is verbal; that is, one individual's statement is followed by another individual's statement. Nonverbal acts also count. A double interact is a set of three statements, a triple

38. B. Aubrey Fisher, *Perspectives on Human Communication* (New York: Macmillan, 1978).

39. B. Aubrey Fisher and Leonard C. Hawes, "An Interact System Model: Generating a Grounded Theory of Small Groups," *Quarterly Journal of Speech* 57 (1971): 444–53.

interact a set of four. Theoretically we could look at any number of statements in a row as a unit of analysis, although in practice single and double interacts generally are all a human observer can process.

Fisher emphasizes two related elements of interaction analysis. The first is the idea of punctuation, the second is stochastic probability. Punctuation of interactional sequences is the natural grouping of interacts. Interaction is not just a string of acts. Rather, acts cluster into groupings that help the observer make sense out of the communication event. For example, suppose that our hypothetical factory worker often tells jokes to the people working around her. Whenever she says, "Have you heard the one about . . . " the others grimace. Her introduction to the joke is followed by nonverbal facial expressions from the others that are taken to mean, "Oh, no, not another corny joke." These two acts are paired because they are a meaningful whole; they constitute a natural interact in this situation.

Stochastic probability refers to the patterned nature of interaction. Remember that one principle of systems is that parts of a system are correlated or constrained in some way or another. Events in a system are not random, but patterned. Thus the system has structure. One of the ways of conceptualizing the patterned nature of the communication system is to note the ways in which acts are connected. A given act has a particular probability of following another act. Or, to flip the coin, an antecedent act will be followed by a subsequent act with predictable frequency. This antecedent-subsequent link is known as a stochastic relationship. In a system certain acts are linked with greater frequency than others. In the preceding example the coworkers' grimaces almost always follow the introduction of a joke. The communication system in the factory is structured or patterned by a large and complex set of interacts that vary in their degree of predictability. Ideally the communication system has enough structure or predictability to remain stable but sufficient freedom to allow for adjustment or adaptation to changing circumstances.

Content and relationship dimensions, the third part of Fisher's application, comes from the early work of relationship theorists (see Chapter 9). Any communication act has two dimensions. The first relays information content; the second provides information about the relationship between the participants. The latter kind of information tells the participants how to interpret the content message. So when our factory worker begins to tell a joke, she not only is preparing the others to hear a funny story but she is projecting her own friendliness. Her coworkers' facial expressions say on the content level, "We are tired of your jokes," but on the relationship level they may be saying, "Yes, go ahead, we like to joke around." This intriguing element of interpersonal communication is discussed in greater detail in Chapter 9.

The final element in Fisher's approach is the *social system*. That communication involves interaction among people should be amply clear by this point. Communication is therefore social. Although machines can assist in the communication system, the human element is its essence. Further, a social system relies on interaction between individuals; it does not rely on their internal states. Thus our factory worker herself is not a communication system in Fisher's eyes. But when she interacts with others, a social system is created.

Further, the social system can be viewed hierarchically. In other words, the system can be understood in terms of at least three levels: subsystem, system, and suprasystem. In Fisher's terms the subsystem is the individual human being, the system is interacting group, and the suprasystem is the larger organization or social context in which the interaction takes place. The system can also be viewed in terms of a hierarchy of repetitive interactions. Acts are part of interacts; interacts proceed in phases over time; and phases are repeated in cycles. For example, the factory workers proceed through various phases of interaction. When a new worker joins the group, for instance, the group may go through a phase of friendly acceptance, followed by a checking-out phase. This period could be followed by a phase of testing the new employee, followed by the phase of full integration into the work group. This series of phases over time would be repeated in cycles as new employees entered the scene.

Criticism of System Theory

System theory has been attacked on several fronts, although its supporters remain undaunted.[40] Six major issues have emerged: (1) Does the breadth and generality of system theory provide the advantage of integration or the disadvantage of ambiguity? (2) Does the theory's openness provide flexibility in application or confusing equivocality? (3) Is system theory merely a philosophical perspective, or does it provide useful explanation? (4) Has system theory generated useful research? (5) Is the system paradigm an arbitrary convention, or does it reflect reality in nature? (6) Does system theory help to simplify, or does it make things more complicated than they really are?

The first issue clearly relates to theoretical scope. From the beginning supporters have claimed that system theory provides a common vocabulary to integrate the sciences. It establishes useful logics that can be fruitfully applied to a broad range of phenomena. Others, however, claim that system theory merely confuses. If it is everything, it is really nothing. If all phenomena follow the same system principles, we have no basis for understanding anything apart from anything else. Along the same line, some critics point out that system theory cannot have its cake and eat it too. Either it must remain a general framework without explaining real-world events, or it must abandon general integration in favor of making substantive claims. Jesse Delia expresses this concern: "General System Theory manifests a fundamental ambiguity in that at points it seems to present a substantive perspective making specific theoretical claims and at other points to present a general abstract language devoid of specific theoretical substance for the unification of alternative theoretical views."[41]

The second issue relates to the first. Does the theory's openness provide flexibility of thought or confusing equivocality? This concern relates to the criterion of theoretical appropriateness. Detractors claim that the theory embodies what Delia calls "a fancy form of the fallacy of equivocation." In other words, by permitting a variety of substantive applications in different theoretical domains, it cannot prevent inconsistencies among these applications. Two theories using a system framework may even contradict each other. Where, then, Delia asks, is the supposed unity brought about by system theory? This problem is exacerbated by the fact that system theories can employ various logics, which are not necessarily consistent with one another.[42] Supporters answer that this openness is one of the main advantages of system theory: It does not bias the researcher with an a priori notion of what to expect. Consequently, it promotes research that looks for things as they are without imposing arbitrary theoretical categories.[43]

The third issue is also a matter of appropriateness. Some critics question whether the systems approach is a theory at all, claiming that it has no explanatory power. While it gives us a perspective or way of conceptualizing, it provides little basis for knowing why things occur as they do. Fisher agrees:

40. For arguments supporting system theory, see especially Bertalanffy, "A Critical Review"; Buckley, *Sociology*; Fisher, *Perspectives*; Monge, "Systems Perspective."

41. Jesse Delia, "Alternative Perspectives for the Study of Human Communication: Critique and Response," *Communication Quarterly* 25 (1977): 51. See also Edgan Taschjan, "The Entropy of Complex Dynamic Systems," *Behavioral Science* 19 (1975): 3.

42. Delia, "Alternative Perspectives," pp. 51–52.

43. Wayne Beach, "Stocktaking Open-Systems Research and Theory: A Critique and Proposals for Action" (Paper delivered at the meeting of the Western Speech Communication Association, Phoenix, Arizona, November 1977).

> These principles are quite abstract (that is to say, general). Consequently, they can be applied in numerous ways by differing theorists with equally different results. In fact, system "theory" is probably a misnomer. . . . In short, system theory is a loosely organized and highly abstract set of principles, which serve to direct our thinking but which are subject to numerous interpretations.[44]

System advocates probably would agree with this assessment of general system theory but point out that any given substantive system theory could be highly explanatory.

The fourth issue relates to system theory's heuristic value, questioning its ability to generate research. According to Donald Cushman, "systems is a perspective which has produced more staunch advocates than theoretical empirical research."[45] Again, critics return to the extreme generality of the approach as the basis of their criticism. They claim that the theory simply does not suggest substantive questions for investigation.

To the contrary advocates claim that the fresh perspective provided by system theory suggests new ways of looking at old problems and thus is highly heuristic. Beach points out, for example, that a great deal of fruitful research followed Fisher and Hawes's 1971 article on small group systems.[46] Fisher himself has done research on small group interaction. This work is presented in Chapter 11.

The fifth issue relates to the validity of system theory. Critics question whether system theory was developed to reflect what really happens in nature or to represent a useful convention for conceptualizing complex processes. In fact, system advocates themselves differ in their views of the function of the approach in this regard. Critics place system theory in a dilemma. If the theory attempts to describe phenomena as they really are, it is invalid. It posits similarities among events that are not really there. If, on the other hand, the theory provides merely a useful vocabulary for ordering a complex world, attributed similarities among events are only semantic and are therefore useless for providing understanding of those events. As Delia points out: "[Events] have different referents; they require different explanations; calling them the same thing . . . does not make them the same."[47] Bertalanffy calls this objection the "so what?" argument: If we find an analogy between two events, it is meaningless.[48]

The final issue of system theory is parsimony. Adherents claim that the world is so complex that a sensible framework such as system theory is necessary to sort out the elements of world processes. Critics generally doubt that events are that complex. They claim that system theory overcomplicates events that are essentially simple. Charles Berger states the case against overcomplication:

> In the behavioral sciences . . . we may be the victims of what I call irrelevant variety. Irrelevant variety is generated by the presence of attributes in a situation which have little to do with the phenomenon we are studying but which give the impression that what we are studying is very complex. . . . Merely because persons differ along a large number of physical, psychological, and social dimensions, does not mean that all of these differences will make a difference in terms of the phenomena we are studying. . . . It is probably the case that relatively few variables ultimately can account for most of the action.[49]

The criticism against system theory boils down to two basic problems. First, system

44. Fisher, *Perspectives*, p. 196. See also Bertalanffy, "Critical Review."

45. Donald Cushman, "The Rules Perspective as a Theoretical Basis for the Study of Human Communication," *Communication Quarterly* 25 (1977): 30–45.

46. B. Aubrey Fisher and Leonard Hawes, "An Interact System Model: Generating a Grounded Theory of Small Group Decision-Making," *Quarterly Journal of Speech* 58 (1971): 4430–53. See also Beach, "Stocktaking."

47. Delia, "Alternative Perspectives," p. 51.

48. Bertalanffy, "Critical Review."

49. Charles Berger, "The Covering Law Perspective as a Theoretical Basis for the Study of Human Communication," *Communication Quarterly* 75 (1977): 7–18. See also Gerald R. Miller, "The Pervasiveness and Marvelous Complexity of Human Communication: A Note of Skepticism" (Keynote address delivered at the Fourth Annual Conference in Communication, California State University, Fresno, May 1977). See also Beach, "Stocktaking.

theory is said to be so general as to be void of theoretical value. Second, there is disagreement and ambiguity about what the role of system theory is or should be in communication inquiry. This latter criticism is perhaps unfair, in that system theory in the general sense is not intended to represent the substance of particular objects of study. We should recognize system theory for what it is, a general approach to the world. Let the critics examine particular theories of communication that have taken a system approach. The following chapters summarize this second kind of criticism as appropriate.

What Do We Know about Communication as a System?

In summary, system theory presents the most direct and complete discussion of communication from a *general process* point of view. Four key elements in system theory highlight the process nature of communication. The first of these is holism, which suggests that parts of the communication process interrelate to form a whole that is not divisible into parts. System theory states that to isolate any single part for study—which, ironically, we do all the time—distorts the nature of the whole. The second major element of communication process is self-regulation, which is accomplished by feedback and adaptation. Third, communication is organized hierarchically. The principle of hierarchy states that whatever is observed is always part of a larger picture. Hierarchical organization has long been used to analyze communication events, as we shall see repeatedly throughout this text. Fourth, dynamism or change is an important aspect of communication. Processual events move; they are not static. Any system, including a communication system, constantly works to maintain homeostasis, but it also realizes morphogenesis or movement from one state to another.

CHAPTER

4 Symbolic Interactionism and Rules Theory

In the previous chapter we reviewed system theory, which represents a popular tool for explaining the process nature of communication. This chapter covers two other general theoretical orientations: symbolic interactionism and rules theory. These bodies of theory, which capture the symbolic nature of communication, are consistent with one another in many respects and thus are easily integrated into a single chapter.

Symbolic interactionism, a formulation primarily from the field of sociology, is the broadest overview of the role of communication in society. It provides an excellent launch pad for scores of other theories of interaction. In fact, proponents of symbolic interactionism maintain that many of the more specific theories of communication, language, and socialization are subsumed under this broader framework. It will become apparent in this chapter that symbolic interactionism is really not *a* theory but a theoretical perspective or orientation under which numerous specific theories may fall. This point is a transition from the previous chapters, for it illustrates that theories cannot be viewed as a series of independent explanations of some phenomenon. Theories interrelate, overlap, and fall into patterns. It is often hard to know where one theory ends and another begins.

The rules perspective became popular in communication circles during the 1970s. Rules theorists have gone beyond symbolic interactionism to discuss the specific mechanisms at work in everyday interaction. They teach that people generate rules for interaction and use these rules to govern social behavior.

Symbolic Interactionism

Symbolic interactionism contains a core of common premises about communication and society. Jerome Manis and Bernard Meltzer published a compilation of articles within the area in which they isolate seven basic theoretical and methodological propositions from symbolic interactionism, each identifying a central concept of the tradition:

1. The meaning component in human conduct: Distinctly human behavior and interaction are carried on through the medium of symbols and their meanings.
2. The social sources of humanness: The individual becomes humanized through interaction with other persons.
3. Society as process: Human society is most usefully conceived as consisting of people in interaction.
4. The voluntaristic component in human conduct: Human beings are active in shaping their own behavior.
5. A dialectical conception of mind: Consciousness, or thinking, involves interaction within oneself.
6. The constructive, emergent nature of human conduct: Human beings construct their behavior in the course of its execution.
7. The necessity of sympathetic introspection: An understanding of human conduct requires study of the actors' covert behavior.[1]

For purposes of discussion the symbolic interaction movement can be divided into trends. First, we will look at the foundations of symbolic interaction in the early oral tradition. Second, we will cover the two competing schools growing out of these earlier foundations. Fi-

1. Jerome G. Manis and Bernard N. Meltzer, eds., *Symbolic Interaction* (Boston: Allyn and Bacon, 1978), p. 437.

nally, we will list specific subareas of symbolic interactionism, one of which—the dramaturgical movement—we will discuss later in the chapter.

Manford Kuhn divides the time line of symbolic interactionism into two major portions. The first, which he calls the *oral tradition*, was the early period when the primary foundations of symbolic interaction developed. Following the posthumous publication of George Herbert Mead's *Mind, Self, and Society*, the second period, which may be termed the *age of inquiry*, came to flower.[2] Of course, the ideas of symbolic interaction did not emerge overnight from the mind of a lone thinker. They can be traced to the early psychology of William James. The primary interactionists in the early tradition were Charles Cooley, John Dewey, I. A. Thomas, and George Herbert Mead. Before Mead's ideas on communication were published, the interactionist perspective found life and sustenance primarily through oral transmission, especially in Mead's classroom. Although Mead did not publish his ideas during his lifetime, he is considered the prime mover of symbolic interactionism.

During this early Meadian period, the important ideas of the theory were developed. Mead and other interactionists departed from earlier sociological perspectives that had distinguished between the person and the society. Mead viewed individuals and society as inseparable and interdependent. Early interactionism stressed both the importance of social development and innate biological factors as well. Further, the early symbolic interactionists were not as concerned with how people communicated as they were with the impact of this communication on society and individuals. Above all, the early interactionists stressed the role of the shared meaning of symbols as the binding factor in society. The early theorists were strongly concerned with studying people in relation to their social situation. They maintained that a person's behavior could not be studied apart from the setting in which the behavior occurred or apart from the individual's perception of the environment. A result of this concern was that these early interactionists favored case histories as a research method.[3]

During the age of inquiry—the years that followed the publication of *Mind, Self, and Society*—two divergent schools began to develop within the arena of symbolic interactionism. The original formulations of Mead were not altogether consistent, leaving room for divergent interpretation and extension. As a result the Chicago and Iowa schools developed. The Chicago School, led primarily by Herbert Blumer, continued the humanistic tradition begun by Mead. Blumer above all believes that the study of humans cannot be conducted in the same manner as the study of things. The goals of the researcher must be to empathize with the subject, to enter the subject's realm of experience, and to attempt to understand the value of the person as an individual. Blumer and his followers avoid quantitative and scientific approaches to studying human behavior. They stress life histories, autobiographies, case studies, diaries, letters, and nondirective interviews. Blumer particularly stresses the importance of participant observation in the study of communication. Further, the Chicago tradition sees people as creative, innovative, and free to define each situation in individual and unpredictable ways. Self and society are viewed as process, not structure; to freeze the process would be to lose the essence of person-society relationships.

The Iowa School takes a more scientific approach to studying interaction. Manford Kuhn, its leader, believes that interactionist concepts can be operationalized. While Kuhn admits the process nature of behavior, he advocates that

2. Manford H. Kuhn, "Major Trends in Symbolic Interaction Theory in the Past Twenty-Five Years," *The Sociological Quarterly* 5 (1964): 61–84.

3. Bernard N. Meltzer and John W. Petras, "The Chicago and Iowa Schools of Symbolic Interactionism," in *Human Nature and Collective Behavior*, ed. Tamotsu Shibutani (Englewood Cliffs, N.J.: Prentice-Hall, 1970).

the objective structural approach is more fruitful than the "soft" methods employed by Blumer. As we will see later in the chapter, Kuhn is responsible for one of the primary measurement techniques used in symbolic interaction research.[4]

Largely because of the basic split that grew out of the attempt to resolve ambiguities left by Mead, a number of tributaries have formed since about 1940. Kuhn lists six major subareas: role theory, reference group theory, social perception and person perception, self-theory, interpersonal theory, and language and culture.[5] Whether all of the theorists in these subareas would pledge allegiance to symbolic interactionism remains to be seen. All of these areas likely have been influenced by the writings of the major symbolic interactionists. In this chapter we will discuss Mead, Blumer, Kuhn, and Burke.

Foundations: George Herbert Mead

Although it would be a mistake to attribute all of the basic ideas behind symbolic interactionism to a single person, George Herbert Mead was no doubt the primary generator of the movement.[6] Like nearly every theorist, Mead was a product of his time, following others in the predominant thought of the day. Following Darwin's theory of biological evolution, philosophers in related disciplines turned their thinking toward the evolutionary perspective. Pragmatists such as Mead attempted to pull together ideas from biology, psychology, and sociology in viewing the person as an evolutionary being. Yet, in fundamental ways Mead departed from and added to the work of these predecessors.

4. Ibid.

5. Kuhn, "Major Trends."

6. Mead's primary work in symbolic interactionism is *Mind, Self, and Society* (Chicago: University of Chicago Press, 1934). For outstanding secondary sources on Mead, see Bernard N. Meltzer, "Mead's Social Psychology," in *Symbolic Interaction*, ed. Jerome Manis and Bernard Meltzer (Boston: Allyn and Bacon, 1972), pp. 4–22; and Charles Morris, "George H. Mead as Social Psychologist and Social Philosopher," in *Mind, Self, and Society*, "Introduction."

All of Mead's work was collected and edited after his death in 1931. As a result his books appear poorly organized. In fact, his best-known work, *Mind, Self, and Society*, was collected from students' class notes. *The Philosophy of the Present*, published in 1932, is a group of lectures on the philosophy of history. *Mind, Self, and Society*, the "bible" of symbolic interactionism, followed in 1934. *Movements of Thought in the 19th Century*, lectures in the history of ideas, followed in 1936. In 1938 *Philosophy of the Act* was published.

The three cardinal concepts in Mead's theory, captured in the title of his best-known work, are society, self, and mind. These categories are not distinct, however. Rather, they are different aspects of the same general process, the social act. Basic to Mead's thought is the notion that people are *actors*, not *reactors*. The social act is an umbrella concept under which nearly all other psychological and social processes fall. The act is a complete unit of conduct, a gestalt, that cannot be analyzed into specific subparts. An act may be short, such as tying a shoe, or it may be the fulfillment of a life plan. Acts interrelate and are built upon one another in hierarchical form throughout a lifetime. Acts begin with an impulse; they involve perception and assignment of meaning, covert rehearsal, weighing of alternatives in one's head, and consummation. In its most basic form a social act involves a three-part relationship: an initial gesture from one individual, a response to that gesture by another (covertly or overtly), and a result of the act, which is perceived or imagined by both parties. In a holdup, for example, the robber indicates to the victim what is intended. The victim responds by giving money, and in the initial gesture and response, the defined result (a holdup) has occurred.

With this outline in mind, let us look more closely at the first facet of Meadian analysis—*society*. Society, or group life, is a cluster of cooperative behaviors on the part of society's members. Lower animals have societies too, but they differ from human society in fundamental ways. Animal societies, such as those of the bee, are based on biological necessity; they are physiologically determined. As a result an animal society behaves in predictable, stable, and unchanging ways. What is it, then, that distinguishes human cooperative behavior?

Human cooperation requires understanding the *intentions* of the other communicator. Since "minding" or thinking is a process of figuring out what actions one will undertake in the future, part of "feeling out" the other person is assessing what that person will do next. Thus cooperation consists of "reading" the other person's actions and intentions and responding in an appropriate way. Such cooperation is the heart of interpersonal communication. This notion of mutual responding with the use of language makes symbolic interactionism a vital approach to communication theory.

Animals may communicate in elementary ways, but symbol-using behavior is what distinguishes human communication. Subhuman species are said to go through a *conversation of gestures*. These gestures, however, are only *signals*, for they elicit predictable, programmed, instinctive responses. For example, a mother hen may cluck and her chicks will run to her. Or a dog will growl and lift the upper lip when encountering another hostile dog. No internal meaning is present in these acts for the animals in question. Animals do not assign conscious meaning to gestures; they do not "think through" their responses. The signal type of communication in animals takes place quickly, without interruption. Humans, on the other hand, use *symbols* in their communication. People consciously conduct a process of mental manipulation, delaying of response, and assigning meaning to the gestures of the other. The symbol is *interpreted* by the receiver. Assume for a moment that two men are sitting next to one another at a bar. The first man accidentally picks up the wrong drink. The other man is incensed; he tightens his fist, draws his arm back, and says, "Why you. . . ." The first man sees the gesture; he perceives the other's intention (to strike him). He interprets the symbols, assigns meaning to them, and plans his own reply. He responds, "Oh, don't hit me. It was an accident." His adaptation prevents an embarrassing, and painful, experience. Of course, this example is of a simple social act, but it illustrates the responsive, adaptive, cooperative nature of conscious, symbol-using behavior. If our two characters had been dogs and one had encroached on the other's territory, the outcome would have been more predictable.

This idea of society as a series of cooperative, symbol-using interactions has another aspect. The symbols used must possess shared meaning for the individuals in society. In Mead's terminology a gesture with shared meaning is a *significant symbol*. In short, society arises in the significant symbols of the group. Because of the ability to vocalize symbols, we literally can hear ourselves and thus can respond to the self, as others respond to us. We can imagine what it is like to receive our own messages, and we can empathize with the listener and take the listener's role, mentally completing the other's response.

This interplay between responding to others and responding to self is an important concept in Mead's theory, and it provides an excellent transition to the second member of the troika—the *self*. To state that a person has a self implies that the individual can act toward self as toward others. A person may react favorably to the self and feel pride, happiness, encouragement; or one may become angry or disgusted with the self. The primary way that a person comes to see self as others see it (possess a self-concept) is through role taking. Of course, this act would not be possible without language (significant symbols), for through language the child learns the responses, intentions, and definitions of others.

Mead describes two explicit phases of self-development and an initial implicit phase. The first stage is the *preparatory stage*.[7] Here the infant imitates others by mirroring. The baby

7. This label is not Mead's. It is supplied by Meltzer in "The Chicago and Iowa Schools."

may pick up the paper, or put on daddy's shoes, or stab at a piece of meat with a fork. This phase is purely preliminary, in which the child does not possess meanings for the acts imitated. Later, in the *play stage*, the child literally plays the role of significant others in the environment. In playing mother and father or fire fighter or nurse, the child empathizes with the definitions of these others. Mead describes how a child in the play stage will pretend to be another person and will act toward a hypothetical receiver who is really oneself. The play stage is sequential in that each role is taken separately, much as an actor playing out prescribed parts. It is marked by disorganization and sporadic movement from one role to another. No unitary viewpoint is maintained, and the child does not develop a singular concept of self. In the *game stage* the individual responds in a generalized way to several others simultaneously. Mead uses the analogy of the baseball game, in which each player must envision simultaneously all nine roles and adapt accordingly. At this stage the person must generalize a composite role of all others' definitions of self.

The concept of the *generalized other* is one of Mead's main contributions. The generalized other is the unified role from which the individual sees the self. It is our individual perception of the overall way that others see us. The self-concept is unified and organized through internalization of this generalized other. Your generalized other is your concept of how others in general perceive you. You have learned this self-picture from years of symbolic interaction with other people in your life.

The self has two facets, each serving an essential function in the human being's life. The *I* is the impulsive, unorganized, undirected, unpredictable part of the person. The *me* is the generalized other, made up of the organized and consistent patterns shared with others. Every act begins with an impulse from the *I* and quickly becomes controlled by the *me*. The *I* is the driving force in action, while the *me* provides direction and guidance. Mead uses the concept of *me* to explain socially acceptable and adaptive behavior and the *I* to explain creative, unpredictable impulses within the person.

The self, or the ability to act toward the self, creates a situation not encountered by lower animals. The ability to use significant symbols to respond to oneself leads to the possibility of inner experience and thought that may or may not be consummated in overt conduct. This latter idea constitutes the third part of Mead's theory—the *mind*. The mind can be defined as the process of interacting with oneself. This ability, which develops along with the self, is crucial to human life, for it is part of every act. "Minding" involves hesitating (postponing overt action) while one consciously assigns meaning to the stimuli. Mind often arises around problem situations in which the individual must think through future actions. The person imagines various outcomes, selecting and testing possible alternative actions.

The reason that mind is important for Mead is that it provides the rationale for seeing persons as actors rather than reactors. Human beings literally construct the act before they consummate it. Responses can be designed and controlled before they are enacted. The rat in the maze goes through a trial-and-error process, whereas in human beings this trial and error can take place covertly through imagination and reflection before the person ever begins to act.

Normally, in the animal world the organism is bombarded by stimuli from the environment, but in human life the organism makes objects out of the stimuli. Because people possess significant symbols that allow them to name their concepts, the person can transform mere stimuli into real objects. Objects do not exist apart from people. The object is always defined by the individual in terms of the kinds of acts that a person might make toward the object. A pencil is a pencil if I can write with it. A seascape is a seascape when I value looking at it. A bottle of bourbon is a liquor when I conceive of drinking it, or not drinking it. Objects become the objects they are through the individual's symbolic minding process; when the individual envisions new or different actions toward an object, the object is changed.

In summary Mead sees the person as a biologically advanced organism with a brain capable of rational thought. Through significant gestures and role taking, the person becomes an object to oneself; that is, one sees the self as others see it. The person internalizes this general self-view and behaves consistently with it. Through the process of mind, the person plans and rehearses symbolic behavior in preparation for interaction with others.

Herbert Blumer and the Chicago School

Herbert Blumer undoubtedly was Mead's foremost apostle. In fact, Blumer coined the term *symbolic interactionism*, an expression Mead himself never used. Blumer refers to this label as "a somewhat barbaric neologism that I coined in an offhand way. . . . The term somehow caught on."[8] Although Blumer published articles throughout his career, not until his 1969 publication of *Symbolic Interactionism: Perspective and Method* did a unified view of his thought become available.[9] In his first chapter Blumer clearly states his debt to Mead and his devotion to furthering the interactionist perspective. Blumer's formulations are consistent with those of his mentor, but he does not merely repeat Mead: "I have been compelled to develop my own version, dealing explicitly with many crucial matters that were only implicit in the thought of Mead and others, and covering critical topics with which they were not concerned."[10]

Blumer begins his writing on symbolic interaction with three premises: (1) "Human beings act toward things on the basis of the meanings that the things have for them"; (2) "the meaning of such things is derived from, or arises out of, the social interaction that one has with one's fellows"; (3) "these meanings are handled in, and modified through, an interpretive process used by the person in dealing with the things he encounters."[11]

As we will see, Blumer has been critical of the mainstream of social science on a number of counts, the first of which is the treatment of meaning. Blumer shows how most theories of behavioral science undercut the importance of the concept of meaning. Many theories ignore meaning completely, and others place it in the general subordinate category of antecedent factors. In symbolic interactionism, though, meaning takes a central role in the social process itself. Meaning is a product of social life. Whatever meaning a person possesses for a thing is the result of interaction with others about the object being defined. A person has no meaning for something apart from the interaction with other human beings.

What is distinctive about the interactionist view of meaning is its stress on conscious interpretation. An object has meaning for the person at the point when the individual consciously thinks about or interprets the object. This process of handling meanings becomes an internal conversaton: "The actor selects, checks, suspends, regroups, and transforms the meanings in light of the situation in which he is placed and the direction of his action."[12] This internal process, as you will recall, is the same as Mead's concept of mind.

Blumer stresses the importance of this definition of meaning for the symbolic interactionist perspective. Blumer's three premises on meaning form the skeleton for his thought, and the meat is provided by what he calls "root images." The root images cover the topics of group life, social interaction, the nature of objects, persons as actors, the nature of human action, and interlinkages of individual actions in society. Let us discuss each of these in turn.

Blumer reiterates Mead's view that society arises from individual interactions. No human

8. Herbert Blumer, *Symbolic Interactionism: Perspective and Method* (Englewood Cliffs, N.J.: Prentice-Hall, 1969), p. 1.

9. Ibid.

10. Ibid.

11. Ibid., p. 2.

12. Ibid., p. 5.

action stands apart from *interaction*. Nearly all that a person is and does is formed in the process of interacting symbolically with others. Society results from each person's coordinating one's own conduct with that of others. Thus both group life and individual conduct are shaped through the ongoing process of symbolic interaction.

Blumer treats objects in essentially the same way as does Mead. For Blumer objects are of three types: physical (things), social (people), and abstract (ideas). Objects come to have meaning through symbolic interaction. Objects may hold different meanings for different people, depending on the nature of others' actions toward the person regarding the defined object. A police officer in a ghetto may mean something different to the citizens of that area than a police officer means to the inhabitants of a posh residential area because of the different interactions among the residents of these two vastly different geographical areas.

Blumer's treatment of action is essentially the same as Mead's. Blumer sees persons as actors, not reactors. People are able to act because they possess a self and, to reiterate Mead, an individual has the ability to act toward self as an object. This capacity to act implies that the individual can deal with problem situations: "Instead of being merely an organism that responds to the play of factors on or through it, the human being is seen as an organism that has to deal with what it notes."[13]

One of the primary areas in which Blumer extends Mead's thinking is group or societal action. Blumer recognizes the importance of group action and takes steps to define it. What is seen as societal or group action is merely the extended process of many individuals fitting their actions to one another. A joint action of a group of people consists of an *interlinkage* of their separate actions, but group action is not a mere summation of the individual actions. Such institutions as marriage, trade, war, and church worship are joint actions. Group action is based in individual acts. Hence it is incorrect to consider group conduct as independent from the individual actions of the participants: "The participants still have to guide their respective acts by forming and using meanings."[14]

Blumer makes three basic observations about linkages. First, he notes that the largest portion of group action in an advanced society consists of highly recurrent and stable patterns. These group actions possess common and preestablished meanings in a society. Because of the high frequency of such patterns, scholars have tended to treat them as structures or entities. Blumer warns us not to forget that new situations present problems requiring adjustment and redefinition. Even in highly repetitious group patterns nothing is permanent. Each case must begin anew with individual action. No matter how solid a group action appears to be, it is still rooted in individual human selves: "It is the social process in group life that creates and upholds the rules, not the rules that create and uphold group life."[15]

The second observation Blumer makes about groups is the pervasive and extended nature of some interlinkages. Individual actions may be connected through complicated networks. Distant actors may be interlinked ultimately in diverse ways, but contrary to popular sociological thinking, "a network or an institution does not function automatically because of some inner dynamics or system requirements: it functions because people at different points do something, and what they do is a result of how they define the situation in which they are called on to act."[16]

Blumer's third observation ties together the first two. With an understanding that groups in a society are based in individual symbolic interaction, we may come to realize that individuals' backgrounds are important in the kind of joint action that occurs. Blumer's main point, repetitiously described, is that societal groups

13. Ibid., p. 14.

14. Ibid., p. 17.

15. Ibid., p. 19.

16. Ibid.

and institutions are not structures all their own. First and foremost they are interlinkages of individual symbolic interactions.

Another broad area in which Blumer goes beyond Mead is methodology. Since methodology is the primary, and dramatic, difference between the Chicago and Iowa schools, reviewing Blumer's ideas on method is particularly important. One cannot read Blumer without realizing how vital this topic is to him. Although Mead does not emphasize method, Blumer maintains that the very nature of symbolic interactionism is captured in its method. Blumer's opinions on this topic are strong.

According to Blumer, the most basic foundation for behavioral science must be the empirical world: "This empirical world must forever be the central point of concern. It is the point of departure and the point of return in the case of empirical science."[17] However, we must not underestimate the role of the observer in empirical testing. Consistent with symbolic interactionist perspective, reality exists only through human experience. In Blumer's words, "It is impossible to cite a single instance of a characterization of the 'world of reality' that is not cast in the form of human imagery."[18]

In this empirical context are two potential dangers for research. The first is the conception that reality in the empirical world is immutable and exists to be "discovered" by science. Another related danger is the belief that reality is best cast in terms of physics. Both conceptions already have played havoc with social science research: "To force all of the empirical world to fit a scheme that has been devised for a given segment of that world is philosophical doctrinizing and does not represent the approach of genuine empirical science."[19]

Inquiry in its ideal form involves six major aspects. First, the researcher must possess and make use of some framework or model of the empirical world. Research cannot be approached on abstract levels that do not include a prior picture of what the real world is like. Second, the researcher needs to ask questions about the world, which eventually must be framed as problems. Third, the kind of data to be sought must be determined and a realistic appraisal made of the ways in which that data can be obtained. Fourth, the researcher needs to ascertain patterns of relationship among the data collected. Fifth, interpretation of the findings is necessary. Sixth, the investigator must conceptualize what has been discovered.

Blumer levels a biting criticism of the mainstream of social science method in the following words:

> The overwhelming bulk of what passes today as methodology is made up of such preoccupations as the following: the devising and use of sophisticated research techniques, usually of an advanced statistical character; the construction of logical and mathematical models, all too frequently guided by the criterion of elegance; the elaboration of formal schemes on how to construct concepts and theories; valiant application of imported schemes, such as input-output analysis, systems analysis, and stochastic analysis; studious conformity to the canons of research design; and the promotion of a particular procedure, such as survey research, as the method of scientific study. I marvel at the supreme confidence with which these preoccupations are advanced as the stuff of methodology. Many of these preoccupations . . . are grossly inadequate on the simple ground that they deal with only a limited aspect of the full act of scientific inquiry, ignoring such matters as premises, problems, concepts, and so on. More serious is their almost universal failure to face the task of outlining the principles of how schemes, problems, data, connections, concepts, and interpretations are to be constructed in the light of the nature of the empirical world under study.[20]

All of these traditional methods use four generalized procedures, according to Blumer. These approaches fail as realistic methods for empirical validation. They are "(a) adhering to a scientific protocol, (b) engaging in replication of research studies, (c) relying on the testing of hypotheses, and (d) employing so-called operational procedures."[21]

17. Ibid., p. 22.
18. Ibid.
19. Ibid., p. 23.
20. Ibid., pp. 26–27.
21. Ibid.

If the usual means of research are inadequate, what does Blumer propose as an alternative? Blumer maintains that researchers must develop firsthand participative knowledge of the phenomena investigated. The scientist may call participative knowledge "soft," but actually it is a rigorous process of finding out what the real world is like. This sort of method consists of two stages.

The first stage Blumer calls *exploration*. Exploration is a flexible scanning technique wherein the investigator uses any ethical method of getting information. In the exploring stage the investigator should move from technique to technique in a flexible and comfortable manner in order to get a broad picture of the area being investigated. Techniques may range from direct observation to interviewing, from listening in on conversations to surveying life histories, from reading letters and diaries to consulting public records. No formal guidelines are followed, and whatever procedures are used should be adapted to the situation. The second stage is more focused. After ascertaining the general nature of the phenomenon, the researcher begins *inspection*. The primary difference between exploration and inspection is depth and focus. Inspection is "an intensive focused examination," according to Blumer. This examination must be done in the context of the area under investigation.

Manford Kuhn and the Iowa School

Manford Kuhn and his students, while maintaining basic interactionist principles, take two new steps not previously seen in the old-line interactionist theory. The first is to make the interactionist concept of self more concrete; the second, which makes the first possible, is the use of quantitative research. In this latter area the Iowa and Chicago schools part company. Blumer strongly criticizes the trend in the behavioral sciences to operationalize; Kuhn makes a point to do just that! As a result Kuhn's work moves more toward microscopic analysis than does the traditional Chicago approach.

Like many of the interactionists, Kuhn never published a truly unified work. The closest may be Hickman and Kuhn's *Individuals, Groups, and Economic Behavior*, published in 1956.[22] (For an excellent short synthesis see Charles Tucker's critique.[23])

Kuhn's theoretical premises are consistent with Mead's thought. Kuhn conceives of the basis of all action as symbolic interaction. The child is socialized through interaction with others in the society into which he or she is born. The person has meaning for and thereby deals with objects in the environment through social interaction. To Kuhn the naming of an object is important, for naming is a way of conveying the object's meaning in communicable terms. Kuhn agrees with his colleagues that the individual is not a passive reactor but an active planner. He reinforces the view that individuals undertake self-conversations as part of the process of acting. Kuhn also reiterates the importance of language in thinking and communicating.

Like Mead and Blumer Kuhn discusses the importance of *objects* in the actor's world. The object can be any aspect of the person's reality: a thing, a quality, an event, or a state of affairs. The only requirement for something to become an object for a person is that the person name it, represent it symbolically. Reality for persons is the totality of their social objects. Kuhn agrees with other interactionists that meaning is socially derived. Meaning is assigned to an object from group norms regulating how people deal with the object in question.

A second concept important to Kuhn is the *plan of action*. A plan of action is a person's total behavior pattern toward a given object, including whether to seek or avoid it, how the object is thought to behave (since this determines how the person will behave toward the object), and feelings about the object as it is defined. Attitudes constitute a subset of the plan of action.

22. C. A. Hickman and Manford Kuhn, *Individuals, Groups, and Economic Behavior* (New York: Holt, Rinehart and Winston, 1956).

23. Charles Tucker, "Some Methodological Problems of Kuhn's Self Theory," *The Sociological Quarterly* 7 (1966), 345–58.

Attitudes are verbal statements that act as blueprints for one's behavior. The attitude indicates the end toward which action will be directed as well as the evaluation of the object. Because attitudes are verbal statements, they can be observed and measured.

A third concept important to Kuhn is the *orientational other*. Orientational others are those who have been particularly influential in a person's life. They possess four qualities. First, they are people to whom the individual is emotionally and psychologically committed. Second, they are the ones who provide the person with general vocabulary, central concepts, and categories. Third, they provide the individual with the basic distinction between self and others, including one's perceived role differentiation. Fourth, the orientational others' communications continually sustain the individual's self-concept. Orientational others may be in the present or past, they may be present or absent. The important idea behind the concept is that the individual comes to see the world through interaction with *particular* other persons who have touched one's life in important ways.

Finally, we come to Kuhn's most important concept—the *self*. Kuhn's theory and method revolve around self, and it is in this area that Kuhn most dramatically extends symbolic interactionist thinking. Kuhn is primarily responsible for a technique known as the "twenty-statements" self-attitudes test. His rationale for developing this procedure is stated succinctly: "If as we suppose, human behavior is *organized* and *directed*, and if, as we further suppose, the organization and direction are supplied by the individual's *attitudes toward himself*, it ought to be of crucial significance to social psychology to be able to identify and measure self-attitudes."[24] A subject taking the "twenty-statements" test would be confronted with twenty blank spaces preceded by the following simple instructions:

24. Manford Kuhn and Thomas McPartland, "An Empirical Investigation of Self-Attitudes," *American Sociological Review* 19 (1954), p. 68.

"There are twenty numbered blanks on the page below. Please write twenty answers to the simple question, "Who am I?" in the blanks. Just give twenty different answers to this question. Answer as if you were giving the answers to yourself, not to somebody else. Write the answers in the order that they occur to you. Don't worry about logic or 'importance.' Go along fairly fast, for time is limited."[25]

A number of potential ways are available to analyze the responses from this test, with each method tapping a different aspect of self. Here are Kuhn's primary theoretical formulations. First, the self-conception is seen as the individual's plans of action toward the self as an object. This self-concept consists of the individual's identities (roles and statuses), interests and aversions, goals, ideologies, and self-evaluations. Such self-conceptions are anchoring attitudes, for they act as one's most common frame of reference for judging other objects. All subsequent plans of action stem primarily from the self-concept.

Two major aspects of the self may be termed the ordering variable and the locus variable. The *ordering variable* is the relative salience of identifications the individual possesses. It is observable in the order of statements listed by the subject in the "twenty-statements" task. For example, if the person lists "Baptist" a great deal higher than "father," the researcher may conclude that the person identifies more readily with religious affiliation than with family affiliation. The *locus variable* is the extent to which the subject in a general way tends to identify with consensual groupings rather than idiosyncratic, subjective qualities.

In scoring the self-attitude test, the analyst may place statements in one of two categories. A statement may be said to be *consensual* if it consists of a discrete group or class identification, such as student, girl, husband, Baptist, from Chicago, premed, daughter, oldest child, studying engineering. Other statements are not descriptions of commonly agreed-on cate-

25. Ibid., p. 69.

gories. Examples of *subconsensual* responses are happy, bored, pretty, good student, too heavy, good wife, interesting. The number of statements in the consensual group is the individual's locus score.

The idea of locus is important to Kuhn: "Persons vary over a rather wide range in the relative volume of consensual and subconsensual components in their self-conceptions. It is in this finding that our empirical investigation has given the greatest advance over the purely deductive and more or less literary formulations of George Herbert Mead."[26]

The conflict between the Chicago and Iowa schools is apparent. In fact, the work of Kuhn and his associates has become so estranged from mainstream symbolic interactionism that it has lost its support among those who espouse the basic tenets of the movement. Kuhn's methods simply are not adequate for investigating *processual* behavior, an essential element of interaction. As a result a group of followers, who believe in both the central ideas of symbolic interactionism and the expressed need to examine social life in concrete ways, has emerged as the "new" Iowa School. One of its leaders, Carl Couch, describes the situation: "By the mid-1960s most of us affiliated with Kuhn had become disenchanted with the use of the TST [twenty-statements test] and allied instruments. There was an increasing awareness that this set of procedures was not generating the data required for serious testing, revision, and elaboration of the theory. Some turned to naturalistic observation. . . . Some gave up the search; others foundered."[27]

Couch and his associates began studying the structure of coordinated behavior by using videotaped sequences. They have produced research on how interaction begins (openings) and ends (closings), how disagreements are negotiated, and how unanticipated consequences that block achievement of interaction objectives are accounted for. By studying these areas, they attempt to isolate general principles of symbolic interaction. Such principles may form the basis for a grounded theory of symbolic interaction in the future.[28]

The Dramatism of Kenneth Burke

The so-called dramaturgical school of symbolic interactionism is distinguished by the use of the dramatic metaphor. The dramaturgists see people as actors on a metaphorical stage playing out roles in interaction with others. Several theorists might be termed dramaturgical in this sense, but dramaturgical theory in actuality lacks the unity required to call it a school. Three dramaturgists seem to lead the movement. The first, Erving Goffman, has written extensively about how individuals present themselves to others in rolelike behavior. His theory is distinctly microscopic and takes a different turn from other interactionists. (Although Goffman is known as a symbolic interactionist, it seems more appropriate to treat his theory at length in Part IV on contextual theories.) The other two primary dramaturgical interactionists, who have taken different approaches from Goffman, are Kenneth Burke and his advocate in the field of sociology, Hugh Duncan.

Although Burke's concepts are consistent with the symbolic interactionist movement, it is doubtful that he would align himself exclusively with the movement. In fact, unlike most of the symbolic interactionists, Burke has not identified with any particular academic discipline. He has written widely in many areas of thought from creative writing, to literary and rhetorical criticism, to social psychology, to linguistic analysis. Also, unlike most other symbolic interactionists, Burke's concepts are not derived from the work of Mead and the

26. Ibid., p. 76.

27. Carl J. Couch, "Symbolic Interaction and Generic Sociological Principles" (Paper presented at the Symposium on Symbolic Interaction, Boston, 1979), p. 9.

28. This work is summarized in Carl J. Couch and Robert Hintz, eds., *Constructing Social Life* (Champaign: Stipes Publishing Co., 1975); and Clark McPhail, "Toward a Theory of Collective Behavior" (Paper presented at the Symposium on Symbolic Interaction, Columbia, South Carolina, 1978).

other early sociologists. Some of his most important works, in fact, appeared concurrently with the publication of Mead's ideas. On the other hand, it would be incorrect to exclude Burke from the mainstream of symbolic interactionist thought, for while he has maintained his independence, his theory is highly consistent with the others presented in this chapter.

Kenneth Burke is no doubt a giant among symbol theorists. He has written profusely over a period of fifty years, and his theory is the most comprehensive of all the interactionists. Hugh Duncan wrote, "It may be said without exaggeration that anyone writing today on communication, however 'original' he may be, is echoing something said by Burke."[29] Burke has published eight major books spanning from 1931 to 1966.[30] Unfortunately, Burke is not noted for clarity of style. His theory is scattered and often appears ambiguous. When a scholar takes the time necessary to know Burke's work, however, the coherence and unity of the theory become apparent. Fortunately, a number of scholars have provided written interpretations of Burke's ideas.[31] In surveying Burke's communication theory, we will begin with a summary of his concept of dramatism; then we will turn to his central concepts of humanity, language, and communication; and finally we will sketch Burke's method.

29. Hugh Duncan, "Communication in Society," *Arts in Society* 3 (1964), 105.

30. Burke's major works include *Counter-Statement* (New York: Harcourt, Brace & Company, 1931); *Permanence and Change* (New York: New Republic, 1935); *Attitudes toward History* (New York: New Republic, 1937); *The Philosophy of Literary Form* (Baton Rouge: Louisiana State University, 1941); *A Grammar of Motives* (1945) and *A Rhetoric of Motives* (1950) (Englewood Cliffs, N.J.: Prentice Hall); *A Rhetoric of Religion* (Boston: Beacon Press, 1961); *Language as Symbolic Action* (Berkeley and Los Angeles University of California Press, 1966).

31. I would like to express my particular appreciation to friend and colleague Peter Coyne for the continued insights he has given me on Kenneth Burke. See Peter Coyne, "Kenneth Burke and the Rhetorical Criticism of Public Address" (Doctoral dissertation, University of Utah, 1973). For a comprehensive overview on Kenneth Burke, see William Rueckert, ed., *Critical Responses to Kenneth Burke* (Minneapolis: University of Minnesota Press, 1969).

Burke sees the act as the basic concept in dramatism. His view of human action is consistent with that of Mead, Blumer, and Kuhn. Specifically, Burke distinguishes between *action* and *motion*. All objects and animals in the universe can be said to possess motion, but only human beings have action. Action consists of purposeful, voluntary behaviors of individuals. *Dramatism* is the study of action in this sense; the study of motion is *mechanism*. Burke believes that a dramatistic (teleological) view of people is needed in all of the "human" disciplines, for human behavior cannot be properly understood without it. With this perspective let us look at Burke's seminal ideas.

Burke views the individual as a biological and neurological being, who possesses all of the animalistic characteristics of lower species. Consistent with Mead, Burke distinguishes humans by their symbol-using behavior, the ability to act. People are symbol-creating, symbol-using, and symbol-misusing animals. They create symbols to name things and situations; they use symbols for communication; and they often abuse symbols—misuse them to their disadvantage. Burke's view of symbols is broad, including an array of linguistic and nonverbal elements as well. Especially intriguing for Burke is the notion that a person can symbolize symbols. One can talk about speech and can write about words. This second-level activity is a distinguishing characteristic of symbol use.

In addition Burke sees people as instrument creators. They create a variety of mechanical and social tools that, unlike lower animals, separate them from their natural condition. People filter reality through the symbolic screen. For an animal reality just is, but for humans reality is mediated through symbols. Burke agrees with Mead that language functions as the vehicle for action. Because of the social need for people to cooperate in their actions, language arises and shapes behavior. Language, as seen by Burke, is always emotionally loaded. No word can be affectively neutral. As a result a person's attitudes, judgments, and feelings invariably are in that person's language. Language is by nature selective and abstract, focusing attention on particular aspects of reality at the expense of others. While language is economical, it is also ambiguous. Further, language is formal in that it tends to follow certain patterns or forms.

An overriding consideration for all of Burke's work is his concept of guilt. The term *guilt* is Burke's all-purpose word for any feeling of tension within a person: anxiety, embarrassment, self-hatred, disgust, and so forth. For Burke guilt is a condition caused only in humans by their symbol-using nature. He identifies three interrelated sources of guilt arising out of language. The first is *the negative*. Through language people moralize (animals do not). They construct a myriad of rules and proscriptions. Now, these rules are never entirely consistent. In following one rule, you necessarily are breaking another, creating guilt. We will see that Burke's concept of guilt in this sense is similar to the idea of cognitive dissonance (see Chapter 8). The second reason for guilt is the *principle of perfection*, or categorical guilt. People are sensitive to their failings. Humans are able to imagine (through language) a state of perfection. Then, by their very nature, they spend their lives striving for whatever degree of this perfection they set for themselves. Guilt arises as a result of the discrepancy between the real and the ideal. A third reason for guilt is the *principle of hierarchy*. In seeking order, people structure society in social pyramids or hierarchies (social ratings, social orderings). This ranking of course, is a symbolic phenomenon. Competitions and divisions result between classes and groups in the hierarchy, and guilt results. For Burke guilt is the primary motive behind all action and communication: We communicate to purge our guilt.

In discussing communication Burke uses several inseparable terms: persuasion, identification, consubstantiality, communication, and rhetoric. Let us see how these concepts are integrated in his theory. The underlying concept behind Burke's ideas on communication is that of *substance*, or in Burke's words the doctrine of substance. Substance is the general nature, fundamentals, or essence of any thing. Substance must be viewed in holistic terms; it is not a mere summation of the parts or aspects of the thing in consideration. Each person is distinct, possessing separate substance. Crucial to Burke's theory is the understanding that the substances of any two persons always overlap to some extent. The overlapping is not perfect, though, and thus prevents ideal communication. Whatever communication occurs between individuals is a direct function of their *consubstantiality* (sharing of common substance). Consubstantiality, or commonality, allows for communication because of the *shared meaning* it creates for the symbols used. When Barney and Joe are relaxing next to the swimming pool on a warm summer morning, they communicate with one another in a free and understanding manner because they share meanings for the language in use. They are, so to speak, consubstantial. On the other hand, when Mary and Bob ask a question of a harried bus boy in a Swiss restaurant, they may feel frustration because of their lack of shared meaning with this individual. To combine Mead and Burke, a significant symbol is one that allows for shared meaning through consubstantiality.

Another important concept of Burke is *identification*. As generally conceived, identification is the same as consubstantiality, or the sharing of substance. The opposite of identification is *division*. Division and the guilt it produces are the primary motives for communication. Through communication, identification is increased. In a spiraling fashion as identification increases, shared meaning increases, thereby improving understanding. Identification thus can be a means to persuasion or improved communication or an end in itself. Identification can be conscious or unconscious, planned or accidental. Three overlapping sources of identification exist between people. Material identification results from goods, possessions, and things. Idealistic identification results from ideas, attitudes, feelings, and values. Formal identification results from the form or arrangement of the act. If two people who are introduced shake hands, the conventional form of handshaking causes some identification to take place. Speakers can identify better with their audiences if they provide a form that is meaningful to the particular audience.

Before we proceed, let us look at a couple of cautions. First, identification is not an either-or occurrence but a matter of degree. Some consubstantiality will always be present merely by virtue of the shared humanness of any two persons. Identification can be great or small, and it can be increased or decreased by the actions of the communicators. Second, although identification and division exist side by side between any two persons, communication is more successful when identification is greater than division.

An interesting phenomenon that might seem to contradict Burke's view of identification is that people of lower strata in a hierarchy often identify with godlike persons at the top of the hierarchy, despite tremendous apparent division. This kind of identification can be seen, for example, in the mass following of a charismatic leader. Two overlapping factors explain its occurrence. First, individuals perceive in others an embodiment of the perfection they themselves strive for. Second, the mystery surrounding the charismatic person simultaneously tends to hide the division that exists. This phenomenon may be called identification through *mystification*.

In striving for happiness, each person adopts certain strategies of identification. Strategies are analogous to Kuhn's concept of plans of action. They are the tactics for living, the plans for communicating with another. Burke does not attempt to outline all available strategies for relating to others, because the list would be indefinitely long. One of the suggestions he makes for analyzing a rhetorical (communicative) act is to assess the strategies the communicators use to increase their identification. Burke provides a full-blown methodology for studying rhetorical acts. His method, in fact, has proved useful in areas such as rhetorical and literary criticism—the analysis of speeches, poems, books, and other rhetorical devices.

Burke's most basic methodological paradigm is the *dramatistic pentad*. Pentad, meaning a group of five, is in this sense an analytical framework for the most efficient study of any act. The first part is the *act*, what is done by the actor. It is a view of what the actor played, what was accomplished. The second part is the *scene*, the situation or setting in which the act was accomplished. It includes a view of the physical setting as well as the cultural and social milieu in which the act was carried out. The third component is the *agent*, the actor, including all that is known about the individual. The agent's substance reaches all aspects of his or her being, history, personality, demeanor, and any other contributing factors. The *agency*, the fourth component, is the means or vehicle the agent uses in carrying out the act. Agency may include channels of communication, devices, institutions, strategies, or messages. Fifth, the *purpose* is the reason for the act—the rhetorical goal, the hoped-for effect or result of the act.

For example, in writing a paper for your communication theory course you, the agent, gather information and present it to the instructor (the act). Your course, your university, your library, your desk and room, the social atmosphere of your school, and more constitute the scene; the format of the paper itself is the agency. You have a variety of purposes, including, in all likelihood, getting a good grade.

Criticism of Symbolic Interactionism

Although many specific objections have been raised against symbolic interactionism, for the most part they can be combined into three major criticisms.[32] First, symbolic interac-

32. For reviews of specific objections to symbolic interactionism, see Jerome G. Manis and Bernard N. Meltzer, "Appraisals of Symbolic Interactionism," in Manis and Meltzer, *Symbolic Interaction*, pt. IV, pp. 393–440; Bernard N. Meltzer, John Petras, and Larry Reynolds, *Symbolic Interactionism: Genesis, Varieties, and Criticism* (London: Routledge and Kegan Paul, 1975).

tionism is said to be nonempirical. That is, one cannot readily translate its concepts into observable, researchable units. Second, it is said to be overly restrictive in the variables it takes into account. Critics have charged that it ignores crucial psychological variables on one end and societal variables on the other. Third, it uses concepts in an inexact, inconsistent way. Let us look at each of these objections more closely. In doing so, we will relate the objections to the categories for evaluating theory outlined in Chapter 2.

The first major criticism of symbolic interactionism has broad implications. Despite Blumer's protestations to the contrary, critics maintain that in actual practice the researcher does not know what to look for in observing interactionist concepts in real life. This problem seems to stem from the vague, intuitive claims of early interactionists. What is mind, for example? How can this concept be observed? We already have noted Kuhn's failure to operationalize interactionist concepts without giving up its assumptions about the process nature of behavior. Most basically, this criticism questions the *appropriateness* of symbolic interactionism to lead to a more complete understanding of everyday behavior. As such, critics believe it to be more appropriately social philosophy, which may guide our thinking about events, but which provides little concrete conceptualization for explaining the events. John Lofland's criticism is especially biting. He claims that interactionists participate in three main activities: "doctrinaire reiteration of the master's teachings, . . . [making] slightly more specific the general imagery, . . . [and connecting] descriptive case studies and interactionism.[33]

As a result of this alleged failure, symbolic interactionism is not thought to be adequately *heuristic*. It has generated few testable hypotheses, and little research has been produced. Interactionist scholars thus have been unable to elaborate and expand their thinking. Carl Couch, a leading proponent (and house critic) of the movement, points out that interactionists do engage in research, but that their observations do not cast light on the theory's key concepts, making revision and elaboration difficult. Couch believes this circumstance need not be so, and the "new" Iowa tradition has emerged out of a need for interactionists to do "serious sociological work."[34]

The second major criticism is that interactionism has either ignored or downplayed important explanation variables. Critics say it leaves out the emotions of the individual on one end and societal organization on the other. These arguments as a whole make clear that interactionism is overly restrictive in *scope*. To cover as much of social life as it pretends to do, interactionism must take into account social structures as well as individual feelings. The problem is not one merely of scope, of course; it casts doubt on the *validity* of the tradition as well.

The failure of symbolic interactionism to deal with social organization is a major concern for interactionists. Social organization or structure removes individual prerogative, a highly valued idea in old-style interactionism. Social structure is normally a matter of power, and interactionists have been loath to admit to power inequality. However, the concept of power can be investigated from an interactionist perspective, and since about 1965 several research programs have begun to look at power.[35]

Somewhat less work has been done in the area of emotions. Interactionists now generally agree that feelings have been neglected by symbolic interactionism, although they claim that

33. John Lofland, "Interactionist Imagery and Analytic Interruptus," in *Human Nature and Collective Behavior*, ed. Tamotsu Shibutani (Englewood Cliffs, N.J.: Prentice-Hall, 1970), p. 37.

34. Couch, "Symbolic Interaction."

35. This line of work is discussed in Peter M. Hall, "Structuring Symbolic Interaction: Communication and Power," in *Communication Yearbook 4*, ed. Dan Nimmo (New Brunswick, N.J.: Transaction Books, 1980), pp. 49–60.

interactionism is not antithetical to the study of feeling or affect.

The third general criticism of symbolic interactionism is that its concepts are not used consistently. As a result such concepts as *I, me, self, role*, and others are vague. This is a problem of both internal *validity* and *parsimony*.[36] However, we must keep in mind that symbolic interactionism is not a unified theory. Rather, it is a general framework, and as we have seen, it has different versions. Therefore, although this is a valid criticism of early interactionism, it is not a fair picture of the movement today.

Interactionists have not been daunted by their critics. The movement has adjusted and matured. It is too early to tell what will happen to symbolic interactionism, although it appears that the grand movement will be replaced by a series of middle-range theories that provide concrete explanations of social behavior consistent with the general tenets of old-line symbolic interactionism. Rules theory shows promise for filling this gap.

The Rules Approach to Communication

In the history of ideas, two different strands of thought sometimes are found to be consistent with one another, and they converge to the benefit of both. Each tradition enhances or improves the other. Such is the case with symbolic interactionism and rules theory. Symbolic interactionism tells us of the importance of interaction and meaning in human experience; the rules approach gives form and substance to this interaction-meaning cycle. Susan Shimanoff discusses the importance of rules in symbolic interaction: "In order for communication to exist, or continue, two or more interacting individuals must share rules for using symbols. Not only must they have rules for individual symbols, but they must also agree on such matters as how to take turns at speaking, how to be polite or how to insult, to greet, and so forth. If every symbol user manipulated symbols at random, the result would be chaos rather than communication."[37]

Unfortunately the rules approach is a loose confederation of ideas that are still evolving as a recognizable body of research and theory. As a result discussing rules theory as a unified approach is not possible. Let us look briefly at the main theoretical branches of the rules approach, emphasizing two recent rules theories of communication.

Despite its diversity the rules approach is held together by certain common assumptions.[38] Although these are not identical to the premises of symbolic interactionism, they are consistent with and add to the latter framework. The action principle, which is central to symbolic interactionist thought, generally is considered to be a primary assumption of the rules approach. Although some human activity is mechanical and determined by uncontrollable factors, the most important behaviors are considered to be actively initiated by the individual. People are thought to choose courses of action within situations to accomplish their intentions. You recall that this action principle is opposed to the motion principle, in which human behavior is seen as determined by prior causes. Rules theorists agree that the motion principle, which gives rise to laws of nature, is appropriate in the science of objects but that it is not useful for understanding human social life. For this reason the rule-

36. As an example of this criticism, see the analysis of the concept of self in Meltzer, Petras, and Reynolds, pp. 94–95.

37. Susan B. Shimanoff, *Communication Rules: Theory and Research* (Beverly Hills: Sage Publications, 1980), pp. 31–32.

38. The similarities and differences among rules theories are discussed in such sources as Donald P. Cushman, "The Rules Perspective as a Theoretical Basis for the Study of Human Communication," *Communication Quarterly* 25 (1977), 30–45; W. Barnett Pearce, "Rules Theories of Communication: Varieties, Limitations, and Potentials" (Paper presented at the Speech Communication Association, New York City, 1980); Stuart J. Sigman, "On Communication Rules from a Social Perspective," *Human Communication Research* 7 (1980), 37–51; and Shimanoff, *Communication Rules*.

governed approach to communication theory often is set in opposition to the law-governed approach.

Another basic assumption of most rules theories is that social behavior is structured and organized. Certain behaviors recur in similar situations. Social interaction patterns, however, vary in different settings. Although these patterns are organized, they are not universal, but highly contextual. Thus most rules theories consider the relationship between the way people act and the culture and situation wherein the action occurs. In fact, rules scholars criticize law-governed theories precisely because of their failure to reflect such variation.

Rules are considered to be the mechanism through which social action is organized. The structure of interaction can be understood in terms of the rules governing it. Rules affect the options available in a given situation. Because rules are thought to be contextual, they explain why people behave similarly in similar situations but differently in different situations.

The rules approach began in the field of philosophy in what has become known as ordinary language philosophy. That tradition, spirited by Wittgenstein, Austin, Searle, and others, is discussed in greater depth in Chapter 6. Other fields of study have taken up the banner, including speech communication, anthropology, linguistics, psychology, and sociology.[39] Discussing all of these applications in depth would be impossible. Fortunately, Donald Cushman has distilled this work into three major research and theory programs, described in the following paragraphs.[40]

In linguistics we find one of the important applications of rules theories. Here the concept of grammatical rules has been developed to explain how speakers can generate any novel sentence from minimal exposure to the language. Sentences are generated and understood on the basis of rules. The native speaker acquires these rules early in life, based on maturation of innate abilities. The generative grammar school, an important aspect of communication theory, will be discussed in Chapter 5.

A second major rules application is that of the previously mentioned philosophers of the action tradition. These scholars relate actions to intentions via rules; people accomplish objectives by applying particular rules. Thus rules are seen as practical tools for accomplishing intentions. One branch of this tradition is ordinary language philosophy, which is responsible for the original work on communication rules. This tradition deals with the ways people create speech to fulfill intentions (see Chapter 6).

A third rules tradition is in cognitive development. Philosophers and psychologists of this tradition study how people conceptualize and solve problems and how their behavior is affected by cognitive processes. These scholars believe that rules are learned gradually during childhood and that an individual's ability to grasp and use rules becomes increasingly complex, allowing the individual to become more behaviorally adaptive.

Approaches to Rules

The rules perspective includes several definitions.[41] Barnett Pearce outlines three main groups of rule conceptions.[42]

Rule-following Approach. In this view rules are seen simply as observed behavioral regularities. A recurring pattern is said to happen "as a rule." Pearce calls such rules weak laws because they are cast in the form of a statement of what is expected to happen under certain circumstances. This approach is highly descriptive but does not explain why particular patterns recur.

39. Shimanoff, *Communication Rules*, pp. 33–34, lists some of the seminal figures in these fields.

40. Cushman, "The Rules Perspective."

41. See Shimanoff, *Communication Rules*, for comparison of various definitions as well as a discussion of the differences between rules and other similar concepts such as norm.

42. Pearce, "Rules Theories." See also Joan Ganz, *Rules: A Systematic Study* (The Hague: Mouton, 1971).

It aims only to catalogue predictable behaviors. Linguistic theories typically are of this type, suggesting that speakers follow rules of grammar with a high degree of regularity. Of all approaches to rules, this group least supports the basic assumptions of the rules tradition.

Rule-governed Approach. Here rules are beliefs about what should or should not be done to achieve an objective in a given situation. The rule-governed approach attempts to uncover people's intentions and to define the socially acceptable ways in which people accomplish their intentions. For example, if a person wishes to engage another person in conversation at a party and the other person is talking with someone else, one would approach the two individuals and not speak until recognized nonverbally. To interrupt or to break in too quickly would be a rules violation that could prevent the desired conversation from occurring. This approach presumes that people know the rules and have the power to follow or to violate them. It also assumes that people usually act consciously, intentionally, and rationally.

Rule-using Approach. This view is consistent with the rule-governed approach except that it posits a more complex social situation. The actor potentially is confronted with a variety of rules for accomplishing various intentions. The actor chooses which rules to follow (or more properly, to use) in carrying out an intention. As a rules critic the individual reflects on rules, following some and discarding others. This approach thereby provides a basis for evaluating what choices a person makes in a social situation and even allows for people to create new options. It also enables the theorist to discuss communication competence by observing how well a person sorts through the matrix of objectives and rules to plan an interaction strategy. In a highly homogeneous situation such as breaking into a cocktail party conversation, the rules are few and simple. Here the rule-governed approach suffices to explain what occurs. The broader rule-using approach is better suited for understanding the preparation of a speech, the organization of a meeting, the writing of a letter, and other heterogeneous rule situations.

Although these approaches may appear to compete for explaining actions, they need not be considered such. Various types of human action can be classified properly under each category. The problem for the theorist is to decide what level is most appropriately defined as communication "rules," and on this matter there is little agreement.

Now that we have discussed the general nature of the rules approach, let us turn to some specific applications of rules. Two recent theories, which are rather different from one another, will illustrate how the rules approach can be applied to communication theory. We will look at Susan Shimanoff's work because it helps us understand the nature of rules in communication, providing an excellent conceptual approach. The second theory, that of Barnett Pearce and Vernon Cronen, is useful for seeing how rules operate in ongoing interaction. Later in the chapter we will examine some of the ways these theories are similar and ways they differ.

Shimanoff's Integrative Approach

Susan Shimanoff's work is presented for several reasons.[43] It is perhaps the most recent general treatment of rules. Shimanoff surveyed the literature on rules and formulated an overview that incorporates what she judges to be the best thinking in the field. She added to rules theory in such a way as to make it particularly applicable to communication. Her work is integrative in that it critically considers and analyzes the divergent literature. Shimanoff does not, indeed could never, incorporate all notions of rules, but she explains her chosen position by comparing and contrasting it with others. Finally, she takes a first step toward developing a rules theory of communication that has the po-

43. Shimanoff, *Communication Rules*.

tential of clarifying and unifying the thought in this area.

Shimanoff defines a rule as "a followable prescription that indicates what behavior is obligated, preferred, or prohibited in certain contexts."[44] This definition incorporates the following four elements.

(1) *Rules must be followable*. This criterion implies that actors can choose whether to follow or to violate a rule. If a person has no choice in a course of action, then a "rule" is not being followed. The laws of nature are not "followed" by the objects under their control; they are fulfilled. For example, you are not following a rule by running out of a burning building. On the other hand, rules must deal with the possible. One cannot follow an impossible rule. This statement does not imply that people are indifferent to rules. Behavior is greatly affected by rules, as the following criterion indicates. (By the way, you perhaps have noticed that Shimanoff uses the word *follow* differently from Pearce's rule-following category described earlier.)

(2) *Rules are prescriptive.* By this Shimanoff means that a course of action is called for and that the failure to abide by the rule can be criticized. Prescriptions may state what is obligated, preferred, or prohibited, but in any case negative evaluation may ensue if the rule is not followed. Thus rules cannot "prescribe" permitted behaviors because no criticism would follow if such behaviors were not chosen. For example, while telling a joke is permissible in certain situations, joke telling is not prescribed and therefore not rule following. One is obligated to apologize, however, after accidentally bumping another person, and the violation of this rule may result in criticism.

(3) *Rules are contextual*. Shimanoff points out that theories vary in the degree of contextuality believed to exist in a rules situation. Some theories state that rules are idiosyncratic, that each situation has its set of rules. Others seek broad, almost universal, rules that cover nearly all situations. Shimanoff takes a position in the middle. Since rules are a vehicle for understanding organized, recurring behavior, they must apply in at least two different occurrences; potentially they may be broad enough to cover many situations. Hence, rules can be understood in terms of their *range* or generalizability. The "apology rule" just mentioned applies in almost all situations and is therefore broad in scope. Still, it is contextual in that it applies only when one person bothers another in some way. In fact, you can probably think of situations in which apologizing is uncalled for and potentially annoying.

(4) *Rules specify appropriate behavior.* They tell us what to *do* or *not do*. They do not specify how we must think, feel, or interpret. For example, a rule may require an apology, but it cannot require the apologizer to feel sorry.

In order to identify a rule properly, an observer must be able to specify its context and its obligated, preferred, or prohibited behavior. The rule also must be stated in a form that demonstrates that it is followable. Shimanoff believes that the if-then format allows the observer to identify rules by specifying four components: If . . ., then one (must, must not, should). . . . The if clause specifies the nature of the prescription and the prescribed behavior. Consider the following examples:

If one is not the owner or guest of the owner, then one is prohibited from being in the land marked off by this sign.

If one is playing bridge and is the dealer, then one must bid first.

If one is wearing a hat and is entering a church, then one must remove his/her hat.

If one is playing chess and one's chess pieces are white, then one must move his/her piece first.[45]

44. Ibid., p. 57.

45. Ibid., p. 79. Shimanoff adapted these rule examples from Gidon Gottlieb, *Logic of Choice: An Investigation of the Concepts of Rule and Rationality* (New York: Macmillan, 1968), p. 11; Max Black, *Models and Metaphors* (Ithaca: Cornell University Press, 1962), p. 106; Raymond D. Gumb, *Rule-Governed Linguistic Behavior* (Paris: Mouton, 1972), p. 21; and Ganz, *Rules*, p. 13.

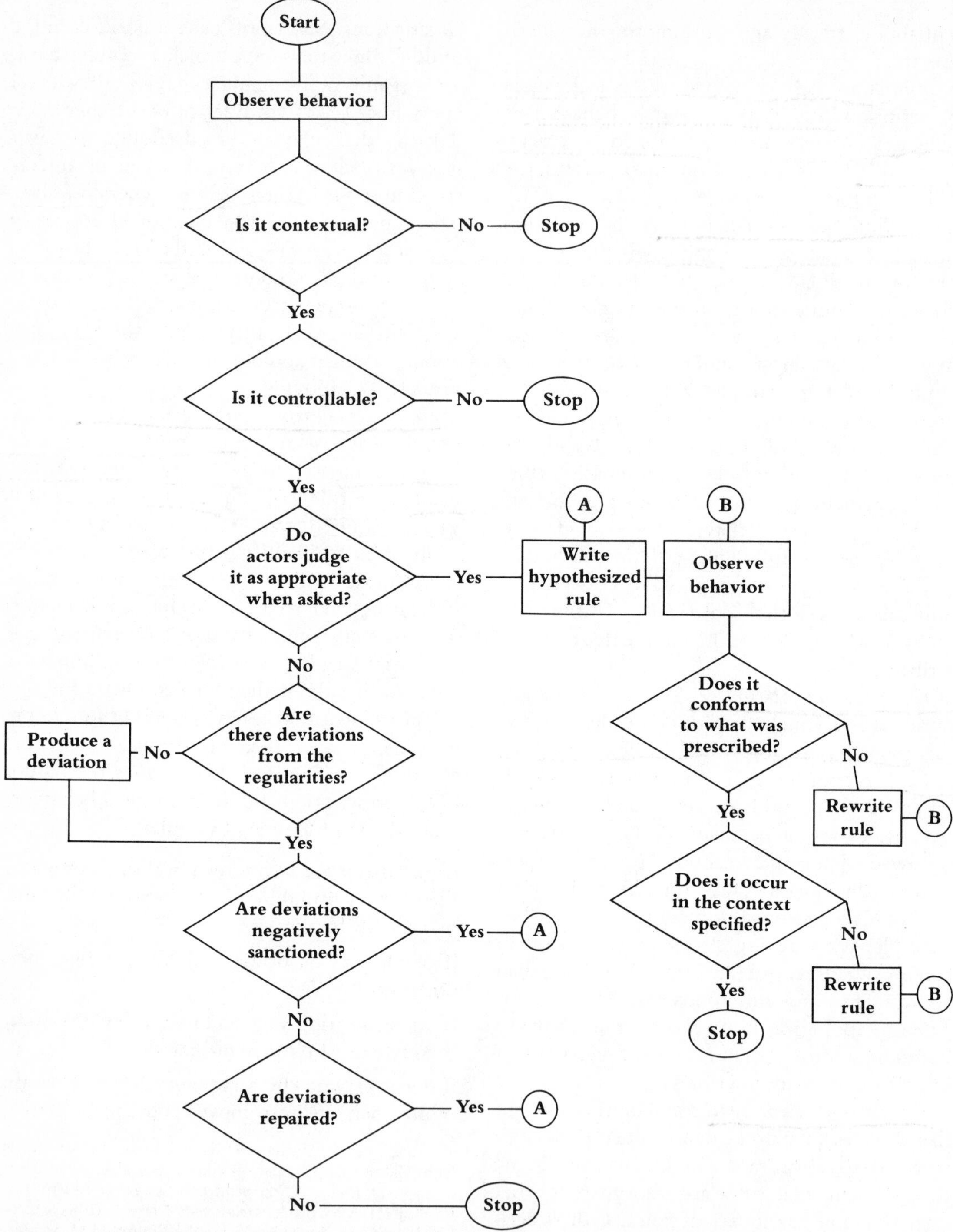

Figure 4.1. Decision tree to identify rules from observed behavior.

Notice that Shimanoff's use of if-then does not imply causal reasoning in which the antecedent causes a consequent. Rather, the antecedent serves as the context in which the rule applies.

To verify a rules theory, a researcher must be able to observe rules in operation in everyday interaction. If Shimanoff's rule model is accurate, one will be able to apply her rule criteria to any episode and thereby identify the rules in force. Some rules are easy to see in operation because they are *explicit*. Such rules are announced, for instance, on a sign or in a game rule book. Most rules are *implicit*, though, and must be inferred from the behavior of the participants. Behavior can be examined in terms of three criteria: (1) Is the behavior controllable (to assess the degree to which the underlying rule is followable)? (2) Is the behavior criticizable (to assess whether the underlying rule is prescriptive)? (3) Is the behavior contextual (to assess whether people behave differently in various situations)?

Applying these criteria is not necessarily easy. For example, consider how difficult it would be to determine whether an action is criticized. We know that rule behavior is open to evaluation and that compliance may be praised while violation is punished. Overt sanctions are easiest to identify in observing interactions because they involve verbal or nonverbal rewards and punishments. Sanctions may range from simple frowns or smiles to a stern lecture about rule violation. In addition to noting sanctions, observers can also look for repairs. Here a rule violator will behave in a way that reveals that a rule was violated. Apologizing is an example. In the absence of overt sanctions or repairs, the observer can ask participants whether a given behavior was appropriate or not. Figure 4.1 is a decision tree illustrating how to identify rules from observed behavior.[46]

One of Shimanoff's most interesting contributions is her model of rule behavior, which indicates the ways people relate to rules in actual interaction (Figure 4.2).[47] This model identifies eight types of rule-related behavior. Four of these are rule conforming, and four are rule deviating. Let us look at these in pairs, beginning toward the center of the figure. *Rule-fulfilling* and *rule-ignorant* behaviors involve acting without knowing the rule. For example, a prevalent rule in some situations is for men to open doors for women. Imagine a little boy who naively opens a door for a woman. He is unaware that he has followed a rule, but the woman might respond by saying, "What a gentleman you are." This behavior is rule fulfilling because the boy didn't know he was following a prescription. On the other hand, had the boy failed to open the door in ignorance of the rule (rule-ignorant behavior), the woman might whisper to the boy's parents, "You need to teach your child good manners."

46. Shimanoff, *Communication Rules,* pp. 106–7.

47. Ibid., p. 127.

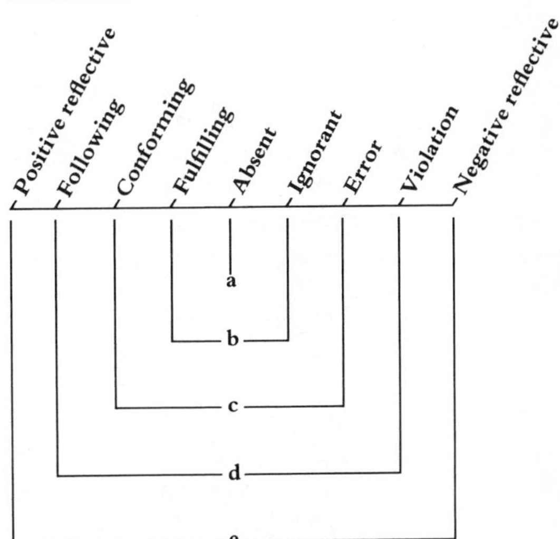

From *Communication Rules: Theory and Research*, by Susan B. Shimanoff. Copyright © 1980 by Sage Publications. Reprinted by permission of the publisher.

Figure 4.2. Rule-related behavior.

Conforming or *error* behaviors definitely are governed by rules, although the rule is not noted consciously by the individual at the time it is followed or not followed. Men often unconsciously open doors for women, and frequently they fail to do so, not out of ignorance but because they are not thinking about it at the moment. The first instance is an example of conforming behavior, the second of error behavior.

Rule-following behavior is conscious compliance with the rule. To pursue our example, rule following would apply when a man intentionally steps ahead of a woman and opens a door. *Rule violation*, on the other hand, is intentional violation of the rule. For instance, a man may be tired and simply may not feel like opening the door for his companion.

Reflective behavior involves *positive reflection* or *negative reflection* (following or violating) of a rule after evaluating it. The women's movement questions many social rules, such as men's opening doors. A feminist male may consciously choose not to open the door for a woman, precisely because of his evaluation of what the gesture implies about sex roles. Or a woman may take the initiative to open a door first. A man who does not espouse feminist values may make a point to open the door because, on reflection, he believes that the rule is a good one.

The primary value of Shimanoff's treatment is the clear, operational definition of rule that it provides. The following treatment of rules is different from Shimanoff's in that it does not center on the definition of rule but on how individuals use rules in communication.

Coordinated Management of Meaning

The theory of the coordinated management of meaning, developed by W. Barnett Pearce, Vernon Cronen, and their colleagues, emerged during the 1970s as a comprehensive theory of communication.[48] A meaning-centered rules theory, it integrates work from symbolic interactionism (Chapter 4), system theory (Chapter 3), speech acts (Chapter 6), and relational communication (Chapter 9). This theory is interesting not only because it integrates and builds on a great deal of previous theoretical work but because it is broadly applicable. It is one of the few general theories of *communication per se*.

Communication as Coordination. An individual is part of many systems, each with its own set of interactional rules. Over time individuals internalize some of these rules and draw on them to guide their actions. The basic problem of communication is that no two individuals enter an interaction knowing precisely what rules the other participants may find salient. Initially, at least, communication events are uncoordinated, and the primary task in all communication is to achieve and later sustain some form of coordination. Such coordination may or may not include mutual understanding (shared meaning), but it must minimally involve a meshing of the rules governing the behavior of participants. In other words, participants must develop a common logic of interactional rules. Any positive outcome of communication, including mutual understanding, depends first and foremost on rules coordination.

Importance of Context. Communication systems must be viewed holistically. Individuals' meanings are part of a hierarchy of meanings. (See Chapter 3 for the concept of hierarchy.) In other words, the person is a whole entity but is part of a larger context as well. Pearce and Cronen envision a rather complex hierarchy of meaning

48. W. Barnett Pearce and Vernon Cronen, *Communication Action and Meaning* (New York: Praeger, 1980); Vernon Cronen, W. Barnett Pearce, and Linda Harris, "The Coordinated Management of Meaning," in *Comparative Human Communication Theory*, ed. Frank E. X. Dance (New York: Harper & Row, 1982); W. Barnett Pearce, "The Coordinated Management of Meaning: A Rules Based Theory of Interpersonal Communication," in *Explorations in Interpersonal Communication*, ed. Gerald R. Miller (Beverly Hills: Sage Publications, 1976), pp. 17–36; Vernon Cronen, W. Barnett Pearce, and Linda Harris, "The Logic of the Coordinated Management of Meaning," *Communication Education* 28 (1979), 22–38.

contexts within which communication takes place. The nature of this hierarchy varies from system to system. Pearce and Cronen's depiction (Figure 4.3) shows the hierarchy as a hypothesized, idealized form.[49] One chooses rules partially on the basis of the perceived context of the interaction. The communicator may use any level of abstraction as the context of the moment; how one behaves depends greatly on the context in operation. Let us explain the levels presented in Figure 4.3, then we will discuss an example.

49. Pearce and Cronen, *Communication*, p. 131.

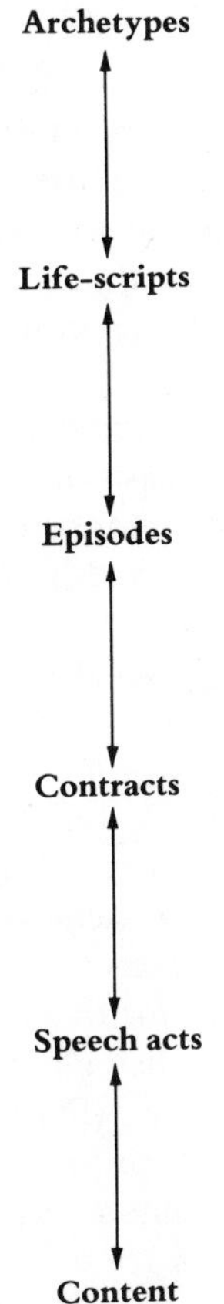

From *Communication Action and Meaning*, by W. Barnett Pearce and Vernon Cronen. Copyright © 1980 by Praeger Publishers. Reprinted by permission of the publisher.

Figure 4.3. A model of hierarchically organized meanings.

The *content* level is the message itself, the actual linguistic and paralinguistic elements of the utterance. *Speech acts* are messages designed to fulfill a simple intention. (Speech act theory is covered in Chapter 6.) *Contracts* are the defined requirements of the relationship. An *episode* is a sequence of speech acts perceived by participants to constitute a unit of interaction. Life-scripts are sets of episodes taken by the individual to be consistent with self-concept. Finally, *archetypes* are accepted images of how things are, a person's basic logic of the universe.

Consider, for example, a marriage in which the husband and wife tend to withdraw from conflict. On the content level an observer would concentrate on the actual utterances of the husband and wife, looking closely at the types of words used and at the grammatical structure. At the speech act level the observer would assess the interactional rules, perhaps discovering that when the wife objected or disagreed with the husband, he would withdraw or fail to respond. At the level of contracts, one might note that the couple maintained an implicit agreement not to argue with each other. In a sense we would say that this agreement was a requirement or "contract" of the relationship. In analyzing episodes one would look for repetitive behavior patterns. The observer might note that the husband's withdrawing in the face of disagreement occurs over and over, and at a higher level one might infer that conflict-avoidance is an important part of his life-script. Finally, as an archetype the couple might believe that harmony and happiness should pervade all human relationships.

Rules. Pearce and Cronen borrow the concept of *constitutive* and *regulative* rules from speech act theory and make them a central part of their treatment. In speech act theory constitutive rules define what a given act should be taken to "count as"; regulative rules refer to how one should behave within a given context. These two kinds of rules are intimately related. Pearce and Cronen take a major step in the development of rules theory by demonstrating how rules are involved in communication and how they are managed by participants in interaction. (Notice that this approach to rules is substantially different from Shimanoff's treatment.)

In order to demonstrate the operation of rules, Pearce and Cronen developed a set of symbols denoting rule structures. Three are important here:

⎤ = in the context of

⟶ = counts as

⊃ = if, then

The first symbol denotes the context of an act, the second applies to a constitutive rule, and the third is used in regard to a regulative rule. Consider the following examples:

play
insult ⟶ joke

In the context of play, an insult is to be taken as a joke.

Constitutive rule: An insult counts as a joke.

conflict
insult ⟶ put-down

In the context of conflict, an insult is to be taken as a put-down.

Constitutive rule: An insult counts as a put-down.

episode of an argument
husband insults wife's family ⊃ wife cries

When arguing, the wife typically cries after the husband insults her family.

Regulative rule: When the husband insults, wife should cry.

episode of playful banter

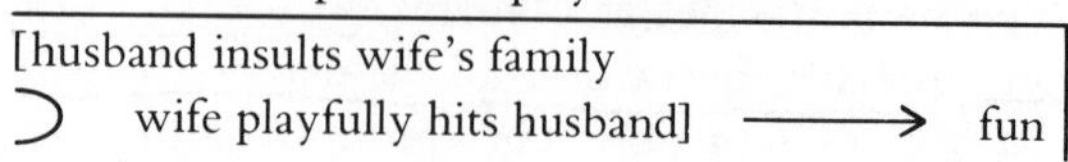

In play it is considered fun for the wife to "hit" the husband after he insults her family.

Regulative rule: Wife should respond to husband's insult by "hitting" him.

Constitutive rule: This sequence of events is to be taken as fun.

These examples are simple, but complex acts may be diagramed in the same fashion. Whereas simple examples are used here for clarity, most significant interactions are far more complex. Notice also that the bracketing of context is important for determining the rules in operation.

One's rule system provides a *logical force* for acting, a pressure to act in certain ways. One behaves in a manner consistent with one's assumptions about the rules in force. Two types of logical force operate in communication. Prefigurative force is an antecedent-to-act linkage in which the individual is "pressured" to behave in certain ways *because of* prior conditions. Practical logical force is an act-to-consequent linkage in which one behaves in a certain way *in order to* achieve a future condition. In any communication encounter an individual's rule system for that context presents a series of "oughts" that guide interpretations, responses, and actions. (Do not become confused by the use of terms here; prefigurative and practical force are similar to the concepts of causal and practical force referred to in Chapter 2, but logical force here is a broader concept than that referred to in the earlier chapter.)

Coordinated Management. The foregoing discussion is preliminary to the heart of coordinated management theory, which deals with how people actually mesh their rules. The key problem of coordination is this: Each individual must use his or her rules to guide interpretation of and response to the actions of others, but within a short time a new interpersonal system must develop so that the interactions are coordinated. At some point participants must become enmeshed for communication to be successful.

Figure 4.4 shows how enmeshment occurs.[50] (The model is perhaps overly simple in order to make the process clear.) Person A acts in a particular way in response to prior conditions (prefigurative force) or to achieve a consequent (practical force). The act is taken as a message by Person B, who uses constitutive rules to interpret the message. Person A's act thus becomes an antecedent event to which Person B responds, based on B's regulative rules. B's act is in turn interpreted by A as a message from the standpoint of A's constitutive rules. B's act as interpreted by A thus becomes a consequent to A's initial act. A will then compare B's act with the intended consequent. If A and B are operating with substantially different rule structures, they quickly will discover that one person's behavior does not represent the consequent intended, and they will readjust their rules until some level of coordination is achieved.

50. Ibid., p. 174.

Consider the simple example of a child trying to get back a ball after accidentally having thrown it through a neighbor's window.[51] The adult begins with the following rule structure:

Constitutive rule: If I say, "Is this ball yours?" in a stern fashion, this act will be taken as anger, a demand for a confession, and a threat.

Regulative rule: My act, taken as anger, will elicit crying and apologies. I in turn will become less angry and will give back the ball.

The child, on the other hand, has a very different set of rules:

Constitutive rule: When the neighbor says, "Is this your ball?" he is asking for information. My statement, "Give it back," will be taken as a request.

Regulative rule: When the neighbor requests information, I will respond with a factual answer, "Yes, it is." I will say, "Give it back," and he will give it back.

Now observe the actual conversation:

Neighbor: "Is this your ball?"

Child: "Yes, it is. Give it back."

51. The example is adapted from Pearce and Cronen, *Communication*, pp. 162–64. Originally it was developed in K. T. Alvy, "The Development of Listener Adapted Communication in Grade-School Children from Different Social Class Backgrounds," *Genetic Psychology Monographs* 87 (1973), 33–104.

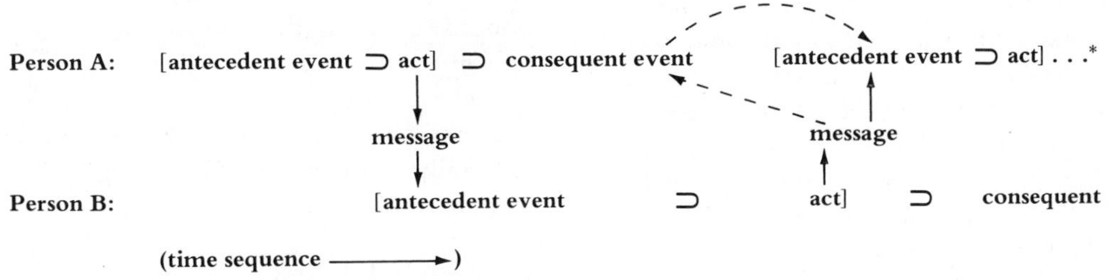

*Solid arrows denote constitutive rules. Broken arrows denote the coorientational state of comparing the subsequent message to the anticipated consequent event in anticipation of the next act.

Figure 4.4. Enmeshment process.

Obviously, the neighbor did not get the expected response and will interpret the child's remark as impudence rather than the simple request intended by the child. At this point the interaction is not coordinated. Now the neighbor must adjust the regulative rule by trying a different approach:

Neighbor: "Give it back? This ball hit my window. Do you know that?"

If the child has a sufficiently complex rule structure to provide options, he may adjust so that a successful outcome can be achieved. If not, coordination may not be achieved. Consider:

Unsatisfactory outcome (no enmeshment):
Child: "Give my ball back. I'll tell daddy if you don't give it back."
Neighbor: "Get out of my yard, kid."

Successful outcome (coordination achieved):
Child: "I'm sorry. I didn't mean to do it, and I will be careful in the future."
Neighbor: "Okay. Here's your ball."

Any communication episode can be evaluated in terms of three variables related to coordinated management. The first is *coherence* or the degree to which participants make sense of the sequence of events in the interaction. Lack of coherence occurs when one or more participants feel they do not know what is going on. Lack of coherence is the epitome of the lack of coordination. The second variable, *control*, is the degree to which one or more participants feel able to make choices that affect the sequence of acts in the interaction. In some situations one or more participants are able to enact a sufficiently complex rule structure so that they may select rules and affect the course of the encounter while still maintaining coordination. In other situations one or more participants (even all participants) may feel highly coordinated but limited or programmed, such that they have little effect on the outcome. The third variable is *valence* or the degree to which participants are happy with the interaction. Consider the two versions of the example of the neighbor and the child. In the unsuccessful version both participants would have felt low coherence, low control, and negative valence. In the successful version both would have felt that the interaction was coherent. The neighbor would have felt a good deal of control, while the child probably would have felt little control. Both parties probably would have felt positive valence.

Communication Competence. The foregoing analysis shows clearly that an individual's ability to manage a variety of rule systems is important in effectiveness as a communicator. People who can choose facilely among rule options in interpreting events and acting within situations will achieve coordination of meaning more often than people who have a more restricted repertoire of rule systems. Pearce and Cronen define this communication competence as "the person's ability to move within and among the various systems s/he is cocreating or comanaging."[52]

Three levels of competence are delineated. *Minimal* competence, the inability to comanage meanings with others in a system within which one must exist, can result from an overly simple cognitive system that has restrictive constitutive rules. It can also result from inability to adapt one's rules to context or from inability to take other individuals' rule systems into account.

Satisfactory competence enables a person to communicate effectively in the system at hand, usually achieving coordination with others. *Optimal* competence is the ability to understand the boundaries, strengths, and weaknesses of a system in comparison with other systems and to actively choose whether to become enmeshed in a particular system or to remain outside. An optimally competent person can enter or exit a system at will.

Criticism of the Rules Approach

Criticism of rules theory typically has centered around two issues: conceptual coherence and explanatory power. Let us consider each of these in turn:

52. Pearce and Cronen, *Communication*, p. 187.

First, is rules theory conceptually coherent? The answer to this question is a resounding no. Even its adherents admit that the rules tradition lacks unity and coherence. Jesse Delia verbalizes this objection in strong terms:

> The terrain covered by notions of "rules," then, is broad, grossly diffuse, and imprecisely articulated. And the real problem for any position purporting to be a general rules perspective is that the meaning of "rule" does not remain constant either within or across these domains. The "rules" territory taken as a whole is, in fact, little short of chaotic. At the least, it is clear that there is no unifying conception of the rule construct, of the domain of phenomena to which the construct has reference, of whether rules have generative power in producing and directing behavior, . . . or of the proper way to give an account of some domain of phenomena utilizing the construct. The idea of "rules" as a general construct represents only a diffuse notion devoid of specific theoretical substance.[53]

The two theories we have covered illustrate this lack of coherence. Shimanoff is firm in stating that a rule must deal with overt behavior. She believes that the concept should not apply to interpretation. Pearce and Cronen, however, place constitutive rules at a central place in their approach. For them rules apply not only to overt behavior but to internal meanings as well.

The second question is, are rules theories sufficiently explanatory? Critics generally believe that rules approaches cannot be explanatory as long as they fail to develop generic principles that cut across contexts. To identify the rules in operation within a particular context is not sufficient to explain communication processes. Berger believes that "at some point one must go beyond the description of 'what the rules are' and ask why some rules are selected over others . . . [and] what social forces produced the kinds of conventions and appropriate modes of behavior we now observe."[54] Berger's view is that a covering law approach is ultimately necessary to provide explanation; attempts of rules theorists to provide generic principles are nothing more than covering laws in disguise.

Most rules advocates do not go along with this argument, of course. Shimanoff points out that most rules explanations, in contrast to laws explanations, are teleological or reason giving. Behaviors are explained in terms of their practical impact on creating desired outcomes. Such explanations can be generalized. While developing universal explanations would not be desirable, and perhaps not possible, rules theories should seek reason-giving explanations that cover relatively broad classes of situations, even to the point of allowing for prediction.[55]

The appropriate question here is not whether rules theories are explanatory but what kind of explanation the critic believes is necessary. Clearly, Berger and Shimanoff disagree on the level of generality necessary for adequate explanation. We must also keep in mind that different rules theories possess different levels of explanatory power.

Recall from Chapter 2 that explanation is made possible by principles of necessity and generality. Barnett Pearce discusses rules approach in terms of these criteria.[56] Rule-following approaches tend not to be explanatory because they merely describe recurring behavior without indicating any form of necessity. Rule-governed approaches explain in terms of practical necessity, although their generality is somewhat limited. Pearce believes that the rule-using approach, while presently limited, has the highest potential for explanatory power in terms of both practical and logical necessity and generality.

Shimanoff's theory is basically descriptive, providing detailed guidelines for identifying rules in a social situation. As such it is highly heuristic from a methodological standpoint. It is also strong in providing conceptual guidance

53. Jesse Delia, "Alternative Perspectives for the Study of Human Communication: Critique and Response," *Communication Quarterly* 25 (1977), 54.

54. Charles R. Berger, "The Covering Law Perspective as a Theoretical Basis for the Study of Human Communication," *Communication Quarterly* 25 (1977), p. 12.

55. Shimanoff, *Communication Rules*, pp. 217–34.

56. Pearce, "Rules Theories."

in understanding rules. Shimanoff's theory, however, does not present much explanation. Little basis exists for understanding why particular kinds of communication behavior occur in various situations. Shimanoff's framework shows potential for developing explanation, but we shall have to see what theorists do with it in the future.

Although Pearce and Cronen do not present firm guides for identifying rule behavior, their theory of coordinated management is a step toward providing explanation of rule-using behavior. The theory appears to be quite heuristic in this way. The authors have demonstrated how it can be tested with a variety of research methods.[57] This theory has potential for stimulating a series of studies that could uncover new dimensions of the communication process.

The power of Pearce and Cronen's theory results primarily from its elaboration of the operations by which coordination is achieved. The theory's concepts help structure an observer's perceptions of what is happening in any communication event. However, the theory has not yet generated a sufficiently complete set of hypotheses to enable the observer to predict the course or outcome of an interaction.

Some critics no doubt will take issue with Pearce and Cronen's subordination of shared meaning. Although shared meaning is important, Pearce and Cronen believe that it is not crucial for successful communication and that coordination always precedes understanding. Their postulate that rules coordination is essential for successful communication may well be valid, but critics will point out that the degree and rapidity with which rules mesh may depend on the degree of shared meaning already established within the system. The research reported by Pearce and Cronen indeed provides strong evidence that rules coordination is necessary for interaction coherence, but these studies do not imply that coordination is sufficient by itself to explain coherence. Of course, shared meaning is largely a function of agreement on constitutive rules, but meaning also has an experiential and referential aspect as we shall see in Chapter 6. This theory could be strengthened by showing how other aspects of meaning enter the coordination process. Instead of assuming, as Pearce and Cronen do, that mutual understanding always follows coordination, the theory could elaborate ways in which mutual understanding may sometimes prefigure coordination.

57. Ten studies ranging widely in method are reported in Pearce and Cronen, *Communication*, chap. 7.

What Do We Know about Communication as Symbolic Interaction?

The unifying idea behind this chapter is symbolic interaction. The term is chosen as an integrating concept because the theories of this domain all deal with ways people interact to create social entities. Society requires social interaction. It also requires social order and shared meaning. The essence of social life is the coming together of human beings in community through the use of symbols. Interaction is both the precursor and the product of shared meaning, and shared meaning makes all aspects of society possible. In short, the work of this domain demonstrates that communication, above all else, is a symbolic, rule-governed activity.

Two groups of theory are presented in this chapter. The first, symbolic interactionism, deals with the ways in which human life, both private and public, is affected by symbols and meaning. The second, rules theory, gives us a means for understanding how social order is maintained among humans, who, unlike lower animals, are able to make choices.

These two sets of theory demonstrate a handful of generalizations that have become so popular as to assume the status of truisms. First, symbolic interaction is the binding force of society. Second, symbolic interaction is vital to human development. The roles we take in society and the images we have of ourselves are shaped through interaction with other people. Third, people create their own worlds through the use of symbols and meanings. Fundamental to most of the theories in this chapter is the belief that people are active builders of their own realities. Fourth, thinking is merely an extension of symbolic interaction with others. Thinking, or internal conversation, is based on meanings learned through interaction with others. Fifth, social behavior is largely governed by rules that, unlike causative laws, are guidelines for individual choice.

The primary objection to theories in this group is that they are abstract and diverse in their claims. Rules theorists do not even agree on what a rule is; their definitions vary from extremely mechanistic to highly humanistic. Symbolic interactionism is sometimes vague and the researcher can never be sure, based on these theories, precisely what to observe in attempting to verify claims. This criticism, shared also with system theory, stems from the general nature of the first two domains (Chapters 3 and 4). Admittedly, most of the theories in these two chapters are not discriminating, for they are designed to capture the general essence of communication without postulating specific relationships within given situations. They have been grouped together because of this shared goal. Do not misinterpret however, that these general theories cannot be applied to specific contexts; indeed, they often are, as you will see repeatedly throughout the text. Evaluations of the specific symbolic interactionist and rules theories related to various themes and contexts are presented in the appropriate chapters. Like general system theory, symbolic interactionism and rules theory are most valuable for guiding our thinking about the nature of communication events rather than for directing our observations of specific finely combed events.

PART

THEMATIC THEORIES

Chapter 5
Theories of Language and Nonverbal Coding

Chapter 6
Theories of Meaning

Chapter 7
Theories of Information and Information Processing

Chapter 8
Theories of Persuasion

CHAPTER

5 Theories of Language and Nonverbal Coding

Essentially every theoretical approach to communication recognizes as a basic fact that communication takes place through the use of signs. Roughly, a sign is a stimulus that embodies a meaning beyond itself. Signs that elicit singular, programmed responses are sometimes known as signals. Other signs are complex, evoking a rich variety of meanings and conceptions. Such signs, important to most of the theories in this chapter, are often referred to as symbols.[1] This chapter and the next are devoted to theories that attempt to describe and explain the role of symbols in communication.

Our discussion in this chapter is divided into two broad areas. The first covers language, the primary element of most human communication. Although language is central to communication, certain nonlinguistic, or nonverbal, elements of communication are also important. The second section of the chapter presents some prominent theories of nonverbal communication. The next chapter covers theories of meaning, a topic that is intimately intertwined with the subject matter of the present chapter.

A casual reading of this chapter may leave the impression that it provides a complete picture of theory in language and nonverbal communication. No brief treatment could ever accomplish such a synthesis. Indeed, the areas of language and nonverbal communication consist of specialties and subspecialties that have produced a copious quantity of research and theory. The issues within these fields are numerous, sometimes subtle, and always more complex than implied here. While this qualification applies to all of the chapters in the book, it is especially pertinent here.

1. This analysis taken from Wallace Fotheringham, *Perspectives on Persuasion* (Boston: Allyn and Bacon, 1966), pp. 52–68.

Theories of Language

Linguistics, the study of language, is one of the most important theoretical areas related to human communication. Language is so central to human behavior that it has captured the interest of social scientists and scholars for centuries. The number of approaches to linguistics is large, and the breadth of the field thus confusingly broad.[2] Basically, linguistics has two large, overlapping branches. *Historical linguistics* is the study of how language changes over time and how it has evolved into language groups in the world. *Descriptive linguistics* is the study of particular languages, how they are structured and how they are used. (Several subbranches also exist.) In this book we will discuss primarily the twentieth-century theories of descriptive linguistics. The theories presented in this section address three significant sets of questions: (1) How is language structured? What are the syntactical units and relations within a sentence? (2) How is language used? What mental or be-

2. There are many fine textbooks on language study. A classic is John B. Carroll, *The Study of Language* (Cambridge: At the University Press, 1953). More recent texts include Lois Bloom, *Language Development: Form and Function in Emerging Grammars* (Cambridge: M.I.T. Press, 1970); B. G. Blount, ed., *Language, Culture, and Society: A Book of Readings* (Cambridge: Winthrop Publishing, 1974): Yuen Ren Chao, *Language and Symbolic Systems* (New York: Cambridge University Press, 1968); Phillip S. Dale, *Language Development: Structure and Function* (Hinsdale, Ill.: Dryden Press, 1972); Joseph A. DeVito, ed., *Language: Concepts and Processes* (Englewood Cliffs, N.J.: Prentice-Hall, 1973); Paul Garvin, *Method and Theory in Linguistics* (New York: Humanities Press, 1970); Archibald Hill, ed., *Linguistics Today* (New York: Basic Books, 1969).

havioral processes are involved in the production and reception of speech? (3) How is language acquired?

Classical Linguistics

A revolution occurred in the study of language after the mid-1950s. Many language scholars came to conceptualize grammar quite differently than they had before. Still, many elements of the old grammar have lived on in various forms. Let us review the salient features of classical linguistics, then turn to the newer generative grammar in the next section.

Structural Linguistics. What has become the standard model of sentence structure was developed between 1930 and 1950 in the classical structural period.[3] Numerous linguists contributed to this model, but the most important include Leonard Bloomfield, Charles Fries, and Zellig Harris.[4] Basically, this model breaks down a sentence into component parts in hierarchical fashion. Sounds and sound groups combine to form word roots and word parts, which in turn combine to form words and phrases. Phrases are put together to make clauses or sentences. Thus language can be analyzed on various levels, roughly corresponding to sounds, words, and phrases.

The first level of sounds involves the study of phonetics. An isolatable speech sound is a *phone*. Phones of a particular type are grouped into a sound family called *phoneme*, which is the basic building block of any language. Any dialect of a language contains a number of phonemes. These phonemes are combined according to rules to produce *morphemes*, the smallest meaningful linguistic unit. Some morphemes are free—they can stand alone as a word in a sentence. Other morphemes are bound—they must be combined with other morphemes to form words. On the syntax level words are combined according to rules to form grammatical phrases, which are linked together into clauses and sentences. This structural approach provides an orderly classification of language parts. Actual observed segments are put into classes of a given type (phoneme, morpheme, and so forth), and these segments are sequenced in a sentence-building process. At each level of analysis is a finite set of classes (for example, phonemes or morphemes) that can be observed in the native language. Sentences are always built up from the bottom of the hierarchy, so that succeeding levels depend on the formation of lower levels.

While this approach provides a useful description of the structure of language, it fails to explain how people use language. This latter question, far more central to communication than language structure, has demanded the attention of psycholinguists since about 1950. We know that people must possess an intuitive knowledge of their language in order to produce meaningful, grammatical speech. What is the nature of this knowledge? How is it acquired? How is it actualized? These important questions have been addressed by psycholinguists in the last three decades. The literature that has emerged from this work is extensive, controversial, and highly technical.

Finite-State Grammar. The earliest attempt to explain how people produced sentences was the finite-state approach. No serious language scholar of today uses this approach because it was proved invalid years ago. Reviewing it briefly is instructive, however, to illustrate the development of language theory and to provide a contrast with modern grammar theory. Basically, finite-state theorists believed that sentences are produced from left to right, one word at a time, with the selection of each word providing a set of choices for the next word.

3. An excellent summary and critique of this period can be found in J. A. Fodor, T. G. Bever, and M. F. Garrett, *The Psychology of Language: An Introduction to Psycholinguistics and Generative Grammar* (New York: McGraw-Hill, 1974).

4. Leonard Bloomfield, *Language* (New York: Holt, Rinehart and Winston, 1933); Charles Fries, *The Structure of English* (New York: Harcourt, Brace & World, 1952); Zellig Harris, *Structural Linguistics* (Chicago: University of Chicago Press, 1951).

The obvious weakness of finite-state grammar is that it provided no simple, parsimonious explanation for how human beings could produce an infinite number of novel sentences. In other words, it allowed for little creativity on the part of speakers.

Phrase-Structure Grammar. This approach, a mainstay in grammar theory for many years, is no longer believed to be adequate by itself to explain the generation of sentences.[5] Its essential features, however, are still used as part of a larger explanatory framework, which is explained in the next section. Phrase structure breaks down a given sentence into phrases. A sentence is a hierarchy of components, with each successively larger component being generated by a set of *rewrite rules*. For example, a sentence may be broken down according to the following rewrite rule:

sentence ↔ noun phrase + verb phrase

Or, to use an actual example:

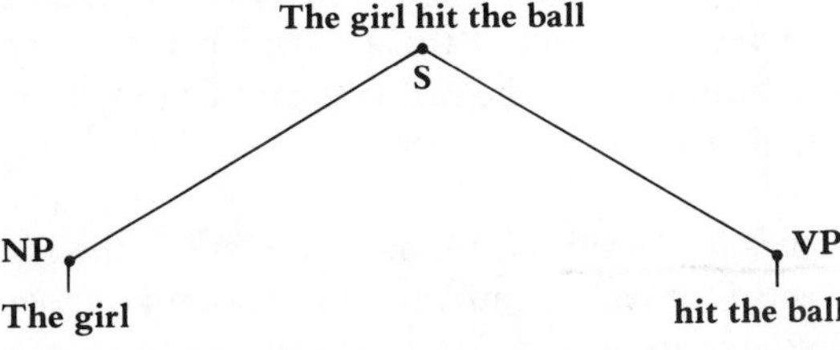

The verb phrase can be broken down further according to the following rewrite rule:

verb phrase ↔ verb + noun phrase

Or, to continue the example:

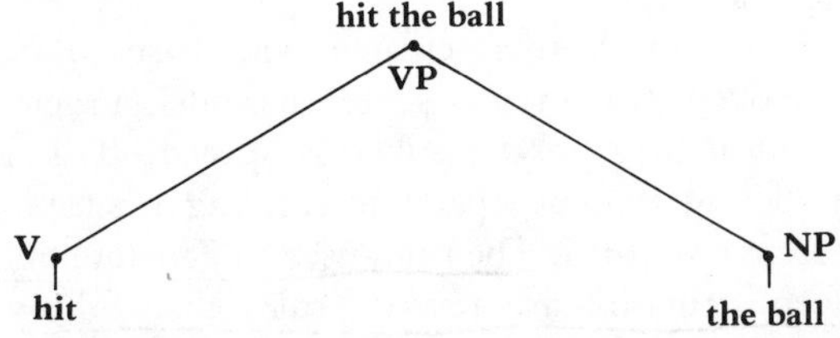

This process continues until all units of the sentence are accounted for, including small parts such as the articles *the* or *an*. These analyses are often illustrated by a tree diagram, as shown in Figure 5.1.

Criticism of Classical Linguistics. The primary objection to classical linguistics is that although it is useful as a taxonomic, or descriptive, approach, it is powerless to explain how language is generated. A simple example will suffice to illustrate this weakness. Phrase-structure grammar would analyze the following two sentences exactly the same way, even though the slightest inspection reveals that their syntactical origins must be different:[6]

John is easy to please.

John is eager to please.

Although *easy* and *eager* have different semantic meanings, these sentences have entirely different syntactical meanings. In the first sentence *John* is the object of the infinitive *to please*. In the second *John* is the noun phrase of the sentence. Regular phrase structure provides no

5. For an explanation and critique of finite-state and phrase-structure grammar, see Noam Chomsky, "Three Models for the Description of Language," *Transactions on Information Theory,* vol. IT-2 (1956): 113–24; and Jerry Fodor, James Jenkins, and Sol Saporta, "Psycholinguistics and Communication Theory," in *Human Communication Theory*, ed. Frank Dance (New York: Holt, Rinehart and Winston, 1967), pp. 160–201.

6. Examples from Gilbert Harmon, *On Noam Chomsky: Critical Essays* (Garden City: Anchor Books, 1974), p. 5.

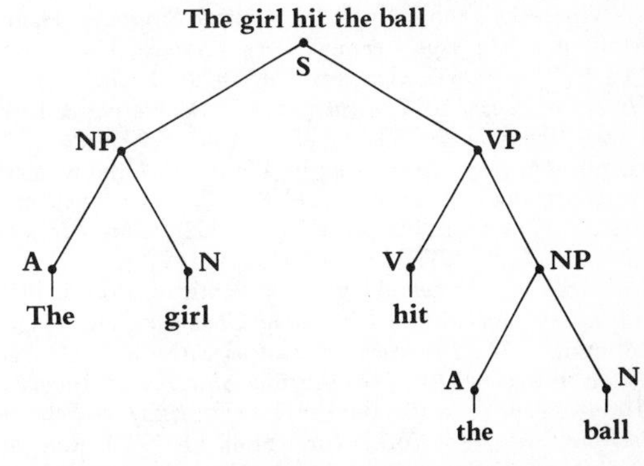

Figure 5.1. A simple tree diagram.

easy way to explain these different grammatical meanings.

Basically, this problem involves theoretical *appropriateness*. The nature of classical linguistics makes it inappropriate as an explanatory device; yet, the most important questions of language demand that the theorist go beyond mere description of sentences as uttered. Questions to be answered include the following: What constitutes a necessary and sufficient grammar, such that a speaker competent in the grammar of a language can produce an infinite number of novel sentences? By what cognitive process are sentences generated and understood? How is syntactical ambiguity to be accounted for? How is language acquired? To answer questions such as these, generative grammar has been developed.

Generative Grammar

Noam Chomsky is the primary force behind generative grammar. As a young linguist in the 1950s, Chomsky parted company with the classical theorists to develop an approach that since has become the foundation of contemporary linguistics.[7] Like any theoretical tradition generative grammar now has several positions within it, although the tradition as a whole is built on a cluster of essential ideas. Three of these ideas warrant discussion.

First, generative grammar rests on the believed centrality of sentence generation, which is seen as far more important than sentence description. Second, the objective of generative grammar is to isolate a set of rules that will parsimoniously explain how any sentence could be generated. Parsimony is the key. Inventing a new rule for each construction is not workable. Indeed, the brain is finite and cannot operate on an infinitely expanding set of linguistic rules. Yet people can produce and understand an infinite number of sentences. An adequate grammar must explain this paradox. The answer lies in a relatively small number of rules that can be used over and over again to produce novel sentences. The third essential feature of generative grammar is the transformation. (In fact, generative grammar is alternatively named *transformational grammar*.) Transformations are the key element in the generative grammar system. We shall see the role of transformations momentarily.

As Chomsky freely admits, transformational grammar does not yet solve all of the mysteries of language. Consequently, various versions have emerged as alternative explanations of language processes. We will cover two of these. The first is standard theory, which for many years represented the mainstream of thought in linguistics.

Standard Theory. Original generative theory posits four basic components of grammar. *Deep structures* are believed to be underlying sentence models constructed by the use of base *phrase-structure rules*. The deep structure of any sentence is modified by *transformation rules*, resulting in an uttered (or utterable) *surface structure*. Sentence generation proceeds along the following lines.

Deep structure is created with base rules. The deep structure is a sentence model, a mental structure, not utterable as speech. It is a model of sentence parts resembling a simple declarative form. The rules used to generate the deep structure are rewrite rules that follow lines originally developed in phrase-structure grammar.

Next, a surface structure is generated by

7. Chomsky's works include: *Syntactic Structures* (Hague: Mouton, 1957); *Aspects of the Theory of Syntax* (Cambridge: M.I.T. Press, 1965); *Cartesian Linguistics: A Chapter in the History of Rationalist Thought* (New York: Harper & Row, 1966); *Topics in the Theory of Generative Grammar* (The Hague: Mouton, 1966); *Language and Mind* (New York: Harcourt Brace Jovanovich, 1968); *The Sound Pattern of English* (New York: Harper & Row, 1968); *Current Issues in Linguistic Theory* (The Hague: Mouton, 1970); *Problems of Knowledge and Freedom* (New York: Pantheon Books, 1971); *Studies on Semantics in Generative Grammar* (The Hague: Mouton, 1972); *Reflections on Language* (New York: Pantheon Books, 1975); *The Logical Structure of Linguistic Theory* (New York: Plenum Press, 1975); *Essays on Form and Interpretation* (New York: North Holland, 1977); *Rules and Representations* (New York: Columbia University Press, 1980).

transformation rules. Unlike rewrite rules transformation rules are instructions of movement: Move component *x* to location *y*. For example, the active transformation moves components so that they appear in the order NP + VP (Sally hit the ball). The passive transformation prescribes NP + auxiliary + VP + NP (The ball is hit by Sally). A sufficient, but parsimoniously small, number of phrase-structure and transformation rules will permit the generation of any proper sentence.

Since this book is not a linguistics text, we will not cover the range of possible transformation rules of English. In order to understand the basics of the theory, however, we will look at an example. Our example uses two transformation rules: the passive transformation and the adjective transformation.[8] The passive transformation inverts the noun phrase and verb phrase, puts the verb in the passive form, and adds the preposition *by*:

8. Several English transformations are explained in brief form by Peter Salus, *Linguistics* (Indianapolis: Bobbs-Merrill, 1969).

John loves Mary.

Mary is loved by John. (passive)

The adjective transformation occurs by deleting the verb form *be* and placing the adjective in front of the noun:

John loves Mary.

Mary is pretty.

John loves pretty Mary. (adjective)

Suppose you wish to generate the sentence, Ripe mushrooms are loved by hobbits.[9] You would do this in two stages. First, with the phrase-structure rules you would generate a deep tree, as shown in Figure 5.2. This deep tree provides the basic semantic interpretation of the sentence. All of the basic logical grammatical relations are present, and the meaning of the sentence is set. Don't worry that this deep structure does not resemble the intended surface structure. The deep structure is an ab-

9. Example from ibid.

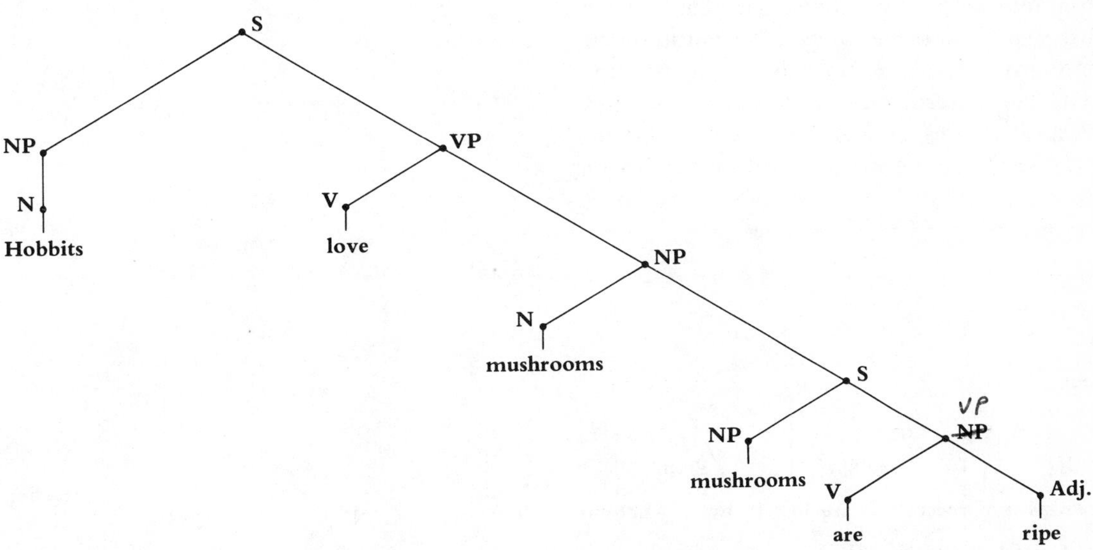

Figure 5.2. An example of deep structure.

stract entity from which the actual sentence will be generated in the next stage.

The surface tree—the actual sentence—is generated by applying the two transformations described above, passive and adjective. Figure 5.3 illustrates the surface tree.

With a relatively small number of rewrite rules and transformation rules, a speaker can generate any novel grammatical sentence. The basic semantic structure is generated on the deep or abstract level with phrase structure, and sentences are generated by subjecting the underlying structure to transformations. In essence this process is what a speaker intuitively "knows" about the language. The two-stage sentence-generation model is a parsimonious and descriptively adequate explanation of how the speaker uses this knowledge.

An essential feature of standard theory is that a singular correspondence exists between a surface structure and its deep structure. Any meaningful sentence structure has one, and only one, deep structure. If an uttered sentence has more than one syntactical meaning, each meaning is derivable from a separate deep structure. For example, the sentence, She is a dancing teacher, has two possible meanings. No analysis of surface structure alone can explain this paradox. The two interpretations stem from separate deep structures with different configurations. One stems from a structure with the following components: NP (She) + VP (teaches dancing). The other is transformed from a deep structure of two clauses—(1) NP (She) + VP (dances), and (2) NP (She) + VP (teaches)—that have been combined into a single deep structure of the following form: NP (She) + S (who dances) + VP (teaches). These deep structures would be diagrammed as indicated in Figure 5.4.

Obviously, this theory explains surface ambiguities, while the classical structure cannot. It also illustrates that in standard theory meaning must always be located at the deep level. Chomsky has come to believe, however, that deep grammar alone is not sufficient to explain all meaning structures. He therefore has developed a new approach, which is as yet undeveloped and controversial.

Trace Theory. Trace theory, or *extended standard theory*, was developed in an attempt to approximate better how people assign interpretations to grammatical structures. Advocates of trace theory, including Chomsky, add an additional

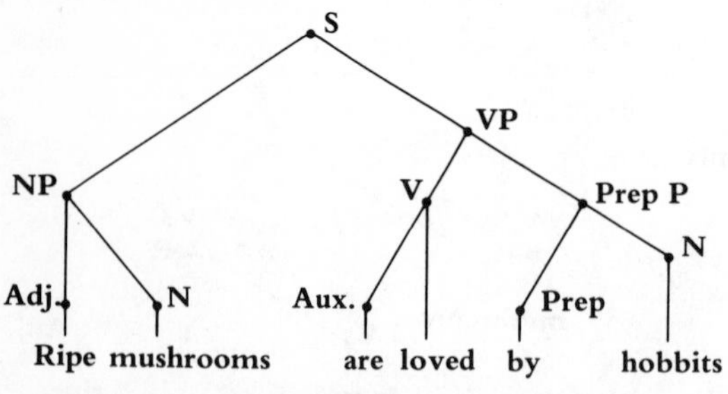

From *Linguistics*, by Peter H. Salus. Copyright © 1969 by The Bobbs-Merrill Company, Inc. Reprinted by permission of the publisher.

Figure 5.3. An example of a surface structure.

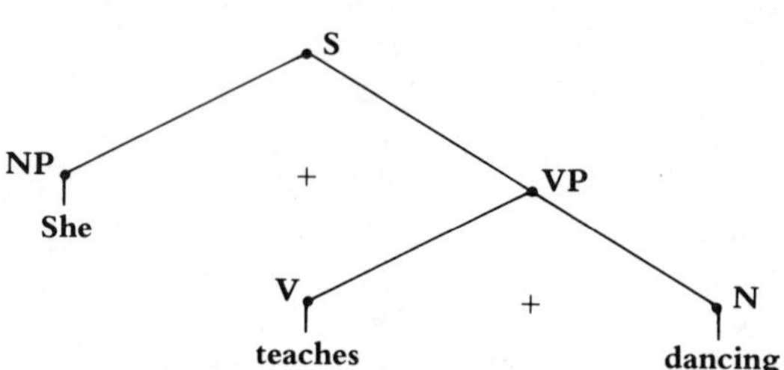

A. *Deep structure for first interpretation.*

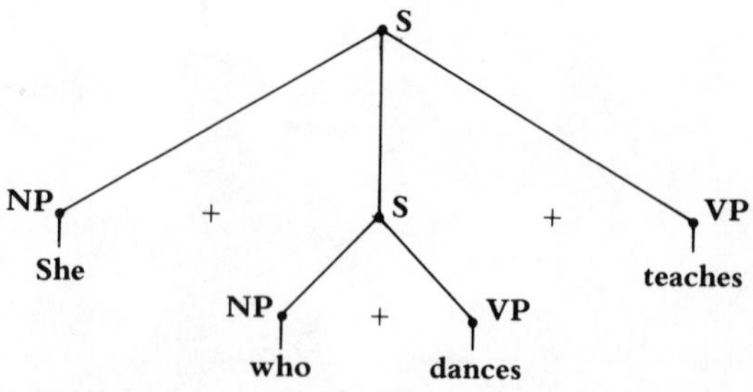

B. *Deep structure for second interpretation.*

Figure 5.4. Two illustrative deep structures.

level to sentence production.[10] Deep structures are generated by base rules, and transformations are applied, resulting in *S-structures.* S-structures possess the basic structure of the uttered sentence, except that they contain "traces" of components in former positions before being moved by transformation rules. Traces are seen strictly as mental representations of deep sentence structure that aid in surface interpretation. S-structures are translated into actual utterable sentences by phonological rules. The resultant spoken sentence is the *logical form* or *LF-structure.*

Consider the following sentence as an example: Who do you want to visit? This question is ambiguous. It could mean (1) What person do you wish to go to? or (2) What person do you wish to come to you? The first interpretation stems from the deep structure, *You wish to visit who.* The second comes from, *You wish who to visit.* Applying transformation rules, the speaker moves the element *who* to the front of the sentence, but a mental trace *(t)* of its former location is left in the S-structure, as follows: (1) *who do you want to visit* ***t***, and (2) *who do you want* ***t*** *to visit.*

In ongoing speech phonological rules allow you to make a distinction between these two meanings in the way you utter the sentences. For example, one such rule allows you to contract *want* and *to* to *wanna*, if and only if these two morphemes are contiguous. In the S-structure of the first sentence they are contiguous and thus you could say, Who do you *wanna* visit? But in the second sentence the trace of the former placement of *who* separates *want* and *to*. Thus to properly get across the second interpretation, you would utter these two words distinctly and avoid using *wanna.*[11]

The important difference between standard theory and trace theory is that in the latter, meaning is attributed at the S-level, not the deep level. In other words, deep elements, through their traces, and surface elements are combined in the attribution of meaning.

Language Acquisition. Some of Chomsky's most revolutionary and controversial ideas relate to language acquisition. Once Chomsky identified the rich system of grammar that constitutes an individual's linguistic knowledge, scholars immediately began to ask where this knowledge comes from.

The behaviorists had a ready answer. For them language is learned in the same fashion as is any other behavior.[12] The child, born with a highly developed, but blank, cerebral cortex, responds randomly to various environmental stimuli. Through a series of associations and reinforcements, the child's responses are repeated and shaped to form language.

Generative theorists find this explanation weak. Chomsky calls it "a dead end, if not an intellectual scandal."[13] The behaviorists' explanation is inadequate on two counts. It cannot adequately account for the extremely rapid acquisition of language in early childhood, and it does not explain the ability to produce and understand novel sentences that the child has never heard before.[14]

Chomsky approaches language acquisition

10. Trace theory is explained in Chomsky, *Rules and Representations*, pp. 155–81.

11. Examples from ibid.

12. The best known behavioristic treatment of language learning is Skinner, *Verbal Behavior* (New York: Appleton-Century-Crofts, 1957). For an integrated learning theory of language, see Arthur Staats, *Learning, Language, and Cognition* (New York: Holt, Rinehart and Winston, 1968). Finally, see H. Hobart Mowrer, "The Psychologist Looks at Language," *American Psychologist*, 9 (1954): 660–92; *Learning Theory and the Symbolic Processes* (New York: John Wiley and Sons, 1960).

13. Chomsky, *The Logical Structure of Linguistic Theory*, p. 40.

14. One learning theory approach, contextual generalization, was developed to explain this phenomenon. See Martin D. Braine, "On Learning the Grammatical Order of Words," *Psychological Review*, 70 (1963): 323–48. For a debate on the basic issues, see ibid.; T. G. Bever, J. A. Fodor, and W. Weksel, "A Critique of Contextual Generalization," *Psychological Review*, 72 (1965): 467–82; Martin Braine, "On the Basis of Phrase Structure: A Reply to Bever, Fodor, and Weksel," *Psychological Review*, 72 (1965): 483–92; T. G. Bever, J. A. Fodor, and W. Weksel, "Is Linguistics Empirical?" *Psychological Review*, 72 (1965): 493–500.

with the assumptions that language is a fundamental cognitive element and that cognition, like any other physiological/anatomical process is a biological function. Thus for Chomsky basic language knowledge is innate. According to Chomsky, the child is born with various kinds of linguistic information.[15] This information is universal and is not related to any particular language. The innate information is the same regardless of the culture into which the child is born. Chomsky believes that the child brings to language learning a basic knowledge of all the possible universal phonetic sequences (as opposed to impossible sequences), all possible deep structure trees (as opposed to impossible trees), and all possible transformations (as opposed to impossible ones). The child knows the difference between what is possible in any language (a *language universal*) and what is not. This amounts to an enumeration of all possible grammars. Further, the child is born with a standard routine for testing the utterances heard. This recognition device allows the child to match what is heard against all possible sequences until the grammar of the native language is "discovered." This sorting process involves the child's hypothesizing about the native grammar and testing the hypothesis. Thus language is not "learned" but develops and is triggered by experience.

Fodor, Bever, and Garrett make an analogy between this process in the child and the work of a field linguist:

> In Chomsky's view, then, the child is faced with a task analogous to that of a field linguist confronted with an alien language. Both are required to construct a characterization of the regularities underlying a certain set of phonetic strings . . . where the relevant form of characterization is a generative grammar. Like the field linguist, the child does not come to his task empty-handed: ideally, both are in possession of a "linguistic theory". . . . In either case the problem is that of discovering which of the infinitely many grammars that satisfy universal constraints on form and content of linguistic rules is the best one for the language from which the corpus is drawn.[16]

Our understanding of language acquisition is primitive. The nativists believe that the language a child acquires in the first few years is too rich to be explained solely in terms of learning. The alternative theory we have just discussed is abstract and vague. In the future we may be able to see advances in understanding of this interesting phenomenon. What will be discovered about language acquisition particularly and language behavior generally may lead to an improved knowledge of basic human thought processes.

Generative grammar affects all fields interested in language. Gilbert Harmon states, "Chomsky has let us see that there is a single subject of language and mind which crosses departmental boundaries."[17] This theory grew out of the field of linguistics but rapidly stimulated interest in other fields as well. It has become especially important in psycholinguistics, since it bears directly on problems of human cognition.

Yet, curiously, generative theory has had little impact on many scholars interested in communication. Chomsky prefers not to conceive of language primarily as a tool of communication but a natural phenomenon of import in and of itself. Needless to say, this claim is controversial, and we shall return to it in the section on criticism.

Chomsky's work is philosophically interesting and complex. Its blend of philosophical views is provocative as Justin Leiber points out:

> [Chomsky's ideas present] a peculiar, but explicable, paradox; . . . namely, that man has a kind of free creative nature that Chomsky believes depends on the highly constraining innateness, and derived mentalistic character, belonging to the human mind. The paradox is resolved by recalling that it is the infinite capacities of human thought, the infinistic and abstract character of man's linguistic competencies, that purport to establish that man is by nature beyond a

15. Chomsky, *Aspects of the Theory of Syntax*, p. 30. An interpretation and summary is provided by Fodor et al., *Psychology of Language*, pp. 470–72.

16. Fodor et al., *Psychology of Language*, p. 472.

17. Gilbert Harmon, *On Noam Chomsky*, p. vii.

behaviorist or determinist viewpoint. One needs a strong, built-in capacity, as it were, before full, free creativity can manifest itself as choice within this infinite, discrete range. . . . The freedom Chomsky wishes to emphasize is the freedom of a being with infinite and reasoned choices when so unrestrained by external force.[18]

In treating the study of mind as a natural science, Chomsky displays some obvious aspects of World View I. (See Chapter 2.) He believes that elements of language and mind are universal and available for discovery. He is analytical in approach, seeking inherent mechanisms of mind. However, in fulfilling his view of the individual as distinctly human and creative, he follows actional assumptions. He strongly believes in the a priori nature of knowledge and that much knowledge is tacit or implicit. He follows the notion that knowledge arises from an application of innate categories onto the world of experience.[19] In short, Chomsky is a champion of a point of view that has not been popular in this century—rationalism. He has revived the basic idea of René Descartes of the seventeenth century, that the mind is given its power by a priori qualities and that knowledge arises from the use of this power in understanding experience.

Criticism of Generative Grammar

Chomskian linguistics has been described as a true Kuhnian revolution (see Chapter 2). It is generally praised as providing answers to questions that classical and behavioristic linguistics could not handle. Its major strengths are usually seen as its parsimony and explanatory power. However, language presents us with one of our most difficult intellectual puzzles, and even generative grammar has its weaknesses. Basically, generative grammar has been criticized on two fronts, its scope and its validity.

Two problems of scope warrant discussion here. First, generative grammar generally ignores or downplays semantics. Primarily it is a theory of grammar, of syntax; problems of individual lexical units and their meanings are ignored as unimportant.[20]

Second, critics are bothered by the failure of generative grammarians to consider problems of language as used in everyday life. Generative grammar treats language as an abstraction, claiming that an understanding of the anomalies of language use is unimportant to an understanding of language itself. This approach makes a sharp distinction between language *competence* and language *performance*. The former is knowledge of grammar; the latter is language use. Generative grammarians steadfastly have maintained that performance is not a linguistic concern. Consequently, they are not interested in how language is used in social interaction. The theory therefore does not account for local and cultural variations of language, nor does it account for the commonly observed phenomenon of ungrammatical speech.

Much of the criticism of generative grammar questions its validity. A good deal of disagreement exists within the generative movement itself about the locus of meaning. Where in the process of sentence generation is meaning established? Chomsky has shown that meaningfulness cannot reside strictly at the surface level, yet deep analysis by itself may not be adequate for the establishment of meaning. Trace theory presents an answer, but as yet it is controversial and sketchy.

Much uncertainty exists, of course, about the innatist arguments of generative grammar. Innatism is a position that cannot be proved, although its strength lies in the fact that it has not yet been disproved. As we already have pointed out, alternative explanations of language acquisition have failed. Even if basic language mechanisms are innate, we are far from understanding their nature or how they oper-

18. Justin Leiber, *Noam Chomsky: A Philosophical Overview* (Boston: Twayne Publishers, 1975), p. 182.

19. Chomsky discusses features of his epistemology in *Rules and Representations*, chapter 6.

20. This criticism is discussed by John Searle, "Chomsky's Revolution in Linguistics," in Harmon, *On Noam Chomsky*, pp. 2–33.

ate. The claims of generative grammar are still speculative.

Transformational theory's key problems result from the difficulty of observing generative processes. Linguists must rely on inferences made from observing spoken sentences. Classical linguistics failed to make this inferential leap from observed behavior to hidden processes, and thus it fell short. As a result of its strong reliance on inference, generative theory operates primarily from logical force (see Chapter 2). Its explanations rest on the strength of the logical connections among inferences. It also relies heavily on reasoning from "residues." In other words, alternative explanations are attacked and shown to be inadequate. What cannot be disproved, the residue, is taken as the best explanation. Linguistic writings are filled with demonstrations of how this or that explanation will not work in explaining a particular construction. The use of inference, logical necessity, and residues in the development of generative theory is not inherently weak, and it is the only available method for developing theory in the absence of direct observation.

Theories of Nonverbal Communication

Most scholars would agree that language is a central element of human communication; yet communication involves much more than language. The signs that are used in communication may be verbal (linguistic) or nonverbal; most communication involves messages that contain a complex web of both verbal and nonverbal signs.

Nonverbal communication, an important aspect of coding and messages, is a cousin area to linguistics. For this reason it has been included in this chapter. In addition, nonverbal communication relates strongly to interpersonal communication and therefore applies to group and organizational communication as well. Students of mass communication are interested in nonverbal aspects of media. One well-known textbook of nonverbal communication, in fact, has isolated "mediated" messages as a special form of nonverbal code.[21] Because of its widespread application in all of these contexts, nonverbal coding is included here as a thematic domain.

Actually, we touch on theories of nonverbal communication in two places in this book. Here we cover five well-known theories of nonverbal coding. The theories that relate nonverbal processes specifically to interpersonal communication are included in Chapters 9 and 10.

Although research and writing on nonverbal communication are copious and diverse, nonverbal scholars have not been quick to produce theory. Judee Burgoon comments on the field:

> If nonverbal communication in the 1950s and 1960s was regarded as the foundling child of the social sciences—disdained, neglected, even nameless—the 1970s marked a transition toward a legitimate and identifiable area of scholarship. An increasing consciousness and conscientiousness regarding nonverbal communication was reflected in the publication of literally thousands of articles related to it, in its emergence as a topic for courses and textbooks, and in its skyrocketing popularity with the lay public.[22]

Nonverbal communication theory is difficult to summarize because it has been plagued by conceptual difficulties. Scholars disagree about what nonverbal communication is. Defining the term is not easy, as Randall Harrison points out:

> The term "nonverbal communication" has been applied to a broad range of phenomena: everything from facial expression and gesture to fashion and

21. Randall Harrison, "Nonverbal Communication," in *Handbook of Communication*, eds. Ithiel de sola Pool et al. (Chicago: Rand McNally, 1973).

22. Judee K. Burgoon, "Nonverbal Communication Research in the 1970s: An Overview," in *Communication Yearbook 4*, ed. Dan Nimmo (New Brunswick, N.J.: Transaction Books, 1980), p. 179. In addition to this excellent review, see also Mark Knapp, *Nonverbal Communication in Human Interaction* (New York: Holt, Rinehart and Winston, 1978); Mark Knapp, John Wiemann, and John Daly, "Nonverbal Communication: Issues and Appraisal," *Human Communication Research*, 4 (1978): 271–80; Robert G. Harper, Arthur Wiess, and Joseph Motarozzo, *Nonverbal Communication: The State of the Art* (New York: John Wiley and Sons, 1978).

status symbol, from dance and drama to music and mime, from the flow of affect to the flow of traffic, from the territoriality of animals to the protocol of diplomats, from extrasensory perception to analog computers, and from the rhetoric of violence to the rhetoric of topless dancers.[23]

Four major conceptual issues are evident.[24] The first is *intent*. Are all communication acts intentional? Are acts that are unintentional communicative? Are acts that are not perceived by a source as intended to be considered as communication? The second issue is *awareness*. Must communicators be aware of communicative acts? Or do acts of which either source, receiver, or both are unaware count as communication? The third issue involves *shared meaning*. To what extent must the meanings of acts be shared to count as communication? Finally, scholars disagree on what constitutes *meaningful units* of analysis. What kinds of signs are to be included in nonverbal communication?

Two analytical problems arise from these issues. First, one is never sure what to count as nonverbal communication. Our discussion will not take sides in this debate, but you will see that the various theories included define somewhat different behaviors and acts as important. Second, classifying or organizing the diversity of work in nonverbal communication presents a problem. One of the most useful classification schemes is that created by Judee Burgoon, who divided the writings in this area into five categories.[25] The first is research in the *variable analytic tradition*. This research attempts to isolate and understand how certain nonverbal variables relate to aspects of communication. Such research tends to be experimental, behavioristic, and nonactional. *Context research* examines the behavior of people in different situations, correlating nonverbal behavior with the demands of the situation. Writings on *skill development* deal with the improvement of nonverbal elements of message sending and receiving. The last two categories are especially useful for theories surveyed in this text. *Structural approaches* classify nonverbal behavior in order to reveal the ways in which nonverbal messages are structured. *Functional approaches*, on the other hand, show how nonverbal actions are used and how they operate in the communication process. Since many of the prominent theories of nonverbal communication fall into these last two categories, this section of the chapter is organized around the structure-function distinction.

Structural Theories

Among the various theories of nonverbal communication, certain structural approaches stand out clearly. These theories can be classified according to Abne Eisenberg and Ralph Smith's three-point analysis: kinesics, the study of bodily activity; proxemics, the study of space; and paralanguage, the study of voice.[26] Two anthropological theories that have become standards in nonverbal communication are Ray Birdwhistell's kinesic theory and Edward Hall's theory of proxemics. A third representative theory is G. L. Trager's on paralanguage. These three views provide an excellent representation of theory on the structure of nonverbal communication.

Birdwhistell's Theory of Kinesics. Ray Birdwhistell, one of the most important theorists and researchers on body movement, has led the field of kinesics for over thirty years.[27] As the inventor of the term, he is considered the father of kinesics. An anthropologist interested in language, Birdwhistell uses linguistics as a model for his kinesic work. In fact, kinesics is popularly referred to as *body language*, although cri-

23. Randall Harrison, "Nonverbal Communication," in *Handbook of Communication*, eds. Ithiel de sola Pool et al. (Chicago: Rand McNally, 1973).

24. This analysis from Burgoon, "Nonverbal Communication Research."

25. Burgoon, "Nonverbal Communication Research."

26. Abne M. Eisenberg and Ralph R. Smith, *Nonverbal Communication* (Indianapolis: Bobbs-Merrill, 1971).

27. Birdwhistell's major works include *Introduction to Kinesics* (Louisville: University of Louisville Press, 1952); *Kinesics and Context* (Philadelphia: University of Pennsylvania Press, 1970).

tics doubt the validity of the language analogy. Let us look at the foundation ideas of Birdwhistell's theory.

Communication, as a complex process, is a multichannel phenomenon. It makes use of all sensory channels, and a complete analysis must encompass all channels in use. Birdwhistell describes the continuous process: "While no single channel is in constant use, one or more channels are always in operation. Communication is the term which I apply to this continuous process."[28] Although developing methodologies for studying each channel is important, the theorist must always keep an eye on the whole. So, while Birdwhistell has concentrated his work on the visual channel, he has also attempted to relate his findings to the larger complex.

In *Kinesics and Context* Birdwhistell lists seven assumptions on which he bases his theory.

1. Like other events in nature, no body movement or expression is without meaning in the context in which it appears.
2. Like other aspects of human behavior, body posture, movement, and facial expression are patterned and, thus, subject to systematic analysis.
3. While the possible limitations imposed by particular biological substrata are recognized, until otherwise demonstrated, the systematic body motion of the members of a community is considered a function of the social system to which the group belongs.
4. Visible body activity, like audible acoustic activity, systematically influences the behavior of other members of any particular group.
5. Until otherwise demonstrated such behavior will be considered to have an investigable communicational function.
6. The meanings derived therefrom are functions both of the behavior and of the operations by which it is investigated.
7. The particular biological system and the special life experience of any individual will contribute idiosyncratic elements to his kinesic system, but the individual or symptomatic quality of these elements can only be assessed following the analysis of the larger system of which he is a part.[29]

28. Birdwhistell, *Kinesics*, p. 70.
29. Ibid., pp. 183–84.

One of the most important connections Birdwhistell found is the link between bodily activity and language, called the linguistic-kinesic analogy. This analogy extends classical linguistics into the realm of kinesics:

> This original study of gestures gave the first indication that kinesic structure is parallel to language structure. By the study of gestures in context, it became clear that the kinesic system has forms which are astonishingly like words in language. The discovery in turn led to the investigation of the components of these forms and to the discovery of the larger complexes of which they were components. . . . It has become clear that there are body behaviors which function like significant sounds, that combine into simple or relatively complex units like words, which are combined into much longer stretches of structured behavior like sentences or even paragraphs.[30]

The similarity of hierarchical structure in kinesics to that of linguistics is striking. The problem of the kinesicist is similar to that of the linguist: "Kinesics is concerned with abstracting from the continuous muscular shifts which are characteristics of living physiological systems those groupings of movement which are of significance to the communicational process and thus to the interactional systems of particular social groups."[31] Out of the thousands of perceptible bodily motions produced in a short period of time, certain of these emerge as functional in communication. Such movements are called *kines*: "A kine is an abstraction of that range of behavior produced by a member of a given social group which, for another member of that same group, stands in perceptual contrast to a different range of such behavior."[32] In other words, it is a range of motions or positions seen as a single motion or position. A perceptible movement of the eyelid or a turn of the hand are examples of kines. What is defined as a kine in one cultural group may not be in another. Kines are further grouped into *kinemes*, elements that display differential communicative function. Like the phoneme in linguistics,

30. Ibid., p. 80.
31. Ibid., p. 192.
32. Ibid., p. 193.

the kineme is a group of relatively interchangeable kines. For example, up to twenty-three different positions (kines) of the eyelids may be discerned, but they can be grouped into about four kinemes. Kinemes, like phonemes, occur in context. A complex combination of kinemes throughout the body may be called a *kinemorph*.

Hall's Theory of Proxemics. If Birdwhistell is the father of kinesics, Edward Hall is surely the father of proxemics.[33] Hall shares the view of his fellow anthropologist Birdwhistell that communication is a multichannel affair. Hall believes that just as language varies from culture to culture, so do the other interacting media. Specifically, *proxemics* refers to the use of space in communication. "Proxemics is the term I have coined for the interrelated observations and theories of man's use of space as a specialized elaboration of culture."[34] A more specific definition is "the study of how man unconsciously structures microspace—the distance between men in conduct of daily transactions, the organization of space in his houses and buildings, and ultimately the layout of his towns."[35] Although this definition of proxemics is broad, most of the work in the area has been limited to the use of interpersonal space.

These definitions make clear that the way space is used in interaction is very much a cultural matter. In different cultures various sensory modalities assume importance. In some cultures, such as the American, sight and hearing predominate; in other cultures, such as the Arabian, smell is also important. Some cultures rely on touching more than do others. In any case, a necessary relation is present between the use of senses in interaction and interpersonal distances. Another reason that proxemic relations vary among cultures involves the definition of the self. People in most western cultures learn to identify the self through the skin and clothes. Arabs, however, place the self deeper in the middle of the body.

For these reasons, then, the people of a particular culture structure their space in particular ways. Hall defines three basic types of space. *Fixed-feature space* consists of the unmovable structural arrangements around us. Walls and rooms are examples. *Semifixed feature space* is the way that movable obstacles such as furniture are arranged. *Informal space* is the personal territory around the body that travels with a person. Informal space determines the interpersonal distance between individuals. American culture utilizes four discernible distances: intimate (zero to eighteen inches), personal (one and one-half to four feet), social (four to twelve feet), and public (over twelve feet).

When people are engaged in conversation, eight possible factors are involved in the distance between them. Hall lists these factors as primary categories:

1. *Posture-sex factors:* These include the sex of the participant and the basic position (standing, sitting, lying).

2. *Sociofugal-sociopetal axis:* The word *sociofugal* implies discouragement of interaction; *sociopetal* implies the opposite. This dimension refers to the angle of the shoulders relative to the other person. The speakers may be facing each other, may be back to back, or may be positioned toward any other angle in the radius.

3. *Kinesthetic factors:* This is the closeness of the individuals in terms of touch-ability. Individuals may be in physical contact or within close distance, they may be outside body contact distance, or they may be positioned anywhere in between these extremes. This factor also includes the positioning of body parts as well as which parts are touching.

4. *Touching behavior:* People may be involved

33. Edward Hall's major works include *Silent Language* (Greenwich, Conn.: Fawcett, 1959); "A System for the Notation of Proxemic Behavior," *American Anthropologist*, 65 (1963): 1003–26; and *The Hidden Dimension* (New York: Random House, 1966). Excellent summaries can be found in Eisenberg and Smith, *Nonverbal Communication*, pp. 85–88; Knapp, *Nonverbal Communication in Human Interaction*, pp. 186–90; and O. Michael Watson, "Conflicts and Directions in Proxemic Research," *Journal of Communication*, 22 (1972): 443–59.

34. Hall, *The Hidden Dimension*, p. 1.

35. Hall, "A System for Notation," p. 1003.

in any of the following tactile relations: caressing and holding, feeling, prolonged holding, pressing against, spot touching, accidental brushing, or no contact.

5. *Visual code:* This category includes the manner of eye contact ranging from direct (eye-to-eye) to no contact.

6. *Thermal code:* This element involves the perceived heat from the other communicator.

7. *Olfactory code:* This factor includes the kind and degree of odor perceived in the conversation.

8. *Voice loudness:* The loudness of speech relates directly to interpersonal space.

Paralanguage. The third category of nonverbal behavior is paralanguage, or the use of vocal signs in communication. It forms the borderline between the verbal and nonverbal aspects of interaction. The sounds we make in speaking relate to language but are not included directly in language. Trager's work in this area is not as well known as the other theories in the chapter, but it is an important contribution to our understanding.[36] Trager divides paralinguistic cues into four types: voice qualities, vocal characterizers, vocal qualifiers, and vocal segregates. *Voice qualities* include such cues as pitch range, quality of articulation (forceful or relaxed), and rhythm. *Vocal characterizers* include such noises as laughing, crying, yelling, yawning, spitting, belching. *Vocal qualifiers* include the manner in which words and phrases are uttered. For example, a word may be spoken softly or with high pitch; a phrase may be drawled or clipped. Finally, *vocal segregates* include the rhythmic factors that contribute to the flow of speech: "uh," "um," pauses, and other interruptions of rhythm.

Functional Theories

Ekman and Friesen. For nearly twenty years Paul Ekman and Wallace Friesen have collaborated on nonverbal research that has led to an excellent general model of nonverbal signs.[37] They have concentrated their work on kinesic behavior (for example, face and hands). Their goal has been ambitious: "Our aim has been to increase understanding of the individual, his feelings, mood, personality, and attitudes, and to increase understanding of any given interpersonal interaction, the nature of the relationship, the status or quality of communication, what impressions are formed, and what is revealed about interpersonal style or skill."[38]

These authors have approached nonverbal activity from three perspectives: origin, coding, and usage. Origin is the source of an act. A nonverbal behavior may be innate (built into the nervous system), species constant (universal behavior required for survival), or variant across cultures, groups, and individuals. As examples, one could speculate that eyebrow raising as a response to surprise is innate, that territoriality is species constant, and that shaking the head back and forth to indicate no is culture specific.

Coding is the relationship of the act to its meaning. An act may be *arbitrary*; that is, no indication of meaning is inherent in the sign itself. Head nodding is a good example. By convention, in our culture we agree that nodding is an indication of yes, but this coding is purely arbitrary. Other nonverbal signs are *iconic*. Iconic signs resemble what is being signified. For instance, we often draw pictures in the air or position our hands to illustrate what we are talking about. The third category of coding is *intrinsic*. Intrinsically coded cues contain their meaning within them; such cues are themselves part of what is being signified. Crying is an example of intrinsic coding. Crying is

36. G. L. Trager, "Paralanguage: A First Approximation," *Studies in Linguistics*, 13 (1958): 1–12.

37. Ekman and Friesen's major works include "Nonverbal Behavior in Psychotherapy Research," in *Research in Psychotherapy*, ed. J. Shlien, vol. III (Washington, D.C.: American Psychological Association, 1968); "The Repertoire of Nonverbal Behavior: Categories, Origins, Usage, and Coding." *Semiotica*, 1 (1969): 49–98; *Emotion in the Human Face: Guidelines for Research and an Integration of Findings* (New York: Pergamon Press, 1972); *Unmasking the Face* (Englewood Cliffs, N.J.: Prentice-Hall, 1975).

38. Paul Ekman and Wallace Friesen, "Hand Movements," *Journal of Communication*, 22 (1972): 353.

a sign of emotion, but it is also part of the emotion itself.

The third way to analyze a behavior is by usage. This category includes variables related to circumstances. It involves such factors as external conditions around the behavior, awareness or nonawareness of the act, reactions from others, and the type of information conveyed. A helpful subanalysis of usage is the degree to which a nonverbal behavior is intended to convey information. A *communicative* act is one used deliberately to convey meaning. *Interactive* acts are those that influence the behavior of the other participants. An act will be both communicative and interactive if it is intentional and influential. For example, if you deliberately wave to a friend as a sign of greeting and the friend waves back, your cue would be communicative and interactive. A third category of behaviors are those not intended to be communicative but that nevertheless provide information for the perceiver. Such acts are said to be *informative*. On a day when you are feeling less than friendly, you may duck into a hallway to avoid meeting an acquaintance coming your way. If the other person sees the avoidance, your behavior has been informative even though you did not intend to communicate.

All nonverbal behavior is one of five types, depending on origin, coding, and usage. The first type is the emblem. *Emblems* have a verbal translation of a rather precise meaning for a social group. They are normally used in a deliberate fashion to communicate a particular message. The victory "V" and the black power fist are examples. The origin of emblems is cultural learning; emblems may be either arbitrary or iconic in coding.

Illustrators are the second kind of nonverbal cues. Illustrators have a high relation to speech since they are used to illustrate what is being said verbally. They are intentional, though we may not always be directly aware of them. They include eight types: *batons* (movements that accent or emphasize), *ideographs* ("sketching" the direction of a thought), *deictic movements* (pointing), *spatial movements* (depicting or outlining space), *rhythmic movements* (pacing motions), *kinetographs* (depicting physical actions), *pictographs* (drawing a picture in the air), and *emblematic movements* (illustrating a verbal statement). These types are not mutually exclusive; some motions are combinations of types. Illustrators are informative or communicative in use and occasionally may be interactive. They are also learned.

The third type of nonverbal behavior is the *adaptor*, which serves to facilitate release of bodily tension. Such actions as hand wringing, head scratching, or foot jiggling are examples of adaptors. *Self-adaptors*, which usually occur in private, are directed to one's own body. They may include scratching, stroking, grooming, squeezing. *Alter-adaptors* are directed to another's body. *Object-adaptors* are directed at things. In any case, adaptors may be iconic or intrinsic. Rarely are they intentional, and one is usually not aware of one's own adaptive behaviors. They may occur when the individual is communicating with another, but they usually occur with greater frequency when the person is alone. Although they are rarely communicative, they are sometimes interactive and often informative.

Regulators, the fourth type of behavior, are used directly to regulate, control, or coordinate interaction. For example, we use eye contact to signal speaking and listening roles in a conversation. Regulators are primarily interactive. They are coded intrinsically or iconically, and their origin is cultural learning.

The final category of behavior is the *affect display*. These behaviors, which may be in part innate, involve the display of feelings and emotions. The face is particularly rich for affect display, although other parts of the body also may be involved. Affect displays are intrinsically coded. They are rarely communicative, often interactive, and always informative.

Dittmann's Theory of Emotional Communication. Allen Dittmann provides an important functional theory of emotional communication. His theory has three parts: emotional information, emotion signs, and channels for communicating emotion.[39]

Following the classical definition of emotion, Dittmann explains emotion in terms of *behavioral deviation*. That is, whether perceived by self or others, an emotional expression is a deviation from some baseline behavior. We judge a person's emotion on the basis of how the behavior is different from what is usually seen in this individual and culture. This explanation, of course, assumes that people have some intuitive knowledge of baseline behavior in relation to various situations in which emotions occur. Such knowledge stems from experience with universal behavior patterns, cultural modes of expression, and social structure, as well as the observed person's idiosyncratic behavioral patterns. Once emotional expression is perceived, it is placed in the category (fear, anger, sadness, and so forth) that the perceiver has learned to associate with the particular behavioral deviation being observed.

What is the nature of emotional signs? Dittmann provides a useful and interesting analysis of nonverbal affect display. His analysis contains three major factors: communicative specificity, level of awareness, and intentional control. These variables extend Ekman and Friesen's concept of sign use.

The first variable, communicative specificity, is a continuum between the extremes of communication and expression. Messages on the communication end of this spectrum possess "coded" or agreed-upon meaning. Communicative cues are relatively specific in terms of what they relay to the perceiver. Messages at the other end have less social meaning and tend to express one's feeling in idiosyncratic terms. In our culture shrugging the shoulders is a sign of uncertainty, possessing a high degree of communicative specificity.

The second dimension in Dittmann's model, level of awareness, actually is two variables. On one end of the spectrum is full awareness; on the other is either subliminal unconscious or repression. A person may be more or less aware of a particular behavior. If the behavior is done without awareness, one of two conditions exists: Either the behavior is psychologically repressed, or the stimulus is not strong enough to be perceived. This dimension of awareness can apply to either the sender, the receiver, or both. Suppose in a conversation a speaker is expressing dislike for another person by a slight frown. If the listener has a strong need for acceptance at that moment, the listener might repress awareness of the frown and fail to realize the other speaker's dislike. Or perhaps the frown is so slight that the listener fails to see it because it is subliminal. At the other end of the scale, however, the listener might be mildly or strongly aware of the frown. In summary, this variable forms two continuums, with awareness as one extreme and either repressed unconscious or subliminal unconscious as the other.

The third dimension of the emotional message is intentional control. In some circumstances a person tends to express feeling fully and spontaneously. At other times emotions are controlled and monitored. (As in the case of the other factors, intentional control is always a matter of degree.) A good illustration of an extreme case of control is when a person has a strong urge to laugh in an inappropriate setting and fakes a cough to cover up the laughter.

The final division of Dittmann's theory deals with channels of emotional communication. In any face-to-face interaction a number of modalities are used. We know that a rich assortment of behaviors is communicated in the form of bodily activity, space, voice, and so forth. In an ongoing conversation these behaviors blend together into a kind of gestalt image. Certain behaviors will be more salient for the receiver than others, depending on the situation and culture. Thus the primary channel of emotional communication in a given conversation de-

39. Allen T. Dittmann, *Interpersonal Messages of Emotion* (New York: Springer Publishing, 1972). Dittmann's approach is based on information theory, which we will not pursue here. See chaps. 2 and 3. Information theory is covered separately in this book in Chapter 7.

pends on what the receiver perceives from the complex stimuli. Dittmann describes three broad classifications of channels: audible, visual, and psychophysiological. *Audible channels* include language and paralanguage; *visual channels* include facial expression and body movement; *psychophysiological channels* are those cues emanating from bodily functions (for example, breathing, eyeblinking, and so forth).

Criticism

Certainly the work of nonverbal communication has helped us realize the complexity and subtlety of communication codes. The various categories suggested by theory have been heuristic in producing an impressive quantity of research. The major problems of nonverbal communication theories lie in their appropriateness for explaining intricacies of the communication process and in their narrowness of scope.[40]

We can express the major criticism of these theories as a series of fallacies. The first is the *fallacy of the linguistic analogy*. Although some superficial similarities may be observed between language and kinesics, probably more differences than similarities exist. Language is presented sequentially and involves discrete signs; nonverbal codes are not presented solely in a sequential manner and rarely consist of discrete behaviors. Although language is organized hierarchically, no good evidence shows that nonverbal acts are organized in this way (despite Birdwhistell's linguisticlike categories). Language is always used consciously; nonverbal codes often are not. Thus we see that the assumptions of language may not be appropriate to the domain of nonverbal behavior.

The second problem is the *fallacy of analysis*. Most of the structural theorists admit that messages consist of inseparable complexes of verbal and nonverbal codes, yet these theories tend strongly to approach a synthetic topic in an analytic way by focusing on particular behaviors to the exclusion of others. Again, this problem is one of appropriateness and scope.

Finally, there is the *fallacy of nonverbal preeminence*. Nonverbal communication is often assumed to be the most important aspect of any message. Language is reduced to a lesser role. Some writers on nonverbal communication have actually stated as much.[41] Most, however, imply undue importance by separating and concentrating on aspects of nonverbal codes apart from the entire coding complex. In most transactions language is absolutely central, but the relative importance of any part of the code varies from situation to situation.

These fallacies are especially apparent in structural theories of nonverbal communication, and they arise from the tendency of such theories to separate and classify bodily activity. The functional approaches tend to be less segmental in their treatment of verbal and nonverbal codes.

The attempt to move from finite description of nonverbal communication behavior to an explanation of how it functions in ongoing interaction is a necessary step. Yet this kind of work is fraught with difficulties. First, accurate observation is a problem. How can we know what functions are being served by nonverbal behaviors? Indeed, at any given moment several functions may be involved.

In short, a more comprehensive theory is needed in nonverbal communication. Heretofore the theoretical work has been fragmented and limited. The functional theories take a step in the right direction, but even these could be more comprehensive in considering the larger issue of coordinated coding in general.

What Do We Know about Language and Nonverbal Coding?

Of all the communication domains language and meaning are perhaps the most elusive; yet

40. For a more complete analysis and critique of several approaches to nonverbal communication, see Judee Burgoon and Thomas Saine, *The Unspoken Dialogue: An Introduction to Nonverbal Communication* (Boston: Houghton Mifflin, 1978), chap. 2. See also Knapp, Wiemann, and Daly, "Nonverbal Communication."

41. A. Mehrabian, "Communication without Words," *Psychology Today*, 2 (1968): 51–52.

ironically they lie at the heart of communication as a symbolic activity. Earlier simplistic models of language no longer are considered adequate to explain how language is acquired and how sentences are generated and understood. Meaning is not simply a matter of individual word denotations and connotations. Grammar, as an organizing link among semantic units, is vital in the communication of meaning. Therefore much work in linguistics has centered on syntax as the key element of language. Generally accepted among linguists today is the belief that the generation and reception of sentences cannot occur on the surface level alone. Deeper coding processes must be examined. Unfortunately, linguists are far from certain what these deep processes are. The mainstream of linguistic thought states that sentences are created and understood by the use of a parsimonious set of rules that can be combined in numerous ways to create or understand an infinite number of sentences.

Language acquisition also remains an unsolved puzzle. Few linguistics still believe that language is strictly a learned behavior. Rather, they believe that children are born with an innate model of linguistic structure that enables the child to acquire a native language with great speed. Although several notions of how this process occurs have been posed, basically it is still unknown.

Nonverbal communication is an important addition to our body of theory because of what it reveals about the coding complex. Although language is the essence of communication, meanings are communicated by messages that consist of a complex set of linguistic and nonlinguistic cues. Words are not uttered in isolation but are part of a bigger set of vocal, facial, bodily, and spatial cues. Some communication takes place without language at all.

Clearly, nonverbal elements of communication are highly functional, relating emotional meaning, facilitating interaction management, and releasing tension. Nonverbal cues also augment the linguistic code, adding nuance to the meaning of verbal messages.

CHAPTER

6 Theories of Meaning

One cannot logically separate the topics of language and nonverbal communication from meaning. Meaning is the concept that connects symbols with human beings. It is an elusive theme, of which several interpretations exist. The theories presented in this section attempt to describe or explain this concept. For purposes of discussion, these theories are divided into several groups according to similar assumptions and claims: representational theories, ordinary language philosophy, and experiential theories.

Representational Theories of Meaning

The first sense of meaning is representational. Here meaning is seen as the "representation" of an object, event, or condition by a sign. Each theory in this section explains how signs are used to stand for things in the minds of people. The first theory is that of I. A. Richards. Richards shows how three elements—the symbol, the referent, and the person—interrelate in establishing meaning. A closely related approach, which stresses the conception of the referent in the person, is that of Suzanne Langer. The section concludes with a discussion of the semantic theory of Charles Osgood, which attempts to define the nature of meaning within the person.

The Approach of Richards

One of the best known approaches to meaning is that of I. A. Richards and his colleague C. K. Ogden in *The Meaning of Meaning*, later elaborated by Richards in other works.[1] Richards, a scholar in the field of English, was most noted for his work in literary criticism and rhetorical theory. His lifelong pursuit of improving communication led him to consider the nature of words, meanings, and understandings in all kinds of discourse. In the introduction to *The Philosophy of Rhetoric* he writes, "We struggle all our days with misunderstandings, and no apology is required for any study which can prevent or remove them."[2]

For Richards language is a system of signs that, because of its centrality to human life, is supremely important as a field of study. A sign is anything that stands for something else. It elicits in the person an image of a broader context in which the sign was originally perceived. Further, as instruments of thought and communication, language signs are designated specially as *symbols*.

To aid in understanding the nature of symbol meaning, Richards and Ogden developed their famous triangle of meaning, illustrated in Figure 6.1.[3] This model stresses three senses of meaning: meaning in the symbol (What does the word mean?), meaning in the referent (What is the meaning of this thing?), and meaning in the person (What does this mean to you?). While there is a direct relationship between the symbol and the thought or the referent and the thought, the relationship between the symbol and the referent is indirect. It is an

1. C. K. Ogden and I. A. Richards, *The Meaning of Meaning* (London: Kegan, Paul, Trench, Trubner, 1923). I. A. Richards, *The Philosophy of Rhetoric* (New York: Oxford University Press, 1936); *Principles of Literary Criticism* (New York: Harcourt, Brace, 1952). For excellent summaries of Richards's work, see Marie Hochmuth Nichols, "I. A. Richards and the New Rhetoric," *Quarterly Journal of Speech* 44 (1958): 1–16; Marie Hochmuth Nichols, *Rhetoric and Criticism* (Baton Rouge: Louisiana State University Press, 1963), chap. 7; Richard L. Johannesen, ed. *Contemporary Theories of Rhetoric* (New York: Harper & Row, 1971), pt. 3.

2. Richards, *Philosophy of Rhetoric*, p. 3.

3. Ogden and Richards, *The Meaning of Meaning*, p. 11.

arbitrary relationship that holds only because of the common denominator of thought in the person. Let's use the word *cat* as an example. The three elements include the animal itself (referent), the symbol *cat*, and the thought or image of the animal that arises in the person's mind when the word is heard. The connection between the sign and the referent can only occur through the image of the animal in the person. The relationship between *cat* and the actual thing is therefore indirect, even though either will elicit the thought in the person.

With this basic three-way distinction as a base, Richards discusses the ways that language is used. When it is used primarily to communicate description of the referent, the statement is *scientific*. When language is used primarily to communicate one's feeling about something, it is *emotive*. And in the middle is a *mixed* range of statements. In any case communication is an attempt to elicit meanings in another person. The goal of communication is to create a similar mental experience in the other, a goal that can be achieved only when the communicators share a certain degree of past experience. This general aim exists for both emotive and scientific communication. With emotive discourse the communicator hopes to elicit similar feelings and attitudes; with scientific description one hopes to elicit an accurate and factual image. According to Richards, rhetorical criticism must involve the detailed study of words and the ways these kinds of understandings occur. In short, it must become a science of meanings in communication.

Richards's most valuable contribution is his notion that the important meaning is *in the person*. The relationship between the person and the symbol is arbitrary and is mediated by the thought of the person. Thus communication must be viewed as a process of eliciting meanings, not giving meanings. This thesis has had a great impact on the study of human communication. It is a view that has been promoted by each of the theories in this section. A further discussion of this notion is that of Suzanne Langer.

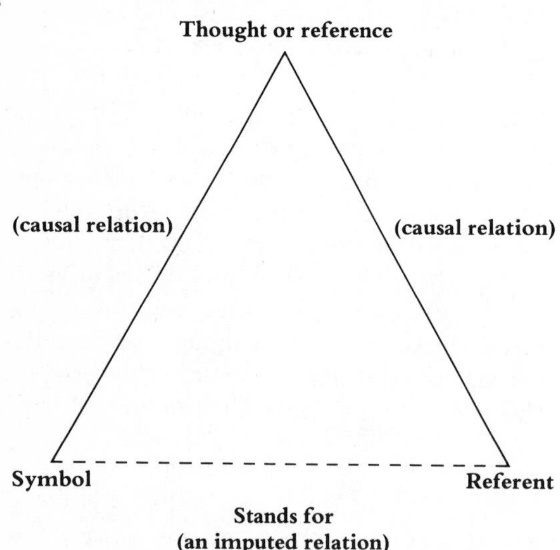

From *The Meaning of Meaning*, by C. K. Ogden and I. A. Richards. Copyright © 1923. Reprinted by permission of Harcourt Brace Jovanovich and Routledge and Kegan Paul.

Figure 6.1. Ogden and Richards's meaning triangle.

Langer's Theory of Symbols

One of the most important topics of philosophy in the past century has been the relationship between language and meaning. It is clear that any investigation of knowledge or epistemology must include a view of these central issues. A most useful concept of language is that of Suzanne Langer, whose *Philosophy in a New Key* has received considerable attention by students of symbolism.[4]

Langer considers symbolism to be the key issue of philosophy, an issue that underlies all human knowing and understanding: "So our interest in the mind has shifted more and more from the acquisition of experience, the domain of sense, to the *uses* of sense-data, the realm of conception and expression."[5] All animal life is

4. Susanne Langer, *Philosophy in a New Key* (Cambridge: Harvard University Press, 1942). See also *Mind: An Essay on Human Feeling* (Baltimore: Johns Hopkins Press), vol. 1, 1967; vol. 2, 1972.

5. Langer, *Philosophy in a New Key*, p. 26.

dominated by feeling, but human feeling includes the additional ability to conceive of objects in their absence via symbols and language.

Langer distinguishes between signs and symbols, using sign in a narrower sense than did our discussion in the last chapter. For her a *sign* is a stimulus that indicates the presence of something else. It corresponds highly with the actual signified event or object. A *symbol* is more complex: "Symbols are not proxy of their objects, but are *vehicles for the conception of objects.*"[6] Symbols allow a person to think about something apart from its immediate presence. Langer therefore calls the symbol "an instrument of thought."[7] We can see how this idea supports Ogden and Richards's idea of meaning in the person. We will return to the function of signs and symbols momentarily. First, let's go back to the broader issue of human mentality.

Not only do people have an increased capacity to use symbols, but the human has a basic need to symbolize apart from the practical necessities of living. Further, the symbol-making process is a continuous function in humans tantamount to eating and sleeping. We therefore must explain a good deal of human behavior in terms of meeting the symbolic need. Symbolic acts involve speech (the use of language) and nonverbal symbolization, which Langer calls *ritual*. In the following passage Langer indicates the importance of studying meaning in symbolism: "In order to relate these two distinct conceptions of symbolism [language and ritual], and exhibit the respective parts they play in that general human response we call *life*, it is necessary to examine more accurately that which makes *symbols* out of anything—out of marks on paper, the little squeaks and grunts we interpret as 'words,' or bended knees—the quality of *meaning*, in its several aspects and forms."[8]

6. Ibid., p. 61. Elsewhere in this book we have treated symbols as a kind of sign. Langer uses the term *sign* more narrowly.

7. Ibid., p. 63.

8. Ibid., p. 52.

Like Richards, Langer conceives of meaning as the complex relation among the symbol, the object, and the person. As she puts it: "If there is not at least one thing meant and one mind for which it is meant, then there is not a complete meaning."[9] Thus we have both a logical and psychological sense of symbol meaning, the logical being the relation between the symbol and referent and the psychological the relation between the symbol and the person.

The real significance of language, however, is not in words, but in *discourse*. Words name things, but "before terms are built into propositions, they assert nothing, preclude nothing . . . say nothing."[10] By tying words together, grammatical structure plays an important symbolic role. A *proposition* is a complex symbol that presents a picture of something. The word *dog* brings up a conception, but its combination with other words in a proposition provides a unified picture: The little brown dog is nestled against my foot.

In this sense language truly makes us human. Through language we communicate, we think, and we feel. The significance of discursive symbolism in human life is captured in the following passage:

> Language draws so many other mental functions into its orbit—very deep and phylogenetically ancient processes of emotive and instinctive character—and lifts them from their animalian state to a new, peculiarly human level. It also engages all sorts of higher, larger cortical mechanisms, producing distinct forms of memory, sequences of recall, logical contradiction, logical entailment, the propositional structure of ideas that is inherent in the conception of fact, and the correlative, largely emotional disposition of the whole mind, belief. The depth to which the influence of language goes in the organization of our perception and apperception becomes more impressive the further one pursues it.[11]

How, then, does language work? Any proposition communicates a common *concept*. The concept is the general idea, pattern, or form

9. Ibid., p. 56.

10. Ibid., p. 67.

11. Langer, *Mind*, p. 324.

embodied by a proposition. It is, in short, common meaning among communicators. But each communicator also will have a private image or meaning, which fills in the details of the common picture. This private image is the person's *conception*. Meaning therefore consists of the individual's conception and the common concept: "A concept is all that a symbol really conveys. But just as quickly as the concept is symbolized to us, our own imagination dresses it up in a private, personal *conception*, which we can distinguish from the public concept only by a process of abstraction."[12] Three terms help to explain Langer's ideas: signification, denotation, connotation.

Signification is the meaning of a sign. A sign, as defined earlier, is a simple stimulus announcing the presence of some object. Signification therefore is a one-to-one relationship between sign and object. *Denotation* is the complex relation of the symbol to its object via the conception in the person. The *connotation* of a symbol is the direct relationship between the symbol and the conception itself. For example, the denotation of the symbol *dog* is its relation to the fluffy little pup at my feet. This relationship occurs only in my mind through conception. Even when the puppy is not present, I can think of it because of the relationship between the symbol and conception—the connotation of the word. Connotation includes all of one's personal feelings and associations attached to a symbol.

Langer notes that humans possess a built-in tendency to *abstract*. Abstraction, which leads to the ability to deal with concepts, is a crucial human function. It is the essence of rationality. Consistent with her notion of meaning, Langer defines abstraction as "a process of recognizing the concept in any configuration given to experience, and forming a conception accordingly."[13] Abstraction is a process of leaving out details in conceiving of an object, event, or situation. For example, the word *dog* brings to mind a conception, a connotation, but this conception is incomplete; it always leaves something out. The more abstract the symbol, the more sketchy the conception: A *dog* is a *mammal*, which is an *animal*; an animal is a *living thing*, which is an *object*. All of these terms can be used to symbolize the furry little puppy, but they constitute a hierarchy of abstraction, each successive term leaving out more details in the conception.

12. Ibid., pp. 71–72.

13. Ibid., p. 72.

Earlier we mentioned that two important types of symbols involve language and ritual. Langer labels these discursive and presentational. *Discursive* symbols involve the combination of smaller units (for example, words and phrases) into larger ones. Individual word meanings are combined into larger concepts. Such symbols are linguistic. In *presentational* symbolism individual units may not have distinct meaning. Such forms may not be translatable or definable in other terms. The meanings of presentational forms are understood only through the whole. Nonverbal rituals and forms constitute "a simultaneous integral presentation."[14] A Catholic mass or commencement ceremony illustrates this idea.

While other philosophers have excluded presentational forms from rationality, Langer believes that all experience, including thought (discursive symbolism) and feeling (presentational symbolism), is rational. Some of the most important human experiences are emotional and are best communicated through presentational forms such as art and music. Langer summarizes her quest in the following passage: "The continual pursuit of meanings—wider, clearer, more negotiable, more articulate meanings—is philosophy. It permeates all mental life; sometimes in conscious form of metaphysical thought, sometimes in the free, confident manipulation of established ideas to derive their more precise, detailed implications, and sometimes—in the greatest creative peri-

14. Ibid., p. 97.

ods—in the form of passionate mythical, ritual, and devotional expression."[15]

Osgood's Theory of Meaning

The other theories in this section define meaning in terms of the association between a symbol and its referent. The theory of Charles Osgood seeks to explain how this association arises and to isolate the psychological dimensions of connotation. As a behaviorist Osgood is especially interested in how meanings are learned and how they relate to internal and external behavior. He is well known for his work on the semantic differential, a method for measuring meaning. His theory is one of the most elaborate of the behavioral theories of language and meaning.[16] Osgood believes that language should not be studied apart from actual ongoing behavior, that language is used in context, and that theories of psycholinguistics should explain the interaction between language and other human activity. Clearly his approach differs significantly from the purely structural approach of Chomsky, which was reviewed in the last chapter.

In order to understand Osgood's theory, you may need a little background in learning theory. Osgood follows the classical learning tradition, which teaches that learning is a process of developing new internal or external behavioral associations. In this tradition learning theory begins with the assumption that individuals respond to stimuli in the environment. The link between stimulus and response is often referred to as S-R. Most learning theorists such as Osgood agree that predispositions in the individual affect how the person will respond to the stimulus, and so they revise the model to read S-O-R, which refers to stimulus-organism-response.

When a new stimulus is paired or associated with the original stimulus, the organism learns to respond to the new stimulus in the same way as to the old. For example, Pavlov's dog learned to salivate to the sound of a bell. By this process new S-R links are established. This model of learning is simple, and psychologists agree that learning does occur in other, more complex ways. Osgood, however, believes that this basic association process is responsible for the establishment of meaning. Although individuals can respond overtly to actual environmental stimuli, they also have a representation of the stimulus and response that is internal in the organism. While the symbols *S* and *R* are used to represent the overt stimulus and response, the lowercase letters *s* and *r* designate the internal representation. Meaning occurs on the internal (s-r) level. Osgood's model of this internal-external relationship is somewhat complex.

He proposes a three-stage behavioral model, illustrated in Figure 6.2.[17] This model can be used to analyze any behavior, but he applies it to language and meaning in particular. Three basic processes are involved: *encoding* (receiving stimuli), *association* (pairing stimuli and responses), and *decoding* (responding). These processes occur on one of three levels, depending on the complexity of the behavior involved. The *projection level* is the simple neural pathway system between sensor and effector organs. Behavior on this level is reflexive, such as knee jerks and eye blinks. Here the stimulus and response are linked automatically and directly. On the *integration level* the stimulus-response link is not automatic. Stimulus and response must be integrated by the brain through perceived association. An example is the routine greeting ritual: "How are you?" "I am fine."

The *representational level* is the level on which meaning occurs. The stimulus from the environment is projected onto the brain, where an internal response leads to an internal stimulus (meaning), which in turn leads to the individual's overt response. The internal response or

15. Ibid., pp. 293–94.

16. Charles Osgood, "On Understanding and Creating Sentences," *American Psychologist* 18 (1963): 735–51.

17. Ibid., p. 740.

meaning is a learned association between certain actual responses to the object and a sign of the object. Thus the sign (a word, perhaps) will elicit a particular meaning or set of meanings, which stem from the association of the sign and the object. To use a rather dramatic example, suppose you sit in a small fragile chair, and it collapses. In the immediate future a picture of the chair, the sight of another similar chair, or the words "small fragile chair" will elicit an image (r_m) in your head that influences how you will respond. This internal response (fear or pain) is part of your meaning for the sign. In real life meanings are more complex than in this example, but they are formed, Osgood believes, through the same basic associational process. In summary, Osgood sees the first level as sensory, the second as perceptual, and the third as meaningful.

The development of meaning by associating a sign with an environmental stimulus is illustrated in Figure 6.3. This figure shows the

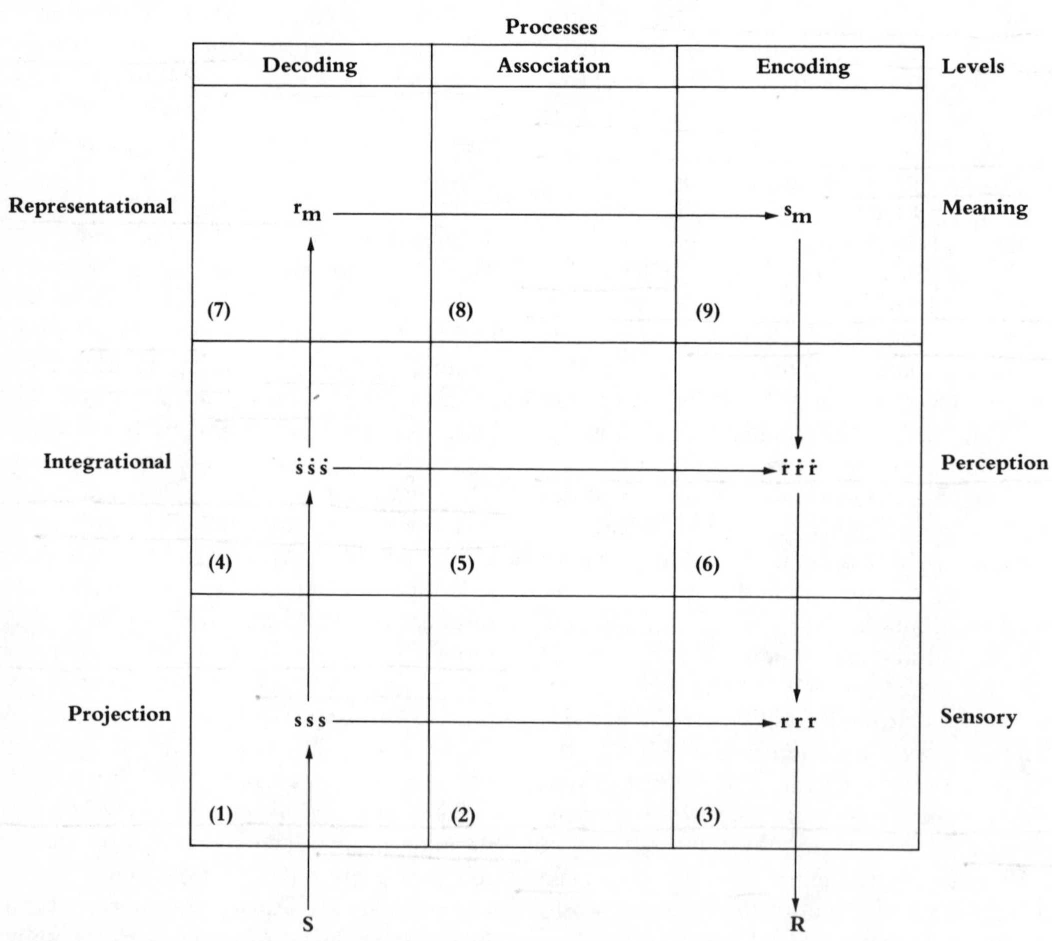

*The symbol *s* refers to internal stimuli, *r* to internal responses, both differentiated by level. *S* and *R* refer to external stimulus and response.

Figure 6.2. Three-stage mediation model of behavior.

development of a sign $\boxed{S}$ as the result of its association with a natural stimulus S. A portion of one's complex response to the natural stimulus R_T becomes represented in the form of an internal response r_m, which in turn becomes an internal stimulus to a new but related overt response R_X. Meaning is the internal mediating process represented in Figure 6.3 as $r_m \longrightarrow s_m$. Such meaning, since it is inside the person and unique to the person's own experience with the natural stimulus, is said to be *connotative*. Osgood presents a good example of this process. For a particular person a spider (S) elicits a complex response R_T. When the word *spider* is associated with the object as it might be in a small child, a portion of the response R_m (fear) becomes associated with the label. This internal meaning mediates the person's response to the word, even when the actual object is not present.[18]

Most meanings are not learned as a result of direct experience with the natural stimulus. In other words, they are learned by associations between one sign and another, a process that may occur in the abstract out of physical contact with the original stimulus. Figure 6.4 is Osgood's illustration of this more complex process.[19] This figure depicts a series of signs, $\boxed{S}$, each of which elicits meanings in the individual because of previous associations (r_m). These signs are associated with another new sign, /S/, and their internal responses (meanings) "rub off" on the new sign (r_{ma}). To continue our example, imagine that the child who had already established internal responses to the words *spider, big*, and *hairy* listened to a story about a tarantula. In the story the tarantula was characterized as a "big, hairy spider." Through association the child will now have a meaning for the new word tarantula. This word may also carry some mixture of the connotations earlier attached to the other words because of its association with these words. If the child associated *spider* with fear, *big* with potentially dangerous, and *hairy* with feeling creepy, then the child might well react to a real or imagined tarantula by running away. In this example the words *spider, big*, and *hairy* are $\boxed{S_1}$, $\boxed{S_2}$, and $\boxed{S_3}$; r_{m1} is fear, r_{m2} is dangerous, and r_{m3} is creepy. The new word /S/ (tarantula), when associated with the other words, comes to elicit the internal response of avoidance (r_{ma}), which itself becomes a stimulus (s_{ma}) to cause the child to run away (R_{xa}) when threatened by a real or imagined tarantula.

18. Osgood, "The Nature and Measurement of Meaning," in *The Semantic Differential Technique*, ed. James Snider and Charles Osgood (Chicago: Aldine, 1969), pp. 9–10.
19. Ibid., p. 11.

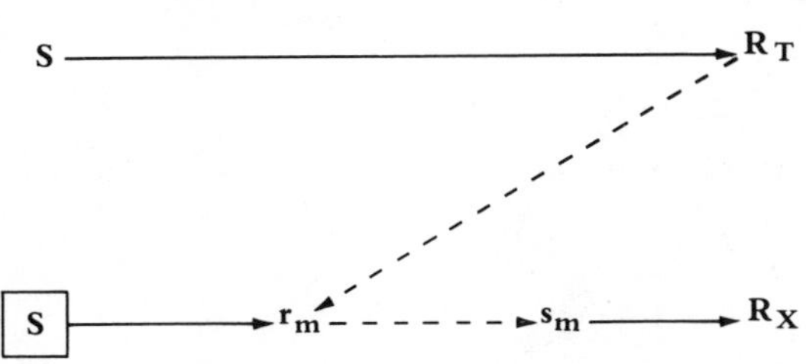

Figure 6.3. Development of a sign.

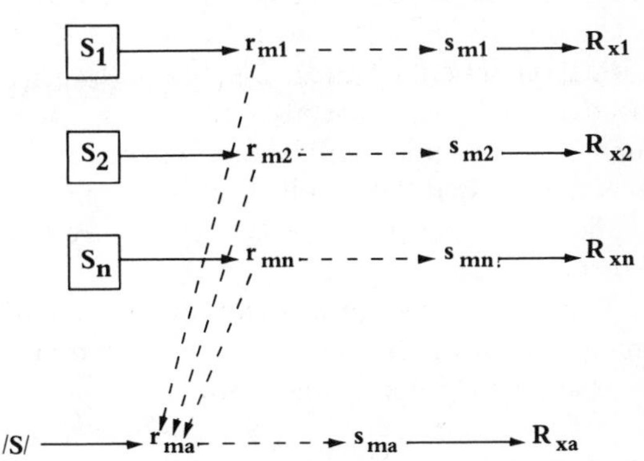

Figure 6.4. Development of an assign.

Osgood is perhaps best known for the *semantic differential technique*, a method for measuring meaning.[20] This measurement technique assumes that one's meanings can be expressed by the use of words. The method begins by finding a set of adjectives that could be used to express individuals' connotations for some stimulus or sign. These adjectives are set against one another as opposites, such as good/bad, high/low, slow/fast. Individuals are given a topic, word, or other stimulus and are asked to indicate on a seven-point scale how they associate the stimulus with the adjective pairs. A sample scale looks like this:

good ——:——:——:——:——:——:—— bad

The subject places a check mark on any space between these adjectives to indicate the degree of good or bad associated with the stimulus. The subject may fill out as many as fifty such scales for each stimulus. Osgood then uses a statistical technique called factor analysis to find the basic dimensions of meaning that are operating in peoples' connotations of the stimulus. His findings in this research have led to the theory of semantic space.[21]

One's meaning for any sign is said to be located in a metaphorical space of three major dimensions: *evaluation, activity*, and *potency*. A given sign, perhaps a word or concept, elicits a reaction in the person consisting of a sense of evaluation (good or bad), activity (active or inactive), and potency or strength. The person's connotative meaning will lie somewhere in this hypothetical space, depending on the responses of the person on the three factors. Figure 6.5 illustrates semantic space.

Take the concept *mother*, for example. For any given person this sign will elicit an internal response embodying some combination of the three factors. One person might judge *mother* as good, passive, weak; another as good, active, and strong. In any case one's connotative meaning for *mother* will depend on learned associations in the individual's life. (Keep in mind that the three dimensions of meaning are not dichotomous but continuous variables.)

Osgood and others have done semantic differential research on a variety of sign types, including word concepts, music, art, and even sonar sounds.[22] In addition they have done research among a number of groups of people representing a wide range of cultures. Osgood believes that the three factors of meaning—evaluation, potency, and activity—apply across all people and all concepts.[23] If this is true, then Osgood has significantly advanced our understanding of meaning.

Osgood's mediational approach has been especially well applied by social psychologists to persuasion and attitude research. Osgood himself has participated in developing a theory

20. Ibid.

21. More recently Osgood has hypothesized that bipolarity is a basic factor in all language and human thought. See Charles Osgood and Meredith Richards, "From Yang and Yin to *and* or *but*," *Language* 49 (1973): 380–412.

22. A sampling of studies illustrating the applications can be found in Snider and Osgood, *Semantic Differential*. This work also includes an atlas of approximately 55 concepts and their semantic profiles.

23. This point of view is expressed in Charles Osgood, "Semantic Differential Technique in the Comparative Study of Cultures," in *The Semantic Differential Technique*, ed. James Snider and Charles Osgood (Chicago: Aldine, 1969), pp. 303–32); and *Cross Cultural Universals of Affective Meaning* (Urbana: University of Illinois Press, 1975).

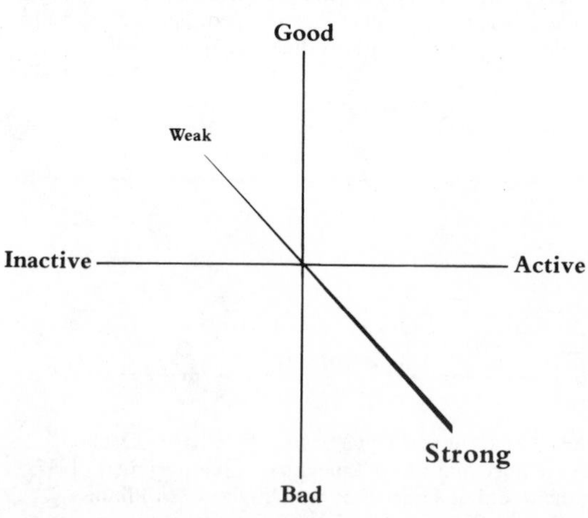

Figure 6.5. Three-dimensional semantic space.

of attitude change. His semantic differential technique has often been used in attitude research because his concept of meaning is similar to that of attitude. We will return to this issue again in Chapter 8.

An interesting epistemological division is found among the theories in this section. Langer and Richards stress the importance of individual interpretation and the personal nature of meaning. Osgood's theory, however, is behavioristic and posits universal factors of meaning. His semantic differential epitomizes the behaviorist penchant for "discovering" and "measuring" dimensions of existing reality. This fundamental difference illustrates clearly how a theorist's assumptions about knowledge shape the sort of claims made and methods used. Richards and Langer, assuming rich individual differences in personal knowledge, attempt to capture idiosyncratic aspects of representational meaning. Osgood, in contrast, seeks the generalized forms of meaning that cut across situations and cultures.

Criticism of Representational Theories

The basic criticism of representational theories as a group is one of scope. No one denies that there is a grain of truth in these theories, but they are indicted for being overly simple. The notion that words are taken to represent referents is obvious and uninteresting, according to critics.[24] These theories are word-centered and tell us little of how meaning arises and develops in the communicative process. Critics believe that the most important aspects of meaning are beyond the word level. Langer identifies the higher discursive level but does not develop it. In the next section theories from ordinary language philosophy represent one attempt to deal with meaning on a higher level.

Osgood's theory of sematic space, because of its method, has incurred a different kind of criticism, related mainly to validity.[25] Although most behavioral researchers admit the usefulness of semantic differential technique for measuring a certain aspect of connotative meaning, they question the view that the factors of meaning—evaluation, potency, and activity—are invariant and universal across situations, concepts, and cultures. Although these factors have appeared in an amazingly diverse set of studies, they do not always appear; to suggest that they are universal is a gross overgeneralization. Problems of validity in the use of semantic differential arise from at least two methodological problems.

First, somewhat similar responses may result from the use of a highly structured stimulus situation. The semantic differential always involves adjective scales, and subjects are often presented with many of the same scales in study after study. Subjects may respond more to the form of the instrument than to the real meanings of the concepts. Second, the semantic differential relies heavily on a statistical procedure called factor analysis. This technique shows how the several scales intercorrelate to form factors, but the researcher must subjectively interpret and name the factors. If a theorist such as Osgood believes that three factors are universal, a strong tendency may develop to interpret the factor structure in just that way. In short, the claim that factors of meaning are universal may be the result of a self-fulfilling prophecy.

Ordinary Language Philosophy

Ordinary language philosophy began as a reaction to two earlier movements. One was the representational approach to meaning, and the other was the tradition of propositional meaning. As you have just seen in the last section, representational theories center on the relation-

24. This criticism is developed extensively by Bernard Harrison, *An Introduction to the Philosophy of Language* (New York: St. Martin's Press, 1979). See also Stanley Deetz, "Words without Things: Toward a Social Phenomenology of Language," *Quarterly Journal of Speech* 59 (1973): 40–54.

25. Criticisms, including both positive and negative evaluations of the semantic differential, are summarized in Donald K. Darnell, "Semantic Differentiation," in *Methods of Research in Communication*, ed. Philip Emmert and William Brooks (Boston: Houghton Mifflin, 1970), pp. 181–96.

ship between symbols and referents. The propositional school looks to the sentence for meaning; it finds the source of meaning to be the logical structure of propositions, or claims. This approach does not consider how a statement is actually being used in interaction. Ordinary language philosophers believe that the most important aspect of meaning is not found in the reference of words or in formal logic but in the way language is used. Speech *acts*, not *forms*, are the most important factors of communication meaning.

Foundations: Wittgenstein and Austin

Ludwig Wittgenstein, a German philosopher, was the originator of ordinary language philosophy. His early works were strongly in the propositional tradition, but he repudiated this approach in one of the most dramatic turnarounds in modern philosophy.[26] He later taught that the meaning of language depends on the context of use. Further, single words by themselves are rarely meaningful. Language, as used in ordinary life, constitutes a *language game*. In other words, people follow rules for accomplishing verbal acts. Giving and obeying orders, asking and answering questions, describing events are examples of ordinary uses of language that follow rules and hence constitute language games.

While the philosophical groundwork of ordinary language philosophy was laid by Wittgenstein, J. L. Austin developed the basic concepts of what his protégé, John Searle, later called speech acts.[27] Austin designates three types of speech acts. A *locutionary act* involves saying something that has referential meaning. It is equivalent to the utterance itself without considering the speaker's intentions. Philosophers of the propositional school center all of their efforts on the analysis of such acts. An *illocutionary act* involves saying something with the force of communicating an intention. An illocution is taken as a warning, a compliment, a reprimand, a promise, and so forth. A *perlocutionary act* is one designed to affect the feelings, attitudes, beliefs, or behaviors of listeners.[28] The latter two types of acts, which are clearly most important for Austin, are marked by the use of certain *performative verbs*. These verbs literally name the act being accomplished by the utterance. Such verbs as *name, assert, promise, ask* or *thank* guide the observer to understand the intentions of the speaker. These concepts are discussed in more detail in the next section on speech acts.

Searle's Theory of Speech Acts

Building on the foundation laid by Wittgenstein and Austin, John Searle developed the well-known theory of speech acts.[29] Although Searle is not solely responsible for speech act theory, he is clearly the leader of the movement, and his name is most often associated with the theory.

The *speech act* is the basic unit of language for expressing meaning. It is an utterance that expresses an intention. Normally the speech act is a sentence, but it can be a word or phrase, so long as it follows the rules necessary to accomplish the intention (or in Wittgenstein's

26. Wittgenstein's best known early work was *Tractus Logico-Philosophicus* (London: Routledge and Kegan Paul, 1922); his later work, which forms the foundation for ordinary language philosophy, is *Philosophical Investigations* (Oxford: Basil Blackwell, 1953). I have relied on the excellent summary by David Silverman and Brian Torode, *The Material Word: Some Theories of Language and Its Limits* (London: Routledge and Kegan Paul, 1980).

27. J. L. Austin, *How to Do Things with Words* (Cambridge: Harvard University Press, 1962); Austin, *Philosophy of Language* (Englewood Cliffs, N.J.: Prentice-Hall, 1964).

28. Perlocutionary acts are undeveloped in speech act literature. For a development of this concept, see Robert N. Gaines, "Doing by Saying: Toward a Theory of Perlocution," *Quarterly Journal of Speech* 65 (1979): 207–17.

29. John Searle, *Speech Acts: An Essay in the Philosophy of Language* (Cambridge: Cambridge University Press, 1969); Searle, "Human Communication Theory and the Philosophy of Language," in *Human Communication Theory*, ed. Frank Dance (New York: Holt, Rinehart and Winston, 1967), pp. 116–29. Good secondary sources include John Stewart, "Concepts of Language and Meaning: A Comparative Study," *Quarterly Journal of Speech* 58 (1972): 123–33; Paul N. Campbell, "A Rhetorical View of Locutionary, Illocutionary, and Perlocutionary Acts," *Quarterly Journal of Speech* 59 (1973): 284–96; Gaines, "Doing by Saying"; and Silverman and Torode, *The Material Word*, pp. 203–25.

terms, to play the language game). We will discuss rules in speech acts momentarily; for now let us turn our attention to the nature of speech acts. When one speaks, one performs an act. The act may involve stating, questioning, commanding, promising, or any of a number of other acts. Speech therefore is conceived of as a form of action or intentional behavior. If we relate this discussion to the previous chapter, we see that while Chomsky is interested in language *competence*, Searle is interested in language *performance*.

What, then, is *meaning* from the standpoint of speech act theory? Meaning is roughly the same as intention. The speaker means something, when he or she performs a speech act, and the performing of a speech act is an attempt to communicate one's intention to another person. An important part of the meaning of a speech act is that the recipient understand the speaker's intention. Unlike the representational view of meaning, speech act theory does not stress the individual referents of symbols but the intent of the act as a whole. If you make a promise, you are communicating an intention about something you will do in the future; but more importantly, you are expecting the other communicator to realize from what you have said what your intention is.

Searle's classification, essentially the same as Austin's but slightly different, divides speech acts into four types. The first is an *utterance act*. Such acts are the simple pronunciation of words, singly or in combination. Here the intention is to utter, nothing more. An example is an actor doing voice exercises. The *propositional act* is what Austin refers to as a locution. It is the utterance of a sentence with the intention of expressing a reference. In other words, the individual wishes to make an association between a subject and verb or to designate an object and refer this object to something else. An *illocutionary act* is designed to fulfill an intention vis-à-vis another person. Here one uses the speech act to elicit response in another. Finally, the *perlocutionary act* is one designed to have effects or consequences in other peoples' behavior. Since the difference between illocution and perlocution is sometimes hard to grasp, let's pursue it a little further.

An illocution is an act in which the speaker's primary concern is that the listener understand the speaker's intention. A perlocution is an act in which the speaker not only expects the listener to understand but to act in a particular way because of that understanding. If I say, "I am thirsty," with the intention of having you understand that I need a drink, I am performing an illocutionary act. If I make the same statement expecting you to bring me a glass of water, my act is perlocutionary. These four kinds of acts are highly interrelated and often are uttered simultaneously.

Now let us pursue propositional acts and illocutionary acts in more detail. The proposition can be understood as one aspect of the content of an illocution. It designates some quality or association of an object, situation, or event. *The cake is good, Salt is harmful to the body, Her name is Karen* are all examples of propositions. Propositions can be evaluated in terms of their truth value. The logical relationship of one proposition to another can also be examined. These are the proper tasks of the propositional school referred to earlier. In speech act theory, however, truth and logic are not considered important. Rather, the question is what a speaker intends to do by uttering a proposition. The meaning of an illocutionary act is determined in part by establishing how the speaker wishes others to take the stated proposition. Hence, for Searle, propositions must always be viewed as part of a larger context, the illocution. Searle would be interested in acts such as the following: I *ask* whether the cake is good; I *warn* you that salt is harmful to the body; I *state* that her name is Karen. What the speaker is doing with the proposition is the speech act, and how the proposition is to be taken by the audience is the *illocutionary force* of the statement. You could, for example, state the proposition *The cake is good* in such a way as to have the listener realize that you were speaking ironically, meaning to imply just the opposite: This cake is the worst I ever ate.

Searle states fundamentally that "speaking a language is engaging in a rule-governed form of behavior."[30] In Chapter 4 we mentioned that speech act theory is one of the primary applications of rules theory. Two types of rules are important. *Constitutive rules* create new forms of behavior; that is, acts are created by the establishment of rules. For example, football as a game exists only by virtue of its rules. The rules constitute the game. When you observe people following a certain set of rules, you know the game of football is being played. These rules therefore tell you what to interpret as football. In speech acts, one's intention is largely understood by another person by virtue of constitutive rules, because these rules tell others what to count as a particular kind of act. An example is provided in the next paragraph. The second kind of rule is regulative. *Regulative rules* provide guidelines for acting out already established behavior. The behaviors are known and available before being used in the act, and the regulative rules tell one how to use the behaviors to accomplish a particular intention. For example, a host often opens the door for a guest who is leaving.

As an example of the use of constitutive rules, let us look at one of Searle's extended analyses of a speech act, the act of making a promise. Promising involves five basic rules. First, promising involves uttering a sentence that indicates the speaker will do some future act (*propositional content rule*). Second, the sentence is uttered only if the listener would rather that the speaker do the act than not do it (*preparatory rule*). Third, a statement is a promise only when it would not otherwise be obvious to the speaker and hearer that the act would be done in the normal course of events (*preparatory rule*). Fourth, the speaker must intend to do the act (*sincerity rule*). Finally, a promise involves the establishment of an obligation for the speaker to do the act (*essential rule*). These five rules "constitute" a sufficient set of conditions for an act to count as a promise.

Any illocutionary act must have the basic kinds of rules named in parentheses above. The propositional content rule specifies some condition of the referenced object. Preparatory rules involve the presumed preconditions in the speaker and hearer necessary for the act to take place. The sincerity rule requires the speaker to mean what is said. (In the case of insincere illocutions, the act is presented in such a way that the listener presumes the speaker actually intends what he or she says is intended.) The essential rule states that the act is indeed taken by the hearer and speaker to represent what it appears to be on the face. Of course, many acts are not successful in these ways, and speech acts can be evaluated in terms of the degree to which they meet these criteria. Searle believes that speech acts may be defective; Austin calls a defective act an infelicity. These constitutive rules are believed to apply to a wide variety of illocutionary acts, including at least requesting, asserting, questioning, thanking, advising, warning, greeting, and congratulating.

Although many speech acts are direct, involving the use of an explicit proposition that clearly states the intention, other speech acts are indirect. For example, in requesting that his family come to the table, a father might say, "Is anybody hungry?" On the face this appears to be a question, but in actuality it is a request.

Searle outlines five types of illocutionary acts. The first is called *assertives*. An assertive is a statement of a proposition that commits the speaker to advocate the truth of the proposition. In direct form such acts might contain such performative verbs as state, affirm, conclude, believe, and so forth. *Directives* are illocutions that attempt to get the listener to do something. They are commands, requests, pleadings, prayers, entreaties, invitations, and so forth. *Commissives* commit the speaker to a future act. They consist of such acts as promising, vowing, pledging, contracting, guaranteeing, and so forth. *Expressives* are acts that communicate some aspect of the speaker's

30. Searle, *Speech Acts*, p. 22

psychological state. They include thanking, congratulating, apologizing, condoling, welcoming, and others. Finally, a *declaration* is designed to create a proposition that, by its very assertion, makes it so. Examples include appointing, marrying, firing, resigning, and so forth.

Criticism of Ordinary Language Philosophy

The obvious strength of ordinary language philosophy is that it takes the analysis of language out of the realm of the formal and structural and into the arena of actual use. Ironically, its primary weakness may be that it has not done enough to show how language-in-use operates in ongoing communication.[31] This problem is discussed in terms of three related criteria of theory evaluation: scope, validity, and heuristic value.

Critics point out that despite its broad claims and qualifications to the contrary, speech act analysis is narrow in scope. It focuses on the structure of utterances as indicators of their intentional meanings. Austin, for example, is more concerned about the apparent inherent implications of performative verbs than he is with speakers' actual purposes in using those verbs or with listeners' actual interpretations.

Although some critics agree that intentions are an important aspect of meaning, that speech constitutes a form of action, and that speech acts are governed by rules, they argue that the conceptual categories of speech act theory are vague or meaningless. Austin's three-fold distinction among locutionary, illocutionary, and perlocutionary acts has been severely criticized from this standpoint. One critic states: "And now Austin has, in my judgment, erected a structure that is in imminent danger of collapse."[32] His three-fold analysis is criticized for being unclear. Critics question the utility of locution as a concept if the utterance of a locution automatically constitutes an illocution, as Austin claims it does. The distinction between illocutionary and perlocutionary acts is equally unclear to many readers, who point out that even if one could observe the difference among these concepts, it is doubtful that they constitute a useful conceptual framework for guiding our understanding of speech acts. It would perhaps be more fruitful to recogize that any given speech act may be fulfilling a variety of intents and may be taken in a variety of different ways by different listeners. Conceptually, the terms *illocution* and *perlocution* may apply more directly to types of force and effects than to types of acts per se.

The distinction between regulative and constitutive rules is equally fuzzy.[33] The problem here is that once any act becomes standardized, as in the case of almost all illocutionary acts, rules no longer are constitutive in the sense of creating new acts. Hence, rules that regulate can be taken as constitutive, and rules that constitute an act also regulate it.

These apparent weaknesses of scope and validity have lessened the heuristic value of these theories. Little research on communication processes has resulted from the ideas of Wittgenstein, Austin, and Searle, even though on the face, language-in-use would seem to be of great interest. Perhaps the main contribution of this line of theory is a basic idea, an idea that awaits future investigation and development.

Language and Experience

Experiential theories of meaning take the position that the most important aspect of meaning is in the relationship between language and experience. All of these theories share the thesis that language strongly influences the ongoing life and experience of the person. Meaning thus is conceived as the person's knowledge of reality, as shaped by language. Unlike the representational approaches, these theories do not separate the sign, the referent, and the person.

31. A thorough and rather biting critique of Austin can be found in Campbell, "Rhetorical View"; see also Gaines, "Doing by Saying." Critical commentary can also be found in Silverman and Torode, *The Material Word*, and Harrison, *Introduction*.

32. Campbell, "Rhetorical View," p. 287.

33. Susan B. Shimanoff, *Communication Rules: Theory and Research* (Beverly Hills, CA: Sage 1980), pp. 84–85.

They place the three as being so closely intertwined that they must be viewed together. There are numerous experiential approaches to meaning. Two major experiential theories are presented here for illustration: Cassirer's theory of symbolic forms and Whorf's theory of linguistic relativity.

Cassirer's Philosophy of Symbolic Forms

Ernst Cassirer is one of the best-known language philosophers of our age. Cassirer was a German philosopher who wrote during the first half of this century. As an epistemologist he believed that the human mind can be understood only through an investigation of symbolic processes, and he devoted his life to exploring this topic. *The Philosophy of Symbolic Forms*, published in the 1920s, is his largest single work and the one most concerned with language and meaning.[34] *An Essay on Man*, perhaps his best known work, also deals in part with symbolism.[35]

For Cassirer language is intimately tied to the human mind. The important human quality of language is *meaning*. Cassirer believes that language cannot be studied from afar as a natural object might be studied. It must be approached phenomenologically through the mind and meanings of the person.

Human beings experience the world through symbols; symbolic representation is inherent to our perception. Languages and other symbolic forms structure reality for us, but we are not stuck in an inflexible position because of some preordained linguistic straitjacket. People must confront natural forces, and thus their language must adapt to "reality." What Cassirer seems to be saying is that language and nature interact. Our language and other symbolic forms influence how we perceive; at the same time, what we perceive may influence our symbolic forms.[36]

A culture's predominant symbolic forms shape both the culture's expression and perception. Cassirer, in *The Philosophy of Symbolic Forms*, discusses four major forms: *myth, art, common language, and science*.[37] Myth and art, like primitive language, are highly personal and feeling-centered forms. Myth is a primitive, nonlogical, value-centered form. The values it expresses include life, power, violence, evil, and death. These values are emotionally charged. Myth, therefore, does not lead to understanding of concepts but to a deep sense of identification among the people of a culture. As Langer describes it: "Mythic symbols do not even appear to be symbols; they appear as holy objects or places or being, and their import is felt as an inherent power."[38] Recalling Cassirer's basic theme of the symbol-mediated nature of reality, Langer continues: "This is not 'make-believe,' not a willful or playful distortion of a radically different 'given fact,' but is *the way phenomena are given* to naive apprehension."[39] At this level the person sees the meaning of the symbol as intrinsic in the form itself: "In savage societies, names are treated as though they were physical proxies for their bearers."[40]

Cassirer did not write much about art, but art is similar to myth—highly personal and feeling centered. Neither myth nor art forms are very abstract. Unlike scientific forms their

34. Ernst Cassirer, *The Philosophy of Symbolic Forms*, 3 vols. (Berlin: Bruno Cassirer, 1923, 1925, 1929). Several secondary sources are available, including Carl H. Hamburg, *Symbol and Reality* (The Hague: Martinus Nijhoff, 1970); Seymour W. Itzkoff, *Ernst Cassirer: Scientific Knowledge and the Concept of Man* (Notre Dame: University of Notre Dame Press, 1971); Paul Schilpp, ed., *The Philosophy of Ernst Cassirer* (New York: Tudor Publishing, 1949). For a short overview see Wilbur Urban, "Cassirer's Philosophy of Language," in Schlipp, *The Philosophy of Ernst Cassirer*, pp. 403–41.

35. Ernst Cassirer, *An Essay on Man* (New Haven: Yale University Press, 1944).

36. This interpretation is further developed in Itzkoff, *Ernst Cassirer*, pp. 115–18, 138.

37. Explanations of these can be found in Susanne K. Langer, "On Cassirer's Theory of Language and Myth," in *The Philosophy of Ernst Cassirer*, ed. Paul Schlipp (New York: Tudor Publishing, 1949), pp. 387–90; Itzkoff, *Ernst Cassirer*, pp. 105–8; Urban, "Cassirer's Philosophy of Language," p. 420–30.

38. Langer, "On Cassirer's Theory," p. 388.

39. Ibid., p. 389.

40. Ibid., p. 390.

meanings are rather fixed in the feeling of the moment.

Science, the highest symbolic form, develops late in the evolution of a culture. Unlike the primitive mythical form, it facilitates abstract thought. Scientific forms mediate reality just as primitive forms do, but the scientist recognizes this fact. Mathematics, the ultimate scientific form, is so distant from the sensory experience that it symbolizes pure relations rather than things.

The fourth form, language, is intimately related to the other three. Cassirer shows how language evolves from a primitive state similar to myth to an advanced state similar to science. Language passes through three stages. In the *mimetic stage*, the language is tied to individual perceptions of the moment. Like mythical forms meaning at this stage varies little and lacks the abstraction necessary for concept formation and logical thinking. The second stage is *analogic*. At this stage the language begins to move away from a strict one-to-one relationship with things. People begin to use sounds more in terms of analogy to the real world rather than identifying objects with sounds.

The most advanced stage in language development is *symbolic*. At the symbolic stage grammar develops. Word meanings are broad enough to allow a range of conceptions to be possible. Thus perception itself is widened. The person becomes more creative and adaptive. Only at this advanced stage can science develop. In summary the history of language is one of ever increasing abstraction. As language develops, meaning is broadened from a strict sensory, here-and-now identification to forms that allow for multiple meanings and interrelationships.

Cassirer's notions on the relationship of language to thought are largely influenced by his observations of aphasics at a neurological institute. Our symbol-processing abilities allow us to see relationships and to think through actions. People who have lost their symbol-processing abilities cannot operate on an abstract level. At low levels of abstraction, the person is bound to the immediate sensory experience. Here is an example: "The contrast between normal man, who lives in a world of mediated signs and meanings, and the apractic, who must aim at a direct goal for his actions, is exemplified by the fact that many apractics who under ordinary conditions could not pour themselves a glass of water when asked, do so spontaneously when thirsty. The multitude of individual and mediated symbolic steps between the request to pour the water and the actual act is too overwhelming for them to integrate and respond normally."[41]

Meaning therefore seems to involve two important attributes, made possible by symbolic processes: gestalt perception (seeing wholes and interrelationships) and thought or mental action apart from the immediate presence of the sensuous object.

In short, Cassirer sees meaning as the individual's perceptual and thought worlds mediated by the predominant linguistic and nonlinguistic symbolic forms of the culture. Cassirer does not break completely with representational theory, but he takes a broader view by showing how symbolic forms create meaning worlds in people by shaping their perception and thinking.

Linguistic Relativity

Another theory that supports this view that language shapes our very being is the *Sapir-Whorf hypothesis*, otherwise known as the theory of *linguistic relativity*. Although the method and origin of the relativity hypothesis is distant from that of Cassirer, its assumptions about language and meaning are much the same. This theory[42] is based on the work of Edward Sapir and his protégé Benjamin Lee

41. Itzkoff, *Ernst Cassirer*, p. 132.

42. Edward Sapir, *Language: An Introduction to the Study of Speech* (New York: Harcourt, Brace & World, 1921); Benjamin Whorf, *Language, Thought, and Reality* (New York: John Wiley and Sons, 1956). In the previous volume the following articles are most helpful: John B. Carroll, "Introduction," pp. 1–34; "The Relation of Habitual Thought and Behavior in Language," pp. 134–359; "Language, Mind, and Reality," pp. 246–69.

Whorf. Whorf is best known for his fieldwork in linguistics; his analysis of the Hopi is particularly well known. In his research Whorf discovered that fundamental syntactical differences are present among language groups. The Whorfian hypothesis of linguistic relativity simply states that *the structure of a culture's language determines the behavior and habits of thinking in that culture*. In the words of Edward Sapir:

Human beings do not live in the objective world alone, nor alone in the world of social activity as ordinarily understood, but are very much at the mercy of the particular language which has become the medium of expression for their society. It is quite an illusion to imagine that one adjusts to reality essentially without the use of language and that language is merely an incidental means of solving specific problems of communication or reflection. The fact of the matter is that the "real world" is to a large extent unconsciously built up on the language habits of the group. . . . We see and hear and otherwise experience very largely as we do because the language habits of our community predispose certain choices of interpretation.[43]

This hypothesis suggests that our thought processes and the way we see the world are shaped by the grammatical structure of the language. As one reviewer reacted, "All one's life one has been tricked . . . by the structure of language into a certain way of perceiving reality."[44]

Whorf spent much of his life investigating the relationship of language and behavior. His work with the Hopi illustrates the relativity hypothesis. Like all cultural groups the Hopi possess a *thought-world microcosm*, which represents their view of the world at large or *macrocosm*. One area of Whorf's extensive analysis of Hopi thought is the analysis of time. While many cultures refer to points in time (for example, seasons) as nouns, the Hopi conceive of time as a passage or process. Thus the Hopi language never objectifies time. A Hopi would not refer to summer as "in the summer." Instead, the Hopi would refer to the passing or coming of a phase that is never here and now but always moving, accumulating. In our culture three tenses indicate locations or places in a spatial analogy: past, present, and future. Hopi verbs have no tense in the same sense. Instead, their verb forms relate to duration and order. In the Standard Average European languages (SAE), including English, we visualize time as a line. The Hopi conception is more complex, as illustrated in the following example.[45]

Suppose that a speaker reports to a hearer that a third person is running: "He is running." The Hopi would use the word *wari*, which is a statement of running as a fact. The same word would be used for a report of past running, "He ran." For the Hopi the statement of fact (validity) is what is important, not whether the event is presently occurring or happened in the past. If, however, the Hopi speaker wished to report a past event of running from memory (the hearer did not actually see it), a different form would be used, *era wari*. The English sentence, "He will run," would translate *warikni*, which communicates running as a statement of expectation. Again, it is not the location in past, present, or future that is important to the Hopi, but the nature of validity (observed fact, recalled fact, or expectation). Another English form, "He runs [on the track team]," would translate *warikngwe*. This latter Hopi form again refers to running, but in the sense of law or condition.

As a result of these linguistic differences, Hopi and SAE cultures will think about, perceive, and behave toward time differently. For example, the Hopi tend to engage in lengthy preparing activities. Experiences (getting prepared) tend to accumulate as time "gets later." The emphasis is on the accumulated experience during the course of time, not on time as a point or location. In SAE cultures, with their spatial treatment of time, experiences are not accumulated in the same sense. Elaborate and lengthy

43. Quoted in Whorf, *Language, Thought, and Reality*, p. 134.

44. Carroll, "Introduction," p. 27.

45. Adapted from Whorf, *Language, Thought, and Reality*, p. 213.

preparations are not often found. The custom in SAE cultures is to record events (space-time analogy) such that what happened in the past is objectified in space (recorded). Whorf summarizes this view: "Concepts of 'time' and 'matter' are not given in substantially the same form by experience to all men but depend upon the nature of the language or languages through the use of which they have been developed."[46]

We have now looked at three senses of meaning. In the first meaning is seen as a representation of some object, occurrence, or condition. The theories that espouse this view outline three distinct elements: the object, the sign, and the person. The second approach views meaning as intention. Theories in the third approach stress the idea that symbols so heavily influence the experience of the person that they cannot be separated from human experience. Here we see a major departure from the traditional view that meaning is in the person and is elicited by signs.

Criticism of Experiential Theory

Experiential theories provide a general attitude toward language and meaning. Their strength is that they remind us of the centrality of individual human experience in meaning.

The problem is that once we understand and accept their premises, we are not sure where to take them to deepen our understanding of the phenomena under study. They keep generalization and development of substantive theory out of reach. If meaning is so wrapped up in personal experience, how do we separate it from individual experience long enough to apprehend it? How do researchers and theorists transcend their own linguistic experience to understand the process as a whole? Experiential theories provide little in the way of substantive understanding of the nature of language as language or of meaning processes.

The strength of Whorfian theory is that it goes beyond philosophical claims to make theoretical generalizations about how language operates in cultural experience. Whorf and Sapir's claims, however, are extreme. One commentator writes that this theory promotes two horrors: the horror of helplessness, that people are helplessly trapped by their language, and the horror of hopelessness, that there is no hope for communication across cultures.[47] A good deal of linguistic research challenges the validity of these claims. Recall the concept of language universals from the last chapter. Chomsky believes that the essential features of language are anything but culturally bound. Osgood too believes that he has found universal factors of meaning and that these definitely are not determined by cultural factors.

46. Ibid., p. 158.

What Do We Know about Meaning?

The human being brings a wealth of experience to any communication event. People use language to share this experience. The correlation between language and experience is *meaning*, which is such a big part of communication studies as to constitute a domain of its own. Scholarship on meaning is highly speculative and rests largely on philosophical argument and anecdotal observation. This is not to suggest that meaning theory is trivial or unimportant. Indeed, some of the greatest minds in philosophy have grappled with the nature of meaning. This area is controversial because a particular idea of meaning often reflects a particular ontology or set of beliefs about the nature of being. Much of this controversy is needless. Meaning itself is an abstract concept; and consequently it can be applied legitimately in a variety of ways. Even in everyday life we use the term in different ways. We say that we had a *meaningful* experience, or we question the *meaning* of a word, or we deny another person's misinterpretation of our intentions by saying that we didn't *mean* it that way.

Most theories of meaning contain a grain (or

47. Joshua Fishman, "A Systemization of the Whorfian Hypothesis," *Behavioral Science* 5 (1960): 323–39.

boulder) of truth. They have greater potential for integrating the various notions of meaning than implied by their advocates. Such an integration can be accomplished by using a multidimensional model of meaning, consisting of at least three factors.

First, meaning has a *referential* aspect. Clearly words and other symbols are taken to represent objects, situations, conditions, or states. Communication itself could not occur without shared symbolic references. The problem in meaning theory is not that the notion of meaning as reference is wrong, but that it is inadequate by itself to explain the complexity of meaning.

Thus a second dimension needs to be added to the model, the *experiential* aspect of meaning. This dimension emphasizes that meaning is largely a matter of experience. How one experiences the world is determined in part by the meanings one attaches to symbols of objects in the world. At the same time that very experience shapes our meanings. We use symbols to affect and adapt to our environment by expressing our experience; at the same time meanings attached to language affect how we experience the environment.

A third dimension complicates our conception even more. This is the *purposive* dimension, which implies that human's intentions vis-à-vis others are an important aspect of meaning. We fulfill purposes in using language and other symbols, and our intentions shape the way symbols are understood.

Given the extensiveness of the domains of language and meaning and their multidisciplinary nature, it is not surprising that these areas are epistemologically mixed. Most philosophical theories of meaning now in vogue treat meaning as relative and subjective, recognizing the individuality of experiential meanings. However, this observation is not true of all philosophical approaches; some philosophers seek universal meaning structures. Some psychologists too have treated meaning as an objective event, attempting to measure it and discover its operational characteristics.

Postscript

Clearly language and meaning are domains that are central to the process of communication, yet difficult to understand. They are multifaceted, involving many different dimensions, and thus they present us with a paradox. They are at the heart of all human communication, yet they seem to be just beyond our grasp to define and explain. It is obvious from the material presented in the last two chapters that controversies abound among theorists of language and meaning. Many of the issues are epistemological; others are substantive. Once again we are faced with the realization that the most fruitful way to gain a fuller understanding and appreciation for elements of human communication is to apply multiple perspectives, each of which presents particular insights that together enlighten the subject.

With the full recognition that evaluative generalizations are difficult and risky in domains as huge as these, we can make some parting judgments. This area of theory contains a wide variety of related concepts. Yet, ironically, the theories of language, nonverbal coding, and meaning remain for the most part isolated and separated from one another. In the domains of language and meaning we see a clear example of the disadvantages of single-discipline and overly specialized approaches to the study of communication. For example, many linguists, in their focus on the complexities of grammar, have ignored obvious connections between linguistic and other social processes. Language often is treated as a phenomenon apart from communication. Likewise, researchers of nonverbal communication too often separate nonlinguistic codes from the larger coding complex, focusing undue attention on small parts of an inseparable whole. Because of the heretofore disjointed nature of this work, integrative theories such as that of Pearce and Cronen (Chapter 4) are especially attractive.

Of course any criticism of language and meaning must be tempered with the qualification that these phenomena are extremely difficult to study. We will never be able to observe deep processes of language generation or meaning directly, making this kind of study a speculative business. Researchers must make inferences about unseen processes based on observable behaviors. The trick is to come up with a picture of underlying phenomena that account for patterns of observed behavior. Thus linguists must provide explanations that account for actual speech. Early language theory failed to do this, but more recent developments in generative grammar have been successful in providing a credible theory of language.

The challenge of meaning theory is somewhat different. Issues in meaning theory are largely semantic. The major disagreements deal with the meaning of meaning. Indeed, meaning theorists have not been able to agree on what to observe to make inferences about meaning because they cannot agree on what meaning is!

Hopefully, these last two chapters have provided a modicum of clarity to an otherwise muddy river. We move now to a discussion of the effects of language and meaning in the realms of information and persuasion.

CHAPTER

7 Theories of Information and Information Processing

Information is an important element in the communication process. The essential feature of all messages is information, and people use the information in messages to reduce uncertainty and thereby adapt to the environment. This chapter is divided into two parts. The first part reviews ideas that have been labeled *information theory*. Although information theory has less direct applicability to communication than do some of the other theories in this book, it establishes certain foundational definitions that lie at the base of much of our current thinking about communication. The second part of the chapter reviews some theories of *information processing*, which deal with how humans handle information they receive from the environment. The first section provides important concepts of information as a commodity, and the second section helps us understand how people use information in their lives.

Information Theory

In an early article on the mathematical theory of communication, Warren Weaver suggests three fruitful areas of concern for information theory.[1] The first, the *technical* level of information, concerns the accuracy and efficiency of information transmission. The second, the *semantic* level, relates to the meanings of information to individuals. Finally, the *effectiveness* level deals with the influence of information on the receiver of communication. The first section of this chapter is organized into three parts corresponding to Weaver's three levels of information. The first part discusses classical information theory, which is designed as a tool for developing transmissional devices. The second part deals with the semantics of information, and the third presents a theory of information effects.

Information theory, which is primarily a mathematical formulation, grew out of the postwar boom in the telecommunications industry. A perspective that focuses on the *measurement* of information, it deals with the quantitative study of information in messages and the flow of information between senders and receivers. It has extremely practical applications in the electronic sciences of communication that have a need for computing information quantities and designing channels, transmitters, receivers, and codes that facilitate efficient handling of information. Before we get into the core concepts of information theory, let's discuss the development of the movement.[2]

Information theory developed out of investigations in physics, engineering, and mathematics, which were concerned with the organization among occurrences. The common thread among these rather independent investigations was the realization that organization is a matter of probability. (One of the developments at this time was cybernetics. As you recall from Chapter 3, Wiener's work in this area relied heavily on communication engineering.[3]) The primary work that crystallized information theory was that of Claude Shannon, a telecommunications

1. Warren Weaver, "The Mathematics of Communication," *Scientific American* 181 (1949): 11–15.

2. Several brief histories of the movement are available. See, for example, Wendell R. Garner, *Uncertainty and Structure as Psychological Concepts* (New York: John Wiley & Sons, 1962), p. 8.

3. Norbert Wiener, *Cybernetics or Control and Communication in the Animal and Machine* (Cambridge: M.I.T. Press, 1948).

engineer at the Bell Telephone Laboratories. His classic book with Warren Weaver, *The Mathematical Theory of Communication*, is the basic source for information theory.[4]

Technical Information Theory

Basic Concepts. Information theory provides a precise definition of *information*. Perhaps it is easier to understand information by starting with a related concept, *entropy*, borrowed from thermodynamics. Entropy is randomness, or lack of organization in a situation. A totally entropic situation is unpredictable. Because of the entropy in the situation, you cannot know what will happen next. Entropy is best thought of as variable. Most of the situations you are confronted with are partially predictable. If black clouds come over the sky, you might predict rain, and you would probably be right. Because weather is an organized system, certain probable relationships (for example, clouds and rain) exist. On the other hand, you cannot predict rain conclusively. The entropy existing in the situation causes some uncertainty. In short, the more entropy, the less organization and predictability.

What does this have to do with information? *Information is a measure of uncertainty, or entropy, in a situation*. The greater the uncertainty, the more the information. When a situation is completely predictable, no information is present. Most people associate information with certainty or knowledge; consequently, this definition from information theory can be confusing. As used by the information theorist, the concept does not refer to a message, facts, or meaning. It is a concept bound only to the quantification of stimuli or signals in a situation.

On closer examination, this idea of information is not as distant from common sense as it first appears. We have said that information is the amount of uncertainty in the situation. Another way of thinking of it is to consider information as the number of *messages* required to completely reduce the uncertainty in the situation. For example, your friend is about to flip a coin. Will it land heads up or tails up? You are uncertain, you cannot predict. This uncertainty, which results from the entropy in the situation, will be eliminated by seeing the result of the flip. Now let's suppose that you have received a tip that your friend's coin is two headed. The flip is "fixed." There is no uncertainty and therefore no information. In other words, you could not receive any message that would make you predict any better than you already have. In short, a situation with which you are completely familiar has no information for you.

We have now related information to uncertainty and to the number of messages necessary to reduce uncertainty. There is yet a third way to view information. Information can be thought of as the number of *choices* or *alternatives* available to a person in predicting the outcome of a situation. In a complex situation of many possible outcomes, more information is available than in a simple situation with few outcomes. In other words, a person would need more messages to predict the outcome of a complex situation than to predict the outcome of a simple one. For example, there is more information in a two-dice toss than in the toss of a single die and more information in a single-die toss than in a coin flip. Since information is a function of the number of alternatives, it reflects the degree of freedom in making choices within a situation. The more information in a situation, the freer you are to choose alternatives within that situation.

The idea of information will become clearer after you understand the unit of information, the *bit*. Bit stands for *binary digit*. A bit is a unit

4. Claude Shannon and Warren Weaver, *The Mathematical Theory of Communication* (Urbana: University of Illinois Press, 1949). For a number of excellent brief secondary sources, see the bibliography. Two sources were particularly helpful in the preparation of this chapter: Allan R. Broadhurst and Donald K. Darnell, "An Introduction to Cybernetics and Information Theory," *Quarterly Journal of Speech* 51 (1965): 442–53; Klaus Krippendorf, "Information Theory," in *Communication and Behavior*, ed. G. Hanneman and W. McEwen (Reading, Mass.: Addison-Wesley, 1975), 351–89.

used for counting alternatives. Technically, the number of bits in a situation of equally possible outcomes is equal to the number of times the outcomes would be halved in order to reduce the uncertainty to zero.

Consider the following family tree. One of the members of this family has committed a murder for a crime syndicate. As far as you can tell, all family members are equally suspect. How much information is in this situation?

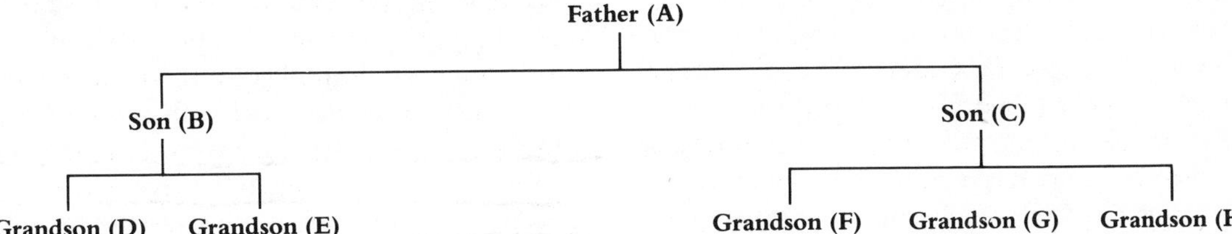

First, you discover that Son (B) and his family (D and E) were on vacation on the other side of the world when the crime took place. They took Father (A) with them. This message provides one bit of information, since it eliminates half of the alternatives (A, B, D, and E). Further, you discover that Son (C) and Grandson (F) were at home, fighting, at the time of the murder. This alibi provides a second bit of information, halving the possibilities again. Then you find out that G died a year ago, providing a third bit of information. Thus you see that this situation has three bits of information.

This example is a *combinatorial* approach to counting bits. The approach, which assumes that each alternative is equally probable, is excellent for getting across the meaning of the information theorist's conception of information, but it is not realistic. Often some alternatives have a higher probability of occurring than others. When this happens, the *statistical* approach is necessary for computing bits.[5] The statistical approach recognizes that as certain alternatives increase in probability, entropy or uncertainty decreases. Thus the less equal the probability of occurrence, the less the information. In the example of the killer, suppose H were a more probable killer than any of the others, based on past record. Hypothetically, you might distribute the probabilities as follows: A = .05, B = .05, C = .05, D = .05, E = .05, F = .05, G = .05, H = .65. Plugging these values into a formula shows that the murder situation contains 1.88 bits of information or uncertainty.

Another important concept is *redundancy*. Redundancy is a function of its sister concept, *relative entropy*. Relative entropy is the proportion of entropy present compared with the maximum amount possible. Entropy is maximum when all alternatives are equally probable. Let's look again at our example. The number of bits of uncertainty is 1.88. The maximum uncertainty possible is 3. Therefore, the relative entropy in this situation is

$$1.88/3 = .62 \text{ or } 62\%$$

The redundancy is

$$1 - .62 = .38 \text{ or } 38\%$$

In qualitative terms redundancy is the proportion of a situation that is predictable; it is a measure of certainty. In a relation if one alternative follows from another, it is predictable and therefore redundant.

Information Transmission. Now that we have summarized the basic concepts of information theory, we can move to the first area of concern, the technical level, which deals primarily with the accurate and efficient transmission of information. Technical information theory is not concerned with the meaning of messages, only with their transmission and reception.

5. For a good distinction between these, see Krippendorf, "Information Theory."

This application is particularly important in electronic communication.

The basic model of communication developed by Shannon and Weaver is shown in Figure 7.1.[6] In this model communication begins at the *source*. The source formulates or selects a message, consisting of signs to be transmitted. The *transmitter* converts the message into a set of signals that are sent over a *channel* to a receiver. The *receiver* converts the signals into a message. This model can be applied to a variety of situations. In the electronic arena a television message is a good example. The producers, directors, and announcers constitute the source. The message is transmitted by air waves (channel) to the home receiver, which converts electromagnetic waves back into a visual impression for the viewer. In the interpersonal arena the speaker's brain is the source, the vocal system the transmitter, and the air medium the channel. The listener's ear is the receiver and the listener's brain the destination.

The final element in Shannon and Weaver's model is noise. *Noise* is any disturbance in the channel that distorts or otherwise masks the signal. The disturbance may be, literally, noise in auditory communication, but any kind of interference is included. We will return to this concept momentarily. First, let us integrate information into the model at this point.

In the last section information was defined as a measure of uncertainty in a situation. This definition is general. In information transmission we are concerned with the special case in which the message itself is the "situation." Like any stimulus field a message, consisting of symbols or signs arranged according to rules, has a degree of uncertainty or entropy. This uncertainty (information) is a result of the *code* or language into which the message is *encoded*. Normally, a message is a sequence of stimuli or signs that hit the receiver serially. Ordinary written language is an example. This idea of information can be applied to the predictability of a sequential arrangement such as a sentence. If the letters in the sentence were arranged randomly, there would be 100 percent entropy. *Decoding* would be difficult because of the great amount of information in the message. But letters (or sounds in speech) are not organized randomly. Various predictable patterns are found. These patterns make decoding easier because there is less information, lower relative entropy, and high redundancy. For example, an adjective has a high probability of being followed by a noun. A *q* is always followed by a *u* in English. Thus the overall arrangement of a sentence is patterned and partially predictable. On the other hand, a sentence does contain some information. Redundancy, predictability, is never 100 percent. If it were, there would be no freedom of choice. Once the first letter was written, all other letters would follow auto-

6. Shannon and Weaver, *Mathematical Theory*, p. 5.

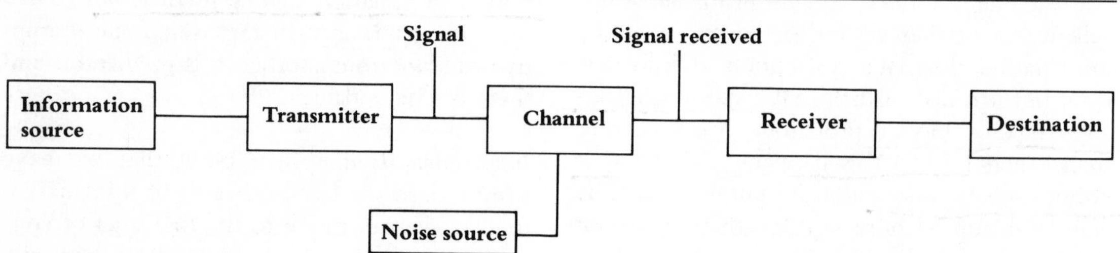

From *The Mathematical Theory of Communication*, by Claude Shannon and Warren Weaver. Copyright © 1949 by the Board of Trustees of the University of Illinois. Reprinted by permission of the University of Illinois Press.

Figure 7.1. Shannon and Weaver's model of communication.

matically. Language is blessed with moderate redundancy, allowing ease in decoding, with freedom of encoding.

Language information is an example of a *Markov process*, in which subsequent alternatives bear a probability relationship to antecedent occurrences in a chain. In a Markov probability situation the probabilities of alternatives occurring vary from moment to moment. In English there is a 100 percent probability that *u* will follow *q*, but the probability is considerably less that an *i* will follow a *t*. Thus in sequential messages we must talk in terms of average relative entropy and average redundancy. The average relative entropy-redundancy of English is about fifty percent.

Whether the message is coded into regular language, electronic signals, or some other verbal or nonverbal code, the problem of transmission is the same—to reconstruct the message accurately at the destination. Any television viewer with poor reception is painfully aware of the problem. Accurate transmission would be no problem were it not for certain factors such as noise.

Now you can begin to see the role of redundancy in a message. Redundancy compensates noise. As noise distorts, masks, or replaces signals, redundancy allows the receiver to correct or fill in missing or distorted stimuli. For example, suppose you receive from a friend a letter that has been smeared by rain. The first sentences might look like this: "How -------yo--? I a--- --ine. Or perhaps because of static, a sentence of radio news comes across as, The Pres----- ----ed States has --clared. . . . You can make some sense out of these distorted sentences because of the predictability or redundancy in the language.

Another factor limiting accurate transmission is channel capacity. Channel capacity is usually defined in terms of the maximum amount of information that can be transmitted over a channel per second.

What, then, is necessary for accurate transmission? Accurate transmission involves coding at a maximum rate that will not exceed channel capacity. It also means using a code with sufficient redundancy to compensate the amount of noise present in the channel. If there is too much redundancy, transmission will be inefficient; if too little, it will be inaccurate.

The major contribution of classical information theory to human sciences is that the latter have used the technical model as an analogue for modeling interpersonal communication. Witness the fact that Shannon and Weaver's model (Figure 7.1) is one of the most frequently reproduced depictions of communication in textbooks.

Except for this analogue function, information theory has little relevance to any domain outside information per se. It does relate to systems theory by suggesting that system parts are connected to one another through information transmission. It also speaks to the technical side of mass communication. However, as will be indicated in the criticism section, these incursions into other domains do not help us much to understand the human side of communication.

Semantic Information

To make information theory more relevant to human communication, the notion of semantic information has been developed.[7] To understand this concept, you must shift your thinking slightly. We know that information is a measure of uncertainty in a situation or message. From technical information theory we learn that such information can be transmitted. Now at the semantic level we concentrate on the *communication* of information, which *reduces* the uncertainty in a situation. The information

7. In addition to the theories presented in this chapter, some notable attempts have been made to expand classical information theory into the semantic area. See Y. Bar-Hillel and R. Carnap, "Semantic Information," *British Journal of the Philosophy of Science* 4 (1953): 147–57; and Krippendorf, "Information Theory." Material in this section is taken from Krippendorf.

conveyed by a message that reduces information is called *semantic information*. What is added to the theory at this point is the human element of interpretation and understanding.

Semantic information always relates to a specific aspect in the situation; it is about something. Further, it always reduces the number of alternatives available in interpreting the situation. The gangland-killing example has eight possible killers. Since all are equally probable, three bits of information are found in the situation. When you receive the message that half of them were around the world on a vacation at the time of the killing, you have received one bit of semantic information, thus reducing the total amount of information in the situation to two bits. When a person receives information about something, a certain amount of uncertainty in a situation has been removed.

Of course, semantic information is always relative to the human being's state of knowledge. Information in this sense must be defined in terms of the *perceived* alternatives of the person receiving the message.

Now that we have defined semantic information, we will see what happens when a person receives a series of messages about a situation. Two possibilities exist. The individual may receive logically independent messages or redundant messages. Logically independent messages about the same situation convey completely different information. Such messages are *additive*. For example, the message that half of the suspects were on vacation provides one bit of information, while the message that two others were home together provides a second bit, equalling a total reduction of two bits.

More often, though, messages overlap in meaning. This occurrence is *semantic redundancy*. For example, you may learn that the vacation took place and then find out in a second message that the father was on vacation while his son and grandson were home together, fighting. The information that the father was on vacation is redundant; it occurs in both messages. Redundancy plays the same role on the semantic level as it does on the technical level. Redundant, or unnecessary, information counteracts noise. It also facilitates learning on the part of the receiver.

To summarize, semantic information is the amount of information in a message that, because it is transmitted to the person, is removed from the situation. The net effect of semantic information (receiving messages) is to reduce the total amount of uncertainty in the situation. Herein we find the contribution of information theory to our common understanding of information.

An Effectiveness Approach to Information

The third of Weaver's three levels of information theory, the effectiveness level, deals with the impact of information on the system. It is here that we see a particularly striking relationship between information theory, systems, and cybernetics. Perhaps the most explicit approach is that of Russell Ackoff.[8]

Ackoff begins his theory with the notion of *purposeful state*. A system, such as a person, is in a purposeful state if some goal is desired and various unequal alternative ways exist for achieving the goal. *Communication via messages affects the system if it changes the purposeful state of the organism*.

Six concepts are related to the notion of purposeful state. The first is the *individual*. This may be any system in a purposeful state, but for simplicity we will refer to it as a person from now on. Second, there is a *course of action* leading to the third element, *outcome*. Thus purposefulness consists, in part, of an individual's choosing to achieve an outcome by taking a particular course of action. The fourth element in the model is the *probability* that the individual will take the particular course of action. Fifth, *efficiency* is the likelihood that the specified out-

8. Russell Ackoff, "Toward a Behavioral Theory of Communication," *Management Science* 4 (1957–58): 218–34; and Russell Ackoff and Fred Emery, *On Purposeful Systems* (Chicago: Aldine, 1972).

come will occur as a result of the course of action. The final concept crucial to the idea of purposefulness is *value*, which is the importance of the outcome to the individual. Next we will define a purposeful state.

A purposeful state requires the following conditions: First, at least two courses of action must be available to the individual. These must be viable *choices* for the person to use in achieving the desired outcome. Further, the courses of action must have some degree of efficiency: There must be a probability that the outcome will be achieved from either of the courses, and the probabilities or efficiencies cannot be equal. Finally, the person must want the outcome: The goal must have value for the person.

The definition of purposeful state can be clarified with a simple example. Suppose a young woman is interested in seeing the world. Visiting foreign lands has value for her. She could take two courses of action to achieve the desired outcome: joining the army or joining the peace corps. If each course really is available to her, and if one has a higher probability of leading to the goal, she then is in a purposeful state. She can make a *choice* that has a chance of getting her to foreign lands. But suppose she fails the physical examination for the army. The army is no longer an available choice. As conceived by this theory, she is no longer in a purposeful state, since no alternative choice is available. Another condition that might occur is for the efficiencies of the courses of action to be equal. In this case there is no basis for choice, and once again the young woman is out of a purposeful state. In short, she must have various ways of seeing the world, and one must be a more likely course. Recall Ackoff's thesis, which is an answer to this third-level problem: Communication via messages affects the system if it changes the purposeful state of the organism.

Messages may affect the purposeful state of the individual in three ways. First, a message may *inform*, in which case the probabilities of choice are altered. Second, the message may *instruct*, changing the efficiencies of the courses of action. Third, the message may *motivate*, changing the value of the outcome. We can easily relate the first kind of effect to semantic information. You will recall that semantic information is equal to the reduction of uncertainty in a situation. If various courses of action are present in a purposeful state and each has a probability of leading to the desired outcome (efficiency), receiving information about the efficiencies reduces the uncertainty involved, which changes the probability that one alternative will be chosen. For example, suppose our young world traveler is leaning toward joining the army when she receives information that most WACs are stationed at bases in the United States. This message regarding the efficiency of the army as her choice now increases the probability that she will join the Peace Corps. By reducing the uncertainty among the perceived efficiencies of the alternatives, information affects the purposeful state by altering the probability that a given course will be chosen.

The second kind of effect is *instruction*. While information provides a clearer basis for choice by making the efficiencies known, instruction directly changes the efficiencies. This change is accomplished by providing the person with knowledge and competencies that will enable that person to achieve the outcome via a particular course of action. In our example the woman may be shown how to manipulate the assignment process in the WACs in order to be assigned overseas. This instruction increases the efficiency of the army for reaching her goal.

The third effect of messages on a system is *motivation*. Motivation is the result of a change in value. The woman in our example would, of course, have several goals (outcomes) of value to her. Let us say that a different goal is owning a restaurant. If the outcome of seeing the world has a higher value than owning a restaurant, she will pursue it with one of the courses of action described. But she may receive a message that increases the desirability of owning a restaurant, thus changing the outcome of her purposeful state.

Ackoff's theory rounds out our brief survey of information theory. Classical information theory, which is primarily technical, deals with the measurement of information for purposes of accurate and efficient transmission. The theory of semantic information shows how the receipt of information in messages reduces uncertainty. Finally, Ackoff's effectiveness theory broadens the scope of coverage to include the effect of messages on purposeful systems.

The extensive literature on information theory has been touched but lightly here. This short summary of some key points briefly illustrates how information theory has added dimensions to our understanding of communication.

Criticism

Clearly information theory is indispensable for developing advanced electronic communication devices. Its problems lie not in its technical usefulness but in the claims made for it by some of the original information theorists, system theorists, and scholars outside of these areas who looked to information theory for answers it cannot provide. Its original formulators, Shannon and Weaver, hoped to use the theory as a covering model for all human and machine communication. However, even Colin Cherry, whose famous 1957 treatise on communication was based largely on information theory, now argues in his 1978 third edition that "the language of physical science is inadequate for discussion of what is essentially human about human communication."[9]

Most criticism of information theory relates to the standard of *appropriateness*.[10] The epistemological assumptions of the theory are not considered appropriate for understanding many aspects of human communication. Roger Conant captures the essence of the argument:

> When Shannon's theory first appeared it provoked a lot of optimism, not only in the telephone company for which it had clear technical applications, but also among biologists, psychologists, and the like who hoped it would illuminate the ways in which cells, animals, people, and perhaps even societies use information. Although the theory has been put to use in these ways, the results have not been spectacular at all. . . . Shannon's theory provides practically no help in understanding everyday communication.[11]

Many critics have centered on the ill-advised use of the term *information* as a symptom of this problem. The usage of the term is at such odds with popular meanings for *information* that a great deal of confusion has resulted. Ironically, information theory is not at all about *information* as we commonly understand it. One critic has suggested that the approach be retitled the "theory of signal transmission."[12] Because the term *information* as used by these theorists is so difficult to apply to human communication, other scholars have developed new definitions of the term under the old rubric of *information theory* that have caused even more befuddlement.[13] Of course, terminological confusion is only a symptom of the problems involved in stretching the concept to fit alien domains. Three such problems have been cited frequently in the literature.

The first is that information theory is designed as a measurement tool based on statistical procedures. Human messages in their full complexity are not easily broken down into

9. Colin Cherry, *On Human Communication* (Cambridge: M.I.T. Press, 1978), p. ix.

10. Criticism of information theory can be found in many sources, including the following, on which my summary relies: Anatol Rapoport, "The Promise and Pitfalls of Information Theory," *Behavioral Science* 1 (1956): 303–9; also reprinted in *Modern Systems Research for the Behaviorist Scientist*, ed. Walter Buckley (Chicago: Aldine, 1968), 137–42; Rollo Handy and Paul Kurtz, "Information Theory," in *American Behavioral Scientist* 7, no. 6 (1964), pp. 99–104; Roger C. Conant, "A Vector Theory of Information," in *Communication Yearbook 3*, ed. Dan Nimmo (New Brunswick, N.J.: Transaction Books, 1979), 177–96.

11. Conant, "A Vector Theory," p. 178.

12. Yehoshua Bar-Hillel, "Concluding Review, in *Information Theory in Psychology*, ed. Henry Quastler (Glencoe, Ill.: Free Press, 1955), p. 3.

13. See, for example, Krippendorf, "Information Theory."

observable, measurable signals. Although the phonetic structure of language is amenable to analysis, when you add paralinguistic cues, not to mention kinesic and proxemic features, information theory becomes virtually useless. Also, many of the codes used in human communication are continuous, not discrete; that is, they do not consist of off-on signals. Such codes are difficult to fit into the mathematical paradigm.

A second problem of applying information theory to human communication is that the theory downplays meaning as the topic was developed in the last chapter. Even if we were able to predict the amount of information received by a listener, we would know nothing of the degree of shared understanding between the communicators or the impact of the message on them.

Finally, information theory does not deal with the contextual or personal factors affecting an individual's channel capacity. For example, individual learning, which changes one's ability to comprehend certain types of messages and ultimately one's capacity to receive signals, is left untouched in classical theory. Newer approaches such as that of Ackoff help to improve in this area.

Theories of Information Processing

This section covers a variety of theories that deal, not with the nature of information, but with the ways persons deal with information—how information is received, organized, stored, and used. For the most part these theories cover processes that occur within the individual. As such they may not appear at first to relate to communication. Keep in mind, however, that the basic commodity of communication is information, and information processing on the intrapersonal level is an integral part of the communication process.

This discussion is divided into two parts. First, standard information processing theory is presented. Next, we move to a topic that has seen particularly fruitful applications in communication research: theories of cognitive complexity.

At this point a qualification stated several times in this text must again be reiterated. The literature of information processing is immense. The theories included here represent only a sampling of this work. So although the theories summarized here are important, they are far from exhaustive.

"Standard Theory"

"Standard theory" is placed in quotation marks because the work summarized in this section does not constitute a single theory. It was not organized by a particular scholar or group of scholars. Rather, this work is a composite of research findings of cognitive psychologists in this century. This work is called "standard" only because it represents the mainstream of psychological thought about the basic processes of cognition. Also, the use of the word *standard* does not imply that the findings reported here are universally accepted. Indeed, cognitive psychology is one of the most dynamic fields in the behavioral sciences.

The following summary is based on the excellent synopsis of C. David Mortensen.[14] His model for organizing information-processing research is three-dimensional: encoding/decoding, stages, and integration. Together these elements constitute a general framework for understanding cognition. Figure 7.2 depicts the three dimensions.[15] We deal with the first two here; integration is taken up separately in the next section under cognitive complexity.

Encoding refers to all of the activities involved in transforming information into messages. Speech (and its derivative, writing) are encoding activities in communication. *Decoding*

14. C. David Mortensen, "Human Information Processing," in *Communication: The Study of Human Interaction* (New York: McGraw-Hill, 1972), 69–124.

15. Ibid., p. 80.

involves the transformation of sensations into meaning. In communication decoding activities include listening and reading. Perception of nonverbal signs is also a decoding activity. Here we see an important distinction between psychological theories of information processing and classical information theory. In classical theory information is thought to exist apart from the individual as a quality of the signal. Most cognitive psychologists, however, would agree that signals merely present sensory stimuli and that information results from the processing activities of encoding and decoding within the individual.

Let us look more closely at the four primary stages of information processing: sensation, central processing, storage, and recall. *Sensation* involves receiving signals from the environment. These signals include energy that stimulates receptor organs such as the eyes and ears. Actually, sensation is a rather complex process. Before any stimulation can enter the nervous system, the receptor nerve fibers must be activated. The level at which a receptor cell "fires" is the arousal threshold. A receptor cell will not activate until a certain minimum level of energy impinges upon it (light, sound, and so forth). For example, auditory nerves normally will not be excited until sound waves reach a level exceeding ten-to-fifteen hertz.

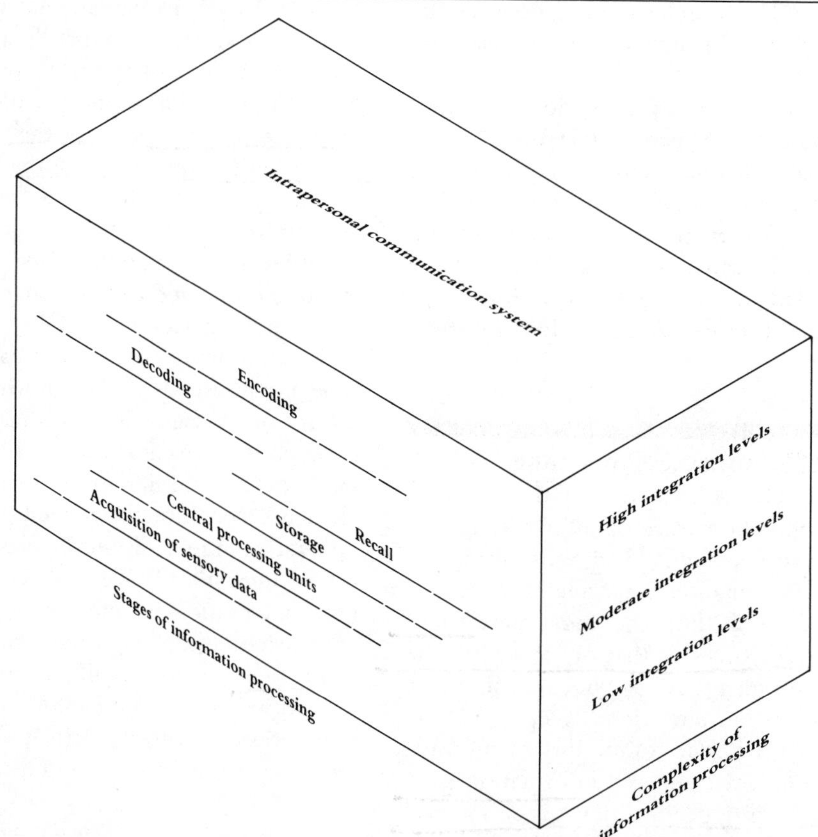

From "Human Information Processing," in *Communication: The Study of Human Interaction*, by C. David Mortensen. Copyright © 1972 by McGraw-Hill. Reprinted by permission of the publisher.

Figure 7.2. Information-processing model.

Our sense organs are almost always being stimulated in one way or another, which means that the sensory systems must cope with a virtual onslaught of stimulation most of the time. The cocktail party situation illustrates this occurrence.[16] In a crowded room one must attend to a single message at a time, separating it from other stimuli. We selectively filter stimulation. Although the research evidence on this point is mixed, stimuli appear to be filtered not only by the sense organs according to stimulus properties (for example, loudness, brightness) but by the brain's use of previous experience to assign meaning and relevance to certain stimuli over others. Without the individual's awareness, the brain apparently screens out irrelevant stimuli and organizes sensations into potentially meaningful units.

For example, when you are talking with someone in a crowded room, your brain filters out extraneous stimulation from other conversations. One of the reasons for this is that your conversation is a coherent and organized interaction, and bits and pieces of other conversations are not meaningful to this organized pattern. However, at times someone standing nearby says something that strikes a familiar note, and your brain takes your attention off your immediate conversation so that you tune into the outside comment. Sometimes you may even fake attention to your partner while you are paying attention to someone else's conversation.

The second stage of information processing is *central processing*, or perception. Here data that have entered the system are assigned meaning and prepared for entry into storage or memory. An important aspect of perception is the organization of the sensory field. Sensations are related to one another and organized into meaningful patterns. It is well known that the context of a stimulus, the background in which it is presented, is important to how the stimulus is perceived. A number of rules or laws of perceptual organization direct the organizing process. Although we do not have space to explain these here, any general psychology text lists them. We are all aware that attitude and motivation affect perception. One's feelings, attitudes, and motives of the moment affect how sensory stimuli are filtered and organized. This truism is well supported by research and common experience. One of the reasons you may find it hard not to listen to someone else's conversation at a cocktail party is that the other conversation "fits" into your attitudinal or motivational state of the moment.

Storage or memory is the third stage of information processing. A great deal of research on memory has been done in psychology. From much of this work it is clear that memory and perceptual organization go hand in hand. Our memories affect central processing, and in turn memory is facilitated by organization. Specific percepts are not stored independently in drawers of the brain. Rather, they are integrated into complex hierarchical webs of knowledge. Memory is thus facilitated by the anchor of context. Likewise, one never remembers just one piece of data; it is remembered by association with something else. In other words, thinking and remembering are intimately tied together. For these reasons certain mnemonic devices, such as making a word out of the first letter of each item in a list, aid memory.

The final stage of information processing is *recall*. Our memories are organized according to event models, with recall being closely tied to our organization of past events. Long-term recall is therefore largely a matter of reconstruction. The individual plugs certain recalled impressions into the model and rebuilds an entire sequence of events. Often what you "remember" about an event is not what really happened but your construction of what logically could have happened under the circumstances.

Recall is a vital link between decoding and encoding. As messages are decoded, they are integrated into an organized structure of memories where they reside in association with other

16. Colin Cherry, "The Cocktail Party Problem," *Discovery*, March 1962, p. 32.

aspects of the memory hierarchy. Encoding involves the stimulation of a part of the memory system so that appropriate data are recalled and used to formulate messages.

Criticism of Standard Theory

Criticizing standard theory as if it were a singular theory would be unfair. In fact, until the past decade or so work in cognitive psychology could be faulted for failing to develop middle-range theories to guide research on information processing. The area of standard theory is a good example of research done in bits and pieces without an overarching theory. In recent years, however, a number of theoretical frameworks for understanding cognition have arisen. We will look at two of these in the next section of this chapter.

Before we leave standard theory, two cautions are in order. Although many researchers who contributed to this field know otherwise, they have a tendency, in looking at the work as a whole, to image information processing as a linear sequence of events that operate in a machinelike fashion. It is a mistake to think of cognition as a series of discrete events occurring over time. "Stages" should be interpreted loosely as overlapping processes that interrelate to form a whole. Also, information processing in humans is highly individual and is not particularly comparable with machine behavior.[17]

Cognitive Complexity

In this section we will look at two theories of cognitive complexity, which is the third factor of information processing listed in Figure 7.2. One theory is attributable to Harold Schroder and his colleagues and the other to Walter Crockett.

An active group of speech communication scholars under the tutelage of Jesse Delia at the University of Illinois has produced an impressive number of studies applying cognitive complexity to interpersonal communication.[18] The concept of cognitive complexity is relevant to several themes of communication. These theories are placed here because of their direct relevance to information processing, although Crockett's work could as easily fit in the chapters on interpersonal communication. Although little work has been done on cognitive complexity outside these two domains, the field is ripe for extensions of research to such areas as persuasion, group communication, organizations, and media effects.

Cognitive complexity theories attempt to uncover processes by which persons make sense of their surroundings. They seek correlations and patterns of behavior, but they do not construct covering laws. Further, they tend to be process oriented, rejecting fine analysis. As Schroder and colleagues write: "As the integrative complexity of the conceptual structure increases in regard to a given stimulus domain, . . . the view of man as purely a product of his past—as a reactive creature warding off diversity—becomes increasingly erroneous."[19]

Levels of Integration. Schroder, Driver, and Streufert have presented an appealing theory of cognitive complexity.[20] This theory states that cognitive functioning involves two types of elements. The first are the content variables, consisting of what an individual knows—the person's thoughts, attitudes, needs, and so forth. The authors identify these elements as dimensions of cognition. The second kind of element consists of structural variables, or how an individual processes the dimensions. The structural variables are rules or programs for

17. For an elaboration of this criticism, see Geoffrey Underwood, "Concepts in Information Processing," in *Strategies of Information Processing,* ed. G. Underwood (New York: Academic Press, 1978), pp. 1–22.

18. This literature is reviewed in part by Claudia Hale, "Cognitive Complexity-Simplicity as a Determinant of Communication Effectiveness," *Communication Monographs* 47 (1980): 304–11.

19. Harold M. Schroder, Michael S. Driver, and Siegfried Streufert, *Human Information Processing: Individuals and Groups Functioning in Complex Social Situations* (New York: Holt, Rinehart and Winston, 1967), p. v.

20. Ibid.

combining or integrating the content variables. In short, dimensions are units of thought, and rules are relations among units.

People vary in terms of the complexity of their cognitive systems. Where dimensions are numerous and levels of integration many, cognitive complexity is said to be high. Where dimensions are few and integration simple, complexity is low. Although a correlation may be present between the number of content elements and the degree of connections among dimensions, integrative complexity primarily is the number of connections, including the variety of rules, among dimensions.

Integration is accomplished through a hierarchy of rules. The hierarchy can be simple

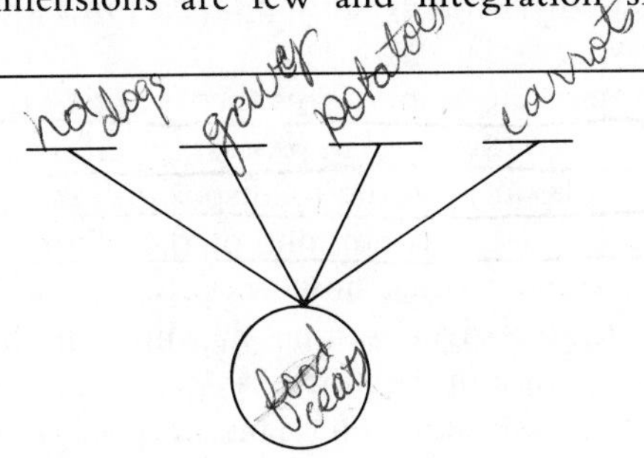

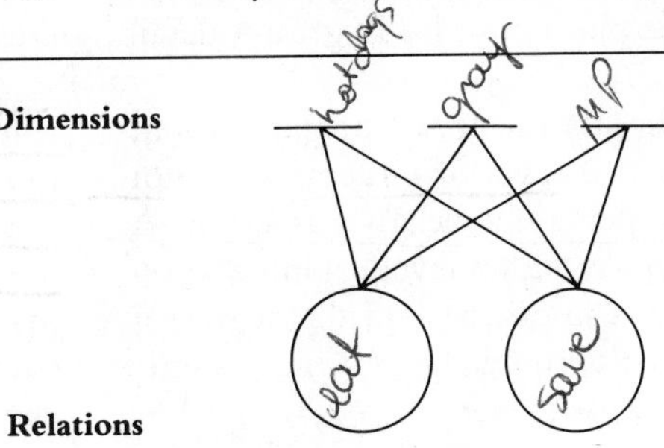

***A.** Low integration index: relatively fixed organization*

***B.** Moderately low integration index: few alternate combinations*

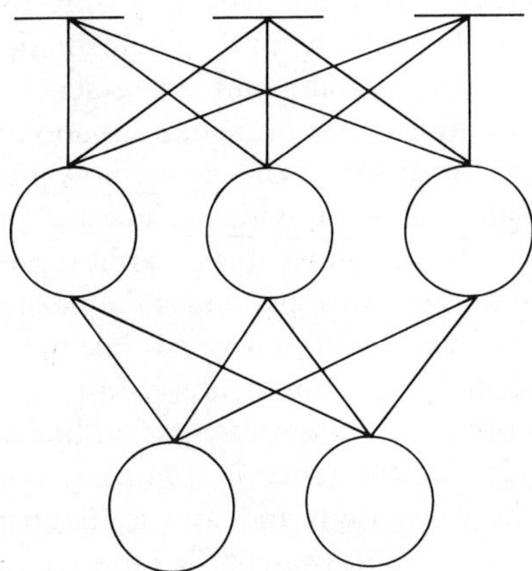

***C.** Moderately high integration index: alternate combinations and higher-order rules*

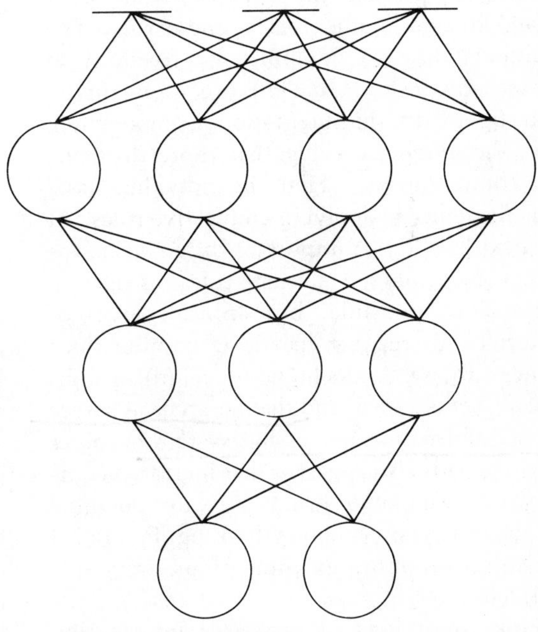

***D.** High integration index: possibilities for complex relationships*

Figure 7.3. Levels of integration.

or complex. The focus of this theory is on differences in integrative complexity. Where integration is low, the dimensions are integrated by a single, simple rule. (For example, Never cross the street; Fat people are jolly.) Where integration is high, numerous rules are used to relate the dimensions, and rules themselves are integrated into an abstract hierarchy of relationships. We will explore this idea in greater detail momentarily.

Before we discuss the levels of integration, we should note that level of integration is not viewed by Schroder and colleagues as a trait. A single individual has higher levels of integration in some areas than in others, and the degree of complexity in one's knowledge, even in a single area, may change over time.

Figure 7.3 contrasts varying levels of integration.[21] These models are not intended to represent discrete types but points along a continuum of complexity. The first figure (a) we see low integration; the dimensions are connected to one another via a single rule. The individual has no flexibility or freedom to choose among alternative interpretations. In the next figure (b) the integration is moderately low, the difference being that more than one rule comes into play. Here the individual has a little flexibility in applying connective rules. At the next level (c) an important difference is apparent. Not only are alternate rules for relating dimensions possible, but another level of metarules for relating first-level combinations comes into use. At the highest level (d) an additional layer is added, and the hierarchical nature of the information-processing system becomes apparent. It is also apparent that increased complexity of integration brings a greater potential for abstract versus concrete thinking. Figure 7.4 presents a simplified example of an integrative hierarchy.

How an individual processes information depends greatly on the level of integration in force. With low integration the person's thinking is quite programmed, and little creativity or self-initiative is possible. Thinking tends to be black and white; conflict among competing stimuli is minimized since differences are not noted; conclusions are concrete; and compartmentalization is rife. With high integration comes freedom of choice, high levels of behavioral adjustment and adaptation, and creativity.

An important claim of this theory is that the level of integration used in processing information depends on both the predisposition of the individual and the conditions of the environment. In other words, how we process information in any given setting depends on the complexity of our cognitive system and the demands of the situation. This idea leads to Shroder and colleagues' U curve hypothesis.

Individuals generally reach their highest level of integration in processing information at some optimal level of environmental complexity. This relationship is illustrated in Figure 7.5. In this figure the highest level of information processing is achieved at point X, which is a moderately complex environmental situation.[22] The shape and position of the curve, however, are not the same for all individuals. The authors hypothesize (1) that individuals with higher levels of integration for a particular theme area will reach their peak of cognitive complexity at a higher point of environmental complexity than will people with lower integration hierarchies; and (2) the difference in complexity of processing between high and low individuals diminishes as the environment becomes either simpler or more complex, as illustrated in Figure 7.6.[23]

Let's look at a simple example. Consider the different ways two drivers would respond to different traffic conditions. One driver is just learning to drive. Assume this individual has a low level of integration in the area of driving. The other driver is experienced, having a high

21. Adapted from ibid., p. 15, 18, 20, 22.

22. Ibid., p. 37.

23. Ibid., p. 40.

level of integration. In an extremely simple situation, say a red light at an intersection in low traffic, both drivers would process the sensory information at a low level. They would also process information at an equally low level in a highly complex situation such as a traffic accident just ahead in heavy traffic in foul weather. At moderate conditions in between these extremes, however, would be vast differences in the degree of integration with which the two drivers would process information.

Cognitive Complexity and Impression Formation. In his well-known treatment of cognitive complexity, Walter Crockett uses a similar concept to that of Schroder and his colleagues.[24] His notion of cognitive complexity is not as ramified, but his main concern is to apply this aspect of information processing to interpersonal perception. Here we see a direct relationship being made between information processing and communication behavior. In fact, a good deal of research has applied Crockett's cognitive complexity idea to other communication variables.

Crockett, like Schroder, recognizes that a

24. Walter H. Crockett, "Cognitive Complexity and Impression Formation," in *Progress in Experimental Personality Research*, ed. Brendon A. Maher (New York: Academic Press, 1965), vol. 2, pp. 47–90.

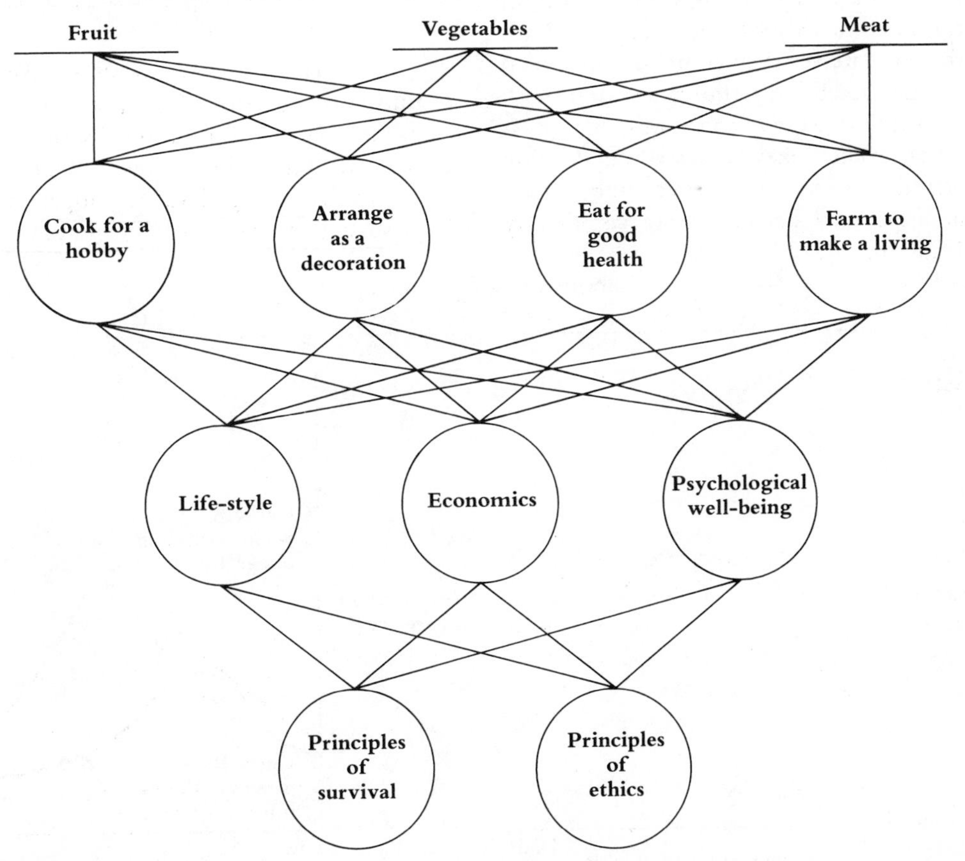

Figure 7.4. Simplified example.

cognitive system consists of content elements and relationships among elements. Complexity or simplicity in the system is a matter of the relative number of constructs (dimensions) and the degree of hierarchical organization of the constructs. The number of constructs used by an individual to organize a perceptual field is the degree of *cognitive differentiation*. More cognitively complex individuals are able to make more distinctions in a situation than cognitively noncomplex people.

Crockett agrees that cognitive complexity is not a general trait. Individuals vary in their own complexity across topics and over time. Further, cognitive complexity is a matter of human development. Small children typically are cognitively simple, processing information in rather global, undifferentiated terms. With growth and maturity they come to understand events with greater discrimination and with more sensitivity to the relationships among aspects of an event. Likewise, as adults develop more familiarity and experience with a new content area, they become more cognitively complex in that area.

Crockett is especially concerned about one realm of information processing in particular, person perception. He is interested in how individuals process information about other people. Since communication involves interpersonal interaction, this line of work is especially relevant. The main hypotheses of the theory follow:

> First, individuals with complex cognitive systems with respect to other people need not necessarily have complex systems with respect to other domains. Second, those individuals for whom interpersonal relations are functionally important should have more complex cognitive systems with respect to other people than those for whom interpersonal relations are less important. Third, a particular individual may show differential complexity in his interpersonal constructs with respect to different categories of other people, depending upon the extent of his interaction with them.[25]

What, then, is the relationship between the cognitive complexity of interpersonal impressions and how information about others is processed? Crockett makes several claims. First, a relationship does not appear to exist between cognitive complexity and the ability to

25. Ibid., p. 54.

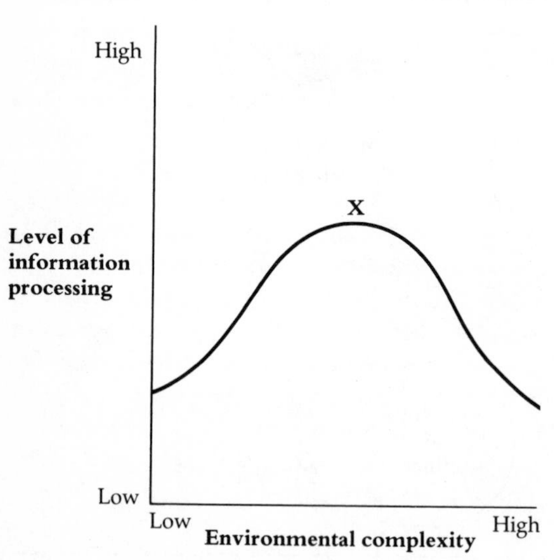

Figure 7.5. U curve hypothesis.

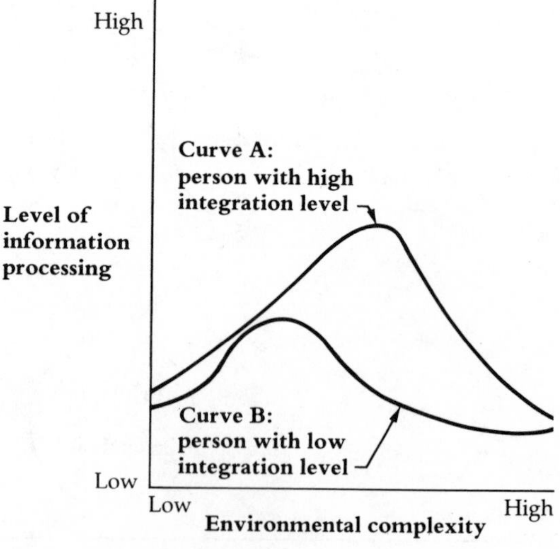

Figure 7.6. Individual differences.

accurately predict another's behavior. However, cognitively complex individuals seem to distinguish more between people in impression formation than do simple individuals. They also assume less similarity between self and others. In brief, cognitively complex individuals seem to be less susceptible to stereotyping than are noncomplex individuals.

In addition, cognitively complex individuals tend to attribute both positive and negative qualities to others, and they are therefore less likely to divide people into good and bad groups than would cognitively noncomplex people. Another correlation involves the reconciliation of discrepant perceptions in another person. Because cognitively complex individuals are able to put perceptions into a broader network of understanding, they have a greater ability to reconcile contradictory attributes of others.

As indicated, much research has sought to discover how cognitive complexity affects interpersonal communication.[26] The general upshot of this research is that cognitively complex individuals are more able than noncomplex individuals to take the perspective of another communicator. Thus their messages to others tend to be adapted to the other communicator's constructs, making communication more effective.

Criticism of Cognitive Complexity

Cognitive complexity theories are appealing for a variety of reasons. They meet almost all of the criteria for good theory. They provide a basis for understanding information processing from an actional or constructivistic point of view. They present a reasonable explanation, without falling into mechanistic reasoning, for how humans differ in conceptualizing events and in making judgments about people. In considering ways these theories might better serve our understanding of cognition, we note two concerns. The first relates to scope, the second to validity.

26. Hale, "Cognitive Complexity-Simplicity."

Although these theories take a step toward understanding the structure of cognition, they do not go far enough in relating cognitive complexity to other facets of information processing. The work of Schroder and his colleagues centers almost entirely on the U curve hypothesis. The work of Crockett and his followers extends the concept into the realm of person perception, which, although a first step in the right direction, is still somewhat limited. Such questions as the following are worth pursuing: How does complexity affect perception of complex stimuli? By what strategies do individuals with high (versus low) integration understand verbal and nonverbal messages? How is complexity of integration related to problem solving? What is the effect of integration on information storage and retrieval? How do developmental factors, including such predispositions as values and attitudes, affect cognitive complexity? Of course, the theorists should not be faulted for failing to touch every base in their original formulations, but the heuristic value of the theory could have been heightened by noting potential connections between cognitive complexity and other information-processing variables. Ironically, these theories could themselves be discussed at a higher level of integrative complexity.

The second concern relates to the notion of hierarchy. Both of the approaches discussed here rest on the central claim that cognitive structure is hierarchical (as illustrated in Figure 7.3). This notion is appealing because it is parsimonious and aesthetically elegant. Yet there is no particular reason to believe that actual cognition is always this neat. In fact, the hierarchy of cognitions is difficult to prove (or disprove, for that matter), and these authors seem to take it as self-evident. There is no doubt that cognitions are organized, but that they are grouped systematically into increasingly abstract sets is uncertain. As an alternative organizational model, consider the possibility of a network of clusters of associated cognitions without definite hierarchical order.

What Do We Know about Information

Classical information theorists define information in terms of uncertainty. They present a theory whereby engineers can develop systems that will transmit messages from one location to another via signals along channels. Although the concepts of the technical theory of information are vital in understanding machine communication, they tell us little of the ways humans use information. More recent developments in information theory help us understand the role of information in human life. We know that semantic information helps individuals reduce uncertainty in the environment, facilitating adaptation to complex situations. This process involves removing unknowns in a stimulus situation. Information of this type has the potential for affecting in a number of ways the choices people make. Information can affect the individual's perception of how well various options will work in achieving goals. It can help people affect systems in such a way as to achieve a goal more readily. Information can also have a direct effect on one's goal priorities, causing a redirection of energy toward new goals.

Information processing consists of a complex set of interrelated processes. Several generalizations about these processes are warranted. First, all cognition seems to be affected heavily by memory; but, second, memory is more than simple recall of stored data. Memory seems to involve organized reconstruction of events. This fact suggests, third, that all cognitive processes are governed by organizing schemes. Thus, for example, perception is structured by certain organizing principles, and memory is consistent with our notions of how events should happen. Fourth, cognitions are never isolated but exist in a complex web of interrelationships. Fifth, most cognitive processes seem to be tied to language. Our linguistic categories affect how we perceive, recall, and think. Sixth, attitudes and emotions cannot be separated from cognition: Perception, memory, problem solving, and other cognitive processes are affected by these.

Unfortunately human information processing is difficult to study. It suffers from some of the same problems as does the work on language and meaning outlined in the last section. The basic problem is that we must infer from observed responses to unobservable processes. The alternative is to assume that human information processing is similar to machine information processing, which can be observed directly. However, great doubt exists as to whether this assumption is valid. Besides, even machines can process information in a variety of ways, and they therefore provide little clue to how humans actually think.

CHAPTER

8 Theories of Persuasion

Until the mid-1970s persuasion was most often conceptualized as a process by which one person or group affects, influences, or changes another person or group. Although social influence is still the central element of most persuasion, the unidirectional, one-person-changes-another-person concept is now generally seen as inadequate.[1] This approach has been replaced by an information-processing approach that focuses more on the information receiver than the message source. In short, personal change is seen as a consequence of information processing.

This chapter divides persuasion into four sections. The first provides a general humanistic background for contemporary theories of persuasion. The second summarizes behavioristic research that springs from the humanistic tradition. The two remaining sections divide the mainstream of contemporary persuasion theory into two basic groups. The first group, found in the third section of this chapter, are theories that link persuasion with information processing. The second group, found in the last section of the chapter, consists of theories of persuasion through cognitive reorganization.[2]

Humanistic Foundations: Rhetorical Theory

The study of communication and persuasion is not a new interest. Humans have been looking at these phenomena for centuries. The roots of our understanding of communication processes in general and persuasion in particular go deep into the historical soil. Typically, persuasion has been examined in two broad ways. The historical scholar has contributed by examining historical artifacts, including treatises, papers, and speeches. With the advent of modern pscyhology and the behavioral sciences in the twentieth century, persuasion began to be studied by behavioral scientists as well. Using empirical methods, psychologists and others have tested many hypotheses that grew out of theories of the past. We will attempt to experience the flavor of both the humanistic theories that began in ancient Greece and the contemporary behavioral theories.

When we think of theory as described in Chapter 1, we normally focus on the scientific type of the present century. Yet it is clear that many of the qualities of theory outlined earlier in the book are present in ancient explanations of communication. The most important historical theory of communication and persuasion is Aristotelian rhetorical theory.

Aristotelian Rhetorical Theory

Aristotle, considered to be a seminal figure in philosophy, laid a classical groundwork for much of modern philosophy. For years Aristotelian theory was the primary conceptual framework used in the field of speech, and many psychological investigations found their original hypotheses in the works of Aristotle and his numerous interpreters.

1. For discussions of this conceptual shift, see Gerald Miller and Michael Burgoon, "Persuasion Research: Review and Commentary," in *Communication Yearbook 2*, ed. Brent Rubin (New Brunswick, N.J.: Transaction Books, 1978), pp. 29–47; and Kathleen Reardon, *Persuasion: Theory and Context* (Beverly Hills: Sage, 1981), chap. 1.

2. This organization and review rely heavily on the excellent integrative work of Mary John Smith, *Persuasion and Human Action* (Belmont, Calif.: Wadsworth, 1982).

Aristotle was a great scientist, philosopher, and social interpreter of his age. During the fourth century B.C., he produced many classical works related to the nature of things and the nature of people. His work that most concerns communication and persuasion is *Rhetoric*.[3] This work is "generally considered the most important single work in the literature of speechcraft."[4] As a manual for speech making, *Rhetoric* relates most centrally to persuasion as a domain. In fact, Aristotle defined rhetoric as the faculty of discovering the available means of persuasion in any case.[5] For many years in the field of speech rhetoric was equated with persuasion. We need to keep in mind, of course, that this theory, along with the other persuasion theories, apply to personal change in all contexts—interpersonal, group, organizational, and mass.

Rhetoric is a description of the processes of speech making as well as a textbook on how to make speeches. It is important to realize that the primary mode of persuasion and mass communication in ancient times was public speaking. As a result theorizing at that time dealt with speech as a communication channel.

For Aristotle rhetoric was essentially the same as persuasion is for us today. In fact, many scholars, particularly in the fields of speech communication and English, still prefer the term *rhetoric* to more recent labels. Aristotle defines rhetoric "as a faculty of discovering all the possible means of persuasion in any subject."[6] In *Rhetoric* Aristotle points out the two broad kinds of proofs or appeals that affect persuasion, *artistic* and *inartistic*. Inartistic proofs are the aspects of the situation and qualities of the speaker that are not directly controlled by the speaker. Although inartistic proofs enter the process of persuasion in important ways, Aristotle and most other rhetorical theorists are primarily concerned with artistic proofs that are directly controlled by the speaker. Artistic proofs include three types: ethos, pathos, and logos. *Ethos*, ethical or personal appeals, includes all of the ways a person projects personal qualities so as to elicit belief on the part of the audience. Such factors as character, knowledge, and goodwill can be projected as ethical proofs. Interestingly, much of the research since the late 1940s on source credibility has tested Aristotle's original hypotheses about ethos. The second proof, *pathos*, consists of the emotional appeals brought to bear in the rhetorical act. The purpose of emotional proofs is to involve the audience's feelings and to call on its sympathies. Aristotle spent considerable time in *Rhetoric* discussing emotions and how they relate to people's lives. The third proof, *logical appeal*, was important to Aristotle and other classical theorists, for it was seen as the essence of reasoned discourse.

Logic consists of the use of *examples* and *enthymemes*. Examples help the audience see the validity of generalizations about the speaker's topic. Enthymemes, partial syllogisms, are important in eliciting audience participation in the reasoning process. A syllogism is defined as a logical device of deduction in which conclusions of a specific nature are inferred on the basis of assumptions or premises. Syllogisms are used to demonstrate the truth or validity of conclusions that a scientist might make. The enthymeme, on the other hand, is a practical device that is particularly useful in persuasion because of its appeal to listeners in the communication process. The enthymeme does not include all premises and conclusions; instead it requires audience members mentally to fill in missing logical steps, and thus it stimulates involvement. Contemporary rhetorical scholars have discussed the enthymeme in depth and have demonstrated that it is a device used in most practical persuasion.

Suppose, for example, that you are involved in a recycling campaign and want members of your community to see the value of recycling

3. Aristotle, *Rhetoric*, trans. W. Rhys Roberts (New York: Oxford University Press, 1924). Other translations are available.

4. Lester Thonssen and A. Craig Beard, *Speech Criticism: The Development of Standards for Rhetorical Appraisal* (New York: Ronald Press, 1948), p. 57.

5. Aristotle, *Rhetoric*, p. 1.

6. Ibid.

aluminum cans. Your reasoning might follow this syllogism: (1) The earth is worth protecting; (2) Saving natural resources protects the earth; (3) Recycling helps save natural resources; (4) Therefore recycling helps protect the earth and is worthy. Since you probably would not state all of the steps in this reasoning, an enthymeme would suffice: (1) The earth is worth protecting, and (2) Recycling saves natural resources. Or, to have the audience think through the reasons for recycling, you might say: Protect the earth: Recycle. The audience will fill in the rest.

In addition to the three kinds of proof, Aristotle also discusses three other aspects of public persuasion: delivery, style (the use of language), and organization. The principles of Aristotle have been discussed and expanded throughout the ages in many ways. Some theorists have focused on style, others on logic, still others on the responsibility of the speaker in different persuasive situations.

Aristotle has been rediscovered periodically.[7] One such rediscovery occurred early in this century. In the last century speeches were treated primarily as literature, but as the contemporary view of communication developed, it became clear to scholars of rhetoric that speeches should be seen from a functional viewpoint. The shift, which stimulated a return to the Aristotelian model, was articulated most clearly by Herbert Wichelns in his classic 1925 article, "The Literary Criticism of Oratory." In the article he repudiates the literary study of speech making and calls for a return to the rhetorical perspective. The following quotation, the heart of his discussion, outlines the basic parameters of neo-Aristotelian rhetorical theory as it is used today:

> Rhetorical criticism is necessarily analytical. The scheme of a rhetorical study includes the element of the speaker's personality as a conditioning factor: it includes also the public character of the man—not what he was, but what he was thought to be. It requires a description of the speaker's audience, and of the leading ideas with which he plied his hearers—his topics, the motives to which he appealed, the nature of the proofs he offered. These will reveal his own judgment of human nature in his audiences, and also his judgment on the questions which he discussed. Attention must be paid, too, to the relation of the surviving texts to what was actually uttered: in case the nature of the changes is known, there may be occasion to consider adaptation to two audiences—that which heard and that which read. Nor can rhetorical criticism omit the speaker's mode of arrangement and his mode of expression, nor his habit of preparation and his manner of delivery from the platform; though the last two are perhaps less significant. "Style"—in the sense which corresponds to diction and sentence movement—must receive attention, but only as one among various means that secure for the speaker ready access to the minds of his auditors. Finally, the effect of the discourse on its immediate hearers is not to be ignored, either in the testimony of witnesses, nor in the record of events. And throughout such a study one must conceive of the public man as influencing the men of his own times by the power of his discourse.[8]

Contemporary Approaches

Rhetorical theory has undergone considerable development in the twentieth century. One of the most important contemporary theorists is Kenneth Burke, whose theory is summarized in Chapter 4. The work of I. A. Richards, presented in Chapter 6, is also associated with rhetorical theory. Several other major figures have presented theories of rhetoric. Scholars often make a sharp distinction between "rhetorical" theory and "communication" theory, a distinction that seems false. We do not have space to pursue rhetorical theories here; several excellent books provide summaries.[9] The following criticism is limited to Aristotelian theory.

7. For a detailed survey of the development of rhetorical theory throughout history, see Nancy L. Harper, *Human Communication Theory: The History of a Paradigm* (Rochelle Park, N.J.: Hayden Book Co., 1979).

8. Herbert A. Wichelns, "The Literary Criticism of Oratory," in *Studies in Rhetoric and Public Speaking in Honor of James Albert Winans* (New York: The Century Company, 1925), pp. 212–13.

9. For excellent summaries of twentieth-century rhetorical theory, see Bernard L. Brock and Robert L. Scott, *Methods of Rhetorical Criticism* (Detroit: Wayne State University Press, 1980); James L. Golden, Goodwin F. Berquist, and William E. Coleman, *The Rhetoric of Western Thought* (Dubuque, Iowa: Kendall Hunt, 1976); Douglas Ehninger, *Contemporary Rhetoric* (Glenview, Ill.: Scott, Foresman, 1972); Richard L. Johannesen, *Contemporary Theories of Rhetoric* (New York: Harper & Row, 1971).

Criticism

Aristotelian theory probably was effective in its day. Its problems result primarily from modern-day applications. Because the theory employs a linear model in which a strong distinction is made between rhetor (source) and audience (receiver), it leaves little room for interaction among communicators. As such it neglects the process nature of communication. This failure is serious because of its adverse effect on much of our recent thinking about communication. In the next section you will see how this linear model is continued even in recent psychological research. This criticism is primarily one of theoretical *appropriateness*.

Aristotelian theory has also been criticized because of its three-fold analysis of ethos, pathos, and logos. In actual practice separating information into these categories is difficult. Any argument or appeal may, and probably does, involve a combination of personal regard, feelings, and logic. Aristotle presents these three elements as descriptors of message parts, but they probably more accurately relate to dimensions of perception that do not correspond perfectly with specific message appeals. This objection relates to our criterion of *validity*.

Contemporary Applications: The Yale Tradition

An Organizing Model

One of the most prolific research programs in persuasion was the Yale Communication and Attitude Change Program, conducted primarily in the 1950s. This work is interesting to study in conjunction with Aristotelian theory because it represents a contemporary operationalization of the classical linear model.[10] The goal of the Yale program was to discover ways that communication variables operate within the attitude change situation. The investigators hypothesized that in addition to the specific communication-bound variables affecting persuasion, certain general persuasibility dimensions were also present. This hypothesis arose out of the relatively commonsensical idea that some people are easier to persuade than others, regardless of the topic or situation.

The model illustrated in Figure 8.1 outlines the major types of persuasion variables investigated by the Yale group.[11] This model is an excellent outline of the antecedent, intermediate, and outcome variables in the persuasion paradigm. The model begins on the left with observable communication stimuli and ends on the right with various kinds of persuasion effects. The two middle blocks are particularly interesting, for they center on the mediating and predispositional factors between cause and effect. These two factors are extremely important in understanding persuasion, because they occur inside the person and facilitate or inhibit persuasion.

The Yale studies, including the theories of persuasibility, illustrate well the deterministic, behavioristic quality of much persuasion research. One immediately perceives a qualitative difference between the theories from cognitive psychology in the previous chapter and theories of social psychology, represented here by the Yale work. The former are concerned with *what people do with* information, while the latter focus on *how people are affected by* information.

Much research on persuasion took place in the Yale program. Summarizing the work is beyond the scope of this book; reviews of the literature are readily available elsewhere.[12]

10. The monographs in the Yale series include Carl I. Hovland, Irving L. Janis, and Harold H. Kelley, *Communication and Persuasion* (New Haven, Conn.: Yale University Press, 1953); Carl I. Hovland et al., *The Order of Presentation in Persuasion* (New Haven, Conn.: Yale University Press, 1959); Milton J. Rosenberg et al., *Attitude Organization and Change* (New Haven, Conn.: Yale University Press, 1960); Muzafer Sherif and Carl I. Hovland, *Social Judgment* (New Haven, Conn.: Yale University Press, 1961).

11. Irving L. Janis et al., *Personality and Persuasibility* (New Haven, Conn.: Yale University Press, 1959).

12. For a brief summary of the findings of the Yale research, see Smith, *Persuasion*, pp. 219–36.

The Persuasibility Problem

Of particular interest in Figure 8.1 is the small block at the top of the second column, labeled *communication-free*. People are hypothesized to vary in terms of their general persuasibility, apart from any other specific communication-related factor.

The original research in this area attempted

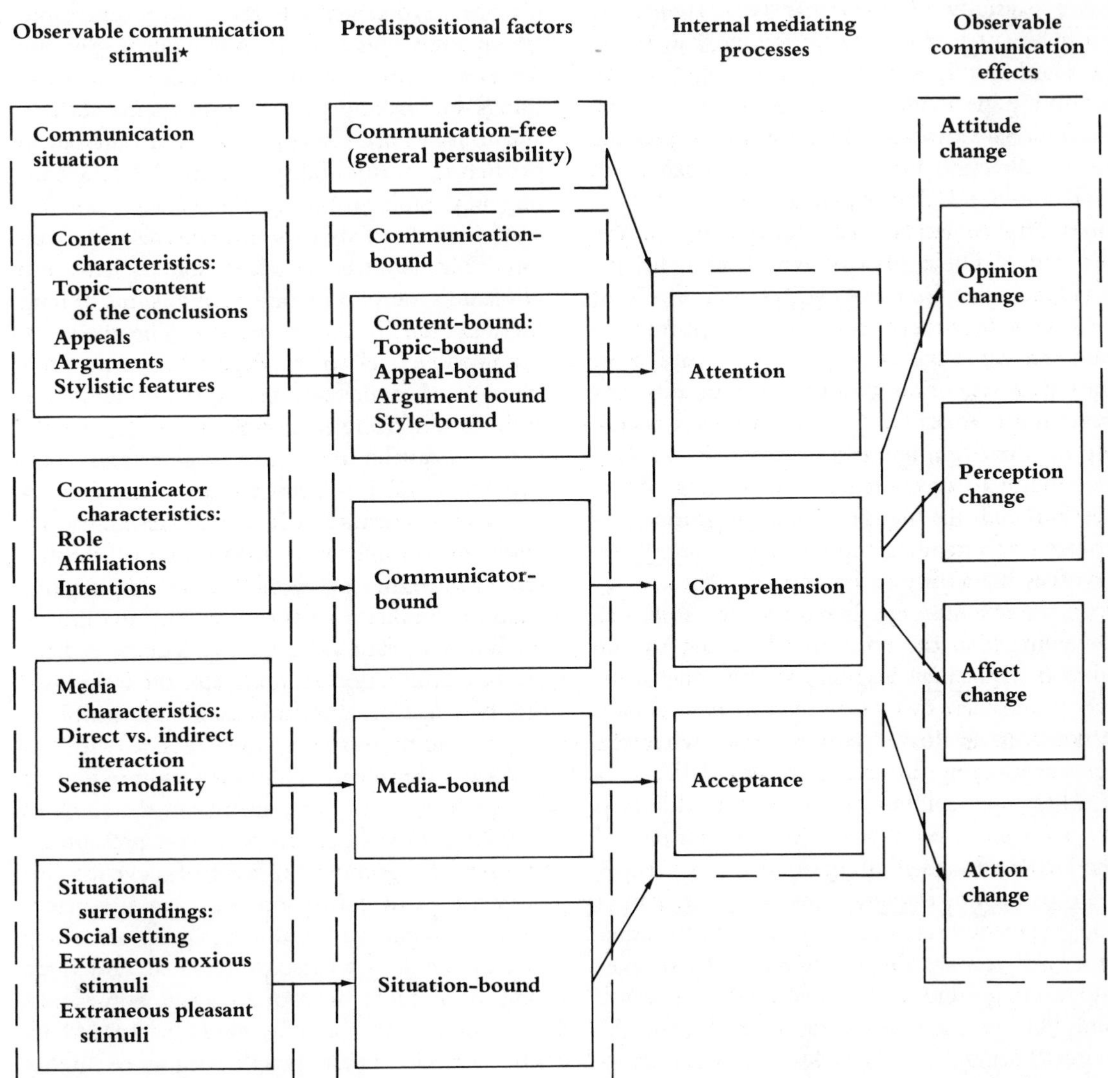

*The categories and subcategories are not necessarily exhaustive but are intended to highlight the main types of stimulus variables that play a role in producing changes in verbalizable attitudes.

Personality and Persuasibility by Irving Janis, et al. New Haven: Yale University Press, 1959. Reprinted by permission of the publisher.

Figure 8.1. Major factors in attitude change produced by means of social communication.

to discover various personality correlates of persuasibility. The researchers wanted to know what kind of person tends to be persuasible or not persuasible. With a few exceptions, though, this line of research reached a dead end. It became painfully obvious that persuasibility is more a matter of internal processes than traits. Persuasibility appears to be a complex matter involving particular interactions among the mediational variables. In attempting to provide clearer direction for research, Irving Janis and Carl Hovland developed a theory of persuasibility to explain the complexity of the problem.[13] These authors hypothesize that individuals vary in their *abilities* and levels of *motivation* to process messages. Communication receivers have varying degrees of ability in four areas: attention, comprehension, anticipation, and evaluation. *Attention* involves focusing on the communication stimuli; it involves the ability to pay attention to aspects of the speaker and the message. *Comprehension* involves understanding the message. *Anticipation* involves the ability to imagine or rehearse acceptance of a message. It requires the ability to see yourself in the position advocated by the speaker. *Evaluation* involves scrutinizing arguments and identifying attempts to manipulate. When you evaluate, you criticize what the speaker is saying, in your own mind at least.

These four abilities can be combined in two ways for purposes of analysis. The first part of the analysis looks at attention and comprehension together as *learning factors* and anticipation and evaluation as *acceptance factors*. In other words, if you are able to attend to the speaker and message and comprehend what is being said, you are more apt to internalize or learn the material being discussed. Likewise, if you anticipate going along with the speaker and you are not too critical of what the speaker is saying, you are more apt to be persuaded. The second kind of analysis considers attention, comprehension, and anticipation as *facilitating factors* and evaluation as an *inhibiting factor*. High abilities to attend, comprehend, and anticipate will promote persuasibility, but a high ability to evaluate will retard persuasibility.

Of course, abilities alone will not determine the degree to which attention, comprehension, anticipation, and evaluation will occur. Because the person must be able not only to do these things but be motivated to do them, abilities and motives are always considered together in predicting persuasibility. Figure 8.2 is a contingency table outlining the various possible combinations of abilities and motives in persuasion. The table is an adaptation of Janis and Hovland's outline of interrelationships among the basic factors in the model. The theorists' assumptions, related to Figure 8.2, are as follows: (1) A deficiency in the three facilitating abilities will decrease persuasibility. (2) A deficiency in evaluation ability will increase persuasibility. (3) Low motivation to use facilitative abilities results in lower persuasibility. (4) High motivation to use the facilitating abilities results in higher persuasibility. (5) High motivation to evaluate leads to lower persuasibility. (6) When all four abilities are adequate and the level of motivation is moderate, the individual will be selective, discriminating, and flexible in responding to persuasive messages.

As an example imagine that you have given a speech to a community group on the topic of recycling. In your speech you have presented a number of arguments in favor of recycling, involving political, economic, and conservationist points. You might expect, according to this theory of persuasibility, to find three kinds of members in your audience. Some audience members would be easily persuaded by your speech. These people would be highly motivated and able to pay attention, to comprehend your speech, and to imagine themselves going to the recycling center. Such individuals probably would not be particularly able or motivated to evaluated your arguments. Another kind of person would be stubborn and resistant to persuasion. Such individuals prob-

13. Janis, *Personality*, chap. 12.

ably would have low motivation and/or ability to attend, to comprehend, and to anticipate. Or these individuals might be highly motivated and able to evaluate your arguments. A third group of people in the audience would be adaptable and flexible. Such individuals would not be automatically persuaded or resistant but would make a decision based on your arguments and their needs. They probably would have a moderate motivation and ability to attend, comprehend, anticipate, and evaluate.

This theory conceives of persuasibility as a condition, not a trait. Persuasibility may be caused by any number of interactions among predispositional and mediating factors. If persuasibility is not a singular type, then it must have several variations, depending on the individual combination of factors present in the persuasible or nonpersuasible person.

In reviewing Hovland and Janis's theory of persuasibility, we must realize that this attempt was the first to systematize an approach for the purpose of structuring research. In a more recent treatment William McGuire further amplifies the complexity of the matter of influenceability. McGuire notes that persuasibility is really part of the larger condition of general *influenceability*, whether in the form of persuasion, conformity, or suggestibility. Again, the issue is important, for it suggests that significant *individual differences* exist in terms of being influenced across situations.[14]

We have already seen that influenceability is the consequence of complex relationships among mediating variables within the person and situation. McGuire further contributes to this view by defining the main principles involved in these mediational relationships. He outlines five such principles. These principles are important for our consideration because they illustrate once again that persuasion—indeed communication—is hardly a simple cause-effect relationship.

The first principle of influenceability is the *mediational* principle. This relatively simple principle restates what we have said above, that persuasibility is mediated by a number of intervening variables. One cannot understand the

14. William J. McGuire, "The Nature of Attitudes and Attitude Change," in *The Handbook of Social Psychology*, vol. 3, ed. Gardner Lindzey and Elliot Aronson (Reading, Mass.: Addison-Wesley, 1969), pp. 136–314; see also McGuire, "Personality and Susceptibility to Social Influence," in *Handbook of Personality Theory and Research*, ed. E. F. Borgatta and W. W. Lambert (Chicago: Rand McNally, 1967); McGuire, "Personality and Attitude Change: An Information-Processing Theory," in *Psychological Foundations of Attitudes*, ed. Anthony G. Greenwald, Timothy C. Brock, and Thomas M. Ostrom (New York: Academic Press, 1968), pp. 171–95.

		Facilitative abilities: Attention, comprehension, and anticipation			**Inhibiting ability: Evaluation**		
		High	**Medium**	**Low**	**High**	**Medium**	**Low**
Motives	**High**	**Persuasible**		**Not persuasible**	**Not persuasible**		**Persuasible**
	Moderate		**Adaptive**			**Adaptive**	
	Low	**Not persuasible**	**Not persuasible**	**Not persuasible**	**Persuasible**	**Persuasible**	**Persuasible**

Figure 8.2. Combinations of abilities and motives as they relate to persuasibility.

relationship between personality and persuasibility without considering the ways various personality factors affect such mediators as intelligence, age, self-esteem, and anxiety.

The second principle is that of *compensation*. This principle states that various mediating factors will have opposing effects, thus tending to compensate or cancel out one another. An important corollary of the compensation principle is that the intermediate levels of compensating variables maximize influenceability. The reason for this is that when a particular person is high on one variable, a compensating low level on another variable may cancel out the effect of the first, but all relevant mediating variables combine optimally at the middle of the range. For an overly simple example, consider the hypothetical relationship among three variables: age, anxiety, and influenceability. Imagine that age is inversely related to influenceability: Younger people are more easily influenced than older people. Imagine further that anxiety is positively related to influenceability: More anxious people are more easily influenced than relaxed people. Now, if age and anxiety are negatively correlated (younger people tend to be more anxious), these variables will cancel each other out at the extremes, and influenceability will be highest in the middle range—among middle-aged people who are moderately anxious.

The third principle is the *situational-weighting* principle, which states that the type of influence affects how much difference will be found in audience influenceability. McGuire discusses three types of influence: suggestion, conformity, and persuasion. By suggestion he means simple messages that require little attention on the part of the listener. Most people are easily influenced by suggestion, and there is little difference between people in their degree of suggestion-influenceability. Conformity is defined as group pressure influence. People vary moderately in the degree to which they will be influenced by conformity pressure. By persuasion McGuire means complex discourse that involves message elements that are more difficult, such as rational argument. Since persuasion requires abilities to attend and comprehend and since people vary in these abilities, a great deal of difference exists among people in terms of how much they will be influenced by persuasive communication.

Fourth, the *confounding* principle states that variables cluster together into syndromes. Another way of saying this is that the mediating variables within a person will correlate with one another in different ways. For example, researchers have found that self-esteem correlates negatively with persuasibility. But since self-esteem correlates differently with other variables such as depression and withdrawal, the investigator cannot really understand the net effect of self-esteem on persuasibility without first knowing how it intercorrelates with the other two variables. Suppose, for example, a person who has low self-esteem is depressed and withdraws. Such a person would not expose himself or herself to many communicative messages and therefore would be a poor message receiver, thus lowering persuasibility.

Fifth is the *interaction* principle, which concerns the mediating variables in the person that create individual persuasibility differences. These variables interact with other external communication variables, such as source and message, to determine the final actual change. This principle, of course, argues against a strictly general persuasibility factor.

What these principles mean to our understanding of persuasion and persuasibility is that the degree to which a person is influenced by a persuasive message depends on a number of specific interrelationships among the factors within that person. We may never be able to find strong singular correlates of persuasibility because of the numerous possible combinations of individual-difference variables within the person. The more fruitful approach thus seems to be to define the broad principles involved in the process, as McGuire has done, and to hypothesize specific types of persuasibility, as did Janis and Hovland. And so, according to McGuire, you could not easily predict who would and who would not be influenced by your recycling speech on the basis of their simple abilities and motives, as suggested in the earlier example.

Criticism

The Yale work has been criticized primarily because of its theoretical *inappropriateness*.[15] Some critics have observed, for example, that the Yale studies represent a modern-day, empirical elaboration of Aristotelian theory. As such the model employed by the Yale group is overly linear, ignoring interaction and feedback. The underlying model of this work suggests a series of causal links from message to receiver to effect. The work leaves little room for human action, since people are seen as behaving primarily in accord with external pressures and internal mediators.

On the other hand, this tradition has been praised for its heuristic value. The original Yale monographs were filled with research ideas that for two decades stimulated a great deal of research on attitude change. Although the Yale studies seem simplistic by today's standards, they were a landmark in taking a first step toward researching actual communication variables.

Information-Processing Theories of Persuasion

Information-Integration Theory

General Background. The information-integration approach centers on the ways people accumulate and organize information about some person, object, situation, or idea to form attitudes toward that concept. The construct *attitude* has been important in persuasion theory. An attitude usually is defined as a predisposition to act in a positive or negative way toward the attitude object, although the correlation between attitude and behavior has been shown to be tenuous. At any rate much persuasion research has focused on *attitude change*. The information-integration approach is one of the most credible models of the nature of attitudes.[16]

According to this theory, an individual's attitude system can be affected by information that is received and integrated into the attitude-information system. All information has the potential of affecting one's attitudes, but the degree to which it affects attitudes depends on two variables. The first is *valence*. Valence is an individual's judgment about the degree to which the information is good news or bad news. If it supports one's beliefs and attitudes, it generally will be viewed as good; if not, it probably will be seen as bad. Of course any particular piece of information will be evaluated in terms of a scale from very bad to very good. The second variable that affects the importance of information to a person is the weight assigned to the information. *Weight* is a function of reliability. If the person thinks the information is probably true, a higher weight will be assigned to the information; if not, a lower weight will be given. Valence affects how information influences attitudes; weight affects the degree to which it does so. When the assigned weight is low, the information will have little effect, no matter what its valence.

For example, suppose that you have two friends, one who is strongly in favor of increasing the United States' nuclear strength and the other who is strongly in favor of unilateral arms reduction. Suppose further that you and your friends are told that the president is about to

15. My criticism of this work and the following theories is heavily influenced by the excellent distillation of Mary John Smith, *Persuasion and Human Action*. I have also relied heavily on Charles A. Kiesler, Barry E. Collins, and Norman Miller, *Attitude Change: A Critical Analysis of Theoretical Approaches* (New York: John Wiley & Sons, 1969).

16. Contributors include Norman H. Anderson, "Integration Theory and Attitude Change," *Psychological Review* 78 (1971): 171–206; Martin Fishbein and Icek Ajzen, *Belief, Attitude, Intention, and Behavior* (Reading, Mass.: Addison-Wesley, 1975); Robert S. Wyer, *Cognitive Organization and Change* (Hillsdale, N.J.: Erlbaum 1974).

announce that the United States will initiate a good-faith arms reduction with the hope that the Soviet Union will respond likewise. How will this information affect your attitudes toward U.S. arms policy? If your two friends accept this information as true, they will assign a high weight to it, and it will affect their attitudes toward the president. One of your friends definitely will define the information as bad news, and his attitude toward the president will likely become more negative. However, your other friend will see this information as good, and her attitude toward the president may become more positive. You, on the other hand, don't believe this information is accurate and therefore you assign it little weight. Consequently, regardless of your initial attitude, the information probably will not affect your attitude toward the president one way or another.

An attitude is considered to be an accumulation of information about the attitude object, each piece of information having been evaluated as we have just indicated. (The exact way that information is accumulated to form an attitude is in dispute.[17]) Thus attitude change occurs because of new information or changing judgments of truthfulness or value.

Fishbein: Beliefs and Attitudes. One of the best-known and respected attitude theorists is Martin Fishbein.[18] Fishbein's contribution is important because it highlights the complex and interactive nature of attitudes. According to Fishbein, there are two kinds of belief, both of which are probability statements. The first is what he terms *belief in* a thing. When one believes *in* something, he or she predicts a high probability of existence. The second kind of belief, *belief about*, is the predicted probability that a particular relationship exists between the belief object and some other quality or thing. Again, this is a probability situation, and one's belief is the predicted probability of the existence of a particular relationship. For example, one may believe *in* God, that God exists. One may also believe that God is omnipotent—a probability statement of a relationship between God and omnipotence.

Attitudes differ from beliefs in that they are *evaluative*. Beliefs are probability statements of evaluation or judgment. Attitudes are correlated with beliefs and predispose a person to behave a certain way toward the attitude object. Attitudes are learned as part of one's concept formation. They may change as new learnings occur throughout life. Furthermore, Fishbein sees attitudes as hierarchically organized. In other words, general attitudes are predicted from specific ones in a *summative* fashion. An attitude toward an object is the sum of the specific factors, including beliefs and evaluations, in the family hierarchy. This formula is represented algebraically as follows.[19]

$$A_o = \sum_{I}^{N} B_i a_i$$

where

A_o = the attitude toward object o
B_i = the strength of belief i about o; that is, the probability or improbability that o is associated with some other concept x_i
a_i = the evaluative aspect of B_i; that is, the evaluation of x_i
N = the number of beliefs about o.

The distinctive feature of Fishbein's formula is that it stresses the interactive nature of attitudes. Attitudes are a function of a complex factor that involves both beliefs (probability predictions) and evaluations. The example in Table 8.1 will

17. For a review of the issues in this dispute, see Smith, *Persuasion*, 245–48.

18. Fishbein has published several articles on this topic. Among these are "A Behavior Theory Approach to the Relations between Beliefs about an Object and the Attitude toward the Object," "A Consideration of Beliefs and Their Role in Attitude Measurement," and "The AB Scales: An Operational Definition of Belief and Attitude." These three articles are reprinted in *Readings in Attitude Theory and Measurement*, ed. Martin Fishbein (New York: John Wiley & Sons, 1967). For an excellent secondary source see David T. Burhans, "The Attitude-Behavior Discrepancy Problem: Revisited," *Quarterly Journal of Speech* 57 (1971): 418–28. For a more recent treatment see Fishbein and Ajzen, *Belief*.

19. Fishbein, "A Behavior Theory," p. 394.

help to clarify this model. According to this conceptualization, attitude change can occur from any of three sources. First, information can alter the believability (weight) of particular beliefs. Second, information can change the value of a belief. Finally, information can add new beliefs to the attitude structure.

Criticism. Most of the negative criticism of information-integration theory relates to the validity of measurement. Although the idea that attitudes consist of accumulated and weighted beliefs is generally accepted, there is quite a bit of doubt that one can measure the overall accumulated weight and value of a belief system

TABLE 8.1
A simplified example of an attitude hierarchy according to the Fishbein model

ATTITUDE OBJECT (o)→ JOGGING N = 6 (NUMBER OF BELIEFS IN SYSTEM)

ASSOCIATED CONCEPTS (x_i)	PROBABILITY OF ASSOCIATION (B_i)	EVALUATION (a_i)
x_1 Cardiovascular health	B_1 Jogging promotes cardiovascular vigor.	a_1 Cardiovascular vigor is good.
x_2 Disease	B_2 Jogging reduces the chance of disease.	a_2 Disease is bad.
x_3 Obesity	B_3 Jogging reduces weight.	a_3 Being overweight is bad.
x_4 Mental health	B_4 Jogging promotes peace of mind.	a_4 Letting off mental tensions is good.
x_5 Friendship	B_5 Jogging introduces a person to new friends.	a_5 Friendship is important.
x_6 Physique	B_6 Jogging builds better bodies.	a_6 A beautiful body is appealing.

Scale for B: 0 = very unlikely association; 1 = highly likely association
Scale for a: 1= strongly disagree; 5 = strongly agree
Scale for A: 0 = very negative attitude; 25 = very positive attitude

X	HYPOTHETICAL NEGATIVE ATTITUDE TOWARD JOGGING		HYPOTHETICAL POSITIVE ATTITUDE TOWARD JOGGING	
	PROBABILITY	EVALUATION	PROBABILITY	EVALUATION
X_1	$B_1 = .30$	$a_1 = 4$	$B_1 = .95$	$a_1 = 5$
X_2	$B_2 = .30$	$a_2 = 5$	$B_2 = .60$	$a_2 = 5$
X_3	$B_3 = .50$	$a_3 = 3$	$B_3 = .80$	$a_3 = 4$
X_4	$B_4 = .10$	$a_4 = 4$	$B_4 = .80$	$a_4 = 4$
X_5	$B_5 = .20$	$a_5 = 3$	$B_5 = .60$	$a_5 = 4$
X_6	$B_6 = .70$	$a_6 = 2$	$B_6 = .50$	$a_6 = 2$
	$A_o = (.30)\,4 + (.30)\,5 + (.50)\,3 + (.10)\,4 + (.20)\,3 + (.70)\,2 = 6.6$		$A_o = (.95)\,5 + (.60)\,5 + (.80)\,4 + (.80)\,4 + (.60)\,4 + (.50)\,2 = 17.55$	

with any degree of reliability. In the natural setting a researcher would first have to isolate beliefs contributing to an attitude, measure them accurately, and factor out the influence of other elements of the system. Since this process is difficult or impossible to do, most research in this tradition is artificial, hypothetical, and controlled. This problem thus casts doubt on the *external validity* of the claims.

The other serious problem among research studies in this area is that serious disagreement exists about the way one accumulates information to form an attitude. The research evidence is equivocal on this point. This controversy casts doubt on the *internal validity* of the approach.

The difficulty with criticizing research methodology is that every method of observation, in the natural setting or in the laboratory, has weaknesses. One can always question the reliability and validity of data collection. The fact is that this theory has been widely acclaimed in the field. Methodological problems aside, this theory provides a useful model for understanding the nature of attitude and attitude change from an information-processing point of view.

Social Judgment Theory

Social judgment theory is primarily a product of the work of the social psychologist Muzafer Sherif and his associates.[20] This theory finds its roots in the early psychophysical research in which persons were tested in their ability to judge physical stimuli. Using this paradigm as an analogy, Sherif investigated the ways individuals judge nonphysical objects or social stimuli. He learned that many principles of psychophysics hold for social judgment as well.

20. The first major work in this area was Muzafer Sherif and Carl Hovland, *Social Judgment*. See also Muzafer Sherif, Carolyn Sherif, and Roger Nebergall, *Attitude and Attitude Change: The Social Judgment-Involvement Approach* (Philadelphia: W. B. Saunders, 1965). For a brief overview of the theory, see Muzafer Sherif, *Social Interaction—Process and Products* (Chicago: Aldine, 1967), chaps. 16, 17, 18. Several secondary sources are also available; see, for example, Kiesler, Collins, and Miller, *Attitude Change*, chap. 6.

Sherif and his colleagues found that individual judgments of things and people are highly situational and depend on one's initial orientation toward the world. The psychological literature shows that people make judgments about things based on anchors or reference points. Suppose that you are involved in an experimental situation in which you are asked to judge the relative weight of five objects. On what would you base your judgment? If the experimenter handed you a weight and told you it was ten pounds, you would first feel the reference weight and then make judgments about the other objects based on the kinesthetic feeling you received from the known weight. In this case the known weight would act as an anchor, influencing your judgment of the others. In fact, with a different initial weight, you would judge the same objects differently. To demonstrate this idea of anchors, you could try a simple experiment. Take three bowls. Fill the first with hot water, the second with cold water, the third with tepid water. Put one hand in the hot water, the other in the cold water; and after a few moments, place both hands in the tepid water. Your perceptions of the tepid water will be different for each hand because each hand had a different anchor, or reference.

Sherif reasons that similar processes operate in judging communication messages. In social perception anchors are internal; they are based on past experience. The internal anchor or reference point is always present and influences the way a person responds in communication with others. The more important the issue is to one's ego, the stronger the anchor will influence what is understood.

We will now look at the central concepts of social judgment theory. These include the *latitude of acceptance, rejection, and noncommitment*. In a social judgment experiment you would be given a large number of statements about some issue. You then would be asked to sort these messages into groups according to similarity of position. You could use as many groups as you wished. Then you would order these groups in terms of position on a negative-positive scale, and you would indicate which groups are acceptable to you personally, which are not acceptable, and which are neutral. The first measures your latitude of acceptance, the second your latitude of rejection, and the third your latitude of noncommitment. We can see that an individual will approach real-life messages in the same way. While a person has a particular attitude about the issue, there will be a range of statements, pro or con, that the person can tolerate; there will also be a range that one cannot accept.

Another important concept from social judgment is *ego-involvement*. Previously, an attitude was thought to be measured primarily in terms of valence (direction, pro or con) and the degree of agreement or disagreement. But Sherif demonstrates that ego-involvement is significant apart from either of these other two dimensions of attitude. Ego-involvement is the degree to which one's attitude toward something affects the self-concept. It is a measure of how important the issue is to the individual. For example, you may have read a great deal of material supporting the viewpoint that marijuana should be legalized. You may feel strongly on the issue because of the literature you have read. Thus you would have a strong positive attitude toward legalization, but your ego-involvement might be very low if your life is relatively unaffected by the issue. But if you are a regular marijuana smoker and have been arrested for possessing the drug, no doubt you would be highly ego-involved. Ego-involvement makes a great deal of difference in how you respond to messages related to the issue. There is a relatively high correlation between involvement and extremity, but it is not a perfect correlation. In fact, it is possible for a person to be neutral on an issue, yet highly ego-involved.

Now let us consider what social judgment theory says about the communication process. The social judgment theory is a fine contribution to our understanding of communication because it explains two important behaviors of audiences in receiving messages. First, we know from Sherif's work that individuals judge the favorability of a message based on their own internal anchors of position and ego-involvement. On a given issue, such as legalization of marijuana, a person will distort the message by *contrast* or *assimilation*. The contrast effect occurs when individuals judge a message to be farther from their point of view than it actually is. The assimilation effect occurs when persons judge the message to be closer to their point of view than it actually is.

Basically, when a message is relatively close to one's own position, that message will be assimilated. In the case of relatively distant messages, contrast is likely to occur. These assimilation and contrast effects are heightened by ego-involvement. For example, if you were strongly in favor of the legalization of marijuana, a moderately favorable statement might seem like a strong positive statement because of your assimilation; while a slightly unfavorable statement might be perceived to be strongly opposed to one's view because of contrast. If you were highly ego-involved in the issue, this effect would be even greater. Suppose, for example, that someone told you that they thought possession and smoking of marijuana should be legal but that growing the plant on a commercial basis should be against the law. If you were highly ego-involved in your belief that the drug should be legalized, you might perceive this statement to be strongly against marijuana, even though it is a rather middle-of-the-road position.

The second area in which social judgment theory aids our understanding of communication is attitude change. The predictions made by social judgment theory are the following: (1) Messages falling within the latitude of acceptance facilitate attitude change. (2) If a message is judged by the person to lie within the latitude of rejection, attitude change will be reduced or nonexistent. In fact, a boomerang effect may occur in which the discrepant message actually reinforces one's own position on the issue. (3) Within the latitude of acceptance and noncommitment, the more discrepant the message from the person's own stand, the greater the expected attitude change. However, once the message hits the latitude of rejection, change will not be expected. (4) The greater one's ego-involvement in the issue, the larger the latitude of rejection, the smaller the latitude of noncommitment, and thus the less the expected attitude change. In summary, social judgment theory predicts a curvilinear relationship between discrepancy and attitude change, as indicated in Figure 8.3.

In our example of the legalization of marijuana, imagine that two people receive the same message opposing legalization. Assume this message is only moderately opposed. Person A believes that the possession of marijuana should not be a crime; Person B adamantly favors legalization and is highly ego-involved. These two people, while both on the positive side of legalization, would respond differently to the message opposing it. The first individual would have a large latitude of acceptance, a relative large latitude of noncommitment, and a very small latitude of rejection. In other words,

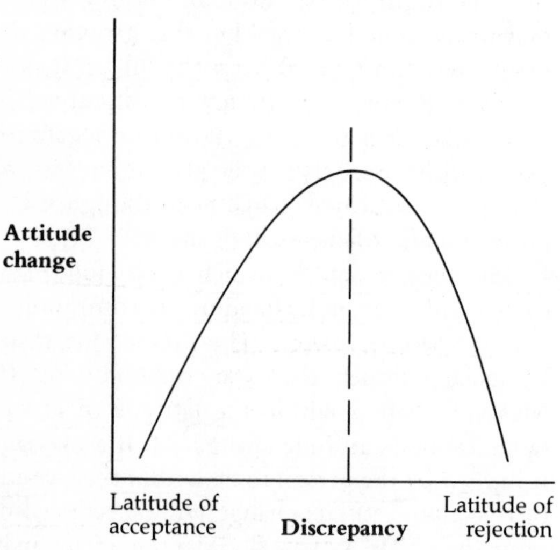

Figure 8.3. Theoretical relationship between discrepancy and change.

Person A would be open to communications ranging from positive to negative on the issue. We would predict that Person A would be influenced to shift the position in the direction of the message. Person B, on the other hand, probably would have a large latitude of rejection. Ego-involvement would cause this person to reject almost all messages discrepant from his or her own. Since the latitude of rejection is so large in Person B, most messages would not be acceptable, and attitude change would not be predicted.

Criticism. The major strength of social judgment theory is its *parsimony*. It presents an intuitively believable set of claims based on just a few important constructs. Although this theory is no longer in vogue, its aesthetic elegance elicited great popularity in the 1960s, and it stimulated a good deal of research, which speaks well for its *heuristic* value. Ego-involvement, which the theory presented as a core construct, has since become a mainstay in persuasion literature.

The basic problem with social judgment theory is that it begs the question on some important claims. It fails to prove certain key assumptions. The theory assumes, for example, that there is a sequential, causal mechanism whereby judgment as a cognitive activity precedes attitude change. All of the claims of the theory follow from this assumption, which may not hold. For example, the theory claims that the judgment process may lead to distortion of a message, affecting latitudes of acceptance and thereby affecting the potential for attitude change. However, the same result could also be explained by other factors. This objection to social judgment theory casts doubt on its validity.

Theories of Cognitive Reorganization and Persuasion

The theories in this section share a common focus on reorganization of the cognitive system. All of these theories conceive of persuasion as largely an intrapersonal event in which self-persuasion is the key. In short, persuasion is strictly a matter of cognitive reorganization. Two types of theory are presented: social learning and cognitive consistency theories.

Social Learning Theory

Traditionally learning theory has been a deterministic approach that presumed that people's behavior is shaped by associations and reinforcers in the environment. Positively reinforced behaviors are thought to increase in frequency, while negatively reinforced behaviors decrease. In traditional learning theory little freedom is accorded individuals to make choices about how to respond in a situation. Behavior is considered to be more or less programmed.[21]

Social learning theory teaches the importance of reinforcers, but unlike traditional learning theory this newer approach postulates not only that people make choices about behavior but that they also control the reinforcers in their environment.

Social learning theory is attributed primarily to Albert Bandura.[22] Bandura's theory is a cognitive approach to learning. The paradigm is stated briefly as follows: (1) People establish goals that entail rewards or positive consequences if achieved. (2) People choose to behave in ways that have the potential for achieving the goals. (3) People interpret the consequences of behavior as rewards or punishments. (4) Choices are affected by the perceived successes and failures of the past as well as by anticipated consequences in the future. In other words, behavior is shaped by interaction between external conditions and internal cognitive processes.

As an example consider a woman who wants to stop smoking. She has the ability within herself to set that as a goal, and she can imagine a number of rewards that would result from not smoking. For instance, she might imagine that her health would improve, that her life would be extended, that her house would not be filled with smoke, and that she would be more pleasant to other people. In other words, this individual would be setting herself up for positive reinforcers that could help her change her own behavior. Next, she would develop a deliberate plan to reduce smoking and then stop altogether. Perhaps she would go to a stop-smoking clinic or other program, or perhaps she would stop cold turkey. She would then become conscious of the consequences of her behavior. If some of the imagined rewards actually happened, she would be induced to remain a nonsmoker; however, if negative consequences were experienced, she might decide to begin smoking again. For example, she might discover that she begins to gain weight as she reduces her smoking. Ultimately, her behavior will be affected one way or another by her own cognitive interpretations of the consequences of her actions. If she fails and returns to smoking, she will probably be reluctant in the near future to try stopping again.

Reinforcement in one's environment serves two functions, according to Bandura. The first is *informational*. The consequences of one's actions help the individual to learn the rules, instructing the person about which actions lead to favorable results and which do not. The learned rules are guides for how to act in the future. Children, for instance, often learn social rules by trial and error. Through this process they come to learn what is proper to say or not say in different situations. The second function of reinforcement is *motivational*; that is, choices are affected by perceived consequences. One is motivated to repeat rewarded actions and to avoid punished actions. An individual, such as the woman in the example about stopping smoking, is motivated to behave in certain ways because of her cognitive understanding of the consequences of behavior.

Clearly information from outside affects our internal cognitions to a large extent. This in-

21. For a summary of traditional approaches to learning, see J. W. Kling, "Learning: Introductory Survey," in *Woodworth and Schlossberg's Experimental Psychology*, ed. J. W. Kling and Lorrin Riggs (New York: Holt, Rinehart and Winston, 1971), pp. 551–613.

22. Albert Bandura, *Social Learning Theory* (Englewood Cliffs, N.J.: Prentice-Hall, 1977).

formation can come from direct experience, role playing, or modeling. In *direct experience* one observes directly what happens as a consequence of a certain action. The smoker referred to put herself through a direct experience to stop smoking. *Role playing* is mental identification with a certain kind of behavior within a particular situation. The person mentally rehearses an action and imagines what the consequences would be. In trying to stop smoking, an individual might imagine what it would be like not to smoke and might anticipate the rewards that could accrue. The difference between direct experience and role playing is that the former is real and direct, while the latter is imagined and indirect. *Modeling*, the third source of social learning, involves actually witnessing another person's actions and the consequences. The woman who wanted to stop smoking might have been motivated because of a good friend who seemed to benefit from stopping. Modeling is perhaps the most common way adults learn.

We have indicated that people often create their own rewards and punishments. This hypothesis is an important part of social learning theory. Our internal standards act as reinforcers. We apply these standards to our behavior, rewarding ourselves when we think we have done a good job and punishing ourselves when we believe we have let down. Self-esteem is an important determinant of self-reinforcement because the higher our self-esteem, the more we value our own choices.

This theory represents a major epistemological shift in the field of social psychology and learning theory. The original formulations of learning and reinforcement on which this theory is based are deterministic; but by shifting the focus to cognitive choice and internal reinforcement, Bandura has adopted a teleological and actional set of assumptions. How an individual construes and interprets events is considered to be all important in determining personal knowledge. Further, a person's understanding of behavioral consequences is largely a result of social knowledge. Both role playing and modeling are mechanisms for the social development of knowledge. This is not to argue that all knowledge is a matter of social consensus. Indeed, this theory stresses idiosyncratic interpretations. The point is that learning occurs as a result of identification with others.

Criticism. The strength of social learning theory is its consistency with current trends in persuasion that emphasize the importance of individual interpretation and choice in making changes. Its external *validity* is generally considered to be strong.

The weakness of the theory is its restricted scope. While it identifies learning as a major source of personal change, it ignores other possible sources of change, including many of the factors identified by other theories summarized in this chapter. From a communication standpoint Bandura's approach does not help us understand how verbal communication affects beliefs, attitudes, and behavior. Surely reinforcement and rule learning must be affected by interaction with others, yet Bandura provides little help in understanding the relationship between what people say to others—their messages—and attitude and behavior change.

Theories of Cognitive Consistency

General Background. The largest portion of work in psychology related to attitude, attitude change, and persuasion undoubtedly is *consistency theory*. All of these theories begin with the same basic premise: People need to be consistent or at least see themselves as consistent. The vocabulary and concepts change from theory to theory, and the hypothesized relationships among variables differ, but the basic assumption of consistency remains. In a *Psychology Today* interview one of the major consistency theorists, Theodore Newcomb, discusses this assumption: "I happen to have studied the tendency toward balance, but that doesn't mean there is anything inherently good or desirable about it. Education, life itself, thrives on imbalances. Without them you would live like an oyster, utterly passive. Most kinds of fun and excitement begin with inconsistency, with the possible exception of unrequited love. The best scientist, for example, looks for the inconsistencies. . . . My point is not that we don't seek inconsistencies, but that we have trouble living with them for very long. The direction of change is very likely to be toward balance."[23] In system language, people seek *homeostatis*. In fact, this theme of consistency can be related well to the system view that the goal of an open system is self-maintenance and balance (Chapter 3).

These theories tend to be nonactional, assuming that individuals basically are responsive to environmental pressures. Behavior change results from information in the environment that disrupts balance of the cognitive system. These theories are also discovery oriented, relying on research that aims to discover precisely what conditions lead to change and to predict the nature and degree of change. In short, knowledge is not something that one participates in actively; rather, one's knowledge of the world results from conditions of balance or imbalance. People are under pressure to see the world in consistent ways.

The consistency theories of attitude and attitude change began in the mid 1940s with the work of Fritz Heider. Over the following decade several additions and modifications were made on the basic idea of balance. Heider's primary contribution to consistency theory is his introduction of the concept of balance and his initiation of research in this area.[24]

One of the first important extensions of Heider's idea was that of Theodore Newcomb. Newcomb has been primarily interested in interpersonal attraction. (We will look again at his ideas in Chapter 10.) Newcomb's contribution is his application of Heider's hypothesis to communication. The model explains the simplest possible communicative act: two people conversing about a topic of mutual interest. Newcomb then analyses this situation in terms of the varying orientations of the communicators toward the topic and its effect on their attitudes and toward each other.[25]

Another theory of cognitive consistency is the congruity model, proposed in 1955 by Osgood and Tannenbaum as one application of their work on the measurement of meaning (see Chapter 6).[26] This theory is in line with the earlier work of Heider and Newcomb but extends these models by applying a measurement technique and attempting more precise prediction of outcome. This model involves three basic elements: a perceiver and two objects of judgment. When the objects of judgment (concepts, people, and so forth) are brought into association with one another, then congruity or incongruity will result. If the perceiver's judgment, or evaluation, of the two elements is consistent, then congruity exists. If it is inconsistent, there is pressure to change.

In the remainder of this section, two prominent theories of cognitive consistency are summarized. These were chosen because of their prominence in the field and their relative completeness of explanation. The first is the theory of cognitive dissonance by Leon Festinger and the second is the theory of attitudes, beliefs, and values of Milton Rokeach.

The Theory of Cognitive Dissonance. Leon Festinger's theory of cognitive dissonance is the most significant and impactful consistency theory. In fact, it is one of the most important theories in the history of social psychology.

23. Carol Tavris, "What Does College Do for a Person? Frankly, Very Little," *Psychology Today*, September 1974, p. 78.

24. Fritz Heider, "Attitudes and Cognitive Organization," *Journal of Psychology* 21 (1946): 107–12; *The Psychology of Interpersonal Relations* (New York: John Wiley & Sons, 1958).

25. Theodore Newcomb, *The Acquaintance Process* (New York: Holt, Rinehart and Winston, 1961); "An Approach to the Study of Communicative Acts," *Psychological Review* 60 (1953): 393–404.

26. Charles E. Osgood and Percy Tannenbaum, "The Principle of Congruity in the Prediction of Attitude Change," *Psychological Review* 62 (1955): 42–55.

Over the years it has produced a prodigious quantity of research as well as volumes of criticism, interpretation, and extrapolation.[27] Festinger broadened the scope of consistency theory to include a range of what he called cognitive elements, including attitudes, perceptions, knowledge, and behaviors. Two cognitive elements (an attitude and a behavior, perhaps) will have one of three kinds of relationships. The first of these is null or *irrelevant*, the second consistent or *consonant*, and the third inconsistent or *dissonant*. Dissonance is a relationship in which one element would not be expected to follow from the other. It is important to note that dissonance is a matter of psychological consistency, not of logical relationships. Dissonance and consonance therefore must be evaluated in terms of a single individual's psychological system. We must always ask what is consonant or dissonant for a person's own psychological system. More formally, Festinger defines cognitive dissonance as a situation in which the opposite of one element follows from the other.

Two overriding premises are found in dissonance theory. The first is that dissonance produces tension or stress that pressures the individual to change so that the dissonance is thereby reduced. Second, when dissonance is present, the individual will not only attempt to reduce it but will avoid situations in which additional dissonance might be produced. These tendencies to reduce dissonance and to avoid dissonance-producing information are a direct function of the magnitude of dissonance present in the system; the greater the dissonance, the greater the need for change. Dissonance is a result of two antecedent variables, the importance of the cognitive elements and the number of elements involved in the dissonant relation. This latter variable is a matter of balance: the more equal the number of elements on the sides of the relation, the greater the dissonance.

Consider two examples of a low-dissonance prediction. On a particular day you may be faced with a decision of whether to eat breakfast. Suppose you are expecting to meet a friend to go shopping, but your alarm didn't go off and you are late. You can skip breakfast and be on time, or you can eat toast and coffee and be a little late. You will quickly decide to do one or the other, but in any case some dissonance will result. This dissonance probably will be small because neither eating breakfast nor being on time is important. But if your situation involves being late for work, a different variable is operating. You probably would choose to skip breakfast and be on time. The prediction is the same (a small amount of dissonance), but the reason is different. The deck is stacked; a number of important cognitive elements lie on the "getting to work on time" side of the relation. Not only do you have a sense of obligation to your work, you also have a need to make a good impression on your boss, to get work done that is stacked up on your desk from the day before, and to avoid having your pay docked.

With these basic concepts in mind, we can now turn to the ways in which we deal with cognitive dissonance. Understanding that dissonance produces a tension for reduction, we can imagine a number of "methods" for reducing the dissonance. First, one might change one or more of the cognitive elements. Second, new elements might be added to one side of the tension or the other. Third, one might come to see the elements as less important than they used to be. Fourth, a person might seek consonant information. Fifth, the individual might reduce dissonance by distorting or misinterpret-

27. Leon Festinger, *A Theory of Cognitive Dissonance* (Stanford, Calif.: Stanford University Press, 1957). Many short reviews of dissonance theory are available, including Kiesler, Collins, and Miller, *Attitude Change*; Robert Zajonc, "The Concepts of Balance, Congruity, and Dissonance," *Public Opinion Quarterly* 24 (1960): 280–96; Roger Brown, "Models of Attitude Change," in *New Directions in Psychology* (New York: Holt, Rinehart and Winston, 1962), pp. 1–85; Roger Brown, *Social Psychology* (New York: Free Press, 1965); chap. 11. For a readable exposition showing the practical applications of cognitive dissonance theory, see Elliot Aronson, *The Social Animal* (New York: Viking Press, 1972), chap. 4. For a detailed examination of the theory and related research, see J. W. Brehm and A. R. Cohen, *Explorations in Cognitive Dissonance* (New York: John Wiley & Sons, 1962).

ing the information involved. One of the most common examples of cognitive dissonance involves smoking. Smoking is a particularly good example because of the extensiveness of the smoking habit coupled with the large amount of information available on smoking and health. Suppose a smoker is reading and hearing a lot of facts about the health hazards of smoking. This occurrence is bound to produce dissonance, which might be very great, depending on the importance of the habit and the person's values on health and life. Here's what a smoker could do. The smoker might change the cognitive elements by stopping smoking or by rejecting the belief that smoking is unhealthy. Or the person might add new cognitive elements, such as smoking filters. The importance of the elements involved in dissonance might be reduced. For example, smokers sometimes say that they want a high quality of life, not a long life. The smoker might seek out consonant information supporting the view that smoking is not all that bad. Finally, the smoker might decide to distort the information received, saying something like, "As I read the evidence, smoking is harmful only for people who are already sick anyway."

Much of the theory and research on cognitive dissonance has centered around the various situations in which dissonance is likely to result. These include decision making, forced compliance, initiation, social support, and effort. Let us consider each of these dissonance-producing situations. The first, decision making, has received a great deal of research attention. Salespeople call this kind of dissonance "buyer's remorse." The popular saying goes, "The grass is always greener on the other side." The amount of dissonance one experiences as a result of a decision depends on four variables, the first of which is the importance of the decision. Certain decisions, such as that to skip breakfast, may be unimportant and produce little dissonance. Buying a house, seeking a new job, or moving to a new community, however, might involve a great deal of dissonance. The second variable is the attractiveness of the chosen alternative. Other things being equal, the less attractive the chosen alternative, the greater the dissonance. Third, the greater the perceived attractiveness of the unchosen alternative, the more the felt dissonance. Fourth, the greater the degree of similarity or overlap between the alternatives, the less the dissonance. If one is making a decision between two similar cars, little dissonance potential exists.

The second situation in which dissonance is apt to result is forced compliance or being induced to do or say something contrary to one's beliefs or values. This situation usually occurs when a reward is involved for complying or a punishment for not complying. Dissonance theory predicts that the less the pressure to conform, the greater the dissonance. If you were asked to do something you didn't like doing but you were paid quite a bit for doing it, you would not feel as much dissonance as if you were paid very little. The less external justification (such as reward or punishment), the more one must focus on the internal inconsistency within the self. This is why, according to dissonance theorists, the "soft" social pressures one encounters may be powerful in inducing rationalization or change.

Other situational predictions are made by dissonance theory. The theory predicts that the more difficult one's initiation to a group, the greater commitment one will have to that group. The more social support one receives from friends on an idea or action, the greater the pressure to believe in that idea or action. The greater the amount of effort one puts into a task, the more one will rationalize the value of that task.

In short, the theory of cognitive dissonance has had a major impact in the field of persuasion. It has won an important place in communication theory because of what it says about messages, information, and persuasion.

Rokeach: Attitudes, Beliefs, and Values. One of the finest recent theories on attitude and change is that of Milton Rokeach. He has developed an extensive explanation of human behavior based on beliefs, attitudes, and values.[28] His theory builds on the theories of the past and provides some pertinent extensions. While Rokeach's theory is definitely a consistency theory, it provides a breadth of explanation and prediction not approached by any of the other theories in the area, with the possible exception of cognitive dissonance.

Rokeach conceives of a highly organized belief-attitude-value system, which guides the behavior of the individual and supports the person's self-regard. Briefly, he describes the system in the following way: "All these conceptually distinct components—the countless beliefs, their organizations into thousands of attitudes, the several dozens of hierarchically arranged terminal values—are organized to form a single, functionally interconnected belief system."[29]

Beliefs are the hundreds of thousands of statements (usually inferences) that we make about self and the world. Beliefs are general or specific, and they are arranged within the system in terms of their centrality or importance to the ego. At the center of the belief system are those well-established, relatively unchangeable beliefs that literally form the core view of self and world. At the periphery of the system lie the many unimportant, changeable beliefs. There are three hypotheses about the belief system. First, beliefs vary in terms of centrality-peripherality. Second, the more central the belief, the more resistant it is to change. Third, a change in a central belief will produce more overall change in the system than will a change in a peripheral belief.

Beliefs are divided into five kinds, ranging in centrality. The most central beliefs are *primitive, with 100 percent consensus*. This group of beliefs are axiomatic; they are taken for granted. Primitive beliefs are learned by direct contact with the object of belief and are reinforced by literally unanimous agreement among one's peers. These beliefs are the truisms one counts on: The sun shines; With money I can buy things; Mothers bear children. The second class of belief, which is somewhat less central than the first, is *primitive beliefs with zero consensus*. These are also learned by direct contact, but they are private and not confirmable by others. They involve personal perceptions lying in a totally subjective realm: I believe in God; I am a stupid person; My son is a good boy. The third type of belief is *authority beliefs*. Children at an early age come to realize that they must rely on the opinions of others in establishing their belief systems. Primitive beliefs only take us so far in rounding out our conceptions of the world. Authority beliefs provide answers to the questions, With whom should I identify? and Whom should I believe? They are less central than primitive beliefs and change from time to time. The fourth type of belief, stemming from authority, is *derived beliefs*. These are the beliefs we get from trusted sources. Finally, on the periphery of the belief system are *inconsequential beliefs*, which are rather arbitrary and changeable. When inconsequential beliefs change, they make little impact on the system. Table 8.2, from Rokeach's book, lists several examples of beliefs.[30]

Groups of beliefs that are organized around a focal object and predispose a person to behave in a particular way toward that object are attitudes. If a belief system has hundreds of thousands of beliefs, it likewise will have perhaps thousands of attitudes, each consisting of a number of beliefs about the attitude object. Figure 8.4 illustrates, in overly simple form, the organization of an attitude.

Rokeach believes attitudes are of two important kinds that must always be viewed together. These are *attitude-toward-object* and *attitude-toward-situation*. One's behavior in a particular situation is a function of these two in combination. If a person does not behave in a given

28. Milton Rokeach, *Beliefs, Attitudes, and Values: A Theory of Organization and Change* (San Francisco: Jossey-Bass, 1969); *The Nature of Human Values* (New York: Free Press, 1973).

29. Rokeach, *Human Values*, p. 215.

30. Rokeach, *Beliefs*, pp. 26–29.

situation congruently with the attitude-toward-object, it is probably because the attitude-toward-situation does not facilitate a particular behavior at that time. A common example of this might be food preference. Your attitude toward red meat may say: Avoid. But your attitude toward eating red meat may say: It is not socially acceptable to refuse food served to you when you are a guest. Thus the vegetarian may eat meat, despite a private, negative attitude toward it. This idea is consistent with Fishbein's conception, summarized earlier. The

TABLE 8.2
Examples of beliefs

Type A: *Primitive beliefs, unanimous consensus*
1. I was born in (real birthplace).
2. I am ____________ years old.
3. My name is __________________.

Type B: *Primitive beliefs, zero consensus*
4. I believe my mother loves me.
5. Sometimes I have a strong urge to kill myself.
6. I like myself.

Type C: *Authority beliefs*
7. The philosophy of Adolph Hitler is basically a sound one, and I am all for it.
8. The philosophy of the pope is basically a sound one.
9. The philosophy of Jesus Christ is basically a sound one.

Type D: *Derived beliefs*
10. People can be divided into two distinct groups: the weak and the strong.
11. Birth control is morally wrong.
12. The ten commandments are of divine origin.

Type E: *Inconsequential beliefs*
13. I think summertime is a much more enjoyable time of the year than winter.
14. I would never walk through a revolving door if I had a choice.
15. The side from which I get out of bed in the morning really does influence how I feel.

From *Beliefs, Attitudes, and Values*, by Milton Rokeach. Copyright © 1972 by Jossey-Bass, Inc. Reprinted by permission of the publisher.

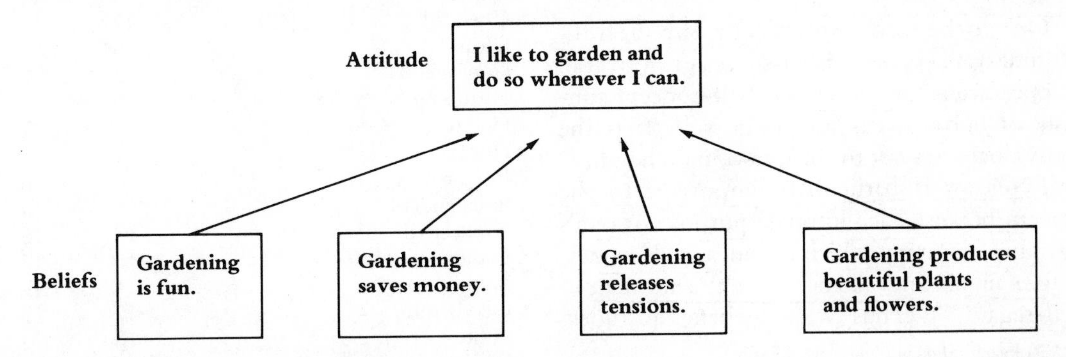

Figure 8.4. A simple example of the belief structure of an attitude.

main point of both models is that behavior is a complex function of sets of attitudes. In Rokeach's theory, then, the system consists of many beliefs ranging in centrality, which are clustered together to form attitudes that predispose the person to behave in certain ways. Attitudes are complex evaluations of objects and situations.

Rokeach believes that of the three concepts in explaining human behavior, value is the most important. Values are specific types of belief that are central in the system and act as life guides. Values are of two kinds: *instrumental* and *terminal*. Instrumental values are guidelines for living on which we base our daily behavior. Terminal values are the ultimate aims of life toward which we work. In his extensive research on values, Rokeach has isolated what he considers the most common values in our society and has developed a ranking scale to assess individuals' value systems. The ranking task is based on the hierarchical nature of the value system, in which values range in importance to the person. Table 8.3 lists the eighteen terminal and instrumental values isolated in the theory.[31] The numbers in the columns indicate the composite rankings for American men and women. A world at peace is the most important terminal value for men and women, and honesty is the most important instrumental value. Rokeach has conducted several studies with his scale and provides a breakdown of attitude rankings into various categories of age, race, and education.[32]

One other component in the belief-attitude-value system that assumes great overall importance is the *self-concept*. Self-concept consists of one's beliefs about the self. It is the individual's answer to the question, Who am I? Self-concept is particularly important to the system because "the ultimate purpose of one's total belief system, which includes one's values, is to maintain and enhance . . . the sentiment of self-regard."[33] Thus while beliefs, attitudes, and values constitute the components of the system, the self-concept is its guiding goal or purpose. With these four concepts Rokeach has tied together the theory into a cohesive pack-

31. Rokeach, *Human Values*, pp. 57–58.

32. Ibid., chap. 3.

33. Ibid., p. 216.

TABLE 8.3
Value rankings (composite) for American men and women

VALUES	MEN	WOMEN
Terminal Values:		
A comfortable life	4	13
An exciting life	18	18
A sense of accomplishment	7	10
A world at peace	1	1
A world of beauty	15	15
Equality	9	8
Family security	2	2
Freedom	3	3
Happiness	5	5
Inner harmony	13	12
Mature love	14	14
National security	10	11
Pleasure	17	16
Salvation	12	4
Self-respect	6	6
Social recognition	16	17
True friendship	11	9
Wisdom	8	7
Instrumental Values:		
Ambitious	2	4
Broadminded	4	5
Capable	8	12
Cheerful	12	10
Clean	9	8
Courageous	5	6
Forgiving	6	2
Helpful	7	7
Honest	1	1
Imaginative	18	18
Independent	11	14
Intellectual	15	16
Logical	16	17
Loving	14	9
Obedient	17	15
Polite	13	13
Responsible	3	3
Self-controlled	10	11

age. At the heart lie one's self-conceptions, and the flesh is filled out by the other components.

Rokeach is basically a consistency theorist. He includes a number of significant hypotheses about attitudes, beliefs, and values, but in the final analysis, he believes that people are guided by a need for consistency and that inconsistency creates a pressure to change. Even in discussing consistency Rokeach has broadened his base far beyond the other consistency theories. Taking the total system into consideration, he sees consistency as extremely complex. An individual may be inconsistent on several different grounds. In all, ten areas in the psychological system interrelate and bear the potential for inconsistency. Table 8.4, reproduced from Rokeach's book, is a matrix of all the possible relations among elements in the belief-attitude-value system.[34] In the cells of the matrix are indications of the areas of study that have focused on various of these relationships. One of the significant impressions we get from this matrix is the number of empty cells that have not been examined in any significant way, according to Rokeach. He criticizes consistency theory:

> None of the theories discussed can be regarded as a comprehensive theory of change. A comprehensive theory should ideally be able to address itself to the conditions that will lead to long-range as well as short-range change, behavioral change as well as cognitive change, personality change as well as cognitive and behavioral change, and a rising or lowering of self-conceptions as well as their maintenance. A major objective of this book is to build a theoretical framework that will, it is hoped, address itself to such issues, one that at least attempts to bridge the current gap between various personality, social-psychological, and behavior theories that for the most part do not speak to each other.[35]

Furthermore, Rokeach believes that the most important inconsistencies in a person's psychological system are those in row A involving cognitions about the self. Only when inconsistencies involve the self-conception will there be significant, lasting change. The reason for this is that such contradictions increase self-dissatisfaction. Since maintenance of the self-regard is the overall aim of the psychological system, it is natural that this should be so. Rokeach's theory of the attitude-belief-value system is complex and lengthy. We have only been able to sketch it here.

Rokeach's theory is somewhat more complex than dissonance theory and its precursors, and its epistemology is less extreme. For example, Rokeach believes that people use values as criteria for making judgments, implying that individuals can be actively involved in defining situations. However, his methods are firmly empirical and scientific. He calls for operational definition of values, analysis that distinguishes values from other cognitive elements, and objective research to find the true structure of values in individuals. He also hypothesizes that the same few values operate in all people. Methodologically, then, Rokeach's work epitomizes the hypothetico-deductive method.

Criticism. Consistency theory has had a major impact on our thinking about attitude and attitude change. A mainstay of social psychology for many years, it is appealing because of its *parsimony* and *heuristic value*. For a twenty-year period it stimulated a great deal of research. The popularity of consistency theory is understandable, given the goal of this field to discover a few important variables that would predict social behavior. Consistency theories do just that. They isolate certain elements of cognition and show how manipulations among these variables can predict a person's feelings, thoughts, or actions. They also appeal to the social scientist's sense of logic, providing an explanation for behavior that makes intuitive sense. At one time consistency theories were so well accepted that debates centered not on whether people respond to dissonance but on ways to improve the precision of predictions based on these theories.

In recent years, however, consistency theory has become less popular. Several weaknesses

34. Ibid., pp. 220–21.

35. Ibid., p. 224.

TABLE 8.4
Matrix of contradictory relations possible within the total belief system

ORGANIZATION OF:	A	B	C	D	E	F	G	H	I	J
A. Cognitions about self	Psychoanalysis					Rational therapy Reality therapy Emotional role playing	Nondirective therapy	Encounter groups T-groups Psychodrama		
B. Terminal value system					Cognitive-affective consistency					
C. Instrumental value system						Achievement motivation				
D. Attitude system				Congruity theory Belief congruence			Balance theory			
E. Attitude					Syllogistic analysis of attitudes	Dissonance theory Attribution theory	Communication and persuasion Innoculation theory Assimilation-contrast theory			
F. Cognitions about own behavior									Modeling and observational learning	
G. Cognitions about significant others' attitudes										
H. Cognitions about significant others' values or needs										
I. Cognitions about significant others' behavior										
J. Cognitions about behavior of nonsocial objects										

have become apparent. These weaknesses revolve around three criteria: appropriateness, validity, and scope. The following comments about these failures center on dissonance theory.

The first objection to dissonance theory relates to its theoretical *appropriateness*. Basically, the dissonance hypothesis for change is overly simple. Chapanis and Chapanis capture this objection in harsh terms: "To condense most complex social situations into two, and only two, simple dissonant statements represents so great an abstraction that the model no longer bears any reasonable resemblance to reality."[36] More recent research on cognition and information processing (see Chapter 7) provides evidence that cognition is too complex to break down to simple consistencies and inconsistencies. For example, cognitive complexity theory posits that cognitions are organized in extensive hierarchies and that the individual's understanding of environment is variable and adaptive.

Another issue related to theoretical appropriateness is the question of whether people are passive in responding to inconsistencies. Most research evidence of recent years indicates that they are not. Cognitions do not come prepackaged in consistent or inconsistent forms. Individuals actively define and redefine situations, depending on the needs of the moment.

The second basis for criticism of dissonance theory is *validity*. The basic standard for any predictive theory—and the theory of cognitive dissonance is precisely that—is to be stated in such a way that contradictory evidence could prove the theory wrong in its predictions. In other words, the theory must be falsifiable. The problem with dissonance theory is that it can be used to explain various, contradictory results and cannot be proved wrong, which creates a situation wherein the dissonance theorist wins no matter how an experiment comes out. If attitude change results from the manipulations, one can argue that the change was caused by dissonance; if attitude change does not occur, one can say that dissonance did not exist. Furthermore, dissonance is such a general concept that it can take any number of forms. Thus the experimenter can claim that a particular result was caused by one kind of dissonance but that an entirely different result was produced by another kind of dissonance. This circular reasoning results from the fact that dissonance researchers do not measure dissonance per se but infer dissonance from behavior. Indeed, there is some question as to whether dissonance is directly observable at all.

The third objection to dissonance theory relates to its *scope*. Originally thought to apply to a wide range of cognitive activity, dissonance theory is now seen as applying to a rather narrow area of behavior.

Rokeach's work has taken a giant step toward improving consistency theory. It overcomes virtually all of the weaknesses of the earlier models. First, it is broadly based, including a variety of cognitive concepts. It explains why cognitions do not always change and why some cognitions are more apt to change than others. The major contribution of Rokeach's theory is that it broadens our understanding of consistency and inconsistency. Rokeach shows that what may appear consistent on one level may be entirely inconsistent on another (see Table 8.3).

The major problem of Rokeach's work is his attempt to operationalize constructs that are not amenable to measurement. His attempt to reduce all values to a standard list and to describe the value system in terms of a simple ranking is unrealistic at best and ludicrous at worst. Still, the power of this theory should not be underestimated. The time may be right to modify Rokeach's approach so that it is consistent with recent action-oriented, rules-based notions of human behavior.

What Do We Know about Persuasion?

A revolution has occurred in the field of persuasion. Until about 1970 persuasion research was

36. Natalia P. Chapanis and Alphonse Chapanis, "Cognitive Dissonance: Five Years Later," *Psychological Bulletin* 61 (1964): p. 21.

deterministic in orientation, assuming that people were passive responders to environmental pressures. The attitude and attitude change research tradition used a linear model that assumed that messages together with certain situational and predispositional factors in the receiver caused change. Now persuasion is being viewed from an actional, teleological position. Old-line attitude research is judged inadequate to explain how people deal with messages. It is viewed as overly simple and not explanatory. New approaches, which emphasize active involvement and information processing, have more potential for uncovering useful conceptions of how communication involves change.

Most of the theory in this section makes clear that persuasion is largely related to information processing. In fact the essence of persuasion is the impact of information on the intrapersonal system. People change by reorganizing their cognitions in the face of messages from others. Several factors enter the persuasion process. These include tension reduction, learning, social judgment, and interpersonal trust. Many theories of persuasion involve the first of these factors, *tension reduction*. Here attitudes, beliefs, and/or values are changed to bring about less tension. One major source of tension referred to by these theories is inconsistency or dissonance. In the past *learning* through interaction with others was thought to be a passive consequence of environmental change, but it now seems to be an active process involving information processing. *Social judgment* is an important part of much communication. People and their stated beliefs, along with information from others, are judged by the receiver in terms of position (degree of positive or negative valence), value, and similarity to one's own position. This process of judgment is an important aspect of the information processing that goes into personal change. Finally, interpersonal *trust* is an important factor in how an individual judges information from another. Our attitudes toward people are closely related to our attitudes toward things and situations. The importance of credibility appears in various ways throughout theories of persuasion.

PART

IV

CONTEXTUAL THEORIES

Chapter 9
Interpersonal Contexts I:
Theories of Relationship, Presentation, and Perception

Chapter 10
Interpersonal Contexts II:
Theories of Disclosure, Attraction, and Conflict

Chapter 11
Interpersonal Contexts III:
Theories of Groups and Organizations

Chapter 12
Mediated Contexts:
Theories of Mass Communication

CHAPTER

9 Interpersonal Contexts I: Theories of Relationship, Presentation, and Perception

Introduction

At this point in the book, let us recap briefly. In Part I you learned about the nature of theory, and in Part II the first set of actual theories was presented. These were general theories of communication related to systems, symbolic interaction, and rules. Part III presented theories that deal with basic communication themes: language and nonverbal coding, meaning, information, and persuasion. In Part IV we will look at prominent theories that focus on contexts of communication. Here two kinds of context are included, interpersonal and mass. In essence these are two end points on a spectrum of contexts.

Contexts of Communication

The theories in this part of the book deal with basic processes common to most communication. Communication always occurs in context, and the nature of communication depends in large measure on this context. In Chapter 1 four main contexts were described: dyadic communication, group communication, organizational communication, and mass communication. These contexts form a hierarchy in which each higher level includes the lower levels but adds something individual of its own. For example, mass communication is distinctive as a context, but it includes many of the features of dyadic, group, and organizational communication as well.

For purposes of discussion these contexts are divided into two broad groups: interpersonal and mediated. Interpersonal contexts primarily include direct face-to-face communication; mediated contexts involve messages that are filtered through channels for mass consumption. For the most part we can say that dyadic, group, and organizational communication tend to be interpersonal and that mass communication is mediated. However, this generalization has exceptions. Some dyadic communication is mediated, as in using the telephone. Organizational communication often uses media (for example, employee newsletters), and mass communication sometimes occurs through word of mouth, which is primarily interpersonal. Grouping the contexts in this way does not imply mutual exclusion; it merely notes the primary emphasis of the contexts.

This chapter discusses theories of relational communication. These theories apply especially to the dyadic context, but they provide insights for group and organizational communication as well. In Chapter 10 theories of disclosure, attraction, and conflict are presented. These theories apply especially well to the dyadic context, although they relate to other contexts too. Chapter 11 presents theories that relate directly to groups and organizations, and Chapter 12 covers theories of mass communication.

What Is Interpersonal Communication?

Dean Barnlund offers the following definition: "The study of interpersonal communication, then, is concerned with the investigation of relatively informal social situations in which persons in face-to-face encounters sustain focused interaction through the reciprocal exchange of verbal and nonverbal cues."[1] This definition includes five criteria. First, there must be two or more people in physical proximity who per-

1. Dean Barnlund, *Interpersonal Communication: Survey and Studies* (Boston: Houghton Mifflin, 1968), p. 10.

ceive the presence of one another. Second, interpersonal communication involves communicative interdependence. In other words, one's communicative behavior is a direct consequence of the other's. Barnlund calls this quality *focused interaction*, which implies concentrated mutual attention. Third, interpersonal communication involves the exchange of messages; fourth, these messages are coded in a variety of verbal and nonverbal ways. The final criterion is that interpersonal communication is relatively unstructured; it is marked by informality and flexibility. This definition is a good general guide, but you will quickly see that not all theories of interpersonal communication conform to these criteria.

The next section presents a theory that explains the functions of interpersonal communication. This theory provides a setting for the remainder of the chapter and for the next two. It helps us understand the role of interpersonal communication in dyadic, group, and organizational contexts of human life.

Functions of Interpersonal Communication

The functional theory of Frank Dance and Carl Larson is a general theory that sets the stage for many of the theories that follow.[2] At first glance this theory presents an irony: It deals with interpersonal communication, but it focuses on the person alone. This apparent paradox is no inconsistency once you understand the authors' intent. They wish to answer the question of what happens when an individual communicates or, to be consistent with the title of the theory: How does communication function in the life of the individual? A function is a strong relationship that occurs naturally between two or more elements. The relationship implies a dependency between one thing and another. Dance and Larson isolate some important functions of communication within the individual. An important assumption of their work, therefore, is that the experience of the individual is affected in a major way by the individual's communication with others. Stated differently: "For in intraperson communication we find those unique characteristics of the human animal that distinguish us from other animal forms. Our position will be that these unique characteristics manifest themselves at the intrapersonal level, but are developed and sustained through interpersonal communication."[3]

The authors name five attributes that characterize interpersonal communication: "(1) symbolic content (2) is produced by one individual, (3) according to a code, (4) with anticipated consumption by other(s), (5) according to the same code."[4] These attributes constitute a definition of communication that guides the theory as a whole. We will discuss the following functions outlined in this theory: linking, mentation, and regulation.

The Linking Function. The first function of communication is to provide a link between the person and the environment. In other words, the individual develops cultural, social, and psychological ties to the world outside the self. As children develop, they begin to distinguish between the self and other objects. This self-other conception arises largely out of interaction with others, who communicate to a child the sense of self-conception. Although we understand the intrapersonal world as separate from the outer world, we learn through communication that the two are linked or related.

Individuals communicate egocentrically (to themselves) and nonegocentrically (to others). Moving back and forth between egocentric and nonegocentric communication helps us organize concepts of the self, the other, and the self-other relationship. An important part of the self-concept is our perception of other peoples' judgments of us. Most communication involves some self-disclosure, and one's disclo-

2. Frank E. X. Dance and Carl E. Larson, *The Functions of Human Communication* (New York: Holt, Rinehart and Winston, 1976).

3. Ibid., pp. 31–32.

4. Ibid., pp. 32–37, 162.

sures to others always risk being judged. As we communicate with others, we often shift our orientations from the content of what is being said to the others' rejections and/or acceptances of that content and, hence, of the self.

Through communication, then, we relate the self to the environment. We do this largely to adapt to or to fit comfortably into the social/cultural surroundings. We accomplish this goal through assimilation and accommodation. Assimilation is primarily a process of changing one's perception or evaluation of aspects of the environment to fit one's perception or evaluation of the self. For example, the theory predicts that an individual will reevaluate another person if that other person has rejected a valued aspect of one's self. Accommodation involves changing aspects of the self to fit one's evaluations of others. For example, one may reevaluate the self in the face of rejection when the rejection is consistent with other responses frequently encountered.

The Mentation Function. Broadly speaking, we can say that humans engage in two kinds of activity. Some behavior is animalistic in the sense of being "unmediated, uncontrolled, necessary responses to environmental properties." Much of our behavior, however, is of a different class, including "conceptual thinking, involving memory, planning, and foresight; and evaluative judgment."[5] These higher activities are called *mentation*. The key to distinguishing mentation from lower forms of behavior is that it involves conscious intent on the part of the actor. Most important at this juncture is the generalization that mentation is made possible by the internalization of speech. We think because we communicate.

Language and meaning enable the individual to possess imagination. In other words people can live a mental life that is not tied to the here and now. We can reflect on the past and we can plan for the future. We can imagine locations other than the place and activities of the moment. The authors refer to this process as *decentering*.

Dance and Larson state that decentering increases the probability that communicators will achieve understanding. Decentering allows one to create a mental image of what one believes is the perspective of the other person. This mental image is the facilitating factor of empathy.

The Regulatory Function. Interpersonal communication also serves to regulate. Regulation occurs on three levels: one's behavior is regulated by others, one regulates one's own behavior, and one regulates the behavior of others. In childhood these functions occur developmentally in sequence. Significant figures in a child's life use language to regulate the child's behavior. The child, in turn, uses the communicated norms and limitations to regulate the self. Soon the child begins to use communication to affect others. In ongoing life all three forms of regulation occur concurrently, and they interrelate to support one another.

Self-regulation is especially important. Our ability to use symbols egocentrically enables us to direct our own behavior. We respond to our own question, What am I going to do next? This question is a natural part of our need to reduce uncertainty. It arises when the proper course of action is not defined from the outside. Routines that we may choose in response to this self-direction are ignoring, delaying, searching for a regulation principle, listening to others, following others, or staging. Staging involves playing a role that is consistent with what others want, despite one's own desires. Dance and Larson theorize that the individual uses these self-regulating routines to influence others as well.

Dance and Larson's theory relates most centrally to interpersonal communication, as they themselves state.[6] However, it has strong connections with other domains as well. First, it is a general theory dealing with the symbolic nature of communication. The theory could easily

5. Ibid., pp. 165–66.

6. Ibid., p. 48.

be labeled symbolic interactionist. As such it would fit well into that section of our domain model (Chapter 4). It also has applicability to language, meaning, information processing, and persuasion. Of these topics the theory, with its concepts of mentation and regulation, relates most strongly to meaning as conceived in Chapter 6.

This interpersonal communication theory is a product of the field of speech communication. Speech communication, once primarily a pedagogical field interested in speech skills, has emerged as a major force in the study of communication. Several theories in this chapter have been developed by individuals associated with this field, for interpersonal communication has become one of its major interests. Much of the work of speech communication scholars, like that of Dance and Larson, tends to be integrative, bridging gaps among traditional disciplines.[7]

Criticism. Dance and Larson's treatise is a welcome addition to communication theory because it directs our attention to aspects that heretofore have been downplayed. Most theories of interpersonal communication are structural, emphasizing what happens in communication. This theory redirects the focus to the consequences of communication. In a fresh way it aims to accomplish what symbolic interactionist theories sought years ago, namely, to define the ways communication affects the most important facets of human life.

An important strength of this theory is its *parsimony*. By relating its theoretical claims to a small set of functions, this theory presents a clear and simple framework in which the interrelationship of variables can be understood.

The weaknesses of this theory arise from its newness. Admittedly, the theory is a first step toward a more elaborate conceptualization. Its limitations relate to scope, theoretical appropriateness, and validity.

Dance and Larson choose to focus on the individual, explaining how communication functions in the psychological life of the person. They leave another side of the coin largely untouched—social and cultural functions. That is, communication could be shown to affect both social structure and cultural values. A whole realm of theory could be developed in this area, expanding its original scope.

A second weakness relates to theoretical appropriateness. Dance and Larson take a relatively actional stance, emphasizing the proactive nature of human life. Yet many of their hypotheses are in the form of predictive covering laws, implying little choice on the part of the individual. This inconsistency is troublesome.

Another weakness is related to validity. Recall that validity is partially determined by the correspondence between a theory's claims and actual observations. Many of this theory's hypotheses are supported by research. Many, however, are speculative, as the authors admit. This criticism is tempered by the fact that no theory can claim perfect validity; initial speculation is a vital part of the theory-building process.

Relational Communication

The essence of interpersonal communication is relationship. Relationships are established and maintained by interpersonal communication, and, inversely, communication patterns between people are shaped largely by the nature of their relationships. Theories of relational communication go back many years. We will cover a brief history of this work in three sections, emphasizing origins of relational theory, extensions, and recent developments.

Theories of relational communication demonstrate clearly how the tenets of system

7. For a sampling of theoretical work in speech communication, see Frank E. X. Dance, ed., *Human Communication Theory: Comparative Essays* (New York: Harper & Row, 1982).

theory, symbolic interactionism, and rules theory can be applied to a particular aspect of our communication experience. Relational theories are firmly planted in the dyadic context, although one can easily extend their implications into the group and organization as well. Although no one, to my knowledge, has done so explicitly, relational research findings could be made relevant to information processing and persuasion as well. Indeed, defining the relationship is an interpersonal information-processing task, and relational control is related to regulation and therefore pertinent to persuasion.

Origins of Relational Theory

Anthropologist Gregory Bateson is founder of the line of theory that has come to be known as relational communication.[8] Bateson's work led to the development of two foundational propositions on which relational theories still rest. The first is the proposition of the dual nature of messages. Every interpersonal exchange bears two messages, a "report" message and a "command" message. The report message contains the substance or content of the communication, while the command message makes a statement about the relationship.[9] These two elements have come to be known as the content message and the relationship message, or communication and metacommunication, respectively. We will explore these concepts in greater detail in upcoming sections.

Bateson's second seminal proposition is that relationships can be characterized by complementarity or symmetry. In complementary relationships the dominant behavior of one participant elicits submissive behavior from the other. In symmetry, dominance is met by dominance, or submissiveness by submissiveness. We will return to these thoughts momentarily.

Although Bateson's ideas originated in anthropological research, they were quickly picked up in psychiatry and applied to pathological relationships. Bateson himself teamed with colleagues in psychiatry to develop relational theory further.[10] Perhaps Bateson's most famous contribution in this regard is the double bind theory of schizophrenia.[11] According to this theory, schizophrenia is caused by social factors, most notable of which is the double bind. Significant persons in the schizophrenic's life send contradictory messages, in which the command and report functions are inconsistent. This situation sets a no-win trap, such that the individual loses no matter what course of action is taken. For example, a parent may state on the report level that he or she wishes to comfort a hurt child, but nonverbally, on the command level, the parent tells the child to stay away. This double bind notion was revolutionary in psychiatry, for it suggested that mental illness may not be caused as much by internal personality factors as by interpersonal social factors.

Bateson would have preferred to keep his work more general, but psychiatry, wanting to apply it to mental health, provided monetary support.[12] Psychiatry and clinical psychology by their nature are interested in communication. Not only do therapeutic procedures often rely on communication, but communication offers a fruitful area of possible etiology in mental health. Several other theories in this chapter

8. Bateson began to formulate his ideas on relationship in his field observations of the Iatmul tribe of New Guinea in the 1930s. See *Naven* (Stanford: Stanford University Press, 1958).

9. This proposition was first presented in the classic theory of communication by Juergen Ruesch and Gregory Bateson, *Communication: The Social Matrix of Society* (New York: Norton, 1951). For space reasons a detailed summary of this theory is not presented here. See the first edition of *Theories of Human Communication* (Columbus: Charles E. Merrill, 1978), pp. 43–47.

10. See, for example, Ruesch and Bateson, *Communication*.

11. Gregory Bateson, Donald Jackson, J. Haley, and J. Weaklund, "Toward a Theory of Schizophrenia," *Behavioral Science* 1 (1956): 251–64.

12. Gregory Bateson, "A Formal Approach to Explicit, Implicit, and Embodied Ideas and to Their Forms of Interaction," in *Double-Bind*, ed. C. E. Sluzki and D. C. Ransom (New York: Grune & Stratton, 1976), p. xii.

also stem from psychiatry and clinical psychology because of their interest in communication.

Extensions: The Palo Alto Group

In the 1950s and 1960s Bateson led an active group of researchers and clinicians in a program to further develop and apply ideas on relational communication. These scholars became known as the Palo Alto Group. Although their interests were primarily clinical, their work has had enormous impact on the study of interpersonal communication in general. About 1960 psychiatrist Paul Watzlawick joined the group and quickly became one of its leaders.

This group's work received wide publicity and popularity through the publication of *Pragmatics of Human Communication.*[13] Although this book does not express a complete picture of the Palo Alto Group, it is the most comprehensive single work of the group and has been treated as its basic statement of theory.

In the book Paul Watzlawick, Janet Beavin, and Don Jackson present a well-known analysis of communication based on system principles. (A system was defined in Chapter 3 as a set of objects that interrelate with one another to form a unique whole.) Part and parcel of a system is the notion of *relationship*, and in defining interaction, the authors stress this idea: "Interactional systems then, shall be *two or more communicants in the process of, or at the level of, defining the nature of their relationship.*"[14]

Relationships emerge from the interaction between people. People set up for themselves interaction rules, which govern their communicative behaviors. By obeying the rules, behaving appropriately, the participants sanction the defined relationship. In a marriage, for example, a dominance-submission relationship may emerge and be reinforced by implicit rules. The husband may send messages of command, which are followed by compliance by the wife, or vice versa. A status relationship in an organization may be observed in a subordinate's nonverbal behavior. The subordinate, for example, may pause at the supervisor's door to await an invitation to enter. Such implicit rules are numerous in any ongoing relationship, be it a friendship, hateship, business relationship, love affair, family, or whatever.

In *Pragmatics of Communication* Watzlawick, Beavin, and Jackson present five basic axioms.[15] First, "one cannot *not* communicate."[16] This axiom has been quoted again and again in textbooks on communication. Its point is important, for the axiom emphasizes that the very attempt to avoid interaction is itself a kind of interaction. It also emphasizes that any perceivable behavior is potentially communicative. Second, the authors postulate that "every communication has a content and a relationship aspect such that the latter classifies the former and is therefore metacommunication."[17] When two people are talking, each is relating information to the other, but simultaneously each is also "commenting" on the information at a higher level. This simultaneous relationship-talk (which often is nonverbal) is what is meant by *metacommunication*. For example, on the content level a teacher may tell you that a test will be given tomorrow. Many possible metamessages may accompany the content level. The instructor may be making any of the following impressions: I am the authority in this classroom; I teach, you learn; What I have lectured about is important; I need feedback on your progress; I have a need to judge you; I want you to think I am fulfilling my role as professor; and so on. This axiom further substantiates the theorists' idea that interaction is a constant process of defining relationships.

The third axiom of communication deals with the punctuation of communication se-

13. Paul Watzlawick, Janet Beavin, and Don Jackson, *Pragmatics of Human Communication: A Study of Interactional Patterns, Pathologies, and Paradoxes* (New York: Norton, 1967).

14. Ibid., pp. 120–21.

15. These axioms are summarized in Joseph DeVito, *The Interpersonal Communication Book* (New York: Harper & Row, 1976).

16. Watzlawick et al., *Pragmatics*, p. 51.

17. Ibid., p. 54.

quences. Interaction sequences, like word sequences, cannot be understood as a string of isolated elements. To make sense, they must be punctuated or grouped syntactically. In raw form an interaction consists of a move by one individual followed by moves from others. The objective observer would see a series of behaviors. Like the series of sounds in a sentence, these behaviors are not simply a chain. Certain behaviors are responses to others. Behaviors are thus grouped or punctuated into larger units, which in the whole help to define the relationship. Of course, any given string of behaviors might be punctuated in various ways. One source of difficulty between communicators occurs when they punctuate differently. For example, consider a marriage involving nagging by the husband and withdrawing by the wife. This sequence can be punctuated in two ways. On the one hand, the wife's withdrawing may be a response to the husband's nagging: nag/withdraw, nag/withdraw. On the other hand, the opposite may be occurring: withdraw/nag, withdraw/nag. In the first case the punctuation of nag/withdraw implies an attack/retreat relationship. But the husband's punctuation of withdraw/nag implies ignoring/imploring.

Fourth, "human beings communicate both digitally and analogically."[18] The authors describe two types of coding used in interpersonal communication. Each has two distinguishing characteristics. *Digital* coding is relatively arbitrary. In other words a digital sign is used to represent a referent that bears no intrinsic relation to the sign. The relationship between the sign and the referent is strictly imputed. Second, the digital signs are discrete; they are "on" or "off," uttered or not uttered. The most common digital code in human communication is language. Sounds, words, and phrases, arranged syntactically, communicate meanings.

The *analogic* code is quite different from digital signs. It also has two distinguishing characteristics. First, an analogic sign is not arbitrary. Either it resembles the significate (for example, photo) or is intrinsic to the thing being signified. Second, an analogue is often continuous rather than discrete; it has degrees of intensity or longevity. Most nonverbal signs are analogic. For example, a facial expression of surprise not only is a sign of a feeling or condition but is actually part of the surprise itself. Its meaning is intrinsic. Further, the facial expression is not an either-or sign. It is a continuous variable between no expression and extreme facial distortion.

While the digital and analogic codes are different from one another, they are used together and cannot be separated in ongoing communication. For example, a word (digital) can be uttered in a variety of paralinguistic ways (loud, soft; high, low; and so forth). The manner of utterance is analogic. Likewise, a written message consisting of letters and words (digital) is presented on paper using various layouts, styles of handwriting or print, and other analogic codes.

Within the stream of behaviors in interaction, both digital and analogic coding blend together. Watzlawick and the others believe that these two serve different functions. Digital signs, having relatively precise meanings, communicate the content dimension; while the analogic code, which is rich in feeling and meaning, is the vehicle for the relationship (metacommunication) level. To relate this axiom to the content-relationship idea of the second axiom, we can say that while people are communicating digitally on the content level, they are commenting about their relationship analogically on the metalevel. For example, suppose a father at a playground sees his daughter fall and scrape her knee. Immediately, he says, "Don't cry. Daddy is coming." The content meaning is clear. The child receives a message stating that her father is going to come to her. Imagine the large number of relationship messages that might be sent analogically with body and voice. The father might communicate his own fear, worry, anger, boredom, or domi-

18. Ibid., p. 67.

nance. At the same time he might communicate a number of possible perceptions of his little girl, including "careless person," "attention getter," "injured child," "provoker," and so on. Truly this axiom captures the complexity of even the simplest interpersonal exchange.[19]

The final axiom of communication expresses a difference between *symmetrical* and *complementary* interaction. When two communicators in a relationship behave similarly, the relationship is said to be symmetrical; differences are minimized. When communicator differences are maximized, however, a complementary relationship is said to exist. In a marriage when two partners both vie for power, they are involved in a symmetrical relationship. Likewise, coworkers are communicating symmetrically when each abdicates responsibility for taking control of the job. A complementary marital relationship would exist when the wife behaves in ways that reinforce her submission, and the husband responds dominantly. In the work setting a complementary relationship would exist when one's feelings of superiority shape the way one responds to another's expressed low self-esteem. Ideally, an ongoing relationship includes an optimal blend of complementary and symmetrical interactions. Flexibility is the key.

Recent Developments

The ideas of the Palo Alto Group in recent years have been removed from a strictly clinical application, and much research has been done on the relational elements of normal interaction. Two relatively formalized statements are summarized below.

Millar and Rogers. Frank Millar and L. Edna Rogers have been actively researching relational communication since the early 1970s. In 1976 they presented a viewpoint in order to "stimulate dialogue about how to conceive of interpersonal relationships." Although the theory was presented as "suggestive rather than definitive," it remains one of the most cogent and heuristically valuable recent statements about relational communication.[20] The theory makes a major step toward codifying heretofore abstract concepts.

Millar and Rogers begin with the assumption that relationships are complex. They use a symbolic interactionist and systems base in assuming that "since a person's 'reality' is largely a function of his or her own making, choice and change . . . are two crucial themes that must be emphasized in any communication theory of human behavior."[21] They also follow earlier relational theorists in advocating that communication is a reciprocal negotiating process of defining the relationship.

Millar and Rogers's model begins with a definition of the three dimensions of relationship: control, trust, and intimacy. *Control* is the distribution of power to direct the character of interaction or to define the nature of the relationship. In other words, control is a question of who holds definitional rights. The second dimension is *trust*, the responsible acceptance of the control dimension. Trusting involves admission of dependence, and trustworthiness is acceptance of the obligation not to exploit control in a dependency situation. *Intimacy* is attachment in the sense of using the other person for self-confirmation. It is reliance on the other person's view of one's own ego to limit one's own behavior.

Since control has received most attention by researchers of relational communication, including Millar and Rogers, we will cover this variable last. Let us now look briefly at the

19. Coding is a complex concept. Two additional sources that reflect the complexity of coding distinctions are Michael Nolan, "The Relationship between Verbal and Nonverbal Communication," in *Communication and Behavior*, ed. Gerhard Hanneman and William McEwan (Reading, Mass.: Addison-Wesley, 1975), pp. 98–118; and Randall Harrison, "Code Systems," in *Beyond Words* (Englewood Cliffs, N.J.: Prentice-Hall, 1974), chap. 4.

20. Frank E. Millar and L. Edna Rogers, "A Relational Approach to Interpersonal Communication," in *Explorations in Interpersonal Communication*, ed. Gerald Miller (Beverly Hills: Sage, 1976), pp. 87–103; quotations from p. 90.

21. Ibid., p. 88.

other two dimensions. Trust can be correlated with three other variables. The first is the *vulnerability pattern*. Vulnerability involves placing oneself in a situation wherein one may get hurt by the choices of the other. As a pattern vulnerability varies in terms of the frequency that one places oneself in a vulnerable position. Millar and Rogers speculate that lower levels of the vulnerability pattern mark suspicion and distrust, that high frequencies in the vulnerability scale mean risk taking, and that middle-range positions reflect trust.

The second correlate of trust is *reward dependability*, or the degree to which one person depends on another in a relationship. The wider the difference in vulnerability patterns between two people in a relationship, the greater the reward dependency of the more vulnerable party. High dependency by one person, relative to the other, may lead to exploitation by the trusted person. As reward dependability between persons becomes more equal, the relationship becomes more interdependent and trust increases.

The third related variable is the *confidence pattern*, the relative degree of confidence in the other person's trustworthiness. In a unilateral relationship one party is far more confident than the other. In a cooperative relationship confidence and trust are mutual.

Consider the example of Mary and Bob. When Bob met Mary, her parents had just died and she was lonely. A shy person, Mary had few friends to confide in. She was swept off her feet by Bob's attention, and soon they were married. Bob was a young entrepreneur in an import-export business and had many associates and a large circle of acquaintances. His high level of sociability gave Mary a false sense of social stimulation, but she remained shy and was not at ease around other people. Bob made fun of Mary to his friends, and she often became the brunt of their social jokes. She went along with their joking, but inside she felt one down. After a while Mary balked at going out with Bob. Rarely would she admit her feelings of embarrassment or shyness, as she did when they were first married. This example illustrates Mary's lack of trust in Bob. In their relationship she was highly vulnerable and therefore greatly dependent. Because of their difference in vulnerability, Bob fell into the habit of exploiting his power over Mary, further reducing her trust. Later when Mary admitted in counseling that she did not trust Bob, he couldn't understand. He responded that he trusted her, and she should trust him. Bob failed to understand that the vulnerability pattern in their relationsip made Mary the vulnerable party, with his having little to risk. Consequently, their confidence pattern was such that Bob was more confident than Mary and was unaware that her ego was risked in her trusting him.

The next dimension of a relationship is intimacy. Two variables are relevant. The *transferable-nontransferable* continuum refers to the degree to which the relationship is unique. In a nontransferable relationship the partners almost always receive self-confirmation only from each other. This kind of relationship is highly intimate. In a transferable relationship one finds several other people with whom confirmation can be achieved. Such a relationship is not unique or intimate. In the example of Bob and Mary, the relationship for Bob was transferable; he had many other people who could as easily have met his needs as did Mary. Mary, however, had no one else to meet her needs in the way that Bob did. For her the relationship was nontransferable.

The second variable of intimacy is *degree of attachment*, or the amount of interdependence in terms of mutual self-confirmation achieved in the relationship. The greater the attachment, the greater the intimacy. In Bob and Mary's relationship little mutual attachment was present. Bob received much ego confirmation outside the relationship, while Mary relied entirely on Bob for her self-confirmation.

The last dimension of relationships, control, seems to be the pivotal dimension. Certainly it has received the most research attention. Millar and Rogers have elaborated this dimension.[22] Control is characterized by two variables. The first is the *rigid-flexible* continuum. The more flexible the relationship, the more control passes back and forth between the two parties. *Stability-instability* relates to the predictability of the control shifts. The more consistent the pattern of control over time, the more stable the control. Obviously, Mary and Bob have a rigid but stable control pattern.

Let us take a closer look at how control operates in a relationship. Following from the work of early relationship theorists, Millar and Rogers define control in terms of complementarity and symmetry. Control cannot be defined by examining a single message. Rather, one must look at the pattern of messages and responses over time. Every message is a stimulus for the next message in the sequence. In other words when A makes a statement, B's response defines the nature of the relationship at that moment. If B responds in a way that asserts control, B's message is said to be *one-up*. If B responds in a way that accepts A's assertion of control, B's message is *one-down*. If B's response neither asserts control nor relinquishes it, the message is *one-across*. A complementary exchange occurs when one partner asserts a one-up message and the other responds one-down. In a complementary relationship this kind of transaction predominates. A symmetrical exchange involves both partners presenting one-up or one-down messages, and a symmetrical relationship is marked by a preponderance of such exchanges. A third state, transition, exists when the partners' responses are different (for example, one-up/one-across) but not opposite. Table 9.1 illustrates nine control states generated by combinations of these types of control messages.[23]

22. Millar and Rogers have relied in part on the work of associates as a basis for this conceptualization. See P. M. Ericson and L. E. Rogers, "New Procedures for Analyzing Relational Communication," *Family Process* 12 (1973): 245–67; L. E. Rogers and R. V. Farace, "Analysis of Relational Communication in Dyads: New Measurement Procedures," *Human Communication Research* 1 (1975): 222–39.

23. Millar and Rogers, "A Relational Approach," p. 97.

Consider the following brief exchanges between Mary and Bob as examples of the nine types of transactions.

1. *Competitive symmetry* (one-up/one-up)

Bob: You know I want you to keep the house picked up during the day.
Mary: I want you to help sometimes!

2. *Complementarity* (one-down/one-up)

Mary: With your help, Bob, I know we can get out of this.
Bob: Yeah.

3. *Transition* (one-across/one-up)

Mary: I'm willing to compromise if you are.
Bob: No, I won't give in.

4. *Complementarity* (one-up/one-down)

Bob: Let's get out of town this weekend, so we can work this thing out. Okay?
Mary: Okay.

5. *Submissive symmetry* (one-down/one-down)

Bob: I'm so tired. What are we ever going to do?
Mary: Bob, don't back out. I need you.

6. *Transition* (one-across/one-down)

Bob: What household chores do you think I should do?
Mary: Whatever you want to do.

7. *Transition* (one-up/one-across)

Bob: I definitely think we should not have any more kids.
Mary: Why?

8. *Transition* (one-down/one-across)

Mary: I'm sorry I don't want to go out very often. What can I do about it?
Bob: Why don't you like to go out?

9. *Neutralized symmetry* (one-across/one-across)

Mary: I think you should stay home more often, but it's really okay if you need to go out.
Bob: Well, I do like to go out, but I should stay home more, I guess.

Parks. The foregoing concepts of complementarity and symmetry are useful for understanding the configuration of relational patterns. Malcolm Parks has presented a set of axioms and theorems, based on research findings and clinical observations. These rely heavily on Millar and Rogers's taxonomy in Table 9.1 and can be viewed as an extension of this theory. At the same time Parks's axioms are based on propositions from earlier theorists as well, including both Bateson and Watzlawick. Since the axioms and theorems are self-explanatory, they are listed without comment:[24]

Axioms

1. The greater the competitive symmetry, the greater the frequency of unilateral action in a relationship.
2. The greater the competitive symmetry, the lower the probability of relationship termination.
3. The greater the role discrepancy, the greater the competitive symmetry.
4. The greater the competitive symmetry, the greater the frequency of open conflict.
5. The greater the competitive symmetry, the greater the frequency of threat and intimidation messages.
6. The greater the competitive symmetry, the greater the frequency of messages of rejection.
7. The less competitive symmetry, the greater the satisfaction with communication.
8. The greater the external threat, the less the competitive symmetry.
9. The greater the role discrepancy, the less frequent is communication about feelings toward the other.
10. The greater the complementarity, the less empathy.
11. The greater the complementarity, the greater the role specialization.
12. The greater the complementarity, the greater the mutual envy.
13. The greater the rigidity, the greater the frequency of disconfirming messages.
14. The greater the rigidity, the greater the probability of psychopathology.
15. The greater the rigidity, the less frequent are attempts to explicitly define the relationship.

Theorems (derived from the above axioms)

1. The greater the role discrepancy, the greater the frequency of unilateral action in the relationship.
2. The greater the role discrepancy, the lower the probability of relational termination.
3. The greater the role discrepancy, the greater the frequency of open conflict.
4. The greater the role discrepancy, the greater the frequency of threat and intimidation messages.
5. The greater the role discrepancy, the greater the frequency of messages of rejection.

24. See Malcolm Parks, "Relational Communication: Theory and Research," *Human Communication Research* 3 (1977): 372–81.

TABLE 9.1
Control configurations

CONTROL DIRECTION OF SPEAKER B'S MESSAGE	CONTROL DIRECTION OF SPEAKER A'S MESSAGE		
	ONE-UP (↑)	ONE-DOWN (↓)	ONE-ACROSS (→)
One-up (↑)	1. (↑↑) Competitive symmetry	4. (↑↓) Complementarity	7. (↑→) Transition
One-down (↓)	2. (↓↑) Complementarity	5. (↓↓) Submissive symmetry	8. (↓→) Transition
One-across (→)	3. (→↑) Transition	6. (→↓) Transition	9. (→→) Neutralized symmetry

6. The greater the role discrepancy, the less satisfaction with communication.

7. The greater the external threat, the greater the frequency of mutual or joint action in a relationship.

8. The greater the external threat, the higher the probability of relationship termination.

9. The greater the external threat, the lower the frequency of open conflict within the relationship.

10. The greater the external threat, the lower the frequency of threat and intimidation messages within the relationship.

11. The greater the external threat, the lower the frequency of messages of rejection within the relationship.

12. The greater the external threat, the greater the satisfaction with communication within the relationship.

Theories of relational communication tend to be actional in ontology.[25] As Millar and Rogers state, their transactional approach to theory "emphasizes a dynamic, emergent, holistic approach to the study of social behavior. It requires social scientists to look for multiple causes and multiplicative effects, rather than unidimensional and additive cause-effect sequences."[26] For the most part the work of the Palo Alto Group relies on clinical interpretation of relationships as experienced by the partners in the relationship. Later research, however, uses objective observation and measurement in search of generalizations. For the most part, however, researchers such as Parks develop general axiomatic propositions that leave wide latitude for individual choice in relational communication.

Criticism

Critics of relational communication have addressed, directly or indirectly, each of the criteria in our critical model: scope, appropriateness, heuristic value, validity, and parsimony. Supporters have defended the work using the same categories. The two groups clash little on substance. Rather, an evaluation of these theories depends on one's epistemological biases and research values.

Supporters of the work on relational communication praise it in all categories. In scope they see it as providing a needed focus on one important aspect of interpersonal communication, the full coverage of the nature of relationships.[27] It validly broadens scope from focus on individual to focus on interaction. Supporters also see it as appropriately humanistic, following Bateson's admonition against experimental, intrusive methods.[28] Although until recently this work had not stimulated much research, it has been heuristic in stimulating clinical application and observation.[29] Its external validity is also supported by the clinical applications, which supporters view as successful.[30] Finally, the theory can be viewed as parsimonious on the grounds that many normal and abnormal relational outcomes are explained by only a few elements of relationship.[31]

Although the critics usually are sympathetic to what relational theorists have begun, they see serious problems in the overall work.[32] Most of the criticism can be boiled down to two main objections. The first is conceptual confusion. Typically, critics point out two difficulties in this regard. The first conceptual problem is the premise, implied by Watzlawick, Beavin, and Jackson's first axiom, that all behavior is communicative. The objection is that by placing no limits on what is communicative, the concept becomes meaningless. Carol Wilder discusses

25. For an excellent discussion of the epistemology of relational communication, see Carol Wilder, "The Palo Alto Group: Difficulties and Directions of the Interactional View for Human Communication Research," *Human Communication Research* 5 (1979): 171–86.

26. Millar and Rogers, "A Relational Approach," p. 90.

27. Ibid.

28. Gregory Bateson, "Slippery Theories," *Interactional Journal of Psychiatry* 2 (1966): 415–17.

29. See Paul Watzlawick and John Weaklund, eds., *The International View: Studies at the Mental Research Institute, Palo Alto, 1965-1974* (New York: Norton, 1977).

30. See Paul Watzlawick, John Weaklund, and Richard Fish, *Change: Principles of Problem Formation and Problem Resolution* (New York: Norton, 1974).

31. Watzlawick, Beavin, and Jackson, *Pragmatics*.

32. The criticism of relational communication is discussed in detail by Wilder, "Palo Alto Group."

this problem with Paul Watzlawick in an interview:

WILDER: The first axiom in *Pragmatics*—"One cannot not communicate"—has a fine aesthetic ring to it and brings to mind some of the tacit dimensions of communication, but some have argued that it expands the boundaries of what constitutes communication beyond any useful or meaningful grounds.

WATZLAWICK: Yes, this has been said. And it usually boils down to the question: "Is intentionality an essential ingredient of communication?" If you are interested in the exchange of information on what we would call a conscious or voluntary, deliberate level then, indeed, the answer is "yes." But, I would say, if you take our viewpoint and say that all behavior in the presence of another person is communication, I should think you have to extend it to the point of the axiom.[33]

Another area of conceptual confusion critics often mention is the distinction between the report and command functions, or metacommunication.[34] One critical treatment calls the concept "muddled and confusing."[35] The problem is that the Palo Alto Group, at different points in their writing, imply as many as three different meanings for metacommunication. (The use of various other labels, such as command message and relational message, is also confusing.) At points metacommunication refers to a verbal or nonverbal classification of the content message, in which one's partner guides the coding of the content. At other times metacommunication refers to nonverbal statements about the relationship itself, such as indicating who is in control. Or, metacommunication sometimes refers to explicit discussion by individuals about the nature of their relationship. To make matters worse, metacommunication has been treated alternately as strictly analogic, analogic and digital, nonverbal, and both verbal and nonverbal.

The accusation that theories of relational communication are conceptually confused strikes primarily at the internal validity or consistency of these theories. At the same time it questions parsimony, noting that the so-called few core concepts are really many.

The second main objection to relational communication theories is that the concepts are difficult to operationalize and therefore are not amenable to verification through research. This objection indirectly questions the appropriateness of the epistemological assumptions of the theories, their heuristic value, and their external validity.

The issue here is whether relational concepts are best tested through the clinical case study method or by objective observation of multiple subjects. This issue is epistemological, not substantive. Researchers who are not members of the Palo Alto Group have attempted to operationalize relational concepts in such a way as to make measurement possible. The work of Millar, Rogers, Parks, and their associates, summarized earlier, exemplifies this approach. While many believe this effort is a step in the right direction, Parks points out that the conceptual distinctions of one-up, one-down, and one-across are still rudimentary and need elaboration.[36]

Theories of Self-Presentation

Most relational theories of communication recognize that people engage in two basic kinds of activities in encounters with others: They attempt to understand others, and they present themselves to others. This is the two-sided coin of perception-presentation. In this section we will look at theories in the latter group. In the next section we will examine the other side of the coin. The following theories present in-

33. Carol Wilder, "From the Interactional View—A Conversation with Paul Watzlawick," *Journal of Communication* 28 (1978): 41–42.

34. This problem is well discussed by William Wilmot, "Meta-communication: A Re-examination and Extension," in *Communication Yearbook 4*, ed. Dan Nimmo (New Brunswick, N.J.: Transaction Books, 1980), pp. 61–69.

35. Arthur Bochner and Dorothy Krueger, "Interpersonal Communication Theory and Research: An Overview of Inscrutable Epistemologies and Muddled Concepts," in *Communication Yearbook 3*, ed. Dan Nimmo (New Brunswick, N.J.: Transaction Books, 1979), p. 203.

36. Parks, "Relational Communication."

teresting contrasting approaches to self-presentation in interpersonal communication.

Schutz's Psychological Approach

In the last section we talked about theories that describe the nature of interpersonal relationships. These theories imply the importance of relationships in human life. Another theory that more clearly explains the need for communication is that of William Schutz: fundamental interpersonal relations orientation theory (FIRO).[37] Schutz writes that the human being has needs for social relationships with other people. Like biological needs social needs must be satisfied to avoid illness and death. Schutz's theory consists of four postulates. We will review each in turn.

The first postulate, which defines interpersonal needs, is the heart of the theory: "Every individual has three important interpersonal needs: inclusion, control, and affection. . . . Inclusion, control, and affection constitute a sufficient set of areas of interpersonal behavior for the prediction and explanation of interpersonal phenomena."[38] This listing of needs is necessary and sufficient to understand interpersonal relations. In other words how one behaves toward others is determined by these three needs.

Each need is conceived as a variable between extremes, some people needing a high degree of the quality, others needing less. If one's need is being met, one will feel psychologically comfortable. Inclusion relates to the degree of association needed. Control is the person's need to affect and have power over others. Affection is the degree of love needed. How a person relates to others will depend on that individual's manner of meeting these needs.

Schutz's analysis of interpersonal needs is reflected in his list of variables in Table 9.2.[39] *Inclusion*, or the need to have satisfactory relations with others, is represented on a continuum between the two extremes of high interaction and no interaction. Acts of inclusion range from always originating or eliciting interaction to never doing so. Feelings of inclusion include being interested in others and eliciting interest from others. A satisfactory self-concept emerging from optimal inclusion is the feeling that one is a worthwhile person. Schutz describes inclusion: "It has to do with interacting with people, with attention, acknowledgement, being known, prominence, recognition, prestige, status, and fame; with identity, individuality, understanding, interest, commitment, and participation. It is unlike affection in that it does not involve strong emotional attachments to individual persons. It is unlike control in that the preoccupation is with prominence, not dominance."[40]

The *control* need is a variable between strong control and no control. Acts of control range from controlling all of the behavior of others (or being controlled by others) to controlling no behavior (or not being controlled by others). On the feeling dimension a healthy relationship involves mutual respect for one's competence and responsibility. The self-concept growing out of the optimal fulfillment of this need is self-respect. As Schutz puts it: "Thus the flavor of control is transmitted by behavior involving influence, leadership, power, coercion, authority, accomplishment, intellectual superiority, high achievement, and independence, as well as dependency (for decision making), rebellion, resistance, and submission. It differs from inclusion behavior in that it does not require prominence. . . . Control behavior differs from

37. See William Schutz, *Firo: A Three-Dimensional Theory of Interpersonal Behavior* (New York: Rinehart, 1958); or *The Interpersonal Underworld* (Palo Alto, Calif.: Science and Behavior Books, 1966); *Here Comes Everybody* (New York: Harper & Row, 1973); *Elements of Encounter* (New York: Bantam, 1975); *Leaders of Schools* (La Jolla, Calif.: University Associates, 1977). For a brief summary of the theory, see Lawrence Rosenfeld, "Conceptual Orientations," in *Human Interaction in the Small Group* (Columbus: Charles E. Merrill, 1973), pp. 16–18, 47–48.

38. Schutz, *Firo*, p. 13.

39. Schutz, *Leaders*, p. 29.

40. Schutz, *Firo*, p. 22.

affection behavior in that it has to do with power relations rather than emotional closeness."[41]

The interpersonal *affection* need is expressed by a spectrum between closeness and distance. Acts of affection range from originating and eliciting much love to originating and eliciting no love. Satisfactory feelings of affection include adequate levels of closeness with others. The resultant self-concept says, I am lovable. "Thus the flavor of affection is embodied in situations of love, emotional closeness, personal confidences, intimacy. Negative affection is characterized by hate, hostility, and emotional rejection."[42]

The task of the person in meeting these three needs is to strike an optimal psychological balance or equilibrium. This involves behaving in such a way that one feels comfortable in terms of inclusion, control, and affection.

41. Ibid., p. 23.
42. Ibid., p. 24.

We have now examined the three needs in terms of observability (acts and feelings) and directionality (originating or receiving). An individual's behaviors and feelings of inclusion, control, and affection exist in one of four states. These states are desired, ideal, anxious, and pathological. *Desired states* are those that optimally meet the individual's needs. *Ideal states* are more than satisfactory; they are the healthiest possible relations. *Anxious states* involve too much or too little inclusion, control, or affection. *Pathological states* involve dysfunctional interpersonal relations and lead to various psychotic, psychopathic, or neurotic conditions.

The ideal, anxious, and pathological

TABLE 9.2
FIRO theory variables

	BEHAVIOR	FEELINGS
Expressed inclusion	I make efforts to include people in my activities and to get them to include me in theirs. I try to belong, to join social groups, and to be with people as much as possible.	Other people are important to me. I have a high regard for people as people, and I am very much interested in them.
Wanted inclusion	I want other people to include me in their activities and to invite me to belong, even if I do not make an effort to be included.	I want others to have a high regard for me as a person. I want them to consider me important and interesting.
Expressed control	I try to exert control and influence over things. I take charge of things. I tell other people what to do.	I want other people to feel that I am a competent, influential person, and to respect my capabilities.
Wanted control	I want others to control and influence me. I want other people to tell me what to do.	I see other people as strong and competent. I trust and rely on their abilities.
Expressed affection	I make efforts to become close to people. I express friendly and affectionate feelings. I try to be personal and intimate.	I feel people are likeable or lovable.
Wanted affection	I want others to express friendly and affectionate feelings toward me and to try to become close to me.	I want people to feel that I am a likeable or lovable person who is very warm and affectionate.

categories yield various types for each need. Within the anxious category are two subtypes: overactive and underactive. In the inclusion category are four subtypes: undersocial, oversocial, social, and psychotic. The *undersocial* person tends to be introverted. He or she is neither interested in others, nor are others interested in him or her. As a result of the inability to meet the inclusion need, the undersocial person may have anxieties of feeling worthless. *Oversocial* persons, on the other hand, are extroverted. By erring in the opposite direction, they are attention getters. The ideal inclusion type is the *social.* This individual is comfortable being with others as well as being alone and has managed to achieve a balance in association with others. In pathological form, failure to meet the inclusion need will lead to *psychosis,* particularly schizophrenia.

For the control category, the subtypes are four: the abdicrat, the autocrat, the democrat, and the psychopath. The *abdicrat* is submissive, avoiding responsibility. Such individuals do not have confidence in their own abilities. On the other extreme is the *autocrat,* who tends to dominate in social situations. Underlying this form of behavior is a basic mistrust of others. The *democrat* is the ideal type, who comfortably controls or is controlled, as appropriate. The pathological type is the psychopath or the obsessive-compulsive.

Likewise there are four affection subtypes: underpersonal, overpersonal, personal, and neurotic. The *underpersonal* individual relates superficially to others, avoiding emotional involvement. Such persons fear being unlovable. The *overpersonal* tends to be manipulative, seeking to win affection. The *personal* relates comfortably in various ways, developing close relationships and giving genuine affection. Personal individuals will maintain a satisfactory distance as appropriate. The pathological form is neurosis.

Table 9.3 illustrates the various interpersonal anxiety types. The following is a description of each cell of Table 9.3.

Anxieties about self-toward-others behavior

Too much:

Inclusion: I am with people too much.

Control: I am too dominating.

Affection: I get too personal.

Too little:

Inclusion: I do not mix with people enough.

TABLE 9.3
Types of interpersonal anxieties

		SELF TOWARD OTHERS		OTHERS TOWARD SELF	
		BEHAVIOR LEVEL	FEELING LEVEL	BEHAVIOR LEVEL	FEELING LEVEL
Too much	Inclusion				
	Control				
	Affection				
Too little	Inclusion				
	Control				
	Affection				

Control: I am not decisive enough.
Affection: I am too cool and aloof.

Anxieties about others-toward-self behavior
Too much:
Inclusion: People do not leave me alone enough.
Control: People boss me around too much.
Affection: People get too personal with me.
Too little:
Inclusion: People do not pay enough attention to me.
Control: People do not help me enough.
Affection: People do not act personal enough with me.

Anxieties about self-toward-others feelings
Too much:
Inclusion: I respect everyone's individuality too much.
Control: I respect everyone's competence too much.
Affection: I do not like people enough.
Too little:
Inclusion: I do not respect people as individuals enough.
Control: I do not trust people's abilities enough.
Affection: I do not like people enough.

Anxieties about others-toward-self feelings
Too much:
Inclusion: People feel I am too important.
Control: People respect my abilities too much.
Affection: People like me too much.
Too little:
Inclusion: People do not feel that I am significant enough.
Control: People do not respect my abilities enough.
Affection: People do not like me enough.

Now that we have discussed the three needs of Schutz's first postulate, we will briefly summarize the other three postulates. The second is the postulate of relational continuity, stated as follows: "An individual's expressed interpersonal behavior will be similar to the behavior he experienced in his earliest interpersonal relations, usually with his parents."[43] This postulate explains that the origin of interpersonal behavior is early parent-child interaction. We tend to pattern behavior in a situation after behavior recalled from a similar childhood situation. We may copy our own childhood behavior or our parents' behavior.

Schutz's third postulate, the postulate of compatibility, states that compatibility is important in the efficient operation of a group.[44] Compatibility is defined in terms of the inclusion, control, and affection behaviors of the group members. Compatibility increases both the desire to communicate and cohesiveness, which in turn increase productivity.

Schutz's fourth postulate relates to group formation. As a group develops, it passes through a sequence of inclusion behavior, control, and affection. If the group anticipates that the association will end, it then reverses the pattern before dissolving, passing again through a control phase and ending with inclusion. Thus a group's history of predominant behavior follows the pattern inclusion-control-affection-control-inclusion.

The focus of Schutz's theory is interpersonal needs. He sees interpersonal behavior as an attempt to fulfill various needs via relating to others. His theory helps to explain why people relate to others in particular ways. Another explanation of how we behave interpersonally is offered by Erving Goffman in his theory of self-presentation.

Goffman's Social Approach

One of the most prolific sociologists of our day is Erving Goffman.[45] As a symbolic interactionist of the dramaturgical tradition, Goffman analyzes human behavior with a theatrical

43. Ibid., p. 81.
44. Ibid., p. 105.
45. See the bibliography for Chapter 9 for a listing of Goffman's works.

metaphor. The ordinary interaction setting is a stage. People are actors, structuring their performances to make impressions on audiences. According to Goffman, interpersonal communication is a presentation through which various aspects of the self are projected. Goffman's analyses in his various books are highly detailed. Presenting all of his concepts here would be impossible. Instead, we will look at his main ideas and premises.

Goffman's observations of nearly twenty years are spread throughout his books, making synthesis difficult. Fortunately, Goffman provides a theoretical framework that outlines his general approach to human behavior.[46] After we review a beginning set of premises, we will go back to material specifically related to interpersonal communication.

Goffman begins his reasoning with the assumption that the person faced with a situation must somehow make sense of or organize the events perceived. What emerges as an organized happening for the individual becomes that person's reality of the moment. This premise states that what is real for a person emerges in that person's *definition of the situation*. (This idea is an elaboration of a key concept from symbolic interactionism as discussed in Chapter 4.

A typical response of a person to a new situation is the question, What is going on here? The person's definition of the situation provides an answer. Often the first definition is not adequate and a rereading may be necessary, as in the case of a practical joke, a mistake, or a misunderstanding. The notion of a rereading is important for Goffman because he has observed that we are often deceived and deceive one another in our relations.

Several terms highlight Goffman's general approach. A *strip* is any arbitrary sequence of activity. A *frame* is a basic element of organization used in defining a situation. *Frame analysis* thus consists of examining the ways experience is organized for the individual. What the frame (or framework) does is allow the person to identify and understand otherwise meaningless events; it gives meaning to the ongoing activities of life. A *natural framework* is an unguided event of nature, with which the individual must cope. A *social framework*, on the other hand, is seen as controllable, guided by some intelligence. Thus humans have a sense of control when they enter the social frame. Of course, these two types of frameworks interrelate, since social beings act on and are in turn influenced by the natural order. Goffman demonstrates the importance of frameworks for culture: "Taken all together, the primary frameworks of a particular social group constitute a central element of its culture, especially insofar as understandings emerge concerning principal classes of schemata, the relations of these classes to one another, and the sum total of forces and agents that these interpretive designs acknowledge to be loose in the world."[47] This view that a culture is defined in part by its definitions of situations is consistent not only with the central ideas of symbolic interactionism but with several theories of meaning presented in Chapter 6.

Primary framework is the basic unit of social life. Goffman points out in detail various ways that primary frames can be transformed or altered so that similar organizational principles are used to meet different ends. A game, for example, is modeled after a fight, but its purpose is different. A large portion of our frameworks are not primary at all, though they are modeled after primary events. Examples include games, drama, deceptions (both good and bad), experiments, and other fabrications. Indeed, what happens in ordinary interpersonal communication often involves this kind of secondary activity, including dramatic presentations, fabrications, and deceptions.

With this general theoretical approach as a base, we come to Goffman's central ideas on communication. Communication activities, like all activities, are viewed in the context of

46. Erving Goffman, *Frame Analysis: An Essay on the Organization of Experience* (Cambridge: Harvard University Press, 1974).

47. Ibid., p. 27.

frame analysis. We will begin with the concept of *face engagement*.[48] A face engagement or *encounter* occurs when people engage in focused interaction. Persons in a face engagement have a single focus of attention and a perceived mutual activity. In unfocused interaction people in public places acknowledge the presence of one another without paying attention to one another. In such an unfocused situation the individual is normally accessible for encounter with others. Once an engagement begins, a mutual contract exists to continue the engagement to some kind of termination. During this time a relationship develops and is mutually sustained. Face engagements are both verbal and nonverbal, and the cues exhibited are important in signifying the nature of the relationship as well as a mutual definition of the situation.

People in face engagements of talk take turns presenting dramas to one another. Story telling—recounting past events—is a matter of impressing the listener by dramatic portrayal. This idea of presenting dramas is central to Goffman's overall theory.

> I am suggesting that often what talkers undertake to do is not to provide information to a recipient but to present dramas to an audience. Indeed, it seems that we spend most of our time not engaged in giving information but in giving shows. And observe, this theatricality is not based on mere displays of feelings or faked exhibitions of spontaneity or anything else by way of the huffing and puffing we might derogate by calling theatrical. The parallel between stage and conversation is much, much deeper than that. The point is that ordinarily when an individual says something, he is not saying it as a bold statement of fact on his own behalf. He is recounting. He is running through a strip of already determined events for the engagement of his listeners.[49]

In engaging others, the speaker presents a particular character to the audience. The person divides the self into a number of parts and like the stage actor presents this or that character in a particular engagement role. Thus in ordinary conversation we have the actor and the character, or the animator and the animation; the listener willingly is involved in the characterization being presented.

Of course, the individual has opportunities to present the self in situations other than conversation. Even in unfocused interaction scenes are presented to others.[50] Goffman believes that the self is literally determined by these dramatizations. Here is how he explains the self:

> A correctly staged and performed scene leads the audience to impute a self to a performed character, but this imputation—this self—is a *product* of a scene that comes off, and is not a cause of it. The self, then, as a performed character, is not an organic thing that has a specific location, whose fundamental fate is to be born, to mature, and to die; it is a dramatic effect arising diffusely from a scene that is presented, and the characteristic issue, the crucial concern, is whether it will be credited or discredited.[51]

In attempting to define a situation, the person goes through a two-part process. First, the person needs information about the other people in the situation. Second, one needs to give information about oneself. This process of exchanging information enables people to know what is expected of them. Usually, this exchange occurs indirectly through observing the behavior of others and structuring one's own behavior to elicit impressions in others. Self-presentation is very much a matter of *impression management*. The person influences the definition of a situation by projecting a particular impression: "He may wish them to think highly of him, or to think that he thinks highly of them, or to perceive how in fact he feels toward them or to obtain no clear-cut impression; he may wish to insure sufficient harmony so that the interaction can be sustained, or to defraud, get rid of, confuse, mislead, antagonize, or insult them."[52]

48. On the nature of face-to-face interaction, see Erving Goffman, *Encounters: Two Studies in the Sociology of Interaction* (Indianapolis: Bobbs-Merrill, 1961); *Behavior in Public Places* (New York: Free Press, 1963); *Interaction Ritual: Essays on Face-to-Face Behavior* (Garden City: Doubleday, 1967); and *Relations in Public* (New York: Basic Books, 1971).

49. Goffman, *Frame Analysis*, p. 508.

50. The best sources on self-presentation are Erving Goffman, *The Presentation of Self in Everyday Life* (Garden City: Doubleday, 1959); and *Relations in Public*.

51. Goffman, *Presentation*, pp. 252–53.

52. Ibid., p. 3.

Since all participants in a situation project images, an overall definition of the situation emerges. This general definition is normally rather unified. Once the definition is set, moral pressure is created to maintain it by suppressing contradictions and doubts. A person may add to the projections but never contradict the image initially set. The very organization of society is based on this principle.

> In consequence, when an individual projects a definition of the situation and thereby makes an implicit or explicit claim to be a person of a particular kind, he automatically exerts a moral demand upon the others, obliging them to value and treat him in the manner that persons of this kind have the right to expect. He also implicitly foregoes all claims to be things he does not appear to be and hence foregoes the treatment that would be appropriate for such individuals. The others find, then, that the individual has informed them as to what is and as to what they ought to see as the "is."[53]

If the presentation falters or is contradicted by later scenes, the consequence to the individual and to the social structure can be severe.

Goffman uses this basic stance in his many analyses of public life. He shows how self-presentation occurs in verbal and nonverbal behavior in all public settings. For us Goffman demonstrates the relevance of self-presentation to interpersonal communication.

In stark contrast to the deterministic epistemology of Schutz, Goffman's epistemology is humanistic.[54] His epistemological biases are best stated in *Frame Analysis*, in which he expresses his belief that knowledge arises out of the interaction between the individual and the world outside the individual. Knowledge for Goffman is not "invested" by the person nor is it "presented" anew by nature. It is a product of both nature and social definition. Still, Goffman's theory leaves wide latitude for choice as well as assuming that cultural forces play a major role. Goffman's methods and his style of reporting observations are interpretive rather than scientific.

53. Ibid., p. 13.

54. For excellent discussions of Goffman's epistemology, see Jason Ditton, ed., *The View from Goffman* (New York: St. Martin's Press, 1980); see especially the following articles: Randall Collins, "Erving Goffman and the Development of Modern Social Theory," pp. 170–209; Steve Crook and Laurie Taylor, "Goffman's Version of Reality," pp. 233–51; Peter K. Manning, "Goffman's Framing Order: Style as Structure," pp. 252–84.

Criticism

Schutz's theory has two clear strengths. First, it is parsimonious, explaining a great deal of interpersonal behavior in terms of a few variables. Second, it has been well validated, though not universally, by several research studies.[55] As a corollary value the theory is rather heuristic.

Problems of the theory are in scope and appropriateness. Many communication scholars would say that we can never adequately explain social behavior on the basis of internal needs, although clearly these do have some explanatory power. The theory can also be faulted on ontological grounds for its failure to provide room for human choice or change. Beyond immediate compatibility, it does not give us a way to understand how people adjust to one another in ongoing interaction. In fairness, however, we must note that no theory can be all-inclusive, and Schutz's work provides a basis for understanding some aspects of a fairly narrow range of behavior.

Goffman's work presents contrasting strengths and faults to Schutz's theory. Goffman's theory is broad in scope, providing insights on numerous aspects of social life. His descriptions and analyses are intuitively valid and appropriate to many scholars and a large segment of the public who read his books.

Goffman's work has been faulted primarily on two grounds. First, it has been viewed as noncumulative, scattered, and unparsimonious. In the extreme he is accused of being atheoretical. Consider the following indictment: "The

55. For a partial summary of research on this theory, see Marvin Shaw, *Group Dynamics: The Psychology of Small Group Behavior* (New York: McGraw-Hill, 1981), pp. 228–31.

non-cumulative look of Goffman's work is puzzling, and some of the blame is due to his continual shifts in concepts. Goffman never re-uses earlier concepts in later works, manifesting a kind of role-distancing from his own previous work; and he very seldom refers to his earlier work in any respect. Thus one never gets from Goffman himself any overview of his own theory, and one is left to figure out for oneself if one is to expect any theoretical unity or only a string of self-contained virtuoso performances."[56]

Although Goffman often fails to take explicit theoretical stands, a close examination of his work reveals that he has indeed integrated important sociological theories, as the same critic points out: "We have seen that he has continually drawn upon powerful intellectual traditions and upon wide-ranging empirical research both of his own rather innovative procurement, and of the best of his contemporaries. But Goffman hides his intellectual elitism behind a theory-deprecating manner, producing a kind of underground, hermetic theorizing beneath a popularistic-seeming surface."[57] *Frame Analysis* does a great deal to integrate Goffman's work into a theoretical framework. For the first time Goffman discusses in an abstract way the nature and principles of social life apart from the substance of specific human actions. For this reason *Frame Analysis* is a significant and pivotal work in Goffman's career.[58]

The second criticism of Goffman's work is ambiguity and inconsistency in using concepts.[59] He tends to create a new set of terms for each project and even uses some of these inconsistently. For example, he sometimes defines *self* as the imputations of others, but at other times he defines it as one's own view of self. This confusion is exacerbated by his applying more than one label to the same thing (for example, person and self). To make matters worse, Goffman's predominant style is metaphorical and lacks precision.

This section has given us an unusually good opportunity to see a diversity of communication theory. Here we have two theories that are vastly different in epistemology, style, and scope, each with its special strengths and weaknesses, but both providing insights into self-presentation in human interaction.

56. Collins, "Erving Goffman," p. 175.

57. Ibid., p. 205.

58. For comments on *Frame Analysis*, see Crook and Taylor, "Reality," and Stephen Littlejohn, "Frame Analysis and Communication," *Communication Research* 4 (1977): 485–92.

59. For an elaboration of this criticism, see Manning, "Framing Order."

Interpersonal Perception and Attribution

In the last section we noted that self-presentation and interpersonal perception are like a two-sided coin. In a social situation people both present the self to others and take in the presentations of others through perception. Much work has been done in social psychology on interpersonal perception, far more than can be summarized here. Renato Tagiuri introduces us to this field: "Person perception refers to the processes by which man comes to know and to think about other persons, their characteristics, qualities, and inner states. The phrase *person perception* is not very satisfactory, the term *perception* here being used in a loose way, most often meaning apperception and cognition. This topical area has been variously named social perception, person perception, and interpersonal perception, to mention only a few of the phrases used."[60]

Broadly, two areas of research have developed in interpersonal perception. The first has focused on the nature and accuracy of judgments made about other persons. The second trend has dealt with the process of interpersonal perception. This latter area interests us in the context of communication theory.

Much of the research work in interpersonal perception is atheoretical. An impressive

60. Renato Tagiuri, "Person Perception," in The *Handbook of Social Psychology*, vol. 3, ed. Gardner Lindzey and Elliot Aronson (Reading, Mass.: Addison-Wesley, 1969), p. 395.

amount of research on perceptual problems has been done but not a great deal of theorizing.[61] The major exception to this general observation is a related field, which matured in the 1970s, known as *attribution theory*. Because of its individual contribution to our understanding of interpersonal perception, we will concentrate on attribution theory here.

Although attribution theories relate most centrally to interpersonal communication, they also apply to information processing because of their cognitive basis. Attribution theory in particular deals with lay epistemology, or the ways that individuals process information in order to generate information about self, others, and situations.

For many years attribution theory went against the grain of mainstream psychology by suggesting that an individual's construction of reality is an important aspect of human behavior. With the shift in social psychology from discovering the real causes of behavior to the interpretation of how people perceive the causes of their own behavior, attribution theory has become firmly planted in social psychology and has become one of the mainstays of the field. Many social psychologists believe that attribution processes lie at the heart of most other social phenomena.[62]

Perception and Metaperception

The axioms of Watzlawick, Beavin, and Jackson provide an excellent general description of the relationship dimension of interpersonal communication. Another theory that adds depth to this analysis is R. D. Laing's. Laing, a British psychiatrist, has written a number of books related to the process of perception in communication.[63] Laing's thesis is that one's communicative behavior is largely shaped by one's perception (experience) of the relationship with the other communicator.

Laing takes a phenomenological approach to the study of human beings: The basic datum for analysis is the *experience* of the person, or reality *as experienced by* a given individual. Laing makes a distinction between experience and behavior. *Behavior*, which is the observable actions of another, is public; experience is private. Experience is the feeling that accompanies behavior or the perception of another's behavior. It consists of imagination, perception, and memory. We can imagine the future; we can perceive the present; we can recall the past. Such experiences are internal in the individual and not directly accessible to anyone else.

Behavior, on the other hand, can be observed, but another's experience cannot. Inferring experience from behavior is the heart of communication, but doing this is difficult, as Laing points out: "I see you, and you see me. I experience you, and you experience me. I see your behavior. You see my behavior. But I do not and never have and never will see your *experience* of me."[64] As implied in this quotation, experience is an intrapersonal matter, but one's experience is also affected largely by relations with others and how one perceives or experiences others. How we behave toward another person is a function of two related experiences, the experience of the other person and the experience of the relationship. Likewise, our experience is further affected by behavior. Interpersonal communication is often marked by a behavior-experience spiral.

The foregoing paragraph states that behavior is related to one's experience of the other and one's experience of the relationship. Laing's message will become clearer as we review his notion of interpersonal perception.[65] A person interacting with another has two levels of expe-

61. This conclusion is supported in ibid.

62. For an excellent compilation of work in attribution, see John K. Harvey, William J. Ickes, and Robert F. Kidd, eds., *New Directions in Attribution Research*, vols. 1 and 2 (New York: John Wiley & Sons, 1976, 1978).

63. Laing's works most concerned with communication include *The Politics of Experience* (New York: Pantheon Books, 1967); *Self and Others* (London: Tavistock Publications, 1969); and R. D. Laing, H. Phillipson, and A. R. Lee, *Interpersonal Perception* (New York: Springer, 1966).

64. Laing, *Politics of Experience*, p. 4.

65. Laing et al., *Interpersonal Perception*. An excellent brief summary can be found in Rosenfeld, "Conceptual Orientations," pp. 31–36.

rience (perception), or *perspectives*. The person experiences the other individual in a *direct perspective*. One also experiences the other's experience. In this second or *metaperspective* the communicator imagines, or infers, what the other person is feeling, perceiving, or thinking. Laing describes the process: "I cannot avoid trying to understand your experience, because although I do not experience your experience, which is invisible to me (and nontastable, nontouchable, nonsmellable, and inaudible), yet I experience you *as experiencing*. I do not experience your experience. But I experience you experiencing. I experience myself as experienced by you. And I experience you as experiencing yourself as experienced by me. And so on."[66] To use Laing's favorite characters, Jack perceives certain behaviors of Jill (direct perspective). He also infers or imagines Jill's perceptions (metaperspective).

A relationship then is defined by the communicator's direct perspectives and metaperspectives. Theoretically, metaperception can proceed indefinitely through higher levels. Jack loves Jill. Jack thinks Jill loves him. Jack thinks that Jill thinks that he loves her, and so on. Further, since experience affects behavior, one often behaves in accordance with his or her metaperspectives. If Jack thinks Jill thinks he does not love her, he may try to change Jill's imaged perception. The *metaidentity* is how the person believes others see one. (You may recall from symbolic interactionism the importance of another's perceptions in establishing the self.)

Of course, metaperspectives may or may not be accurate, and the health of a relationship is much determined by perceptual accuracy. Three concepts are pertinent at this point. *Understanding* is the agreement or conjunction between Jack's metaperspective and Jill's direct perspective. If Jack correctly infers that Jill loves him, understanding results. *Being understood* is the inverse. It is the conjunction of Jack's meta-metaperspective and Jill's metaperspective. If Jack correctly infers that Jill believes Jack loves her, he is understood. But being understood is not the same as *feeling understood*. The latter is defined as the conjunction between Jack's direct perspective and his own metaperspective. If Jack infers that Jill believes he loves her, and he does, then he feels understood.

Since communicators attempt to behave in ways that, according to their metaperspectives, will affect others, *spirals* can develop wherein each person acts toward the other in such a way that particular metaperspectives (for example, mistrust) become accentuated. This idea of spiral has been important for Laing as a psychiatrist because it explains various pathological relationships. For example, Jack, as a paranoid, mistrusts Jill. He does not believe she loves him. He then accuses her of having affairs with other men. Jill, in her metaperception of Jack's mistrust, attempts to prove her love. Jack sees this attempt as covering up her lack of love. Now he perceives Jill as a liar. The spiral will continue until the relationship is destroyed. This example is of a *unilateral spiral*. Jack's mistrust of Jill becomes more and more accentuated. A *bilateral spiral* occurs when both parties move toward increasingly extreme metaperceptions. For example, Jack believes Jill wants too much from him. He judges her as greedy. At the same time Jill sees Jack as selfish. Both feel the other is withholding what he or she needs. Since both parties feel misunderstood, they retaliate, causing their metaperceptions of greed and selfishness to increase. Such spirals need to be broken before the system (dyad or person) is destroyed.

Now that we have discussed Laing's basic ideas of experience, perception, and metaperception, we can move to another part of his theory, which also adds to our understanding of interpersonal communication. In the second half of *Self and Others*, Laing presents a helpful analysis of the forms of interpersonal action.[67] Some of these forms are growthful and positive; others are dysfunctional and therefore harmful.

66. Laing, *Politics of Experience*, p. 5.

67. Laing, *Self and Others*, part II.

The first form of action is *complementarity*, the aspect of a relationship that allows one to fulfill one's identity. A person's identity cannot be complete without complementary relations with others. Motherhood is not possible without a child. You cannot be a lover without someone to love. One cannot be an oppressor without the complementarity of submission. Laing defines this aspect of interpersonal relations: "One speaks of a gesture, an action, a feeling, a need, a role, an identity, being the complement of a corresponding gesture, action, feeling, need, role, or identity of the other."[68] A failure to find appropriate complementarity in a relationship is extremely frustrating and can lead to pathology. Laing's concept of complementarity is consistent with that of the Palo Alto Group.

A second important form of relating involves *confirmation*, or the affirmation of one's identity. In an interaction communicators behave in ways and send messages that confirm the other's self-perception. A simple smile may do it, as might a host of verbal and nonverbal reinforcers. If Jack loves Jill and Jill recognizes and accepts his love, confirmation takes place. On the other hand, many interactions involve *disconfirmation*, as in the following example: "A little boy of five runs to his mother holding a big fat worm in his hand, and says, 'Mummy, look what a big fat worm I have got.' She says, 'You are filthy—away and clean yourself immediately.'"[69] Since communication occurs on multiple levels, one can confirm another on one level and disconfirm simultaneously on yet another level. A parent may console a hurt child verbally, while tactilely and kinesically communicating irritation and annoyance. Here Laing's conception is similar to Bateson's notion of the double bind.

Another form of relationship is *collusion*. Collusion is mutual self-deception, which necessarily involves more than one person. Laing describes it as an unstated game. Another definition of collusion is false confirmation. Here is how it happens: "Two people in relation may confirm each other or genuinely complement each other. Still, to disclose oneself to the other is hard without confidence in oneself and trust in the other. Desire for confirmation from each is present in both, but each is caught between trust and mistrust, confidence and despair, and both settle for counterfeit acts of confirmation on the basis of pretence. To do so *both* must play the game of collusion."[70] Thus Jack and Jill continue to date long after they have fallen out of love. Neither wishes to hurt the other. Both fake love, thus faking confirmation of the other's "love."

Another form of relationship involves *false and untenable positions*. This condition occurs when one behaves incongruently with needs and feelings. It happens when a person does not feel like oneself. A person can put oneself into an untenable position, but one can also be put there by another person in a relationship. Laing uses everyday expressions to capture the essence of this kind of relation: "To put someone on the spot; to give someone [no] room to move; to have no elbow room; to be put in an awkward position; to make someone feel small; to know where one is with someone; to pull someone or to be pulled in opposite directions; to turn the screw on; to know where one stands; to have the ground taken from under one's feet; to be boxed in, tied in a knot, caught, sat upon, cornered, entangled, trapped, smothered."[71]

The final class of interpersonal actions discussed by Laing is *attributions and injunctions*. Attributions are statements telling a person how to be; injunctions tell a person how to behave. Attributions and injunctions are harmful when they contradict the individual's own self-attributions and self-injunctions. This class of behavior is closely related to confirmation and disconfirmation as well as to false positions. The previous example of two people in a rela-

68. Ibid., p. 67.

69. Ibid., p. 85.

70. Ibid., p. 91.

71. Ibid., p. 118.

tion talking about their "love" is an excellent illustration of the effect of attribution. (Be careful not to confuse Laing's concept of attribution with that of the attribution theorists summarized in the next section.)

Heider's Attribution Theory

Specifically, attribution theory deals with the ways people infer the causes of behavior. This theory is alternatively known as naive psychology. It explains the processes by which most people come to understand their own behavior and that of others. Scientific psychology attempts to ascertain the actual causes of behavior; naive psychology centers on the perceived causes of behavior in ongoing interaction.

Attribution theory has three basic assumptions.[72] First, people attempt to determine the causes of behavior. When in doubt, they look for information that will help them answer the question, Why is he doing that? Harold Kelley puts it this way: "In the course of my interaction with other people, I often wonder why they act as they do. I may wonder how to interpret a compliment a student makes of a lecture I recently gave, why my friend is so critical of a certain common acquaintance, or why my colleague has not done his share of work on our joint project. These are questions about the attribution of the other person's behavior—what causes it, what is responsible for it, to what is it to be attributed?"[73] The second assumption of attribution theory is that people assign causes systematically. Kelley likens this occurrence to the scientific method: "The lay attributor . . . generally acts like a good scientist, examining the covariation between a given effect and various possible causes."[74] The third assumption is that the attributed cause has impact on the perceiver's own feelings and behavior. The communicator's attributions determine in large part the meaning for the situation.

Thus, attribution theory, while it relates directly to interpersonal communication, is supportive of several previous topics in this book, including symbolic interaction, meaning, and information processing. It also supplements some of the previous theories of this chapter, notably those of Laing and Goffman.

Fritz Heider could easily be called the father of attribution theory. It was he who coined the term *naive psychology*. Heider's early work has been extended by a number of later theorists.

In Chapter 8 you saw that Heider's balance theory is a classic in social psychology. The notion of balance is further elucidated and placed in the larger context of naive psychology in *The Psychology of Interpersonal Relations*.[75] Heider summarizes the main points of his theory:

> According to naive psychology people have an awareness of their surroundings and the events in it (the *life space*), they attain this awareness through *perception* and other processes, they are *affected* by their personal and impersonal environment, they *cause* changes in the environment, they are able to (*can*) and *try* to cause these changes, they have wishes (*wants*) and *sentiments*, they stand in unit to other entities (belonging), and they are accountable according to certain standards (*ought*). All these characteristics determine what role the other person plays in our own life space and how we react to him.[76]

Thus in the major concepts of his theory, Heider presents the important attributes perceived in interpersonal communication. These are the commonly perceived causes of behavior: being affected by, causing, can, trying, wanting, sentiments, belonging, ought, and may.

As Laing, Heider distinguishes between direct and indirect perception. Indirect perception occurs when one infers from overt behavior the

72. The basic assumptions in attribution theory are outlined in Edward E. Jones et al., *Attribution: Perceiving the Causes of Behavior* (Morristown, N.J.: General Learning Press, 1972), p. xi.

73. Harold H. Kelley, "Attribution in Social Interaction," in *Attribution: Perceiving the Causes of Behavior* (Morristown, N.J.: General Learning Press, 1972), p. 1.

74. Ibid., p. 2.

75. Fritz Heider, *The Psychology of Interpersonal Relations* (New York: John Wiley & Sons, 1958).

76. Ibid., p. 17.

causes of that behavior. Such causal perception is mediated by psychological variables in the perceiver. There is not a one-to-one relationship between the observed behavior and the cause. A variety of behaviors may be perceived as stemming from a single cause, or, conversely, one behavior may be thought to arise from multiple possible causes. One of the tasks of the perceiver is to resolve such ambiguities inherent in the situation. For example, a supervisor in a company may notice that one employee is particularly industrious. The supervisor must decide whether the employee's drive can be attributed to personal dedication or to a desire to seek personal favors, since either of these elements could be the cause.

Of course, every behavior is *embedded* in a situation, and the naive psychologist makes the most of the context in resolving ambiguities. For one thing, we usually have the benefit of exposure over time, as Heider points out: "It is probably fair to say that the stimulus fields basic for person perception are usually *more extended in time* than those relevant to thing perception. . . . In most cases we cognize a person's traits, and especially his wishes, sentiments, or intentions from what he does and says, and we know considerably less when we are limited to what we can see of him as a static object."[77]

The most important factor in resolving ambiguity is meaning. The attributor's meanings for stimuli are crucial in interpersonal perception, especially because of the use of language and speech, although Heider makes it clear that we have meanings for nonlinguistic acts as well. Basically, meanings are integrators in perception, organizing percepts into patterns that help us make sense of the world. Heider would agree with Goffman that the person sees situations in terms of well-integrated frames. From a need for consistency, the perceiver aligns meanings in such a way that causal attribution makes logical sense. In short, the total attribution process becomes integrated and consistent.

The lack of one-to-one correspondence between behavior and motive makes multiple interpretations of a given event possible. Thus it is reasonable to expect idiosyncratic patterns of perception, which Heider calls *perceptual styles*. This notion introduces another variable in perception, namely, individual manners of perception. (Because we are not dealing here with scientific or objective analysis, it is not appropriate to speak of accurate or erroneous perception.) Heider recognizes that any state of affairs may give rise to a number of interpretations, each of which seems true to the perceiver.

Although Heider does not use the same terminology as does Laing, he recognizes the significance of metaperception in communication. In interpersonal perception one individual perceives the perceptions of another. Bob recognizes that Mary is an active perceiver and that her perceptions affect her. This recognition on Bob's part also affects him. He may attempt to influence Mary's perception in order to bring about results that are favorable to him. In addition his expectations of Mary are affected by his assessment of how she perceives the situation. Thus his own attributions of Mary are affected.

One of the most important attributions involves *purposive action*. When one perceives an action to be purposive, two underlying attributes are recognized: ability (*can*) and attempt (*try*). These causal agents are necessary and sufficient conditions to explain purposeful behavior. Trying means intention and exertion. Suppose, for example, that your friend fails to show up for a meeting. According to this theory, you will wonder why. Here are the possibilities as outlined by the naive analysis of action. Either your friend was not able to make it (couldn't), or she didn't try. If she wasn't able, something would have been wrong with her (for example, illness), or some environmental factor (for example, snowstorm) prevented her appearance. If she did not try, she either didn't want to (intention) or was too lazy (exertion). Now you can see what happens in interpersonal perception. In this instance you will infer the causes of your friend's behavior

77. Ibid., p. 39.

according to your overall experience, your meanings, the situational factors, as well as your own perceptual style.

This example of the naive analysis of action is included to illustrate Heider's conception of the perceptual process. In this case the realm of attribution is can and try. The same basic process is used in attributions dealing with desire and pleasure, sentiments, ought and value, benefit and harm, and others. Two of these attributional areas will be expanded further.

The area of sentiments is important because it relates to Heider's earlier work on balance (see Chapter 8). Basically, the sentiments we attribute to another person are consistent with our sentiments toward the other person and toward certain objects that we hold in common with the other. In interpersonal relationships we have a need to balance our various interrelated sentiments. In fact, Heider believes that people have a general tendency to balance the entire perceptual picture, a notion we will return to in a moment. First, let us look at the attributions of ought and value.

The *ought* attribution is particularly interesting because it departs from the normal patterns of attribution. The ought is seen by the person as a demand from some suprapersonal source. The perceiver views the ought as an impersonal, objective demand, a truism. Further, the ought has interpersonal validity in that most people would agree that the demand is present. As Heider puts it, "One might say that ought rises out of a tendency to equalize the life spaces of different persons as well as the different moments of the same life space."[78] Thus a person says, "You ought to go to the dentist," or "I ought to report the theft."

But oughts do not necessarily correspond with *values*. I may dread going to the dentist even though I think I ought to. However, people seek congruity among attributions; especially they feel a need for balance between oughts and values: "There exists a tendency to be in harmony with the requirements of the objective order. Thus the situation is balanced if one likes to do what one ought to do, if one likes and enjoys the entities one believes are valuable, if happiness and goodness go together, if *p* admires the person he likes and likes the person with whom he shares values, if what ought to be conforms with what really is, etc."[79]

78. Ibid., p. 222.

Kelley's Attribution Theory

One of the most prominent theories of the process of attribution is that of Harold Kelley.[80] Kelley developed two postulates about causal attribution, which apply to both self-perception and perception of others.

The first postulate is the *covariation principle:* "An effect is attributed to one of its possible causes with which, over time, it covaries."[81] This principle applies to situations in which the perceiver has information from more than one observation. The person sees which effects are associated (covary) with which causes. The second principle, which applies in the case of single observations, is the *discounting effect*: "The role of a given cause in producing a given effect is discounted if other plausible causes are also present."[82] In other words, the perceiver tends to weigh possible causes in relation to one another. These two postulates describe attribution as a rational process in which the individual carefully examines the various causal possibilities and generalizes on the basis of the best available data.

The covariation principle applies when the person has multiple observations from which to generalize. The perceiver goes through a naive version of *analysis of variance*. Analysis of variance is a statistical procedure often used in experimental research. It allows the researcher to weigh the various sources of variation in such a

79. Ibid., p. 233.

80. See the bibliography for Chapter 9 for a list of Kelley's works.

81. Harold Kelley, "The Processes of Causal Attribution," *American Psychologist* 28 (1973): 108.

82. Ibid., p. 113.

way as to determine the causes in operation. Analogically, the perceiver uses the same basic pattern, treating possible causes as independent variables and effects as dependent variables. Figure 9.1 illustrates a three-way contingency model used in causal influence.[83] The three dimensions in this model include the several persons observed, the various times in which observation took place, and some other objects (entities) that enter the situation.

Suppose you learn that your friend likes a particular record. Why? A number of reasons are possible. Perhaps your friend generally likes recorded music and enjoys many records. This attribution is to the person, as illustrated in Figure 9.2(a). If this record is especially good and is enjoyed by most people, the attribution is to the entity, as in Figure 9.2(b). A third possibility is that something about the time is causing your friend's enjoyment of the music. Perhaps this is final exam week, and you have observed that most of your friends like music at this time of the semester since music tends to soothe anxieties. The attribution to time is illustrated in Figure 9.2(c). All of these attributions are *main effects*. In other words one of the three primary dimensions is inferred to be the cause.

83. Ibid., p. 110.

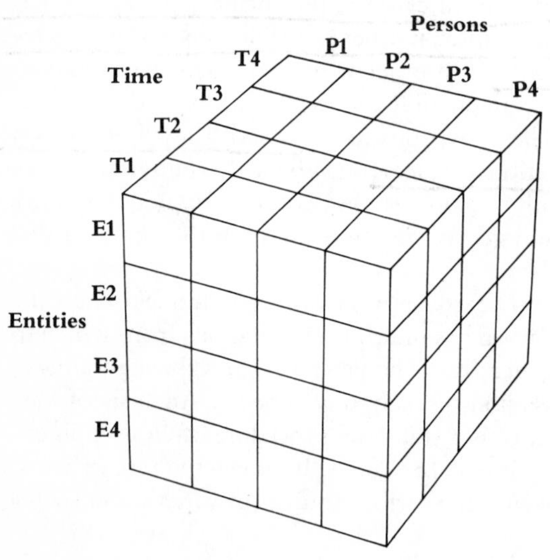

From *American Psychologist*, "The Process of Causal Attribution," by Harold Kelley. Copyright © 1973 by the American Psychological Association. Reprinted by permission of the publisher and the author.

Figure 9.1. Analysis of variance model of attribution.

Sometimes attribution is not so simple. In the parlance of analysis of variance, you may infer *interaction effects*. You might infer that the primary causal agents combine in certain ways to achieve effects. For example, you might have observed that your friend likes only one record, but that no one else likes that record. Thus you have attributed interaction between entity (record) and person (your friend), as illustrated in Figure 9.2(d). You are reasoning that peculiar aspects of the record interact with particular qualities in your friend to produce liking. A more complex three-way interaction, illustrated in Figure 9.2(e), is what you might call attribution to circumstances. In this attribution you believe that your friend is enjoying this particular record *at this time*. Your friend didn't enjoy it at any other time, and no one else enjoys it at this or another time.

In all of these cases the perceiver observes the covariation (association) of particular causes and effects in different situations over time. By putting these various observations together, the observer sees patterns emerge, and the causal inferences outlined above occur. Much of the time, however, we do not make multiple observations. We do not have the advantage of a complete data block such as that shown in Figure 9.1. Ergo, we use the discounting principle.

The discounting effect applies when the perceiver must rely on a single observation. The various possible causes of an observed effect are weighed against one another, and an inferred causal structure emerges. The process itself is no different from the analysis of variance paradigm above. What is different is the way the data block is filled in. In the discounting model most of the data (that is, causal patterns) is assumed, not observed. One makes assumptions about cause-effect relationships on the

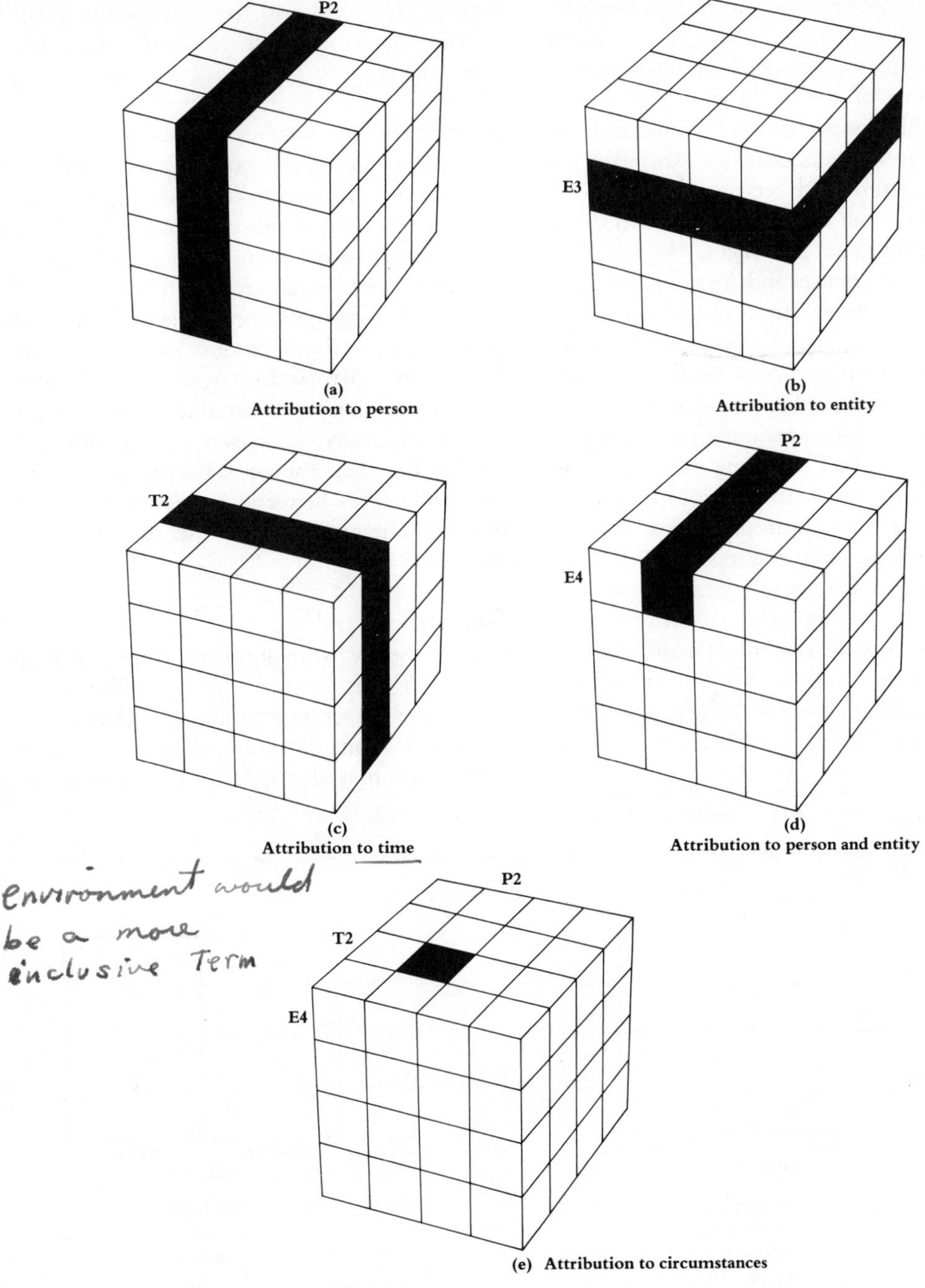

Figure 9.2. Various attribution possibilities.

basis of past experience and learnings. As Kelley puts it: "The mature individual . . . has a repertoire of abstract ideas about the operation and interaction of causal factors. These conceptions [enable one to make an] economical and fast attributional analysis, by providing a framework within which bits and pieces of relevant informtion can be fitted in order to draw reasonably good causal inferences."[84]

By using experience and learning, the attributor brings various causal assumptions into play. The result is *a causal schema* in which assumed causes are placed in a contingent relation. A particularly good example of this occurs when you have both an assumed internal cause (in the person) and a competing external cause (in the situation). For example, your friend has just received an A on a term paper. You assume that this outcome occurred because of your friend's ability or because the assignment was easy. A couple of causal schemata are possible here. If you follow the schema of *multiple necessary causes*, you will reason that your friend got the A because he is able and the task was easy. This schema is illustrated in Figure 9.3(a). Or perhaps you will use the schema of *multiple sufficient causes*, in which you reason that either your friend is able or the task was easy or both. Figure 9.3(b) illustrates this possibility. Other more complex schemata have been studied by Kelley, but these simple ones provide sufficient illustration of the process for our purposes here. Kelley summarizes the importance of the attribution process: "There is much evidence . . . that attributions do matter. Man's concern with the reasons for events does not leave him 'lost in thought' about those reasons. Rather, his causal explanations play an important role in providing his impetus to action and in his decisions among alternative courses of action. When the attributions are appropriate, the person undoubtedly fares better in his decisions and actions than he would in the absence of the causal analysis."[85]

Criticism

Laing's theory is an intuitively appealing approach. It sensitizes one to the difference between the direct perception of behavior and inferences about the perceptions of others. Its weakness is that of scope. The theory is sugges-

84. Harold Kelley, *Causal Schemata and the Attribution Process* (Morristown, N.J.: General Learning Press, 1972), p. 2.

85. Kelley, "Processes," p. 127.

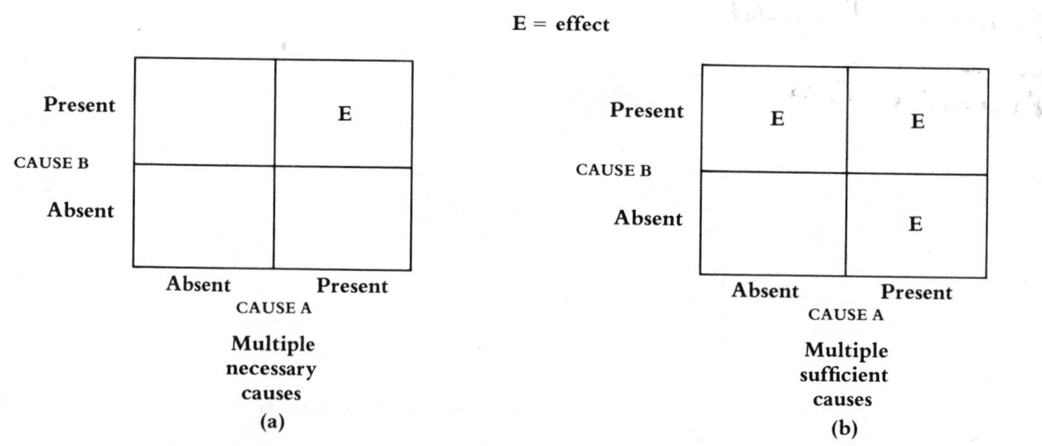

From *American Psychologist*, "The Process of Causal Attribution," by Harold Kelley. Copyright © 1973 by the American Psychological Association. Reprinted by permission of the publisher and the author.

Figure 9.3. Causal schemata.

tive of problems in interpersonal communication, but it gives little basis for understanding what choices people will make in various situations. Its failure to operationalize concepts limits its heuristic utility.

On the other hand, attribution theory provides an excellent set of operational concepts for describing and explaining a broad range of social perceptions. It has been immensely popular in social psychology because of its wide applicability in various social phenomena and its tremendous heuristic value.[86]

The major weakness of attribution theory for the field of communication is one of scope. Ironically, this work is largely interpersonal, yet it has dealt little with interaction. The field is ripe for scholars to theorize and conduct research on the relation of messages to attribution. In addition, the theory is almost exclusively based on the model of the rational person, yet we know that much of our perception is affected by emotional factors. Jones says these are "phenomena that I don't think attribution theory is well designed to handle."[87]

What Do We Know about Relational Communication?

Interpersonal communication functions in important ways in the life of the individual. Three such functions are linking the individual to the environment, facilitating thinking, and regulating behavior. Social functions are also fulfilled by interpersonal communication, most notably the establishment, maintenance, and modification of relationships.

86. Harvey, Ickes, and Kidd, *New Directions*, vol. 2, 376–77.

87. Ibid., p. 384.

Clearly the key concept that provides unity to the theory presented in this chapter is *relationship*. The theories recognize that communication is the essence of relationships. From relational theory we know that people use communication to define the nature of the relationship and that relationships are complementary or symmetrical, depending on the distribution of power between the participants.

Communicating in a relationship consists of self-presentation and interpersonal perception. One's presentation of self to others is governed in part by interpersonal needs for inclusion, control, and affection. People define the situations they encounter, and they adapt to those situations as defined. Much communication—direct and indirect, verbal and nonverbal—is designed to present various aspects of the self that the communicator believes to be appropriate to the situation.

Interpersonal perception is a process of knowing other people by making inferences about qualities of others and the causes of their behavior. Communicators not only make direct inferences about other people's behavior, but they also infer what other people are perceiving and thinking. Attribution, or the inference of the causes of behavior, is based on information about the person and the situation. Given a certain amount of experience with another individual, one will attribute certain causes to the other's behavior by integrating information about the individual's motives and about the situation in which the behavior occurs.

Relationships consist of a number of factors in addition to self-presentation and interpersonal perception. Some of these, which are taken up in the next chapter, include disclosure and understanding, attraction and relational maintenance, and conflict.

CHAPTER

10 Interpersonal Contexts II: Theories of Disclosure, Attraction, and Conflict

Interpersonal communication, the topic of chapters 9 and 10, is considered by most communication scholars to be highly central to the study of communication. Consequently, it generates much interest, and a substantial body of theory has been developed to explain it. The last chapter was devoted to theories that deal with relationship as a central concept. Those theories deal most directly with relationships, although the theories presented in this chapter also contribute to this topic. The division between these two chapters is somewhat arbitrary; consequently, they should be read together to provide a fuller understanding of interpersonal processes.

In this chapter we will look at a number of theories centering on three major topics: (1) understanding as a goal of communication and disclosure as a means of achieving that goal, (2) interpersonal attraction and other factors that lead to the development and maintenance of relationships, and (3) social conflict and the special role of communication in conflict situations. The theories here, as those in the previous chapter, deal most centrally with dyadic communication, but they also apply to group and organizational contexts.

Theories of Disclosure and Understanding

An important contribution to theory in interpersonal communication is that of humanistic psychology. Humanistic psychology arose in response to a perceived inadequacy in the two giant branches of psychology, the psychoanalytic and the behavioristic. As such humanistic psychology has come to be known as "the third force."[1] Today it retains its identity as one subdiscipline among several in psychology. The clinical orientation of most humanistic psychologists remains the primary focus of this group.

Humanistic theories stand in opposition to the deterministic epistemology of behaviorism. They always stress subjective response over objective discovery.[2] The key epistemological point of the humanistic school is that variable analysis and generalizations about human behavior are trivial compared with the richness of individual human experience.

Johari Window

We begin with Joseph Luft's model of human interaction because it provides a basic introduction to the ideas of disclosure and understanding.[3] This model, known as the *Johari Window*, is widely used in textbooks on interpersonal communication.[4] The model, illustrated in Figure 10.1, contains four quadrants that represent the person in relation to others. It is an awareness-understanding-disclosure model. Quadrant 1, the open quadrant, contains all the aspects (for example, feelings and behaviors) known to self and others. Quadrant 2, the blind quadrant, is known to others but not to self. The Hidden quadrant is known to self but not

1. Abraham H. Maslow, *The Farther Reaches of Human Nature* (New York: The Viking Press, 1971), p. 4.

2. For an excellent analysis of the epistemology of humanistic psychology, see Harold G. Coward and Joseph R. Royce, "Toward an Epistemological Basis for Humanistic Psychology," in *Humanistic Psychology: Concepts and Criticisms*, ed. Joseph Royce and Leendert P. Mos (New York: Plenum, 1981), pp. 109–34.

3. Joseph Luft, *Of Human Interaction* (Palo Alto: National Press Books, 1969).

4. *Johari* refers to the first names of the model's creators, Joseph Luft and Harry Ingham.

to others. A fourth, unknown quadrant is also presumed to exist, although it cannot be observed directly.

Luft's model is based on eight assumptions about human behavior. These assumptions are worth repeating here because they underlie most of the humanistic thinking, including all theories in this section. First, human behavior should be approached holistically. What is important in analyzing behavior is the whole person in context. Second, what is happening to a person or group is best understood subjectively in terms of the individual's perceptions and feelings. Because of this premise, the humanists are sometimes considered to be phenomenologists. Third, behavior is primarily emotional, not rational. This assumption explains the emphasis on feelings in the humanistic approach. Fourth, the person and the group tend to operate without awareness of the sources of their behavior. Thus the humanists stress the need for increased awareness of how one affects and is affected by others. Fifth, qualitative factors such as acceptance, conflict, and trust are highly important, even though they are difficult to quantify. Sixth, the most important aspects of behavior are found in process and change rather than structure. As a result of this assumption, the humanists stress change and growth in their various teachings. Seventh, principles governing behavior should be discovered inductively by examining personal experience rather than by applying abstractions deductively. Again, we see a phenomenological orientation stressing personal experience over abstraction. Eighth, behavior should be understood in its complexity rather than in rigid simplicity. This final assumption brings us full circle back to the holistic nature of the person, as expressed in the first assumption.

	Known to self	**Not known to self**
Known to others	1 **Open**	2 **Blind**
Not known to others	3 **Hidden**	4 **Unknown**

From *Of Human Interaction*, by Joseph Luft. Copyright © 1969 by the National Press. Reprinted by permission of Mayfield Publishing Co., formerly National Press Books.

Figure 10.1. Johari Window.

The Johari Window calls attention to those aspects of the person that are known and those that are out of awareness. More importantly from a communication point of view, it stresses the changes in awareness that occur over time. Ideally, quadrant 1 should increase in size with communication. If communication is good, disclosure occurs, moving feelings and behavior from quadrant 3 to quadrant 1. Good communication also involves feedback, which causes feelings and behaviors to go from quadrant 2 to quadrant 1. The unknown area of quadrant 4 is difficult to discover, but it can become known in retrospect through reflection, the use of certain drugs, projective technique, and dreaming.

Luft summarizes the importance of understanding in the following excerpt. His words also justify the work of the entire humanistic school:

> Efforts over time to increase man's understanding of the world and of life have apparently not significantly reduced his doubts about meaningfulness in the universe. Perhaps it is true that unless he derives from human interaction the special quality of feeling understood, he will suffer the despair of meaninglessness no matter what he achieves and how well he understands everything else. Feeling understood appears then to be a necessary though perhaps not a sufficient condition for man to come to terms with the world and with himself. Hypothetically,

every man can offer the gift of really feeling understood to someone, provided he can relate with him in a way that makes it possible to co-experience what is going on within.

Being understanding, when one is able to do so, is rewarding in its own right even though it is not the same as feeling understood. But when it is mutual, when you and I understand as well as feel understood simultaneously, then for that moment the world is home and bread is baking in the oven.[5]

Rogers's Theory of Congruence

The Johari Window provides an excellent introduction to the theories that focus on disclosure and understanding. With this introduction we move to the full-blown theory of interpersonal relations by Carl Rogers.[6] Rogers is known as the father of client-centered therapy and of the encounter group. He is a giant in the field of psychology and one of the leaders of the "third force" of humanism. The self-theory of Carl Rogers is the most comprehensive theoretical statement relating the humanistic approach to interpersonal communication.

Rogers begins his theory from a phenomenological position. The *organism* is the locus of all experience. The *phenomenal field* is the totality of one's experience, and it resides in the person (organism). It is completely private and can only be inferred by others. Rogers believes with Laing (Chapter 9) that one can never experience another's experience. Thus the person's behavior results most directly from the internal experience—reality as perceived and felt by the individual. At any moment one's phenomenal field consists of those aspects that are conscious by virtue of symbolization and those that are unconscious. Rogers points out, however, that a particular experience need not be conscious at the moment to affect behavior. Consistent with the system approach, Rogers describes the organism as a system in which change in one part affects the whole.

As the child matures, a portion of the phenomenal field becomes identified as the *self*. This concept is central to Rogers's theory. The self is "the organized, consistent conceptual gestalt composed of perceptions of the characteristics of the 'I' or 'me' and the perceptions of the relationships of the 'I' or 'me' to others and to various aspects of life, together with the values attached to these perceptions."[7] Rogers depicts an actual self and an ideal self.

Rogers's key concept is *congruence*, a correspondence or consistency between the conscious self and the phenomenal field. This congruence thus is a kind of internal consistency in the organism at a given moment. Incongruence occurs when the person does not fully behave or feel consistently with the totality of experience. Incongruence is much like Laing's notion of the false and untenable position. Incongruence leads to maladjustment; congruence reflects maturity and adjustment.

All of us have a tendency to actualize the self. In other words we seek experiences that will enhance the self, leading to autonomy and growth. This growth process is frustrated by the confusion stemming from incongruence. When our choices are not adequately symbolized (unclear), we cannot distinguish growthful from regressive behavior. Both the cause and cure of this consequence lie in interpersonal communication.

In communicating with others, we project positive and negative evaluations of the other's self. Negative attributions and injunctions tend to create an incongruity between the person's self and the phenomenal field. For example, if a child is told that overeating is wrong or is punished for overeating, the child may develop an untrue self-feeling. "Overeating is wrong" is incongruent with the experience of wanting to eat more. Two voices tug at the child. One

5. Luft, *Human Interaction*, p. 145.

6. The theory is best summarized in Carl Rogers, *Client-centered Therapy* (Boston: Houghton Mifflin, 1951), chap. 11; and "A Theory of Therapy, Personality, and Interpersonal Relationships, as Developed in the Client-centered Framework," in *Psychology: A Study of Science*, ed. S. Koch (New York: McGraw-Hill, 1959), vol. 3, 184–256. An excellent secondary source is Gardner Lindzey and Calvin S. Hall, *Theories of Personality* (New York: John Wiley & Sons, 1970), chap. 13.

7. Rogers, "A Theory," p. 200.

says, "You love to eat." The other says, "Don't eat." Confusion results, which frustrates the actualizing tendency.

What is needed in interpersonal relations, therefore, is what Rogers calls *unconditional positive regard*. Such an interpersonal attitude removes the threat to congruency, thus promoting the actualizing tendency. Two formal settings in which change of this sort can occur are client-centered therapy and the encounter group. Rogers would like to see all interpersonal relations become more supportive.

Now let us look more closely at this process of growth via communication. First, Rogers postulates that the threat-free environment promoted by positive regard allows the person to examine internal inconsistencies and restructure the self-concept without fear of judgment. At the same time the person increases the ability to be accepting of others. Here lies the connection between self-regard and regard for others. People who tend to be defensive (incongruent) lack self-regard as well as regard for others. As one becomes more self-accepting (congruent), one more readily accepts the behaviors of others. A threat-free environment marked by acceptance allows the person to continually examine the self and to change throughout life.

Congruence is contagious through communication. If one person in a relationship behaves openly and congruently, with positive regard and acceptance for the other, the other person will follow suit. Thus we have the main postulate in Rogers's theory:

> Assuming (a) a minimal willingness on the part of two people to be in contact; (b) an ability and minimal willingness on the part of each to receive communication from the other; and (c) assuming the contact to continue over a period of time; then the following relationship is hypothesized to hold true.
>
> The greater the congruence of experience, awareness and communication on the part of one individual, the more the ensuing relationship will involve a tendency toward reciprocal communication with a quality of increasing congruence; a tendency toward more mutually accurate understanding of the communications; improved psychological adjustments and functioning in both parties; mutual satisfaction in the relationship.[8]

When one person enters a relationship with the intent of facilitating growth on the part of the other, a *helping relationship* results. In his classic article "The Characteristics of a Helping Relationship," Rogers outlines ten qualities of a good helping relationship.[9] These are also the ideal qualities of interpersonal communication generally.

1. The communicators are perceived by one another as trustworthy, or consistently dependable.
2. They express their separate selves unambiguously.
3. They possess positive attitudes of warmth and caring for the other.
4. Each partner keeps his or her own separate identity.
5. Each partner permits the other to have a separate identity.
6. The helping relationship is marked by empathy. (Each communicator attempts to understand the feelings of the other.)
7. The helper accepts the various facets of the other's experience as communicated by the other.
8. The partners respond with sufficient sensitivity to allay threat.
9. They are able to free themselves from the threat of evaluation by the other.
10. Each person, recognizing that the other is changing, is flexible enough to permit change.

Self-Disclosure

Foundations: Sidney Jourard. The picture we have just discussed of the ideal relationship is one of disclosure and understanding in a threat-free environment. A theorist who has investigated this process of self-disclosure is

8. Carl Rogers, *On Becoming a Person* (Boston: Houghton Mifflin, 1961), p. 344.

9. Ibid.

Sidney Jourard.[10] Jourard is at once social philosopher, clinical psychologist, and empirical researcher. He has written at length about the human condition. As a clinician he has related the healthy state of the person to a willingness to explore the world openly, and as a researcher he has conducted numerous investigations of disclosing behavior. Jourard's prescription for the human being is openness or *transparency*.

Transparency is a two-sided coin, involving in part the individual's willingness to let the world of things and other people disclose themselves. Jourard sees the world in its many forms as constantly disclosing itself, but the person as receiver may or may not be open to perceiving this multiple world view. Being transparent means, on one side, allowing the world to disclose itself freely. The other side of the coin is the person's willingness to disclose oneself to others. Thus the ideal interpersonal relationship is such that people allow others to experience them fully and are open to experiencing others fully.

Jourard conceived this philosophical position after observing that his patients tended to be closed to the world. He found that they became healthy as a result of their willingness to disclose themselves to the therapist. Thus Jourard equates sickness with closedness and health with transparency.

Jourard sees growth, a person's moving toward new ways of behaving, as a direct result of openness to the world. The sick person is not willing to experience the world in various ways and is therefore fixed or stagnant. The growing person, being transparent, will come to new life positions. Such change is the essense of personal growth. "The awareness that things are different is not growth, though it is a necessary condition of growth. A growth cycle calls for (a) an acknowledgement that the world has changed, (b) a shattering of the present experienced 'world structure,' and (c) a restructuring, retotalization, of the world-structure which encompasses the new disclosure of changed reality."[11]

Growth in this fashion relates closely to interpersonal communication, since the disclosing world is largely social. Ideally, growing communicators self-disclose to one another their many changing faces. To accept one's own changes requires verification via acceptance on the part of others. It is difficult to grow if others around you are not open to your disclosures of change. "But if you suspend any preconceptions you may have of me and my being, and invite me simply to be and to disclose this being to you, you create an ambience, an area of 'low pressure' where I can let my being happen and be disclosed, to you and to me simultaneously—to me from the inside, and to you who receive the outside layer of my being."[12] This notion, of course, is strikingly like Rogers's view; it is an extension of the basic humanistic idea. In Jourard's work you may also detect the influence of Laing. Jourard, in fact, studied with Laing for a time.

Jourard summarizes transparency in the following passage:

> Transparency, thus, is a multifaceted mode of being—it calls for a courage and a willingness to let the world be what it is, to let the other be who he is, and to let oneself be who one is. It calls as well for a commitment to truth, as it changeably presents itself. It calls for a readiness to suspend concepts and beliefs about self, others, and world, and to perceive what is. It calls for a willingness to suspend imagination, wish, and fantasy, a readiness to inform and revise concepts with fresh inputs of perception. That it calls for courage to disclose oneself *to* the world is self-evident.[13]

Elaborations. Since Jourard's ideas on self-disclosure were published, he and several others

10. Sidney Jourard, *Disclosing Man to Himself* (New York: Van Nostrand, 1968); *Self-Disclosure: An Experimental Analysis of the Transparent Self* (New York: John Wiley & Sons, 1971); *The Transparent Self* (New York: Van Nostrand Reinhold, 1971).

11. Jourard, *Disclosing*, p. 154.

12. Ibid., p. 162.

13. Jourard, *Self-Disclosure*, p. 182.

have conducted research that elaborates the rudimentary notions.[14] Here are some of these research findings in general form: (1) Disclosure increases with increased relational intimacy. (2) Disclosure increases when rewarded. (3) Disclosure increases with the need to reduce uncertainty in a relationship. (4) Disclosure tends to be reciprocal (dyadic effect). (5) Women tend to be higher disclosers than men. (6) Women disclose more with individuals they like, whereas men disclose more with people they trust. (7) Disclosure is regulated by norms of appropriateness. (8) Attraction is related to positive disclosure but not to negative disclosure. (9) Positive disclosure is more likely in nonintimate or moderately intimate relationships. (10) Negative disclosure occurs with greater frequency in highly intimate settings than in less intimate ones. (11) Satisfaction and disclosure have a curvilinear relationship; that is, relational satisfaction is greatest at moderate levels of disclosure (see Figure 10.2).[15]

14. I have relied on the excellent analysis and summary of Shirley J. Gilbert, "Empirical and Theoretical Extensions of Self-Disclosure," in *Explorations in Interpersonal Communication*, ed. Gerald Miller (Beverly Hills, Calif.; Sage Publications, 1976), pp. 197–216. See also P. W. Cozby, "Self-Disclosure: A Literature Review," *Psychological Bulletin* 79 (1973): 73–91.

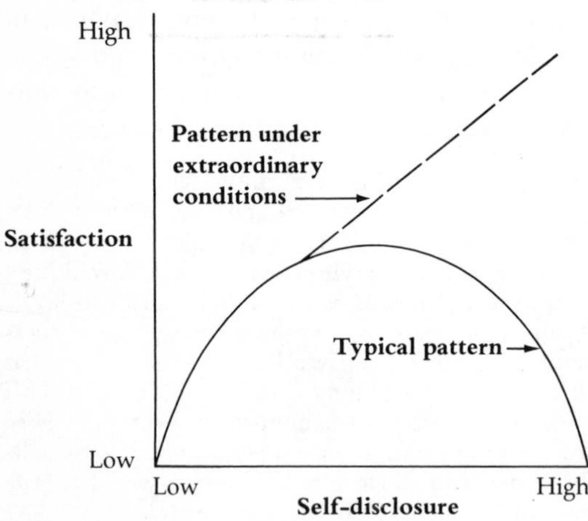

Adapted from Shirley J. Gilbert, "Empirical and Theoretical Extensions of Self-Disclosure," pp. 197–216 in Gerald R. Miller, ed., *Explorations in Interpersonal Communication*, © 1976 Sage Publications, Inc., with permission.

Figure 10.2. Linear and curvilinear patterns in self-disclosure.

This last finding, which seems to be supported by several studies, is interesting in that it paints a different picture than Jourard's ideal. The humanists call for a linear relationship between satisfaction and disclosure, such that the greater the disclosure the higher the satisfaction in the relationship. This difference between curvilinear and linear arises from the distinction between normative theory and descriptive theory. The former states what should be, the latter what is. Shirley Gilbert suggests three conditions necessary for Jourard's ideal to occur in a relationship. First, the participants must have healthy self-concepts. Second, they must be willing to take relational risks. Third, they must be committed to unconditional positive regard in the relationship. Gilbert describes intimacy in these terms:

> There are interpersonal price tags attached to intimate relationships. Intimacy, as a dimension of affection, may not be a unidimensional construct. It seems to be comprised of not only feelings (satisfaction) but also commitment (willingness to risk). Intimacy refers not only to the depth of exchange, both verbally and nonverbally, but also to the depth of acceptance or confirmation which characterizes a relationship. Thus, "intimate disclosure" and "intimate relationships" need to be clearly conceptualized and differentiated in future disclosure studies. While disclosure has been established as an index of communicative depth in human relationships, it does not guarantee an intimate relationship.[16]

Criticism

As you can imagine, these theories have been controversial. Generally speaking, they have been challenged on two fronts: theoretical appropriateness and validity. First, their prescriptive and holistic approach prevents productive investigation of actual communication process-

15. Adapted from Gilbert, "Empirical," p. 210.
16. Ibid., pp. 212–13.

es. These theories tell us in a general way how we ought to communicate with others, but they say little about the nature of ordinary communication. This criticism also indirectly questions the heuristic value of these theories. (The work on self-disclosure is an exception here.) One critic levels this objection in harsh terms: "Humanistic psychologists make statements intended as contributions to psychological knowledge, as well as discussing the nature of psychological knowledge and how it should be sought. But this is not all that they do. They organize various forms of psychotherapy. They also publish a great deal of exhortatory and inspirational literature which is designed to help its readers live more satisfactory lives. It thus amounts to attempted psychotherapy of a mass audience."[17]

The validity criticism has two forms. The first is that the humanistic movement is based on incorrect assumptions about the needs of scholarship on behavior. Calling humanistic psychology a "protest movement," Daniel Berlyne believes that these theories are misguided in their protesting of five elements of traditional psychology: the scientific method, empirical methodology, behaviorism, lack of holistic orientation, and inappropriate research questions.[18] He criticizes these protests as overstatements, if not as totally wrong.

The second validity challenge is more serious. Critics state that the prescriptions for improved communication are wrong. One of the strongest statements of this point of view is that of Roderick Hart and Don Burks.[19] Calling humanistic theories "the school of 'expression, joy, and metaphor,'" Hart and Burks criticize them for preaching dysfunctional practices; namely, insensitivity to roles, stylized language, lack of rhetorical adaptation, insensitivity to information propriety, and inability to express ideas in multiple ways. Humanists predictably respond by accusing such critics of failing to understand the humanistic approach and oversimplifying it.[20] (This criticism led to the formulation of a competing theory, which we will summarize in the following section.)

Rhetorical Sensitivity as an Alternative View

In criticizing humanistic approaches to understanding, Roderick Hart and his colleagues have created an alternative conceptualization.[21] For these theorists effective communication does not arise from congruence and disclosure but from *rhetorical sensitivity*. Relying on the categories of Donald Darnell and Wayne Brockriede, Hart contrasts three general types of communicators.[22] *Noble selves* conform to Carl Rogers's image. These people stick to their personal ideals without variation and without adapting or adjusting to others. *Rhetorical reflectors* are individuals who, at the opposite extreme, are molding themselves to others' wishes, with no personal scruples to follow.

Rhetorically sensitive individuals, as a third type, moderate these extremes. Rhetorical sensitivity embodies concern for self, concern for others, and a situational attitude. The theorists outline five attributes of rhetorical sensitivity. First, rhetorically sensitive people accept personal complexity; that is, they understand that each individual is a composite of many selves. Second, such individuals avoid rigidity in communicating with others. Third, the rhetorically sensitive person attempts to balance

17. Daniel E. Berlyne, "Humanistic Psychology as a Protest Movement," in *Humanistic Psychology: Concepts and Criticisms*, ed. Joseph Royce and Leendert P. Mos (New York: Plenum, 1981), p. 261.

18. Ibid.

19. Roderick P. Hart and Don M. Burks, "Rhetorical Sensitivity and Social Interaction," *Speech Monographs* 39 (1972): 75–91. See also Abraham Wandersman, Paul Poppen, and David Ricks, eds., *Humanism and Behaviorism: Dialogue and Growth* (Elmsford, N.Y. Pergamon Press, 1976).

20. Alan L. Sillars, "Expression and Control in Human Interaction: Perspectives on Humanistic Psychology," *Western Speech* 38 (1974): 269–77.

21. Roderick P. Hart, Robert E. Carlson, and William F. Eadie, "Attitudes toward Communication and the Assessment of Rhetorical Sensitivity," *Communication Monographs* 47 (1980): 1–22.

22. Donald Darnell and Wayne Brockriede, *Persons Communicating* (Englewood Cliffs, N.J.: Prentice-Hall, 1976).

self-interests with the interests of others, a sensitivity called *interaction consciousness*. Fourth, rhetorically sensitive people are aware of the appropriateness of communicating or not communicating particular ideas in different situations. Fifth, such persons realize that an idea can be expressed in many ways, and they adapt their message to the audience in the particular situation.

In order to better understand the rhetorically sensitive person in contrast with the noble self and rhetorical reflector, Hart and his colleagues created a questionnaire called RHETSEN and administered it to over 3000 students at 49 universities and to other groups as well. They recognize that most people have varying degrees of all three types within themselves but that a given type predominates. They summarize their findings as follows:

> Our findings amount to at least this: (1) people vary greatly from one another in their attitudes toward encoding interpersonal messages; (2) some of these variances are partly a function of specific philosophical, economic, geographic, and cultural forces impinging upon people; (3) certain subcultural systems (families, ethnic groups, religious assemblages, etc.) reinforce and inhibit certain attitudes toward communication; (4) exceptionally "liberal" systems foster Noble Self predilections while especially "conservative" persons embrace Rhetorical Reflector attitudes; (5) rhetorical sensitivity seems to thrive in those middle-class environments which do not demand ideological zeal from members.[23]

The theory of rhetorical sensitivity is placed here because of its obvious and direct contrast with the theories of humanistic psychology. In addition Hart and Burks themselves apply their concept to interpersonal communication. However, their theory also applies to the domain of persuasion and, by extension, to all communication contexts, including mass communication.

Hart and his colleagues work in the discipline of speech communication. This fact is significant because it helps us to understand the orientation of this theory. As we saw in Chapter 8, speech communication is rooted in the rhetorical tradition. The term *rhetorical sensitivity* itself implies a particular view of communication as adaptive, which would not be expected in many other communication-related disciplines. This view leads to one of the strengths of this approach; namely, that it is framed entirely from within the communication process. Many theories from other fields, as we have seen, cast light on communication, but in actuality they deal with secondary concerns. Speech communication is one of the few disciplines that has communication as its central focus.

Criticism. As mentioned above, one of this theory's strengths is that it deals specifically with message sending, a central communication concern. Another strength is that it provides a set of sensible principles that can be used by the communicator to achieve more effective communication. The theory is also heuristic because of its involvement of the RHETSEN scale. A final advantage of the theory is its parsimony; it is elegant in the sense of presenting a small cluster of concepts from which much elaborative theorizing can follow in the future.

The theory's main weaknesses involve its epistemology. The theory has an interesting and not altogether consistent set of epistemological assumptions. It treats rhetorical sensitivity as a *trait*, implying that individuals may exercise little choice over whether they are noble selves, rhetorical reflectors, or rhetorically sensitive individuals. Also the theory includes a method for measuring—that is, objectively discovering—an individual's rhetorical tendencies.

This theory's aim of classifying individuals into one of three groups is overly simple. In what ways can the individual change in rhetorical orientation, and how much of a role does proactive choice play? Another problem with the trait approach to rhetorical sensitivity is that it does not allow us to understand whether, or under what conditions, a single individual may

23. Ibid., p. 19.

act as noble self, rhetorical reflector, or rhetorically sensitive person.

Interpersonal Attraction and Relational Maintenance

This section summarizes theories related to why people form relationships and why relationships are maintained or dissolved. Four approaches are discussed: Mehrabian's theory of immediacy, Newcomb's cognitive approach, Byrne's learning theory, and Thibaut and Kelley's social exchange theory.

Mehrabian's Concept of Immediacy

Albert Mehrabian has proposed an insightful analysis of communication behavior, which places attraction in a larger interactional context.[24] According to Mehrabian, communication behaviors can be classified by a three-dimensional framework. The factors include liking (immediacy), dominance (power), and responsiveness. These factors are considered to be universal across cultures. Actual verbal and nonverbal behaviors in any act of interpersonal communication can be understood in terms of these dimensions.

Most relationships have a dominance or status dimension, which explains certain behaviors by the participants. Such behaviors constitute the *power metaphor*. For example, power may be correlated with standing upright, using large gestures, or being relaxed. Lack of power or status may be observed in hunched shoulders, cramped gestures, or bodily tension. Like Mehrabian's other two dimensions, this metaphor is standard across cultures, even though specific cultural behaviors may vary.

The second communication factor is the *responsiveness metaphor*. Basically, this factor is correlated with emotional arousal and stimulation. As Mehrabian points out, responsiveness is primarily a matter of speed and loudness. "In reacting to another person, we shift the direction of our look, our facial expression changes, and we converse, which in turn involves how fast we speak, our vocal expressiveness . . . and our speech volume. So, responsiveness to another is simply indexed by the amount of change in facial and vocal expressions, the rate at which one speaks . . . and the volume of speech."[25]

The dimension most related to interpersonal attraction is the *immediacy metaphor*. Here is Mehrabian's immediacy principle: "A basic and transcultural element of human life is that people approach and get more involved with things they like, things that appeal to them and they avoid things that do not appeal to them, or that induce pain and fear."[26] In interpersonal communication, immediacy is reflected by many verbal and nonverbal behaviors. Liking is seen in a number of behaviors that increase the closeness and directness of the participants. Avoidance, on the other hand, can be seen in behaviors that decrease openness and directness between the communicators.

There are several obvious immediacy behaviors. The most common relate to interpersonal distance. We tend to stand closer to people we like. Leaning forward, as opposed to leaning back, is a sign of attraction. Touching behavior is definitely part of the immediacy dimension. In addition attraction elicits greater sensory stimulation between people, which explains why higher incidence of eye contact and face-to-face stances accompany liking and why various avoidance behaviors, such as angular axes of body position, accompany dislike. The media chosen for communication may also relate to immediacy. For example, a telephone conversation is less immediate than face-to-face talking, but communicating via letters is less immediate than conversing by telephone.

Less obvious, perhaps, are the verbal aspects of immediacy. More immediate statements tend to reflect closer distance in time and space. For

24. Albert Mehrabian, *Silent Messages* (Belmont, Calif.: Wadsworth, 1971.)

25. Ibid., p. 118.

26. Ibid., p. 113.

example, "Here's Kathy" is more immediate than "There's Kathy." Ambiguity is related to lower immediacy in that ambiguous statements tend to be overinclusive. Thus "It was a pleasant evening" is less immediate than "I really enjoyed your company." Another sign of immediacy is the apparent willingness of the speaker to take responsibility for what is said. Such speech has fewer qualifiers and conditional statements. For example, "I want to stay" is more immediate than "I suppose it might be all right if I stay a bit longer."

Mehrabian's ideas are helpful in two respects. First, they *describe* the behaviors of attraction; second, they place liking in the broader context of three-dimensional communication. What Mehrabian has not done is *explain* the phenomenon of attraction. For this purpose we look to other theories. There are two general approaches to explaining interpersonal attraction. The *cognitive approach* uses a system paradigm to explain the interrelationships among the elements of the person's cognitive system, one of which is orientations toward other people. The *reinforcement approach* explains attraction as a learned behavior based on stimulus-response relationships. These approaches are not necessarily inconsistent with one another. Both contribute to our understanding of the process, as Byrne points out: "With respect to theoretical differences, it may be noted that the established empirical relationships . . . are interpretable in either cognitive or reinforcement terms. In fact, the two theoretical approaches do not constitute alternative and mutually exclusive explanatory systems. Instead, we have two broadly different interpretational schemas which utilize different languages and which apparently lead to somewhat different types of empirical research."[27]

Newcomb's Cognitive Approach

You encountered the theory of Theodore Newcomb in Chapter 8. That chapter mentions his notion of straining toward symmetry as one of the consistency theories of change. Newcomb's work in its more elaborated form is a theory of interpersonal attraction. In this broader context we can see the important contribution of his ideas.[28] His view is a well-known cognitive approach to attraction.

Newcomb envisions a cognitive system in which various personal orientations interrelate. An *orientation* is a relationship between a person and some aspect of the environment. Orientation involves directedness, selectivity, and attention. If I am oriented toward something, I tend to be directed to it, attend to it in a selective way. One can be oriented to a number of personal, concrete, or abstract objects. A person has orientations toward other people, things, and concepts or ideas. An orientation has a number of qualities, including *sign* (positive or negative) and *intensity* (strong or weak). Orientations also possess what Newcomb calls *cognitive content*, or attributions made about the object of orientation. Newcomb offers the following example of cognitive content: "One parent's attraction toward a child may have strong cognitive components of pride and resemblance to himself, while for the other parent warmth of personal response may be a more important component."[29]

One's orientations interrelate to form a cognitive system. Specifically, three sorts of orientations interact. First, we have orientations of *attraction*. These are interpersonal orientations. Newcomb uses the term *attraction* generally here to imply both positive and negative orientations toward objects or concepts. Finally, there are one's *perceived orientations of others*. Here Newcomb recognizes the concept of metaperception that we have encountered so often in the theories of interpersonal communication.

Basically, two kinds of systems exist within Newcomb's framework. The *individual* system is the person's phenomenal system of orientation toward another person and a relevant ob-

27. Donn Byrne, *The Attraction Paradigm* (New York: Academic Press, 1971), p. 266.

28. Theodore Newcomb, *The Acquaintance Process* (New York: Holt, Rinehart and Winston, 1961).

29. Ibid., p. 6.

ject. Such a system is viewed through the eyes of the perceiver. The second type of system is *collective* and is viewed from outside the individuals involved. In both cases three elements are present: person A, person B, and object X. In the individual system, illustrated in Figure 10.3(a), four orientations interact. These include A's attraction toward B, B's attraction toward A, A's attitude toward X, B's perceived attitude toward X. The collective system, illustrated in Figure 10.3(b), includes not only A's orientations, but B's orientations as well. The broad bands in Figure 10.3(b) indicate the interrelationships between the pairs of orientations as explained next.

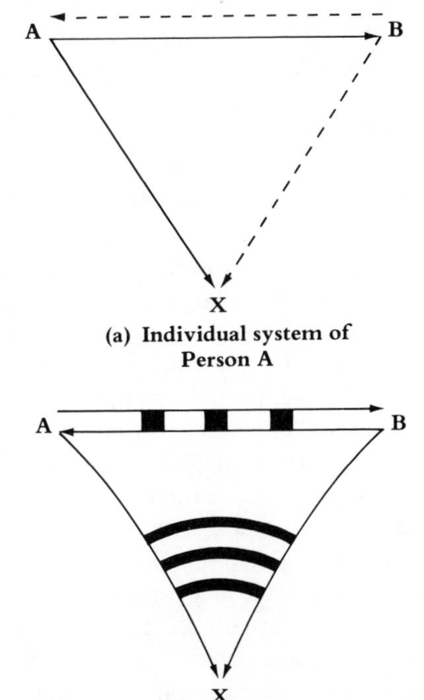

(a) Individual system of Person A

(b) Collective system of Persons A and B

From *The Acquaintance Process* by Theodore M. Newcomb. Copyright © 1961 by Holt, Rinehart and Winston, Inc. Reprinted by permission of Holt, Rinehart and Winston, CBS College Publishing.

★Arrows point from orienting person to person or object of orientation. Broken lines refer to orientations attributed by A to B; solid lines refer to own orientations of person from whom arrow stems. Broad bands refer to relationships between orientations connected by bands.

Figure 10.3. Schematic representation of systems.★

In the individual system certain conditions must be met. An individual system requires that the perceiver regard the object as relevant to the self as well as to the other person. The perceiver must attribute an attitude to B. In the individual system whether A has an accurate perception does not matter. It is only necessary for the perceiver to believe that coorientation exists. If both parties see the coorientation, then the collective model may be used. The collective model usually presumes *communication*, either verbal or nonverbal, between the persons in regard to X.

For example, suppose a man has recently met a woman in the library. He is attracted positively to her and admires her apparent interest in reading. In addition he believes she is positively attracted to him. Here we have an example of an individual system. This man has orientations toward the woman and toward reading. He also attributes orientations to his new acquaintance. If the woman shares the perception of attraction and coorientation to reading, a collective system exists.

You will recall from Chapter 3 that one of the qualities of systems is that they tend to be homeostatic (balanced). Changes that cause imbalance create pressures for other changes that will return the system to balance. In this way a system maintains itself. Such is the case with the cognitive systems described by Newcomb. He explains this phenomenon: "In propositional form, the stronger A's attraction toward B the greater the strength of the force upon A to maintain minimal discrepancy between his own and B's attitude, as he perceives the latter, toward the same X; and, if positive attraction remains constant, the greater the perceived discrepancy in attitude the stronger the force to reduce it. We shall refer to this force as strain."[30]

Thus strain toward symmetry is a function of the attraction of one person toward the other. Two other factors also relate. The *importance* of

30. Ibid., p. 12.

the object to the person is positively related to the amount of strain, as is the perceived *relevance* of the object to the relationship between the persons. To continue our example, if the man is highly attracted to the woman, if he values reading and sees it as important to his relationship with the woman, pressure is thus created for him to attribute interest in reading to the woman. If he finds out that the woman does not read—she was only visiting her friend the librarian—something will change in the system. The man may come to value reading less, changing his attitude toward X. He may distort his perception such that he continues to believe the woman likes to read. He may reduce the importance of his interest in reading. He may reduce the perceived relevance of reading to the relationship. Finally—and most important for the topic of this section—he may become less attracted to the woman. Attraction is thus explained in terms of the system dynamics involving the participants' various interrelated orientations.

This analysis suggests that new information has great impact on the system. New information, if congruent with one of a person's relevant and important orientations, will cause changes throughout the system. Newcomb calls such pressures *reality forces*. On the other hand are *balance forces* in the system that create pressure to minimize discrepancies. Thus the system is in a state of dynamic tension under which new information either will be distorted, or it will cause change.

Newcomb's primary contribution is that he places attraction in the context of the system of interrelated orientations. Attraction is, therefore, not an isolated attitude toward another person. It is part of a complex of elements that demand to be viewed as a whole. Further, Newcomb shows how the individual's orientational system is part of larger collective systems, in which interpersonal communication plays a major role.

Byrne's Reinforcement Approach

The reinforcement approach, notably that of Donn Byrne and his associate G. L. Clore, calls our attention to the ways in which attraction develops. Byrne maintains that attraction is a learned behavior. We looked briefly at learning theory in Chapter 6 when we discussed theories of meaning and in Chapter 8 when we viewed the ways persuasion can be explained by learning theory. You may recall from those discussions that reinforcers in the environment change the probability that certain behaviors will be evoked. If a behavior is rewarded, it increases in frequency; if punished, it decreases.

Byrne applies this basic law of learning to attraction. We tend to be attracted to a person when our experiences with that person involve more rewards than punishments. The opposite is true in the case of dislike. Here is what happens: A reinforcer in the environment (*unconditional stimulus*) brings about pleasant or unpleasant feelings in the person (*implicit affective response*). This internal response or feeling is an intervening variable leading to an evaluation of the stimulus as good or bad. Now, if another person is associated or paired with the original reinforcer, that person comes to elicit similar affective and evaluation responses. To illustrate this explanation, Byrne cites an experiment in which photographs of people were paired with statements that supported or opposed the subjects' attitudes. The negative or positive evaluations elicited by the statements "rubbed off" on the photographs, so that these pictures came to elicit similar evaluations.

In reality any given encounter with another person will take place in a context of numerous stimuli. The various stimuli associated with the encounter will have positive and negative reinforcing qualities. The ultimate attraction of one person to another will be determined more or less by a simple combination of stimuli, each weighed in terms of its strength.

Let us return to our example of the man and woman in the library. The man will be attracted to the woman if his association with her occurs in the presence of a number of rewarding stimuli. For example, the fact that they meet in the library, which is a rewarding stimulus for

31. Byrne, *Attraction Paradigm*.

him, will contribute to attraction. Perhaps they will go to a restaurant in which the atmosphere and food are rewarding. As these positive experiences mount, his attraction increases. On the other hand, if their acquaintance is marked with various negative experiences, dislike may occur.

The theories of Mehrabian, Newcomb, and Byrne deal with interpersonal attraction, and they provide a basis for understanding the stimuli that bring people together in relationships. Ongoing relationships, however, obviously are more complex than simple attraction. One of the most prominent explanations of relational maintenance is the economic approach, that emphasizes the costs and rewards of maintaining a relationship. The next section takes up perhaps the best known of these theories.

Thibaut and Kelley's Theory of Exchange

John Thibaut and Harold Kelley argue that interpersonal relationships, like other kinds of behavior, are evaluated by the person in terms of the value of the consequences.[32] The essence of relationship is interaction, which involves dyadic behavior: One's behaviors affect the other person.

If you could imagine all of the behaviors a person is apt to produce, you could define the individuals' *behavior repertoire.* When people come together in a relationship, they choose various of these behaviors as part of their interaction. The extent to which a behavior is valued depends on the relative costs and rewards, or *outcomes*. Rewards include the pleasure and gratifications associated with the behavior; costs include such inhibitory factors as physical or mental effort, anxiety, or perhaps embarrassment. Such consequences follow all individual actions, but the situation is made more complex when interaction, which necessarily involves more than one person, takes place.

In dyadic interaction the behaviors of the participants are paired. Each person's action yields a particular *goodness of outcome*, based on rewards and costs, and each participant must value the mutual activity above a particular level in order for the relationship to be sustained. The consequences of the actions involved in a relationship may be endogenous or exogenous. *Exogenous* consequences are those external to the relationship. Such consequences, stemming from the person's individual needs and values, would accrue from the action whether another person were involved or not. *Endogenous* factors, however, stem from the unique pairing of actions of both individuals in interaction. For example, in studying this book, you might anticipate the reward of a high score on the test. If this were an exogenous reward, it would result whether you studied by yourself or with another person. However, an added reward of studying with others might be a sense of gratification received if the other person gave you positive feedback (such as stating that he learned from you). Since such a reward depends on the established relationship, it is endogenous.

Endogenous costs may result as well. One's behavior may inhibit the performance of the other person. In the study group, for example, the failure of one member to read the material ahead of time could slow down the entire group. This analysis leads to the thesis of Thibaut and Kelley's work: "Whatever the nature of the early exchanges between A and B, they will voluntarily continue their association only if the experienced outcomes (or inferred but as yet unexperienced outcomes) are found to be adequate."[33]

But what determines adequacy? Here the theorists bring in two important concepts. The *comparison level* (CL) is the criterion or standard

32. J. W. Thibaut and H. H. Kelley, *The Social Psychology of Groups* (New York: John Wiley & Sons, 1959). For an extension and elaboration of their theory, see H. H. Kelley and J. W. Thibaut, *Interpersonal Relations: A Theory of Interdependence* (New York: John Wiley & Sons, 1978). For commentary on this theory, see John J. La Gaipa, "Interpersonal Attraction and Social Exchange," in *Theory and Practice in Interpersonal Attraction*, ed. Steve Duck (New York: Academic Press, 1971), pp. 129–64.

33. Thibaut and Kelley, *Social Psychology*, pp. 20–21.

of attractiveness used to judge the group. However, even if the person does not like a group (the costs are judged too high relative to rewards), association with the group still may be more desirable than any of the alternatives. Therefore the second concept to be considered is the *comparison level of alternatives* (CLalt), which is the lowest level of outcomes tolerated considering other alternatives. Thus CL is the level above which the person is satisfied with the relationship. CLalt is the level of outcome above which the individual will remain in the relationship. CL is a measure of attraction; CLalt is a measure of dependency.

Outcomes vary over time, of course, and one's judgment of a relationship also varies depending on the salient outcomes. As the CL goes up and down, the individual changes standards of judgment: "In other words, the person adapts to the presently experienced levels: after a shift upward to a new level, the once longed for outcomes gradually lose their attractiveness; after a downward shift to a new lower level, the disappointment gradually wears off and the once dreaded outcomes become accepted."[34]

As indicated above, endogenous rewards and costs result from the contingent relations between the behaviors of participants. A number of endogenous factors affect the outcome of the interaction. Some of those discussed by Thibaut and Kelley include power and dependence, norms and roles, tasks, and frustration and deprivation. Let us look at each of these briefly.

The authors indicate that power results from interpersonal dependency. One person has power over another to the extent that he or she can manipulate the outcome of the other's behavior. If the outcome of one's behavior is contingent on the other's behavior, a dependency is said to exist. In such a relationship the controller has *fate control* over the controlled. For example, in your study arrangements with another person you may discover that because you have more grasp of the material you have power over the other person. The outcome for the other person is dependent on your actions.

Norms and roles also affect the perceived outcome of a relationship. A *norm* is a rule of behavior adopted by the members (or most of the members) of a group. Norms are functional because they help to regulate group behavior without the costs of "unrestrained *ad hoc* use of interpersonal power."[35] By following norms, a person does not have to readjust and rethink each behavior anew, and the result is that overall costs are reduced in the interaction. A *role* is a cluster of norms applying to a particular person or task. Like norms, roles help organize a person's behavior, thus reducing costs, unless the person has multiple roles and must expend much energy reconciling the various norms involved.

The person also encounters various costs and rewards in dealing with the *tasks* at hand. Ideally one centers on an optimal manner of handling a task so that rewards can be maximized and costs minimized. However, when the individual repeatedly suffers an unsatisfactory outcome from working on a task, he or she is particularly susceptible to social influence. When more than one person works on such a task, additional costs are added to the relationship.

Sometimes people are forced to remain in an undesirable relationship, in which the outcome of the interaction is below CL (comparison level). Such a situation may lead to *frustration* and *deprivation*. Under these circumstances the person may lower the CL so as to better cope with the outcome. If the individual perceives a good chance of succeeding, he or she may attack the group powers that have prevented rewards or increased costs. Coalitions may develop; perhaps ultimately the nature of the group will change.

As groups grow in size, the complexity of relationships increases. Basically the same principles by which a dyadic relationship is judged (CL and CLalt) are used to judge group relationships. However, in groups of three or more the possibility always exists that subgroups will

34. Ibid., p. 98.

35. Ibid., p. 147.

develop. In making comparisons, the members of a group will consider the relative outcomes of subgroup possibilities. Whenever they perceive that mutual dependence will be more satisfying in the smaller subgroup, the cohesiveness of the larger group will suffer.

Also, as groups become larger, they bring increased possibilities for enhancing rewards. By cooperation and interaction, joint cost cutting may occur. Members can produce rewards for each other, and they can enhance social facilitation of enjoyment. A number of contingent situations may exist, each leading to a different power relationship. First, in a situation of *perfect correspondence of outcomes*, the joint efforts of all will lead to joint rewards. The problem for this kind of group situation is synchronization of efforts. Synchronization of members' behaviors can be difficult, and the larger the group the more difficult it becomes. Second, in a situation of *partial correspondence of outcomes*, the members may receive similar outcomes if they are willing to mesh their efforts. Otherwise, different outcomes may arise. Cooperation is necessary to maximize the outcome for all. The third situation involves *low correspondence of outcomes*. At the extreme only one person can achieve a favorable outcome; in the less extreme case some people may achieve an outcome at the expense of others. Queuing is typical in such groups, in which persons take turns receiving the favorable outcome. These three situations are illustrated by a rowing team, a problem-solving group, and a debate team, respectively.

The theory of Thibaut and Kelley recognizes that interactional patterns depend on the perceived rewards and costs. Groups are functional for people to the degree that they result in outcomes more favorable than group members would expect from other alternative relationships.

Criticism

The theories in this section are representative of the several theories of interpersonal attraction. They are chosen to give an idea of the different approaches that have been employed. The theories also illustrate the key weakness of most theories of interpersonal attraction, that of limited *scope*. Each theory we have discussed focuses on only one element of attraction, putting aside all others. Mehrabian's theory deals with signs of attraction without explaining the nature of liking or immediacy in relationships. Newcomb relies on the idea of cognitive balance. Byrne stresses learning and reinforcement, and Thibaut and Kelley see attraction and relational maintenance entirely from the framework of economics. Doesn't it seem likely that each of these factors enters into attraction and relational maintenance? This body of theory, perhaps more than any other in this book, illustrates the basic admonition about theory presented in Chapter 2, that theories are constructions and abstractions; each focuses on some aspect of the communication process to the neglect of other aspects.

Mehrabian's theory is valuable from the standpoint of relating attraction, and other variables, to communication behavior. Unlike any other, his theory shows us how people behave differently depending on the degree of immediacy, power, and responsiveness present in the communication situation. By providing a clear operationalization of communication behaviors, Mehrabian's theory is heuristic, producing beneficial research ideas.

Unfortunately, Mehrabian's theory is narrow in scope and fails to provide any explanation of communication patterns. One might infer that the use of nonimmediate behavior would reduce attraction, or vice versa, but this is a chicken-egg issue that remains unresolved. In addition we can question the validity of Mehrabian's claim that the three factors of interaction are universal and cross-cultural. This conclusion flies in the face of much research in anthropology that indicates that few behaviors are universal. If they are universals, one wonders how significant they are. For example, responsiveness as a universal state may reflect only certain psychological and anatomical universals that reveal little about internal meanings. That all people, regardless of culture, would express liking in the same ways is extremely suspect, as Hall has shown (see Chapter 5). As a final challenge to the validity of Mehrabian's claims, we cannot be sure about the claimed correlations between immediacy behaviors and actual attraction. Although Mehrabian's theory is parsimonious, it may be overly simple. Surely additional variables enter into attraction. One variable, for example, might be the developmental stage of a relationship. Intimacy and familiarity may lead to immediacy behaviors that are somewhat unconnected with actual liking. At the same time people involved in the early stages of a relationship may not communicate with the directness characterized by immediacy, despite extreme attraction for one another. In short Mehrabian's ideas are too simple to adequately explain the complexities of social life.

Consistency theories such as Newcomb's present an intriguing hypothesis, one we examined in some detail in Chapter 8. The assumption of balance or consistency is appealing because it provides a parsimonious explanation for why people change or remain stable. To inject the notion of coorientation and attraction into this paradigm makes intuitive sense. Another strength of Newcomb's theory is that it involves communication in the process of attraction in a central way. People become aware of their coorientations and make inferences about the other's attitudes through the exchange of messages. According to Newcomb, messages therefore have a direct effect on the cognitive system.

Newcomb's approach, however, has all of the weaknesses of the consistency theories outlined in Chapter 8. It takes away any power of choice on the part of the individual, employing deterministic explanation. It is also overly simple in its claim that the imbalance among cognitions will have great force in changing attraction and attitude.

Byrne's theory also relies completely on determinism. Little active choice is afforded the individual. Although reinforcers in the environment must have some effect on our feelings toward other people, suggesting a primary effect between learning and attraction is surely a simplification of reality. Of all the theories in this section, this one has least to do with communication, ignoring one of the most central elements of social life. There is serious doubt as to whether social behavior is conditioned in the same ways as is physical behavior. Remember the ideas of Albert Bandura, presented in Chapter 8, that suggest a more actional role of the individual creating one's own social reinforcers.

Thibaut and Kelley present an appealing theory of interpersonal attraction and relational maintenance. This theory is highly explanatory because it presents a rationale for understanding many elements of relational behavior. Using a few basic concepts, Thibaut and Kelley explain just about any aspect of social behavior. The criticism is that this theory relies on the assumption of the rational person. Such factors as reinforcement and balance do not seem to enter the system. The theory suggests that people weigh costs and rewards in a deliberate and rational way to decide whether to sustain or dissolve a relationship. This theory relies on game theory as a base. (We will discuss game theory in more detail in the next section.) In brief it suggests that people make moves in a relationship, based on expected rewards and costs, just as they would in a game or war. Another criticism of this theory is that it is based on research that is artificial. This research, typically done in a laboratory, examines the choices people make in response to different reward and cost contingencies, using points or tokens as game outcomes. We are not at all sure whether social rewards work in this way.[36] Finally, the theory, though highly relevant to communication, says little about it. Thibaut and Kelley's ideas could easily be related to interaction, messages, and information, and the time is right for someone to do so.

36. La Gaipa, "Interpersonal Attraction."

Social Conflict

The final section of this chapter covers theories of social conflict. Like most topics in the chapter, conflict is rooted in interpersonal interaction, but it is also seen in other contexts. Most of the material presented here relates directly to the interpersonal context. Keep in mind, though, that it can also be applied to the higher levels of group and mass communication as well.

Over the years many approaches to the study of conflict have emerged, and as in most theoretical areas, this work is not altogether consistent.[37] As a result defining conflict is difficult. Charles Watkins offers an analysis of the essential conditions of conflict, which form an operational definition:[38]

1. Conflict requires at least two parties capable of invoking sanctions on each other.
2. Conflicts arise due to the existence of a mutually desired but mutually unobtainable objective.
3. Each party in a conflict has four possible types of action alternatives:
   a. to obtain the mutually desired objective,
   b. to end the conflict,
   c. to invoke sanctions against the opponent,
   d. to communicate something to the opponent.
4. Parties in conflict may have different value or perceptual systems.
5. Each party has resources which may be increased or diminished by implementation of action alternatives.
6. Conflict terminates only when each party is satisfied that it has "won" or "lost" or believes that the probable costs of continuing the conflict outweigh the probable costs of ending the conflict.

One of the advantages of Watkins's definition is that it includes the possibility for communication. Ironically, many approaches to conflict have neglected the communication aspect. In part to deal with this anomaly, the Speech Communication Association commissioned a conference on communication and conflict. The theoretical approaches included in this section are guided by the work of that conference.[39] Three major approaches to communication and conflict are chosen for discussion. First, we talk about a game theoretic view. Then we move to a transactional model and finally to a theory based on persuasion in conflict. These three approaches provide a fair representation of the ways communication in conflict can be conceptualized.

Game Theory

Game theory was developed many years ago by Von Neumann and Morgenstern as a tool to study economic behavior.[40] Since its inception game theory has provided a base for popular research tools in several disciplines. For researchers studying the processes of decision making or choice making and goal competition or cooperation, game theory provides a possible paradigm. As a result it has been used extensively to study conflict.

Game theory includes several kinds of games. Two-person games, which are particularly useful in conflict research, consist of structured situations where two players take turns making choices that lead to payoffs. In all games the rational decision-making process is stressed. A key question is how players behave

37. A number of reviews are available. An excellent analysis of the diverse assumptions of conflict theories can be found in Leonard Hawes and David Smith, "A Critique of Assumptions Underlying the Study of Communication in Conflict," *Quarterly Journal of Speech* 59 (1973): 423–35. See also Thomas Steinfatt, "Communication and Conflict: A Review of New Material," *Human Communication Research* 1 (1974): 81–89; and David Johnson, "Communication and the Inducement of Cooperative Behavior in Conflicts: A Critical Review," *Speech Monographs* 41 (1974): 64–78.

38. Charles Watkins, "An Analytic Model of Conflict," *Speech Monographs* 41 (1974): 1–5.

39. Gerald Miller and Herbert Simons, eds., *Perspectives on Communication in Conflict* (Englewood Cliffs, N.J.: Prentice-Hall, 1974).

40. J. Von Neumann and O. Morgenstern, *The Theory of Games and Economic Behavior* (Princeton, N.J.: Princeton Unviersity Press, 1944). Numerous secondary sources are also available. See, for example, Morton Davis, *Game Theory: A Non-technical Introduction* (New York: Basic Books, 1970).

in order to gain rewards or goals. Types of games vary in several ways, including the amount of information provided to players, the amount of communication permitted between players, and the extent of cooperation versus competitive incentive built into the payoff matrix. Thomas Steinfatt and Gerald Miller show how game theory is useful in studying conflicts: "Game theory is concerned with how to win a game, with strategies of move sequences that maximize the player's chance to gain and minimize his chance for loss. Because a major ingredient in conflict situations is the desire to gain something one does not possess and to hold onto that which one does possess, certain games are analogous to particular conflict situations and game theory serves as a model to predict the behavior of persons in such conflict situations attempting to gain those ends."[41] Since game theory stresses rational decision making, it involves games of strategy. In such games a player makes moves (choices) that lead to rewards or punishments based on the moves of others. The object is to maximize gains and minimize losses.

One of the most commonly used games is the Prisoner's Dilemma.[42] This simple game is extremely useful because it illustrates a number of salient features of games in general. Also, it is interesting as a *mixed-motive game* since players may choose between cooperating or competing, and genuine reasons are present for choosing either. Here is the situation: Two people are arrested for a crime. After being separated, each must choose whether to confess. If one confesses and the other does not, the confessor will be allowed to go free, and this person's testimony will send the other to prison for twenty years. If both confess, both will be sent to prison for five years. If neither confesses, both will go to prison for one year on a lesser charge. Figure 10.4 illustrates the choices. With no communication between players, they will not know the choice of the other. Each is in a dilemma on whether to trust and cooperate by remaining silent or to compete by confessing. If both are willing to cooperate by not confessing, the long-term payoff is maximized for both. But if one does not behave cooperatively, the other cannot cooperate. Over several trials most players will move ultimately toward the noncooperative strategy.

Steinfatt and Miller reviewed the literature in which games were used to investigate the process of communication in conflict. Their generalizations are a step toward a game theoretic analysis. Using games as an analogue, Steinfatt and Miller list three ways in which parties in conflict come to assess each other's strategies. The first way is to observe the opponent's moves over several trials. In games such as the Prisoner's Dilemma, subjects play through a number of trials of the game. Typically a player will observe the opponent's moves and will thereby judge one's own subsequent moves. The second way of assessing strategy is to observe the total conflict situation. In so doing a player makes inferences from the

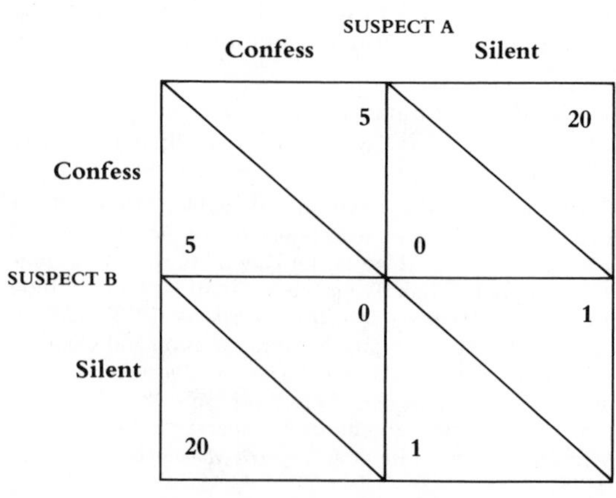

Figure 10.4. Prisoner's dilemma.

41. Thomas Steinfatt and Gerald Miller, "Communication in Game Theoretic Models of Conflict," in *Perspectives on Communication in Conflict*, ed. Gerald Miller and Herbert Simons (Englewood Cliffs, N.J.: Prentice-Hall, 1974), pp. 14–75.

42. This game is explained in Davis, *Game Theory*, pp. 93–107. This book is an excellent source of real-world analogues for many types of games.

situation to the opponent's strategy. In a game the player would study the matrix and try to figure out what the opponent's strategy is likely to be.

The third approach is direct communication. The authors point out: "Ideally, communication makes it possible to conduct the entire conflict at the symbolic level, with each player stating how he would respond to the stated, rather than the actual, moves of the other. . . . Besides avoiding the hostility, disruption, and subsequent losses resulting from actual moves, negotiations allow the parties to move away from a winner-take-all position toward a solution that provides some rewards for everyone."[43] If the players in the Prisoner's Dilemma game could communicate and agree to cooperate, both would receive lesser sentences.

Steinfatt and Miller developed a three-point model of communication in conflict, as reflected in the following definition: "We employ the word 'communication' to indicate the use of mutually understood symbolic behavior such that the probability of engaging in a particular behavior (making a given move) is altered via the exchange of symbolic move sequences which carry no *necessary* consequences for the situation (the formal game matrix)."[44] The first point in this definition is that the communication is *symbolic* in the sense that the stated intention does not carry the actual consequence of the real move. Although real moves might "communicate" in the broader sense, it is necessary to limit the definition here to distinguish between a real move with payoff consequences and symbolic moves. Second, communication changes the probability of moves. If a player receives and understands a message from the other, this will change the likelihood that "rational" competitive moves will take place. If a change in probability does not occur, the message is said to constitute an *attempt to communicate*. The third aspect of the model is that communication may result in nonsituational consequences. We have already seen that symbolic exchanges do not affect the payoff matrix per se. What is affected by communication is the behavior of the person in the situation.

43. Steinfatt and Miller, "Communication in Game Models," pp. 32–33.

44. Ibid., p. 37. This definition is based on the work of T. C. Schelling, *The Strategy of Conflict* (Cambridge: Harvard University Press, 1960). Schelling was one of the first to deal with communication in the game theoretic perspective.

Thus people in conflict are in a situation that has the potential of providing mutually exclusive payoffs. By communicating the parties may reduce their own tendencies to behave chauvinistically. In fact studies have shown that this is what tends to happen. Pregame discussions increase cooperation. The greatest effect occurs when communication exists from the beginning of the conflict. Studies also show that the fuller the communication, the more open the channels, and the greater the resultant cooperation.

Now that we have examined the basic game theoretic concepts of communication and conflict, we turn to two theories that attempt to explain the process of communication in real conflict situations. The first is David Mortensen's *transactional paradigm*.[45]

Transactional Approach

Unlike the reductionistic, behavioristic approach of game theory, the transactional paradigm explains situations and processes as they emerge in the holistic *experience* of the person. We have encountered this philosophical division in several communication areas discussed earlier in this book. Do we conceive of the person as primarily responding to the world as presented or defining and acting on the world? This division is now apparent in the conflict literature as well.

Game theory presents conflict-inducing situations to subjects in order to observe their responses. In ongoing life, according to Morten-

45. C. David Mortensen, "A Transactional Paradigm of Verbalized Social Conflict," in *Perspectives on Communication in Conflict*, ed. Miller and Simons (Englewood Cliffs, N.J. Prentice-Hall, 1974), pp. 90–124.

sen, conflicts are not presented to people but emerge out of situations *as defined by participants*: Conflicts are not objective situations; conflicts exist when the participants believe they exist.

A number of assumptions lie behind this approach. First, the participants in a conflict actively define the communication as conflict. Second, the conflict emerges naturally from the communication between the participants. Third, the communicators are relatively free to define their own rules.

What, then, are the dimensions that give rise to the definition of conflict? Mortensen names five. The first is individual disposition. People vary in the degree to which they expect conflict. At one extreme are people who typically anticipate conflict regardless of the social situation. This form of disposition is *situation-free* or *generalized*. At the other extreme are individuals who possess a completely *situation-bound* disposition. These individuals do not begin to define conflict until particular situational circumstances call for it.

The second dimension is orientation. Here Mortensen relies primarily on the work of Newcomb, summarized in the previous section of this chapter. In short, as one's orientations become increasingly social, the chance that the person will experience conflict becomes greater. As a person becomes more and more aware of one's orientations toward objects and other people, conflict is more likely to arise.

The last three dimensions of conflict are intertwined. These include time, frequency, and salience or intensity. Basically, the more frequent and compressed in time a person experiences or thinks about coorientation with another person, the greater the anticipation of conflict.

According to this theory, these dimensions give rise to conflict communication. Of particular concern in the experience of the person are perceived shifts from generalized to situation-bound states, from intrapersonal to social orientations, and from low to high occurrence of conflict cues. As such changes occur, pressure increases in the person to perceive and verbalize conflict.

For example, suppose that two people become interested in an antique chair at a sale. As each becomes aware of the other's interest in the chair, both move toward increased social orientation. The potential buyers shift from a personal orientation to an awareness of each other and the other's desire for the chair. At this point the parties may become aware of the conflict potential of the sale. They become sensitive to the fact that conflict may arise in the situation. The more they think about it the more salient this possibility becomes, and conflict communication is likely to occur.

Mortensen believes that conflict comunication behaviors can be described in terms of three dimensions: intensity, affect, and orientational behaviors. *Intensity* is the strength or potency of the behavior. As conflict escalates, behaviors increase in rate, loudness, and other signs of intensity. The second dimension is *affect*. In short, people in conflict become more emotional. The third factor is *orientation*. Participants in conflict tend to verbalize their orientations, stressing comparisons and incompatibilities between their direct orientations and their perceptions of the other's orientations. As Mortensen expresses it, "Most of the claims are comparative, evaluative, accusatory, disjunctive, and polarized."[46]

Mortensen summarizes the major propositions of this approach as follows. You can see how these eight behavioral statements relate to the three dimensions described above.

1. Pressures to verbalize inner conflict increase with shifts (a) from generalized to highly differentiated conflict-laden cues, (b) from intrapersonal to social objects of orientation, and (c) from low-salient to high-salient conflict-laden cues.

2. The higher the level of verbal conflict, the greater the frequency of verbalization, the shorter the duration, the greater the amplitude and rate, and the less the level of fluency.

3. The higher the level of verbal conflict, the more

46. Ibid., p. 119.

variable and less synchronized the distribution of verbal acts becomes.

4. The higher the level of verbal conflict, the greater the degree of verbal disequilibrium (as measured by the variability of speech acts, the asymmetricality of reaction times, and the dysfunctionality of overt changes between decoding and encoding).

5. Changes in verbal intensity lead to corresponding shifts in perceptual and substantive indicants of social conflict as manifested by characteristic levels of language intensity and the structure of the claims expressed by the conflict agents.

6. The higher the level of verbal conflict, the more affect display will shift from shows of pleasantness, rejection, and low activation to those of unpleasantness, attention, and higher activation.

7. The higher the level of verbal conflict, the greater will be the variability in primary affects, looking behavior, and dissynchronization between shows of affect and intensity.

8. The higher the level of verbal conflict, the more frequent become the (a) shows of social comparison, (b) polarized social disjunctions, and (c) mentions of rejection and noncommitment (with corresponding decreases in expressions of agreement).[47]

Persuasion and Conflict

Herbert Simons has presented an analysis that adds even greater depth to our understanding of conflict.[48] Simons believes that communication in conflict situations is marked by attempts to influence. While Mortensen explains the conditions and behaviors of conflict, Simons explores the strategies of influence typically used. Simons's analysis includes interpersonal conflict, and it extends to the levels of intergroup and institutional conflict as well.

Behind Simons's theory lie four basic assumptions:

1. All human acts and artifacts constitute potential or actual messages. Thus, even physical acts such as riots, bombings, and political payoffs may have symbolic meaning, apart from whatever direct impact they may have.

2. All communicated messages have potential or actual suasive effects. Thus, there is a rhetorical dimension to all human behaviors.

3. Persuasive messages in social conflicts always take on meaning from their social contexts. Repeatedly . . . we have seen that acts such as confrontational protests made little sense apart from their contexts.

4. Influence in mixed-motive conflicts is neither a matter of the raw imposition of power nor of a friendly meeting of minds; instead, it is an inextricably intertwined combination of persuasive arguments backed up by constraints and inducements. In these social conflicts, once again, rhetoric serves power and power serves rhetoric.[49]

The last assumption is particularly important in that it reflects Simons's major thesis. In conflict situations the various types of influence strategies are used together and cannot be separated from one another. Traditionally, however, three types of influence are distinguished. *Inducements* are promised rewards used to bait one's counterpart into doing what is desired. *Constraint* or *coercion* is used to force an opponent into a particular action. Simons calls these the carrot and the stick; commonly they are known as threats and promises. *Persuasion* traditionally has been defined as a different strategy in which genuine, voluntary choice is extended to the other party. Persuasive influence is most often conceived as relying on information and argumentation.

While this three-fold distinction may be appropriate for various other communication situations, Simons believes it is inappropriate for conflict. As he says: "I shall argue here that in conflict situations, persuasion, broadly defined, is not so much an alternative to the power of constraints and inducements as it is an instrument of that power, an accompaniment to that power, or a consequence of that power."[50] Conflict occurs when the parties' interests are so incompatible that a struggle results. In such situations "power serves rhetoric and rhetoric serves power."[51] How is this so? Simons for-

47. Ibid., p. 121.

48. Herbert Simons, "The Carrot and Stick as Handmaidens of Persuasion in Conflict Situations," in *Perspectives on Communication in Conflict*, ed. Miller and Simons (Englewood Cliffs, N.J.: Prentice-Hall, 1974), pp. 172–205.

49. Ibid., p. 200.

50. Ibid., p. 177.

51. Ibid., p. 178.

wards two basic arguments. First, apparent acts of coercion or inducement must be supported by persuasion. At least, the receiver must be persuaded that the sender can and will institute sanctions. Second, apparent acts of persuasion are supported by an underlying power to constrain or induce. Influence in conflict situations is a two-sided coin. Persuasion supports power, and power supports persuasion. In practice the coin cannot be split.

Simons discusses a number of ways in which power and persuasion interact. An agent using coercion or inducement must establish one's own credibility; one must persuade the recipient that he or she has enough power to carry out the stated promise or threat and is willing to do so. On the other hand, coercion and inducement may be necessary to gain the authority or ethos necessary to persuade effectively. Also, the ends or consequences of power and of persuasion are often mutually supportive. Each may create obligations, pacify opponents, or create attitude change through dissonance reduction. A final area of overlap occurs when potential persuaders use coercive and reward influence to "buy" valuable communication resources. For example, effective persuasion often requires money, access to decision centers, control of media, and other factors.

Criticism

Each approach summarized in this section adds a different slant to our understanding of communication in conflict. The game theoretic approach is structural, outlining the parameters of conflict and the nature of decision-making contingencies among conflict participants. The transactional approach is tactical, stressing the dimensions that give rise to conflict and the nature of conflict communication behaviors. The influence model is strategic in that it stresses the complex interrelationships among the strategies of influence occurring in conflict. As is often the case in the communication realm, we come to understand the phenomenon better by a multitheoretical view.

Another advantage of these theories is that each makes communication a central concept. This treatment is not universally the case in theories of conflict. As a product of the speech communication field, these theories stress the importance of communication as a precursor to, aspect of, or consequence of conflict. The game theoretic approach, as modified by Steinfatt and Miller, points out the role that communication can take in modifying the moves people make in conflict games. The transactional approach of Mortensen indicates that conflict itself is defined through communication among participants. Simons's influence approach states that conflict inherently involves attempts to influence through communication.

We have discussed the game theory approach in terms of relational maintenance. The advantage of this approach to communication and conflict is that it helps us conceptualize the nature of conflict, the relation of conflict to decision making, and the effects of communication on conflict-producing or conflict-ameliorating choices. The approach's disadvantage is that it does not *explain* the process and behaviors of communication in conflict. As Steinfatt and Miller state in their conclusion: "In the daily political, economic, and social conflicts we all face, mutually advantageous solutions are seldom this sharply defined, and in seeking an acceptable solution, communication serves a myriad of cognitive and affective functions."[52]

As we have seen, game theory relies on the assumption that people are always rational in making decisions, that they always want to maximize positive outcomes. However, in actual social life establishing exactly what outcomes people are seeking is not this simplified. How people behave in real social conflict depends in part on their self-concept, motives,

52. Steinfatt and Miller, "Communication," p. 70. For an excellent debate on the value of game theory in communication research, see Robert Bostrom, "Game Theory in Communication Research," *Journal of Communication* 18 (1968): 369–88; and Thomas Beisecker, "Game Theory in Communication Research: A Rejoinder and a Reorientation," *Journal of Communication* 20 (1970); 107–20.

mental health, individual life goals, and an array of other complex factors. Also, as indicated before, game theory relies on rather artificial laboratory research, since analysis of actual life moves in the natural setting is extremely difficult.

The transactional view is an exceptionally fine approach to conflict and communication. It is actional in orientation and avoids universalist definitions of conflict. However, this approach stems from an experiential, phenomenological orientation to reality, which many communication scholars avoid. The criticism of the transactional approach is that in its holism, analysis of variables is difficult. This approach suffers some of the problems of system theory as covered in Chapter 3 and of experiential theories of meaning as explained in Chapter 6. Transactional theories provide an excellent general view of processes, but they keep understanding of actual variable relationships out of touch. Mortensen presents some propositions in his theory. These are presented in the form of lawlike statements, yet as laws they are inconsistent with the basic assumptions of the theory that individuals vary in the degree to which they define conflict and that they are relatively free to choose the rules by which conflict is expressed. This inconsistency points out the basic problem of the transactional approach in making propositional statements about events that are valid in all situations.

The major strength of Simons's strategy approach is that it recognizes that conflict typically is marked by a great deal of communication designed to influence other people. To remove this dimension, as many noncommunication theories do, is to eviscerate conflict as it occurs in real life. (Game theory is weak in this way, but Mortensen's transactional approach recognizes the importance of communication in the conflict situation.) Simons's approach actually centers on this dynamic. Another strength of Simons's theory is its recognition that types of influence cannot be realistically separated from one another in a conflict situation. Persuasion in conflict consists of coercion, sanctions, and argumentation. Unfortunately, this theory is just a beginning. It introduces us to the idea of persuasion in conflict, but it does not develop specific propositions in any detail. It is hoped that communication scholars will move into this area and continue the analysis of communication and conflict through research and theory building.

What Do We Know about Factors of Interpersonal Communication

We are considering theories of interpersonal communication in three parts. The first group of theories, related most directly to relationship, was presented in the last chapter. The present chapter deals with theories related to disclosure and understanding, attraction and relational maintenance, and conflict. In the next chapter we will cover theories related to groups and organizations.

The theories we have summarized in this chapter present an interesting and important body of knowledge about interpersonal communication. We know from these theories that one of the goals of interpersonal communication is understanding. Understanding is achieved by assimilating information about others and disclosing information about oneself. The nature of one's disclosures to others and the receptivity of people to one's disclosures appear to be strongly related to individual growth and personal adjustment. Disclosure, however, to be effective, must be adapted to the situation in which it occurs. The amount and kind of disclosure that occurs between people depends in part on the stage of the relationship and the nature of trust between the participants. Rhetorical sensitivity is the ability of the individual to judge the situation and to make disclosures in a way that others will understand and accept. This quality also involves a recognition that an individual consists of many selves; how one communicates in a situation depends on the self that is appropriate for that situation.

Attraction is related to the establishment and maintenance of relationships. Attraction is a function of a variety of factors, including at least cognitive balance, reinforcement, and cost-reward outcomes. Attraction in a relationship is relative to the partners' aspirations and the perceived outcomes of alternative relationships.

The final element of relationships in this chapter is social conflict. Communication is a central aspect of conflict. Conflict is marked by certain kinds of communication, and communication between parties in a conflict situation can affect the outcome. Although conflict communication tends to be emotional and to involve attempts to influence, it can bring about mutually desirable solutions and a sense of cooperation rather than competition.

Interpersonal communication is the basis for all other contexts of communication. It is fundamental to group and organizational communication; even mass communication depends in part on interpersonal contacts. In upcoming chapters we will consider these higher levels of communication in turn. In the next chapter we will discuss several theories related to communication in formal or structured situations—the group and the organization.

CHAPTER

11 Interpersonal Contexts III: Theories of Groups and Organizations

Interpersonal communication includes dyadic, group, and organizational settings. In the last two chapters we discussed theories related directly to dyadic interaction. This chapter presents theories that apply particularly well to group and organizational settings. Remember, however, that the levels of communication—dyadic, group, organizational, and mass—are not discrete categories. Rather, they are a hierarchy in which each higher level includes apsects of the lower levels. Therefore organizational communication includes many of the elements of group communication, and group communication involves dyadic interaction as a foundation.

Theories of Group Communication

In the last two chapters we looked at a number of the theories related to face-to-face interaction. One important setting for interpersonal communication is the small group. A number of contemporary source books on small groups reflect the breadth of work in this area.[1] Theory and research related to small group communication is scattered and varied. Critics have singled out small group communication as a confusing area of study.[2] Yet several good theories of small group processes have emerged over the years. In this chapter we will look at some of the most interesting and insightful. There can be no doubt that the study of small group communication is important. For one thing the small group is a crucial part of society. As Clovis Shepherd points out, the group is "an essential mechanism of socialization and a primary source of social order." People derive their values and attitudes largely from the groups with which they identify. As a result "the small group serves an important mediating function between the individual and the larger society."[3] In essential agreement with Shepherd, Dorwin Cartwright and Alvin Zander outline four basic assumptions of groups:

1. Groups are inevitable and ubiquitous. . . .
2. Groups mobilize powerful forces that produce effects of utmost importance to individuals. . . .
3. Groups may produce both good and bad consequences. . . .

1. See, for example, Joseph E. McGrath and Irwin Altman, *Small Group Research: A Synthesis and Critique of the Field* (New York: Holt, Rinehart and Winston, 1966); Bernard L. Hinton and H. Joseph Reitz, eds., *Groups and Organizations* (Belmont, Calif.: Wadsworth, 1971); A. Paul Hare, Edgar F. Borgatta, and Robert Bales, eds., *Small Groups: Studies in Social Interaction* (New York: Knopf, 1966); Lawrence Rosenfeld, *Human Interaction in the Small Group Setting* (Columbus, Ohio: Charles E. Merrill, 1973); Marvin E. Shaw, *Group Dynamics: The Psychology of Small Group Behavior* (New York: McGraw-Hill, 1981); Clovis R. Shepherd, *Small Groups: Some Sociological Perspectives* (San Francisco: Chandler, 1964); Dorwin Cartwright and Alvin Zander, eds., *Group Dynamics: Research and Theory* (New York: Harper & Row, 1968); Robert S. Cathcart and Larry A. Samover, eds. *Small Group Communication: A Reader* (Dubuque, Iowa: Brown, 1974).

2. See, for example, McGrath and Altman, *Small Group Research*; Ernest G. Bormann, "The Paradox and Promise of Small Group Research," *Speech Monographs* 37 (1970): 211–17; C. David Mortensen, "The Status of Small Group Research," *Quarterly Journal of Speech* 56 (1970): 304–9; Carl E. Larson, "Speech Communication Research on Small Groups," *Speech Teacher* 20 (1971): 89–107. A number of scholars have responded to this criticism by attempting to provide focus. See, for example, B. Aubrey Fisher and Leonard Hawes, "An Interact System Model: Generating a Grounded Theory of Small Groups," *Quarterly Journal of Speech* 57 (1971): 444–53; Dennis Couran, "Group Communication: Perspectives and Priorities for Future Research," *Quarterly Journal of Speech* 59 (1973): 22–29.

3. Shepherd, *Small Groups*, p. 1.

4. A correct understanding of group dynamics (obtainable from research) permits the possibility that desirable consequences from groups can be deliberately enhanced.[4]

What, then, distinguishes the group? After summarizing several other definitions stressing different aspects of groups, Marvin Shaw provides his own *interactional* definition: "A group is defined as two or more persons who are interacting with one another in such a manner that each person influences and is influenced by each other person. A *small* group is a group having twenty or fewer members, although in most instances we will be concerned with groups having five or fewer members."[5] This definition is a good one for our purposes because it includes a communication as the essential characteristic of the group. Shaw points out that the most interesting groups are those that endure for a relatively long period of time, have a goal or goals, and have a degree of interactional structure.

In their classical treatment of group dynamics, Cartwright and Zander also stress the interactional quality of groups. In particular these authors point out a number of characteristics of small groups:

> It seems likely, then, that when a set of people constitutes a group, one or more of the following statements will characterize them: (a) they engage in frequent interaction; (b) they define themselves as members; (c) they are defined by others as belonging to the group; (d) they share norms concerning matters of common interest; (e) they participate in a system of interlocking roles; (f) they identify with one another as a result of having set up the same model—object or ideals in their super-ego; (g) they find the group to be rewarding; (h) they pursue promotively interdependent goals; (i) they have a collective perception of their unity; (j) they tend to act in a unitary manner toward the environment.[6]

For Cartwright and Zander groupness is a variable, and the more of the foregoing characteristics that exist, the closer the body comes to being a group.

4. Cartwright and Zander, *Research and Theory*, p. 23.
5. Shaw, *Group Dynamics*, p. 10.
6. Cartwright and Zander, *Research and Theory*, p. 48.

Shepherd also uses interaction as the defining quality of the small group.[7] In addition he provides four qualifications. First, as an organized entity the group lies somewhere between the informality of social relations and the formality of organizations. Second, as groups increase in size, their character tends to change. Groups of four or more may appear quite different from dyads and triads. Third, there seems to be an upper size limit to the small group. After reaching a certain size, groups tend to establish formal rules, which characterize organizations. Fourth, small groups possess purposes or goals, role structure, norms, shared values, and communication patterns.

Group Dynamics

Most of what we know about groups and group communication stems from empirical research in social psychology. Collectively this work is known as *group dynamics*. This work is summarized in the three following sections. First, the seminal ideas of Kurt Lewin are presented. The next section includes a general organizing model by Harold Guetzkow and Barry Collins, and the final section presents a catalog of hypotheses arising from empirical research.

Foundations: Lewin's Field Theory. Kurt Lewin was one of the most prominent psychologists of our century. Gardner Lindzey and Calvin Hall have written: "Lewin is considered by many of his peers to be one of the most brilliant figures in contemporary psychology. His theoretical writings and experimental work have left an indelible mark upon the development of psychology."[8] As a social psychologist interested in the nature of individual and group behavior, he is responsible for one of the most influential approaches to the study of behavior. Field theory is an organic approach that in its holistic orientation is consistent with the systems point of view. Lewin was also a phenomenologist in

7. Shepherd, *Small Groups*.
8. Calvin S. Hall and Gardner Lindzey, "Lewin's Field Theory," in *Theories of Personality* (New York: John Wiley & Sons, 1970), chap. 6.

that he viewed behavior from the perspective of the person. Lewin's work is important for two other reasons as well. He believed that social research should delve into the practical affairs of people's lives. As a result he is responsible for much *action research* in which practical problems of groups and organizations are probed. In addition Lewin believed in the overriding value of theory. Good research must be guided by theory, and theory must be constantly built up by research.[9]

We are interested in Lewin because of his work in group dynamics. Lewin was one of the first in the long line of researchers in this area. There can be no doubt that he was influential in shaping much of our thought about the nature of groups. In this section we first consider Lewin's orientation to the person; then we discuss how people relate to groups.

Lewin begins his thought with five assumptions about people. First, what is important to study is the perceptions of the person, or the individual's *psychological field* or *life space*. Second, the person at any moment occupies a position in the life space that can be best conceptualized in its distance from the other objects of the field. Third, the person has goals toward which one moves in the life space. Fourth, the person's behavior can be explained in terms of attempting to reach the goals. Fifth, the field also contains barriers to the goals, barriers that the individual must surpass.[10]

Lewin's theory leads us to see the person moving about in a psychological space, called the life space. This field is not an objective world, but the subjective world of the person. In this field are a number of objects that the individual wishes to approach or avoid, and in striving for goals, the person encounters various barriers. How the person behaves or moves within the life space is governed by *tensions* arising from the individual's needs and wants. For example, consider a girl at play. As the child moves about among her toys, she will behave in accordance with the tensions arising out of the need to achieve some goal or goals. Suppose that she drops a ball into a hole so deep that she cannot reach the bottom. Her immediate behavior will be seen as attempts to solve the problem. She may get a stick or perhaps call for an adult. After the ball is recovered, she will continue playing, seeking new goals in the life space.

The life space is a complex, interdependent, fluid field in which the person moves on the basis of the tensions of the moment. Another way of conceiving this space is as a field of energy. The forces in the field depend on the pressures of the environment and the wants of the person, two aspects that must be viewed as interacting variables. This approach demands that behavior be examined holistically; it also demands that behavior be examined in the here and now.

We must remember that the individual's life space includes groups. Individuals cannot be separated from the groups with which they identify. Groups, too, have a kind of life space. Lewin developed a theory that can be applied to all kinds of groups ranging from families to work groups. His analysis includes large social groups such as communities or institutions as well. The term *group dynamics* implies that groups are products of various forces and tensions. Lewin studied groups from the perspective of their positive and negative forces, especially the ways in which these forces influence the person as a group member.

While a group is a set of people, it is more than the sum of its members. When people join together in a group, a resulting structure evolves with its own goals and life space. The group is an excellent example of a system as outlined in Chapter 3 of this book. As Lewin puts it: "A group can be characterized as a 'dynamical whole'; this means that a change in the state of any subpart changes the state of any other subpart. The degree of interdependence of the subparts of members of the group varies

9. For an interesting biography of Lewin, see Alfred Marrow, *The Practical Theorist: The Life and Work of Kurt Lewin* (New York: Basic Books, 1969).

10. These assumptions are summarized by Shepherd, *Small Groups*.

all the way from loose mass to a compact unit. It depends, among other factors, upon the size, organization, and intimacy of the group."[11] Individuals are members of many groups at one time, which means that a person's groups are an important part of the life space. Consequently, one's groups will create tensions in the life space and therefore influence the movement of the person. Since the life space is fluid, the potency of a group for a particular person will vary from moment to moment. For example, when a person is at home, the family group generally exerts more influence than does the work group. Such may not be the case when the person is at work.

At this point we begin to see one of Lewin's most important themes—the impact of groups on individual life. This impact has four qualities. First, the group provides stability to the person's life. As Lewin states, "The speed and determination with which a person proceeds, his readiness to fight or to submit, and other important characteristics of his behavior depend upon the firmness of the ground on which he stands and upon his general security. The group a person belongs to is one of the most important constituents of this ground."[12] Second, the group provides the person with a means for achieving valued goals. It is a vehicle for approaching or avoiding objects in the life space. Third, the person's values and attitudes are greatly influenced by the values and norms of the groups to which he or she belongs. Fourth, as part of the life space, the person moves about within the group; the person aims for various goals in the group itself.

While group pressures constrain the individual, the person also has some degree of freedom. Group values and norms never coincide completely with individual needs. Groups seem to have an optimal level of freedom. If the individual does not have enough freedom to pursue goals outside the group, dissatisfaction will result, and the individual may leave the group. On the other hand, if the influence of the group is too weak, it will be less functional in helping the individual achieve goals in the life space. Thus the person in face-to-face interaction with groups is constantly adjusting and adapting individual needs and group demands. As a result of this interaction between person and group, both personal needs and behavior and group norms and demands will change.

The most important attribute of groups is *cohesiveness*. Cohesiveness is the degree of mutual interest among members. In a highly cohesive group, a strong mutual identification is found among members. This quality is what keeps a group together. Without it the group will dissolve. Mutual identification is a function of the degree to which members are mutually attracted to certain goals or mutually repulsed by certain negative forces. Cohesiveness is a result of the degree to which all members perceive that their goals can be met within the group. This does not require that the members have similar attitudes, but that they are interdependent, that they must rely on one another to achieve certain mutually desired goals. The more cohesive a group, the more force it exerts on its members. The person is pressured by the group to conform to the group code. This theme has been elaborated over the years throughout small group research and theory.

Lewin is placed first in this chapter because his theory provides an excellent introductory approach to the study of groups. Field theory respects the needs of the individual, at the same time demonstrating how people and groups interact. The group is influenced by personal needs; the person is affected by group standards. While Lewin did not dwell on communication per se, he provides an excellent general orientation toward group and organizational behavior. We cannot begin to understand communication in groups without this more general orientation to the nature of groups and the group-person relationship.

A General Organizing Model. Most of the work on group dynamics centers on task groups. In

11. Kurt Lewin, *Resolving Social Conflicts: Selected Papers on Group Dynamics* (New York: Harper & Row, 1948), p. 94.
12. Ibid., p. 86.

fact most of the theories in this part of the chapter deal directly with task groups. To help guide your thinking about the nature of task accomplishment in groups, the integrative model of Harold Guetzkow and Barry Collins has been included (Figure 11.1).[13] Although this model is dated, it is still useful in outlining general components of the group decision-making process. The model may look complicated at first glance, but it is simple.

Any task group is confronted with two types of problems: task obstacles and interpersonal obstacles. Task obstacles are the difficulties presented to the group as the problem to be solved. Group members deal directly with the problem—analyzing it, suggesting possible solutions, and weighing alternatives. Such efforts are task-related group behaviors. However, whenever two or more people join together to handle a problem, interpersonal obstacles also arise. Such obstacles include the need to make one's ideas clear to others, to deal with conflict among participants, to handle individual member differences, and so forth. Thus in any group discussion members will be dealing simultaneously with task and interpersonal obstacles.

The basic distinction between task work and interpersonal relations has been an overriding concern in the research and theory on small group communication. Both types of behavior are important in accomplishing the task or in achieving group productivity. Any analysis of group problem solving must deal with both task and interpersonal demands. The outputs of a group are affected by members' task and interpersonal efforts.

Interpersonal and task factors interrelate, and group productivity results from both. Interpersonal relations can inhibit problem solving as well as enhance it. The performance of a group

13. Barry Collins and Harold Guetzkow, *A Social Psychology of Group Processes for Decision Making* (New York: John Wiley & Sons, 1964), p. 81.

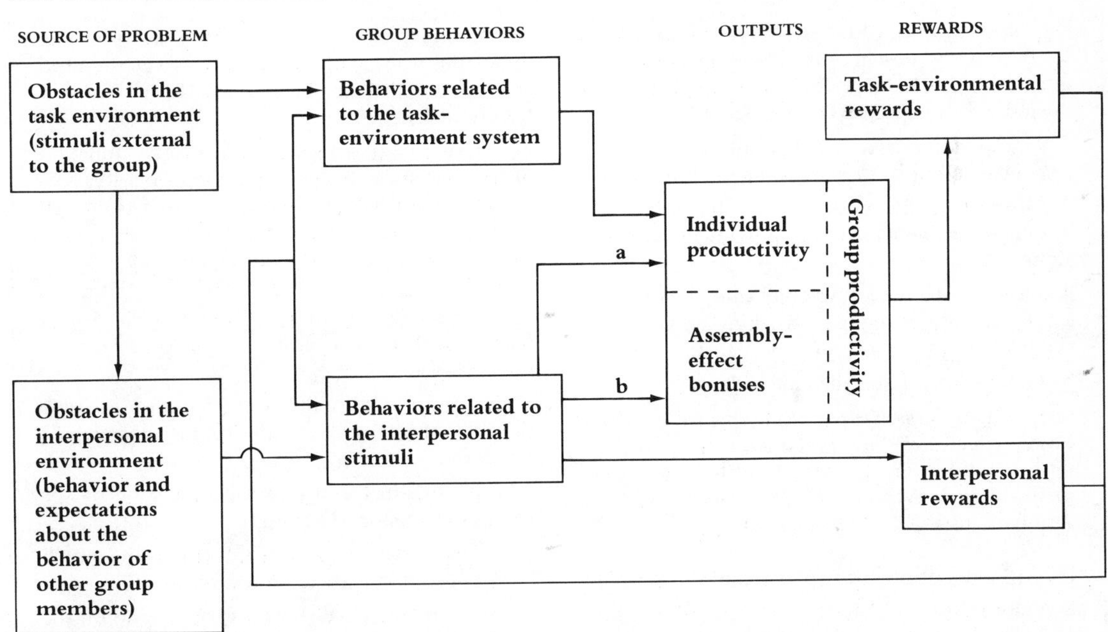

From *A Social Psychology of Group Processes for Decision-Making* by Barry Collins and Harold Guetzkow, John Wiley and Sons, publisher.

Figure 11.1. A simple working model of decision-making groups.

depends primarily on its ability to integrate and organize the individual skills and resources of the members. When this integration is done effectively, an *assembly effect* occurs in which the group solution or product is superior to the individual work of even the best member. We will return to this notion when we discuss ideas on syntality and the groupthink hypothesis later in the chapter.

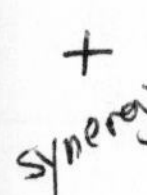

Group rewards can be positive or negative. Successful goal achievement is usually positively rewarding to group members. In addition the resolution of conflict and successful communication often reap interpersonal rewards. On the other hand, "rewards" may also be negative. In any case outcomes are evaluated by group members as positive or negative rewards, and these in turn affect future task and interpersonal efforts in the group, as indicated by the feedback arrows in Figure 11.1.

Research Findings. The disadvantage of the work in group dynamics is that it consists largely of a vast, often unconnected body of research. Although there are several recognized theories related to certain aspects of group communication, some of which were presented in the last two chapters, there are very few theories of group communication as a whole. Certainly we have no recent theories that attempt to bring together this research into a single integrated framework.

Fortunately, Marvin Shaw has taken a step in this direction by creating a series of hypotheses about groups. His integration of the research data is excellent, for it presents a relatively simple and clear summary of what is known in the field of group dynamics. Because the list of hypotheses is long and because they are self-explanatory, they are quoted in the following box on pages 222–226 without comment:

Small Group Research Hypotheses[14]

Hypotheses about Individuals and Groups

1. The mere presence of others increases the motivation level of a performing individual when the individual expects to be evaluated.

2. Group judgments are superior to individual judgments on tasks that involve a random error.

3. Groups usually produce more and better solutions to problems than do individuals working alone.

4. Groups usually require more time to complete a task than do individuals working alone, especially when time is measured in man-minutes.

5. Groups learn faster than individuals.

6. Group discussion often produces group polarization effects, leading to either more risky or more cautious group decisions than decisions made by the average group member prior to group discussion. Groupthink

Hypotheses about Group Formation and Development

1. People join groups in order to satisfy some individual need.

2. Proximity, contact, and interaction provide an opportunity for individuals to discover the need satisfactions that can be attained through affiliation with others.

3. Interpersonal attraction is a positive function of physical attractiveness, attitude similarity, personality similarity, economic similarity, racial similarity, perceived ability of the other person (his or her success or failure), and need compatibility.

4. Individuals desire to affiliate with others whose abilities are equal to or greater than their own.

5. An individual will join a group if he or she finds the activities of the group attractive or rewarding.

6. An individual will join a group if he or she values the goals of the group.

7. There exists a need for affiliation which renders group membership rewarding.

8. An individual will join a group if he or she perceives it to be instrumental in satisfying needs outside the group.

9. Group development follows a reasonably consistent pattern that involves a period of orienta-

14. Shaw, *Group Dynamics*, pp. 76–80, 114–17, 161–66, 202–9, 256–61, 307–14, 343–45, 383–89.

tion, resolution of conflicts about authority and personal relations, and a productive period.

10. Coalitions form in situations in which two or more persons can achieve greater rewards through joint action than can either acting alone.

Hypotheses about the Physical Environment of Groups

1. The physical aspects of the environment interact with attitudes and beliefs to help determine group process.

2. Individuals and groups typically assume a proprietary orientation toward certain geographical areas which they defend against invasion.

3. The size of group territories varies with the density of the locale and the interpersonal relationships among group members.

4. Individuals typically have personal standards concerning appropriate interpersonal distances for various interpersonal relationships and activities.

5. Reactions to unwanted approach by others vary with the personalness of the situation, the intimacy of the person-other relationship, and the status of the person relative to the other.

6. Unwanted proximity of another person evokes discomfort and negative feelings which are revealed by various defensive reactions on the part of the victim, the person whose space is invaded.

7. Male and female groups react differently to variations in population density.

8. High density results in decrements in group performance under some conditions.

9. There is a positive relationship between status and the favorability of spatial position in the group.

10. Communication patterns in groups are determined, in part, by the seating arrangement in the group.

11. Seating arrangement influences the quality of group interaction.

12. A leader is more likely to emerge in a centralized communication network than in a decentralized network.

13. Organizational development occurs more rapidly in a centralized than a decentralized communication network.

14. Group members have higher morale in decentralized than in centralized communication networks.

15. A decentralized communication network is most efficient when the group must solve complex problems, whereas a centralized network is most efficient when the group must solve simple problems.

16. A centralized communication network is more vulnerable to saturation than a decentralized network.

Hypotheses about Personal Characteristics of Group Members

1. The total amount of participation in the group decreases with increasing group size.

2. Differences in relative participation by group members increases with increasing group size.

3. The probability that a leader will emerge increases with increasing size of group.

4. Smaller groups are usually evaluated more positively than larger groups by group members.

5. Conformity to a unanimous majority increases with increasing group size, at least up to some maximum.

6. The effects of group size upon group performance are a function of the kind of task that the group must complete.

7. Social participation increases with increasing chronological age to some maximum level.

8. Social interaction becomes more highly differentiated and complex with increasing chronological age to some maximum.

9. There is a tendency for the group leader to be older than other group members.

10. Conformity behavior increases with chronological age to about age 12, and decreases thereafter.

11. Women are less assertive and less competitive in groups than are men.

12. Women use eye contact as a form of communication more frequently than men.

13. Women usually talk more in groups than men.

14. Females conform to majority opinion more than males.

15. There is a slight tendency for physically superior individuals to become leaders.

16. Leaders are usually more intelligent than nonleaders.

17. The more intelligent group member is usually more active in the group than less intelligent group members.

18. The more intelligent group member is usu-

ally more popular than less intelligent group members.

19. More intelligent persons are less conforming than less intelligent persons.

20. The individual who possesses special skills (abilities, knowledge, information) relative to the group task usually is more active in the group, makes more contributions toward task completion, and has more influence on the group decision.

21. The authoritarian is autocratic and demanding of others in the group.

22. The authoritarian conforms to the majority opinion more than does the nonauthoritarian.

23. Individuals who are positively oriented toward other people enhance social interaction, cohesiveness, and morale in groups, whereas individuals who are positively oriented toward things inhibit social interaction, cohesiveness, and morale.

24. Socially sensitive persons behave in ways which enhance their acceptance in the group and group effectiveness.

25. Ascendant individuals are dominating and self-assertive in groups and generally facilitate group functioning.

26. The more dependable the group member, the more probable it is that he or she will emerge as a leader and will be successful in helping the group achieve its goal.

27. The unconventional group member inhibits group functioning.

28. The anxious group member inhibits effective group functioning.

29. The well-adjusted group member contributes to effective group functioning.

Hypotheses about Group Composition

1. Individuals contribute differently to the group product, depending upon the particular other individuals in the group.

2. Members of high-cohesive groups communicate with each other to a greater extent than members of low-cohesive groups.

3. The pattern and content of interaction are more positively oriented in high-cohesive than in low-cohesive groups.

4. High-cohesive groups exert greater influence over their members than do low-cohesive groups.

5. High-cohesive groups are more effective than low-cohesive groups in achieving their respective goals.

6. Members of high-cohesive groups are generally better satisfied than members of low-cohesive groups.

7. Compatible groups are more effective in achieving group goals than are incompatible groups.

8. Members of compatible groups are better satisfied than members of incompatible groups.

9. Other things being equal, groups composed of members having diverse, relevant abilities perform more effectively than groups composed of members having similar abilities.

10. The interaction styles of men and women are affected differently by the sex composition of the group.

11. Sexually heterogeneous groups are more effective than sexually homogeneous groups.

12. Members conform more in mixed-sex groups than in same-sex groups.

13. Racial heterogeneity tends to create interpersonal tension which is reflected in the feelings and behaviors of group members.

14. Groups whose members are heterogeneous with respect to personality profiles perform more effectively than groups whose members are homogeneous with respect to personality profiles.

Hypotheses about Group Structure

1. The perception that organization facilitates goal achievement is a determinant of group structure.

2. The formation of group structure is facilitated to the extent that group members have a need for structure.

3. The kind of structure that the group develops is influenced by the particular needs of the group members.

4. The kind of structure that the group develops is influenced by the physical environment of the group.

5. A high-status group member may deviate from group norms without being sanctioned if his or her deviancy contributes to goal attainment.

6. The high-status person both initiates and receives more communications than the low-status person.

7. Communications directed upward in the status hierarchy have more positive content than communications directed downward.

8. Role specifications may bias the perceptions and judgments of the role occupant by others.

9. Role conflicts will ordinarily be resolved in favor of the group that is most important to the role occupant.

10. Individuals differ in their predisposition toward conformity to group norms.

11. The more ambiguous the stimulus situation, the greater the probability that a group member will conform to the perceived norms of the group.

12. A group member is more likely to conform to group judgment when other members are in unanimous agreement than when they are not.

13. Greater conformity occurs in groups with decentralized communication networks than in groups with centralized communication networks.

14. Conformity varies positively with the perceived competence of the majority relative to the individual's perception of his or her own competence.

15. The effects of personality, situational, and stimulus variables are additive within the normal ranges of conformity behavior.

16. Conformity introduces order into the group process and provides for the coordination of individual behavior.

17. Under certain circumstances, conformity frees the individual from the coercive influence of authority.

18. Deviation from group norms usually elicits sanctioning behavior by other group members. Continued or habitual deviation may lead to rejection by other group members.

19. High-power group members are usually better liked than low-power group members.

20. The high-power group member is the target of more deferential, approval-seeking behavior than low-power group members.

21. The high-power person has greater influence upon the group than low-power group members.

22. The high-power group member is more highly attracted to the group than are low-power group members.

23. The more power a group member has, the greater the probability that he or she will use it.

Hypotheses about Leadership

1. Persons who actively participate in the group are more likely to attain a position of leadership than those who participate less in the group's activities.

2. Possession of task-related abilities and skills enhances attainment of a position of leadership.

3. Emergent leaders tend to behave in a more authoritarian manner than elected or appointed leaders.

4. The source of the leader's authority influences both the leader's behavior and the reactions of other group members.

5. Effective leaders are characterized by task-related abilities, sociability, and motivation to be a leader.

6. Democratic leadership results in greater member satisfaction than autocratic leadership.

7. Leaders tend to behave in a more authoritarian manner in stressful than in nonstressful situations.

8. The degree to which the leader is endorsed by group members depends upon the success of the group in achieving its goals.

9. A task-oriented leader is more effective when the group-task situation is either very favorable or very unfavorable for the leader, whereas a relationship-oriented leader is more effective when the group-task situation is only moderately favorable or unfavorable to the leader.

Hypotheses about Group Task and Group Goals

1. Individuals establish goals for their groups which influence their behavior in ways similar to the influence of personal goals.

2. Tension systems can be aroused for goals which the individual holds for the group.

3. Tension systems can be aroused for avoidances which the individual holds for the group.

4. Group success is followed by choice of a more difficult task; failure is followed by selection of an easier task.

5. Group members select relatively more difficult tasks if they learn that their past performance is worse than the average for groups like their own; they choose relatively less difficult tasks if they learn that their past performance is better than the average of groups like their own.

6. The greater the group members' desire for group success, the greater the preference for tasks

perceived to be in the intermediate range of difficulty; the stronger the desires to avoid group failure, the greater the preference for tasks at the extremes of the difficulty range.

7. Groups composed wholly of persons with desires to achieve success stronger than their desires to avoid failure more often select tasks in the intermediate range of difficulty than groups composed wholly of persons whose desires to avoid failure exceed their desires to achieve success.

8. The quality of group performance, as measured by time and errors, decreases with increasing task difficulty.

9. Reaction time decreases with increased task difficulty.

10. Group members attempt leadership more frequently when the task is difficult than when it is easy.

11. When task difficulty is low or moderate, conformity is curvilinearly related to the self-esteem of the group member.

12. The quality of group performance decreases with increasing task demands.

13. The characteristics of group products vary with the difficulty of the group task.

14. On difficult tasks, group performance is facilitated to the extent that group members can freely communicate their feelings of satisfaction with the group's progress toward goal achievement.

15. The kinds of leadership abilities that are required for effective group action vary with the type of task.

16. The characteristics of group products are a function of the kind of task faced by the group.

17. The activity of group leaders varies with the kind of task faced by the group.

18. Group performance is better when the task is disjunctive than when it is conjunctive.

19. The style of leadership that is most effective varies with task solution multiplicity.

20. The quality of group performance, as measured by time and errors, is negatively correlated with the cooperation requirements of the group task.

21. Goal clarity and goal-path clarity are positively related to motivational characteristics of group members.

22. Goal clarity and goal-path clarity are positively correlated with the efficiency of group members.

23. Interpersonal relations are generally more positive in cooperative than in competitive situations.

24. Homogeneous group goals facilitate effective group functioning, whereas heterogeneous group goals hinder effective group functioning.

Criticism. Ironically, the work of Kurt Lewin, which remains a foundation for contemporary research on group dynamics, is epistemologically and ontologically different from its latter-day counterparts. Lewin's theory is holistic, phenomenological, and field oriented. Social psychological research since Lewin for the most part has been analytic, scientific, and laboratory oriented. Lewin took a systems view of group life, noting the integrated and interdependent nature of group variables. Most group researchers today are from the variable-analytic tradition, in which distinct factors are isolated for close scrutiny. Therefore these two groups of theories must be criticized separately.

Lewin is recognized as a giant in the field of social psychology. Not only did he present certain fundamental concepts and findings that remain viable today, but he was instrumental in motivating social psychology as a field. Hall and Lindzey have written of him:

> Lewin's theory was one of those that helped to revive the conception of man as a complex energy field, motivated by psychological forces, and behaving selectively and creatively. The hollow man was replenished with psychological needs, intentions, hopes, and aspirations. The robot was transformed into a living human being. The crass and dreary materialism of behaviorism was replaced by a more humanistic picture of man. While "objective" psychology tailored many of its empirical propositions to be tested on dogs, cats, and rats, Lewin's theory led to research on human behavior as expressed in more or less natural settings. Children at play, adolescents in group activities, workers in factories, housewives planning meals, these were some of the

natural life situations in which hypotheses derived from Lewin's field theory were empirically tested.[15]

Lewin's work was just a beginning, and although he made significant contributions to our understanding of groups, most of these were general orientations and provided little substance about how groups actually operate. For a greater understanding of the variables of group dynamics, we must rely on more recent research.[16]

No doubt, social psychological research on groups has contributed much to our understanding of group process and problem solving. The lengthy list of hypotheses by Shaw illustrates at a glance the tremendous scope and power of much of this research. Unfortunately, this work is nontheoretical. It consists of a large number of research findings in search of an integrating framework. Consequently, Shaw's list is extremely unparsimonious. Most of the hypotheses relate two or three variables with no connecting thread. General theories of groups have the potential of providing parsimony by reducing the vast array of variables to certain basic factors and explanatory structures.

Another criticism of social psychological work is that it consists largely of laboratory research on artificial groups. Much more research on natural groups in the field setting is required. Most group research studies center on two or three variables, ignoring the holistic nature of group operations. This fault is a natural condition of the limitations of our research tools. Observing more than a few variables at a time is difficult and leads to other kinds of error in making conclusions about what is observed. What is needed, and it is needed badly in the small group field, is a kind of triangulation between the laboratory and the natural setting. Ironically, research in this area needs to return to the type of work conducted by Lewin forty-five years ago.

15. Hall and Lindzey, "Lewin," pp. 254–55.

16. For criticism of group dynamics, see Shaw, *Group Dynamics*, pp. 445–51.

Theories of Group Interaction

Group outcome depends greatly on the nature of interaction in the group. Theories of group interaction are especially important in this book because of the central concern for communication as the base of group productivity. We will look at two theories of group interaction. The first, an old standard, is Bales's interaction process analysis. The second, more recent theory, modifies Bale's notion of interaction and takes interaction analysis in a different direction.

Interaction Process Analysis. One of the most prominent small group theories is Robert Bales's interaction process analysis.[17] Bales's theory concentrates on interaction or communication per se. Using his many years of research as a foundation, Bales has created a unified and well-developed theory of small group interaction. It is centered around the idea that people act and react in groups. As one person makes a comment, another person responds to the comment. Bales's aim, then, is to explain the pattern of responses in the small task group. Bales explains the value of his system: "Interaction process analysis is built on a very simple common-sense base, and much that one intuitively believes about everyday conversation can be confirmed by it. The surprising thing, perhaps, is that it goes much further than one would suspect in revealing basic attitudes of people, their personalities, and their positions in a group."[18]

Figure 11.2 illustrates the categories of interaction. These twelve categories are grouped into four broader sets, as outlined at the left of the figure. In addition the behavior types are paired according to typical action-response expectations. Each of these pairs implies a particular problem area for groups, as labeled. The

17. Robert F. Bales, *Interaction Process Analysis: A Method for the Study of Small Groups* (Reading, Mass.: Addison-Wesley, 1950; *Personality and Interpersonal Behavior* (New York: Holt, Rinehart and Winston, 1970).

18. Bales, *Personality*, p. 95.

figure also reflects the approximate percentage of comments in each category, according to gross norms.

The four sets of behavior in the model can be further synthesized into two classes of group behavior. We have seen these in the earlier theories in this chapter. The first and fourth categories, positive actions and negative actions, constitute the *socioemotional area,* which relates to the interpersonal relations in the group. In addition to accomplishing a task, the group must mesh psychologically, a goal that can be aided or impeded by socioemotional communication. The second and third classes can be considered the *task area.* The interactions in this section relate to the problem or task of the group. In investigating leadership, Bales has found that typically the same group will have two different kinds of leaders. The task leader, who facilitates and coordinates the task-related comments, directs energy toward getting the job done. The emergence of the task leadership role is important in group problem solving. Equally important is the emergence of a socioemotional leader. Usually a second leader takes this role. This individual works for improved relations in the group, concentrating on interactions in the positive and negative sectors.

The way a person behaves in a group depends on the role the individual takes and the person's personality. Role is situational. It depends on the demands of the interpersonal dynamics of the group, including the expectations of others. The way a person behaves will lead to certain perceptions by the other group members. "One might expect utter chaos with all this relativism of definition, but in many operating groups there is a surprising amount of consensus on the way in which most individual members are perceived and evaluated."[19] Bales has shown how the perception of an individual's position in a group is a function of three dimensions. These include the extent to which the individual is seen as striving for *success and power* (as opposed to devaluation of the

19. Ibid., p. 4.

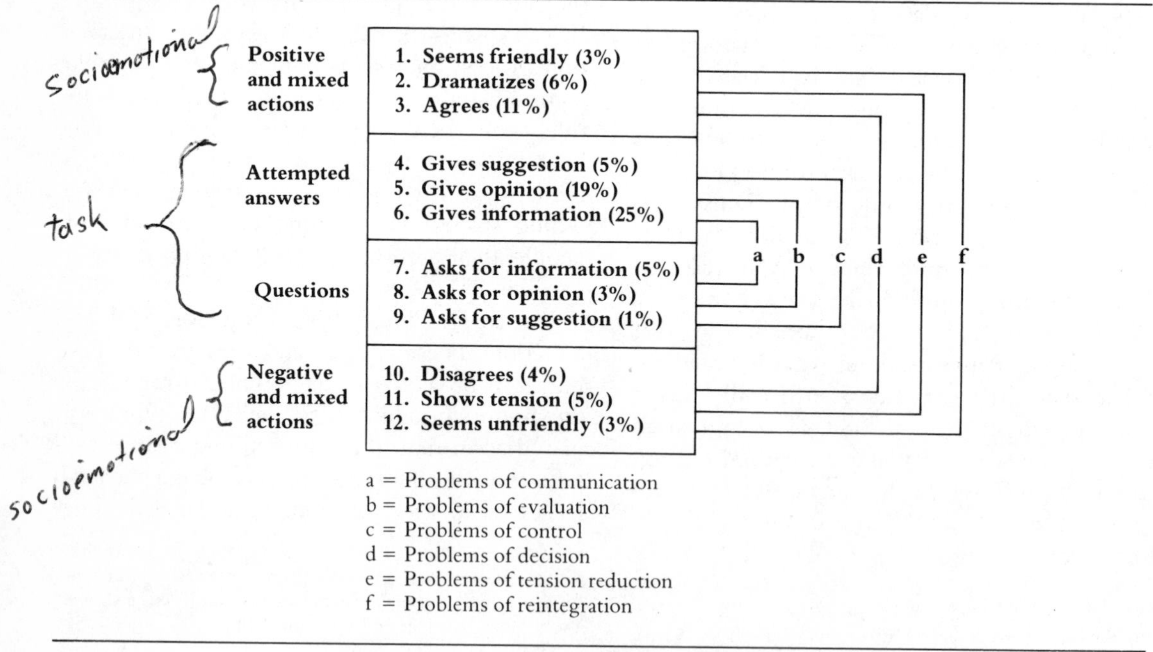

Figure 11.2. Categories for interaction process analysis.

self), the degree of *equalitarianism* expressed (as opposed to individualistic isolationism), and the extent to which the individual supports *conservative group beliefs* (as opposed to rejecting authority). These factors are visualized in a three-dimensional space, as shown in Figure 11.3. The axes of the space are labeled positive-negative, upward-downward, and forward-backward. Bales uses these spatial labels to name the various position types in his theory.

Within a particular group any member can be placed in this three-dimensional space, depending on how the individual's behavior relates to the factors. The direction of an individual's position depends on the quadrant in which that individual appears (for example, UPF); one's position within the quadrant is determined by the degree of each dimension represented. Thus, for example, a UPF could appear at various points in the space, depending on the degree of U, of P, and of F. Table 11.1 lists the behavior types and their value directions. When all of the group's members are plotted on the spatial graph, their interrelationships and networks can be seen. The larger the group, the greater the tendency for subgroups of coalitions to develop. These subgroups consist of individuals with similar value dimensions. Obviously,

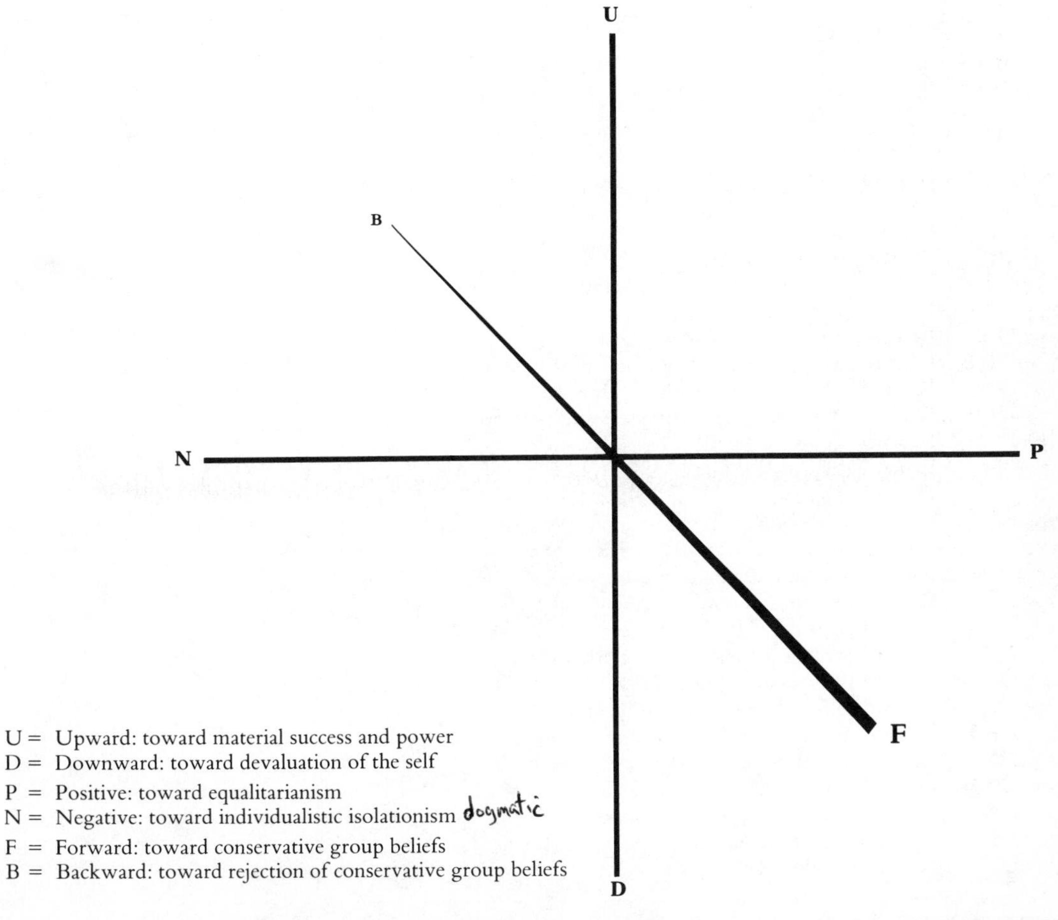

Figure 11.3. A spatial model of interpersonal behavior.

affinity exists between individuals who are close in value dimension and direction, while distant individuals are not connected. Bales describes the typical pattern:

> No self-analytic group so far has shown a completely integrated network of all members. There are normally three or four networks in a group of about twenty-five members, the largest one in the group ranging from about seven to sixteen members, the second largest from five to ten members, the third from three to six members, and the fourth from two to four members. All groups have had some isolates, ranging in number from three to five per group. The isolates are more likely to appear on the thinly populated negative side of the space, but they may appear in any region.[20]

Not only can we predict the coalitions and networks of a group from a knowledge of the distribution of types, but Bales has shown that behavior type is related to the nature of interaction in groups. The interaction that a person initiates and receives depends in part on his or her behavior type. Keep in mind at this point that one's behavior in a group is determined by both personality and role. Table 11.2 shows how interaction is related to value directions.[21]

Bales's theory is valuable in studying small group *communication* because it stresses *interac-*

20. Ibid., p. 47.
21. Ibid., pp. 86–97.

TABLE 11.1
Types of group roles and value directions

Type AVE:	Toward a balanced average of all directions
Type U:	Toward material success and power
Type UP:	Toward social success
Type UPF:	Toward social solidarity and progress
Type UF:	Toward group loyalty and cooperation
Type UNF:	Toward autocratic authority
Type UN:	Toward tough-minded assertiveness
Type UNB:	Toward rugged individualism and gratification
Type UB:	Toward value-relativism and expression
Type UPB:	Toward emotional supportiveness and warmth
Type P:	Toward equalitarianism
Type PF:	Toward altruistic love
Type F:	Toward conservative group beliefs
Type NF:	Toward value-determined restraint
Type N:	Toward individualistic isolationism
Type NB:	Toward rejection of social conformity
Type B:	Toward rejection of conservative group beliefs
Type PB:	Toward permissive liberalism
Type DB:	Toward trust in the goodness of others
Type DPF:	Toward salvation through love
Type DF:	Toward self-knowledge and subjectivity
Type DNF:	Toward self-sacrifice for values
Type DN:	Toward rejection of social success
Type DNB:	Toward failure and withdrawal
Type DB:	Toward withholding of cooperation
Type DBP:	Toward identification with the underprivileged
Type D:	Toward devaluation of the self

tion. He emphasizes the ways people respond to one another verbally. We have seen how the character of interaction is manifest in social and task comments and in value statements. In the next section you will see that the way a group develops—the phases through which it passes—depends greatly on the interactional patterns within the group.

Fisher's Interaction Analysis. B. Aubrey Fisher and his associates have developed a theoretical perspective on group phases and decision emergence that stresses *interaction* and uses a system orientation. Since their theory is communication-oriented and incorporates much material of previous theories, we will study it in some detail. In preview we will look at the general orientation of the interact system model. Next, we will discuss Fisher's scheme for interaction analysis and the phases of decision emergence. We will conclude the section by recapping Fisher's notion of decision and modification. The thrust of this discussion is the process by which groups deal with decision-making tasks.

Often the unit of analysis in group research is the individual's behavior. Fisher and Hawes refer to this as the *human system model*.[22] The human system approach has yielded a number of analyses of individual behavior variables. Many of the findings reported by Shaw, as summarized in the last section, are based on this approach. Clearly Bales's method of analysis, though it is presented as "interaction" analysis, is really a human system approach. It focuses on single acts of individual group participants.

Fisher and Hawes believe that a more sensible approach for the study of group communication is the *interact system model*, in which the basic unit of analysis is not an individual act, but an *interact*. An interact is the verbal or nonverbal act of one person followed by a reaction from another. Here the unit for analysis is a contiguous pair of acts. Fisher and Hawes explore the nature of behavior-response sets. Par-

22. Fisher and Hawes, "An Interact System."

TABLE 11.2
Relationship between interaction and type

CATEGORY	LOW INITIATION	HIGH INITIATION	LOW RECEPTION	HIGH RECEPTION
Seems friendly	N	P	N	P
Dramatizes	DF	UB	NF	PB
Agrees	NB	PF	B	F
Gives suggestion	DB	UF	DN	UP
Gives opinion	B	F	NB	PF
Gives information	U	D	N	P
Asks for information	DN	UP	UF	DB
Asks for opinion	N	P	UP	DN
Asks for suggestion	UB	DF	B	F
Disagrees	P	N	DPB	UNF
Shows tension	UF	DB	DPF	UNB
Seems unfriendly	P	N	DPB	UNF

ticularly, they have observed that interacts seem to be organized over time in a hierarchical fashion. Three levels are defined.

The first level involves *interact categories*. These are the specific classes or types of interacts observed in groups. For example, an asserted interpretation of a proposal might be followed by a comment seeking clarification of the proposal. Over the entire discussion the frequency of such interact categories would be studied to determine how they tend to group into *interact phases*, the second level of analysis. A study of interact phases reveals the pattern of development in the group as it progresses toward task accomplishment. The third level of analysis is *cycles*. As the group proceeds through a number of tasks, the phases repeat themselves in cyclical fashion.

Let's take a closer look at Fisher's method of interaction analysis. Fisher concentrates on interacts in groups. In other words, he looks at pairs of contiguous acts. What his system classifies is an act and its response. Interacts can be classified on two dimensions, the content dimension and the relationship dimension. This conceptualization is similar to that of the relational theories summarized in Chapter 9. You may recall that these theorists state that all communication messages have a content or information dimension and a relationship or metacommunication dimension. While a person is making a statement, the individual is also reflecting on the relationship in some way. The most common scheme for understanding relational messages, and Fisher follows suit here, is the three-fold analysis of one-up, one-down, and one-across messages. In interaction analysis group members would be observed in terms of their complementary (for example, one-up, one-down), symmetrical (for example, one-up, one-up), and transitional (for example, one-up, one-across) responses. (You may find it useful at this point to review relational theory from Chapter 9.)

Despite the potential utility of an interaction analysis of the relational dimension in groups, Fisher has concentrated on the content dimension. Following the hypothesis that almost all comments in a task group are related in one way or another to a *decision proposal*, Fisher classifies statements in terms of how they respond to a decision proposal. The following outline is his classification scheme:[23]

1. Interpretation
   - f. Favorable toward the decision proposal
   - u. Unfavorable toward the decision proposal
   - ab. Ambiguous toward the decision proposal, containing a bivalued (both favorable and unfavorable) evaluation
   - an. Ambiguous toward the decision proposal, containing a neutral evaluation
2. Substantiation
   - f. Favorable toward the decision proposal
   - u. Unfavorable toward the decision proposal
   - ab. Ambiguous toward the decision proposal, containing a bivalued (both favorable and unfavorable) evaluation
   - an. Ambiguous toward the decision proposal, containing a neutral evaluation
3. Clarification
4. Modification
5. Agreement
6. Disagreement

Two essential differences exist between Bales's and Fisher's theories. First, Bales classifies a given act strictly in terms of its task or socioemotional function. Fisher assumes that any given act may fulfill either or both functions simultaneously. (Actually, Fisher finds it more appropriate to look at the content and relational dimensions of acts, although these divisions may in some ways be close to Bales's task and socioemotional categories.) Second, Bales classifies only single acts, while Fisher classifies interacts. In observing a group, Fisher will create a matrix with twelve rows and twelve columns, corresponding to the twelve categories in his system. This matrix thus contains 144 cells, one for each potential type of interact. In other words the observer will clas-

23. B. Aubrey Fisher, *Small Group Decision Making: Communication and the Group Process* (New York: McGraw-Hill, 1980), p. 117.

sify the first act and the second act, placing a mark in the appropriate cell between the two. In this way the researcher can actually see the character and frequency of act pairs in a group discussion. Fisher believes this kind of data is useful for understanding how groups function, how decisions are made, and how groups pass through phases as decisions emerge. For our purposes this approach is exciting because it focuses directly and completely on *interpersonal communication* as no other group theory does.

In his theory of decision emergence, Fisher outlines four phases through which task groups tend to proceed: orientation, conflict, emergence, and reinforcement.[24] In observing the distribution of interacts across these phases, Fisher notes the ways interaction changes as the group decision formulates and solidifies. The *orientation phase* involves getting acquainted, clarifying, and beginning to express points of view. A high level of agreement characterizes this stage, and comments are often designed to test the group. Thus positions expressed are both qualified and tentative. In this phase people grope for direction and interpersonal understanding. The following excerpt from a jury deliberation in a mock trial illustrates many orientational qualities. The trial involves an auto-pedestrian accident.

A: First of all, we decide whether it's a case of liability or negligence.
B: Yeah, . . . negligence.
A: It's the same thing. In other words, you all feel that Roger Adams alone was negligent without the contributory negligence of Derby—or was it Derby's fault as much as Adam's fault—or was it either's fault—or was it just plain accident.
C: Guilty or not guilty.
A: It's not just those two choices, though. We've got three choices.
D: What else can there be, though? I mean. . . .
A: It's not a criminal action like whether he robbed a store. It's just whether he is negligent, both of them are negligent, or whether. . . .
D: Yeah, I see. But there are still only two verdicts. Do we give the plaintiff any money or not?
A: First of all, how many people here feel that just Roger Adams alone was negligent and that Alfred Derby, the person who was hit, in no way contributed to this negligence and therefore should receive compensation?[25]

The *conflict* phase includes a great deal of dissent. People in this second phase begin to solidify their attitudes, and much polarization results. The interacts in this phase tend to include more disagreement and unfavorable evaluation. As an observer you would notice that members argue and attempt to persuade at this point. Members also tend to form coalitions in the conflict phase. As people group together according to their common stands on the issues, polarization grows. Observe the nature of the interaction in the following excerpt:

A: The thing to decide is: Was Roger Adams in a hurry and did he act in such a manner that a reasonable, adult, mature person would?
C. You have to consider him a reasonable, prudent person. He was waved on by another person who was going to make the turn, regardless of whether he was in a hurry or not.
A: I would say that if he is reasonable, he wouldn't take another person's word for it.
C: Oh, come on now! There is only one car on the street.
A: I certainly wouldn't do it.
C: Do you consider yourself reasonable?
A: I'm not reasonable. I'll admit it, too. But what does that have to do with it? I wouldn't want to use myself as an example. That doesn't say that he wasn't reasonable.
B: Then we're not going to get any place. You have to give some criteria. You can't just say he wasn't reasonable and let it go at that.[26]

These coalitions tend to disappear in the third phase. In the *emergence* phase the first inklings of cooperation begin to show. People are less tenacious in defending their viewpoints. As they soften their positions and undergo attitude change, ambiguity becomes apparent in their interaction. Comments are more equivocal as ambiguity functions to mediate the attitude

24. B. Aubrey Fisher, "Decision Emergence: Phases in Group Decision Making," *Speech Monographs* 37 (1970): 53–66; Fisher, *Decision Making*.

25. Fisher, *Decision Making*, p. 298.

26. Ibid., p. 300.

shifts the members are going through. The number of favorable comments increases until a group decision begins to emerge. The ambiguity characterizing this phase can be seen in the following excerpt:

A: Let me ask one more question. Do you think Derby (the plaintiff) was in the crosswalk?
D: I don't think so.
C: No, I don't. I don't think that has too much to do with it, though.
D: I agree.
C: I know there are some statutes about the crosswalk, but I mean the fact that he was in . . . I don't know. That might be kind of important.
D: He was on the roadway is really the issue.
C: I don't think it really happened exactly the way the defendant described it. I think he embellished it a little toward his side. I think it happened close enough to it, though.
F: As far as that goes, Derby may have his own story too. I mean each would be looking out for himself. That's only natural.
D: Of course you are going to get this in any situation.
F: That's just it. Both of them. You can't use the two prime subjects. You have to try and go on the witnesses. Of course they are witnesses, too, and you have to consider them. And they are important, too, but . . .[27]

In the final phase, *reinforcement*, the group decision solidifies and receives reinforcement from group members. The group unifies, standing behind its solution. Comments are almost uniformly positive and favorable, and more interaction occurs on matters of interpretation. The ambiguity that marked the third phase tends to disappear. The following excerpt illustrates the interaction typical of phase four:

E: Everybody saw the car coming.
B: Besides that, he said his lights were on.
C: His turn signal was on. It was obvious that he was coming. That would make it all the more easier to see the car coming.
D: Practically everybody saw that car coming. His lights turning.
E: That guy that was on the sidewalk. . . . He saw all this traffic, and he also saw Adams coming. That's why he didn't go. Why did Derby go? He has to be at some fault.
C: I feel sorry for him, and I'd like to help him out, but I just don't think I can.
D: I agree.
B: You can't base it on an emotion . . .
D: Of course not.
C: I don't think we should take into any account what they told us at the beginning, either—about Adams being a drunkard and that.
B: No. Don't even mention that.
F: No. Don't worry about it.
C: No.[28]

Fisher shows us in the preceding analysis that groups go through phases of development in their decision-making interaction. These phases characterize the nature of interaction as it changes over time. An important related topic is that of *decision modification*.[29] Fisher finds that groups typically do not introduce a single solution and pursue that solution until all members agree. Nor do they introduce a single proposal and continue to modify it until consensus is reached. Rarely is parliamentary format the typical pattern in small group discussion. Fisher theorizes on the basis of his group observations that decision modification is cyclical; several proposals are made, each discussed briefly, and certain of them reintroduced at a later time. Discussion of proposals seems therefore to proceed in spurts of energy. Proposal A will be introduced and discussed. Suddenly the group will drop this idea and move to proposal B. After discussing this, the group may introduce and discuss other proposals. Then someone will revive proposal A, perhaps in modified form. The group finally will settle on a modified plan that was introduced earlier in the discussion in a different form.

Why does discussion usually proceed in such an erratic fashion? Probably because the interpersonal demands of discussion require "breaks" from task work. In effect the attention span of a group is short because of the intense nature of group work. Such an explanation

27. Ibid., pp. 303–4.

28. Ibid., p. 306.

29. Ibid.; also B. Aubrey Fisher, "The Process of Decision Modification in Small Discussion Groups," *Journal of Communication* 20 (1970): 51–64.

suggests that "flight" behavior helps manage tension and conflict. The group's need to work on interpersonal dynamics is supported by other theories as well, including Collins and Guetzkow's ideas on interpersonal barriers and Bales's notion of socioemotional (versus task) interaction.

Fisher finds that in modifying proposals, groups tend to follow one of two patterns. If conflict is low, the group will reintroduce proposals in less abstract, more specific language. For example, in a discussion of a public health nursing conference, an original idea to begin "with a non-threatening something" was modified to "begin with a history of the contributions which public health has made to the field of nursing."[30] A group, as it successively returns to a proposal, seems to follow the pattern of stating the problem, discussing criteria for solution, introducing an abstract solution, and moving finally to a concrete solution. Keep in mind, however, that the group most likely will not move through these four steps with continuity. Rather, it will deal sporadically with these themes as members depart from and return to the proposal in a stop-and-start fashion.

The second typical pattern of modification occurs when conflict is higher. Here the group does not attempt to make a proposal more specific. Because disagreement exists on the very nature of the proposal, the group introduces substitute proposals of the same level of abstraction as the original. In the first pattern, which involves making proposals more specific, the group task seems to be one of mutual discovery of the best specific implementation of a general idea. In this social conflict pattern the task is more of debate and persuasion among various alternative proposals.

Criticism: In general Bales's and Fisher's theories share a common strength and a common weakness. The strength is that interaction analysis, whether of the Bales or Fisher type, allows us to look carefully at the communication behavior of groups, correlating interpersonal messages with other group factors. In other words interaction analysis provides a way to analyze group communication. Thus these theories are both appropriate and heuristic. These advantages, however, have been gained at the price of a trade-off, which leads to their common weakness. When individual acts (or interacts) are analyzed according to a classification scheme, rich idiosyncratic meanings are glossed over. The value of understanding general group trends is bought at the price of depth understanding of particular events in groups.[31]

Bales's theory is an excellent beginning for understanding interaction in groups. His theory is highly parsimonious and internally consistent. It is built on a sensible and intuitively appealing conceptual base, from which a number of propositions about group interaction are derived. The theory's heuristic value is evidenced by the numerous studies based on the Bales categories, including Bales's own research over a twenty-year period at Harvard University.

Bales's system has been criticized for two weaknesses. First the theory is strictly act oriented. In other words it fails to describe interaction response. It presumes that any statement will stand on its own apart from contiguous statements by other people. Fisher, in contrast, shows how analyses that stop at the act level are not adequate. The second problem of Bales's system is that it separates the task and socioemotional areas of group discussion. Careful examination of groups in action shows that task and socioemotional functions are thoroughly mixed. One can fulfill both task and social functions in a single statement, and in classifying group behavior it is difficult to validly separate these functions. True, a given statement may be mostly task, or mostly social, but to separate them completely would be a mistake. Consequently Bales envisions the group as a body that swings between discussion of task matters to discussion of social matters, back and forth.

30. Fisher, *Decision Making*, p. 155.

31. Ibid., p. 322.

Fisher, on the other hand, finds that groups do not operate in this way. Such criticism casts doubt on the validity of Bales's approach.

Fisher takes a major step toward correcting these problems, but his theory too has weaknesses. Although Fisher's theory admits to the existence of the relational dimension of interaction, it makes no attempt to correlate the content and relational aspects of group discussion. Its second weakness is related to the first. Fisher's method does not accommodate nonverbal elements of messages. (Bales's method shares this weakness.) Consequently many of the most central aspects of relational messages are ignored. Anyone who has participated in a group discussion knows that the nonverbal element is a powerful form of communication, both of content and relational dimensions. To be fair, of course, we must note how difficult it would be to accurately code nonverbal interaction, which undoubtedly is the reason Fisher has not attempted to do so.

Theories of Interpersonal Effects in Groups

The theories discussed so far in this chapter present a variety of factors interacting to create an interpersonal dynamic in group communication. These factors include roles, norms, interaction patterns, phases, and others. We will now consider two theories that concentrate on the nature of interpersonal effects in groups and integrate much of what already has been discussed. The first is Cattell's theory of group syntality, and the second is Janis's groupthink hypothesis. Both theories attempt an answer to the question: What is the outcome of interpersonal communication in groups? Cattell offers a general answer, while Janis suggests a specific negative effect.

Cattell's Theory of Group Syntality. Raymond Cattell's theory of group syntality (group personality) has been influential in the history of group dynamics.[32] He suggests three defining aspects or *panels* for group description: syntality traits, internal structure, and population traits. While personality describes the predictable behavior of an individual, *syntality* is the predictable pattern of group behavior. Thus a group may appear aggressive, efficient, isolated, energetic, reliable. The second panel, *internal structure*, is defined in terms of the interpersonal relations among the group members. Such characteristics may deal with status structure, internal subgroupings, modes of government, and patterns of communication. The third panel is *population traits*, the traits of a group's individual members. In defining a group's population traits, you would discuss the modal or typical characteristics, including intelligence, attitudes, and so forth.

These three panels are interrelated; syntality is a function of population traits and internal structure. This notion reinforces points made by Lewin about the interrelationships between the group and the individual. The theory as a whole can be summarized as follows: People with individual personalities and traits come together to achieve their goals more efficiently. In so doing, they commit their energies to achieving group tasks and to maintaining the group. What the group accomplishes is a direct function of the amount of energy invested by the separate members. The total group effect is a result of its energy input and output. Let us look more closely at these relationships.

The key concept in group effect is *synergy*. Group synergy is the total energy input of the members. However, much of the energy put into a group does not directly support its goals. Because of interpersonal demands, energy must be expended to maintain relationships and overcome interpersonal barriers. *Effective synergy* is the group energy remaining after *intrinsic* or *group maintenance synergy* is subtracted. While such intrinsic energy is productive in the sense that it works toward group cohesiveness, it does not contribute directly to task accomplishment.[33]

32. Raymond Cattell, "Concepts and Methods in the Measurement of Group Syntality," *Psychological Review* 55 (1948): 48–63.

33. This discussion helps us better understand Collins and

The synergy of a group results from the attitudes of the members toward the group. To the extent that members have different attitudes toward the group and its operations, conflict will result, increasing the proportion of energy needed for group maintenance. Thus the more that individuals possess similar attitudes, the less the need for intrinsic investment, and the greater the effective synergy.

Let's use a simplified example to see how Cattell's theory explains real events. Suppose that in forming a study group, you discover that the members have varying attitudes toward the subject matter and differing manners of study. In your meetings you argue a lot about how to organize your efforts and how to learn the material. Much time and energy is spent working out these interpersonal problems. This is your intrinsic synergy. Now, after getting your test grade back, if you sense that the study group failed to achieve the goal of mutual benefit, you will withdraw your energy and join another group or study alone. In this case the effective synergy of the group was so low that it did not accomplish more than you could have accomplished yourself. Next suppose that you join another group. This group agrees immediately on how to proceed and gets down to work. Since there are few interpersonal barriers to overcome, the group is cohesive. The effective synergy is high, and everyone does better on the examination than they would have done had they studied alone.

Janis's Groupthink Theory. Cattell's theory gives us one kind of answer to the question of interpersonal effects in groups. The groupthink hypothesis of Irving Janis is much different.[34] Janis examines in some detail the adequacy of decisions made by groups. He shows how certain conditions can lead to high group satisfaction but ineffective output. Janis's ideas give us a more concrete explanation of synergistic factors, and at the same time they demonstrate how actual practice may vary from predictions made by syntality theory.

Unlike the other theories presented in this chapter, Janis's theory is normative and applied. It is normative in that it provides a base for diagnosing problems and remediating weaknesses in group performance; it is applied to actual political groups. Janis has relied heavily on social-psychological research on group dynamics, integrating concepts such as cohesiveness in explaining actual observed group practices. Janis describes groupthink: "I use the term groupthink as a quick and easy way to refer to a mode of thinking that people engage in when they are deeply involved in a cohesive in-group, when members' strivings for unanimity override their motivation to realistically appraise alternative courses of action. . . . The invidiousness is intentional: Groupthink refers to a deterioration of mental efficiency, reality testing, and moral judgment that results from in-group pressures."[35]

Janis's approach is intriguing. He uses historical data to support his theory by analyzing six political decision-making episodes in which outcomes were either good or bad, depending on the extent of groupthink.[36] These interesting historical analyses once again illustrate how communication theory may be generated in a variety of arenas. One of the finest qualities of Janis's approach is that his theory involves small group communication at the interface of psychology, political science, and history.

Groupthink can have six negative outcomes:

1. The group limits its discussion to only a few alternatives. It does not consider a full range of creative possibilities.

2. The position initially favored by most

Guetzkow's idea of assembly effects and Thibaut and Kelley's conception of costs and rewards.

34. Irving Janis, *Victims of Groupthink: A Psychological Study of Foreign Decisions and Fiascos* (Boston: Houghton Mifflin, 1967).

35. Ibid., p. 9.

36. These include the Bay of Pigs, the Korean War, Pearl Harbor, and the escalation of the Vietnam War, as negative examples. Positive examples include the Cuban Missile Crisis and the Marshall Plan.

members is never restudied to seek out less obvious pitfalls.

3. The group fails to reexamine those alternatives originally disfavored by the majority.

4. Expert opinion is not sought.

5. The group is highly selective in gathering and attending to available information.

6. The group is so confident in its chosen alternative that it does not consider contingency plans.

Janis maintains that groupthink is marked by a number of symptoms. The first symptom of groupthink is an *illusion of invulnerability*, which creates an undue air of optimism. Second, the group creates *collective efforts to rationalize* the course of action decided on. Third, the group maintains an *unquestioned belief in the group's inherent morality*, leading to a soft pedaling of ethical or moral consequences. Out-group leaders are *stereotyped* as evil, weak, or stupid. In addition direct *pressure* is exerted on members not to express counteropinions. Dissent is quickly squelched. This leads to the sixth symptom, the *self-censorship* of deviations. Thus there is a shared *illusion of unanimity* within the group. Finally, groupthink involves the emergence of *self-appointed mindguards* to protect the group and its leader from adverse opinion and unwanted information. The mindguard typically suppresses negative information by counseling participants not to "rock the boat."

Groupthink is a direct result of cohesiveness in groups. Most small group research and theory indicate that cohesiveness is functional in group performance. Lewin writes that cohesiveness is a reflection of the degree to which all group members share common goals and values. According to Cattell, the amount of effective synergy in groups results from cohesiveness, since cohesive groups need expend little intrinsic synergy. Although Janis does not deny the value of cohesiveness in decision-making groups, he shows how highly cohesive groups may still invest a lot of energy on maintaining goodwill in the group to the detriment of decision making.

The element that can make cohesiveness negative is the person's need to maintain self-esteem. Such rewards as friendship, prestige, and mutually recognized competence are received in highly cohesive groups. With such rewards at stake, it is not surprising that group members invest intrinsic synergy to maintain solidarity. The doubts or uncertainties that arise may lead to an undermining of group confidence and hence of individual members' self-esteem. Janis summarizes the problem as follows: "The greater the threats to the self-esteem of members of a cohesive decision-making body, the greater will be their inclination to resort to concurrence-seeking at the expense of critical thinking. If this explanatory hypothesis is correct, symptoms of groupthink will be found most often when a decision poses a moral dilemma, especially if the most advantageous course of action requires the policy-makers to violate their own standards of humanitarian behavior."[37]

Thus cohesiveness is a necessary but not sufficient condition for groupthink. Under conditions of low cohesiveness, factors may be present that prevent the illusion of unanimity. The natural conflict in noncohesive groups leads to much debate and consideration of all sides of an issue. Unfortunately such conflict is itself dysfunctional in decision making, as several theorists have pointed out. The amount of synergy absorbed by conflict significantly reduces group output.

What is the answer to this dilemma? Janis believes that decision-making groups need to recognize the dangers of groupthink. He suggests steps to prevent groupthink:

1. The leader of a policy-forming group should assign the role of critical evaluator to each member, encouraging the group to give high priority to airing objections and doubts.

2. The leaders in an organization's hierarchy, when assigning a policy-planning mission to a group,

37. Janis, *Groupthink*, p. 206.

should be impartial instead of stating preferences and expectations at the outset.

3. The organization should routinely follow the administrative practice of setting up several independent policy-planning and evaluation groups to work on the same policy question, each carrying out its deliberations under a different leader.

4. Throughout the period when the feasibility and effectiveness of policy alternatives are being surveyed, the policy-making group should from time to time divide into two or more subgroups to meet separately, under different chairmen, and then come together to hammer out their differences.

5. Each member of the policy-making group should discuss periodically the group's deliberations with trusted associates in his own unit of the organization and report back their [sic] reactions.

6. One or more outside experts or qualified colleagues within the organization who are not core members of the policy-making group should be invited to each meeting on a staggered basis and should be encouraged to challenge the views of the core members.

7. At every meeting devoted to evaluating policy alternatives, at least one member should be assigned the role of devil's advocate.

8. Whenever the policy issue involves relations with a rival nation or organization, a sizable bloc [sic] of time (perhaps an entire session) should be spent surveying all warning signals from rivals and constructing alternative scenarios of the rivals' intentions.

9. After reaching a preliminary consensus about what seems to be the best policy alternative, the policy-making group should hold a "second-chance" meeting at which every member is expected to express as vividly as he can all his residual doubts and to rethink the entire issue before making a definitive choice.[38]

After our review of several basic theories of small group communication, Janis's applied and prescriptive theory may seem out of place, yet it is not. This groupthink theory involves in a practical setting some of the important concepts from previous research and theory. It demonstrates the viability of group dynamics. In addition, it provides new understandings in its own right. Janis's approach is valuable because, like Lewin's theory, it provides a multidisciplinary view.

38. Ibid., pp. 209–19.

Criticism. The value of Cattell's theory is that it presents a basic idea, synergy, that is useful in understanding groups. Although Cattell does not develop this idea of group energy to any appreciable degree, it has been applied repeatedly and developed in detail in the group dynamics literature summarized earlier. Janis's groupthink theory, in fact, is nothing more than application of the synergy notion. The problem with Cattell's representation of synergy is that it implies that intrinsic synergy is bad and that the more effective the synergy in a group, the better the group's output will be. Clearly Janis's work shows that this is not the case. The thrust of Janis's hypothesis is that in highly cohesive groups where intrinsic synergy is low, group output may in fact be inadequate. Groupthink occurs precisely because not enough conflict (intrinsic energy) is present in the group.

Janis's theory is appealing. It stems not only from laboratory research but from field application and historical case study as well.[39] It is a theory that demonstrates the utility of group dynamics ideas in understanding actual groups at work. As we have seen repeatedly in this book, one of the failings of most communication theories is that they are based on limited perspectives or on limited types of research. Theories such as Janis's are like a breath of fresh air in this regard.

Janis's theory is different also because of its applied nature. It is a normative, or prescriptive theory, providing guidelines for improved group functioning. However, this aspect of the theory leads to one of its weaknesses, namely, that it does not take us very far in understanding or explaining how groups function. It suggests a way of guarding against one particular danger in groups, but it does not help us understand the nature of cohesiveness, conflict, roles, or communication. For this reason some scholars would be reluctant to call Janis's work

39. For a laboratory test of the groupthink hypothesis, see John A. Courtright, "A Laboratory Investigation of Groupthink," *Communication Monographs* 45 (1978): 229–246.

a theory at all. Janis himself refers to this application merely as a hypothesis.

The groupthink hypothesis appears to have validity. Not only is it internally consistent in terms of congruence with other known aspects of groups, but its external validity, established through application to actual cases and laboratory test, also appears to be high. On the negative side the theory is somewhat narrow in scope and is not heuristic in producing a range of research ideas.

Theories of Organizational Communication

According to sociologist Amatai Etzioni: "Our society is an organizational society. We are born in organizations, educated in organizations, and most of us spend much of our lives working for organizations. We spend much of our leisure time playing and praying in organizations. Most of us will die in an organization, and when the time comes for burial, the largest organization of all—the state—must grant official permission."[40]

We know that a great deal of communication takes place in the context of the organization. A large body of literature and theory has been written about human communication in organizations. In our search to understand the communication process, it is important for us to browse along the way in the area of organization theory.

Bernard Berelson and Gary Steiner outline four characteristics of an organization that distinguish it from other social groupings.[41] The first is *formality*. The typical organization has a set of goals, policies, procedures, and regulations that give it form. The second quality of organizations is *hierarchy*, typically expressed in terms of pyramidal structure. Third, organizations tend to consist of *many people*, "enough so that close personal relations among all are impossible."[42] Fourth, organizations usually last longer than a human lifetime.

The second definition of organization is George Strother's. According to Strother, organizations consist of two or more people involved in a cooperative relationship, which implies that they have collective goals. The members of the organization differ in terms of function, and they maintain a stable hierarchical structure. Strother also recognizes that the organization exists within an environment or milieu.[43]

Organizations may be viewed from many perspectives, only one of which is the communication perspective. Many theories and much of the literature on organizations ignore this aspect, but some of the writing both recognizes the importance of communication and covers it in detail. University departments of business and speech communication reflect this concern in their curricula. A survey on organizational communication indicates that a large portion of speech communication graduate programs offers courses in organizational communication stressing theory, research, and application.[44]

In this section we will survey some important theories of human organization, emphasizing their contributions to our understanding of interpersonal communication. Most reviewers divide this theory into three broad groups.[45] The first, *classical theory*, rests on assumptions that organizational members are instruments of management or, more broadly, of the bureaucracy. Classical theories attempt to answer questions such as the following: "How is the work divided? How is the labor force divided? How many levels of authority and control

40. Amatai Etzioni, *Modern Organizations* (Englewood Cliffs, N.J.: Prentice-Hall, 1964), p. 1.

41. Bernard Berelson and Gary Steiner, *Human Behavior: An Inventory of Scientific Findings* (New York: Harcourt, Brace, 1964), p. 364.

42. Ibid.

43. George B. Strother, "Problems in the Development of a Social Science of Organization," in *The Social Science of Organizations: Four Perspectives*, ed. H. J. Leavitt (Englewood Cliffs, N.J.: Prentice-Hall, 1963), p. 23.

44. Gerald Goldhaber, *Organizational Communication* (Dubuque, Iowa: William C. Brown, 1974), p. 8.

45. Ibid., p. 24. See also James March and Herbert Simon, *Organizations* (New York: John Wiley & Sons, 1958), p. 6.

exist? How many people exist at each level? What are the specific job functions of each person?"[46] One of the weaknesses of classical theory is that it deals little with communication. For this reason we will look at it only briefly, focusing on the most prominent and pertinent of the classical approaches, Weber's theory of bureaucracy.

The second school of thought on organizational communication is usually termed *human relations*. It rests on propositions asserting that people's attitudes, values, and personal needs are all important. Fundamental human relations questions include: "What roles do people assume in the organization? What status relationships exist as a result of various roles? What is the morale and attitude of the people? What social and psychological needs exist for the people? What informal groups exist within the organization?"[47]

A third branch of thought in organizational theory may be called the *social systems* school. This group of theories, which assumes that organizations are based on decision making and problem solving, tends to answer the following kinds of questions: "What are the key parts of the organization? How do they relate interdependently to each other? What processes in the organization facilitate these interdependent relationships? What are the main goals of the organization? What is the relationship between the organization and its environment?"[48] The systems approach is the most popular perspective for viewing organizations. Here we summarize two important system theories of organizations that emphasize communication as the basis for system relationships.

Weber's Classical Bureaucratic Theory

Certainly Max Weber was one of the most prominent sociology and economics theorists of all time. In his lifetime, from 1864 to 1930, he produced a quantity of work on the nature of human institutions. One of the areas for which he is best known is his theory of bureaucracy. This theory is part of a larger work found in *The Theory of Social and Economic Organization*, edited by Talcott Parsons.[49] Weber's concepts form the heart of what is commonly known as structuralism. These ideas, developed at the beginning of the century, relate to the early classical theory of organization.

Weber defines organization as follows: "An 'organization' is a system of continuous, purposive activity of a specified kind. A 'corporate organization' is an associative social relationship characterized by an administrative staff devoted to such continuous purposive activity."[50] A central part of Weber's theory of bureaucracy is his concepts of power, authority, and legitimacy. For Weber power is the ability of a person in any social relationship to influence others and to overcome resistance. Power in this sense is fundamental to most social relationships. When power is legitimate, compliance is effective and complete. Etzioni summarizes this concept: "Weber's study of legitimation introduces a whole new dimension to the study of organizational discipline. He used *power* to refer to the ability to induce acceptance or orders; *legitimation* to refer to the acceptance of the exercise of power because it is in line with values held by the subjects; and authority to refer to the combination of the two—i.e., to power that is viewed as legitimate."[51] This idea of legitimate

46. Goldhaber, *Organizational Communication*, p. 7.

47. Ibid.

48. Ibid.

49. Max Weber, *The Theory of Social and Economic Organizations*, trans. A. M. Henderson and Talcott Parsons (New York: Oxford University Press, 1947). A lengthy interpretation and discussion of Weber's theory can be found in Parson's introduction to the above book. Other secondary sources include: Strother, "Problems"; Dwight Waldo, "Organizational Theory: An Elephantine Problem," *General Systems* 7 (1962): 247–60; March and Simon, *Organizations;* Etzioni, *Modern Organizations*; Reinhard Bendix, *Max Weber: An Intellectual Portrait* (Garden City, N.Y.: Doubleday, 1962); Julien Freund, *The Sociology of Max Weber* (New York: Pantheon Books, 1968). For a more complete bibliography of primary and secondary sources on Weber, see S. N. Eisenstadt, *Max Weber on Charisma and Institution Building* (Chicago: University of Chicago Press, 1968).

50. Weber, *Social and Economic Organizations*, p. 151.

51. Etzioni, *Modern Organizations*, p. 51.

power is a central communication concern. Whether communications will be accepted in an organization hinges on the degree to which the superior has legitimate authority.

Weber outlines three types of authority.[52] The first is *traditional authority.* Traditional authority occurs when orders of the superior are perceived as justified by tradition. One's power is seen as legitimate because "it has always been legitimate." The second form of authority is *bureaucratic* or *rational-legal authority.* This form is most relevant in bureaucracies. The authorities in a bureaucracy derive their power from the bureaucracy's rules, which govern and are accepted by all organization members. Weber sees bureaucracy as the most efficient pattern for mass administration: "Experience tends to show that the purely bureaucratic type of administrative organization—that is, the monocratic variety of bureaucracy—is, from a purely technical point of view, capable of attaining the highest degree of efficiency and is in this sense formally the most rational known means of carrying out imperative control over human beings. It is superior to any other form in precision, in stability, in the stringency of its discipline, and in its reliability."[53]

Weber's view of bureaucracy rests on a number of well-defined principles.[54] First, bureaucracy is based on rules. Such rules allow the solution of problems, standardization, and equality in the organization. Second, bureaucracies are based on the concept of *sphere of competence.* Thus there is a systematic division of labor, each role having clearly defined rights and powers. Third, the essence of bureaucracy is hierarchy. Fourth, administrators are appointed on the basis of their knowledge and training. They are not generally elected, nor do they inherit their positions. Fifth, the members of the bureaucracy must not share in the ownership of the organization. Sixth, bureaucrats must be free to allocate resources within their realms of influence without fear of outside infringement. Seventh, a bureaucracy requires carefully maintained records. This final criterion is important in terms of communication. Weber puts it this way: "Administrative acts, decisions, and rules are formulated and recorded in writing, even in cases where oral discussion is the rule or is even mandatory. This applies to preliminary discussions and proposals, to final decisions, and to all sorts of orders and rules. The combination of written documents and a continuous organization of official functions constitutes the 'office' which is the central focus of all types of modern corporate action."[55]

Another feature of a bureaucracy is that it is usually headed by a nonbureaucrat. Nonbureaucratic heads are often elected or inherit their positions. They include presidents, cabinets, boards of trustees, and kings. Bureaucrats are dispensable; they may be replaced by similarly trained individuals, but the succession of the nonbureaucratic head may well be a crisis, precipitating innovation and change.

The first two types of authority are traditional and bureaucratic forms. The third is *charismatic authority.* Under this type of authority, power is justified through the charismatic nature of the superior individual's personality. Unlike bureaucratic authority charisma defies order and routine. The charismatic leader is revolutionary and establishes authority in opposition to the traditions of the day. One's leadership as a prophet or demagogue comes about through the demonstration of magical powers and heroism. Weber does not have much faith in this kind of mass persuasion.

Criticism. Weber's theory is included here primarily as a general backdrop for other theories to come. In this regard it serves two functions. First, it provides a "classical" or

52. Weber, *Social and Economic Organizations*, pp. 330–32.

53. Ibid., p. 337.

54. Ibid., pp. 330–34. See also Etzioni, *Modern Organizations*, pp. 53–54.

55. Weber, *Social and Economic Organizations*, p. 332.

standard picture with which the other theories can be contrasted. Second, it presents the common traditional view of organizations, relating the essence of the classical notion of organizations. Notice that communication and human behavior are downplayed in the theory; the thrust is structure and task factors. For our purposes this facet is the theory's greatest weakness. The theory gives implicit ideas of what communication is like in organizations, but communication is not treated as an explanatory variable, nor is it seen as the essence of organizational life. As the upcoming sections will indicate, this failure is significant.

Like most other classical treatments, Weber's theory is prescriptive or normative. It does not explain how or why organizations operate the way they do. Hence we do not get an adequate idea of how organizations operate. While the claims of classical theories have some validity, the philosophical appropriateness of the assumptions of these theories is not adequate, nor is their heuristic value high.

Precisely because of the failure of classical theory to deal with communication in a central way, the human relations movement began in the 1930s.

Human Relations School

The human relations school of organization theory developed partially as a reaction to the sterile classical theories and partially as a reaction to the depression of the 1930s. World War II pushed the movement onward, and by the mid-1940s it had become very popular. Human relations theory originated with the Hawthorne studies, which received considerable attention in the 1920s and 1930s.[56] These extensive studies were directed by F. J. Roethlisberger, a Harvard industrial psychologist, and R. Dickson, a Western Electric manager. Elton Mayo of the Harvard Business School later acted as a consultant. Under the direction of this team, some three hundred interviewers talked with Western Electric employees about their problems and perceptions. These original interviews led to additional research on group functioning. *Management and the Worker* was published as a summary of the Hawthorne work.[57] Because of his impact on the beginnings of human relations, Elton Mayo is considered the founder of the movement. Kurt Lewin is also an important early contributor.

Charles Perrow describes two general branches in the human relations movement.[58] The first deals primarily with leadership in organizations. The thesis of the leadership school is that leadership facilitates morale, which in turn leads to increased productivity. One of the most important manifestations of this branch is leadership training and T-groups (training groups). The second branch of the human relations movement is more general, dealing with organizational climate as a whole. Again, productivity and worker welfare are stressed. Etzioni points out that "above all, the Human Relations School . . . emphasized the role of communication, participation, and leadership."[59]

The basic tenets of human relations include the following: First, productivity is determined by social norms, not physiological factors. Second, noneconomic rewards are all important in motivating workers. Third, workers usually react as group members rather than individuals. Fourth, leadership is extremely important and involves both formal and informal aspects. Fifth, human relationists stress communication as the most important facilitator of shared decision making.[60]

Argyris and Interpersonal Competence. The reaction of this school against classical theory is

56. For an excellent brief description of the Hawthorne studies, see Charles Perrow, *Complex Organizations: A Critical Essay* (Glenview, Ill.: Scott, Foresman, 1972), p. 97.

57. F. Roethlisberger and W. Dickson, *Management and the Worker* (Cambridge: Harvard University Press, 1939).

58. Perrow, *Complex Organizations,* p. 97.

59. Etzioni, *Modern Organizations,* p. 32.

60. Ibid., p. 38.

perhaps best illustrated by the theory of Chris Argyris, which stresses the individual-organization relationship.[61] Recognizing that organizations are complex, Argyris has chosen to focus on one source of energy in organizations—human psychological energy. Specifically, he has been interested in interpersonal competence and interpersonal relationships.

For Argyris there is a lawful unity in every individual, which defines the self. This self or personality develops interpersonally from interaction with others. The person sees the world through this self-filter, accepting stimuli that are congruent with the self and distorting, denying, or rejecting stimuli that cannot be integrated readily into the self. Thus threatening stimuli arouse defensiveness, which blocks the person's ability to become aware of new possibilities. Persons have a basic need to increase self-acceptance and acceptance of others, a need that is hard to fulfill in the presence of threat and defensiveness. Argyris shows that this is an interpersonal problem: "We come to the conclusion that it is impossible for a human being to enhance his awareness and acceptance of (aspects of) his self without simultaneously creating the conditions for others to do the same. Put in another way, an individual's growth and learning (on the interpersonal level) is inexorably tied up with his fellow man."[62] An authentic relationship is one in which both parties can increase their sense of self-worth and self-awareness. Such a relationship is marked by a high degree of descriptive (nonevaluative) feedback, trust, and experimentation. It is low in defensiveness and threat.

This view of interpersonal communication is grounded in humanistic psychology (see Chapter 10). Argyris's contribution is the application of these postulates to organizational life. The relationship between the person and the organization involves what Argyris calls "the basic dilemma between the needs of individuals aspiring for psychological success and self-esteem and the demand of the pyramidal structure."[63] The strategies typically viewed as necessary to achieve organizational objectives conflict with the needs of the individual. Here we see a direct manifestation of human relations' reaction against classical theory. Argyris believes that traditional organizational assumptions require the person to separate from important dimensions of the self. This separation happens in six ways. First, the person is required to behave "rationally," thus divorcing the self from feelings. Second, the principle of specialization prohibits the worker from pursuing the need to utilize the range of abilities. Third, the mechanisms used by individuals to compensate (or escape), including daydreaming, absenteeism, turnover, trade unions, and noninvolvement, further drive the person from the need to be a producing, growing person. Fourth, the principle of power places the individual in subordinate, passive, and dependent states. This condition worsens the lower the level in the chain of command. Fifth, the same principle removes the worker from self-responsibility. Sixth, the principle of control (separation) places the evaluation of one's work in the hands of another.

In summary the traditional strategies used in organizations to "get the job done" defeat individual growth. To make matters worse, the pattern is cyclical. As the individual self is suppressed, people are forced to take on organizational values, which deepens the problem. In Argyris's words, while technical competence is high, interpersonal competence is reduced. The destructive cycle is illustrated in Figure 11.4.[64]

Obviously Argyris's work refutes classical and structuralist theories of organization. He envisions a much different kind of organization

61. The core of Argyris's framework is found in Chris Argyris, *Personality and Organization: The Conflict between System and the Individual* (New York: Harper & Brothers, 1957). It is updated in part I of *Integrating the Individual and the Organization* (New York: John Wiley & Sons, 1964). Shorter versions are available in part I of *Interpersonal Competence and Organizational Effectiveness* (Homewood, Ill.: Richard D. Irwin, 1962) and "Understanding Human Behavior in Organizations," in *Modern Organization Theory*, ed. Mason Haire (New York: John Wiley & Sons, 1959).

62. Argyris, *Interpersonal Competence*, pp. 20–21.

63. Argyris, *Integrating*, p. 58.

64. Argyris, *Interpersonal Competence*, p. 43.

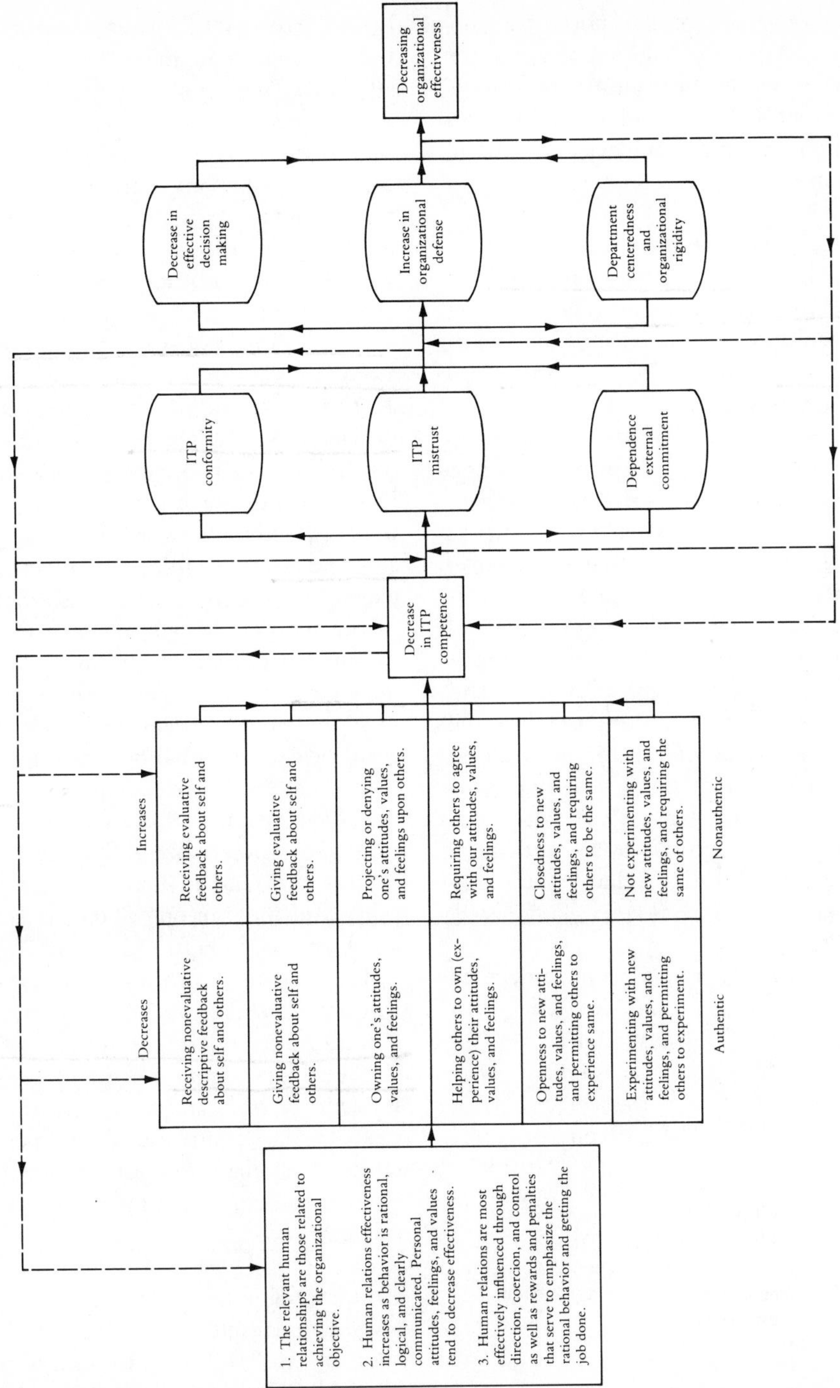

Figure 11.4. Argyris's model of human relations.

in which human values are as important as production values. Argyris would not abandon the pyramid structure, but he would encourage other concurrent forms in which individuals participate in organizational decision making and evaluation.[65]

The Managerial Grid. Another popular human relations model is *The Managerial Grid*® of Robert Blake and Jane Mouton.[66] These authors describe three important dimensions of organizations: purpose (production), people, and hierarchy. The Managerial Grid, illustrated in Figure 11.5, outlines the various contingencies in a superior's attitude for production and people. Each dimension is scaled from low to high, and possible outcomes are described.[67] In their book Blake and Mouton relate communication directly to each of the managerial styles described in Figure 11.5. Following the general human relations pattern, they describe communication as increasingly open, two way, and adaptive, as the style moves along the diagonal from 1,1 to 9,9. At point 9,1 communication is highly formal, task oriented, and one way. At 1,9 it is very informal, social, and approval oriented. At 9,9 "the goal is open, authentic, and candid communication; that is full disclosure."[68]

Likert's Four Systems. Perhaps the most detailed theory of human relations, and surely the most explanatory, is that of Rensis Likert.[69] This rather elaborate theory can be found in *New Patterns of Management* and, more recently, in *The Human Organization*.[70] Likert outlines three broad groups of organizational variables. *Causal variables* are those that can be changed or altered. In this sense they may be considered as the independent variables in the model. *Intervening variables* are those that lead to the results of the causal manipulations. They reflect the general internal state and health of the organization. The *end-result variables*, the dependent variables or outputs, reflect organizational achievement.

An organization can function at any point along a continuum of four systems. System 1, at the extreme of the continuum, is the *exploitative-authoritative* system. Under this system the executive manages with an iron hand. Decisions are made by the executive, with no use of feedback. System 2, or *benevolent-authoritative* leadership, is similar to system 1, except that the manager is sensitive to the needs of the worker. Moving farther along the continuum, we come to system 3, which is *consultative* in nature. The authority figures still maintain control, but they seek consultation from below. At the other extreme of the spectrum, system 4 management or *participative* management, allows the worker to participate fully in decision making. System 4 leads to high performance and an increased sense of responsibility and motivation. These interrelationships are illustrated in Figures 11.6 and 11.7.[71]

Obviously communication is included throughout Likert's model. However, Likert especially considers communication to be an intervening variable, related to the interaction-influence system and a subpart of the category of attitudinal, motivational, and perceptual variables. The relationship of communication variables with management systems is illustrated in Table 11.3.[72]

Criticism. The human relations movement became popular in the 1940s and 1950s, generating a great deal of both ideological support and research data. The movement helped prac-

65. For a detailed exposition of Argyris's ideas on changing organizations, see parts II and III of *Integrating*.

66. *Robert Blake and Jane S. Mouton, The Managerial Grid* (Houston: Gulf Publishing, 1964). This book describes the nature of a number of managerial styles in some detail.

67. Ibid., p. 10.

68. Ibid., pp. 160–61.

69. Perrow, *Complex Organizations*.

70. *Rensis Likert, New Patterns of Management* (New York: McGraw-Hill, 1961); Likert, *The Human Organization* (New York: McGraw-Hill, 1967).

71. Likert, *Human* Organization, pp. 76–137.

72. Ibid., pp. 16–19.

titioners and scholars understand that human beings have needs and values related to organizational functioning and that communication and group process are important aspects of organizational life. It has provided thought on the nature of organizational communication, group dynamics, and leadership, and it has produced a useful set of guidelines for improving interpersonal communication in organizations. However, the movement was basically extreme and

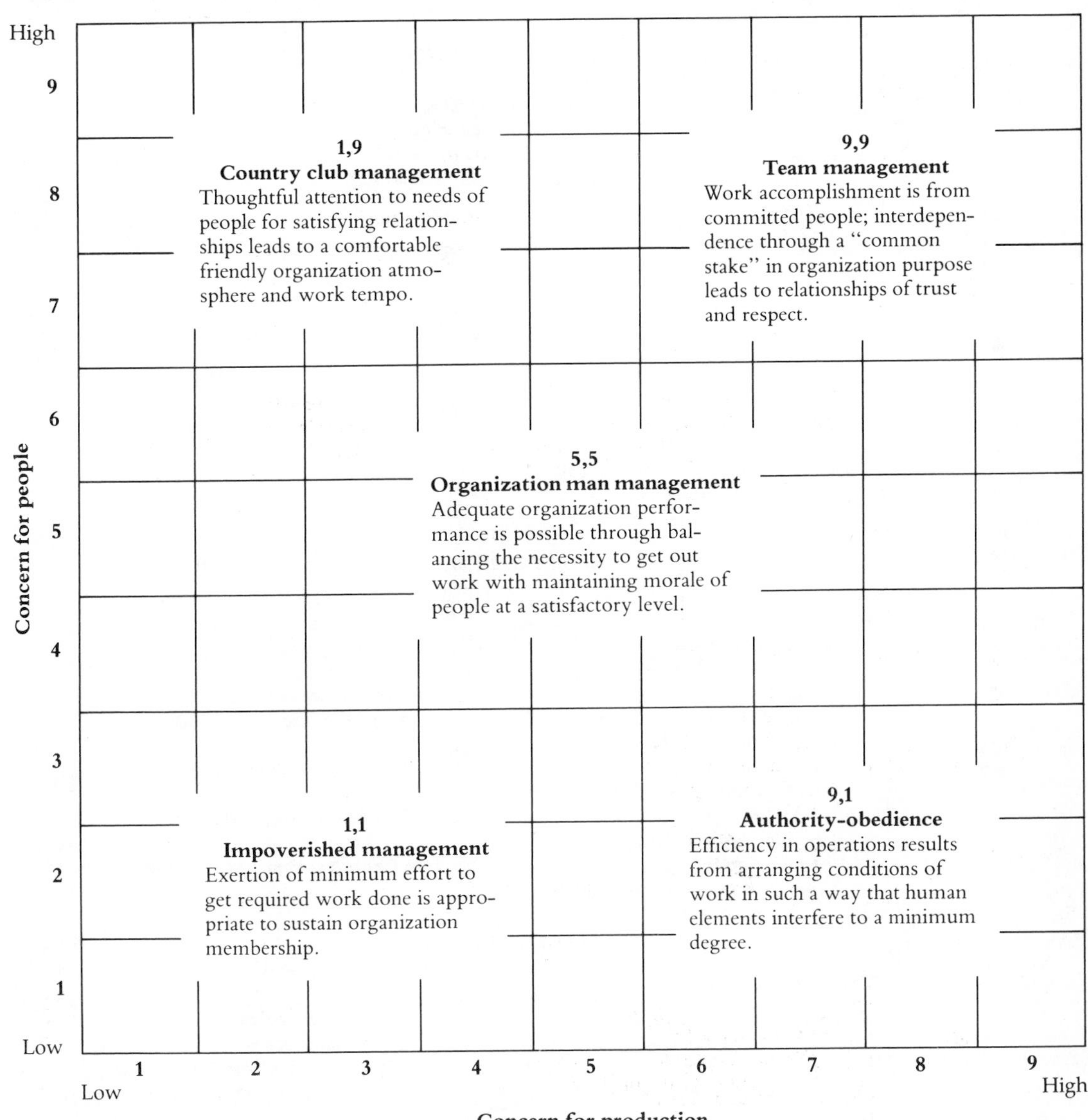

Figure 11.5. The Managerial Grid®.

embodied a number of serious problems, as outlined next.

Human relations was severely criticized almost from its beginning.[73] Its problems are primarily attributable to its extreme position and simplistic view that high morale improves productivity. The correlations claimed to exist between human relations factors and organiza-

73. For a comprehensive critique, see Perrow, *Complex Organizations*.

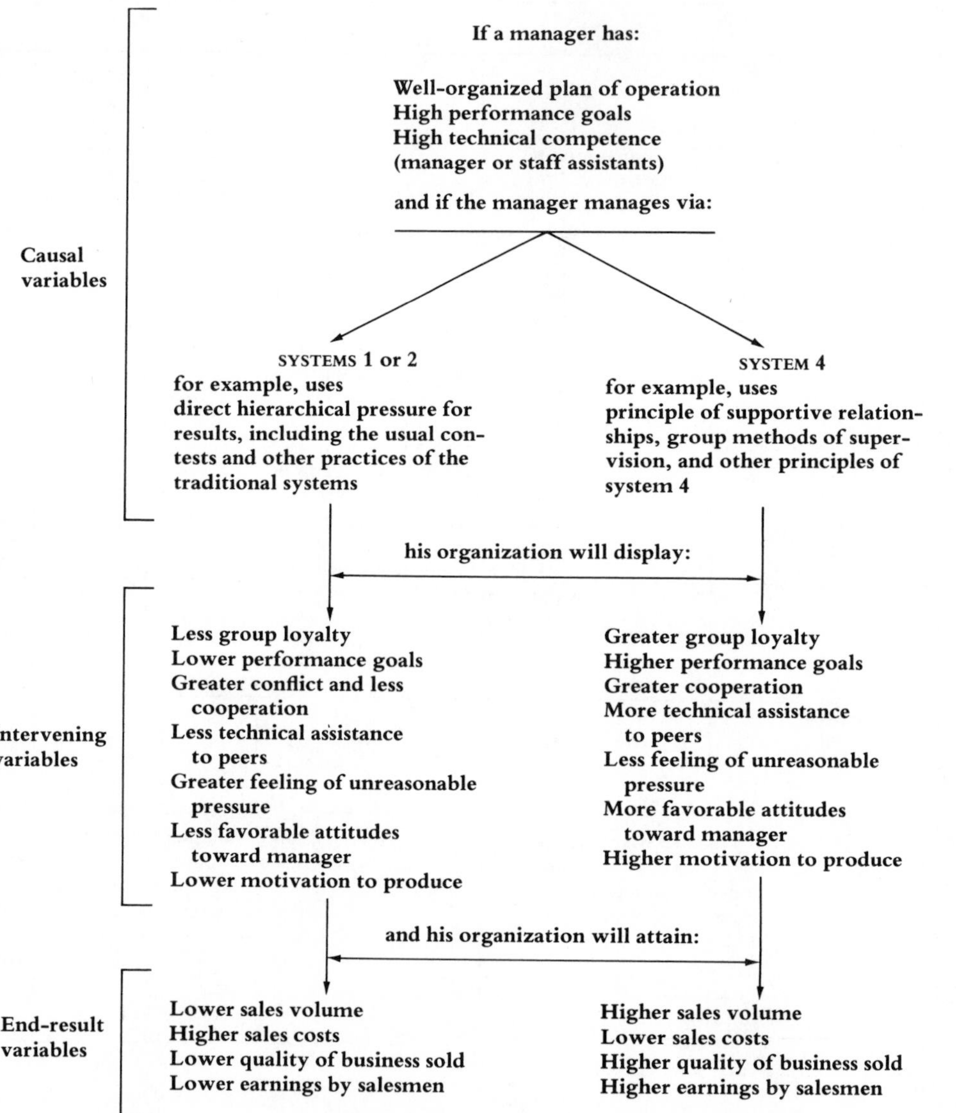

From "New Patterns in Sales Management," in *Changing Perspectives in Marketing Management*, ed. Martin Warshaw.

Figure 11.6. Sequence of developments in a well-organized enterprise, as affected by use of System 2 or System 4.

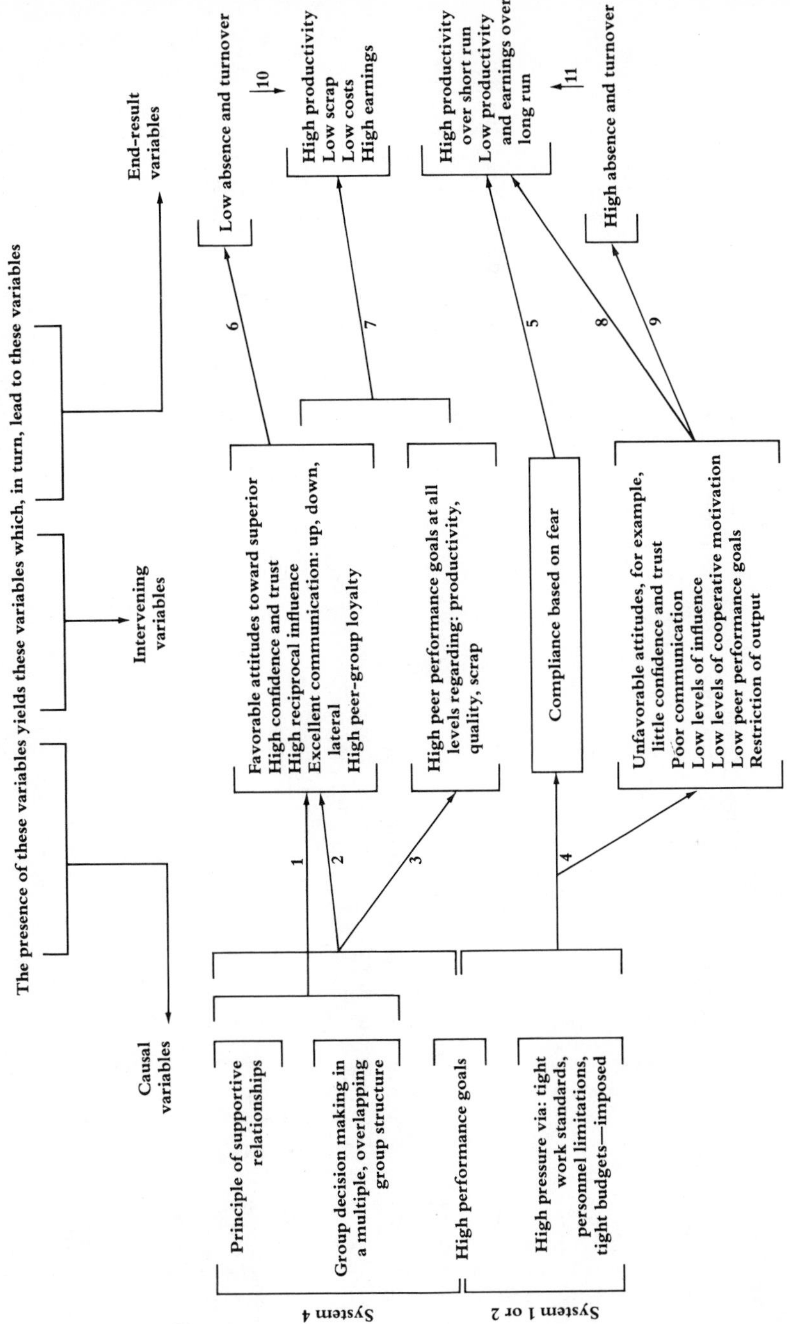

Figure 11.7. Simplified diagram of relationships among variables for system 1 or 2 and system 4 operations.

TABLE 11.3
Organizational and performance characteristics of different management systems based on a comparative analysis

OPERATING CHARACTERISTICS	SYSTEM OF ORGANIZATION			
	AUTHORITATIVE		PARTICIPATIVE	
	EXPLOITATIVE AUTHORITATIVE	BENEVOLENT AUTHORITATIVE	CONSULTATIVE	PARTICIPATIVE GROUP
a. Amount of interaction and communication aimed at achieving organization's objectives	Very little	Little	Quite a bit	Much with both individuals and groups
b. Direction of information flow	Downward	Mostly downward	Down and up	Down, up, and with peers
c. Downward communication				
1. Where initiated	At top of organization or to implement top directive	Primarily at top or patterned on communication from top	Patterned on communication from top but with some initiative at lower levels	Initiated at all levels
2. Extent to which communications are accepted by subordinates	Viewed with great suspicion	May or may not be viewed with suspicion	Often accepted but at times viewed with suspicion. May or may not be openly questioned	Generally accepted, but if not, openly and candidly questioned
d. Upward communication				
1. Adequacy of upward communication via line organization	Very little	Limited	Some	A great deal
2. Subordinates' feeling of responsibility for initiating accurate upward communication	None at all	Relatively little, usually communicates "filtered" information but only when requested. May "yes" the boss	Some to moderate degree of responsibility to initiate accurate upward communication	Considerable responsibility felt and much initiative. Group communicates all relevant information

3. Forces leading to accurate or distorted information	Powerful forces to distort information and deceive superiors	Occasionally forces to distort; also forces for honest communication	Some forces to distort along with many forces to communicate accurately	Virtually no forces to distort and powerful forces to communicate accurately
4. Accuracy of upward communication via line	Tends to be inaccurate	Information that boss wants to hear flows; other information is restricted and filterd	Information that boss wants to hear flows, other information may be limited or cautiously given	Accurate
5. Need for supplementary upward communication system	Need to supplement upward communication by spy system, suggestion system, or some similar devices	Upward communication often supplemented by suggestion system and similar devices	Slight need for supplementary system; suggestion system may be used	No need for any supplementary system
e. Sideward communication, its adequacy and accuracy	Usually poor because of competition between peers and corresponding hostility	Fairly poor because of competition between peers	Fair to good	Good to excellent
f. Psychological closeness of superiors to subordinates (that is, how well does superior know and understand problems faced by subordinates?)	Far apart	Can be moderately close if proper roles are kept	Fairly close	Usually very close
1. Accuracy of perceptions by superiors and subordinates	Often in error	Often in error on some points	Moderately accurate	Usually quite accurate

tional effectiveness have, for the most part, failed the test of empirical study. In many cases the correlations have not been found in research, and where they do appear, serious methodological objections have been raised. One of the biggest apparent weaknesses of human relations theories is that they ignore many nonhuman variables that affect the outcome of an organization. Such theories often fail to take into account the interrelationships among various structural and functional elements of organizational output.

Since much of human relations is based on the humanistic school of psychology, it shares many faults of the latter (see Chapter 10). For instance human relations envisions an organization in which conflict is minimal, suggesting that anything that might frustrate workers will stifle creativity and understanding. Yet we know that the natural conflict that occurs in groups and organizations can be functional, both for individual human growth and for organizational vigor, as Janis shows.

Human relations, like its cousin humanistic psychology, is prescriptive in approach and does not provide much explanation of ongoing organizational processes as they occur in natural organizations. It has values for teaching and for developing certain practical strategies, but it has little theoretical value in the sense of helping us understand how and why individuals organize. Ironically, the ideology of the right, classical structural theory, and the ideology of the left, human relations, share this fault: Each calls for particular kinds of practices to improve organizational functioning without providing a basis for understanding how organizations operate. The group of theories we will discuss next has come into existence primarily with this goal in mind.

The Systems Approach

In the three schools of organizational theory, we see a clear case of thesis-antithesis-synthesis. The classical approach stresses structure above all else. Human relations emphasizes human needs. The system theorists, recognizing the holistic and process nature of organizations, brings these two together. System theories tend to be found among human and structural organizational elements.

Several system theories of organizations have been devised. One of the first was that of Chester Barnard. The work of Barnard was truly a phenomenon. As president of the New Jersey Bell Telephone Company, Barnard was not only a practicing executive but produced one of the most influential treatises on management and organization. Barnard provided two theories, one on organization and one on communication as well. His book, *The Functions of the Executive*, written in 1938, at that time filled a theory void.[74] Barnard's thesis is that organizations can only exist through human cooperation and that cooperation is the medium through which individual capabilities can be combined to achieve superordinate tasks.

Charles Perrow writes the following of Barnard: "This enormously influential and remarkable book contains within it the seeds of three distinct trends in organizational theory that were to dominate the field for the next three decades. One was the institutional school [systems approach]; . . . another was the decision-making school as represented by Herbert Simon; . . . the third was the human relations school. . . . The leading theorists of these schools freely acknowledged their debt to Barnard."[75] Calling him the last of the "practical theorists," Strother writes: "He draws on the work of the classical theorists, psychologists, sociologists, and institutional economists, as well as his own wealth of experience, to develop a closely reasoned, almost Euclidean treatment of industrial organization."[76]

One of the most impactful theories of organization is that presented by James March and Herbert Simon in *Organizations*.[77] This techni-

74. Chester Barnard, *The Functions of the Executive* (Cambridge: Harvard University Press, 1938).

75. Perrow, *Complex Organizations*, p. 75.

76. Strother, "Problems," p. 16.

77. March and Simon, *Organizations*. A helpful secondary source is the interpretive work of Perrow, *Complex Organizations*.

cal treatise exemplifies theory in its purest form. Throughout their text March and Simon present hundreds of propositions related to decision making and organizational functioning. Charles Perrow recognizes this work as an important extension of human relations and classical theories. March and Simon themselves make it clear in the beginning of their book that their work was conducted for the purpose of providing a more complete conceptualization than that found in the "machine" models of the past. Perrow writes: "Herbert Simon and James March have provided . . . the muscle and flesh for the Weberian skeleton, giving it more substance, complexity, and believability without reducing organizational theory to propositions about individual behavior [as the human relations movement has done]."[78] As a result of this fuller view, March and Simon's conceptualization provides a more complex picture of the person than does the human relations school and a more complex picture of organizations than does the classical school.

Another example of a systems approach to organizations is the work of Daniel Katz and Robert Kahn.[79] They present a clear and strong argument in favor of the open system model. Unlike a physical system the organization is social, created by people and bonded by psychological forces. Organizations as social systems are unique in their need for maintenance inputs or control mechanisms to keep human variability in check. Like Barnard, Katz and Kahn teach that the system involves overriding goals that necessitate the subordination of individual needs. Such is the nature of rule enforcement, accomplished through role behavior, norms, and values. These interrelated components provide a necessary integration within the system.

Two representative theories of the system genre have been chosen for discussion because of their central concern with communication as the binding element of organizational systems and because of their impact on the field of communication. Because space necessitates that certain choices be made, the elaboration of the following theories by no means should be taken as a statement that the works of such theorists as Barnard, March and Simon, or Katz and Kahn are unimportant.[80] They are, perhaps, only less central and current to the study of interpersonal communication than are the theories of Weick and Farace, Monge, and Russell.

Weick: The Process of Organizing. One of the most influential theories of organizational communication is that of Carl Weick.[81] Weick's theory of organizing is significant in the communication field because it uses communication as a basis for human organizing and because it provides a rationale for understanding how people organize. In short, Weick's theory is one of the few truly organizational *communication* theories. Since its inception in 1969, it has received wide acclaim and some criticism as well.

Weick sees organizations not as structures or entities but as activities. It is more proper to speak of *organizing* than of *organizations*, because organizations are something that people accomplish, via a process that must be constantly reenacted. Thus when people do what they do in an organization, their activities create organization, so that organizing is continual.

The essence of any organization is that people are acting in such a way that their behaviors are *interlocked*; one person's behavior is contingent on another's. All organizing activities consist of interlocked behaviors. A fundamental quality of interlocking is that communication takes place among the people in the organization. Thus organizing activities consist of *double interacts*, a concept defined earlier in the section on groups. Remember that an act is a statement of communicative behavior

78. Perrow, *Complex Organizations*, p. 146.

79. Daniel Katz and Robert Kahn, *The Social Psychology of Organizations* (New York: John Wiley & Sons, 1966).

80. For a more detailed summary of these theories, see the first edition of this book, Stephen W. Littlejohn, *Theories of Human Communication* (Columbus: Charles E. Merrill, 1978), pp. 303–20.

81. Carl Weick, *The Social Psychology of Organizing* (Reading, Mass.: Addison-Wesley, 1969).

of one individual. An interact involves an act followed by a response. A double interact consists of an act followed by a response and then an adjustment or follow-up act by the first person. Weick believes that all organizing activities are double interacts. Consider an executive and a secretary as an example. The executive asks the secretary to undertake an activity (act); the secretary then asks for clarification (interact); and the executive explains (double interact). Or the executive asks the secretary a favor (act), and the secretary follows through (interact), after which the executive responds with a thank you (double interact). Simple? Yes, but these activities are exactly the kind that Weick believes organizations are built on.

Of course interlocked behaviors do not occur for their own sake. Rather, they fulfill an important function, which is the essence of organizing. Organizing activities fulfill the function of reducing the equivocality of information received from the environment. Equivocality is ambiguity or uncertainty. All information from the environment, according to Weick, is equivocal; organizing activities are instituted by the members of the organization to make the information unequivocal. Of course equivocality is a matter of degree, and the organizing is done to reduce equivocality in the direction of unequivocality.

Let's return to the example of the executive again. Suppose the executive receives a directive from the firm's president to solve a problem of plant safety. What is the nature of this problem, and how should the executive go about solving it? The answers to these questions are not clear, inasmuch as the problem can be defined and solved in a number of ways. In other words the executive is faced with equivocal information.

At this point you probably notice that certain notions from information theory fit in (Chapter 7). Recall that information is a measure of uncertainty in a stimulus situation and that messages or communication reduce the uncertainty. Weick is saying that organizing activities, which consist of double interacts, interlocked behavior, or communication, are designed to make such situations clearer. Of course the importance of information and the degree of equivocality in the information vary. The executive's asking the secretary a favor is an example of an insignificant piece of information, whose equivocality is low; but the example of solving safety problems illustrates a more significant problem that has a great deal of equivocality. This difference is not important to Weick. What is important is that organizing is accomplished through processes that are developed to deal with equivocal information. The exact nature of that information is irrelevant to the fact that the organization members engage in the processes to maintain organization. Interaction serves to achieve common meanings among group members, which is the mechanism by which equivocality is reduced. This idea is further developed next.

We have discussed how individuals interact to deal with equivocal information from the environment. But what is the environment? Traditional theories of organization imply that the environment is a known entity outside the organization. This dualistic notion pits the organization against the environment as if each were somehow preexistent. Weick has a substantially different idea of environment. Organizers are always surrounded by a mix of stimuli to which they must respond, but the "environment" has no meaning apart from what the individual makes of it. In other words the environment is a product of the person, not something outside the person. What makes the environment salient for the individual is the person's attention to particular aspects of the stimuli. People are selective in what they attend to in any situation, and what is attended to at any moment is the environment. Indeed, information from the environment is equivocal precisely because different people attend to different aspects of it. The interaction process (interlocking) is the mechanism by which the individuals in the group reduce this equivocality.

Hence, environments are not preexistent; they are *enacted* by the humans in the organization. People are continually reenacting their environments, depending on their attitudes, values, and experiences of the moment.

For example, the executive of our example is faced with a situation in which interpretation is necessary. Immediately, he or she will attend to certain aspects of the "safety problem." In enlisting the aid of others, for example the secretary, the executive is beginning processes that will enable the group to treat the safety problem as its environment of the moment. To deal with this equivocal environment, group members make proposals (acts) to which others respond (interacts) so that the proposers can refine their initial proposals (double interacts). For example, the executive may ask the secretary to check the files for accident records. This constitutes a proposal, an attempt to reduce the equivocality. The secretary may comply, pulling the appropriate file, so that the executive can be assured that the company knows the extent of the safety problem. Here the sequence of the double interact would be as follows: request file (act), provide file (interact), take file and review it (double interact). Notice how the participants' behaviors are interlocked. The secretary's activity of the moment depends on the executive's request, and the executive's subsequent behavior depends on the secretary's compliance.

Weick views organizing as an evolutionary process that relies on a series of three major processes: enactment, selection, and retention. *Enactment* is the definition of the situation or the registering of equivocal information from outside. Enactment is a process of attending to stimuli in such a way as to acknowledge that equivocality exists. The mere acceptance of certain aspects of the environment removes some equivocality. Accepting the task of dealing with safety problems narrows the field for the executive so that some uncertainty already is removed.

The second process is *selection*. Selection is a process that enables the group to admit certain aspects of information and reject others. It narrows the field, eliminating alternatives with which the organization does not wish to deal. This process therefore removes even more equivocality from the initial information. For example, in dealing with the safety problem, the organization may decide to consider only the aspects of safety that management can control, eliminating all factors that relate to worker predispositions.

The third process of organizing is *retention*. Here further equivocality is removed by decision about what aspects of the initial information will be saved for future use. Retained information is integrated into the existing body of information on which the organization operates. To continue our example, the safety group may decide to deal with safety problems that are caused strictly by machinery, rejecting all other kinds of problems. As you can see, the problem has become much less ambiguous; it has, in Weick's parlance, moved from equivocality toward unequivocality.

After retention occurs, organization members face a choice point. They must make two kinds of decisions. The first is whether to reenact the environment in some way. Here they address the question: Should we (or I) attend to some aspect of the environment that was rejected before? The executive may decide, for example, to have the group go back and check out the rate of accidents that are not related to machinery. The second kind of choice is whether to modify one's behavior or actions. Here the question is: Should I take a different action than I did before? For example, the executive may decide that solutions for both machinery and nonmachinery accidents should be developed.

So far this summary may lead you to believe that organizations move from one process of organizing to another in lockstep fashion: enactment, selection, retention, choice. Such is not the case. Individual subgroups in the organization are continually working on activities in all of these processes for different aspects of the environment. Although certain segments of the organization may specialize in one or more of the organizing processes, nearly everybody undertakes all of them in one form or another most of the time. Such is the essence of organizing.

Knowing the evolutionary stages of organizing helps us see how organizing occurs on a general scale, but this knowledge does not provide an explanation for how equivocality is removed from the information. To address this problem, Weick outlines two elements that occur within each of the three organizing processes. These are assembly rules and interlocked behavior cycles. *Assembly rules* guide the choice of routines that will be used to accomplish the process being conducted (enactment, selection, or retention). Rules are sets of criteria on which organizers decide what to do to reduce equivocality. The question answered by assembly rules is this: Out of all the possible behavior cycles in this organization, which shall we use now? For example, in the selection process the executive might invoke the assembly rule that "two heads are better than one" and on this basis call a meeting of plant engineers. *Behavior cycles* are sets of interlocked behaviors that enable the group to come to an understanding about which meanings should be included and which rejected. Thus the safety meeting called by the executive would enable interested individuals to discuss the safety problem and decide how to proceed in defining and solving it. Assembly rules and behavior cycles are a natural part of each of the three processes of organizing. Remember that a behavior cycle consists of double interacts on the part of participating group members.

Now we have completed the basic elements of Weick's model. They are environment, equivocality, enactment, selection, retention, choices, assembly rules, behavior cycles, and equivocality removed. Weick envisions these elements working together in a system, each element related to the others.

An abstract theory, Weick's model is not designed to explain the substance of activity that one might encounter in an organization but to present in a general way the means by which all organizing occurs. In contrast the following theory is a theory of substance that addresses a variety of communication problems. The two theories are not inconsistent with one another; together they present an excellent system view of communication in organizations.

Structural Functionalism. The last theory to be included in this section is that of Richard Farace, Peter Monge, and Hamish Russell.[82] Their *structural-functional* theory (the most recent of the theories in this chapter) is an eclectic system approach, drawing from the best insights of previous work. Like Weick's this is one of the few strictly organizational *communication* theories. Most other theories summarized in this chapter deal indirectly with communication or include communication as part of a larger theory, but this approach is directed entirely at explaining communication processes in organizations. Thus this theory provides an excellent capstone for the chapter.

Although Farace, Monge, and Russell prefer not to call their work a theory in the narrow sense, it certainly provides a coherent perspective and explanation of communication in organizations. This perspective is consistent with system theory generally and with other system approaches to organizations. The authors define an organization as a system of at least two people (usually many more), with interdependence, input, throughput, and output. This group communicates and cooperates to produce some end product by using energy, information, and materials from the environment.

One of the most important resources in organizations is *information*. Using information theory as a base, Farace and colleagues define information in terms of the reduction of uncer-

82. Richard V. Farace, Peter R. Monge, and Hamish Russell, *Communicating and Organizing* (Reading, Mass.: Addison-Wesley, 1977).

tainty. As a person becomes able to predict which patterns will occur in the flow of matter and energy, uncertainty is reduced and information is gained. (This concept parallels that of semantic information defined in Chapter 7.) Communication is in part the reduction of uncertainty via information. Communication, however, also involves the use of common *symbolic forms* that refer to mutually understood referents.

At this point we encounter one of the most useful distinctions in this theory. The authors delineate two types of communication, which correspond to two types of information. *Absolute information* consists of all the pieces of knowledge present in the system. Thus the totality of communicated information in an organization is absolute communication. On the other hand, *distributed information* is that which has been diffused through the organization. The fact that information exists in an organization does not guarantee that it will be communicated adequately in the system. Questions of absolute information deal with what is known; questions of distribution deal with who knows it. The practical implication of this theoretical distinction is that "failures in distribution policies are due to failures by managers to identify which groups of personnel need to know certain things, or to establish where these groups are supposed to be able to obtain the information they need."[83]

The structural-functional framework for organizational communication rests on three analytic dimensions. The first of these is the *system level*, which is made up of four sublevels: individual, dyadic, group, and organizational. Here the principle of system hierarchy (as discussed in Chapter 3) is manifest. Individuals communicate with others in dyads; dyads cluster together into groups. The organization as a whole is a system of interconnected groups forming a macronetwork.

At each of these levels of analysis, we can examine the *functions* of communication, which is the second dimension. Among the variety of communication functions that exist, these authors stress three: production, innovation, and maintenance. *Production* refers to the direction, coordination, and control of activities. *Innovation* generates change and new ideas in the system. *Maintenance* preserves individual values and interpersonal relations necessary to keep the system together.

The third dimension in the framework is *structure*. While function deals with the content of messages, structure deals with the emergent patterns or regularities in the transmission of messages. For every level in the organization—individual, dyadic, group, and organizational—we may investigate the way communication functions and how it is structured.

In their book Farace and colleagues address in some detail each of the four levels of organizing. We will go over the individual, dyad, and group briefly, highlighting some generalities. Actually, the authors incorporate much of the thinking summarized earlier in this chapter and in the last two chapters into their discussion of these levels. Since their discussion of the macronetwork is such an important contribution of this theory, we will spend more time on it.

The key concept related to individual communication is *load*. Communication load is the rate and complexity of information inputs to a person. Rate is the quantity of inputs such as messages or requests, while complexity is the number of factors that must be dealt with in processing the information. Two problem areas relate to load. *Underload* occurs when the flow of messages to a person falls below the person's ability to process them. *Overload* occurs when the load exceeds the person's capacity. While the notions of load, underload, and overload relate optimally to communication received by single individuals, these concepts also apply to all other levels, including dyadic, group, and organizational. Thus, for example, an entire organization might be underloaded or overloaded.

The key concept applicable to the dyad level

83. Ibid., p. 28.

of communication is *rules*. Members of dyads relate according to patterned expectations. Within organizations there are explicit and implicit rules for communicating. Such rules constitute the explicit or implicit communication policy of the organization. They tell one how to communicate, when to communicate, with whom to communicate, and what to communicate about. Some common rule topics include the following: who initiates interactions; how delays are treated; what topics are discussed and who selects them; how topic changes are handled; how outside interruptions are handled; how interactions are terminated; and how frequently communication occurs.

Through everyday contact between people in an organization, individuals in *groups* tend to work, interact, and communicate together. In fact, the structure of the overall organization depends on these groupings. Since people work together in different groups for different functions, different kinds of groups exist in an organization; a given individual simultaneously may be a member of several groups. Carrying this analysis one step further, we must realize that the organization consists of multiple structures. For example, structures may be built on task relations, power relations, liking, and others. We will return to this idea of organizational structure in a moment. First, let's look at some aspects of individual groups.

First, we note that groups themselves tend to have internal structures. Farace and colleagues outline three types of structure. The first, the *communication structure* or *micronetwork*, is the pattern of interaction in the group. The question here is who communicates with whom within the group. The second kind of structure is the *power structure*. Here the question is who has what kind of power over whom? The third type of structure stressed in this theory is *leadership*. Leadership structure deals with role distribution in the group, specifically the distribution of roles related to interpersonal influence of group members.

We have outlined some key concepts related to the individual, dyad, and group levels of communication. We can move now to perhaps the most significant contribution of these authors, their notion of macronetwork.

A *macronetwork* is a repetitive pattern of information transmission among the groups in an organization. It represents the organization's overall structure. Several types of networks may be overlaid upon an organization, each providing a major function for the organization. Perhaps the most commonly understood network is the formal organization chart, which is the prescribed task network. In addition a number of informal networks may also exist. Any network consists of two fundamental parts: the members and their links.

Links are characterized by five properties. The first is *symmetry*, or the degree to which the members connected by a link interact on an equal basis. In a symmetrical relationship the members give and take information relatively equally. An asymmetric link is one way, with a distinct information sender and receiver. The second property of links is *strength*, which is a simple function of interaction frequency. Members who communicate more often have a stronger link, while those who communicate less often have a weaker link.

Reciprocity, the third property of links, is the extent to which members agree about their links. If one person believes that he or she often communicates with another, but the other denies it, the link is unreciprocated. The fourth property of links is the predominant *content of the interaction*. Is the communication primarily about work, social matters, or some other content area? By probing the content of links in a network, we can discern the network's overall function. The final property of links is *mode*. Here the question is: How is communication achieved, by what channel? Modes may be face-to-face conversations, group meetings, or communication via letter or telephone.

Thus a network consists of members linked together in various ways to share information. To adequately understand a network, we must look at additional factors. Organization members take different network roles. One role is the *isolate.* Before we get into the network itself, we are able to establish those who are not in the network. Isolates have no links with other network members. Of those who are linked to others, some cluster into *groups*. In network terminology a group is characterized by four criteria: (1) More than half of the group's communication is within the group; (2) each person must be linked with all others in the group; (3) the group will not break apart with the exit of one person or the destruction of one link; (4) the group must have at least three members. These criteria, as you can see, make groups relatively stable structures.

A network thus is a series of groups and members who are interlinked. Two other roles are crucial in the network structure: liaison and bridge roles. *Bridges* are group members who also are linked to other groups. *Liaisons* are not members of any group, yet they link two or more groups. Figure 11.8 illustrates these aspects of the network structure.[84] This network concept provides a sensible way of looking at organizational structure and function *in terms of communication*.

Criticism. These two theories, indeed many system theories of organizations, are exciting and quite different from classical and human

84. Ibid., p. 192.

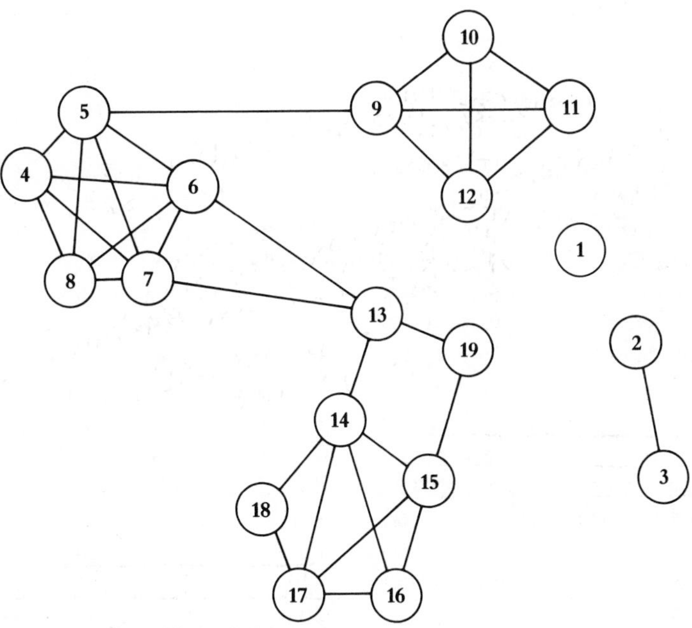

Groups:
Group 1—4, 5, 6, 7, 8
Group 2—9, 10, 11, 12
Group 3—14, 15, 16, 17, 18

Group Linkers:
Bridges—5, 9
Liaison—13
Other—19

Isolates:
True isolate—1
Isolated dyad—2, 3

Figure 11.8. Illustration of communication network roles.

relations theory. They are valuable for us because they stress communication in organizations, emphasizing the ways transfer of information binds elements into holistic organization. With system theory the emphasis changes from components and structure to relations and interactions. This shift of emphasis is captured by Weick: "The word, organization, is a noun and it is also a myth. If one looks for an organization one will not find it. What will be found is that there are events, linked together, that transpire within concrete walls and these sequences, their pathways, their timing, are the forms we erroneously make into substances when we talk about an organization."[85] Thus a key strength of most system theories of organization is that they are highly appropriate for studying the nature of the phenomenon under consideration.

Still, system theories have been criticized.[86] Although a number of objections have been raised against various individual system theories, we will look at only those that apply to the two theories presented. First, however, a general observation is in order. Recall from Chapter 3 on system theory that a major criticism of general system theory as an approach to communication is that it is so abstract that it can be applied in numerous ways, even to the same theme area. The two theories chosen for inclusion here could not illustrate this problem better. Weick's theory presents a view of the most general organizing processes, with little attention to the actual activities that can occur. The theory of Farace and his colleagues, however, looks at how people are grouped into organizational structures by virtue of their information links. Although these theories are not inconsistent with one another, they are hardly comparable. Even though both theories are system approaches, and even though both relate to organizational communication, they cannot be compared in terms of power or utility. They also illustrate that system concepts are slippery and difficult to pin down when they are applied to particular observed events. System concept is more a way of thinking than a theory per se.

System theories of organizations have been criticized specifically for their oversimplification of organizations. This objection is ironic because system theory is touted for its supposed ability to deal with a wide variety of variables in an organism. The problem is two fold. First, system theories tend to exaggerate the system claims in regard to an organization, ignoring aspects of the organization that are not systemlike. Second, along a similar vein, certain variables are downplayed because they do not fit well into the system paradigm. Weick calls for a tempered approach that would address questions such as the following: "When will a set of related entities—the standard definition of a system—act like a system and when will they not; what conditions tighten and loosen interdependencies; what conditions freeze or extend the range of values a variable will take; what conditions diffuse or intensify boundaries?"[87]

The basic problem is that system approaches rarely are specific enough to explain or to predict individual variation. Consequently they are not often falsifiable. Most philosophers of science agree that the validity of a theory that is not falsifiable never really can be known and that such theories therefore should be rejected as inadequate. For example, both theories summarized in this section downplay the individual human as an important factor in organizational functioning. The interactional structure is emphasized over the needs of the individual. This quality is in part a reaction against the hyperbole of the human relations school about the role of human needs.

Another criticism is that these theories are ahistorical, ignoring the developmental course

85. Carl Weick, "Middle Range Theories of Social Systems," *Behavioral Science* 19 (1974): 358.

86. Ibid.; see also Bengt Abrahamsson, *Bureaucracy or Participation: The Logic of Organization* (Beverly Hills, Calif.: Sage, 1977).

87. Weick, "Middle Range," p. 357.

of organizations. The theories also downplay the role of power in the organization, suggesting that system outcomes are a natural result of the mechanism of interactional structure and not of the influence of individuals and groups.

What Do We Know about Communication in Groups and Organizations?

The distinguishing characteristic of communication in groups and organizations is that individuals become linked into a structure by virtue of communication. The concept of macronetwork, as presented in the last section, captures the general idea of this linkage. Dyads become linked into groups, and groups are linked into organizations. The most important generalization for our purposes is that the essential binding element of groups and organizations is information sharing. Without sending and receiving messages, groups and organizations would not exist. Further, it is clear that groups and organizations are constantly being recreated or sustained by continual communication. Therefore communication can be viewed as a process of organizing.

Most theorists agree that organizations, as interlinked groups, constitute a system and exhibit such system qualities as interrelatedness of parts, hierarchy, equifinality, homeostasis, and morphogenesis (see Chapter 3). Most important, the system operates and is sustained through the passage of information along the lines of the system network.

Virtually all of the theories in this chapter stress the functional nature of groups and organizations. In other words the communication that binds individuals to one another accomplishes certain end results. Group and organizational communication functions both on personal and group levels. Individual needs are met by interaction in the group, groupness is maintained through communication, and certain supraordinate group goals are also made achievable through communication. At the same time groups and organizations, through the rules, norms, and values that arise in interaction, constrain the individual. Group membership, in other words, causes a loss of freedom. Communication in groups and organizations makes possible the achievement of otherwise unattainable goals, while paradoxically erecting new barriers that must be dealt with by the individual.

Communication functions in part to enable people to deal with the task and interpersonal barriers that naturally arise as part of joint action. Normally individuals in groups and organizations exert energy to solve problems, make decisions, or accomplish objectives, but the concomitant need to relate to others in the group requires that energy also be directed toward interpersonal objectives as well. Effective group functioning can only occur when optimal levels of task and interpersonal efforts are reached.

Individuals behave in various ways in groups and organizations, giving rise to role division. Roles, including emergent leadership, are established and maintained through communication. The patterns of communication that occur are largely responsible for individual role behavior. Part of the role division in groups and organizations involves the allocation of power. Power is rarely, if ever, equally distributed, and the locus of power depends not only on legitimate or assigned authority but also on information attribution.

This chapter concludes our discussion of interpersonal contexts of communication. In the last three chapters we have studied theories related to dyadic, group, and organizational settings. In the next chapter we move to the fourth major setting: mass communication. As you will discover, mass communication is distinguished primarily because of its mediated form.

CHAPTER

12 The Mediated Context: Theories of Mass Communication

We are living in what Marshall McLuhan calls the "global village." Modern communication media make it possible for millions of people throughout the world to be in touch with nearly any spot on the globe. The omnipresent media present an important challenge to students in many disciplines, for the potential impact of the media is mind boggling. We live in an environment of constant mass communication, which we experience hourly and daily. Yet because we take this environment for granted, we may have lost touch with the reality of its influence. The very essence of society in most countries of the world has been affected by mass communication.

Melvin DeFleur captures the importance of the study of communication: "No student of human nature, whatever his disciplinary identification or theoretical orientation, can study human behavior without recognizing at the outset that man's communication processes are as vital to him as a human being as are his biological processes."[1] George Gerbner adds the following: "This broad 'public-making' significance of mass media of communications—the ability to create publics, define issues, provide common terms of reference, and thus to allocate attention and power—has evoked a large number of theoretical contributions. Other theories of mass media have their origins in political thought, social-economic analysis, and historical-artistic-literary scholarship."[2]

What characterizes the mediated context? Several writers have discussed mass communication as a concept.[3] Most center on four primary criteria of the mass context. First, the audiences of mass communication tend to be large and heterogeneous, and messages tend to be public and open. The second quality of mass communication is that it is primarily one way. The audience is anonymous and impersonal, and feedback is limited. Third, modern electronic technology makes transmission of information to mass audiences rapid. Fourth, most mass communication messages originate from large organizations rather than

1. Melvin DeFleur, *Theories of Mass Communication* (New York: David McKay, 1966), p. xiv.

2. George Gerbner, "Mass Media and Human Communication Theory," in *Human Communication Theory*, ed. Frank Dance (New York: Holt, Rinehart and Winston, 1967), p. 45. There are numerous short surveys of mass communication research and theory such as Gerbner's article. See, for example, David M. White, "Mass Communications Research: A View in Perspective," in *People, Society and Mass Communication*, ed. L. A. Dexter and D. M. White (New York: Free Press, 1964), pp. 521–46; Walter Weiss, "Mass Communication," *Annual Review of Psychology* (Palo Alto, Calif.: Annual Review Press, 1971); Sidney Kraus, "Mass Communication and Political Socialization: A Reassessment of Two Decades of Research," *Quarterly Journal of Speech* 59 (1973): 390–400; Wilbur Schramm, *Men, Messages, and Media: A Look at Human Communication* (New York: Harper & Row, 1973); James A. Anderson, "Mass Communication Theory and Research: An Overview," in *Communication Yearbook I*, ed. Brent Ruben (New Brunswick, N.J.: Transaction Books, 1977), pp. 279–90; Joseph M. Foley, "Mass Communication Theory and Research: An Overview," in *Communication Yearbook II*, ed. Brent Ruben (New Brunswick, N.J.: Transactions Books, 1978), pp. 209–14; Joseph M. Foley, "Mass Communication Theory and Research: An Overview," in *Communication Yearbook III*, ed. Dan Nimmo (New Brunswick, N.J.: Transaction Books, 1979), pp. 263–70; Werner J. Severin and James W. Tankard, *Communication Theories: Origins, Methods, Uses* (New York: Hastings House, 1979); Dennis K. Davis and Stanley J. Baran, *Mass Communication and Everyday Life: A Perspective on Theory and Effects* (Belmont, Calif.: Wadsworth, 1981).

3. See, for example, Theodore Peterson, Jay W. Jensen, and William L. Rivers, *The Mass Media and Modern Society* (New York: Holt, Rinehart and Winston, 1965).

from individuals. Everett Rogers provides the excellent summary of distinction between interpersonal and mass communication shown in Table 12.1.[4] Of course, we must be careful not to separate "public" communication completely from interpersonal channels. While there are some rather broad and important differences, it is helpful to realize that "massness" is a matter of degree. For example, mass communication in the extreme sense is illustrated by a television news broadcast, which is less personalized than reading a specialized article in a journal. Additionally, as we will see later in the chapter, mass and interpersonal channels interrelate in important ways.

Theories of mass communication are exceedingly difficult to integrate and to organize. The theories chosen for this chapter represent the mainstream of thought on mass communication, although this compilation is necessarily incomplete. Since most of the work in mass communication relates to the ways in which the media affect the public, the theories included here reflect this bias.[5] The theories summarized in this chapter are divided into two sections. The first section relates to the nature of audiences and the ways mediated information is distributed among members of the public. The second section relates to media effects and functions, which is the most popular research area in the field.

Theories of Audience and Diffusion

Although the question of how information is diffused in society is approached in many ways, two main kinds of thinking can be isolated. The first consists of a mass audience approach, in which society is thought of as a large amorphous mass that is influenced as a whole by mass communication. The alternative approach is a group mediation model, in which the audience is not viewed as a mass, but as an amalgam of small groups. These two kinds of thought are represented in the two sections that follow.

Theories of Mass Society

The Mass Society Concept. The theory of mass society is a concept growing out of the large, complex and bureaucratic nature of the modern state.[6] The theory envisions a malleable mass of people in which small groupings, community life, and ethnic identity are replaced by society-wide depersonalized relations. As William Kornhauser says, "All members of mass society are equally valued as voters, buyers, and spectators. Numerical superiority therefore tends to be the decisive criterion of success."[7] Great power comes to those who are effective in manipulating the mass.

The conception of society has led to widespread criticism of modern life. Critics of the mass society have suggested several propositions, summarized by Daniel Bell as follows.[8] First, rapid developments in transportation and communication have increased human contact, and economic considerations have made people more and more interdependent. Thus, like a giant system, imbalance in one part affects everybody. The catch is that while we are all

4. Everett M. Rogers, "Mass Media and Interpersonal Communication," in *Handbook of Communication*, ed. Ithiel de sola Pool et al. (Chicago: Rand McNally, 1973), p. 291.

5. For a discussion of other aspects of mass communication, including the ways in which society affects its media and the process by which mediated communication operates, see Melvin L. DeFleur and Sandra Ball-Rokeach, *Theories of Mass Communication* (New York: Longman, 1982).

6. The most prominent critics of mass society are José Ortega y Gasset, Karl Mannheim, Karl Jaspers, Paul Tillich, Gabriel Marcel, and Emil Lederer. The best synthesis can be found in two critiques of the theory: Daniel Bell, "The Theory of Mass Society," *Commentary*, July 1956, pp. 75–83; and R. A. Bauer and A. H. Bauer, "America, Mass Society, and Mass Media," *Journal of Social Issues* 16 (1960): 3–66. Other sources used in the preparation of this section include Eliot Freidson, "Communications Reserach and the Concept of the Mass," in *The Process and Effects of Mass Communication*, ed. Wilbur Schramm and Donald Roberts (Urbana: University of Illinois Press, 1971), pp. 197–208; and W. Kornhauser, "Mass Society," in *International Encyclopedia of the Social Sciences*, vol. 10 (New York: Macmillan, 1968), pp. 58–64.

7. Kornhauser, "Mass Society," p. 59.

8. Bell, "The Theory of Mass Society."

more interdependent, we have become increasingly estranged from one another. Community and family ties are broken and old values questioned. In addition, because society is no longer believed to be led by the elites, morals, tastes, and values decline. Rapid changes in society hurl men and women into multiple role situations, causing a loss of the sense of self. People become more anxious, and a charismatic leader ultimately may be required to lift society out of the abyss.

This dismal view has several implications for the mass media of communication. Critics of mass society fear that minds will be pounded and altered by propagandistic forces behind the media. Paul Lazarsfeld and Robert Merton express this fear: "There is the danger that these technically advanced instruments of mass communication constitute a major avenue for deterioration of aesthetic tastes and popular cultural standards."[9]

9. Paul F. Lazarsfeld and Robert K. Merton, "Mass Communication, Popular Taste, and Organized Social Action," in *The Process and Effects of Mass Communication*, ed. Wilbur Schramm and Donald Roberts (Urbana: University of Illinois Press, 1971), p. 557.

The theory of mass society remains popular in some circles. In the following paragraphs we will review two examples of prominent contemporary theories of mass communication that follow the mass society approach. Notice that these theories are different from one another in content and form, but that they share the common assumption that modern society consists of a large undifferentiated public that is affected as a whole by communication technology.

Marshall McLuhan. Marshall McLuhan is perhaps the best known writer on mass communication among the general public. In fact he may be the most popular communication "theorist" of our time. He has received acclaim primarily because of his interesting and bizarre style and his startling and impactful ideas. At the same time McLuhan has become one of the most controversial writers in the arena of pop culture. Whether one agrees with him or not, his ideas have received too much publicity to be ignored.

McLuhan published for many years, writing such books as the *Gutenberg Galaxy* and *The*

TABLE 12.1
Differences between mass and interpersonal channels

CHARACTERISTICS	INTERPERSONAL CHANNELS	MASS MEDIA CHANNELS
1. Message flow	tends to be two way	tends to be one way
2. Communication context	face to face	interposed
3. Amount of feedback readily available	high	low
4. Ability to overcome selective processes (primarily selective exposure)	high	low
5. Speed to large audience	relatively slow	relatively rapid
6. Possible effect	attitude formation and change	knowledge change

From "Mass Media and Interpersonal Communication," by Everett M. Rogers, in *Handbook of Communication*, ed. Ithiel de Sola Pool et al.

Mechanical Bride.[10] However, it was *Understanding Media*, published in 1964, that brought McLuhan to public attention.[11] Later, his book, *The Medium is the Massage* provided an interesting exposition of his "probes" about our communication environment.[12] His later works consist primarily of a series of articles.[13]

Many students of mass communication—and McLuhan himself—would agree that his works hardly constitute a "theory." Yet an examination of his ideas reveals that he does have a somewhat systematic outline of propositions about the relationship between various media types and culture as a whole. McLuhan's effect on the public arises as much from what people have said about him as from his own writings. Some of this commentary is summarized later under criticism.

McLuhan's ideas changed considerably in the last decade or so of his life. We will begin by summarizing his earlier ideas, then we will move to his later thinking.[14] McLuhan's early ideas on the media of communication stem from his mentor, Harold Adams Innis.[15] Both Innis and McLuhan treat communication media as the essence of civilization, and both see the course of history as a manifestation of the predominant media of the age. Innis was a Canadian economist and historian. In his most important works, *The Bias of Communication* and *Empire and Communications*, he traces the influence of communication throughout the ages.[16] Innis sees communication media as extensions of the human mind. He teaches that the primary interest of any historical period is a bias growing out of the predominant media in use. Heavy media such as parchment, clay, or stone are time-binding, providing a bias toward tradition. Space-binding media such as paper and papyrus, on the other hand, tend to foster empire building, large bureaucracy, and military interests. Speech as a medium encourages temporal thinking, which values knowledge and tradition and supports community involvement and interpersonal relationships. Written media produce different kinds of culture. The space-binding effect of writing produces interests in political authority and the growth of empires in a spatial sense. Predating McLuhan's expoundings on this point, Innis teaches that the essence of Western culture has been shaped by a strong print or spatial bias. His own viewpoint is expressed as follows: "Mechanization has emphasized complexity and confusion; it has been responsible for monopolies in the field of knowledge. . . . The conditions of freedom of thought are in danger of being destroyed by science, technology, and the mechanization of knowledge, and with them, Western civilization. My bias is with the oral tradition, particularly as reflected in Greek civilization, and with the necessity of recapturing something of its spirit."[17]

10. Marshall McLuhan, *The Gutenberg Galaxy: The Making of Typographic Man* (Toronto: University of Toronto Press, 1962); *The Mechanical Bride* (New York: Vanguard Press, 1951).

11. Marshall McLuhan, *Understanding Media* (New York: McGraw-Hill, 1964),

12. Marshall McLuhan and Quentin Fiore, *The Medium is the Massage* (New York: Banton, 1967).

13. Implications of Cultural Uniformity," in *Superculture: American Popular Culture and Europe*, C. E. E. Bigsby, ed. (Bowling Green: Bowling Green University Popular Press, 1975); "At the Moment of Sputnik the Planet Became a Global Theatre in Which There Are No Spectators but Only Actors," *Journal of Communication* 24 (1974): 48–58; "Communication: McLuhan's Laws of the Media," *Technology and Culture* 16 (1975): 74–78; "At the Flip Point of Time—The Point of More Return?" *Journal of Communication* 25 (1975): 102–6; "Misunderstanding the Media's Laws," *Technology and Culture* 17 (1976): 263; "The Violence of the Media," *The Canadian Forum*, September 1976, pp. 9–12; "Laws of the Media," *Et Cetera* 34 (1977): 173–79; "The Rise and Fall of Nature," *Journal of Communication* 27 (1977): 80–81; "The Brain and the Media: The 'Western' Hemisphere," *Journal of Communication* 28 (1978): 54–60.

14. I have relied on the synthesis of Bruce Gronbeck, "McLuhan as Rhetorical Theorist," *Journal of Communication* 31 (1981): 117–28; this article clearly summarizes the differences between McLuhan's early and later ideas.

15. J. W. Carey, "Harold Adams Innis and Marshall McLuhan," *The Antioch Review* 27 (1967): 5–39.

16. Harold A. Innis, *The Bias of Communication* (Toronto: University of Toronto Press, 1951); *Empire and Communications* (Toronto: University of Toronto Press, 1950, 1972).

17. Innis, *The Bias of Communication*, pp. 190–91.

One can easily see the connection between McLuhan's ideas and those of his predecessor, but McLuhan clearly has gone beyond the ideas of Innis in discussing the impact of media on society. In essence McLuhan's early theory can be broken down into a few basic propositions.[18]

McLuhan's most basic hypothesis is that people adapt to their environment through a certain balance or ratio of the senses, and the primary medium of the age brings out a particular sense ratio. McLuhan sees every medium as an extension of some human faculty, with the media of communication thus exaggerating this or that particular sense. In his words, "The wheel . . . is an extension of the foot. The book is an extension of the eye. . . . Clothing, an extension of the skin. . . . Electric circuitry, an extension of the central nervous system."[19] Whatever media predominate will influence human beings by affecting the way they perceive the world.

Before printing was invented, tribal people were primarily hearing-oriented communicators. They were emotionally and interpersonally close. For the tribal person "hearing was believing." But the invention of the printing press changed this. The Gutenberg age brought a new sense ratio into being, in which sight predominated. McLuhan's basic premise about the development of Western culture is that the nature of print forced people into a linear, logical, and categorial kind of perception. For McLuhan the use of the alphabet "fostered and encouraged the habit of perceiving all environment in visual and spatial terms—particularly in terms of a space and of a time that are uniform,

c,o,n,t,i,n,u,o,u,s and
c-o-n-n-e-c-t-e-d."[20]

We have entered a new age, though, according to McLuhan. Electronic technology has brought back an aural predominance. The Gutenberg technology created an explosion in society, separating and segmenting individual from individual; the electronic age has created an implosion, bringing the world back together in a "global village." As a result "it is forcing us to reconsider and reevaluate practically every thought, every action, and every institution formerly taken for granted.[21] McLuhan describes this impact: "Electric circuitry profoundly involves men with one another. Information pours upon us, instantaneously and continuously. As soon as information is acquired, it is very rapidly replaced by still newer information. Our electrically configured world has forced us to move from the habit of data classification to the mode of pattern recognition. We can no longer build serially, block-by-block, step-by-step, because instant communication insures that all factors of the environment and of experience coexist in a state of active interplay."[22]

Thus we come to the main thesis of McLuhan's work: "The medium is the message."[23] This catch phrase, at once curious and thought provoking, refers to the general influence that a medium has apart from its content. Tom Wolfe puts it this way: "It doesn't matter if the networks show twenty hours a day of sadistic cowboys caving in people's teeth or twenty hours of Pablo Casals droning away on his cello in a pure-culture white Spanish drawing room. It doesn't matter about the content."[24] And here, of course, is where McLuhan parts company from most contemporary researchers in mass communication. McLuhan claims that the content of communication is irrelevant. What really makes a difference in people's lives is the predominant media, not content, of the period: "They are so pervasive in their personal,

18. Good brief summaries of McLuhan's theory can be found in the following: Kenneth Boulding, "The Medium"; Tom Wolfe, "The New Life Out There," in *McLuhan: Hot and Cool*, ed. Gerald E. Stearn (New York: Dial, 1957), pp. 56–34; Carey, "Innis and McLuhan."

19. McLuhan and Fiore, *The Medium is the Massage.*

20. Ibid.

21. Ibid.

22. Ibid.

23. McLuhan, *Understanding Media*, p. 7.

24. Wolfe, "New Life," p. 19.

political, economic, aesthetic, psychological, moral, ethical, and social consequences that they leave no part of us untouched, unaffected, unaltered."[25]

McLuhan makes a distinction between the *hot* and the *cool* media of communication. These concepts are the most confusing and probably the most controversial in his writing. McLuhan describes media in terms of the degree to which they involve people perceptually. Hot media are those that contain relatively complete sensory data, or high redundancy in the information-theory sense. With hot media the perceiver has less need to become involved by filling in missing data. McLuhan refers to hot media as low in participation. Hot media, because they give us everything, create a dulling or somnambulism in the population. Cool media, on the other hand, require the individual to participate perceptually by filling in missing data. This participation creates healthy involvement. It is important to realize that McLuhan's use of participation or involvement does not refer to the degree of interest or time spent attending to a particular medium of communication. Rather he refers to the completeness (hot) or incompleteness (cool) of the stimulus. Film, for example, is considered to be a hot medium because the image projected on the screen is complete in every detail. The viewer of a film is not required perceptually to fill in anything. In an information-theory sense (Chapter 7) we could say that the film has high redundancy, low information. Television, on the other hand, provides the viewer with only a sketch through the illumination of tiny dots. Perceptually the viewer must fill in between these visual dots. In short the viewer must become involved perceptually with the stimulus. This distinction is crucial, for McLuhan sees it as a fundamental point of impact on society. As he puts it, "So the hotting-up of one sense tends to effect hypnosis, and the cooling of all senses tends to result in hallucination."[26]

25. McLuhan, *The Medium is the Massage.*

26. McLuhan, *Understanding Media*, p. 32.

Given his definition of cool media, you can see why McLuhan believes that television is changing the fabric of society. But the advent of television brings its own problems. McLuhan makes clear that a shift from one kind of medium to another creates tremendous stresses in society. For example, if a hot medium such as radio is introduced into tribal or nonliterate cultures, which are accustomed to cool media, a violent reaction may occur. Likewise, the reorientation required for hot societies such as our own to adapt to the introduction of cool media such as television has been upsetting.

In *Understanding Media* McLuhan comments on several media. The following quotations highlight his ideas:

Speech:

Language does for intelligence what the wheel does for the foot and body. It enables them to move from thing to thing with greater ease and speed and ever less involvement. Language extends and amplifies man but it also divides his faculties. His collective consciousness or intuitive awareness is diminished by this technical extension of consciousness that is speech. . . . Speech acts to separate man from man, and mankind from the cosmic consciousness.[27]

The Written Word:

The phonetic alphabet is a unique technology. There have been many kinds of writing, pictographic and syllabic, but there is only one phonetic alphabet in which semantically meaningless letters are used to correspond to semantically meaningless sounds. This stark division and parallelism between a visual and an auditory world was both crude and ruthless, culturally speaking; . . . it is the result of the sudden breach between the auditory and the visual experience of man. Only the phonetic alphabet makes such a sharp division in experience, giving to its user an eye for an ear, and freeing him from the tribal trance of resonating word magic and the web of kinship.[28]

Print:

Repeatability is the core of the mechanical principle that has dominated our world especially since the Gutenberg technology. . . . With typography, the principle of movable type introduced the means of mechanizing any handicraft by the process of segmenting and fragmenting an integral action. What

27. Ibid., pp. 79–80.

28. Ibid., pp. 83–84.

had begun with the alphabet as a separation of the multiple gestures and sights and sounds in the spoken word, reached a new level of intensity, first with the woodcut and then with typography.[29]

> *Film:*
> The close relation, then, between the reel world of film and the private fantasy experience of the printed word is indispensable to our Western acceptance of the film form. . . . Film, both in its reel form and in its scenario or script form, is completely involved with book culture.[30]

> *Radio:*
> Radio affects most people intimately, person-to-person, offering a world of unspoken communication between writer-speaker and the listener. That is the immediate aspect of radio. A private experience. The subliminal depths of radio are charged with the resonating echoes of tribal horns and antique drums.[31]
>
> The power of radio to retribalize mankind, its almost instant reversal of individualism into collectivism. . . .[32]

> *Television:*
> TV will not work as background. It engages you. You have to be *with* it. . . . The cool TV medium promotes depth structures in art and entertainment alike, and creates audience involvement in depth as well. . . . There is scarcely a single area of established relationships, from home and church to school and market, that has not been profoundly disturbed in its pattern and texture.[33]

In the 1970s McLuhan's teachings changed substantially. In his earlier works he strongly implies that the form of media in society *affects* or causes certain modes of perception on the part of society's members. In his later teaching he seems much less certain of this causal link. Instead, McLuhan says that media resonate with or reflect the perceptual categories of individuals. Instead of envisioning a causal link between media and personal perception, he later saw a simultaneous outpouring of certain kinds of thought on the part of the media and the person. Media forms do not cause but bring out modes of thought that are already present in the individual. The problem occurs when the individual is not familiar with the patterns of person-environment relationships depicted in media. The lack of consonance between the individual's perceptual categories and the depictions of the media creates stress in society.

This shift in McLuhan's later years involves a change in ontology. Whereas he once saw the human being as a passive responder, he came to believe that people are active creators in their environments.

Jacques Ellul. One of today's foremost critics of the mass society is Jacques Ellul.[34] Ellul has much to say about mass communication and the media of communication, but he does not separate the two from other social forces, such as education. He takes a holistic approach, claiming that all forces of society interact and create a giant mass system from which the individual cannot escape. At the center of this theory is the concept of *technology*, or *la technique*. The evils of mass society arise because of technology and its amoral, lifeless, emphasis on efficiency above all else. Society's primary problem is that, despite the illusion to the contrary, individuals do not make critical choices based on individual values. They are prevented from doing so by the system, which creates uniformity and thoughtless compliance.

In contrast to the amorality of the technological society, Ellul points to the original goals of democracy. True democracy is not possible, however, because technology has subverted individual human choice. The vehicle through which the technological society perpetuates the mass society is *propaganda*. Ellul redefines propaganda to include all mechanisms, intentional and unintentional, that constrain individuals. As Conrad Kellen remarks in the introduction

29. Ibid., p. 160.
30. Ibid., p. 286.
31. Ibid., p. 299.
32. Ibid., p. 304.
33. Ibid., p. 312.

34. For an excellent brief summary see Clifford G. Christians and Michael R. Real, "Jacques Ellul's Contributions to Critical Media Theory." *Journal of Communication* 29 (1979): 83–93.

to Ellul's book: "The principal difference between his thought ediface and most other literature on propaganda is that Ellul regards propaganda as a sociological phenomenon rather than as something *made* by certain people for certain purposes. Propaganda exists and thrives; it is the Siamese twin of our technological society."[35] As implied in this quotation, Ellul sees propaganda as a universal phenomenon of technological society. Furthermore, he takes the point of view that propaganda is necessary, in fact essential, in modern societies.

The technological system requires propaganda in order to keep individuals in line, and individuals rely on it as a source of security. Thus the media are not channels of information used by individuals as a basis for critical thinking, but a means of propaganda that creates general uniformity throughout society by removing individuals from their cultural foundations. As Ellul puts it: "What these media do is exactly what propaganda must do in order to attain its objectives. In reality propaganda cannot exist without these mass media."[36] In using the media of communication, the propagandist must organize and coordinate the involvement of different kinds of media much as a composer uses a keyboard to write a symphony.

Ellul sees propaganda as necessarily ubiquitous and continuous. It must pervade the individual's daily routine, and it must continue for long periods of time. Since propaganda must be based on the public sentiments and opinions of the day to effect the action for which it aims, the propagandist must be familiar with the psychological and sociological tenor of the audience. Along the same line propaganda must be timely in order to mesh with the thoughts and feelings of the average person.

Several kinds of propaganda are found, according to Ellul. He expresses these in terms of distinctions between opposing types. The first distinction is between political and sociological types. Political propaganda is employed by a government or political party to bring about change in the actions of the public. Sociological propaganda is more difficult to define, for its purpose is to integrate individuals into the mass, to unify group behavior; it arises not from the top of the societal structure but from within it. A second distinction can be made between agitation and integration. Agitation is highly visible and calls attention to itself. Usually it is subversive and is utilized by opponents of the primary order. Propaganda by integration, on the other hand, attempts to stabilize and unify. One may also distinguish between vertical and horizontal propaganda. Vertical propaganda is the classical type, in which the leader or group at the top attempts to affect the masses below. Horizontal propaganda originates from within the group and spreads in lateral fashion. Finally, one may distinguish between rational and irrational propaganda, although Ellul points out that propaganda is becoming increasingly rational and almost always is based on facts.

Several conditions are necessary for the spread of propaganda. As already mentioned, it succeeds in societies that have a dual mass-individual character. As society moves toward massness, the common group bonds that formerly held people together begin to break up. In a modern mass culture the individual is apt to find oneself alone face to face with the entire mass: "Precisely because the individual claims to be equal to all other individuals, he becomes an abstraction and is in effect reduced to a cipher."[37] People are thus susceptible to propaganda only after being cut off from their reference groups. Once this separation happens, once people lose their roots, they become more manipulatable.

In mass society public opinion plays an important role. When channels of information are institutionalized, people receive common information and thus take common positions.

35. Conrad Kellen, "Introduction," in Jacques Ellul, *Propaganda—The Formation of Men's Attitudes* (New York: Knopf, 1965), p. v.

36. Ellul, *Propaganda*, p. 9.

37. Ibid., p. 90.

Ellul believes that public opinion is always a step away from reality. The mass media, for example, allow the propagandist to structure "reality" in consistent ways.

Other conditions are required for propaganda to succeed. The most notable is literacy. Propaganda cannot succeed in societies that do not have the educational base of Western cultures. Since propaganda relies on the manipulation of symbols and the development of stereotypes, the population must have a high degree of receptivity to verbal messages. To the extent that a large number of individuals receive the same information, they will react in similar ways. Propaganda requires two basic conditions: loss of group identification and mass receptivity to common information.

One of Ellul's most startling conclusions is that propaganda is necessary in modern society. This fact is true, according to the theorist, on several grounds. First, propaganda is a necessity of the government. The following quotations illustrate this point of view:

> Ergo: even in a democracy, a government that is honest, serious, benevolent, and respects the voter *cannot follow* public opinion. But it *cannot escape* it either. The masses are there; they are interested in politics. The government cannot act without them. So what can it do?
>
> Only one solution is possible: as the government cannot follow opinion, opinion must follow the government. One must convince this present, ponderous, impassioned mass that the government's decisions are legitimate and good and that its foreign policy is correct.[38]

> But there is more: in democracy, the citizens must be tied to the decisions of the government. This is the greatest role propaganda must perform. It must give the people the feeling—which they crave and which satisfies them—to have wanted what the government is doing.[39]

Aside from the state's need for propaganda, the individual needs it. Here are some of the functions propaganda serves for people: It provides psychological support in facing the complexities of modern life. It simplifies these complexities in ways that make the world more understandable to humankind. Propaganda combats loneliness. It promotes feelings of involvement and meaning to common people. Propaganda boosts self-esteem, making people feel important and involved.

The actual effects of propaganda are discussed at length in Ellul's treatise. Among the psychological effects are the following: crystallization or the solidification of public opinion; alienation from self; psychic disassociation of thought from action (uncritical behavior); perpetuation of the need for propaganda. If you have detected an inconsistency among the various needs and effects surrounding propaganda, you have correctly perceived the picture Ellul intended to paint. Propaganda simultaneously produces opposite effects. It can create as well as ease tension. It can create self-justification, but it may also produce guilt. It can promote cohesion, although disassociation can result too. Propaganda may promote political activism or withdrawal.

Propaganda has important sociopolitical effects as well. Today it is not the voice of an ideology as it has been in the past. More often the propagandist (a nonbeliever, really) uses ideologies as a tool to manipulate the public. Propaganda thus affects public opinion by crystallizing it, by simplifying, by separating private and public opinion, and by mobilizing public opinion to action. Another sociopolitical result of propaganda is the partitioning of subgroups in society, creating various we-they confrontations. This separation occurs on many levels, including unions, religious groups, political parties, national lines, and international blocks.

Criticism. The idea of mass society has been rather severely criticized.[40] Clearly the biggest problem with this idea is that it oversimplifies the nature of society. Consequently the claim that the mass public is at the mercy of those

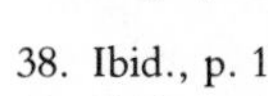

38. Ibid., p. 126.

39. Ibid., p. 127.

40. Bell, "The Theory": Bauer and Bauer, "America."

who control the media has been refuted repeatedly by empirical research in mass communication effects. The topics of mass media influence and mass society in general are complex. In contrast to the theory of mass society is the newer concept of the audience as a complex mediator between media and effect. Raymond Bauer, in observing the failure of many attempts at persuasion, refers to this phenomenon as the *obstinate audience*.[41] He denies the idea that a direct hypodermic needle effect operates between communicator and audience. Instead, many variables involved in the audience interact to shape effects in various ways.[42] (Many of these dynamics were discussed in Chapter 8.) Two of the more important areas of audience mediation are group or interpersonal effects and selectivity. Studies have shown that audience members are selective in their exposure to information.[43] In its simplest form the hypothesis of selective exposure predicts that people in most circumstances will select information consistent with their attitudes and other frames of reference. Thus in opposition to the theory of mass society, the social-psychological approach, while agreeing that certain effects occur, denies the mass-sheep effect commonly feared. This point of view is further elaborated by the multistep flow hypothesis, presented in the next section.

In addition the critics of mass society tend to concentrate on the negative. As critical or normative theory this approach fails to provide a clear understanding of the actual variables at work in advanced societies. Consequently these theories have had little impact or heuristic value in the social sciences. Although many ideas worth pursuing may be found in the work of such theorists as McLuhan, Ellul, and others, researchers have not been open to investigating these ideas, precisely because of their dogmatic and negative nature. Now let us turn our attention to McLuhan and Ellul specifically.

McLuhan is in a world apart. His theory is not only unorthodox but is rarely classified with other theories of a certain genre. However, to the extent that McLuhan conceives of media as affecting society in a general way without discriminating various kinds of effects among different groups, he must be considered among the critics of mass society. His ideas are almost impossible to criticize using standard categories of theory criticism. The reason for this difficulty is that his work is mostly an artistic-historical-literary treatment and does not constitute a theory in the standard sense. Yet there has been no lack of criticism and commentary about the man. To give an idea of the variety of comments that have been published about McLuhan, several quotations are listed:

> Therefore his scholarly stance is somewhat oracular; like the priests of Delphi he produces messages that can be interpreted in different ways but do stimulate thought and in many cases have considerable impact on the people who consult the oracle.[44]

> A man like McLuhan has wit, erudition, and the ability to cross not only academic fields, but fields in the professional community and the academic. He has a fund of history and a sense of tradition which few possess these days. He represents a willingness to confront the present and yet not to reject the past. Yet he often approaches this area with the stance of a huckster, the techniques of a propagandist, the strategies of a con man.[45]

> Again, to vary the medium and to mix the metaphor, the McLuhan books are the skyrocket that came out

41. Raymond A. Bauer, "The Obstinate Audience: The Influence Process from the Point of View of Social Communication," *American Psychologist* 19 (1964): 319–28.

42. Raymond Bauer, "The Audience," in *Handbook of Communication*, ed. Ithiel de sola Pool et al. (Chicago: Rand McNally, 1973), pp. 141–52.

43. Studies on selectivity are well summarized in David O. Sears and Jonathan I. Freedman, "Selective Exposure to Information: A Critical Review," *Public Opinion Quarterly* 31 (1967), reprinted in Wilbur Schramm and Donald F. Roberts, *The Process and Effects of Mass Communication* (Urbana: University of Illinois Press, 1971).

44. Schramm, *Men, Messages, and Media*, p. 125.

45. Donald F. Theall, *The Medium Is the Rear View Mirror: Understanding McLuhan* (Montreal: McGill University Press, 1971), p. xvii.

of this ferment, and one feels almost that if one lit a match they would soar up into the sky and explode into a thousand stars.[46]

His writing is deliberately antilogical: circular, repetitious, unqualified, gnomic, outrageous.[47]

There are people whose fate it is to be read in this spirit: not because of what they have to say, which is meager or foolish, but because of the bleaker measure they provide of their society's quality of mind and conscience. And it is in this spirit that Marshall McLuhan must be approached: as one who has little that is substantial to say but who reveals a very great deal about the cultural permissiveness of mid-century America.[48]

McLuhan writes about himself:

I am an investigator. I make probes. I have no point of view. I do not stay in one position.

Anybody in our culture is regarded as invited as long as he stays in one fixed position. Once he starts moving around and crossing boundaries, he's delinquent, he's fair game.

The explorer is totally inconsistent. He never knows at what moment he will make some startling discovery. And consistency is a meaningless term to apply to an explorer. If he wanted to be consistent, he would stay home. . . .

I don't explain—I explore.[49]

This last quotation captures the qualities of McLuhan's writings that make criticism so difficult—the tendency to use art as evidence, the use of aphorisms or catch phrases in place of clearly defined terms, and the quality of being inconsistent and ambiguous. McLuhan's goal often seems to be to stimulate thought rather than to make clear claims. Bruce Gronbeck relates the frustration of many critics: "To enter the world of Marshall McLuhan with a view to evaluating his contributions to the theoretical literature on rhetoric and communication is an act not unlike taking on Hercules' Hydra; each blow one strikes for propositonal clarity requires two qualifications and a simultaneous assault on at least eight other conceptual quagmires. . . . McLuhan all but defies conceptual synopsis."[50] You can see why such an approach would frustrate social scientists (while delighting many humanists). McLuhan's comment, "I don't explain—I explore," expresses the main reason social scientists have such difficulty using his ideas.[51]

McLuhan's ideas are useful for stimulating a fresh look at the subject matter, but they provide little guidance on how to understand the process of mass communication. They are valuable in that they point to the importance of media forms in society, but they do not give a realistic picture of the variables involved in the effects of media forms. In sum Kenneth Boulding points out: "It is perhaps typical of very creative minds that they hit very large nails not quite on the head."[52]

Ellul can hardly be compared with McLuhan. In contrast to McLuhan's ambiguous, probing technique, Ellul's works are of a single mind and clearly expressed. However, he shares the faults of the critics of mass society spelled out earlier in this section. Basically his tenet that technology is at the base of all social ills is reductionistic. He tends to ignore many complex issues and variables of social life in favor of an overly simple view of mass society. His involvement of *propaganda* as the central concept of communication is an unfortunate usage. It is probably invalid to imply, as Ellul does, that the negative connotations attached to the term *propaganda* apply equally well to all forms of public communication in society.

The positive contribution of the critics of mass society is that they provide an important alternative view to the approach normally taken

46. Kenneth Boulding, "The Medium is the Message," in *McLuhan: Hot and Cool*, Gerald Stearn, ed. (New York: Dial, 1967), p. 57.

47. George P. Elliott, "Marshall McLuhan: Double Agent," in Stearn, *McLuhan*, p. 67.

48. Theodore Roszak, "The Summa Popologica of Marshall McLuhan," in *McLuhan: Pro and Con*, ed. Raymond Rosenthal (New York: Funk & Wagnalls, 1968), p. 257.

49. Stearn, *McLuhan*, p. xiii.

50. Gronbeck, "McLuhan," pp. 117–18.

51. Stearn, *McLuhan*, p. xiii.

52. Boulding, "The Medium," p. 68.

by social scientists. Typically social scientists take an administrative or pragmatic approach to media research. Their aim is to understand how media work so that media can be better used. The social scientists' methods attempt to be objective. Little insight is provided, though, into the values or failings of the media. In contrast the critical approach allows consumers to ask the question: How are communication media falling short in serving society? In the overall picture both critical and pragmatic approaches are necessary. As Clifford Christians and Michael Real state of Ellul: "Unwilling to hide behind the mask of pseudo-objectivity, he steps into the value vacuum of academic analysis with 'must' and 'should.' In being prescriptive as well as descriptive, he reduces the gap between the theory and action."[53]

Theories of Diffusion

The Two-Step Flow. In 1940 a classic voting study was conducted by Paul Lazarsfeld and his colleagues in Elmira, New York.[54] The researchers found an unexpected occurrence that, although unconfirmed, implied a possible strong involvement of interpersonal communication in the total mass communication process. This effect, which came to be known as the *two-step flow hypothesis*, was startling, and it had a major impact on the conception of mass communication.

Since the original Elmira study, much additional data have come in, and the hypothesis has received substantial support.[55] Lazarsfeld hypothesized that information flows from the mass media to certain *opinion leaders* in the community, who facilitate communication through discussions with peers. For example, Lazarsfeld found that voters seem to be more influenced by their friends during a campaign than by the media. One of the most prominent adherents to the two-step flow theory describes how it contradicts the earlier mass society idea:

> The hypothesis aroused considerable interest. The authors themselves were intrigued by its implications for a democratic society. It was a healthy sign, they felt, that people were still most successfully persuaded by give-and-take with other people and that the influence of the mass media was less automatic and less potent than had been assumed. For social theory, and for the design of communication research, the hypothesis suggested that the image of modern urban society needed revision. The image of the audience as a mass of disconnected individuals hooked up to the media but not to each other could not be reconciled with the idea of a two-step flow of communication implying, as it did, networks of interconnected individuals through which mass communications are channeled.[56]

This view expounds the supremacy of the small group in society. More recently it has been shown that small groups interconnect in a web of networks running throughout the "mass."

The two-step flow theory is best summarized in Katz and Lazarsfeld's classic work, *Personal Influence*.[57] Central to the theory is the concept of opinion leaders—individuals in the community who receive information from the media and pass it to their peers. Opinion leaders are distributed in all groups: occupational, social, community, and others. The opinion leader typically is hard to distinguish from other group members, because opinion leadership is not a trait. Instead, it is conceived as a role taken within the process of interpersonal communication. An important aspect is that opinion leadership changes from time to time and from issue to issue. Katz and Lazarsfeld find that it differs in such areas as marketing, fashion, and public affairs. Interest in a particular issue is certainly an important determinant of

53. Christians and Real, "Jacques Ellul's Contributions," p. 92.

54. Paul Lazarsfeld, Bernard Berelson, and H. Gaudet, *The People's Choice* (New York: Columbia University Press, 1948).

55. The best summary of this hypothesis is Elihu Katz, "The Two-Step Flow of Communication," *Public Opinion Quarterly* 21 (1957): 61–78. A more recent treatment is Katz, "Diffusion III: Interpersonal Influence," in *International Encyclopedia of the Social Sciences*, vol. 4, ed. David Sills (New York: Macmillan, 1968).

56. Katz, "Two-Step Flow," p. 61.

57. Elihu Katz and Paul Lazarsfeld, *Personal Influence: The Part Played by People in the Flow of Mass Communications* (New York: Free Press, 1955).

opinion leadership, but leaders can be influential only when interest is shared by all members of the group.

In any case the implication is that groups provide the key for mass communication influence. They do this by providing direction to the individual in terms of opinions, attitudes, values, and norms. Groups also give ready access to communication.

In recent years most theorists have moved to the newer multiple-step model of diffusion.[58] The multiple-step model is similar to the two-step hypothesis; it simply admits to more complex possibilities. Research has shown that the ultimate number of relays between the media and final receivers is variable. In the adoption of an innovation, for example, certain individuals will hear about the innovation directly from media sources, while others will be many steps removed.

However, the basic concept of opinion leadership remains unchanged. Everett Rogers and Floyd Shoemaker provide a list of theoretical generalizations about opinion leadership, which should help round out this theory for us.

> Opinion leaders have greater exposure to mass media than their followers. . . .
>
> Opinion leaders are more cosmopolite than their followers. . . .
>
> Opinion leaders have greater change-agent contact than their followers. . . .
>
> Opinion leaders have greater social participation than their followers. . . .
>
> Opinion leaders have higher social status than their followers. . . .
>
> Opinion leaders are more innovative than their followers. . . .
>
> When the system's norms favor change, opinion leaders are more innovative, but when the norms are traditional, opinion leaders are not especially innovative.[59]

58. One of the best summaries of this extension can be found in Everett M. Rogers and F. Floyd Shoemaker, *Communication of Innovations, A Cross-Cultural Approach* (New York: Free Press, 1971), chap. 6.

59. Ibid., pp. 218–19.

Opinion leaders may be of two kinds: those influential on one topic and those influential on a variety of topics. These types have been called *monomorphic* and *polymorphic*. It has been hypothesized that monomorphism becomes more predominant as systems become more modern. "As the technological base of a system becomes more complex, a division of labor and specialization of roles result, which in turn lead to different sets of opinion leaders for different issues."[60]

The Diffusion of Innovations. One of the most fruitful theoretical areas contributing to our understanding of diffusion stems from the innovation research in rural agriculture, developing nations, and organizations. The diffusion of an innovation occurs when an idea spreads from a point of origin to surrounding geographical areas or from person to person within a single area.[61] Several prominent American and foreign researchers have been responsible for this line of research. The broadest and most communication-oriented theory is that of Everett Rogers and his colleagues.[62]

Rogers began his theory by relating it to the process of social change in general. Social change consists of invention, diffusion (or communication), and consequences. Such change can occur internally from within a group or externally through contact with outside change agents. In the latter case contact may occur spontaneously or accidentally, or it may result from planning on the part of outside agencies.

60. Ibid., p. 224.

61. For a general summary see Torsten Hagerstrand, "Diffusion II: The Diffusion of Innovations," in *International Encyclopedia of the Social Sciences*, vol. 4, ed. David Sills (New York: Macmillan, 1968).

62. Everett M. Rogers, *Diffusion of Innovations* (New York: Free Press, 1962); Rogers and Shoemaker, *Communication of Innovations*; Everett M. Rogers and Ronny Adhikarya, "Diffusion of Innovations: An Up-to-Date Review and Commentary," in *Communication Yearbook III*, ed. Dan Nimmo (New Brunswick, N.J.: Transaction Books, 1979), pp. 67–82; Everett M. Rogers and D. Lawrence Kincaid, *Communication Networks* (New York: Free Press, 1981).

Diffusion of innovations is a time-consuming process. Many years may be required for an idea to spread. Rogers states, in fact, that one of the purposes of diffusion research is to discover the means to shorten this lag. Once established, an innovation will have consequences, be they functional or dysfunctional, direct or indirect, manifest or latent. Change agents normally expect their impact to be functional, direct, and manifest, although this outcome does not always occur.

The diffusion of innovations depends on four broad elements: the innovation, the communication, the channels, the time. An innovation is any new idea in a social system. The perceived newness of the idea is what counts, not its objective newness. Any idea perceived as new by the citizens of the community applies to this process. Rogers's views on communication channels and opinion leaders already have been summarized in the previous section. To review let us note that Rogers sees the diffusion process occurring through both mass and interpersonal channels.

The innovation-decision process consists of the four stages outlined in Figure 12.1.[63] This diagram lists three important interacting determinants of the rate of diffusion. First, the people within a system have certain attributes, including personality, social characteristics, and needs. Second, the social system itself relates significantly to the process of decision. Third are the perceived characteristics of innovations.

There are three different sorts of innovation decisions. The first is the *optional decision*. Farmers, for example, may grow any kind of corn they wish, regardless of the practice of their neighbors. Physicians, among whom considerable diffusion research has been conducted, may decide to use this or that new drug, regardless of decisions made by their peers. On other kinds of issues, such as water fluoridation, *collective decisions* are required. The third kind of decisions are *authority decisions*, or decisions made by force. The fastest rates of adoption usually occur in this last category, although optional decisions can be rapid also. Collective decisions are probably the slowest. Figures 12.2 and 12.3 illustrate the differences between collective and authority decision processes.[64]

The diffusion process just described may appear linear, seeming to occur in discrete steps or stages over time. Rogers now criticizes this linear view, showing that the diffusion of innovations is less linear than he previously thought. Some of his objections to earlier notions are presented in the criticism section that follows. His later thinking is in a somewhat different direction, concentrating on *networks* as the primary mechanism for change.[65] Although mass communication channels may play significant roles in diffusion, interpersonal networks are most important. Networks are more than a simple information linkage between opinion leader and follower, which is implied in the flow models just described. How individuals understand ideas and the degree to which ideas are accepted and modified depend in large measure on the *interaction* along the links in the network. Interaction is important, for diffusion appears to be a product of give and take rather than the simple sending and receiving of information. One new insight of this approach is that individuals modify innovations as part of adoption. Another insight is that innovations are often sought out or created in the system without the intrusion of a change agent. It is a fallacy to think that an innovation is simply injected into a system and adopted or rejected. Communication is a *convergence* of meaning achieved by symbolic interaction. The adoption, rejection, modification, or creation of an innovation is a product of this convergence process. Rogers obviously makes liberal use of symbolic interactionism, system theory, and network theory, which were covered in previous chapters of this book.

Criticism. Beginning with the work of Paul Lazarsfeld, the research and theory of diffusion

63. Rogers and Shoemaker, *Communication of Innovations*, p. 102.

64. Ibid., pp. 276, 305.

65. Rogers and Kincaid, *Communication Networks*.

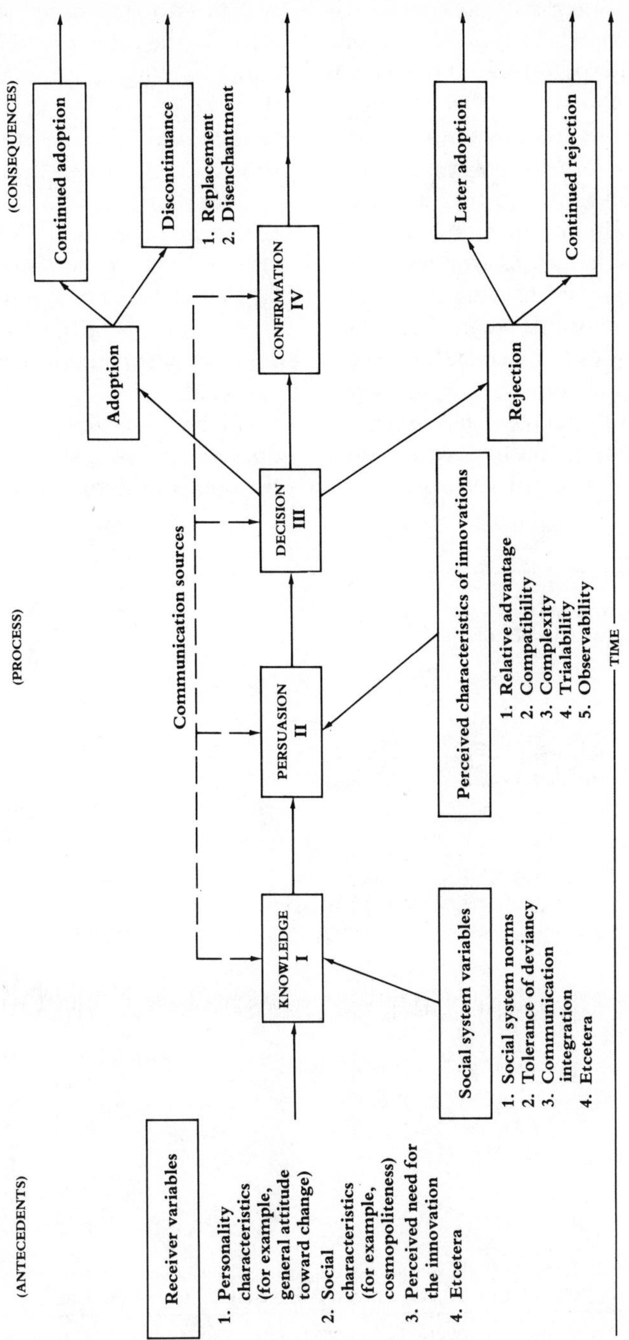

Figure 12.1. Paradigm of the innovation-decision process.

has been immensely successful. Dennis Davis and Stanley Baran remark of Lazarsfeld: "If one person deserves the title of founder of the field of mass communication research, that person is Paul Lazarsfeld. No one has done more to determine the way in which theory and research methods would be developed to aid our understanding of mass communication."[66] The work of Lazarsfeld and his successors has been influential in guiding our thinking about the process of mass communication. The parsimony of these theories has enabled observers to deal with a huge and complex phenomenon with relative ease. Additionally, these theories have been highly heuristic and have produced a large body of research. For many years the idea of the two-step flow (and later multiple-step flow) in the diffusion of information and innovation was a mainstay of mass communication theory, but diffusion theory is undergoing change and is quite unsettled at the present time.[67]

Much criticism of diffusion research and theory arose in the 1970s. Generally, this criticism relates to the simplicity and consequent lack of explanatory power of these theories. Critics now believe that these theories cannot adequately explain the complexities of diffusion processes.

We have realized for some time that diffusion does not follow a strictly two-step process, but the logic of the two-step flow is still a standard

66. Davis and Baran, *Mass Communication*, p. 27.

67. Rogers and Adhikarya, "Diffusion."

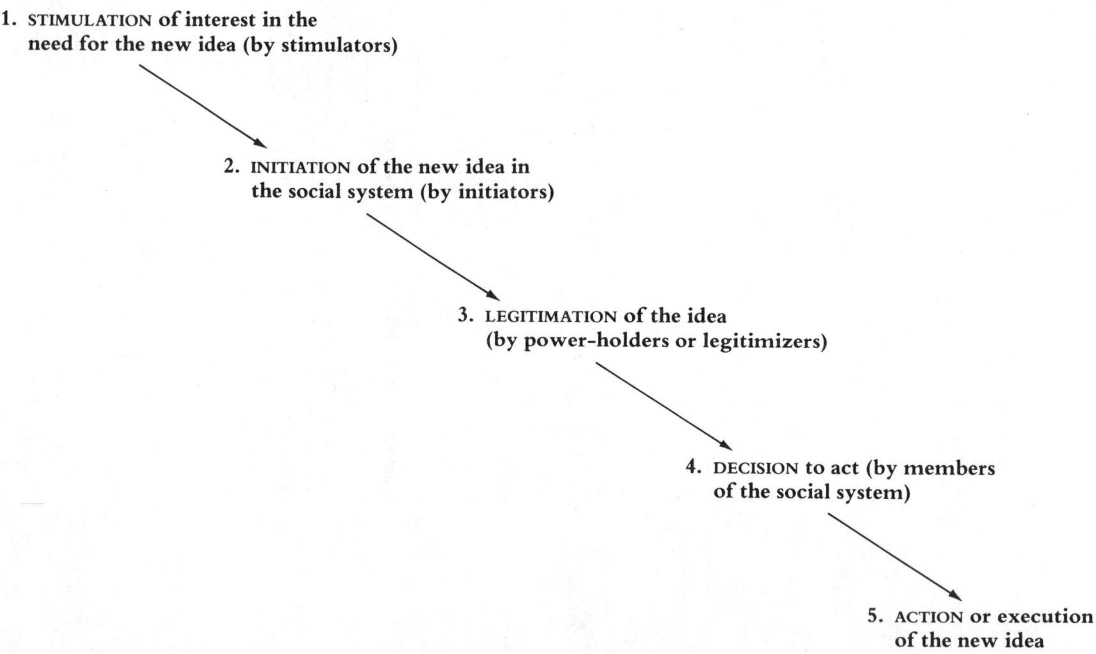
1. STIMULATION of interest in the need for the new idea (by stimulators)
2. INITIATION of the new idea in the social system (by initiators)
3. LEGITIMATION of the idea (by power-holders or legitimizers)
4. DECISION to act (by members of the social system)
5. ACTION or execution of the new idea

Reprinted with permission of Macmillan Publishing Co., Inc. from *Communication of Innovations* by Everett M. Rogers and F. Floyd Shoemaker. Copyright © 1971 by The Free Press, A Division of The Macmillan Company.

Figure 12.2 Paradigm of the collective innovation-decision-making process. The collective innovation-decision-making process is usually conceived as five or more steps or subprocesses from original realization of a need for the new idea (stimulation) to final action or carrying out the new idea in the social system. This conception has mainly evolved from research on community decision making . . . , but it should be generally applicable to most other types of social systems, such as bureaucracies, committees, and families.

explanation. In this explanation diffusion is seen as a process of spreading information or innovation in a linear fashion from media to opinion leader to members of the public; the number of steps is considered irrelevant to the basic process. This logic does not explain enough, however. Research has not consistently supported this notion of how diffusion occurs. At times the media appear to inform the public directly, with little interpersonal involvement; at other times different forms of diffusion are revealed. Rogers believes that for the most part diffusion is a network-oriented process. The strict dichotomy between opinion leaders and followers is overly simple.

The problems of this linear model are many. It tends to be one-way, implying a unidirectional flow of information and one-way causation. The implication that information and influence flow neatly from one person to another is not supported by research, which indicates that a good deal of two-way interaction is involved in the spread of information. Further, the one-way model suggests that receivers are

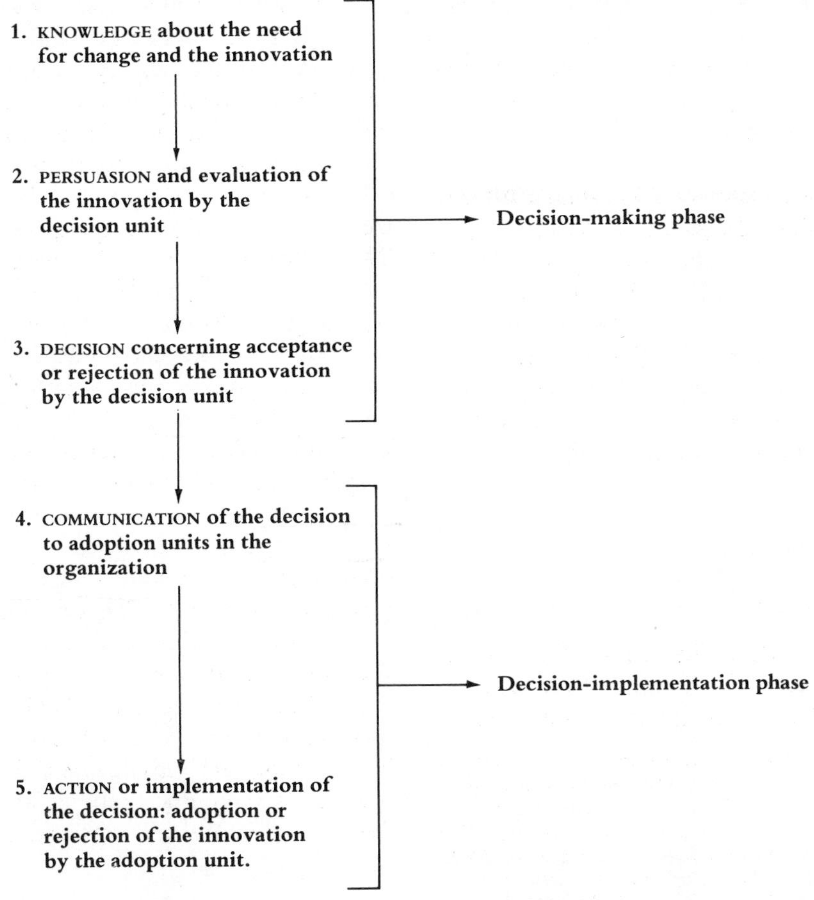
1. KNOWLEDGE about the need for change and the innovation
2. PERSUASION and evaluation of the innovation by the decision unit
3. DECISION concerning acceptance or rejection of the innovation by the decision unit
Decision-making phase
4. COMMUNICATION of the decision to adoption units in the organization
5. ACTION or implementation of the decision: adoption or rejection of the innovation by the adoption unit.
Decision-implementation phase

Reprinted with permission of Macmillan Publishing Co., Inc. from *Communication of Innovations* by Everett M. Rogers and F. Floyd Shoemaker. Copyright © 1971 by The Free Press, A Division of The Macmillan Company.

Figure 12.3. Paradigm showing functions in the authority innovation-decision process.

dependent on information sources, when in actuality individuals in the social group are interdependent. In the give and take of everyday conversation, people exchange information, question it, argue about it, and come to a shared understanding. Another problem with the linear model of diffusion is that it downplays context, but the actual circumstances under which diffusion occurs may have a great deal to do with the pattern of dissemination used by individuals in sharing information and innovations. Since context creates variability in diffusion patterns, research based on the simplistic linear model will be inconsistent. Additionally, linear models tend to stress influence rather than interpersonal understanding. Yet, as Rogers points out, diffusion is more a matter of convergence or the achievement of shared meaning than of strict influence.

Communication Effects and Functions

One of the earliest and best-known theorists of mass communication is Harold Lasswell. Lasswell, a great political scientist of our time, wrote an article entitled "The Structure and Function of Communication in Society." This 1948 treatise presents the simple and often-quoted model of communication:[68]

Who
Says What
In Which Channel
To Whom
With What Effect.

This model outlines the basic elements of communication that have received the most research attention. Although this model can be applied to any kind of communication, most often it is applied to mass communication. Indeed, mass communication effects, the last element in Lasswell's model, has been the most-researched topic in mass communication in the last fifty years.

In the preceding section we discussed the models of media-audience relationships: how audiences receive information and influence. Here we cover more specifically the effects and functions of media communications in society. While the last section stressed the process of dissemination, this section focuses on the outcomes of this dissemination.

The theory of mass communication effects has undergone a curious evolution in this century. Early in the century researchers believed in the "magic bullet" theory of communication effects. Individuals were believed to be directly and heavily influenced by media messages. In other words media were considered to be extremely powerful in shaping public opinion. Then, during the 1950s when the two-step flow hypothesis was popular, media effects were considered to be minimal. Later, in the 1960s, we discovered that the media have effects on audience members but that these effects are mediated by audience variables and are therefore only moderate in strength. Now, after research in the 1970s, scholars have returned to the powerful-effects model, in which the public is considered to be heavily influenced by media. This later research centers on television as the powerful medium.[69] The theoretical basis of this research is still under development, and for the most part theorists remain with the moderate-effects models of the 1960s. Among the most prominent theories of mass media effects and functions are reinforcement theory, agenda setting, uses and gratifications, and the dependency model. We will consider each of these in turn.

68. Harold D. Lasswell, "The Structure and Function of Communication in Society," in *The Communication of Ideas*, ed. Lyman Bryson (New York: Institute for Religious and Social Studies, 1948), p. 37. For information regarding Lasswell's contribution to political science, see Arnold A. Rogow, ed., *Politics, Personality, and Social Science in the Twentieth Century: Essays in Honor of Harold D. Lasswell* (Chicago: University of Chicago Press, 1969), especially the following articles: Heinz Eulan, "The Maddening Methods of Harold D. Lasswell: Some Philosophical Underpinnings," pp. 15–40; Bruce Smith, "The Mystifying Intellectual History of Harold Lasswell," pp. 41–105.

69. For information on the powerful-effects model, see Elisabeth Noelle-Neumann, "Return to the Concept of Powerful Mass Media," in *Studies of Broadcasting*, ed H. Eguchi and K. Sata (Tokyo: The Nippon Hoso Kyokii, 1973), pp. 67–112.

The Reinforcement Approach

Early empirical research on the reinforcement approach integrated most clearly by Joseph Klapper in *The Effects of Mass Communication*.[70] Klapper, in surveying the literature on mass communication effects, develops five broad generalizations or theoretical propositions:

1. Mass communication *ordinarily* does not serve as a necessary and sufficient cause of audience effects, but rather functions among and through a nexus of mediating factors and influences.

2. These mediating factors are such that they typically render mass communication a contributory agent, but not the sole cause, in a process of reinforcing the existing conditions. . . .

3. On such occasions as mass communication does function in the service of change, one of two conditions is likely to exist. Either:

a. the mediating factors will be found to be inoperative and the effect of the media will be found to be direct; or

b. the mediating factors, which normally favor reinforcement will be found to be themselves impelling toward change.

4. There are certain residual situations in which mass communication seems to produce direct effects, or directly and of itself to serve certain psychophysical functions.

5. The efficacy of mass communication, either as a contributory agent or as an agent of direct effect, is affected by various aspects of the media and communications themselves or of the communication situation.[71]

The first generalization is that persuasive attempts in the mass media probably tend to reinforce existing attitudes in the audience. If attitude change occurs at all, it will probably be minor; conversion is rare. This reinforcement effect is probably caused by a number of interacting variables. The first of these is the audience predisposition, which causes selective exposure, selective perception, and selective retention. People, it seems, attend to and recall information that supports existing views. Unsympathetic material may be avoided or distorted. Another mediating variable in the process of reinforcement is group norms. Individuals are influenced by the groups to which they belong; hence, mass persuasion will be mediated by group interaction. This idea was well developed in the multiple-step theories of diffusion, as we have seen. A third broad mediating variable is the process of dissemination itself. Following the lead of earlier researchers such as Katz and Lazarsfeld, Klapper points out the interpersonal nature of mass media dissemination. Along the same line, opinion leadership also influences the effects of mass media. Finally, Klapper lists the nature of media in a free society as an intervening factor. Because media are commercial enterprises carried out to make a profit, they are sensitive to audience needs, and they attempt to utilize preexisting attitudes and opinions in their appeals. In short the tendency of media to reinforce rather than convert may result from a number of interacting variables.

It is possible for attitude change to occur, particularly when group norms and other intra-audience factors are already conflicting. The third generalization in Klapper's synthesis is that predictable antecedent conditions accompany attitude change. The first of these preconditions is that the mediating factors in the audience may be inoperative, and the second is that the mediating factors themselves created pressure toward change. Such direct effects will be particularly noticeable among the neutrals, who do not hold previous opinions on the topic.

Generalization number four relates directly to the previous one. The situations in which direct persuasive effects may occur are itemized as follows: an abatement of selective processes, conflicting or reduced group norms, reduced personal influence, and high persuasibility as a personality trait.

The fifth generalization is that mass effects are influenced by a number of media, message, and situational factors. The previous generalizations dealt primarily with factors in the audience; this final proposition alerts the reader to the presence of mediating factors in the source,

70. Joseph T. Klapper, *The Effects of Mass Communication* (Glencoe, Ill.: Free Press, 1960).

71. Ibid., pp. 8–9.

message, and situation. Such factors include source credibility, media credibility, message organization, two-sided versus one-sided presentations, repetition, and so forth.

Criticism. The reinforcement approach, which is often referred to as the limited-effects model, was a definite step in the right direction at the time it was in vogue. Compared with the bullet theory, the reinforcement approach viewed mass communication as more complicated than had previously been imagined. It envisioned an audience and situation ripe with mediating variables that would inhibit media effects. The research in this tradition did identify some important mediating variables, completing a more elaborate puzzle than had previously been constructed.

The problem of the limited-effects model is that it maintained a linear, cause-to-effect paradigm for research and theory.[72] It failed to take into account the social forces on the media or the ways that individuals might affect the process. The model remained one of active media and passive audience. In addition the limited-effects model concentrated almost exclusively on attitude and opinion effects, ignoring other kinds of effects and functions. Finally, true to past tradition, such research focused on short-term effects of mass communication without questioning whether repeated exposure or time latency might affect the audience.

During the 1960s and 1970s scholars attempted to overcome these difficulties. In the later period we can see an effort to expand the notions of communication effects and to assess functions other than direct audience effects. One of the most popular areas of research centered on the agenda-setting function of mass communication.

The Agenda-setting Function

Writing on the agenda-setting function is not new. Scholars have long known that media have the potential for structuring issues for the public. One of the first writers to formalize this idea was Walter Lippman, a foremost American journalist. Lippman is known for his journalistic writing, his speeches, and his social commentary.[73] Basically, Lippman takes the view that the public responds not to actual events in the environment but to a pseudoenvironment or, as he describes it, "the pictures in our heads."[74] Lippman's model interposes an image between the audience and the actual environment: "For the real environment is altogether too big, too complex, and too fleeting for direct acquaintance. We are not equipped to deal with so much subtlety, so much variety, so many permutations and combinations. And altogether we have to act in that environment, we have to reconstruct it on a simpler model before we can manage with it."[75]

In recent years the agenda-setting function has been most completely described by Donald Shaw, Maxwell McCombs, and their colleagues.[76] In their major work on this subject, Shaw and McCombs write about the agenda-setting function:

> Considerable evidence has accumulated that editors and broadcasters play an important part in shaping our social reality as they go about their day-to-day task of choosing and displaying news. . . . This impact of the mass media—the ability to effect cognitive change among individuals, to structure their thinking—has been labeled the agenda-setting function of mass communication. Here may lie the most important effect of mass communication, its ability to mentally order and organize our world for us. In short, the mass media may not be successful in telling us what to think, but they are stunningly successful in telling us what to think about.[77]

72. Criticism of the reinforcement approach can be found in Severin and Tankard, *Communication Theories*, p. 249.

73. See, for example, M. Childs and J. Reston, eds., *Walter Lippmann and His Times* (New York: Harcourt Brace, 1959); Phillip L. Bright, "The Speaking of Walter Lippman as a Critic of the New Deal," (Doctoral dissertation, University of Washington, 1968).

74. Walter Lippmann, *Public Opinion* (New York: MacMillan, 1921).

75. Ibid., p. 16.

76. Donald L. Shaw and Maxwell E. McCombs, *The Emergence of American Political Issues* (St. Paul: West, 1977).

77. Ibid., p. 5.

In other words agenda setting establishes the salient *issues* or *images* in the minds of the public. This theory obviously is applicable to political campaigns; consequently, nearly all research on agenda setting has used campaigns as case studies.

Agenda setting occurs because the press must be selective in reporting the news. The news outlets, as gatekeepers of information, make choices about what to report and how to report it. Therefore, what the public knows about the state of affairs at any given time is largely a product of media gatekeeping. Further, we know that how a person votes is determined mainly by what issues the individual believes to be important. For this reason some researchers have come to believe that the issues reported during a candidate's term in office may have more effect on the election than the campaign itself.

Figure 12.4 depicts the key variables in the agenda-setting process according to McCombs and Shaw.[78] The first variable consists of the events and issues as they actually occur. These events provide a sea of possibilities for the reporter. Certain events naturally are defined as news; others have a narrower chance of being selected. Selection, or news choices, is the second variable in the model. Journalists experience strong pressures from their teachers, their editors, and their peers to look for certain kinds of events for reporting. In fact news media often agree about the important events and issues on which to report, indicating that journalistic standards are strong.

The third variable, type of news media, also plays a role in the agenda-setting function. For example television seems to have a short-term agenda-setting effect, while newspapers are slower, but longer lasting, in their effects. The type of story, the fourth variable in the model, shapes the nature of the information communicated. The way the information is presented and the placement of the story (for example, front page) affect the salience of an item for the public. The next variable, degree of emphasis, relates to how frequently an item is reported. Evidence suggests that the public generally ranks an issue as more important when it has been discussed frequently in the media.

The model includes some audience mediating variables, shown on the right of the figure. Audience interest and knowledge is one such

78. Ibid., p. 21.

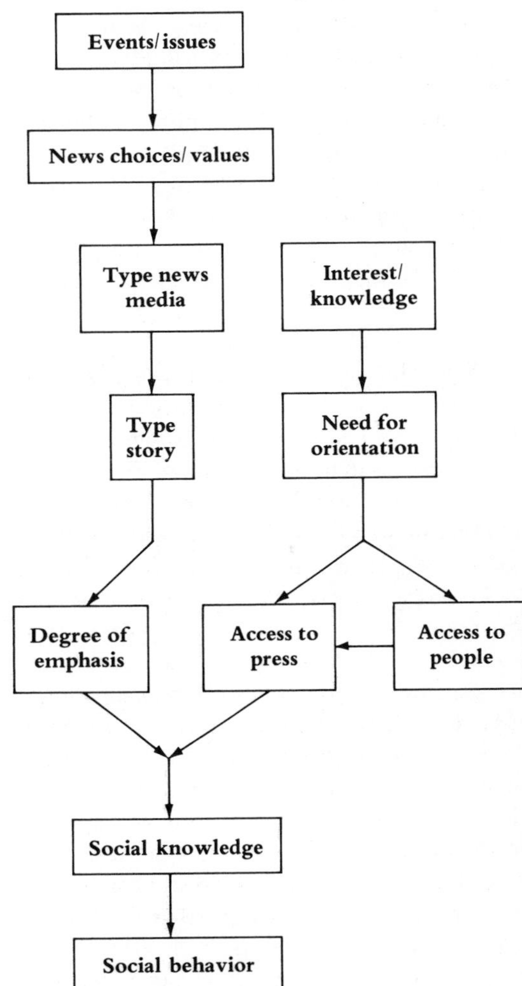

Reprinted by permission from *The Emergence of American Political Issues* by Donald L. Shaw and Maxwell E. McCombs, © 1977 West Publishing Co. All rights reserved.

Figure 12.4. The agenda-setting process.

variable. Typically, the greater the interest in an issue and the less the knowledge about it, the higher will be the need for orientation on that issue. Audience need for orientation will lead to greater media exposure and to more interpersonal communication about related events. Probably those people who are more isolated from others will be more directly influenced by the media in terms of issue salience. The outcome of the agenda-setting process is a kind of consensus on issue importance, which constitutes social knowledge. As David Shaw states: "We always have known the press is a messenger but we are just beginning to obtain a glimpse of how that messenger himself can shape the message and, perhaps, in a small and largely unconscious way help shape our common social destiny. That glimpse, of course, is the major challenge of agenda-setting research."[79]

Criticism. The agenda-setting theory is appealing for two reasons. First, it returns a degree of power to the media after an era in which media effects were thought to be minimal. Second, its focus on cognitive effects rather than attitude and opinion change adds a badly needed dimension to effects research. The idea of issue salience as a media effect is intriguing and important.

The basic problem with this line of work is that although the theory is clear in positing a causal link between media and issue salience, the research evidence on this point is not convincing.[80] Research has uncovered a strong correlation between audience and media views on the importance of issues, but it does not demonstrate that media choices cause audience salience. In fact one would argue that the emphasis given to issues in the media is a reflection, not a cause, of audience agendas. This is a chicken-egg issue. A more likely possibility is that there is an interaction between media and public in terms of the issue agenda. Perhaps Figure 12.4 could be improved by having an arrow going back from social knowledge and behavior to the media variables that purportedly affect agenda setting.

The two theories explained above—the reinforcement approach and agenda setting—are of the direct-effects tradition. Another way effects have been viewed is the *functional approach*. Here the question is not, How are people affected by the media? but, What personal and social functions are fulfilled by the media? In reality agenda-setting research lies on the border between effects and functions. Agenda setting is referred to as a function, but to the extent that media affect issue salience in the minds of individuals, agenda setting is also an effect. Generally speaking, the functional approach does not center on one-way cause-effect but looks to the system as a whole in terms of how media and society interact to achieve system functions. The next three sections present theories that fall within this functionalist tradition.

Early Functional Theories

One of the earliest formal treatments of media functions was that of Harold Lasswell, whose simple linear model is presented earlier in the chapter. Lasswell's work is paradoxical because it implies a linear process of mass communication, yet it also presents a set of functions fulfilled by mass communication, which are not easily classed as causal effects. Lasswell identifies three functions of the media of communication. These are "surveillance of the environment" (knowing what is going on), "correlation of the parts of society in responding to the environment" (having options or solutions for dealing with societal problems), and "the transmission of the social heritage of one generation to the next" (socialization and education).[81]

Charles Wright has expanded on Lasswell's model. Starting with Lasswell's three basic

79. Ibid., p. 29.

80. Criticism of this work can be found in Severin and Tankard, *Communication Theories*, pp. 253–54.

81. Lasswell, "Structure and Function."

functions, he developed a twelve-category model and a functional inventory for mass communication as shown in Figure 12.5 and Table 12.2.[82] The model is set up as a question, probing the various functions and dysfunctions of mass-communicated messages. Such functions are broken down according to social levels. The skeleton provided by the basic functional model is filled in, the questions answered, on the inventory. In Figure 12.5 we see a number of functions and dysfunctions of Lasswell's categories according to social level. Notice that Wright added a fourth function, entertainment, to Lasswell's list.

Criticism. Lasswell's three functions and Wright's elaboration of this theory have been quoted frequently in the literature on mass communication. They provide an excellent simple outline of some functions and dysfunctions of mass communication. As such they are a useful pedagogical device. However, one must stretch to call this work theoretical in the standard sense because it does not help us understand when and how these various functions and dysfunctions operate. They constitute a good observational aid but are not powerful for explanation.

82. Charles R. Wright, "Functional Analysis and Mass Communication," *Public Opinion Quarterly* 24 (1960): 605–20.

One of the criticisms of the functional approach in general is its inherent ambiguities in regard to explanation. Although the following two theories do not solve this problem, they take a step toward providing a different kind of explanation than that found in effects research.

Uses and Gratifications Approach

In recent years, there has been growing dissatisfaction with the direct-effects theories outlined earlier. The problem is that this approach is primarily linear, positing a causal relationship from message to effect. This model takes the form message–audience–mediating variables–effect. Perhaps the paradigm is backward. The approaches we will summarize in this section and the next abandon the message-to-effect model in their search for other explanations.

The uses and gratifications approach focuses on the consumer, the audience member, rather than the message. This approach begins with the person as an active selector of media communications, a viewpoint different from that which sees the person as a passive receiver.[83]

83. The material for this section comes from Elihu Katz, Jay Blumler, and Michael Gurevitch, "Uses of Mass Communication by the Individual," in *Mass Communication Research: Major Issues and Future Directions*, ed. W. Phillips Davidson and Frederick Yu (New York: Praeger, 1974), pp. 11–35. See also Jay Blumler and Elihu Katz, eds., *The Uses of Mass Communication* (Beverly Hills, Calif.: Sage Publications, 1974). See also the entire issue of *Communication Research* 6, January 1979.

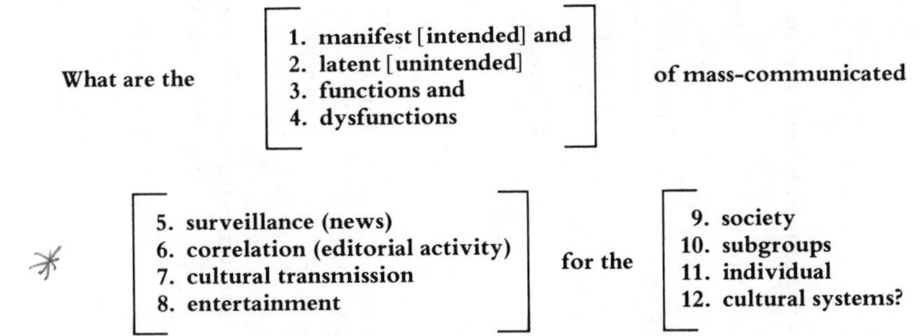

What are the
1. manifest [intended] and
2. latent [unintended]
3. functions and
4. dysfunctions
of mass-communicated
5. surveillance (news)
6. correlation (editorial activity)
7. cultural transmission
8. entertainment
for the
9. society
10. subgroups
11. individual
12. cultural systems?

Figure 12.5. Wright's functional model.

TABLE 12.2
Partial functional inventory for mass communications

	SYSTEM UNDER CONSIDERATION			
	SOCIETY	INDIVIDUAL	SPECIFIC SUBGROUP (E.G. POLITICAL ELITE)	CULTURE
1. Mass communicated activity: surveillance (news)				
Functions (manifest and latent)	Warning: Natural dangers Attack; war	Warning Instrumental	Instrumental: Information useful to power	Aids cultural contact Aids cultural growth
	Instrumental: News essential to the economy and other institutions	Adds prestige: Opinion leadership	Detects: Knowledge of subvers-sive and deviant behavior	
	Ethicizing	Status conferral	Manages public opinion: Monitors Controls	
			Legitimizes power: Status conferral	
Dysfunctions (manifest and latent)	Threatens stability: News of "better" societies Fosters panic	Anxiety Privatization Apathy Narcotization	Threatens power: News of reality "Enemy" propaganda Exposés	Permits cultural invasion
2. Mass-communicated activity: correlation (editorial selection, interpretation, and prescription)				
Functions (manifest and latent)	Aids mobilization	Provides efficiency: Assimilating news	Helps preserve power	Impedes cultural invasion Maintains cultural consensus
	Impedes threats to social stability	Impedes: Overstimulation Anxiety Apathy Privatization		
	Impedes panic			

Dysfunctions (manifest and latent)	Increases social conformism: Impedes social change if social criticism is avoided	Weakens critical faculties Increases passivity	Increases responsibility	Impedes cultural growth
3. Mass-communicated activity: cultural transmission				
Functions (manifest and latent)	Increases social cohesion: Widens base of common norms, experiences, etc. Reduces anomie Continues socialization: Reaches adults even after they have left such institutions as school	Aids integration: Exposure to common norms Reduces idiosyncrasy Reduces anomia	Extends power: Another agency for socialization	Standardizes Maintains cultural consensus
Dysfunctions (manifest and latent)	Augments "mass" society	Depersonalizes acts of socialization		Reduces variety of subcultures
4. Mass-communicated activity: entertainment				
Functions (manifest and latent)	Respite for masses	Respite	Extends power: Control over another area of life	
Dysfunctions (manifest and latent)	Diverts public: Avoids social action	Increases passivity Lowers "tastes" Permits escapism		Weakens aesthetics: "Popular culture"

The basic stance is summarized as follows:

> Compared with classical effects studies, the uses and gratifications approach takes the media consumer rather than the media message as its starting point, and explores his communication behavior in terms of his direct experience with the media. It views the members of the audience as actively utilizing media contents, rather than being passively acted upon by the media. Thus, it does not assume a direct relationship between messages and effects, but postulates instead that members of the audience put messages to use, and that such usages act as intervening variables in the process of effect.[84]

Thus the paradigm for this approach follows the order person–chosen messages–usage–effect. Unfortunately, this theory is still incomplete and rather sketchy. Research findings have not been fully integrated into an explanatory framework, but the basic ideas are worth reviewing.

The individuals most commonly associated with the uses and gratifications approach are Jay Blumler and Elihu Katz. These authors have outlined a number of basic theoretical and methodological assumptions. Three theoretical assumptions warrant discussion. The first is that the audience of mass communication is active and goal directed. Unlike most effects theories uses and gratifications theory assumes that audience members are not passive but take a proactive role in deciding how to use media in their lives. Second, the audience member is largely responsible for choosing media to meet needs. Audience members know their needs and seek out various ways to meet these needs. The third assumption, related to the other two, is that media compete with other sources of need gratification. In other words out of the options that media present, the individual chooses ways to gratify needs.

Although uses and gratifications researchers have not yet agreed on a unifying explanatory framework, the model in Figure 12.6 is one scholar's depiction of the basic process envisioned by most researchers in this area.[85] This figure is self-explanatory, but a brief description of it may be helpful. The approach always begins with basic needs. Individuals act on the basis of needs, and media choices are made in an attempt to deal with these needs. Media selection, which attempts to gratify needs, is affected by social forces as well as by individual characteristics. The degree of gratification or nongratification resulting from one's media choices in turn affects future choices as well as social options made available in the future.

One of the results of uses and gratifications research has been the establishment of needs typologies, or lists of basic need categories that can be gratified through media choices. A number of such typologies have been developed. One of the most parsimonious and sensible is that of Jay Blumler and his colleagues, who divide needs into four categories. The first is surveillance, or the cognitive ordering of the environment. The second is curiosity, or the need to know about particular events or phenomena. The third is diversion, or escape. The fourth is personal identity, or sense of self-meaning. Blumler and his associates have found that these needs are met differently by different kinds of people. Individuals who are outgoing and self-determined tend to meet needs through reading, while individuals who are less socially active and who compensate for a lack of life experience will favor viewing.

Criticism. The uses and gratifications approach was like a breath of fresh air in media research. For the first time scholars in this tradition focused on receivers as active participants in the communication process. This research program was perhaps the first in mass communication to get away from the passive, unthinking audience viewpoint. Here we see an important philosophical shift: The approach changed from a nonactional to an actional view of human be-

84. Katz, Blumler, and Gurevitch, "Uses of Mass Communication," p. 12.

85. Karl Erik Rosengren, "Uses and Gratifications: A Paradigm Outlined," in *The Uses of Mass Communication*, ed. Jay Blumler and Elihu Katz (Beverly Hills, Calif.: Sage, 1974), pp. 270–71.

86. Jay Blumler, "The Role of Theory in Uses and Gratifications Studies," *Communication Research* 6 (1979): 9–34.

1. Certain basic human needs of lower and higher order — under interaction with
2. Differential combinations of intra- and extraindividual characteristics — and also with
3. The structure of the surrounding society, including media structure — result in
4. Differential combinations of individual problems, being more or less strongly felt; — as well as
5. Perceived solutions to these problems; — the combination of problems and solutions constituting
6. Differential motives for attempts at gratification-seeking or problem-solving behavior, — resulting in
7. Differential patterns of media consumption — and
8. Differential patterns of other behavior, — both behavior categories giving
9. Differential patterns of gratifications or nongratifications — and, possibly, affecting
10. The individual's combination of intra- and extraindividual characteristics — as well as, ultimately,
11. The media structure and other social, political, cultural, and economic structures in society.

(a)

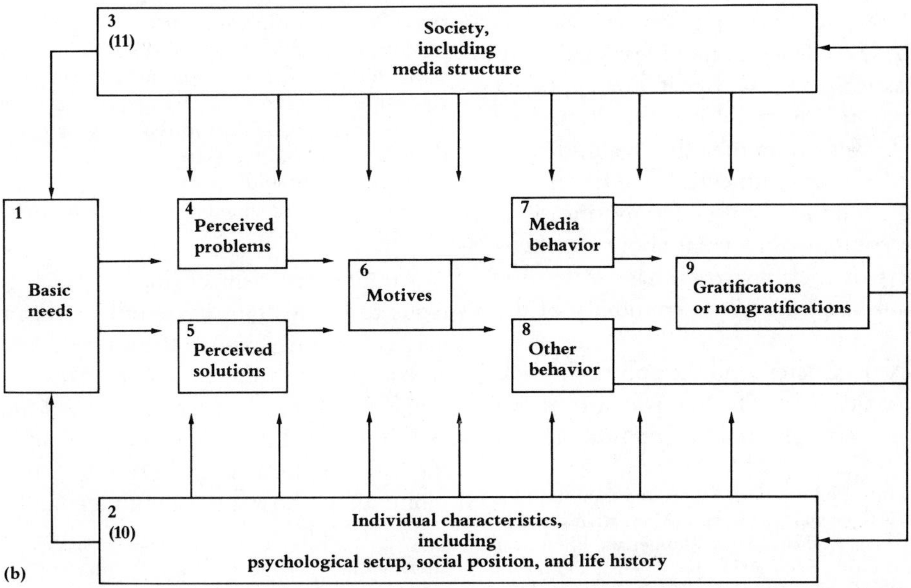

3 (11) Society, including media structure

1 Basic needs

4 Perceived problems

5 Perceived solutions

6 Motives

7 Media behavior

8 Other behavior

9 Gratifications or nongratifications

2 (10) Individual characteristics, including psychological setup, social position, and life history

(b)

Reprinted from Karl Erik Rosengren, "Uses and Gratifications: A Paradigm Outlined," pp. 269–286 in Jay G. Blumler and Elihu Katz, eds., *The Uses of Mass Communications: Current Perspectives on Gratification Research*, © 1974 Sage Publications, Inc., with permission.

Figure 12.6. Visualized paradigm for uses and gratifications research.

ings. Although we have seen this movement from nonactional to actional models in other areas of communication, the nonactional approach was predominant in mass communication research until the uses and gratifications tradition became popular. Indeed, today this approach is perhaps the most popular framework for the study of mass communication. Because of its functional nature, it is also broader in scope than the earlier theories. By focusing on functions rather than causal effects, the scholar has a wider vision of what can happen in mass communication.

The uses and gratifications approach is still new and underdeveloped. There are disagreements and uncertainties among researchers about what the movement should include. Consequently, a good deal of stiff criticism has been leveled against it.[87]

First and foremost is the serious question about what the uses and gratifications model is and ought to be. Some advocates believe that it was never intended to be a unitary theory at all but simply an approach. Blumler himself argues that the uses and gratifications view is merely a loose confederation of ideas guided by common assumptions and that the approach leaves room for many different alternative theories.[88] Swanson, on the other hand, doubts the value of a loose framework.[89] He believes that the unwillingness of uses and gratifications scholars to come to agreement about the theoretical tenets of their approach has led to ambiguities and has reduced the credibility of the movement.

This lack of coherence in the approach gives rise to two objections. The first is that uses and gratifications has appeared atheoretical. It is a compilation of research findings that are not altogether consistent with one another, rather than a set of explanatory propositions. Consequently, the explanatory power of the approach is in doubt. For example, it is unclear whether needs constitute an independent variable, a mediating variable, or a dependent variable. Do needs lead to media use, or does media use cause gratification of needs? The argument is circular: Felt needs cause people to seek methods of gratification; use of media results in gratification of needs. (Such circular explanations usually are considered appropriate in the functional tradition, although critics doubt their utility.)

The second problem arising from the approach's lack of coherence is ambiguity of terms. We are never quite certain what is meant by terms such as *function, use, gratification, need,* or *motive*. The critics' frustration over this ambiguity is expressed by Swanson:

> How may we investigate whether media consumption is necessarily gratifying if we cannot specify: (a) what a gratification is; (b) what the relation is between a gratification and a use; (c) whether a use is a motive, the result of a need, the statement of a function, all three of these, or none of these; (d) what the relation is between a use and its necessary antecedent state—need, problem, motive, or whatever—if, indeed, a use has a necessary antecedent state; and (e) what exactly would count as a negative case which could not be explained ex post facto by these ill-defined concepts.[90]

Another criticism of this appraoch is that it tends to be mentalistic, assuming that individuals consciously know their needs and act in accordance with these internal states. Ironically while the theory centers on internal individual states, it does little to advance our understanding of the human interpretive process that would guide how a person understands or perceives the self, others, and the environment. If a theory claims that individuals act on the basis of self-perceptions, then the mechanism by which perceptions are translated into action should be elucidated.

87. See especially Philip Elliott, "Uses and Gratifications Research: A Critique and Sociological Alternative," in *The Uses of Mass Communication*, ed. Jay Blumler and Elihu Katz (Beverly Hills, Calif.: Sage, 1974), pp. 249–68; and David L. Swanson, "Political Communication Research and the Uses and Gratifications Model: A Critique," *Communication Research* 6 (1979): 37–53.

88. Blumler, "The Role of Theory."

89. Swanson, "Political."

90. Ibid., p. 40.

Further, uses and gratifications has been criticized for its insensitivity to the social situation in which media choice is made. It is an individualistic approach in that it centers on the person without considering the influence of context on the person's choices. In this regard the approach has been criticized for being divorced from social processes and for not making use of any social theory.

Finally, the approach has been criticized for promoting the use of inappropriate research methods. Although the ontology of uses and gratifications is actional, traditional data collection methods are employed. Such methods involve relating one variable to another (the variable analytic tradition.) Critics charge that such methods cannot adequately uncover actional processes. Instead, critics call for more investigative, interpretive, and participative data collection methods. In short the theory's epistemology contradicts its ontology (see Chapter 2).

Dependency Theory

Another recent formulation related to the effects of mass communication is the dependency model of S. J. Ball-Rokeach and M. L. DeFleur.[91] This model takes a step toward filling in the skeleton provided by the needs and gratifications approach. Like its predecessor this approach also rejects the causal assumptions of the early reinforcement hypothesis. To overcome this weakness, these authors take a broad system approach. In their model they propose an integral relationship among audiences, media, and the larger social system: "It is through taking these sets of variables into account individually, interactively, and systematically that a more adequate understanding of mass communications effects can be gained."[92]

91. S. J. Ball-Rokeach and M. L. DeFleur, "A Dependency Model of Mass-Media Effects," *Communication Research* 3 (1976): 3–21. See also DeFleur and Ball-Rokeach, *Theories of Mass Communication*, pp. 240–51.

92. Ball-Rokeach and DeFleur, "A Dependency Model," p. 5.

At the center of this theory is the notion that audiences depend on media information to meet needs and attain goals. We see here that this approach is consistent with the basic ideas of the uses model, but unlike the latter the dependency model assumes a three-way *interaction* among media, audiences, and society. This system interaction is illustrated in Figure 12.7.[93] This diagram indicates that the degree of audience dependency on media information varies. Two sources of variation are outlined. The first is the degree of *structural stability* in the societal system, and the second is the *number and centrality* of information functions being served.

We know that the media serve a gamut of functions such as monitoring governmental activities and providing entertainment. For any given group some of these functions are more central or important than others. A group's dependence on information from a medium increases as that medium supplies information that is more central to the group. Another source of dependency variation is social stability. When social change and conflict are high, established institutions, beliefs, and practices are challenged, forcing people to make reevaluations and choices. At such times reliance on the media for information increases.

The dependency theory includes three types of effects: cognitive, affective, and behavioral. Mass communication effects within these three areas are a function of the degree to which audiences are dependent on media information. Ball-Rokeach and DeFleur outline five types of cognitive effects. The first of these is *ambiguity resolution*. Events in the environment often create ambiguities, leading to a need for additional information. The media themselves often create ambiguity. When ambiguity is present, dependence on media increases. At such times the power of mediated messages to structure understanding or to define situations may be great. At other times when the ambiguity is lessened, this effect may be much reduced.

The second cognitive effect is *attitude forma-*

93. Ibid., p. 8.

tion. The selectivity and other mediational processes outlined by Klapper and the diffusion theorists probably come into play in this effect. Third, media communications create *agenda setting*. At this point people use the media to decide what the important issues are, to decide what to be concerned about. Agenda setting is an interactional process. Topics are chosen by the media and disseminated through mass channels. From these topics people sort out information according to their individual interests and psychological and social characteristics.

The fourth cognitive effect is *expansion of the belief system*. Information may create a broadening of the number of beliefs within such categories as religion or politics, and it may also increase a person's number of categories or beliefs. The fifth cognitive effect, *value clarification*, may occur, for example, when the media precipitate value conflict in such areas as civil rights. Faced with conflicts, audience members are motivated to clarify their own values.

Affective effects relate to feelings and emotional responses. Such states as fear, anxiety, morale, or alienation may be affected by mediated information. Effects may also occur in the *behavior* realm. *Activation*, initiating new behavior, and *deactivation*, ceasing old behaviors, may occur as a result of information received from the media.

The important point from dependency theory is that mediated messages affect people only to the degree that persons depend on media information. In a nutshell, "when people do not have social realities that provide adequate frameworks for understanding, acting, and escaping, and when audiences are dependent in these ways on media information re-

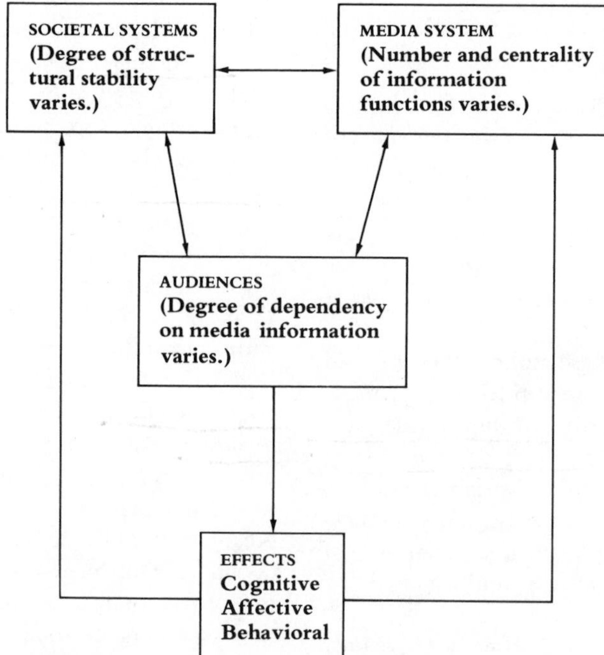

From *Communication Research*, "A Dependency Model of Mass-Media Effects," by S. J. Ball-Rokeach and M. L. DeFleur.

Figure 12.7. Society, media, audience: reciprocal relationships.

ceived, such messages may have a number of alteration effects."[94]

In their book *Theories of Mass Communication*, Ball-Rokeach and DeFleur present an integrated model of mass-communication effects that incorporates many of the ideas of the effects and functions literature summarized in this section.[95] Theirs is an excellent theory with which to end this chapter because it provides an integrated summary of much of the thinking on mass communication. The model is depicted in Figure 12.8. For the most part it is self-explanatory. Notice that the model depicts media as a social system and denotes some of the ways in which aspects of the individual, media, and society interrelate.

94. Ibid., p. 19.

95. DeFleur and Ball-Rokeach, *Theories*, p. 252.

Criticism. As a recent formulation dependency theory and the appended integrative model provide an excellent summary of variables and their interrelationships. As such these models represent taxonomies of factors and variables. They also indicate that many aspects of individuals, society, and media interrelate to form a whole system. Dependency theory shows some of the ways these factors interrelate, although for the most part the fine details of correlations are left open for future research and develop-

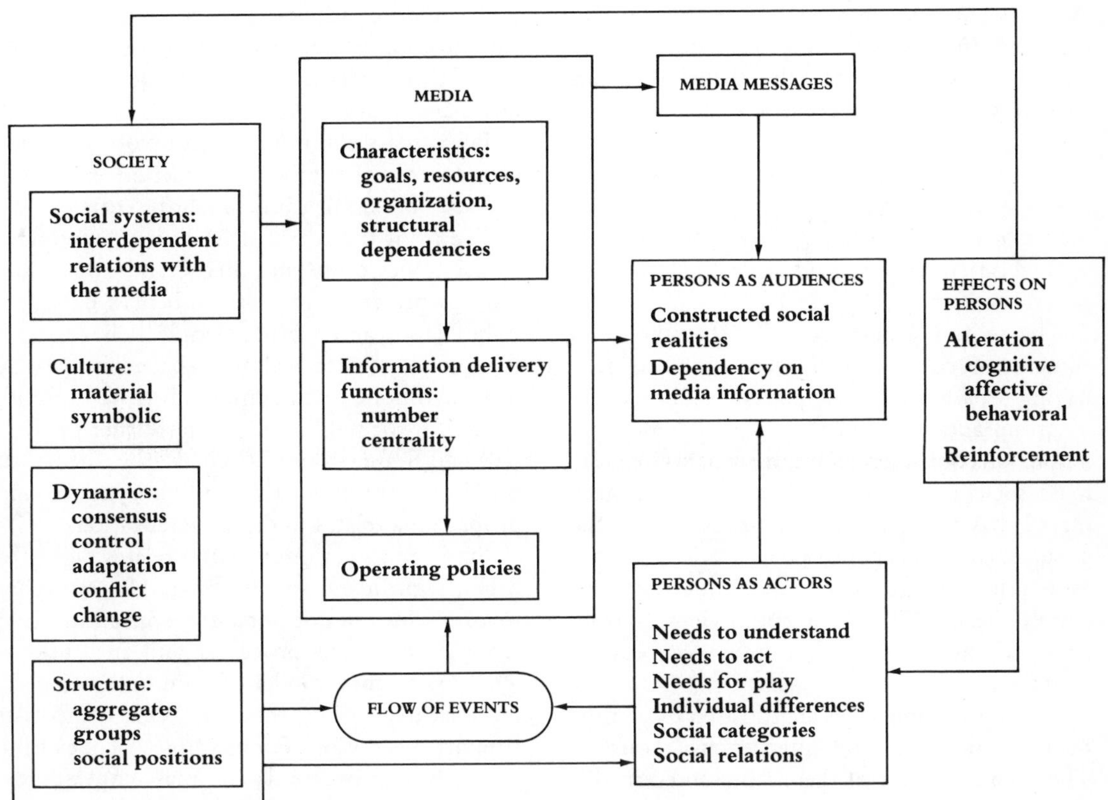

Figure 12.8. Mass media effects on individuals: an integrated model.

ment. These models provide an excellent general picture, but they do not provide much understanding of the precise nature of interactions between the separate variables of communication. Once again we are reminded that a complete understanding of communication requires that we shift our thinking back and forth between general models such as that of Ball-Rokeach and DeFleur and more discriminating work such as the reinforcement and agenda-setting research.

What Do We Know about Mass Communication?

Obviously mass communication is an elusive field. Much controversy and uncertainty exists about how mass communication works and about its effects and the ways it relates to other aspects of society. From the theories in this chapter we can make some broad generalizations.

First, mass communication involves public messages from organizational sources sent via media to large audiences. This process as described is rich indeed, as we see in the following generalizations.

The second generalization is that the mass audience is composed of many publics, each having separate response patterns. The degree of group autonomy in the mass audience is a matter of controversy. We have seen that the mass society theorists tend to assume a large mass behaving as a single mind. However, the group-mediational approach treats the audience as a system of groups bound by interpersonal communication. If this second view is true, processes of diffusion and influence become complex.

Third, mass messages are diffused by a combination of media and interpersonal sources. The preponderance of theory presented in this chapter supports this generalization. Diffusion theorists such as Rogers typically follow a multiple-step flow model of diffusion and influence, recognizing the importance of interpersonal communication. With the exception of McLuhan, Ellul, and a few others, most theorists of communication effects realize that group identification and support are important in media influence processes. Even the uses and dependency approaches note that people actively seek a variety of sources for meeting their needs and goals.

Fourth, media forms, apart from content, affect society. McLuhan is responsible for the aphorism "The medium is the message." While his various ideas are controversial, McLuhan has tuned us to the importance of media technology in modern society. This generalization does not deny the significance of message content; the bulk of theory presented here simply would not support such a denial. Still it is clear from most approaches to mass communication that media technology by itself has great impact.

Fifth, mass communication involves a complex process of symbolic interaction, including the use of significant symbolic forms. We realize from the work of McLuhan, Lippman, Rogers, McCombs and Shaw, and others that what is presented to mass audiences has symbolic significance. What people believe, how they conceptualize reality is shaped in part by these symbols. Such symbols help to simplify reality for the public and to meet other political and social functions. Much of the theory in political communication, public opinion, and propaganda relates to this generalization.

Sixth, mass communication relates highly to other significant social forms. In studying media, you cannot separate communication from other social processes and institutions. The dependency model of communication effects clearly points this out. Other theorists support this notion. For example, Jacques Ellul shows how propaganda and mass communication are related.

In the last four chapters we have seen the ways in which the process of communication occurs in context. We have looked at theories related to interpersonal, group, organizational, and mass communication. We have also seen how all communication involves certain basic processes. By now it should be clear that understanding human communication is not an easy task. Rather, it involves a multidisciplinary and multitheoretical effort, as we will see in the final chapter.

PART

V

CAPSTONE

CHAPTER

13 The Status of Human Communication Theory

You have now completed a lengthy and somewhat detailed survey of communication theories. At this point you undoubtedly realize that communication is an exceedingly broad concept and that theories of communication and related processes are diverse and numerous. This book presents just a sampling of such theories, selected to represent the mainstream of thought about human symbolic interaction. One might wish to complete the puzzle of communication in this final chapter, but that is not possible; no chapter or book could ever present a complete picture of the processes involved in communication. The goal of this chapter is to present a personal assessment of the status of communication theory at this point in its development. Please keep in mind that this analysis is one scholar's judgment; others may not agree.

The Study of Human Communication

The Multitheoretical Tradition

Three approaches can be followed in relating to a large body of theory in an area of study. The first of these is to take hold of the theory or theoretical area that seems intellectually tasty and to work to understand it, defend it, and further develop it. This course is the usual route of graduate students, researchers, and many practitioners. Such individuals, following the lead of their mentors, survey the field, learn research tools suited to their personal aptitudes and interests, and conduct concentrated study or practice in their chosen theoretical area.

A second approach is that of the maverick, who, after working in the field for a while, decides that traditional categories are not satisfactory. The maverick then proceeds to develop a virgin field, to expand the breadth of approaches to a problem area. Both of these avenues reap benefits. Concentrating on a single theoretical area helps a person develop specialized understanding of the chosen theory. Breaking new ground is a creative process, rare, but precious in expanding horizons.

Unfortunately, these two avenues to complex fields of study also carry disadvantages. They can breed defensiveness as well as tunnel vision. In this book we have taken a third road to understanding, a multitheoretical or eclectic approach. This view does not deny the contribution of the specialist and the maverick, but it calls for more. The eclectic approach enables us to develop frameworks within which the work of many disciplines may be integrated around a single issue, problem, or theme.

Communication is such a theme, and at present it requires a multitheoretical viewpoint. A multitheoretical approach respects the integrity of a variety of theoretical and methodological stances. With this eclectic mind we are able to look for the best contributions of those who have chosen to specialize in a particular aspect of communication. We are further able to see patterns and generalizations not apparent from narrower perspectives. We are also able to better define true theoretical controversies. A number of favorable arguments can be given for this kind of approach to studying communication.

First, communication is a ubiquitous and complex process. To conceive of the area as a unified, solid chunk of knowledge would be absurd. As a result we will come to understand the process of communication in its full richness only by viewing it from various perspectives. Any attempt to limit our view to a single, unified perspective is to wear restrictive blinders.

Second, because communication is a process, we will never find the ultimate and true theory. This statement does not imply that all theories are equally valid or useful; investigators may find a specific theory or theories more relevant to their purposes. Rather, communication consists of a number of kinds of events and behaviors, and each theory provides insights of its own.

Third, as pointed out in the second chapter, theories are constructions of reality. They define the way the theorist structures reality, not reality itself. The same sensory experience may be conceived in numerous ways. A single theory will point to certain aspects of an event to the exclusion of others. Only through a multitheoretical approach can we become cognizant of the range of meanings for a given communication event.

Fourth, attempts to develop a best theory will surely be scarred by methodological defensiveness. For researchers and theorists to possess self-respect and confidence in their methods is a healthy sign, but when this confidence turns into parochialism that denies the positive contributions of various methodologies, the state of the art is less than healthy. In fact, the kind of theory sought by a researcher will follow naturally from the particular method used. No single method is a direct pipeline to truth. A multitheoretical approach is necessarily a multimethods approach, providing a kind of convergent validity to what we know about communication.

Of course, theoretical controversies cannot be avoided by an eclectic approach. We dialogue about such controversies, and persons resolve these controversies to their own satisfaction with whatever methods are available. But often, if we keep both eyes open in our search, we see the many ways that various theories support one another, fill gaps in one another, and extend beyond one another. Although the eclectic approach has several advantages—and the field will probably remain eclectic in the future—communication scholars need to develop more unified, integrative theory. This problem is discussed in some detail later in the chapter.

Multidisciplinary Roots

The body of theories related to communication has been produced by a variety of disciplines. Over the years four primary fields have been responsible for most of the work on communication: psychology, sociology, anthropology, and philosophy. Speech communication in recent years has also become a leader in producing research and theory. Of course, many other disciplines have contributed to our understanding of communication, including management, journalism, speech sciences, political science, mathematics, engineering, and others.

In most of these fields, communication has been treated as an implicit process. The majority of fields have been interested in topics that include communication as important but usually subsidiary and tacit variable. Consequently much of our understanding of communication has arisen indirectly from the investigation of other related processes, such as social institutions, norms and values, personality, human relations, organizational behavior, language, and systems. Many of the theories reported in this book really are indirect theories of communication.

Although some explicit theories of communication almost always have been in vogue, scholars interested in communication usually have had to rely mostly on indirect or implicit treatments of communication as a basis for understanding many facets of the process. Such scholars typically were trained in traditional disciplines, although teachers of rhetoric and journalism have long been directly interested in applied communication in group, public speaking, and mediated contexts. Since about 1950 scholars from various disciplines have been increasingly aware of work proceeding in other disciplines on communication themes. In 1949 the National Society for the Study of Communication was born; it thrives today under its newer name of the International Communicaiton Association. This organization is an interdisciplinary group of scholars who share a common interest in communication as a focal, rather than a subsidiary, concern. In addition the Speech Communication Association and its regional associations have become prominent in promoting research and theory on a gamut of communication concerns. Although the study of communication has been and remains a multidisciplinary field, an identifiable, unitary discipline focusing primarily on communication is growing.

The Emergence of Communication as a Field

The 1970s and the 1980s appear to be an era in which the study of communication has come of age. Scholars whose primary interest is communication have produced a great deal of research. As a result we now see a number of recent *communication* theories. Several journals on communication are published, and books about the field have proliferated. In addition new departments of communication in universities around the world have been created. Many of these consist of combinations of such long-standing departments as speech communication, speech sciences, journalism, and mass communication.

The natural result of this increased attention to communication is that our understanding of the process has grown. Much of what is now taught is based more on research data and theoretical foundations than ever before. However, many divisions and issues remain unsolved among communication scholars.

The Status of Communication Theory

This section is an assessment of communication theory—major philosophical issues, communication definitions, and strengths and weaknesses.

Types of Theory

As indicated earlier, one evidence of the increasing maturity of the field of communication is the growing number of serious attempts to create theory. Before about 1975, much of what passed for theory in communication was simple models or taxonomies of concepts. Many of these were presented in visual form. We discussed them in previous chapters. Today fewer of these simple models are being produced, and in their place truly explanatory theories are being created. Scholars still consider models useful but more as pedagogical devices than as explanations of communication processes. As an example of this development, consider the theory of relational communication (Chapter 9). In the 1950s and 1960s when relational theory originally was developed, it consisted of a simple taxonomy of concepts (for example, content dimension, relationship dimension) and a handful of axioms, such as "One cannot not communicate." Although rudimentary relational theory did provide some explanation, as in the case of the double bind, basically it was a series of truisms. Today we understand relations better than we did earlier because of the work done by clinicians and researchers in providing a substantive foundation for the abstractions of relational theory. Park's summary, presented in Chapter 9, outlines the kinds of propositions now being tested. Much is left to accomplish in relational communication, but the difference between what is known now versus even a decade ago shows phenomenal growth and maturity.

Another change in theory between the former infant field of communication and its present childhood is the degree to which theorists have applied abstract approaches. In earlier periods communication theory was largely populated by general theories or abstract propositions. General system theory and symbolic interactionism are examples. Such approaches provided a way of thinking about communication but gave us few substantive propositions about actual phenomena. We explored the weakness of these general approaches in the criticism sections of previous chapters. Today, theorists tend to reify these general theories by pointing to actual communication events. As an example the work of Farace, Monge, and Russell (Chapter 11) is a clearly applied system theory of organizations that presents a unified and internally consistent set of propositions. This theory shows much more sophistication than its general systems precursor.

The 1970s saw a vocal reaction against causal analytic theory. This revolution mirrored a general movement away from deterministic models throughout the behavioral and social sciences. Hence, several serious attempts have been made to create theories based on teleological explanation. Attempts have also been made to ground theories based in the phenomenologic experiences of real people in the natural setting. Still, a careful survey of the theories in this book reveals that there remains a major reliance on causal analytic theories of communication. The bulk of theories still in vogue lie in this camp, although significant theories of the logical and practical types can also be found. As an example of a theory of the causal analytic type, refer to the work of Hart and his colleagues on rhetorical sensitivity (Chapter 10). For an example of a theory utilizing logical necessity as a base for explanation, review Weick's theory of organizing (Chapter 11). Refer to developments in relational theory (Chapter 9) as an example of a theory with practical necessity as an explanatory base.

Philosophical Issues

Some of the differences among theories just noted are a reflection of philosophical issues, namely, issues of epistemology and ontology. In the beginning of this book (Chapter 2) we looked at two basic epistemological groups called World View I and World View II. Remember that these are general opposing kinds of thought and that, in fact, many different epistemological positions exist. World View I theories are those that stress the world as discoverable and that rely on research data that is empirical, quantitative, and analytical. World View II theories stress interpretation as a way of knowing and emphasize holism and synthesis. Interestingly, communication theories now in vogue are rather evenly split between these two types of thinking. In almost every chapter of this book, theories of both types can be found. For example, in mass communication theory, such approaches as that of McLuhan and Ellul illustrate World View II epistemology, while much of the communication effects literature falls under World View I.

Another philosophical split is between theories that rely on actional versus nonactional assumptions. Recall that an actional approach envisions individuals as choice making, subjective, and proactive beings, while nonactional stances envision human behavior as largely determined by forces outside the individual's control. Again, communication theory is rather evenly split between these two types of premises. In persuasion, for example, Bandura's social learning view is basically an actional theory, while attitude theories such as those of Sherif and Rokeach tend to be nonactional.

The third kind of philosophical issue is perspective. Recall from Chapter 2 that perspective relates to the focus of a theory. Depending on the epistemology and ontology of the theorist, the theory will emphasize different aspects of the observed world. While behavioristic theories remain popular, an increasing number are interactional or transactional in orientation. Very few transmissional theories are now popular. A behavioristic theory that has received attention is Crockett's theory of cognitive complexity (Chapter 7). An example of a transmissional theory is Hart's theory of rhetorical sensitivity (Chapter 10). Fisher's theory of the interact (Chapters 3 and 11) is clearly interactional, and Dance and Larson's theory of communication functions is transactional (Chapter 9).

Definitions of Communication

Dance's analysis of communication definitions (Chapter 1) remains the single most comprehensive discussion of the many ways communication has been defined. Dance factored out three basic dimensions of communication definitions. These are level, or the scope of behaviors defined as communicative; intentionality, or whether conscious intent must be present for communication to take place; and normative judgment, or whether the definition includes the criterion of success or quality. Many of the theories in this book do not have explicit definitions of communication, but in most cases such a definition can readily be inferred. In applying Dance's dimensions to the explicit or implicit definitions of communication, we find that while level and intentionality remain viable factors in the definition of communication, the judgment dimension is virtually nonoperative in a contemporary communication theory. There is a lesson in this; namely, most communication theory today is basically descriptive in approach, attempting to describe and explain behaviors that are communicative, regardless whether the behavior results in a successful outcome.

When we look at the other dimensions of communication definitions, we find that definitions are evenly split between those of a high level (define a wide scope of behavior as communicative) and of a low level (specific in identifying certain behaviors as communicative). Among meaning theorists (Chapter 6), for example, Langer and Cassirer include a range of symbols that can communicate meanings, while Richards, Whorf, and the ordinary language theorists center almost entirely on language forms. We also note a relatively even split between theories that require intention as part of communication and those that do not. For example, in Chapter 5 we found that most of the nonverbal communication theorists look at the communicative functions of nonintended bodily and vocal activity, while most of the language theorists center on the intended generation and reception of language.

Strengths and Weaknesses

Generalizing about the strengths and weaknesses of contemporary theories of communication is difficult. As you are aware, there are many differences among theories in terms of their strengths and weaknesses. Still, a survey such as this reveals certain trends.

First, communication theory remains fragmented. Although the field of communication is becoming more unified than ever before, what we know about communication as a theme derives from many separate research and theory traditions. While an eclectic approach has advantages, as we have just spelled out, it has disadvantages as well. The fragmented nature of communication theory detracts from a well-coordinated effort to understand the basic or central processes common to all communication. Fragmentation also creates terminology confusion. Within the coming twenty or thirty years, we will no doubt see an increasing unity among communication theories, such that their work becomes more coordinated and interrelated. In the meantime, books such as this one will serve the function of providing a degree of integration.

Within the field of communication is an amazing lack of middle-range theory. Theories either tend to be highly abstract, as are such general approaches as system theory or symbolic interactionism, or they tend to be inappropriately analytical and myopic, as are such theories as kinesics or information theory. As communication scholars become increasingly aware of each other's work and cross-disciplinary lines, their theories will become appropriately broad, yet capable of explaining a range of phenomena.

As we noted previously, one of the signs of growing maturity in communication scholarship is less reliance on general approaches and more development of actual explanatory theory. This change shows a strength, but we still have a long way to go in this regard. A strong tendency still exists, despite the work of scholars to the contrary, to promote an approach or general confederation of ideas as if it were an explanatory theory. General systems theory, symbolic interaction, rules theory, ordinary language philosophy, information theory, relational theory, the transactional approach, interaction analysis, and the uses and gratifications approach are some examples of fruitful frameworks that should not be considered explanatory theory yet are taken to be so by many writers. One of the biggest steps the field needs to take is to subdivide these traditions into theoretical structures. Eventually, we should have a clear conception of the differences between traditions of thought, theoretical frameworks, approaches, and theories. As yet we have not achieved consensus on this kind of differentiation. In this book the term *theory* has been defined broadly to include any conceivable cluster of ideas that helps us understand the process. Eventually, a finer distinction should be possible.

Despite this indictment, a surge of good theory has been developing. Some of these theories provide a basis for understanding a range of communication-related phenomena in differing contexts. Others exemplify social science theory at its best. Such theories can be found in almost all areas of communication. What these theories share is that they explain a range of phenomena, meeting the criterion of generality, in a way that isolates key explanatory concepts, meeting the criterion of necessity (Chapter 2). They are sufficient in scope, parsimony, heruistic value, and philosophical appropriateness, and they have the potential of displaying high validity.

Major Issues in Communication Theory

This section outlines what appear to be the unresolved substantive issues in communication theory. These issues admittedly are general. They are intended to provide an overview of the broadest areas of disagreement in communication theory without providing a specific analysis of the numerous research and theory issues in each area of communication. You should also note that the issues listed will not necessarily be settled in the near future. Because of the difference in philosophical orientation among communication scholars, some issues may never be settled. For purposes of organization, we will look at these issues in terms of the areas of communication theory represented by chapters in this book. Each issue is stated as a question.

General System Theory and Cybernetics

To what extend does communication operate as a system? This question is about the degree to which communication involves interrelatedness of variables, wholeness or inseparability of parts, homeostasis or balance-seeking behavior, morphogenesis or change, feedback or self-monitoring, and equifinality or variable goal achievement. The issue is not really one of whether communication is or is not a system but the degree of systemlike behavior displayed by communication.

Under what circumstances does communication operate as a system? Some theorists suspect that at times communication is very much a system, but that at other times it is not. This issue deserves research treatment, since circumstances probably dictate to a large extent the degree of systemness of a transaction. If we are to get beyond the truism that communication is a system, then we must probe the ways in which it is so and the circumstances under which it is systemlike.

Symbolic Interaction and Rules

To what extent is meaning created by the social group through interaction? This issue relates to the degree to which meaning is a dependent or an independent variable. Is meaning inherent in language? Is meaning negotiated as part of interaction? Most symbolic interactionists take the position that meaning is created in social interaction and is not a structural given in society. Many other scholars, especially those in mainstream linguistics, see language processes as embedded in culture or possibly even genetically inherited.

Does behavior arise from meanings that are internal to the individual, or is it a response to other pressures in the environment outside of the individual? Symbolic interactionism generally believes that our behavior is created with the intent of fulfilling particular meanings that are internalized through symbolic interaction. Behaviorists are often skeptical about this conclusion, stating that meanings are a mentalistic construct and not useful in understanding why people behave as they do. Here the issue relates to the degree to which meanings are internal "behaviors" that respond to environmental pressures or socially internalized forces that give rise to proactive behavior on the part of the individual.

What are rules? A controversy remains about the nature of rules. Are rules internal interpretive mechanisms similar to meanings? Are they guides for overt behavior only? Are they prescriptive? As we saw in Chapter 4, much disagreement exists about what constitutes a useful definition of the rules concept.

Do rules determine, regulate, govern, or guide? A related issue involves the amount of power in rules. Some theorists believe that rules are tantamount to laws, since they describe lawlike behavior. Others believe that they are powerful forces, but that the individual maintains the ability to override rules. Still other theorists believe that rules are optional guides that individuals choose in adapting to situations. Rules probably play all of these roles in different instances. In the future scholars may find it necessary to discriminate between types of rules or to define rules in a particular way, with the recognition that other forces are also at work in shaping behavior.

How do rules arise? Are rules negotiated in each situation? Are they immutable, embedded in culture? Are they created through symbolic interaction? Rules theories typically are unclear about the way communication functions in creating and/or maintaining rules.

Language

By what process are sentences generated? We simply do not understand how sentences are created. Although linguists have struggled with this question and have created theories that explain a great deal of language behavior, their theories are speculative at best. On the most fundamental level, an issue still remains about the degree to which sentence generation is a sentence-building process or a deeper cognitive process. Most linguists now follow the latter approach, but there is much disagreement even among those who favor the deep-process approach.

How is language acquired? Is language strictly learned? Are basic language building blocks innate? Or is some combination of innate and learning factors at work? Most linguists believe that language cannot be learned strictly according to reinforcement paradigms, but much uncertainty still exists about exactly how children acquire it.

How much meaning is conveyed by nonverbal cues? The question of how important nonverbal symbols are in face-to-face interaction is a strong issue in communication theory. Some scholars maintain that almost all meaning is conveyed nonverbally. Many believe that little of what is conveyed comes via nonverbal cues—that language is most important. The situation itself probably affects the degree to which nonverbal cues elicit meanings in conversation or other forms of communication. Individual differences may also be present regarding the degree to which nonverbal cues are relied on both in sending and receiving messages.

To what extent does bodily activity possess syntactic structures? Here the question is the degree to which body actions are coordinated or organized to form "messages." Some scholars believe that bodily activity in communication is organized in ways that are understood by others and that this organization approximates linguistic syntax. Although most scholars would agree that some kind of organization is probably apparent in nonverbal activity, a question remains as to the degree to which this organization functions in the same sense as syntax or the degree to which such activity communicates meanings that are widely understood.

Meaning

What is meaning? Oddly enough, the most fundamental theoretical issue in the literature is the definition of the term *meaning*. The word has been used in three different ways. The first definition regards meaning as the correspondence between a symbol and individuals' conceptions brought to mind by the symbol. The second definition relates meaning to deep-seated feelings arising out of experience. The third definition sees meaning as purpose or intention about the kind of effect desired in a transaction. Meaning theorists either need to refine their conceptual terms or to recognize that a variety of types of meaning exist and to begin to elucidate these types.

Some of the other issues of meaning were covered earlier in this section under symbolic interaction.

Information

What is information? The concept of information is one of the most confusing in all of communication literature. The classical information theorists present a clear, though narrow, definition. Others, in an attempt to broaden the concept and make it more useful, have bent it to conform to different applications.

Is information a quality of messages, stimuli, or meanings? At what point does a stimulus or set of stimuli become information? Is information a product of perception or cognition, or is it an inherent part of the stimulus field? Actually, this issue is a subset of the larger issue of what defines information. Theorists thus disagree over the locus of information.

In what ways are processes of cognition interconnected? Although all researchers interested in cognition recognize that the aspects of cognition—for example, sensation, perception, recall, encoding, decoding, memory, and so forth—are interconnected, how they related to one another is much less clear. This research area is one of the most dynamic in contemporary psychology, with results that have major implications for language and communication processes.

Persuasion

What are the most important elements of behavior to change as a result of messages from others? This question is a long-term issue in the research of persuasion. Several important elements of behavior have been identified as changeable, including overt behavior, attitudes, beliefs, and values, among others. The question is which of these best identifies the central variable in a change paradigm. We know, for example, that attitudes are correlated with behaviors, and yet research shows that attitude change is not necessarily followed by expected behavior change. Some research even suggests that attitude change follows behavior change. How important are values? Some believe that values are the key to personal change.

By what process do messages lead to change in people? Why do people change or not change in the face of messages that oppose their attitudes, beliefs, values, or behaviors? Does change involve inconsistency resolution, learning, a trust bond, value shifts, group conformity, or some combination of these and other factors? We have clues to the answers to these questions from persuasion research, but firm answers are not easily found.

How active is the recipient in determining how, when, and under what conditions change will occur? Early persuasion theory treated the receiver as a passive individual. Change was thought to occur because of forces out of the individual's control. Later persuasion theorists have taken a more actional stance, suggesting that people vary in the amount and nature of change they undergo as a result of messages, not only between one another but from one time to another. The assumption is that people are selective in choosing the nature and extent of change they will undergo and in choosing media, messages, and sources that will help them resist or facilitate change.

Interpersonal Contexts: Dyadic Communication

What are the relative degrees of influence of socially-derived rules versus internal needs and personality in determining how an individual will communicate with others? This issue is an old one that has reappeared in many guises. Basically it involves a debate between those who look to internal, predispositional factors and those who look to the external situation in deciding what affects behavior.

Is self-disclosure or adaptive communication behavior more functional in producing growthful relationships? This question is normative, and normative issues have always been a big part of the dialogue in this area. The issue centers around the desired degree of self-orientation versus other-orientation in communication. It also relates to questions of interpersonal understanding, trust, and relational maintenance. Perhaps a more productive approach would be to investigate the conditions under which these orientations are most appropriate.

What factors give rise to relational development and maintenance? This issue is abstract, consisting of a number of areas. For example, there is the question of why individuals are attracted to one another. A clear answer has not been forthcoming, although several interesting theories, which are not inconsistent with one another, have been developed. Also, there is the question of why and when relationships dissolve. Is relational maintenance a matter of rational comparison of alternatives, or are other, more subtle relational dimensions involved? Under what circumstances is conflict productive in a relationship and when is it destructive? To what extent is conflict a product of or a determiner of relational change?

What factors in the self, the other, and the situation affect one's perceptions and attributions of others? What are the relative roles of an individual's communicative behavior, predispositions and self-concept, and situational influences on how one will perceive another and how one analyzes or understands the behavior of another? Especially important is the question of how communication patterns affect interpersonal perception.

What forms of communication give rise to conflict? This issue deals with the ways communication affects conflict. Do certain kinds of communication behaviors lead to conflict more often than others? Oddly enough, the relationship between communication and conflict has not been well researched, and much work remains to be done.

What forms of communication direct or abate conflict? This issue has received relatively more attention than has the preceding issue, but still we are uncertain as to the nature of communication necessary to redirect, manage, control, or reduce conflict. Although practitioners such as negotiators and counselors have intuitive and clinically researched notions of the relationship between conflict and communication, not much research and theory building have been done in this area.

Interpersonal Communication: Groups and Organizations

What is the optimal balance of maintenance-related communication to task-related communication for group productivity? Most contemporary theorists of group communication recognize that group productivity depends on communication both for interpersonal maintenance and for task accomplishment, but they disagree about the necessary balance between these. Some theorists believe that a great deal of maintenance energy is necessary in order to critically evaluate task ideas; others think that more than a little is too much and inhibits group functioning.

To what extent does open communication in organizations lead to satisfaction on the part of organization members? To what extent does satisfaction, assumed to be enhanced by open communication, improve organization productivity? These two questions are considered together because they are the dubious premises of much of the human relations movement. As you know from the critiques summarized in Chapter 11, these are major issues among organizational theorists.

To what extent and in what ways do organizations operate as systems? That organizations are systems is a truism, but critics of this claim point out that organizations are not always systemlike. A relatively uninvestigated question is the degree to which and the conditions under which organizations do or do not behave as systems.

Mass Communication

What are the relative effects of media content and media forms? McLuhan has led us to believe that media forms apart from content have had an immense impact on society, but this claim is controversial. We need more research and theory that deals with the nature of the effects of media forms vis-a-vis media content.

To what extent are media effects mediated by audience-related variables? This issue is surely one of the oldest in twentieth-century media communication. As we saw in the last chapter, great uncertainty exists about the conditions under which media effects are direct and when they are indirect. Uncertainy also exists about the conditions that give rise to direct or indirect effects.

What factors affect the conditions under which individuals are active in selecting media communications and when they are not, and on what basis do individuals choose or use media? This question is the basic issue surrounding the uses and gratifications approach. Scholars generally agree that individuals do have an active role in determining how media affect them, but at the same time they are uncertain about the conditions under which individuals are active in this way and the degree to which media effects are out of the control of individuals.

The Future of Communication Theory

Earlier in this chapter we emphasized that although communication theory is based on multiple approaches generated in several disciplines, the field is becoming increasingly unified as an organization of scholars. Before the chapter ends, we should consider a question that has been asked repeatedly throughout the brief history of communication as a field of study. Is it possible and desirable to develop a general theory of communication? In the early 1960s the widely held belief was that the field needed a master theory to guide research on communication. Then, in the decade following scholars generally believed that a single theory not only would be impossible, but undesirable. By the mid-1970s, however, certain scholars had begun to develop such theories.

Although we probably will never have a master theory of communication, three or four competing theories likely will emerge within the coming decade or two. These theories probably will differ in terms of philosophy, contrasting on points of epistemology, ontology, and perspective. Most likely they will provide explanations of the basic processes of communication in all settings. They will not deal solely with isolated aspects or contexts but will center on the process of communication as a focal and general theme. On the other hand, they will not be so general as to serve only as guiding frameworks, nor will they be so broad as to apply to all social and behavioral phenomena. They will be true theories of the middle range.

Let us look at two theories that have potential, with additional development, to become theories of this type. We discuss these only as examples; there are others. The first is the theory of the coordinated management of meaning by Pearce, Cronen, and their colleagues (Chapter 4). This theory attempts to explain basic processes by which individuals mesh their rules of interaction. The theory is general enough to cover nearly all forms and levels of communication, although the authors have not yet extended it to many contexts other than face-to-face interaction. The second example is the functional theory of Dance and Larson (Chapter 9). This theory, also most relevant to interpersonal communication, outlines three basic functions of communication for the individual and presents a number of propositions that are explained in terms of these functions. With additional development this theory could be extended to cover all contexts and social functions as well as individual functions.

We will not take sides here on which philosophical presuppositions should guide the development of general theories. Rather, let us note that any general theory should address at least the following substantive areas.

First, a general theory must address symbols and meanings as the foundation for all communication. Such a theory must move beyond the level of the truism of communication as a symbolic activity that elicits meanings in communicators. It must define the symbols used in communication, including, but not solely, language. Such a theory should explain the ways language and other symbol forms achieve a consensus of understanding of common meanings.

Second, a general theory must deal with human interdependence or interaction. It must show how communication functions to create a social structure beyond the person. Such an explanation might be in terms of communication interacts, system interdependence, interpersonal understanding, coordinated rules, or any of a number of other possible paradigms.

Third, a general theory of communication must also deal with the ways communication enables the individual to adapt to, accommodate, or assimilate the social, cultural, and physical environment. Such concepts as information, persuasion, cognition, cooperation, and conflict might be used in such an explanation.

Fourth, a theory of communication must take into account the context in which communication occurs. No single theory can account for all contexts, but some explanatory mechanism must be developed to help us understand how communication will vary from one situation to another. Preferably, such a theory would provide a basis for understanding the basic factors at work in enabling, allowing, or governing how communication changes from setting to setting. Recent elaborations of rules theory are an attempt to do just this. Other mechanisms for accomplishing the task may also be available.

If communication theory changes in these ways, a text such as this one will take a different form in the future. It will not be a book of theories related to communication; instead, it will present basic theories and show how they can be used to understand a variety of communication in different settings. Whether this prediction will come to pass remains to be seen.

Bibliography

Chapters 1 & 2
The Nature of Communication Theory
Theory in the Process of Inquiry

Achinstein, P. *Laws and Explanation.* New York: Oxford University Press, 1971.

Allport, G. W. *Personality: A Psychological Interpretation.* New York: Holt, 1937.

Anderson, Barry F. *The Psychology Experiment: An Introduction to the Scientific Method.* Monterey, Calif.: Brooks/Cole Publishing Company, 1967.

Arnold, Carroll C. "Rhetorical and Communication Studies: Two Worlds or One?" *Western Speech* 36 (1972):74–81.

Barnlund, Dean C. *Interpersonal Communication: Survey and Studies.* New York: Houghton Mifflin, 1968.

Berger, Charles R. "The Covering Law Perspective as a Theoretical Basis for the Study of Human Communication." *Communication Quarterly* 25 (1977):7–18.

Berger, Peter, and Luckmann, Thomas. *The Social Construction of Reality.* Garden City, N.Y.: Doubleday, 1966.

Berlo, David K. *The Process of Communication.* New York: Holt, Rinehart and Winston, 1960.

Black, Max. *Critical Thinking: An Introduction to Logic and Scientific Method.* Englewood Cliffs, N.J.: Prentice-Hall, 1946.

———. *Models and Metaphors.* Ithaca, N.Y.: Cornell University Press, 1962.

Bormann, Ernest G. *Communication Theory.* New York: Holt, Rinehart and Winston, 1980.

———. *Theory and Research in the Communicative Arts.* New York: Holt, Rinehart and Winston, 1965.

Bowers, John W. *Designing the Communication Experiment.* New York: Random House, 1970.

Bowers, John Waite, and Bradac, James J. "Issues in Communication Theory: A Metatheoretical Analysis." In *Communication Yearbook 5.* Edited by Michael Burgoon. New Brunswick, N.J.: Transaction Books, 1982, pp. 1–28.

Bross, Irwin B. J. *Design for Decision.* New York: Macmillan, 1953.

Brummett, Barry. "Some Implications of 'Process' or 'Intersubjectivity': Postmodern Rhetoric." *Philosophy and Rhetoric* 9 (1976): 21–51.

Clevenger, Theodore, and Matthews, Jack. *The Speech Communication Process.* Glenville, Ill.: Scott, Foresman, 1971.

Cohen, Morris. "Reason in Social Science." In *Readings in the Philosophy of Science.* Edited by H. Feigl and M. Brodbeck. New York: Appleton-Century-Crofts, 1953, pp. 663–73.

Collins, L., ed. *The Uses of Models in the Social Sciences.* Boulder, Col.: Westview Press, 1976.

Cronen, Vernon E., and Davis, Leslie K. "Alternative Approaches for the Communication Theorist: Problems in the Laws-Rules-Systems Trichotomy." *Human Communication Research* 4 (1978):120–28.

Cushman, Donald P. "The Rules Perspective as a Theoretical Basis for the Study of Human Communication." *Communication Quarterly* 25 (1977):30–45.

Cushman, Donald P., and Pearce, W. Barnett. "Generality and Necessity in Three Types of Theory about Human Communication, with Special Attention to Rules Theory." *Human Communication Research* 3 (1977):344–53.

Dance, Frank E. X. "The 'Concept' of Communication." *Journal of Communication* 20 (1970):201–10.

Dance, Frank E. X., and Larson, Carl E. *The Functions of Human Communication: A Theoretical Approach.* New York: Holt, Rinehart and Winston, 1976.

Deutsch, Karl W. "On Communication Models in the Social Sciences." *Public Opinion Quarterly* 16 (1952):356–80.

Feigl, Herbert. "The Scientific Outlook: Naturalism and Humanism." In *Readings in the Philosophy of Science.* Edited by H. Feigl and M. Brodbeck. New York: Appleton-Century-Crofts, 1953, pp. 8–18.

Fisher, Aubrey B. *Perspectives on Human Communication.* New York: Macmillan, 1978.

Glazer, Nathan. "The Social Sciences in Liberal Education." In *Philosophy of the Curriculum.* Edited by Sidney Hook. Buffalo: Prometheus Books, 1975, pp. 145–58.

Gordon, George M. *The Languages of Communication*. New York: Hastings House, 1969.
Hall, Calvin S., and Lindzey, Gardner. *Theories of Personality*. New York: John Wiley & Sons, 1970.
Hanson, N. R. *Patterns of Discovery*. Cambridge: At the University Press, 1961.
Hawes, Leonard C. "Elements of a Model for Communication Processes." *Quarterly Journal of Speech* 59 (1973):11–21.
———. *Pragmatics of Analoguing: Theory and Model Construction in Communication*. Reading, Mass.: Addison-Wesley, 1975.
Hempel, C. G. *Fundamentals of Concept Formation in Empirical Science*. Chicago: University of Chicago Press, 1952.
Holton, Gerald. "Science, Science Teaching, and Rationality." In *The Philosophy of the Curriculum*. Edited by Sidney Hook. Buffalo, N.Y.: Prometheus Books, 1975, pp. 101–18.
Hoover, K. R. *The Elements of Social Scientific Thinking*. New York: St. Martin's Press, 1976.
Houna, Joseph. "Two Ideals of Scientific Theorizing." In *Communication Yearbook 5*. Edited by Michael Burgoon. New Brunswick, N.J.: Transaction Books, 1982, pp. 29–48.
Jabusch, David M., and Littlejohn, Stephen. *Elements of Speech Communication*. Boston: Houghton Mifflin, 1981.
Jarrett, James L. *The Humanities and Humanistic Education*. Reading, Mass.: Addison-Wesley, 1973.
Kaplan, Abraham. *The Conduct of Inquiry*. San Francisco: Chandler, 1964.
Keat, R., and Urry, J. *Social Theory as Science*. London: Routledge & Kegan Paul, 1975.
Kinch, John W. "A Formalized Theory of the Self-Concept." *The American Journal of Sociology* 68 (1963):481–86.
King, Stephen W. "Theory Testing: An Analysis and Extension." *Western Speech* 37 (1973):13–22.
Knower, Franklin H. "The Development of a Sound Communicology." Unpublished Manuscript.
Kuhn, Thomas S. *The Structure of Scientific Revolutions*. Chicago: University of Chicago Press, 1970.
Littlejohn, Stephen W. "Epistemology and the Study of Human Communication." Speech Communication Association, New York City, 1980.
———. "An Overview of Contributions to Human Communication Theory from Other Disciplines." *In Human Communication Theory: Comparative Essays*. Edited by Frank E. X. Dance. New York: Harper & Row, 1982, pp. 247–82.
MacIntyre, Alasdair. "Ontology." In *The Encyclopedia of Philosophy*. Edited by Paul Edwards. New York: Macmillan, 1967, vol. 5, pp. 542–43.
Marrow, Alfred J. *The Practical Theorist: The Life and Work of Kurt Lewin*. New York: Basic Books, 1969.
Mehrabian, Albert. *An Analysis of Personality Theories*. Englewood Cliffs, N.J.: Prentice-Hall, 1968.
Miller, Gerald. "The Current Status of Theory and Research in Interpersonal Communication." *Human Communication Research* 4 (1978):175.
———. *An Introduction to Speech Communication*. Indianapolis, Ind.: Bobbs-Merrill, 1972.
———. *Speech Communication: A Behavioral Approach*. New York: Bobbs-Merrill, 1966.
Miller, Gerald E., and Nicholson, Henry. *Communication Inquiry*. Reading, Mass.: Addison-Wesley, 1976.
Monge, Peter R. "The Systems Perspective as a Theoretical Basis for the Study of Human Communication." *Communication Quarterly* 25 (1977):19–29.
———. "Theory Construction in the Study of Communication: The System Paradigm." *Journal of Communication* 23 (1973):5–16.
Mortensen, C. David. *Communication: The Study of Human Interaction*. New York: McGraw-Hill, 1972.
Murray, Elwood. "Future Directions in Communication Research: An Assessment of the Possible Use of Analogues." *Journal of Communication* 11 (1969):3–12.
Nilsen, Thomas R. "On Defining Communication." *Speech Teacher* 6 (1957):10–17.
Pearce, W. Bennett. "Metatheoretical Concerns in Communication." *Communication Quarterly* 25 (1977):3–6.
Pepper, Stephen. *World Hypotheses*. Berkeley and Los Angeles: University of California Press, 1942.
Polanyi, Michael. *Knowing and Being*. Chicago: University of Chicago Press, 1969.
———. *Personal Knowledge*. London: Routledge & Kegan Paul, 1958.
Polanyi, Michael, and Prosch, H. *Meaning*. Chicago: University of Chicago Press, 1975.
Schutz, Alfred. *The Phenomenology of the Social World*. Translated by George Walsh and Frederick Lehnert. Evanston, Ill.: Northwestern University Press, 1967.

Sereno, Kenneth, and Mortensen, C. David. "A Framework for Communication Theory." In *Foundations of Communication Theory.* Edited by Kenneth Sereno and C. David Mortensen. New York: Harper & Row, 1970.

Smith, David H. "Communication Research and the Idea of Process." *Speech Monographs* 39 (1972):175–82.

Smith, Dennis R., and Kearney, Lawrence. "Organismic Concepts in the Unification of Rhetoric and Communication." *Quarterly Journal of Speech* 59 (1973):30–39.

Smith, Raymond G. *Speech Communication: Theory and Models.* New York: Harper & Row, 1970.

Smith, Ronald L. "General Models of Communication." Communication Research Center, Department of Speech, Purdue University, Lafayette, Ind.; Special Report no. 5, August 1962.

Stegmuller, W. *The Structure and Dynamics of Theories.* New York: Springer-Verlag, 1976.

Thayer, Lee. *Communication and Communication Systems.* Homewood, Ill.: Richard D. Irwin, 1968.

———. "On Theory-Building in Communication: Some Conceptual Problems." *Journal of Communication* 13 (1963):217–35.

von Wright, Georg H. *Explanation and Understanding.* Ithaca, N.Y.: Cornell University Press, 1971.

Williams, Kenneth R. "Reflections on a Human Science of Communication." *Journal of Communication* 23 (1973):239–50.

Zeigler, B. P. *Theory of Modeling and Simulation.* New York: John Wiley & Sons, 1976.

Chapter 3
General Systems Theory and Cybernetics

Ackoff, Russel L., and Emery, Fred. *On Purposeful Systems.* Chicago: Aldine, 1972.

Allport, Gordon W. "The Open System in Personality Theory." *Journal of Abnormal and Social Psychology* 61 (1960):301–11.

———. "The Open System in Personality Theory." In *Modern Systems Research for the Behavioral Scientist.* Edited by Walter Buckley. Chicago: Aldine, 1968, pp. 343–50.

Ashby, W. Ross. "Principles of the Self-Organizing System." In *Principles of Self-Organization.* Edited by Heinz von Foerster and George Zopf. New York: Pergamon Press, 1962, pp. 255–78.

Beach, Wayne. "Stocktaking Open-Systems Research and Theory: A Critique and Proposals for Action." Western Speech Communication Association, Phoenix, Arizona, November 1977.

Berger, Charles. "The Covering Law Perspective as a Theoretical Basis for the Study of Human Communication." *Communication Quarterly* 75 (1977):7–18.

Berlo, David. *The Process of Communication.* New York: Holt, Rinehart and Winston, 1960.

Berrien, F. Kenneth. *General and Social Systems.* New Brunswick, N.J.: Rutgers University Press, 1968.

Bertalanffy, Ludwig. "A Biologist Looks at Human Behavior." *Scientific Monthly* 82 (1956):33–41.

———. "General Systems Theory: A Critical Review." *General Systems* 7 (1962):1–20.

———. *General System Theory: Foundations, Development, Applications.* New York: Braziller, 1968.

———. "On the Definition of the Symbol." In *Psychology and the Symbol.* New York: Random House, 1965.

———. *Robots, Men, and Minds.* New York: Braziller, 1967.

Boulding, Kenneth. "General Systems Theory—The Skeleton of Science." *Management Science* 2 (1956):197–208.

Broadhurst, Allan R., and Darnell, Donald K. "An Introduction to Cybernetics and Information Theory." *Quarterly Journal of Speech* 51 (1965):442–53.

Buckley, Walter, ed. *Modern System Research for the Behavioral Scientist.* Chicago: Aldine, 1968.

Buckley, Walter. "Society as a Complex Adaptive System." In *Modern Systems Research for the Behavioral Scientist.* Edited by Walter Buckley. Chicago: Aldine, 1968, pp. 490–513.

———. *Sociology and Modern Systems Theory.* Englewood Cliffs, N.J.: Prentice-Hall, 1967.

Cadwaller, Mervin. "The Cybernetic Analysis of Change in Complex Social Organizations. *American Journal of Sociology* 65 (1959):154–57.

Cherry, Colin. *On Human Communication.* New York: Science Editions, 1961, 1978.

Churchman, C. W., and Ackoff, R. L. "Purposive Behavior and Cybernetics." *Social Forces* 29 (1950):32–39.

Clevenger, Theodore, and Matthews, Jack. *The Speech Communication Process.* Glenview, Ill.: Scott Foresman, 1971.

Cronen, Vernon, and Mihevec, Nancy. "The Evaluation of Deductive Argument: A Process

Analysis." *Speech Monographs* 39 (1972):124–31.

Cushman, Donald. "The Rules Perspective as a Theoretical Basis for the Study of Human Communication." *Communication Quarterly* 25 (1977):30–45.

Delia, Jesse. "Alternative Perspectives for the Study of Human Communication: Critique and Response." *Communication Quarterly* 25 (1977):51–52.

Deutsch, Karl. "Toward a Cybernetic Model of Man and Society." In *Modern Systems Research for the Behavioral Scientist*. Edited by Walter Buckley. Chicago: Aldine, 1968, pp. 387–400.

Fisher, B. Aubrey. *Perspectives on Human Communication*. New York: Macmillan, 1978.

Fisher, B. Aubrey, and Hawes, Leonard C. "An Interact System Model: Generating a Grounded Theory of Small Groups." *Quarterly Journal of Speech* 57 (1971):444–53.

Gardiner, James C. "A Synthesis of Experimental Studies of Speech Communication Feedback." *Journal of Communication* 21 (1971):17–35.

General Systems: Yearbook of the Society for General Systems Research, 1956–present (annual).

Grinker, Roy R., ed. *Towards a Unified Theory of Human Behavior*. New York: Basic Books, 1967.

Guilbaud, G. T. *What Is Cybernetics?* New York: Grove Press, 1959.

Hall, A. D., and Fagen, R. E. "Definition of System." *General Systems* 1 (1956):18–28.

Handy, Rollo, and Kurtz, Paul. "A Current Appraisal of the Behavioral Sciences: Communication Theory." *American Behavioral Scientist* 7 (1964), no. 6, supplement.

Hawes, Leonard. "Elements in a Model for Communication Processes." *Quarterly Journal of Speech* 59 (1973):11–21.

Hawes, Leonard, and Foley, Joseph M. "A Markov Analysis of Interview Communication." *Speech Monographs* 40 (1973):208–19.

Ivey, Allen E., and Hurst, James C. "Communication as Adaptation." *Journal of Communication* 21 (1971):199–207.

Johnson, F. Craig, and Klare, George R. "Feedback: Principles and Analogies." *Journal of Communication* 12 (1962):150–59.

Klir, George J. *An Introduction to General System Theory*. New York: Van Nostrand, 1970.

Koestler, Arthur. *The Ghost in the Machine*. New York: Macmillan, 1967.

Krippendorff, Klaus. "Scope of the Information Systems Division." *Systemletter* 1 (1972):2–4.

La Rossa, Ralph. "Interpreting Hierarchical Message Structure." *Journal of Communication* 24 (1974):61–68.

Laszlo, Erwin. *Introduction to System Philosophy*. New York: Gordon and Breach, 1972.

———. *The System View of the World*. New York: Braziller, 1972.

"Ludwig von Bertalanffy." *General Systems* 17 (1972):219–28.

McClelland, Charles A. "General Systems and the Social Sciences." *E. T. C.* 18 (1962):449–68.

Maruyama, Magoroh. "The Second Cybernetics: Deviation-Amplifying Mutual Causal Processes." *American Scientist* 51 (1963):164–79.

Melcher, A. J., ed. *General Systems and Organization Theory*. Kent, Ohio: Kent State University Press, 1975.

Miller, Gerald R. "The Pervasiveness and Marvelous Complexity of Human Communication: A Note of Skepticism." Keynote address, Fourth Annual Conference in Communication, California State University, Fresno, May 1977.

Miller, James G. "Living Systems: Basic Concepts; Structure and Process; Cross-Level Hypothesis." *Behavioral Science* 10 (1965):193–237.

———. "Toward a General Theory for Behavioral Sciences." *American Psychologist* 10 (1955):513–31.

Monge, Peter. "The Systems Perspective as a Theoretical Basis for the Study of Human Communication." *Communication Quarterly* 25 (1977):19–29.

———. "Theory Construction in the Study of Communication: The System Paradigm." *Journal of Communication* 23 (1973):5–16.

Mowrer, O. H. "Ego Psychology, Cybernetics, and Learning Theory." In *Learning Theory and Clinical Research*. Edited by D. K. Adams. New York: John Wiley & Sons, 1954, pp. 81–90.

Pask, Gordon. *An Approach to Cybernetics*. New York: Harper, 1961.

Pfaff, M., ed. *Frontiers in Social Thought: Essays in Honor of Kenneth Boulding*. New York: North-Holland Publishing, 1976.

Powers, W. T.; Clark, R. K.; and McFarland, R. I. "A General Feedback Theory of Human Behavior." In *Communication and Culture*. Edited by Alfred Smith. New York: Holt, Rinehart and Winston, 1966, pp. 333—43.

Rapoport, Anatol. "Forward." In *Modern System Research for the Behavioral Scientist*. Edited by Walter Buckley. Chicago: Aldine, 1968, pp. xiii–xxv.

Rosenbleuth, Arturo; Wiener, Norbert; and Bigelow, Julian. "Behavior, Purpose, and Teleology." *Philosophy of Science* 10 (1943):18–24.

Ruesch, Juergen, and Bateson, Gregory. *Communication: The Social Matrix of Psychiatry.* New York: Norton, 1951.

Shibutani, Tamotsu. "A Cybernetic Approach to Motivation." In *Modern System Research for the Behavioral Scientist.* Edited by Walter Buckley. Chicago: Aldine, 1968, pp. 330–36.

Taschjan, Edgan. "The Entropy of Complex Dynamic Systems." *Behavioral Science* 19 (1975): p. 3.

Thayer, Lee. *Communication and Communication Systems.* Homewood, Ill.: Irwin, 1968.

———. "Communication and Organization Theory." In *Human Communication Theory.* Edited by Frank Dance. New York: Holt, Rinehart and Winston, 1967, pp. 40–115.

Toda, Masanao, and Shuford, Emir H. "Logic of Systems: Introduction to a Formal Theory of Structure." *General Systems* 10 (1965):3–27.

Vickers, Geoffrey. "Is Adaptability Enough?" *Behavioral Science* 4 (1959):219–34.

Wiener, Norbert. *Cybernetics or Control and Communication in the Animal and the Machine.* New York: M.I.T. Press, 1961.

———. *The Human Use of Human Beings: Cybernetics and Society.* Boston: Houghton Mifflin, 1954.

Wilson, Donna. "Forms of Hierarchy: A Selected Bibliography." *General Systems* 14 (1969):3–15.

Young, O. R. "A Survey of General Systems Theory." *General Systems* 9 (1964):61–80.

Chapter 4
Symbolic Interactionism and Rules Theory

Alvy, K. T. "The Development of Listener Adapted Communication in Grade-School Children from Different Social Class Backgrounds." *Genetic Psychology Monographs* 87 (1973):33–104.

Berger, Charles R. "The Covering Law Perspective as a Theoretical Basis for the Study of Human Communication." *Communication Quarterly* 25 (1977):12.

Black, Max. *Models and Metaphors.* Ithaca, N.Y.: Cornell University Press, 1962.

Blumer, Herbert. "Attitudes and the Social Act." *Social Problems* 3 (1955):59–65.

———. *Symbolic Interactionism: Perspective and Method.* Englewood Cliffs, N.J.: Prentice-Hall, 1969.

Burke, Kenneth. *Attitudes toward History.* New York: New Republic, 1937.

———. *Counter-Statement.* New York: Harcourt, Brace, 1931.

———. *A Grammar of Motives.* Englewood Cliffs, N.J.: Prentice-Hall, 1945.

———. *Language as Symbolic Action.* Berkeley and Los Angeles: University of California Press, 1966.

———. *Permanence and Change.* New York: New Republic, 1935.

———. *The Philosophy of Literary Form.* Baton Rouge: Louisiana State University Press, 1941.

———. *A Rhetoric of Motives.* Englewood Cliffs, N.J.: Prentice-Hall, 1950.

———. *A Rhetoric of Religion.* Boston: Beacon Press, 1961.

Combs, J. E., and Mansfield, M. W., eds. *Drama in Life: The Use of Communication in Society.* New York: Hastings House, 1976.

Couch, Carl J. "Symbolic Interaction and Generic Sociological Principles." Paper presented at the Symposium on Symbolic Interaction, Boston, 1979.

Couch, Carl J. and Hintz, Robert, eds. *Constructing Social Life.* Champaign, Ill.: Stipes Publishing Co., 1975.

Coyne, Peter M. "Kenneth Burke and the Rhetorical Criticism of Public Address." Doctoral Dissertation, University of Utah, 1973.

Cronen, Vernon: Pearce, W. Barnett; and Harris, Linda. "The Logic of the Coordinated Management of Meaning." *Communication Education* 28 (1979):22–38.

———. "The Coordinated Management of Meaning." In *Comparative Human Communication Theory.* Edited by Frank E. X. Dance. New York: Harper & Row, 1982.

Cushman, Donald P. "The Rules Perspective as a Theoretical Basis for the Study of Human Communication." *Communication Quarterly* 25 (1977):30–45.

Delia, Jesse. "Alternative Perspectives for the Study of Human Communication: Critique and Response." *Communication Quarterly* 25 (1977):54.

Denzin, Norman K. *The Research Act.* Chicago: Aldine, 1970.

Duncan, Hugh D. *Communication and Social Order.* New York: Bedminster Press, 1962.

———. "Communication in Society." *Arts in Society* 3 (1964):105.

———. "The Search for a Social Theory of Communication in American Sociology." In *Human Communication Theory.* Edited by Frank Dance. New York: Holt, Rinehart and Winston, 1967.

———. *Symbols and Society.* New York: Oxford University Press, 1968.

Ganz, Joan. *Rules: A Systematic Study.* The Hague: Mouton, 1971.

Gottlieb, Gidon. *Logic of Choice: An Investigation of the Concepts of Rule and Rationality.* New York: Macmillan, 1968.

Gumb, Raymond D. *Rule-Governed Linguistic Behavior.* Paris: Mouton, 1972.

Hall, Peter M. "Structuring Symbolic Interaction: Communication and Power." In *Communication Yearbook 4.* Edited by Dan Nimmo. New Brunswick, N.J.: Transaction Books, (1980), pp. 49–60.

Hickman, C. A., and Kuhn, Manford. *Individuals, Groups, and Economic Behavior.* New York: Holt, Rinehart and Winston, 1956.

Kuhn, Manford H. "Major Trends in Symbolic Interaction Theory in the Past Twenty-Five Years." *The Sociological Quarterly* 5 (1964):61–84.

———. "The Reference Group Reconsidered." *The Sociological Quarterly* 5 (1964):6–21.

———. "Self-Attitudes by Age, Sex, and Professional Training." *The Sociological Quarterly* 1 (1960):39–55.

Kuhn, Manford H., and Hickman, C. A. *Individuals, Groups, and Economic Behavior.* New York: Holt, Rinehart and Winston, 1956.

Kuhn, Manford H., and McPartland, Thomas S. "An Empirical Investigation of Self-Attitudes." *American Sociological Review* 19 (1954):68–76.

Lofland, John. "Interactionist Imagery and Analytic Interruptus." In *Human Nature and Collective Behavior.* Edited by Tamotsu Shibutani. Englewood Cliffs, N.J.: Prentice-Hall, 1970, p. 37.

McPhail, Clark. "Toward a Theory of Collective Behavior." Paper presented at the Symposium on Symbolic Interaction, Columbia, South Carolina, 1978.

Manis, Jerome G., and Meltzer, Bernard N., eds. *Symbolic Interaction.* Boston: Allyn and Bacon, 1978.

Mead, George H. *Mind, Self, and Society.* Chicago: University of Chicago Press, 1934.

———. *Movements of Thought in the Nineteenth Century.* Chicago: University of Chicago Press, 1936.

———. *The Philosophy of the Act.* Chicago: University of Chicago Press, 1938.

———. *The Philosophy of the Present.* Chicago: University of Chicago Press, 1932.

Meltzer, Bernard N. "Mead's Social Psychology." In *Symbolic Interaction.* Edited by Jerome Manis and Bernard Meltzer. Boston: Allyn and Bacon, 1972, pp. 4–22.

Meltzer, Bernard N., and Petras, John W. "The Chicago and Iowa Schools of Symbolic Interactionism." In *Human Nature and Collective Behavior.* Edited by Tamotsu Shibutani. Englewood Cliffs, N.J.: Prentice-Hall, 1970.

Meltzer, Bernard N.; Petras, John; and Reynolds, Larry. *Symbolic Interactionism: Genesis, Varieties, and Criticism.* London: Routledge & Kegan Paul, 1975.

Morris, Charles. "George H. Mead as Social Psychologist and Social Philosopher." In *Mind, Self, and Society* (Introduction). Chicago: University of Chicago Press, 1934, pp. ix–xxxv.

Natanson, Maurice. *The Journeying Self: A Study in Philosophy and Social Role.* Reading, Mass.: Addison-Wesley, 1970.

Pearce, W. Barnett. "The Coordinated Management of Meaning: A Rules Based Theory of Interpersonal Communication." In *Explorations in Interpersonal Communication.* Edited by Gerald R. Miller. Beverly Hills, Calif.: Sage, 1976, pp. 17–36.

———. "Rules Theories of Communication: Varieties, Limitations, and Potentials." Paper presented at the Speech Communication Association, New York City, 1980.

Pearce, W. Barnett, and Cronen, Vernon. *Communication Action and Meaning.* New York: Praeger, 1980.

Petras, John W., ed. *George Herbert Mead: Essays on His Social Philosophy.* New York: Teachers College Press, 1968.

Pfeutze, Paul E. *The Social Self.* New York: Bookman Associates, 1954.

Rose, Arnold M., ed. *Human Behavior and Social Processes.* Boston: Houghton Mifflin, 1962.

Rueckert, William, ed. *Critical Responses to Kenneth Burke.* Minneapolis: University of Minnesota Press, 1969.

Shimanoff, Susan B. *Communication Rules: Theory and Research.* Beverly Hills, Calif.: Sage, 1980.

Sigman, Stuart J. "On Communication Rules from a Social Perspective." *Human Communication Research* 7 (1980):37–51.

Stevens, Edward. "Sociality and Act in George Herbert Mead." *Social Research* 34 (1967):613–31.

Strauss, Anselm, ed. *George Herbert Mead: On Social Psychology*. Chicago: University of Chicago Press, 1964.

Strong, Samuel W. "A Note on George H. Mead's 'The Philosophy of the Act.'" *American Journal of Sociology* 45 (1939):71–76.

Swanson, Guy E. "On Explanations of Social Interaction." *Sociometry* 28 (1965):101–23.

Tucker, Charles W. "Some Methodological Problems of Kuhn's Self-Theory." *The Sociological Quarterly* 7 (1966):345–58.

Vaughan, Ted R., and Reynolds, Larry T. "The Sociology of Symbolic Interactionism." *The American Sociologist* 3 (1968):208–14.

Vernon, Glenn M. *Human Interaction: An Introduction to Sociology*. New York: Ronald Press, 1965.

Chapter 5
Theories of Language and Nonverbal Coding

Allen, J. P. B., and Van Buren, Paul, eds. *Chomsky: Selected Readings*. New York: Oxford University Press, 1970.

Benthall, J., and Polhemus, T., eds. *The Body as a Medium of Expression*. New York: Dutton, 1975.

Bever, T. G.; Fodor, J. A.; and Weksel, W. "A Critique of Contextual Generalization." *Psychological Review* 72 (1965):467–82.

———. *"Is Linguistics Empirical?" Psychological Review* 72 (1965):493–500.

Birdwhistell, Ray. *Introduction of Kinesics. Louisville: University of Louisville Press, 1952.*

———. *Kinesics and Context*. Philadelphia: University of Pennsylvania Press, 1970.

Bloom, Lois. *Language Development: Form and Function in Emerging Grammars*. Cambridge: M.I.T. Press, 1970.

Bloomfield, Leonard. *Language*. New York: Holt, Rinehart and Winston, 1933.

Blount, B. G., ed. *Language, Culture, and Society: A Book of Readings*. Cambirdge, Mass.: Winthrop Publishing, 1974.

Braine, Martin D. "On the Basis of Phrase Structure: A Reply to Bever, Fodor, and Weksel." *Psychological Review* 72 (1965):483–92.

———. "On Learning the Grammatical Order of Words." *Psychological Review* 70 (1963):323–48.

Burgoon, Judee K. "Nonverbal Communication Research in the 1970s: An Overview." In *Communication Yearbook 4*. Edited by Dan Nimmo. New Brunswick, N.J.: Transaction Books, 1980, p. 179.

Burgoon, Judee K., and Saine, Thomas. *The Unspoken Dialogue: An Introduction to Nonverbal Communication*. Boston: Houghton Mifflin, 1978.

Carroll, John B. *The Study of Language*. Cambridge: At the University Press, 1953.

Chao, Yuen Ren. *Language and Symbolic Systems*. New York: Cambridge University Press, 1968.

Chomsky, Noam. *The Acquisition of Syntax in Children from 5 to 10*. Cambridge: M.I. T. Press, 1969.

———. *Aspects of the Theory of Syntax*. Cambridge: M.I.T. Press, 1965.

———. *Cartesian Linguistics: A Chapter in the History of Rationalist Thought*. New York: Harper & Row, 1966.

———. *Current Issues in Linguistic Theory*. The Hague: Mouton, 1970.

———. *Essays on Form and Interpretation*. New York: North Holland, 1977.

———. *Language and Mind*. New York: Harcourt Brace Jovanovich, 1972.

———. *The Logical Structure of Linguistic Theory*. New York: Plenum Press, 1975.

———. *Problems of Knowledge and Freedom*. New York: Pantheon Books, 1971.

———. *Reflections on Language*. New York: Pantheon Books, 1975.

———. *Rules and Representations*. New York: Columbia University Press, 1980.

———. *The Sound Pattern of English*. New York: Harper & Row, 1968.

———. *Studies on Semantics in Generative Grammar*. The Hague: Mouton, 1972.

———. *Syntactic Structures*. The Hague: Mouton, 1957.

———. "Three Models for the Description of Language." *Transactions on Information Theory* vol. IT-2 (1956):113–24.

———. *Topics in the Theory of Generative Grammar*. The Hague: Mouton, 1966.

Cohen, D., ed. *Explaining Linguistic Phenomena*. Washington, D.C.: Hemisphere, 1974.

Dale, Philip S. *Language Development: Structure and Function*. Hinsdale, Ill. Dryden Press, 1972.

Davis, Martha. *Understanding Body Movement: An Annotated Bibliography*. New York: Arno Press, 1972.

DeVito, Joseph A., ed. *Language: Concepts and Proc-*

esses. Englewood Cliffs, N.J.: Prentice-Hall, 1973.

———. *The Psychology of Speech and Language*. New York: Random House, 1970.

Dittmann, Allen T. *Interpersonal Messages of Emotion*. New York: Springer, 1972.

Eisenberg, Abne M., and Smith, Ralph R. *Nonverbal Communication*. Indianapolis, Ind.: Bobbs-Merrill, 1971.

Ekman, Paul, and Friesen, Wallace. *Emotion in the Human Face: Guidelines for Research and an Integration of Findings*. New York: Pergamon Press, 1972.

———. "Hand Movements." *Journal of Communication* 22 (1972):353–74.

———. "Nonverbal Behavior in Psychotherapy Research." In *Research in Psychotherapy*. Edited by J. Shlien, vol. III. Washington, D.C.: American Psychological Association, 1968, pp. 179–216.

———. "The Repertoire of Nonverbal Behavior: Categories, Origins, Usage, and Coding." *Semiotica* 1 (1969):49–98.

———. *Unmasking the Face*. Englewood Cliffs, N.J.: Prentice-Hall, 1975.

Fodor, J. A.; Bever, T. G.; and Garrett, M. F. *The Psychology of Language: An Introduction to Psycholinguistics and Generative Grammar*. New York: McGraw-Hill, 1974.

Fodor, J. A.; Jenkins, James; and Saporta, Sol. "Psycholinguistics and Communication Theory." In *Human Communication Theory*. Edited by Frank Dance. New York: Holt, Rinehart and Winston, 1967, pp. 160–201.

Fotheringham, Wallace. *Perspectives on Persuasion*. Boston: Allyn and Bacon, 1966.

Frentz, Thomas S. "Toward a Resolution of the Generative Semantics/Classical Theory Controversy: A Psycholinguistic Analysis of Metaphor." *Quarterly Journal of Speech* 60 (1974):125–33.

Fries, Charles. *The Structure of English*. New York: Harcourt, Brace & World, 1952.

Garvin, Paul. *Method and Theory in Linguistics*. New York: Humanities Press, 1970.

Greenberg, Joseph H. "The Linguistic Approach." In *Psycholinguistics: Survey of Theory and Research Problems*. Edited by C. E. Osgood and T. A. Sebock. Bloomington, Indiana University Press, 1954, pp. 8–16.

Hall, Edward T. *Handbook for Proxemic Research*. Washington, D.C.: Society for the Anthropology of Visual Communication, 1974.

———. *The Hidden Dimension*. New York: Random House, 1966.

———. *The Silent Language*. Greenwich, Conn.: Fawcett, 1959.

———. "A System for the Notation of Proxemic Behavior." *American Anthropologist* 65 (1963): 1003–26.

Handy, R., and Kurtz, P. "A Current Appraisal of the Behavioral Sciences. Communication: Information Theory, Cybernetics, Linguistics, Sign Behavior. *American Behavioral Scientist* 7 (1964): no. 6, supplement.

Harmon, Gilbert. *On Noam Chomsky: Critical Essays*. Garden City, N.Y.: Anchor Books, 1974.

Harper, Robert G.; Wiess, Arthur; and Motarozzo, Joseph. *Nonverbal Communication: The State of the Art*. New York: John Wiley & Sons, 1978.

Harris, Zellig. *Structural Linguistics*. Chicago: University of Chicago Press, 1951.

Harrison, Randall. "Nonverbal Communication." In *Handbook of Communication*. Edited by Ithiel de sola Pool et al. Chicago: Rand McNally, 1973.

Harrison, Randall, and Knapp, Mark. "Toward an Understanding of Nonverbal Communication Systems." *Journal of Communication* 22 (1972):339–52.

Harrison, Randall, et al. "The Nonverbal Communication Literature." *Journal of Communication* 22 (1972):460–76.

Hill, Archibald, ed. *Linguistics Today*. New York: Basic Books, 1969.

Holtzman, Paul, ed. *The Journal of Communication. A Special Issue of Nonverbal Communication* 22 (1972):338–477.

Katz, Jerrold. *The Underlying Reality of Language and Its Philosophical Import*. New York: Harper & Row, 1971.

Kess, J. *Psycholinguistics: Introductory Perspectives*. New York: Academic Press, 1976.

Knapp, Mark. *Nonverbal Communication in Human Interaction*. New York: Holt, Rinehart and Winston, 1978.

Knapp, Mark; Wiemann, John; and Daly, John. "Nonverbal Communication: Issues and Appraisal." *Human Communication Research* 4 (1978): 271–80.

Leiber, Justin. *Noam Chomsky: A Philosophical Overview*. Boston: Twayne Publishers, 1975.

McCormack, William, and Wurm, Stephen A., eds. *Language and Man: Anthropological Issues*. Chicago: Aldine, 1976.

McNeill, David. *The Acquisition of Language: The*

Study of Developmental Psycholinguistics. New York: Harper & Row, 1970.
Mehrabian, A. "Communication without Words." *Psychology Today* 2 (1968):51–52.
Moore, Timothy E. *Cognitive Development and the Acquisition of Language.* New York: Academic Press, 1973.
Morris, Charles. "Foundation of the Theory of Signs." In *International Encyclopedia of Unified Science.* Vol. I. pt. I. Chicago: University of Chicago Press, 1953, p. 84.
———. *Signification and Significance.* Cambridge: M.I.T. Press, 1964.
———. *Signs, Language, and Behavior.* New York: Braziller, 1946.
Mowrer, H. Hobart. *Learning Theory and the Symbolic Processes.* New York: John Wiley & Sons, 1960.
———. "The Psychologist Looks at Language." *American Psychologist* 9 (1954):660–92.
Nolan, Michael J. "The Relationship between Verbal and Nonverbal Communication." In *Communication and Behavior.* Edited by Gerhard Hanneman and William McEwen. Reading, Mass.: Addison-Wesley, 1975, pp. 98–119.
Osgood, Charles. "On Understanding and Creating Sentences." *American Psychologist* 18 (1963):735–51.
Parrett, H., ed. *History of Linguistic Thought and Contemporary Linguistics.* New York: Walter de Gryter, 1976.
Puhvel, Joan. *Substance and Structure of Language.* Berkeley and Los Angeles: University of California Press, 1969.
Salus, Peter H. *Linguistics.* Indianapolis, Ind.: Bobbs-Merrill, 1969.
Searles, John. "Chomsky's Revolution in Linguistics." In *On Noam Chomsky: Critical Essays.* Edited by Gilbert Harmon. Garden City, N.Y.: Anchor Books, 1974, pp. 2–33.
Skinner, B. F. *Verbal Behavior.* New York: Appleton-Century-Crofts, 1957.
Slobin, Dan L. *Psycholinguistics.* Glenview, Ill.: Scott, Foresman, 1971.
Staats, Arthur. *Learning, Language, and Cognition.* New York: Holt, Rinehart and Winston, 1968.
Stockwell, Robert P. *Foundations of Syntactic Theory.* Englewood Cliffs, N.J.: Prentice-Hall, 1977.
Stockwell, Robert P., and Macauley, Ronald K. S., eds. *Linguistic Change and Generative Theory.* Bloomington: Indiana University Press, 1972.
Taylor, I. *Introduction to Psycholinguistics.* New York: Holt, Rinehart and Winston, 1976.
Trager, G. L. "Paralanguage: A First Approximation." *Studies in Linguistics* 13 (1958):1–12.
Vendler, Zeno. *Res Cognitans.* Ithaca, N.Y.: Cornell University Press, 1972.
Vetter, Harrold. *Language Behavior and Communication.* Itaska, Ill.: F. E. Peacock 1969.
Watson, O. Michael. "Conflicts and Directions in Proxemic Research." *Journal of Communication* 22 (1972):443–59.
Williams, Frederick. *Language and Speech.* Englewood Cliffs, N.J.: Prentice-Hall, 1972.

Chapter 6
Theories of Meaning

Alexander, Dennis. "A Construct of the Image and a Method of Measurement." *Journal of Communication* 21 (1971):170–78.,
Alexander, Hubert. *Language and Thinking.* Princeton, N.J.: Van Nostrand, 1967.
———. *Meaning in Language.* Glenview, Ill.: Scott, Foresman, 1969.
Alston, W.P. *Philosophy of Language.* Englewood Cliffs, N.J.: Prentice-Hall, 1964.
Austin, J. L. *How to Do Things with Words.* Cambridge: Harvard University Press, 1962.
———. *Philosophical Papers.* Oxford: Clarendon Press, 1962.
———. *Philosophy of Language.* Englewood Cliffs, N.J.: Prentice-Hall, 1964.
Binkley, Timothy. *Wittgenstein's Language.* The Hague: Martinus Nijhoff, 1973.
Bois, J. Samuel. *The Art of Awareness.* Dubuque: W. C. Brown, 1966.
Boulding, Kenneth. *The Image.* Ann Arbor: University of Michigan Press, 1956.
Bourne, Lyle. *Human Conceptual Behavior.* Boston: Allyn and Bacon, 1966.
Brown, C. H. *Wittgensteinian Linguistics.* Paris: Mouton, 1974.
Bruner, J. S.; Goodnow, Jacquelin J.; and Austin, G. A. *A Study of Thinking.* New York: John Wiley & Sons, 1956.
Campbell, Paul N. "A Rhetorical View of Locutionary, Illocutionary, and Perlocutionary Acts." *Quarterly Journal of Speech* 59 (1973):284–96.
Carroll, John B. "Introduction." In *Language, Thought, and Reality.* New York: John Wiley & Sons, 1956, pp. 1–34.
Cassirer, Ernst. *An Essay on Man.* New Haven, Conn.: Yale University Press, 1944.

———. *The Philosophy of Symbolic Forms.* 3 vols. Berlin: Bruno Cassirer, 1923, 1925, 1929.

Cohen, L. J. *The Diversity of Meaning.* London: Metheren, 1962.

Darnell, Donald K. "Semantic Differentiation." In *Methods of Research in Communication.* Edited by Philip Emmert and William Brooks. Boston: Houghton Mifflin, 1970, pp. 181–96.

Deetz, Stanley. "Words without Things: Toward a Social Phenomenology of Language." *Quarterly Journal of Speech* 59 (1973):40–51.

Dewey, John. *Art as Experience.* New York: Minton, Balch, 1934.

———. *Essays in Experimental Logic.* Chicago: University of Chicago Press, 1916.

———. *Experience and Nature.* Chicago: Open Court, 1925.

———. *How We Think.* Boston: Heath, 1910.

———. *The Quest for Certainty.* New York: Minton, Balch, 1929.

Engel, S. Morris. *Wittgenstein's Doctrine of the Tyranny of Language.* The Hague: Martinus Nijhoff, 1971.

Evans, G., and McDowell, J. eds. *Truth and Meaning: Essays in Semantics.* Oxford: Clarendon Press, 1976.

Fann, K. T. *Wittgenstein's Conception of Philosophy.* Berkeley and Los Angeles: University of California Press, 1969.

Fishman, Joshua. "A Systemization of the Whorfian Hypothesis." *Behavioral Science* 5 (1960):323–39.

Flavell, J. H. *The Developmental Psychology of Jean Piaget.* New York: Van Nostrand, 1963.

Furth, H. G. *Piaget and Knowledge: Theoretical Foundations.* Englewood Cliffs, N.J.: Prentice-Hall, 1969.

Gadamer, Hans-Georg. *Truth and Method.* New York: Herder and Herder, 1975.

Gaines, Robert . "Doing by Saying: Toward a Theory of Perlocution." *Quarterly Journal of Speech* 65 (1979):207–17.

Hamburg, Carl H. *Symbol and Reality.* The Hague: Martinus Nijhoff, 1970.

Haney, William. *Communication and Organizational Behavior.* Homewood, Ill.: Irwin, 1973.

Harrison, Bernard. *An Introduction to the Philosophy of Language.* New York: St. Martin's Press, 1979.

Hayakawa, S. I. *Language in Thought and Action.* New York: Harcourt, Brace, 1952.

Heidegger, Martin. *An Introduction to Metaphysics.* Garden City, N.Y.: Doubleday, 1961.

———. *On the Way to Language.* New York: Harper & Row, 1971.

Henle, Paul, ed. *Language, Thought, and Culture.* Ann Arbor: University of Michigan Press, 1958.

Itzkoff, Seymour W. *Ernst Cassirer: Scientific Knowledge and the Concept of Man.* Notre Dame, Ind.: University of Notre Dame Press, 1971.

Johannesen, Richard L., ed. *Contemporary Theories of Rhetoric.* New York: Harper & Row, 1971.

Johnson, Wendell. *People in Quandaries.* New York: Harper & Brothers, 1946.

Johnson, Wendell, and Moeller, Dorothy. *Living with Change: The Semantics of Coping.* New York: Harper & Row, 1972.

Kapferer, B., ed. *Transaction and Meaning: Directions in the Anthropology of Exchange and Symbolic Behavior.* Philadelphia: Institute for the Study of Human Issues, 1976.

Katz, Jerrold J. *The Philosophy of Language.* New York: Harper & Row, 1966.

———. "The Realm of Meaning." In *Communication, Language, and Meaning.* Edited by George Miller. New York: Basic Books, 1973, pp. 36–48.

Kenny, Anthony. *Wittgenstein.* Cambridge: Harvard University Press, 1973.

Klausmeier, J. H.; Chatala, E. S.; and Frayer, D. A. *Conceptual Learning and Development: A Cognitive View.* New York: Academic Press, 1974.

Kockelmans, Joseph J., ed. *On Heidegger and Language.* Evanston; Ill.: Northwestern University Press, 1972.

Korzybski, Alfred. *Science and Sanity: An Introduction to Non-Aristotelian Systems and General Semantics.* Lancaster, Penn.: International Non-Aristotelian Library Publishing, 1933.

Langer, Susanne. *Mind: An Essay on Human Feeling.* 3 vols. Baltimore: Johns Hopkins Press, 1967, 1972, and forthcoming.

———. "On Cassirer's Theory of Language and Myth." In *Ernst Cassirer: Scientific Knowledge and the Concept of Man.* Edited by Seymour W. Itzkoff. Notre Dame, Ind.: University of Notre Dame Press, 1971, pp. 387–90.

———. *Philosophy in a New Key.* Cambridge: Harvard University Press, 1942.

Lee, Irving J. *Language Habits in Human Affairs.* New York: Harper & Brothers, 1941.

Manis, Melvin. *Cognitive Processes.* Monterey, Calif.: Brooks/Cole, 1966.

Miller, George, ed. *Communication, Language, and Meaning.* New York: Basic Books, 1973.

Miller, George; Galanter, Eugene; and Pribram, Karl H. *Plans and the Structure of Behavior.* New York: Holt, Rinehart and Winston, 1960.

Needham, Rodney. *Belief, Language, and Experience.* Chicago: University of Chicago Press, 1973.

Nichols, Marie Hochmuth. "I. A. Richards and the New Rhetoric." *Quarterly Journal of Speech* 44 (1958):1–16.

———. *Rhetoric and Criticism.* Baton Rouge: Louisiana State University Press, 1963.

Ogden, C. K., and Richards, I. A. *The Meaning of Meaning.* London: Kegan, Paul Trench, Trubner, 1923.

Osgood, Charles. *Cross Cultural Universals of Affective Meaning.* Edited by James Snider and Charles Osgood. Urbana, University of Illinois Press, 1975.

Osgood, Charles. "The Nature and Measurement of Meaning." In *The Semantic Differential Technique.* Edited by James Snider and Charles Osgood. Chicago: Aldine, 1969, pp. 9–10.

———. "On Understanding and Creating Sentences." *American Psychologist* 18 (1963):735–51.

———. "Semantic Differential Technique in the Comparative Study of Cultures." In *The Semantic Differential Technique.* Edited by James Snider and Charles Osgood. Chicago: Aldine, 1969, pp. 303–34.

Osgood, Charles; May, William H.; and Miron, Murray S. *Cross-Cultural Universals of Affective Meaning.* Urbana: University of Illinois Press, 1975.

Osgood, Charles, and Richards, Meredith. "From Yang and Yin to *and* or *but*." *Language* 49 (1973):380–412.

Osgood, Charles; Suci, George; and Tannenbaum, Percy H. *The Measurement of Meaning.* Urbana: University of Illinois Press, 1957.

Palmer, Richard D. *Hermeneutics.* Evanston, Ill.: Northwestern University Press, 1969.

Passmore, John. "Wittgenstein and Ordinary Language Philosophy." In *A Hundred Years of Philosophy.* New York: Basic Books, 1966.

Piaget, Jean. *The Construction of Reality in the Child.* New York: Basic Books, 1954.

———. *The Early Growth of Logic in the Child.* London: Routledge & Kegan Paul, 1964.

———. *The Language and Thought of the Child.* New York: Harcourt, Brace, 1926.

———. *Logic and Psychology.* New York: Basic Books, 1957.

———. *Mental Imagery in the Child.* London: Routledge & Kegan Paul, 1970.

———. *On the Development of Memory and Identity.* Barre, Mass.: Clark University Press, 1968.

———. *The Origins of Intelligence in Children.* New York: International University Press, 1952.

———. *The Psychology of Intelligence.* London: Routledge & Kegan Paul, 1947.

———. *Structuralism.* London: Routledge & Kegan Paul, 1971.

Piaget, Jean, and Inhelder, B. *The Growth of Logical Thinking from Childhood to Adolescence: An Essay on the Construction of Formal Operational Structures.* New York: Basic Books, 1958.

Pfaff, M., ed. *Frontiers in Social Thought: Essays in Honor of Kenneth Boulding.* New York: North-Holland, 1976.

Radford, J., and Burton, A. *Thinking: Its Nature and Development.* New York: John Wiley & Sons, 1974.

Ratner, Joseph, ed. *Intelligence in the Modern World: John Dewey's Philosophy.* New York: Random House, 1939.

Reeves, Joan W. *Thinking about Thinking.* London: Martin Secher and Warburg, 1965.

Reitman, Walter R. *Cognition and Thought.* New York: John Wiley & Sons, 1965.

Richards, I. A. *The Philosophy of Rhetoric.* New York: Oxford University Press, 1936.

———. *Principles of Literary Criticism.* New York: Harcourt, Brace, 1952.

Sapir, Edward. *Language: An Introduction to the Study of Speech.* New York: Harcourt, Brace, & World, 1921.

Schilpp, Paul, ed. *The Philosophy of Ernst Cassirer.* New York: Tudor, 1949.

Searle, John. "Human Communication Theory and the Philosophy of Language: Some Remarks." In *Human Communication Theory.* Edited by Frank Dance. New York: Holt, Rinehart and Winston, 1967, pp. 116–29.

———. *Speech Acts: An Essay in the Philosophy of Language.* Cambridge: Cambridge University Press, 1969.

Seidel, George. *Martin Heidegger and the Pre-Socratics.* Lincoln: University of Nebraska Press, 1964.

Shimanoff, Susan B. *Communication Rules: Theory and Research.* Beverly Hills, Calif.: Sage, 1980.

Silverman, David, and Torode, Brian. *The Material Word: Some Theories of Language and Its Limits.* London: Routledge & Kegan Paul, 1980.

Snider, James, and Osgood, Charles, eds. *The Semantic Differential Technique*. Chicago: Aldine, 1969.

Solso, R. L., ed. *Theories in Cognitive Psychology*. Hillsdale, N.J.: Erlbaum, 1974.

Stewart, John. "Concepts of Language and Meaning: A Comparative Study." *Quarterly Journal of Speech* 58 (1972):123–33.

Urban, Wilbur. "Cassirer's Philosophy of Language." In *The Philosophy of Ernst Cassirer*. Edited by Paul Schilpp. New York: Tudor, 1949, pp. 403–41.

Weimer, W. B., and Palermo, D. S., eds. *Cognition and the Symbolic Process*. Hillsdale, N.J.: Erlbaum, 1974.

Whorf Benjamin L. *Language, Thought, and Reality*. New York: John Wiley & Sons, 1956.

Wittgenstein, Ludwig. *The Blue and Brown Books*. Oxford: Basil Blackwell, 1958.

———. *Philosophical Investigations*. Oxford: Basil Blackwell, 1953.

———. *Tractus Logico-Philosophicus*. London: Routledge & Kegan Paul, 1922.

Chapter 7
Theories of Information and Information Processing

Ackoff, Russell. "Toward a Behavioral Theory of Communication." *Management Science* 4 (1957–58):218–34.

Ackoff, Russell, and Emery, Fred. *On Purposeful Systems*. Chicago: Aldine, 1972.

Attneave, Fred. *Applications of Information Theory to Psychology*. New York: Holt, 1959.

Bar-Hillel, Yehoshua. "Concluding Review." In *Information Theory in Psychology*. Edited by Henry Quastler. Glencoe, Ill. Free Press, 1955, p. 3.

———. "An Examination of Information Theory." *Philosophy of Science* 22 (1955):86–105.

Bar-Hillel, Yehoshua, and Carnap, R. "Semantic Information." *British Journal of the Philosophy of Science* 4 (1953):147–57.

Bellow, Francis. "The Information Theory." *Fortune* December 1953, pp. 136–40.

Broadhurst, Allan R., and Darnell, Donald K. "An Introduction to Cybernetics and Information Theory." *Quarterly Journal of Speech* 51 (1965):442–53.

Buckley, Walter, ed. *Modern Systems Research for the Behavioral Scientist*. Chicago: Aldine, 1968.

Cherry, Colin. "The Cocktail Party Problem." *Discovery*, March 1962, p. 32.

———, ed. *Information Theory*. London: Butterworth, 1961.

———. *On Human Communication*. Cambridge: M.I.T. Press, 1978.

Conant, Roger C. "A Vector Theory of Information." In *Communication Yearbook 3*. Edited by Dan Nimmo. New Brunswick, N.J.: Transaction Books, 1979, pp. 177–96.

Crockett, Walter H. "Cognitive Complexity and Impression Formation." In *Progress in Experimental Personality Research*. Edited by Brendon A. Maher. New York: Academic Press, 1965, vol. 2, pp. 47–90.

Darnell, Donald K. "Information Theory." In *Communication Concepts and Processes*. Edited by Joseph A. DeVito. Englewood Cliffs, N.J.: Prentice-Hall, 1971, pp. 37–45.

Dittmann, Allen T. "The Theory of Communication." In *Interpersonal Messages of Emotion*. New York: Springer, 1972, chap. 2.

Frick, F. C. "The Application of Information Theory in Behavioral Studies." In *Modern Systems Research for the Behavioral Scientist*. Edited by Walter Buckley. Chicago: Aldine, 1968, pp. 182–85.

Garner, Wendell R. *Uncertainty and Structure as Psychological Concepts*. New York: John Wiley & Sons, 1962.

Hale, Claudia. "Cognitive Complexity-Simplicity as a Determinant of Communication Effectiveness." *Communication Monographs* 47 (1980):304–11.

Handy, Rollo, and Kurtz, Paul. "A Current Appraisal of the Behavioral Sciences: Information Theory." *American Behavioral Scientist* 7 no. 6 (1964), pp. 99–104.

———. "Information Theory." *American Behavioral Scientist* 7 (1964):99–104.

Kolmogoroff, A. N. "Three Approaches to the Quantitative Definition of Information." *Problemy Peredachi Informatisii* 1 (1965):3–11.

Krippendorf, Klaus. "Information Theory." In *Communication and Behavior*. Edited by Gerhard Hanneman and William McEwen. Reading, Mass.: Addison-Wesley, 1975, pp. 351–89.

Lin, Nan. "Encounter: The Frame of Communication." In *The Study of Human Communication*. Indianapolis, Ind.: Bobbs-Merrill, 1973, chap. 2.

MacKay, Donald. "The Informational Analysis of Questions and Comments." In *Information*

Theory: Fourth London Symposium. Edited by Colin Cherry. London: Butterworth, 1961.

Miller, George. "What Is Information Measurement?" *American Psychologist* 8 (1963):3–11.

Mortensen, C. David. "Human Information Processing." In *Communication: The Study of Human Interaction*. New York: McGraw-Hill, 1972, pp. 69–124.

Pierce, J. R. *Symbols, Signals, and Noise*. New York: Harper Torchbook, 1961.

Rapoport, Anatol. "The Promises and Pitfalls of Information Theory." *Behavioral Science* 1 (1956): 303–9.

———. "What Is Information? *Et Cetera* 10 (1953):247–60.

Rosenfeld, Lawrence. *Aristotle and Information Theory*. The Hague: Mouton, 1971.

Schroder, Harold M.; Driver, Michael S.; and Streufert, Siegfreid. *Human Information Processing: Individuals and Groups Functioning in Complex Social Situations*. New York: Holt, Rinehart and Winston, 1967.

Shannon, Claude, and Weaver, Warren. *The Mathematical Theory of Communication*. Urbana: University of Illinois Press, 1949.

Singh, Jagjit. *Great Ideas in Informaton Theory, Language, and Cybernetics*. New York: Dover, 1966.

Underwood, Geoffrey. "Concepts in Information Processing." In *Strategies of Information Processing*. Edited by G. Underwood. New York: Academic Press, 1978, pp. 1–22.

Weaver, Warren. "The Mathematics of Communication." *Scientific American* 181 (1949):11–15.

Wiener, Norbert. *Cybernetics or Control and Communication in the Animal and the Machine*. Cambridge: M.I.T. Press, 1948.

Young, John F. *Information Theory*. New York: John Wiley & Sons, 1971.

Chapter 8
Theories of Persuasion

Abelson, Robert P., et al., eds. *Theories of Cognitive Consistency: A Sourcebook*. Chicago: Rand McNally, 1968.

Allport, Gordon W. "Attitudes." In *Handbook of Social Psychology*. Edited by C. Murchison. Worcester, Mass.: Clark University Press, 1935, pp. 798–884.

Anderson, Norman H. "Integration Theory and Attitude Change." *Psychological Review* 78 (1971):171–206.

Aristotle. *Rhetoric*. Translated by Lane Cooper. New York: Appleton-Century, 1932.

———. *Rhetoric*. Translated by W. Rhys Roberts. New York: Oxford University Press, 1924.

Aronson, Elliot. *The Social Animal*. New York: Viking, 1972.

Bandura, Albert. *Social Learning Theory*. Englewood Cliffs, N.J.: Prentice-Hall, 1977.

Beisecker, Thomas D., and Parson, Donn W., eds. *The Process of Social Influence*. Englewood Cliffs, N.J.: Prentice-Hall, 1972.

Bem, Daryl J. *Beliefs, Attitudes, and Human Affairs*. Monterey, Calif.: Brooks/Cole, 1970.

Brehm, J. W., and Cohen, A. R., *Explorations in Cognitive Dissonance*. New York: John Wiley & Sons, 1962.

Brock, Bernard L., and Scott, Robert L. *Methods of Rhetorical Criticism*. Detroit: Wayne State University Press, 1980.

Brockriede, Wayne. "Dimensions of the Concept of Rhetoric." *Quarterly Journal of Speech* 54, (1968):1–12.

———. "Toward a Contemporary Aristotelian Theory of Rhetoric." *Quarterly Journal of Speech* 52 (1966):33–40.

Brown, Roger. "Models of Attitude Change." In *New Directions in Psychology*. New York: Holt, Rinehart and Winston, 1962, pp. 1–85.

———. *Social Psychology*. New York: Free Press, 1965.

Burhans, David T. "The Attitude-Behavior Discrepancy Problem: Revisited." *Quarterly Journal of Speech* 57 (1971):418–28.

Chapanis, Natalia P., and Chapanis, Alphonse. "Cognitive Dissonance: Five Years Later." *Psychological Bulletin* 61 (1964):21.

Cohen, Arthur. *Attitude Change and Social Influence*. New York: Basic Books, 1964.

Cronkite, Gary. *Persuasion-Speech and Behavioral Change*. Indianapolis, Ind.: Bobbs-Merrill, 1969.

Ehninger, Douglas. *Contemporary Rhetoric*. Glenview, Ill.: Scott, Foresman, 1972.

Festinger, Leon. *A Theory of Cognitive Dissonance*. Stanford, Calif.: Stanford University Press, 1957.

Festinger, Leon, and Aronson, Elliot. "The Arousal and Reduction of Dissonance in Social Contexts." In *Group Dynamics*. Edited by Dorwin Cartwright and Alvin Zander. New York: Harper & Row, 1960, pp. 214–31.

Fishbein, Martin. "A Behavior Theory Approach

to the Relations between Beliefs about an Object and the Attitude Toward the Object." In *Readings in Attitude Theory and Measurement.* Edited by Martin Fishbein. New York: John Wiley & Sons, 1967, pp. 389–400.

———. "A Consideration of Beliefs, and Their Role in Attitude Measurement." In *Readings in Attitude Theory and Measurement.* Edited by Martin Fishbein. New York: John Wiley & Sons, 1967, pp. 257–66.

———, ed. *Readings in Attitude Theory and Measurement.* New York: John Wiley & Sons, 1967.

Fishbein, Martin, and Ajzen, Icek. *Belief, Attitude, Intention, and Behavior.* Reading, Mass.: Addison-Wesley, 1975.

Fishbein, Martin, and Raven, Bertram H. "The AB Scales: An Operational Definition of Belief and Attitude." In *Readings in Attitude Theory and Measurement.* Edited by Martin Fishbein. New York: John Wiley & Sons, 1967, pp. 183–89.

Fotheringham, Wallace C. *Perspectives on Persuasion.* Boston: Allyn and Bacon, 1966.

Golden, James L.; Berquist, Goodwin F.; and Coleman, William E. *The Rhetoric of Western Thought.* Dubuque, Iowa: Kendall Hunt, 1976.

Greenwald, Anthony G.; Brock, Timothy; and Ostrom, Thomas, eds. *Psychological Foundations of Attitudes.* New York: Academic Press, 1968.

Harper, Nancy L. *Human Communication Theory: The History of a Paradigm.* Rochelle Park, N.J.: Hayden, 1979.

Heider, Fritz. "Attitudes and Cognitive Organization." *Journal of Psychology* 21 (1946):107–12.

———. *The Psychology of Interpersonal Relations.* New York: John Wiley & Sons, 1958.

Hovland, Carl I.; Janis, Irving; and Kelley, Harold. *Communication and Persuasion.* New Haven; Conn.: Yale University Press, 1953.

Hovland, Carl I., et al. *The Order of Presentation in Persuasion.* New Haven, Conn.: Yale University Press, 1959.

Insko, Chester. *Theories of Attitude Change.* New York: Appleton-Century-Crofts, 1967.

Janis, Irving, et al. *Personality and Persuasibility.* New Haven, Conn.: Yale University Press, 1959.

Johannesen, Richard L. *Contemporary Theories of Rhetoric.* New York: Harper & Row, 1971.

Katz, Daniel. "The Functional Approach to the Study of Attitudes." *Public Opinion Quarterly* 24 (1960):163–204.

Kiesler, Charles A.; Collins, Barry E.; and Miller, Norman. *Attitude Change: A Critical Analysis of Theoretical Approaches.* New York: John Wiley & Sons, 1969.

Kling, J. W. "Learning: Introductory Survey." In *Woodworth and Schlossberg's Experimental Psychology.* Edited by J. W. Kling and Lorrin Riggs. New York: Holt, Rinehart and Winston, 1971, pp. 551–613.

McGuire, William. "Inducing Resistance to Persuasion: Some Contemporary Approaches." In *Advances in Experimental Social Psychology.* Edited by L. Berkowitz. New York: Academic Press, 1964, pp. 191–229.

———. "The Nature of Attitudes and Attitude Change." In *The Handbook of Social Psychology,* vol. 3. Edited by Gardner Lindzey and Elliot Aronson. Reading, Mass.: Addison-Wesley, 1969, pp. 136–314.

———. "Personality and Attitude Change: An Information-Processing Theory." In *Psychological Foundations of Attitude.* Edited by Anthony G. Greenwald, Timothy C. Brock, and Thomas M. Ostrom. New York: Academic Press, 1968, pp. 171–95.

———. "Personality and Susceptibility to Social Influence." In *Handbook of Personality Theory and Research.* Edited by E. F. Borgatta and W. W. Lambert. Chicago: Rand McNally, 1967.

Miller, Gerald, and Burgoon, Michael. "Persuasion Research: Review and Commentary." In *Communication Yearbook 2*, edited by Brent Rubin. New Brunswick, N.J.: Transaction Books, 1978, pp. 29–47.

Newcomb, Theodore. *The Acquaintance Process.* New York: Holt, Rinehart and Winston, 1961.

———. "An Approach to the Study of Communicative Acts." *Psychological Review* 60 (1953):393–404.

Newcomb, Theodore; Turner, Ralph; and Converse, Philip. *Social Psychology: The Study of Human Interaction.* New York: Holt, Rinehart and Winston, 1965.

Osgood, Charles E., and Tannenbaum, Percy H. "The Principle of Congruity in the Prediction of Attitude Change." *Psychological Review* 62 (1955):42–55.

Reardon, Kathleen. *Persuasion: Theory and Context.* Beverly Hills, Calif.: Sage, 1981.

Rokeach, Milton. *Beliefs, Attitudes, and Values: A Theory of Organization and Change.* San Francisco: Jossey-Bass, 1969

———. *The Nature of Human Values.* New York: Free Press, 1973.

———. "Persuasion that Persists." *Psychology Today*, September 1971, p. 68.

Rosenberg, Milton J., et al. *Attitude Organization and Change.* New Haven, Conn.: Yale University Press, 1960.

Rosnow, Ralph L., and Robinson, Edward J., eds. *Experiments in Persuasion.* New York: Academic Press, 1967.

Sherif, Muzafer. *Social Interaction—Process and Products.* Chicago: Aldine, 1967.

Sherif, Muzafer, and Cantril, H. *The Psychology of Ego-Involvements.* New York: John Wiley & Sons, 1947.

Sherif, Muzafer, and Hovland, Carl I. *Social Judgment.* New Haven; Conn.: Yale University Press, 1961.

Sherif, Muzafer; Sherif, Carolyn; and Nebergall, Roger. *Attitude and Attitude Change: The Social Judgment-Involvement Approach.* Philadelphia: W. B. Saunders, 1965.

Simons, Herbert W. "Psychological Theories of Persuasion: An Auditor's Report." *Quarterly Journal of Speech* 57 (1971):383–92.

Smith, M. Brewster. *Social Psychology and Human Values.* Chicago: Aldine, 1969.

Smith, Mary John. *Persuasion and Human Action.* Belmont, Calif.: Wadsworth, 1982.

Tavris, Carol. "What Does College Do for a Person? Frankly, Very Little." *Psychology Today*, September 1974, pp. 73–80.

Thonssen, Lester, and Baird, A. Craig. *Speech Criticism: The Development of Standards for Rhetorical Appraisal.* New York: Ronald Press, 1948.

Wagner, Richard V. and Sherwood, John H. *The Study of Attitudes.* Monterey, Calif.: Brooks/Cole, 1969.

Weiss, Robert. "An Extension of Hullian Learning Theory to Persuasive Communication." In *Psychological Foundations of Attitudes.* Edited by Anthony Greenwald, Timothy Brock, and Thomas Ostrom. New York: Academic Press, 1968, pp. 109–45.

———. "Persuasion and the Acquisition of Attitudes: Models from Conditioning and Selective Learning." *Psychological Reports* 11 (1962):709–32.

Wichelns, Herbert A. "The Literary Criticism of Oratory." In *Studies in Rhetoric and Public Speaking in Honor of James Albert Winans.* New York: Century, 1925.

Wicklund, Robert A., and Brehm, Jack W. *Perspectives on Cognitive Dissonance.* Hillsdale, N.J.: Erlbaum, 1976.

Wyer, Robert S. *Cognitive Organization and Change.* Hillsdale, N.J.: Erlbaum, 1974.

Zajonc, Robert. "Attitudinal Effects of Mere Exposure." *Journal of Personality and Social Psychology* 9 (1968):1–27.

———. "The Concepts of Balance, Congruity, and Dissonance." *Public Opinion Quarterly* 24 (1960):280–96.

Chapter 9

Interpersonal Contexts I: Theories of Relationship, Presentation, and Perception.

Barnlund, Dean, ed. *Interpersonal Communication: Survey and Studies.* Boston: Houghton Mifflin, 1968.

Bateson, Gregory. "A Formal Approach to Explicit, Implicit, and Embodied Ideas and to Their Forms of Interaction." In *Double-Bind.* Edited by C. E. Sluzki and D. C. Ransom. New York: Grune & Stratton, 1976, p. xii.

———. "Slippery Theories." *International Journal of Psychiatry* 2 (1966):415–17.

———. *Naven.* Stanford, Calif.: Stanford University Press, 1958.

Bateson, Gregory; Jackson, Donald; Haley, J.; and Weaklund, J. "Toward a Theory of Schizophrenia." *Behavioral Science* 1 (1956):251–64.

Berscheid, E., and Walster, E. *Interpersonal Attraction.* Reading, Mass.: Addison-Wesley, 1969.

Bochner, Arthur, and Krueger, Dorothy. "Interpersonal Communication Theory and Research: An Overview of Inscrutable Epistemologies and Muddled Concepts." In *Communication Yearbook 3.* Edited by Dan Nimmo. New Brunswick, N.J.: Transaction Books, 1979, p. 203.

Dance, Frank E. X., ed. *Human Communication Theory: Comparative Essays.* New York: Harper & Row, 1982.

Dance, Frank E. X., and Larson, Carl E. *The Functions of Human Communication.* New York: Holt, Rinehart and Winston, 1976.

Dawe, Allan. "The Underworld-View of Erving Goffman." *British Journal of Sociology* 24 (1973):246–53.

DeVito, Joseph. *The Interpersonal Communication Book.* New York: Harper & Row, 1976.

Ditton, Jason, ed. *The View from Goffman.* New York: St. Martin's Press, 1980.

Ericson, P. M., and Rogers, L. E. "New Procedures for Analyzing Relational Communication." *Family Process* 12 (1973):245–67.

Goffman, Erving. *Behavior in Public Places.* New York: Free Press, 1963.

———. *Encounters: Two Studies in the Sociology of Interaction.* Indianapolis, Ind.: Bobbs-Merrill, 1961.

———. *Frame Analysis: An Essay on the Organization of Experience.* Cambridge: Harvard University Press, 1974.

———. *Interaction Ritual: Essays on Face-to-Face Behavior.* Garden City, N.Y.: Doubleday, 1967.

———. *The Presentation of Self in Everyday Life.* Garden City, N.Y.: Doubleday, 1959.

———. *Relations in Public.* New York: Basic Books, 1971.

Goldhaber, Gerald. "Dyads in Organizations: A Transactional Analysis Perspective." In *Organizational Communication.* Dubuque, Iowa: Brown, 1976, chap. 6.

Goldhaber, Gerald, and Goldhaber, Marylyn, eds. *Transactional Analysis: Principles and Applications.* Boston: Allyn and Bacon, 1976.

Harrison, Randall. "Code Systems." In *Beyond Words.* Englewood Cliffs, N.J.: Prentice-Hall, 1974, chap. 4.

Harvey, John K.; Ickes, William J.; and Kidd, Robert F., eds., *New Directions in Attribution Research.* 2 vols. New York: John Wiley & Sons, 1976, 1978.

Heider, Fritz. *The Psychology of Interpersonal Relations.* New York: John Wiley & Sons, 1958.

Jones, Edward E., et al. *Attribution: Perceiving the Causes of Behavior.* Morristown, N.J.: General Learning Press, 1972.

Keadon, A.; Harris, R. M.; and Key, M. R., eds. *Organization of Behavior in Face-to-Face Interaction.* Paris: Mouton, 1975.

Kelley, Harold. *Attribution in Social Interaction.* Morristown, N.J.: General Learning Press, 1971.

———. "Attribution in Social Interaction." In *Attribution: Perceiving the Causes of Behavior.* Morristown, N.J.: General Learning Press, 1972, pp. 1–26.

———. "Attribution Theory in Social Psychology." In *Nebraska Symposium on Motivation,* vol. 15. Edited by David Levine. Lincoln: University of Nebraska Press, 1967, pp. 192–240.

———. *Causal Schemata and the Attribution Process.* Morristown, N.J.: General Learning Press, 1972.

———. "Causal Schemata and the Attribution Process." In *Attribution: Perceiving the Causes of Behavior.* Morristown, N.J.: General Learning Press, 1972, pp. 151–74.

———. "The Processes of Causal Attribution." *American Psychologist* 28 (1973):107–28.

Laing, R. D. *The Politics of Experience.* New York: Pantheon, 1967.

———. *Self and Others.* London: Tavistock, 1969.

Laing, R. D.; Phillipson, H.; and Lee, A. R. *Interpersonal Perception.* New York: Springer, 1966.

Littlejohn, Stephen. "Frame Analysis and Communication." *Communication Research* 4 (1977):485–92.

Millar, Frank E., and Rogers, L. Edna. "A Relational Approach to Interpersonal Communication." In *Explorations in Interpersonal Communication.* edited by Gerald Miller. Beverly Hills, Calif.: Sage, 1976, pp. 87–103.

Miller, Gerald R., ed. *Explorations in Interpersonal Communication.* Beverly Hills, Calif.: Sage, 1976.

Newcomb, Theodore. *The Acquaintance Process.* New York: Holt, Rinehart and Winston, 1961.

Noland, Michael. "The Relationship between Verbal and Nonverbal Communication." In *Communication and Behavior.* Edited by Gerhard Hanneman and William McEwen. Reading, Mass.: Addison-Wesley, 1975, pp. 98–118.

Parks, Malcolm. "Relational Communication: Theory and Research." *Human Communication Research* 3 (1977):372–81.

Rogers, L. E., and Farace, R. V. "Analysis of Relational Communication in Dyads: New Measurement Procedures." *Human Communication Research* 1 (1975):222–39.

Rosenfeld, Lawrence. "Conceptual Orientations." In *Human Interaction in the Small Group.* Columbus, Ohio: Charles E. Merrill, 1973, pp. 31–36.

Ruesch, Juergen, and Bateson, Gregory. *Communication: The Social Matrix of Society.* New York: Norton, 1951.

Schutz, William. *Elements of Encounter.* New York: Bantam, 1975.

———. *Firo: A Three-Dimensional Theory of Interpersonal Behavior.* New York: Rinehart, 1958.

———. *Here Comes Everybody.* New York: Harper & Row, 1973.

———. *The Interpersonal Underworld.* Palo Alto, Calif.: Science and Behavior Books, 1966.

———. *Leaders of Schools.* La Jolla, Calif.: University Associates, 1977.

Shaw, Marvin. *Group Dynamics: The Psychology of Small Group Behavior.* New York: McGraw-Hill, 1981.

Tagiuri, Renato. "Person Perception." In *The Handbook of Social Psychology*, vol. 3. Edited by Gardner Lindzey and Elliot Aronson. Reading, Mass.: Addison-Wesley, 1969, pp. 395–449.

Tedeschi, J. T.; Schlenker, B. R.; and Bonoma, T. V. *Conflict, Power, and Games*. Chicago: Aldine, 1973.

Watzlawick, Paul; Beavin, Janet; and Jackson, Don. *Pragmatics of Human Communication: A Study of Interactional Patterns, Pathologies, and Paradoxes*. New York: Norton, 1967.

Watzlawick, Paul, and Weaklund, John, eds. *The Interactional View: Studies at the Mental Research Institute, Palo Alto, 1965–1974*. New York: Norton, 1977.

Watzlawick, Paul; Weaklund, John; and Fish, Richard. *Change: Principles of Problem Formation and Problem Resolution*. New York: Norton, 1974.

Wilder, Carol. "From the Interactional View—A Conversation with Paul Watzlawick." *Journal of Communication* 28 (1978):41–42.

———. "The Palo Alto Group: Difficulties and Directions of the Interactional View for Human Communication Research." *Human Communication Research* 5 (1979):171–86.

Wilmot, William. "Meta-communication: A Reexamination and Extension." In *Communication Yearbook 4*. Edited by Dan Nimmo. New Brunswick, N.J.: Transaction Books, 1980, pp. 61–69.

Chapter 10
Interpersonal Contexts II: Theories of Disclosure, Attraction, and Conflict

Beisecker, Thomas. "Game Theory in Communication Research: A Rejoinder and a Reorientation." *Journal of Communication* 20 (1970):107–20.

Berlyne, Daniel E. "Humanistic Psychology as a Protest Movement." In *Humanistic Psychology: Concepts and Criticisms*. Edited by Joseph Royce and Leendert P. Mos. New York: Plenum, 1981, p. 261.

Berne, Eric. *Games People Play*. New York: Grove Press, 1964.

———. *The Structure and Dynamics of Organizations and Groups*. Philadelphia: Lippincott, 1963.

———. *Transactional Analysis in Psychotherapy*. New York: Grove Press, 1961.

Bostrom, Robert N. "Game Theory in Communication Research." *Journal of Communication* 18 (1968):369–88.

Bowers, John W., ed. *Speech Monographs, Special Issue: Communication and Conflict* 41 (1974):1–84.

Byrne, Donn. *The Attraction Paradigm*. New York: Academic Press, 1971.

Coward, Harold G., and Royce, Joseph R. "Toward an Epistemological Basis for Humanistic Psychology." In *Humanistic Psychology: Concepts and Criticisms*. Edited by Joseph Royce and Leendert P. Mos. New York: Plenum, 1981, pp. 109–34.

Cozby, P. W. "Self-Disclosure: A Literature Review." *Psychological Bulletin* 79 (1973):73–91.

Darnell, Donald, and Brockriede, Wayne. *Persons Communicating*. Englewood Cliffs, N.J.: Prentice-Hall, 1976.

Davis, Morton D. *Game Theory: A Nontechnical Introduction*. New York: Basic Books, 1970.

Dedring, Juergen. *Recent Advances in Peace and Conflict Research: A Critical Survey*. Beverly Hills, Calif.: Sage, 1976.

Gilbert, Shirley J. "Empirical and Theoretical Extensions of Self-Disclosure." In *Explorations in Interpersonal Communication*. Edited by Gerald Miller. Beverly Hills, Calif.: Sage, 1976, pp. 197–216.

Hall, Calvin, and Lindzey, Gardner. "Roger's Self-Theory." In *Theories of Personality*. New York: John Wiley & Sons, 1970, chap. 13.

Harris, Thomas. *I'm OK—You're OK*. New York: Harper & Row, 1969.

Hart, Roderick P., and Burks, Don M. "Rhetorical Sensitivity and Social Interaction." *Speech Monographs* 39 (1972):75–91.

Hart, Roderick P.; Carlson, Robert E.; and Eadie, William F. "Attitudes toward Communication and the Assessment of Rhetorical Sensitivity." *Communication Monographs* 47 (1980):1–22.

Hawes, Leonard C., and Smith, David H. "A Critique of Assumptions Underlying the Study of Communication in Conflict." *Quarterly Journal of Speech* 59 (1973):423–35.

James, Muriel, and Jongeward, Dorothy. *Born to Win*. Reading, Mass.: Addison-Wesley, 1973.

Jandt, F. *Conflict Resolution through Communication*. New York: Harper & Row, 1973.

Johnson, David W. "Communication and the Inducement of Cooperative Behavior in Conflicts: A Critical Review." *Speech Monographs* 41 (1974): 64–78.

Jourard, Sidney. *Disclosing Man to Himself.* New York: Van Nostrand Reinhold, 1968.

———. *Self-Disclosure: An Experimental Analysis of the Transparent Self.* New York: John Wiley & Sons, 1971.

———. *The Transparent Self.* New York: Van Nostrand, 1971.

Kelley, Harold. *Attribution in Social Interaction.* New York: General Learning Press, 1971.

Kelley, Harold, and Thibaut, J. W. *Interpersonal Relations: A Theory of Interdependence.* New York: John Wiley & Sons, 1978.

La Gaipa, John J. "Interpersonal Attraction and Social Exchange." In *Theory and Practice in Interpersonal Attraction.* Edited by Steve Duck. New York: Academic Press, 1971, pp. 129–64.

Lindzey, Gardner, and Hall, Calvin S. *Theories of Personality.* New York: John Wiley & Sons, 1970.

Luce, R. D., and Raiffa, H. *Games and Decisions.* New York: John Wiley & Sons, 1957.

Luft, Joseph. *Of Human Interaction.* Palo Alto, Calif.: National Press Books, 1969.

Maslow, Abraham. *The Farther Reaches of Human Nature.* New York: Viking, 1971.

Mehrabian, Albert. *Silent Messages.* Belmont, Calif.: Wadsworth, 1971.

Miller, Gerald, and Simons, Herbert, eds. *Perspectives on Communication in Conflict.* Englewood Cliffs, N.J.: Prentice-Hall, 1974.

Mortensen, C. David. "A Transactional Paradigm of Verbalized Social Conflict." In *Perspectives on Communication in Social Conflict.* Edited by Gerald Miller and Herbert Simons. Englewood Cliffs, N.J.: Prentice-Hall, 1974, pp. 90–124.

Newcomb, Theodore. *The Acquaintance Process.* New York: Holt, Rinehart and Winston, 1961.

Nolan, Michael. "The Relationship between Verbal and Nonverbal Communication." In *Communication and Behavior.* Edited by Gerhard Hanneman and William McEwen. Reading, Mass.: Addison-Wesley, 1975, pp. 98–118.

Rapoport, Anatol. "Conflict Resolution in Light of Game Theory and Beyond." In *The Structure of Conflict.* Edited by P. Swingle. New York: Academic Press, 1970, pp. 1–44.

———. *Fights, Games, and Debates.* Ann Arbor: University of Michigan Press, 1960.

Rogers, Carl. *On Becoming a Person.* Boston: Houghton-Mifflin, 1961.

———. *Client-centered Therapy.* Boston: Houghton Mifflin, 1951, chap. 11.

———. *Counselling and Psychotherapy.* Boston: Houghton Mifflin, 1942.

———. "A Theory of Therapy, Personality, and Interpersonal Relationships, as Developed in the Client-centered Framework." In *Psychology: A Study of Science.* Edited by S. Koch. New York: McGraw-Hill, 1959, vol. 3, pp. 184–256.

Schelling, T. C. *The Strategy of Conflict.* Cambridge: Harvard University Press, 1960.

Sillars, Alan L. "Expression and Control in Human Interaction: Perspectives on Humanistic Psychology." *Western Speech* 38 (1974):269–77.

Simons, Herbert. "The Carrot and Stick as Handmaidens of Persuasion in Conflict Situations." In *Perspectives on Communication in Social Conflict.* Edited by Gerald Miller and Herbert Simons. Englewood Cliffs, N.J.: Prentice-Hall, 1974, pp. 172–205.

Steiner, Claude. *Scripts People Live.* New York: Grove Press, 1974.

Steinfatt, Thomas M. "Communication and Conflict: A Review of New Material." *Human Communication Research* 1 (1974):81–89.

Steinfatt, Thomas M., and Miller, Gerald. "Communication in Game Theoretic Models of Conflict." In *Perspectives on Communication in Social Conflict.* Edited by Gerald Miller and Herbert Simons. Englewood Cliffs, N.J.: Prentice-Hall, 1974, pp. 14–75.

Tedeschi, J. T.; Schlenker,. B. R.; and Bonoma, T. V. *Conflict, Power, and Games.* Chicago: Aldine, 1973.

Thibaut, J. W., and Kelley, H. H. *The Social Psychology of Groups.* New York: John Wiley & Sons, 1959.

Von Neumann, J., and Morgenstern, O. *The Theory of Games and Economic Behavior.* Princeton, N.J.: Princeton University Press, 1944.

Wandersman, Abraham; Poppen, Paul; and Ricks, David; eds. *Humanism and Behaviorism: Dialogue and Growth.* Elmsford, N.Y.: Pergamon Press, 1976.

Watkins, Charles. "An Analytic Model of Conflict." *Speech Monographs* 41 (1974):1–5.

Chapter 11
Interpersonal Contexts III: Theories of Groups and Organizations

Abrahamsson, Bengt. *Bureaucracy or Participation: The Logic of Organization.* Beverly Hills, Calif.: Sage, 1977.

Allport, G. W. "The Genius of Kurt Lewin." *Journal of Personality* 16 (1947):1–10.

Argyris, Chris. *Integrating the Individual and the Organization*. New York: John Wiley & Sons, 1964.

———. *Interpersonal Competence and Organizational Effectiveness*. Homewood, Ill.: Irwin, 1962.

———. *Management and Organizational Development*. New York: McGraw-Hill, 1971.

———. *Personality and Organization: The Conflict between System and the Individual*. New York: Harper & Brothers, 1957.

———. "Understanding Human Behavior in Organizations." In *Modern Organization Theory*. Edited by Mason Haire. New York: John Wiley & Sons, 1959, pp. 115–54.

Azumi, Koya, and Hage, Jerald. *Organizational Systems: A Text Reader in the Sociology of Organizations*. Lexington, Mass.: Heath, 1972.

Bales, Robert F. *Interaction Process Analysis: A Method for the Study of Small Groups*. Reading, Mass.: Addison-Wesley, 1950.

———. *Personality and Interpersonal Behavior*. New York: Holt, Rinehart and Winston, 1970.

Barnard, Chester. *The Functions of the Executive*. Cambridge: Harvard University Press, 1938.

Bendix, Reinhard. *Max Weber: An Intellectual Portrait*. Garden City, N.Y.: Doubleday, 1962.

Benne, Kenneth, and Sheats, Paul. "Functional Roles of Group Members." *Journal of Social Issues* 4 (1958):41–49.

Bennis, W. G., and Shepard, H. A. "A Theory of Group Development." *Human Relations* 9 (1956):415–37.

Berelson, Bernard, and Steiner, Gary A. *Human Behavior: An Inventory of Scientific Findings*. New York: Harcourt, Brace, 1964.

Blake, Robert, and Mouton, Jane S. *The Managerial Grid*. Houston: Gulf Publishing, 1964.

Borgatta, Edgar; Cottrell, Leonard; and Meyer, Henry. "On the Dimensions of Group Behavior." *Sociometry* 19 (1956):222–40.

Bormann, Ernest G. "The Paradox and Promise of Small Group Research." *Speech Monographs* 37 (1970):211–17.

Bormann, Ernest G.; Howell, William S., Nichols, Ralph G.; and Shapiro, George L. *Interpersonal Communication in the Modern Organization*. Englewood Cliffs, N.J.: Prentice-Hall, 1969.

Cartwright, Dorwin. "Lewinian Theory as a Contemporary Systematic Framework." In *Psychology: A Study of Science,* vol. 2. Edited by S. Koch. New York: McGraw-Hill, 1959, pp. 7–91.

Cartwright, Dorwin, and Zander, Alvin, eds. *Group Dynamics: Research and Theory*. New York: Harper & Row, 1968.

Cathcart, Robert S., and Samovar, Larry A., eds. *Small Group Communication: A Reader*. Dubuque, Iowa: Brown, 1974.

Cattell, Raymond. "Concepts and Methods in the Measurement of Group Syntality." *Psychological Review* 55 (1948):48–63.

Collins, Barry, and Guetzkow, Harold. *A Social Psychology of Group Processes for Decision Making*. New York: John Wiley & Sons, 1964.

Cooper, C. L., ed. *Theories of Group Processes*. New York: John Wiley & Sons, 1975.

Courtright, John A. "A Laboratory Investigation of Groupthink." *Communication Monographs* 45 (1978):229–46.

Deutsch, Karl. "On Communication Models in the Social Sciences." *Public Opinion Quarterly,* Fall 1952, pp. 356–80.

Eisenstadt, S. N. *Max Weber on Charisma and Institution Building*. Chicago: University of Chicago Press, 1968.

Eldgridge, J. E. T., and Crombie, A. D. *A Sociology of Organizations*. New York: International Publishing Service, 1975.

Etzioni, Amatai. *Complex Organizations*. New York: Free Press, 1961.

———. *Modern Organizations*. Englewood Cliffs, N.J.: Prentice-Hall, 1964.

Evan, William M. *Organization Theory: Structures, Systems and Environments*. New York: John Wiley & Sons, 1976.

Farace, Richard V.; Monge, Peter R.; and Russell, Hamish. *Communicating and Organizing*. Reading, Mass. Addison-Wesley, 1977.

Fayol, Henri. *General and Industrial Management*. Translated by Constance Storrs. London: Sir Isaac Pitman & Sons, 1949.

Filley, Alan C., and House, Robert J. *Managerial Process and Organizational Behavior*. Glenview, Ill.: Scott, Foresman, 1969.

Fisher, B. Aubrey. "Decision Emergence: Phases in Group Decision Making." *Speech Monographs* 37 (1970):53–66.

———. "The Process of Decision Modification in Small Discussion Groups." *Journal of Communication* 20 (1970):51–64.

———. *Small Group Decision Making: Communication and the Group Process*. New York: McGraw-Hill, 1980.

Fisher, B. Aubrey, and Hawes, Leonard. "An

Interact System Model: Generating a Grounded Theory of Small Groups." *Quarterly Journal of Speech* 57 (1971):444–53.

Freund, Julien. *The Sociology of Max Weber.* New York: Pantheon Books, 1968.

Goldhaber, Gerald. *Organizational Communication.* Dubuque, Iowa: Brown, 1974.

Gouldner, A. W. "Organizational Analysis." In *Sociology Today.* Edited by R. K. Merton, L. Broom, and L. S. Cottrell. New York: Basic Books, 1958, pp. 400–28.

Gouran, Dennis. "Group Communication: Perspectives and Priorities for Future Research." *Quarterly Journal of Speech* 59 (1973):22–29.

Gulick, Luther, and Urwick, L., eds. *Papers on the Science of Organizations.* New York: Institute of Public Administration, Columbia University, 1937.

Haas, J. Eugene, and Drabek, Thomas E. *Complex Organizations: A Sociological Perspective.* New York: Macmillan, 1973.

Haire, Mason. "Introduction—Recurrent Themes and General Issues in Organization Theory." In *Modern Organization Theory.* Edited by Mason Haire. New York: John Wiley & Sons, 1959, pp. 1–15.

———, ed. *Modern Organization Theory.* New York: John Wiley & Sons, 1959.

Hall, Calvin S., and Lindzey, Gardner. "Lewin's Field Theory." In *Theories of Personality.* New York: John Wiley & Sons, 1970, chap. 6.

Hare, A. Paul. *Handbook of Small Group Research.* New York: Free Press, 1976.

Hare, A. Paul; Borgatta, Edgar F.; and Bales, Robert; eds. *Small Groups: Studies in Social Interaction.* New York: Knopf, 1966.

Hawes, Leonard C. "Social Collectivities as Communication: Perspective on Organizational Behavior." *Quarterly Journal of Speech* 60 (1974):497–502.

Heider, Fritz. "On Lewin's Methods and Theory." *Psychological Issues* 1 (1959):123.

Hinton, Bernard, and Reitz, Joseph, eds. *Groups and Organizations.* Belmont, Calif.: Wadsworth, 1971.

Homans, George C. *The Human Group.* New York: Harcourt, 1950.

———. *Social Behavior: Its Elementary Forms.* New York: Harcourt, 1961.

Huseman, Richard; Logue, Cal; and Freshley, Dwight. *Readings in Interpersonal and Organizational Communication.* Boston: Holbrook Press, 1969.

Janis, Irving. *Victims of Groupthink: A Psychological Study of Foreign Decisions and Fiascos.* Boston: Houghton Mifflin, 1967.

Katz, Daniel, and Kahn, Robert. *The Social Psychology of Organizations.* New York: John Wiley & Sons, 1966.

Kelley, H. H., and Thibaut, J. W. "Group Problem Solving." In *The Handbook of Social Psychology.* Edited by G. Lindzey and E. Aronson. Reading, Mass.: Addison-Wesley, 1969, pp. 1–101.

Knapp, Mark. "A Taxonomic Approach to Organizational Communication." *Journal of Business Communication* 7 (1969):37–47.

Koontz, Harold. "Making Sense of Management Theory." In *Toward a Unified Theory of Management.* New York: McGraw-Hill, 1964, pp. 2–17.

———. *Toward a Unified Theory of Management.* New York: McGraw-Hill, 1964.

Larson, Carl E. "Speech Communication Research on Small Groups." *Speech Teacher* 20 (1971):89–107.

Leavitt, H. J., ed. *The Social Science of Organizations: Four Perspectives.* Englewood Cliffs, N.J.: Prentice-Hall, 1963.

Lewin, Kurt. *A Dynamic Theory of Personality.* New York: McGraw-Hill, 1935.

———. *Field Theory in Social Science.* New York: Harper & Row, 1951.

———. "Frontiers in Group Dynamics: Concept, Method and Reality in Social Science, Social Equilibria, and Social Change." *Human Relations* 1 (1947):5–41.

———. *Resolving Social Conflicts: Selected Papers on Group Dynamics.* New York: Harper & Row, 1948.

Likert, Rensis. *The Human Organization.* New York: McGraw-Hill, 1967.

———. *New Patterns of Management.* New York: McGraw-Hill, 1961.

Littlejohn, Stephen W. *Theories of Human Communication.* Columbus, Ohio: Merrill, 1978.

McGrath, Joseph E., and Altman, Irwin. *Small Group Research: A Synthesis and Critique of the Field.* New York: Holt, Rinehart and Winston, 1966.

McGregor, Douglas. *The Human Side of Enterprise.* New York: McGraw-Hill, 1960.

March, James G., ed. *Handbook of Organizations.* Chicago: Rand McNally, 1965.

March, James G., and Simon, Herbert. *Organizations.* New York: John Wiley & Sons, 1958.

Marrow, Alfred. *The Practical Theorist: The Life and*

Work of Kurt Lewin. New York: Basic Books, 1969.

Massie, Joseph L. "Management Theory." In *Handbook of Organizations.* Edited by James G. March. Chicago: Rand McNally, 1965, pp. 387–422.

Melcher, A. J., ed. *General Systems and Organization Theory.* Kent, Ohio: Kent State University Press, 1975.

Mills, Theodore. *The Sociology of Small Groups.* Englewood Cliffs, N.J.: Prentice-Hall, 1967.

Mortensen, C. David. "The Status of Small Group Research." *Quarterly Journal of Speech* 56 (1970):304–9.

Parsons, Talcott. "Introduction." In *The Theory of Social and Economic Organization,* by Max Weber. New York: Oxford University Press, 1947, pp. 3–86.

Perrow, Charles. *Complex Organizations: A Critical Essay.* Glenview, Ill.: Scott, Foresman, 1972.

Redding, W. Charles. *Communication within the Organization.* New York: Industrial Communication Council, 1972.

Redding, W. Charles, and Sanborn, George. *Business and Industrial Communication–A Sourcebook.* New York: Harper & Row, 1964 .

Rice, George H., and Bishoprick, Dean W. *Conceptual Models of Organization.* New York: Appleton-Century-Crofts, 1971.

Riecken, Henry W., and Homans, George C. "Psychological Aspects of Social Structure." In *Handbook of Social Psychology.* Edited by Gardner Lindzey. Reading, Mass.: Addison-Wesley, 1954.

Roethlisberger, F., and Dickson, W. *Management and the Worker.* Cambridge: Harvard University Press, 1939.

Rosenfeld, Lawrence. *Human Interaction in the Small Group Setting.* Columbus,Ohio: Merrill, 1973.

Rubenstein, Albert H., and Haberstroh, Chadwick J., eds. *Some Theories of Organization.* Homewood, Ill.: Irwin-Dorsey, 1966

Scheidel, Thomas M., and Crowell, Laura. "Idea Development in Small Groups." *Quarterly Journal of Speech* 50 (1964):140–45.

Schein, Edgar H. *Organizational Psychology.* Englewood Cliffs, N.J.: Prentice-Hall, 1965.

Scott, William G. *Organization Theory.* Homewood, Ill.: Irwin, 1967.

———. "Organization Theory: An Overview and an Appraisal." *The Journal of the Academy of Management*, April 1961, pp. 15–16.

Shaw, Marvin. *Group Dynamics: The Psychology of Small Group Behavior.* New York: McGraw-Hill, 1981.

Shepherd, Clovis. *Small Groups: Some Sociological Perspectives.* San Francisco: Chandler, 1964.

Silverman, David. *The Theory of Organizations. A Sociological Framework.* New York: Basic Books, 1970.

Strother, George B. "Problems in the Development of a Social Science of Organization." In *The Social Science of Organizations: Four Perspectives.* Edited by H. J. Leavitt. Englewood Cliffs, N.J.: Prentice-Hall, 1963, pp. 1–38.

Taylor, F. *Principles of Scientific Management.* New York: Harper & Row, 1919.

Thayer, Lee. "Communication and Organization Theory." In *Human Communication Theory.* Edited by Frank Dance. New York: Holt, Rinehart and Winston, 1967, pp. 70–115.

Thibaut, John W., and Kelley, Harold H. *The Social Psychology of Group.* New York: John Wiley & Sons, 1959.

Tuckman, B. W. "Developmental Sequence in Small Groups." *Psychological Bulletin* 63 (1965):384–99.

Waldo, Dwight. "Organization Theory: An Elephantine Problem." *General Systems* 7 (1962):247–60.

Weber, Max. *The Theory of Social and Economic Organizations.* Translated by A. M. Henderson and Talcott Parsons. New York: Oxford University Press, 1947.

Weick, Carl. "Middle Range Theories of Social Systems." *Behavioral Science* 19 (1974):358.

———. *The Social Psychology of Organizing.* Reading, Mass.: Addison-Wesley, 1969.

Whyte, William Foote. *Man and Organization: Three Problems in Human Relations Training.* Homewood, Ill.: Irwin, 1959.

Chapter 12
The Mediated Context: Theories of Mass Communication

Anderson, James A. "Mass Communication Theory and Research: An Overview." In *Communication Yearbook I.* Edited by Brent Ruben. New Brunswick, N.J.: Transaction Books, 1977, pp. 279–90.

Ball-Rokeach, S. J., and DeFleur, M. L. "A Dependency Model of Mass-Media Effects." *Communication Research* 3 (1976):3–21.

Bauer, Raymond A. "The Audience." In *Handbook of Communication*. Edited by Ithiel de sola Pool et al. Chicago: Rand McNally, 1963, pp. 141–52.

———. "The Obstinate Audience: The Influence Process from the Point of View of Social Communication." *American Psychologist* 19 (1964):319–28.

Bauer, Raymond A., and Bauer, Alice H. "America, Mass Society, and Mass Media." *Journal of Social Issues* 16 (1960):3–66.

Beal, George M.; Rogers, Everett M.; and Bohlen, Joe M. "Validity of the Concept of Stages in the Adoption Process." *Rural Sociology* 22 (1957):166–68.

Bell, Daniel. "The Theory of Mass Society." *Commentary* July 1956, pp. 75–83.

Berg, David M. "Rhetoric, Reality, and Mass Media." *Quarterly Journal of Speech* 58 (1972):255–63.

Bloch, M., ed. *Political Language and Oratory in Traditional Society*. London: Academic Press, 1975.

Blum, Eleanor. *Basic Books in the Mass Media*. Urbana: University of Illinois Press, 1972.

Blumler, Jay. "The Role of Theory in Uses and Gratifications Studies." *Communication Research* 6 (1979):9–34.

Blumler, Jay, and Katz, Elihu, eds. *The Uses of Mass Communication*. Beverly Hills, Calif.: Sage, 1974.

Bohlen, Joe M. "Research Needed on Adoption Models." *North Central Regional Research Bulletin, 1968*. Reprinted in *The Process and Effects of Mass Communication*. Wilbur Schramm and Donald F. Roberts. Urbana: University of Illinois Press, 1971, pp. 798–815.

Boorstin, Daniel J. *The Image, or What Happened to the Ameican Dream*. New York: Atheneum, 1962.

Boulding, Kenneth. "The Medium is the Message." In *McLuhan: Hot and Cool*. Edited by Gerald E. Stearn. New York: Dial, 1967, pp. 56–64.

Breed, W. "Social Control in the Newsroom." *Social Forces* 33 (1955):326–35.

Bright, Philip Lewis. "The Speaking of Walter Lippman as a Critic of the New Deal." Doctoral dissertation, University of Washington, 1968.

Carey, J. W. "Harold Adams Innis and Marshall McLuhan." *The Antioch Review* 27 (1967):5–39.

Chaffee, Steven, ed. *Political Communication: Issues and Strategies for Research*. Beverly Hills, Calif.: Sage, 1976.

Childs, M., and Reston, J. eds. *Walter Lippman and His Times*. New York: Harcourt, Brace, 1959.

Christrans, Clifford G., and Real, Michael R. "Jacques Ellul's Contributions to Critical Media Theory." *Journal of Communication* 29 (1979):83–93.

Clarke, P., ed. *New Models for Mass Communication Research*. Beverly Hills, Calif.: Sage, 1973.

"Communication: McLuhan's Laws of the Media." *Technology and Culture* 16 (1975):74–78.

Davidson, W. Phillips; Boylan, James; and Yu, Frederick. *Mass Media: Systems and Effects*. New York: Praeger, 1976.

Davis, Dennis K., and Baran, Stanley J. *Mass Communication and Everyday Life: A Perspective on Theory and Effects*. Belmont, Calif.: Wadsworth, 1981.

DeFleur, Melvin. *Theories of Mass Communication*. New York: McKay, 1966.

DeFleur, Melvin, and Ball-Rokeach, Sandra. *Theories of Mass Communication*. New York: Longman, 1982.

Dexter, L. A., and White, D. M. *People, Society and Mass Communication*. New York: Holt, Rinehart and Winston, 1948.

Edelman, Murray. "The Language of Participation and the Language of Resistance." *Human Communication Research* 3 (1977):159–70.

———. *Politics as Symbolic Action*. New York: Academic Press, 1971.

———. *The Symbolic Uses of Politics*. Urbana: University of Illinois Press, 1964.

Elliott, George P. "Marshall McLuhan: Double Agent." In *McLuhan: Hot and Cool*. Edited by Gerald E. Stearn. New York: Dial, 1967, pp. 65–73.

Elliott, Philip. "Uses and Gratifications Research: A Critique and Sociological Alternative." In *The Uses of Mass Communication*. Edited by Jay Blumler and Elihu Katz. Beverly Hills, Calif.: Sage, 1974, pp. 249–68.

Elliott, Philip, and Swanson, David L. "Political Communication Research and the Uses and Gratifications Model: A Critique." *Communication Research* 6 (1979):37–53.

Ellul, Jacques. *Propaganda—The Formation of Men's Attitudes*. New York: Knopf, 1965.

Fagen, Richard. *Politics and Communication*. Boston: Little, Brown, 1966.

Finkelstein, Sidney. *Sense and Nonsense of McLuhan*. New York: International Publishers, 1968.

Fischer, Heinz D. "Forms and Functions of Supranational Communication." In *International Communication*. Edited by Heinz-Dietrich Fischer and

John C. Merrill. New York: Hastings House, 1970.

———. *International Communication.* New York: Hastings House, 1970.

Foley, Joseph M. "Mass Communication Theory and Research: An Overview." In *Communication Yearbook II.* Edited by Brent Ruben. New Brunswick, N.J.: Transaction Books, 1978, pp. 209–14.

———. "Mass Communication Theory and Research: An Overview." In *Communication Yearbook III.* Edited by Dan Nimmo. New Brunswick, N.J.: Transaction Books, 1979, pp. 263–70.

Freidson, Eliot. "Communications Research and the Concept of the Mass." *American Sociological Review* 1953. Reprinted in *The Process and Effects of Mass Communication.* Wilbur Schramm and Donald F. Roberts. Urbana: University of Illinois Press, 1971, pp. 197–208.

Frey, Frederick. "Communication and Development." In *Handbook of Communication.* Edited by Ithiel de sola Pool et al. Chicago: Rand McNally, 1973, pp. 337–461.

Gerbner, George. "Mass Media and Human Communication Theory." In *Human Communication Theory.* Edited by Frank Dance. New York: Holt, Rinehart and Winston, 1967, pp. 40–60.

———. "Toward a General Model of Communication." *Audio-visual Communication Review* 14 (1956):171–99.

Gieber, Walter. "News is What Newspapermen Make It." In *People, Society, and Mass Communications.* Edited by L. A. Dexter and D. M. White. New York: Free Press, 1964, pp. 173–82.

Golding, Peter. "Media Role in National Development: Critique of a Theoretical Orthodoxy." *Journal of Communication* 24 (1974):39–53.

Graber, D. *Verbal Behavior in Politics.* Urbana: University of Illinois Press, 1976.

Gronbeck, Bruce. "McLuhan as Rhetorical Theorist." *Journal of Communication* 31 (1981):117–28.

Hagerstrand, Torsten. "Diffusion II: The Diffusion of Innovations." In *International Encyclopedia of the Social Sciences.* Vol. 4. Edited by David Sills. New York: Macmillan, 1968.

———. *Innovation Diffusion as a Spatial Process.* Chicago: University of Chicago Press, 1967.

Hansen, Donald A., and Parsons, J. Herschel. *Mass Communication: A Research Bibliography.* Santa Barbara, Calif.: Glendessary Press, 1968.

Hennessy, B. C. *Public Opinion.* North Scituate, Mass.: Duxbury Press, 1975.

"Implications of Cultural Uniformity." In *Superculture: American Popular Culture and Europe.* Edited by C. E. E. Bigsby. Bowling Green, Ohio: Bowling Green University Popular Press, 1975.

Innis, Harold A. *The Bias of Communications.* Toronto: University of Toronto Press, 1951.

———. *Empire and Communication.* Toronto: University of Toronto Press, 1972, 1950.

Katz, Elihu. "Diffusion III: Interpersonal Influence." In *International Encyclopedia of the Social Sciences.* Vol. 4. Edited by David Sills. New York: Macmillan, 1968.

———. "The Two-Step Flow of Communication." *Public Opinion Quarterly* 1957. Reprinted in *Mass Communications.* Wilbur Schramm. Urbana: University of Illinois Press, 1960, pp. 346–65.

Katz, Elihu; Blumler, Jay; and Gurevitch, Michael. "Uses of Mass Communication by the Individual." In *Mass Communication Research: Major Issues and Future Directions.* Edited by W. Phillips Davidson and Frederick Yu. New York: Praeger, 1974, pp. 11–35.

Katz, Elihu, and Lazarsfeld, Paul F. *Personal Influence: The Part Played by People in the Flow of Mass Communications.* New York: Free Press, 1955.

Kecskemeti, Paul. "Propaganda." In *Handbook of Communication.* Edited by Ithiel de sola Pool et al. Chicago: Rand McNally, 1973, pp. 844–70.

Klapper, Joseph T. *The Effects of Mass Communication.* Glencoe, Ill.: Free Press, 1960.

Kornhauser, W. "Mass Society." In *International Encyclopedia of the Social Sciences.* Vol. 10. New York: Macmillan, 1968, pp. 58–64.

Kraus, Sidney. "Mass Communication and Political Socialization: A Reassessment of Two Decades of Research." *Quarterly Journal of Speech* 59 (1973):390–400.

Lasswell, Harold D. "Propaganda." In *The Encyclopedia of the Social Sciences.* Vol. 12. New York: Macmillan, 1934.

———. "The Structure and Function of Communication in Society." In *The Communication of Ideas.* Edited by Lyman Bryson. New York: Institute for Religious and Social Studies, 1948.

"Laws of the Media." *Et Cetera* 34 (1977):173—79.

Lazarsfeld, Paul F. "Public Opinion and the Classical Tradition." *Public Opinion Quarterly* 1957. *Mass Media and Communication.* Edited by Charles S. Steinberg. New York: Hastings House, 1966, pp. 79–93.

Lazarsfeld, Paul F.; Berelson, Bernard; and Gaudet, H. *The People's Choice*. New York: Columbia University Press, 1948.

Lazarsfeld, Paul F., and Merton, Robert K. "Mass Communication, Popular Taste, and Organized Social Action." In *The Communication of Ideas*. Edited by Lyman Bryson. New York: Institute for Religious and Social Studies, 1948.

Lerner, Daniel. *The Passing of Traditional Society*. Glencoe, Ill.: Free Press, 1958.

———. "Toward a Communication Theory of Modernization: A Set of Considerations." In *Communication and Political Development*. Edited by Lucian W. Pye. Princeton, N.J.: Princeton University Press, 1963, pp. 327–50.

Lewin, Kurt. "Channels of Group Life." *Human Relations* 1 (1947):145.

Lippman, Walter. *Public Opinion*. New York: Macmillan, 1921.

McLeod, J.; Becker, L.; and Byrnes, J. "Another Look at the Agenda-setting Function of the Press." *Communication Research* 1 (1974):131–66.

McLuhan, Marshal. "At the Flip Point of Time—The Point of More Return?" *Journal of Communication* 25 (1975):102–6.

———. "At the Moment of Sputnik the Planet Became a Global Theatre in Which There Are No Spectators but Only Actors." *Journal of Communication* 24 (1974):48–58.

———. "The Brain and the Media: The 'Western' Hemisphere." *Journal of Communication* 28 (1978):54–60.

———. "Communication: McLuhan's Laws of the Media." *Technology and Culture* 16 (1975):74–78.

———. *The Gutenberg Galaxy: The Making of Typographic Man*. Toronto: University of Toronto Press, 1962.

———. "Implications of Cultural Uniformity." In *Superculture: American Popular Culture and Europe*. Edited by C. E. E. Bigsby. Bowling Green: Bowling Green University Popular Press, 1975.

———. "Laws of the Media." *Et Cetera* 34 (1977):173–79.

———. *The Mechanical Bride*. New York: Vanguard Press, 1951.

———. "Misunderstanding the Media's Laws." *Technology and Culture* 17 (1976):263.

———. "The Rise and Fall of Nature." *Journal of Communication* 27 (1977):80–81.

———. *Understanding Media*. New York: McGraw-Hill, 1964.

———. "The Violence of the Media." *The Canadian Forum,* September 1976, pp. 9–12.

McLuhan, Marshall, and Fiore, Quentin. *The Medium is the Message. New York: Bantam, 1967.*

McQuail, Denis. Toward a Sociology of Mass Communication. London: Collier-Macmillan, 1969.

Merton, Robert K. *Social Theory and Social Structure*. Glencoe, Ill.: Free Press, 1957.

Noelle-Neumann, Elisabeth. "Return to the Concept of the Powerful Mass Media." In *Studies of Broadcasting*. Edited by H. Eguchi and K. Sata. Tokyo: Nippon Kyokii, 1973, pp. 67–112.

Peterson, Theodore; Jensen, Jay W.; and Rivers, William L. *The Mass Media and Modern Society*. New York: Holt, Rinehart and Winston, 1965.

Pool, Ithiel de sola. "Public Opinion." In *Handbook of Communication*. Edited by Ithiel de sola Pool et al. Chicago: Rand McNally, 1973, pp. 779–835.

Riley, J. W., and Riley, Matilda W. "Mass Communication and the Social System." In *Sociology Today*. Edited by Robert K. Merton. New York: Basic Books, 1959, pp. 537–78.

Rogers, Everett M. *Diffusion of Innovations*. New York: Free Press, 1962.

———. "Mass Media and Interpersonal Communication." In *Handbook of Communication*. Ed. Ithiel de sola Pool et al. Chicago: Rand McNally, 1973, pp. 290–310.

Rogers, Everett M., and Adhikarya, Ronny. "Diffusion of Innovations: An Up-to-Date Review and Commentary." In *Communication Yearbook III*. Edited by Dan Nimmo. New Brunswick, N.J.: Transaction Books, 1979, pp. 67–82.

Rogers, Everett M., and Kincaid, D. Lawrence. *Communication Networks*. New York: Free Press, 1981.

Rogers, Everett M., and Shoemaker, F. Floyd. *Communication of Innovations, A Cross-Cultural Approach*. New York: Free Press, 1971.

Rogow, Arnold A., ed. *Politics, Personality, and Social Science in the Twentieth Century: Essays in Honor of Harold D. Lasswell*. Chicago: University of Chicago Press, 1969.

Rosengren, Karl E. "International News: Time and Type of Report." In *International Communications: Media, Channels, and Functions*. New York: Hastings House, 1970, pp. 74–80.

———. "Uses and Gratifications: A Paradigm Outlined." In *The Uses of Mass Communication*. Edited by Jay Blumler and Elihu Katz. Beverly Hills, Calif.: Sage, 1974, pp. 270–71.

Rosenthal, Raymond, ed. *McLuhan: Pro and Con*. New York: Funk and Wagnalls, 1968.

Roszak, Theodore. "The Summa Popologica of Marshall McLuhan." In *McLuhan: Pro and Con*.

Edited by Raymond Rosenthal. New York: Funk & Wagnalls, 1968, pp. 257–69.

Schramm, Wilbur. "Channels and Audiences." In *Handbook of Communication*. Edited by Ithiel de sola Pool et al. Chicago: Rand McNally, 1973, pp. 116–40.

———. *Mass Communications*. Urbana: University of Illinois Press, 1960.

———. *Mass Media and National Development*. Stanford, Calif.: Stanford University Press, 1964.

———. *Men, Messages, and Media: A Look at Human Communication*. New York: Harper & Row, 1973.

Schramm, Wilbur, and Roberts, Donald F. *The Process and Effects of Mass Communication*. Urbana: University of Illinois Press, 1971.

Sears, David O., and Freedman, Jonathan L. "Selective Exposure to Information: A Critical Review." *Public Opinion Quarterly* 1967. Reprinted in *The Process and Effects of Mass Communication*. Wilbur Schramm and Donald F. Roberts. Urbana: University of Illinois Press, 1971, pp. 209–34.

Sears, David O., and Whitney, Richard E. "Political Persuasion." In *Handbook of Communication*. Edited by Ithiel de sola Pool et al. Chicago: Rand McNally, 1973, pp. 253–89.

Severin, Werner J., and Tankard, James W. *Communication Theories: Origins, Methods, Uses*. New York: Hastings House, 1979.

Shaw, Donald L., and McCombs, Maxwell E. *The Emergence of American Political Issues*. St. Paul: West Publishing, 1977.

Siebert, Fred S.; Peterson, Theodore; and Schramm, Wilbur. *Four Theories of the Press*. Urbana: University of Illinois Press, 1956.

Stearn, Gerald E., ed. *McLuhan: Hot and Cool*. New York: Dial, 1967.

Steinberg, Charles S., ed. *Mass Media and Communication*. New York: Hastings House, 1966.

Stephenson, William. *The Play Theory of Mass Communication*. Chicago: University of Chicago Press, 1967.

Subcommittee for the Study of the Diffusion of Farm Practices, North Central Rural Sociological Committee. *How Farm People Accept New Ideas*. North Central Regional Extension Publication no. 1. Ames, Iowa: Agricultural Extension Service, November 1955.

Swanson, David L. "Political Communication Research and the Uses and Gratifications Model: A Critique." *Communication Research* 6 (1979):37–53.

Theall, Donald F. *The Medium Is the Rear View Mirror: Understanding McLuhan*. Montreal: McGill University Press, 1971.

Weiss, Walter. "Effects of the Mass Media of Communication." In *The Handbook of Social Psychology*. 2d ed. Edited by Gardner Lindzey and Elliot Aronson. Reading, Mass.: Addison-Wesley, 1969, pp., 77–195.

———. "Mass Communication." *Annual Review of Psychology*, Palo Alto, Calif.: Annual Review Press, 1971.

Westley, Bruce, and MacLean, Malcolm. "A Conceptual Model for Communication Research." *Journalism Quarterly* 34 (1957):31–38.

White, David M. "The 'Gate Keeper': A Case Study in the Selection of News." *Journalism Quarterly* 27 (1950):383–90.

———. "Mass Communications Research: A View in Perspective." In *People, Society, and Mass Communications*. Edited by L. A. Dexter and D. M. White. New York: Free Press, 1964, pp. 521–46.

Wolfe, Tom. "The New Life Out There." In *McLuhan: Hot and Cool*. Edited by Gerald Stearn. New York: Dial, 1967, pp. 15–34.

Wright, Charles R. "Functional Analysis and Mass Communication." *Public Opinion Quarterly* 24 (1960):605–20.

———. *Mass Communication: A Sociological Perspective*. New York: Random House, 1959.

Author Index

Subject Index